The Literate Writer

A Rhetoric with Readings across Four Genres

David J. Kann

*California Polytechnic State University,
San Luis Obispo*

Tues/Thurs.
#12F

Mayfield Publishing Company
Mountain View, California
London • Toronto

To Lois, without whom I couldn't have,
and to Rachel, Jennie, Ben, and Arielle, for whom I did.

Copyright © 1995 by Mayfield Publishing Company

Library of Congress Cataloging-in-Publication Data
Kann, David J.
   The literate writer : a rhetoric with readings across four genres
/ David J. Kann.
     p.   cm.
   Includes index.
   ISBN 1-55934-372-9
   1. English language—Rhetoric. 2. College readers. I. Title.
PE1408.K275   1995
808'.042—dc20
                                   94-38168
                                      CIP

Manufactured in the United States of America
10 9 8 7 6 5 4 3 2

Mayfield Publishing Company
1280 Villa Street
Mountain View, California 94041

Sponsoring editor, Thomas V. Broadbent; production editor, April Wells-Hayes; manuscript editor, Beverley J. DeWitt; art director, Jeanne M. Schreiber; text designer, Linda M. Robertson; illustrators, Jean Mailander and Robin Mouat; cover designer, Susan Breitbard; manufacturing manager, Aimee Rutter. The text was set in 11/12 Bembo by G&S Typesetters, Inc., and printed on 45# Glatfelter Restorecote by The Maple-Vail Book Manufacturing Group.

Cover image: *Four Seasons,* Jose Ortega/SIS.

Acknowledgments appear on pages 815–819, which constitute an extension of the copyright page.

 This book is printed on acid-free, recycled paper.

Preface

We read so that we know we're not alone.

—C. S. LEWIS

Some years ago, a number of bureaucratic decisions on the campus where I teach resulted in the elimination of the introduction to literature courses for both English majors and other students. The result was predictable and troubling. Students entering more specialized literature courses either did not know or vaguely remembered the nature and the limits of the genres and had little or no vocabulary for talking about literature.

In my freshman composition course, therefore, I experimented with using "literary" readings interchangeably with "traditional" essays as a way of preparing my students for later literature courses.

I realized that I was not teaching a literature course and that among all the students in a class none might be English majors. I also began with the conviction that a person writes best when he or she is interested in the subject. Consequently, I avoided assigning papers that asked my students to explicate a poem, short story, or play. Instead, I devised assignments that asked the students to engage the ideas and events in writers' works by examining their own comparable experiences and to look for an idea that seemed important enough to them to make them want to tell another person about it.

Believing that this effort could only be successful if students were able to relate a reading to their own thoughts, feelings, and experiences, I chose works—essays, poems, prose fiction, and drama—that were accessible through relatively familiar language and allusions. I also favored works whose subjects or themes were more or less familiar, either directly or analogically. These choices are most emphatically not the same thing as "dumbing down" the readings. They provide a common basis from which to begin. I found that because students are generally comfortable with the demands made by the readings, they discover their competence in matters such as figures of speech and symbols. Once convinced of their competence, they move comfortably toward more challenging work.

The results fascinated me. I found, for example, students relating their readings of Roethke's "My Papa's Waltz" and Anderson's "Discovery of a Father" to their own experiences with parents (or with children, if they themselves were parents) and writing about the conflict between autonomy and obedience. Similarly, Browning's "My Last Duchess," Marvell's "To His Coy Mistress," Lawrence's "Tickets, Please," Atwood's "Pornography," and Glaspell's *Trifles* led some to consider their own experiences with issues of gender.

We discovered that no matter what the genre, at the core of a work was the desire to make a dominant idea clear to an audience separated from the writer by space and quite possibly by time. Along the way, we found that in every genre the writer (a person) writes with the aim of telling something to his or her audience (other people) about the challenges and pleasures of being a person in a particular time and place. We found that writers use observations and conclusions growing from their real or imagined experience to lead their audience to a dominant idea or attitude.

As the students and I learned to test and redefine the limits of "appropriate" writing in a composition class, we also discovered (or rediscovered) approaches to shaping writing. In their groups, the students (and I) searched for strategies for organizing ideas and observations. We found ourselves returning to the traditional organizational schemes I thought I had given up years before, but from a different angle. We began to see organizational approaches emerging from our struggles with dominant ideas and supporting material. In order to talk to each other about these issues and to identify the organizational possibilities emerging from a draft, we found that we needed a common vocabulary and a common set of models that reflected the available choices. We began talking about organizational models as a set of options, none intrinsically better than any other but only more or less appropriate to the shape of the idea that emerged as the students drafted their work. Essentially, the strategies returned to their original form as Aristotle's *topoi*. They became ways a writer queried a draft as to what form it wanted to take.

Once we became comfortable talking about organizational strategies, we began to discover them in our readings, no matter what the genre. For example, Auden's "Musée des Beaux Arts" or Poe's "The Fall of the House of Usher" made sense as descriptions in support of a central, dominant idea. Thomas Nashe's "Song in Time of Plague" and a portion of Freud's *The Interpretation of Dreams* employed classification and analysis to make their points. There did not seem to be any loss of rigor or seriousness in speaking of "literary" works in terms of organizational strategies. And if we granted those strategies as natural ways of arranging thoughts, we found that they could not help but be there. Rather than trivializing the readings, this approach gave the students ways of understanding the assignments more clearly, made the texts more accessible to them, and, most important, led these beginning writers to see the voices and devices of experienced writers as resources they already had available and as possibilities for their own writing.

All of these small surprises led us to a larger discovery. One of my students handed in what I thought was a particularly good essay. When I spoke with her about it, she somewhat shamefacedly confessed that she had made most of it up. It was still a very, very good essay. Or was it a short story? We spoke some more, and we began to talk about what she meant by "making things up." Actually, this student had made none of it up, a point so obvious that it had escaped me. Nothing comes from nothing. This student had combined her observations, her experiences, and what she had heard from other people. She had used all of this experience to lead herself and her reader to an idea.

This discovery called into question the traditional distinction between writing that is thought to be "creative" (fiction, poetry, and drama) and writing thought to be "non-literary" (most nonfiction prose—especially, for the purposes of this book, the student expository and argumentative essay). The conventional distinction between "creative" writing and the catch-all category that lies outside the boundary set by that term establishes a sort of ghetto that limits the resources available to students as long as they think exclusively of their writing as traditional nonfiction prose.

The idea of "telling the truth" became far more elastic than either I or my students had assumed at the beginning of the term. Looking at what happened during drafting and group discussions, we discovered that there are too many processes of selection occurring at any moment of writing to allow us to speak comfortably of "the truth" contained in a piece of writing. We take what is available to construct a usable model of our place in the world, and on that basis we act. Our perceptions and the actions we take based on those perceptions are an interpretive act based on the creative perception of our place in the world, our experiences, the purposes for which we write, and the audience we invoke. All writing is creative.

The next step was as logical as it was unexpected. Grasping the idea that these rhetorical elements transcend the limits of genre, some students asked whether they might write short stories, poems, or short plays instead of essays. I found it difficult to say no and to remain consistent with the way the course was shaping itself. What was left of my orthodox composition teacher self cringed at what I thought might be the consequences of my license. After all, where I teach, freshman composition is supposed to be a course in expository writing. It appeared clear to me that with the latitude I had allowed my students in their writing, they would never learn the skills I was supposed to teach them.

I was wrong. Instead of having turned out a group of inadequate expository writers, I found that their writing was stronger than the writing I was accustomed to seeing at the end of a freshman composition course. The devices the students had learned and experimented with found their way into the essays. Their writing was more vital; it reflected the sort of pleasure that comes with pushing the limits and finding that the limits are an illusion after all.

The result of these first discoveries led me to see that my students had rhetorical and grammatical competence that exceeded my expectations. I found that my task was not to teach them at the point where they were already competent. Instead, it was to create situations that made them conscious of their competence and of their strengths as readers and writers. And, as they gained confidence and control over their abilities, they discovered resources and choices in their own and in others' writing.

This book is the result of those explorations with my students. It aims not so much to teach students how to write and read sensitively and effectively—it grants them that competence—as to create opportunities for them to discover their own resources as writers and readers and apply to their own writing what they have discovered. The book could not have come to be without them.

ACKNOWLEDGMENT

To all the people at Mayfield, but especially to Tom Broadbent, April Wells-Hayes, Pamela Trainer, and Beverley DeWitt: You are all, collectively, *il miglior fabbro*.

Contents

PART 1

You and Your Writing

What This Book Assumes about You and Your Writing

Kharmic actions that cannot be avoided, OR change. FATE

Every writer of a book about writing bases it on a set of assumptions about his or her readers and about how writing happens. A number of ideas regarding you and your writing ability have shaped this book:

All writing is creative writing.
You already talk and write grammatically.
You already use rhetoric.
There is strength in numbers.
Effective writing springs from a reason to write.
Writing is messy and keeps turning back on itself.
You know effective organizational strategies.
You already know and use figurative language.
You already have some knowledge of argument.

This chapter explains the first four assumptions. The remainder are discussed later in the book.

ALL WRITING IS CREATIVE WRITING

Look at the following piece of writing done by a freshman student during the first weeks of class. He was asked to write whatever came to mind for five minutes without going back to revise or to correct his spelling and punctuation. Here is the unedited result:

It's almost summer again. Summer evenings are something I always enjoy. There is nothing more pleasurable than taking an evening stroll when the sun has sunk behind the rows of rooftops and the sultry heat has gone with it to be replaced by a pleasant coolness. As I walk barefoot down the sidewalk in a T-shirt and shorts, I see men home from work sitting on their front porch steps after dinner enjoying a beer.

The water sprinkler is turned on quenching the lush green grass with its ever changing shower of droplets. I walk a little further and see an old man on his porch in a lawn chair escaping the heat of the house with a frosty glass full of cold lemonade. Water is running from his garden hose onto the sidewalk giving off the peculiar smell of dust and evaporating water. A young couple walk by enjoying the evening respite from the heat. I say hi to them and they smile in return as they stroll past me. And the old man with his lemonade, and the lush, green grass. And the man enjoying his beer. And into a cool breeze carrying the scents of a summer evening.

Of course, there are a few flaws in this description of a summer evening. After all, the writer had no time to revise. However, the description also shows many of the strengths that readers associate with effective writing. It sets a clear scene, time, and location. It uses precise, concrete words rather than vague, abstract terms to tell you about the scene. It is logically organized, moving you in a natural sequence through the neighborhood and through time. Its imagery speaks to your senses, putting you in the place. At its close, this piece of writing does a nice job of reminding you what the writer saw, heard, and smelled.

A student like you wrote this piece in his unedited, unrevised voice in a five-minute exercise. Although what you write about and the way you shape your writing might be very different from this example, think what you can do when you take your natural power over your language and your ideas and learn to control it.

Do you think that the writer was really where he says he was or that he had to have been there to write his description? Do you think that everything he describes was at the same place at one time? Do you think he is lying to you? It's possible that he took one experience from here, another from there, an observation from his past, and something that he simply imagined, and combined and shaped them in his own way. Everybody takes remembered and imagined events and arranges them to suit his or her purposes.

Furthermore, nobody tells *all* the truth. To do so would be pointless. If you told a friend about an auto accident you had seen, you probably would not bother to mention the flowers in the window box in the front window of the house across the street from the crash—that is, unless you thought that the accident might have been caused by one of the drivers admiring those flowers. Probably you would not mention the colors of the cars unless those colors also had something to do with the crash.

You've probably been taught that the difference between "factual" writing and "creative" writing is that people who deal in "facts" tell the truth and people who write poetry, drama, or prose fiction—"creative" writers—make things up. However, if you look more closely at the writing you read, that distinction begins to disappear. For example, consider the first two paragraphs of a column that appeared in the *New York Times* in May 1988:

The escalating drug crisis is beginning to take its toll on many Americans. And now growing numbers of well-intentioned officials and other opinion leaders are saying that the best way to fight drugs is to legalize them. But what they're really admitting is that they're willing to abandon a war that we have not even begun to fight.

For example, the newly elected and promising Mayor of Baltimore, Kurt Schmoke, at a meeting of the United States Conference of Mayors, called for a full-scale study of the feasibility of legalization. His comments could not have come at a worse time, for we are in the throes of the worst drug epidemic in our history.

—CHARLES B. RANGEL, "Legalize Drugs? Not on Your Life"

These paragraphs are clear. There is no question about the position Rangel takes. His language is plain and direct. Nevertheless, consider the facts that Rangel has chosen to leave out: How tall is Mayor Schmoke? Where was the conference held? What did the room where Schmoke gave his speech look like? How many people heard the speech? How many mayors attended the conference? Furthermore, is the statement attributed to Mayor Schmoke *exactly* what he said? Is that statement *everything* he said?

If you think that these questions are stupid and have nothing to do with the point Rangel aims to make, you're right, in a way. But the questions do make a point: Rangel carefully selects only the facts that are related to the idea he intends to communicate.

No writer ever tells the *whole* truth. Instead, writers shape their material—their information and their language—to focus the reader's attention on the facts that they consider most important. Another writer with another aim might write a different report of Mayor Schmoke's speech.

Most readers would say that Rangel tries to be truthful. He has decided what truth he wants to convey to his readers, and so he selects elements of the scene and the speech that he considers essential to his purposes, allows others to recede into the background, and ignores the rest.

Now read the following report:

Excerpt from the Proceedings in the Court-Martial of Benjamin L. Harwood, Col., U.S.A., Fort Meyer, VA., June 8, 2038

JUDGE ADVOCATE: I have no further questions, colonel.

DEFENSE COUNSEL: May it please the Court. Rather than recalling Colonel Harwood to the stand later, I would like to establish one point by cross-examination which properly should be made at this time.

J.A.: You may proceed.

D.C.: Colonel Harwood, going back to May 4th of this year, will you tell the Court how you received your orders from General Fairbank?

DEFENDANT: How?

D.C.: In what manner were they communicated to you?

DEF: Verbally. There was no time, you understand, for any confirmation. I was told all General Fairbank knew about the ship in ten hurried sentences and given my orders.

D.C.: Can you recollect them?

DEF: Of course. Not *verbatim,* perhaps, but certainly their substance. Would you like me to repeat them?

D.C.: (*To the Court*) I should like the Court to understand this is merely to introduce in proper order the point we wish to make.

J.A.: On that understanding, the defendant may proceed.

DEF: I was ordered to find out who were the country's leading students of language and communication, considering the problem of the visitors as General Fairbank knew it; to find out where these students were; to get the necessary credentials from the Office of the Chief of Staff; and to bring the persons in question to the landing site immediately.

D.C.: In other words, colonel, your choice was to depend solely on the qualifications of these persons as students?

DEF.: That's right.

D.C.: And nothing was said with reference to their emotional or political outlook?

DEF.: I don't think Army regulations provide for either of those things. (*Laughter*)

J.A.: Order! The colonel will restrain his mordant wit.

DEF.: I beg the Court's pardon. No sir, no mention was made of those factors.

D.C.: That is all, colonel. You may step down. (*To the Court*) This is the very nub of our defense. We contend that Colonel Harwood well and faithfully carried out his orders. No man can be accused of willful neglect simply because of the warped mentality of another.

—JOHN BERRYMAN, "Berom"

Unless you read carefully enough to notice the date on which this transcript was supposed to have been recorded (if you didn't, go back now and read it), there is no reason for you to doubt that what you just read is a real transcript of a real court-martial. The author drew on his knowledge of military procedure and courts-martial to transform reality into fiction—in this case, science fiction. He selected aspects of reality to create the illusion of a real world with real people in conflict with each other.

Now here is a poem:

Blackberry Eating

I love to go out in late September
among the fat, overripe, icy, black blackberries
to eat blackberries for breakfast,
the stalks very prickly, a penalty
they earn for knowing the black art

of blackberry-making; and as I stand among them
lifting the stalks to my mouth, the ripest berries
fall almost unbidden to my tongue,
as words sometimes do, certain peculiar words
like *strengths* or *squinched*,
many-lettered, one-syllabled lumps,
which I squeeze, squinch open, and splurge well
in the silent, startled, icy, black language
of blackberry-eating in late September.

—GALWAY KINNEL

Did the poet really go out in late September to eat blackberries? Did he
feel everything he tells you about in the poem at the moment he writes of?
Of course, there's no way of knowing the answer without interviewing the
writer, and writers don't always remember (or know, or tell) what led to
their writing. In another sense, these questions make no more sense than
the ones asked of Rangel's piece or those that ask whether the court-martial
really happened. The poet took his experiences, and possibly others' experiences that he had heard about or read about, and combined them into a
piece of writing that was true for him, whether or not it was fact.

Like the science fiction writer and the poet, we select from our impressions, our memories of past experiences, and what is happening to us right
now to make some sense of our situation. This complex combination of
memories, assumptions, and experiences causes us to select and arrange our
observations to reflect the world we assume surrounds us.

The poet, the dramatist, and the writer of fiction are no less truthful
than the nonfiction writer. They also take the material available to them,
select from it, and shape it. They highlight those elements that advance their
purposes, and they altogether eliminate others or make them part of the
background. You might object that the poet, the dramatist, or the writer of
fiction made up his or her "facts," whereas the nonfiction writer actually
observed the reality. However, even that assumption is not strictly true. A
writer could not write at all without somehow experiencing or at least observing a *version* of the locations, events, and responses that he or she wraps
in words. Nothing comes from a vacuum; experience feeds imagination.
One writer makes a story, poem, or drama out of his or her experiences;
another writes an essay that supposedly reports, develops, and draws conclusions from facts. Nevertheless, both writers select and shape their facts to
support and to communicate the particular truths they had gathered from
their observations. In a way, all writers write fiction. And all writers tell a
truth.

Any writer approaches his or her expression of the truth with a reason
to write, a drive to create order from what seems to be disorder. Sometimes
that sense of disorder may be difficult to define, and the writer must work
hard to discover what he or she needs to say. At other times, the sense of
disorder may be very specific—perhaps the need to write a letter to the

editor of a local paper protesting a law regulating bicycle riding in town. Once the writer has discovered a reason to write, he or she uses words, sentences, and paragraphs to arrange the essential facts. The writer collects and connects observations and experiences to lead his or her readers to a dominant idea that speaks to their experiences, intellect, and emotions. Every writer concerned with making his or her writing powerful chooses from everything that is available, selecting only those elements that make his or her particular truth clear to the readers.

Thus all writing is "creative" writing. A story, a poem, or a play is no more or less "creative" than an essay or a letter. The difference is in the shape each takes—the form and the language the writer uses to express the truth at the core of the piece. That is why the discussions of the readings in this book do not distinguish between "creative" and "factual" writing. That is also why the writing invitations in this book suggest that you experiment with various forms of written expression—essays, fiction, poetry, and drama—to convey your dominant idea. The more resources you master for expressing yourself, the more powerful writer and reader you will be.

✒ Working with the Readings

Read the three selections that follow: One is a short story, one an essay, and one a poem. The essay seems to be based on the writer's direct observation and her thoughts about what she saw. The short story, being fiction, is "made up"—and is science fiction, as well. But is it devoid of facts? Finally, the poem may or may not refer to a "real" experience. After you have read the selections, answer the questions on page 31, either on your own or in discussion with your group.

THE COLD EQUATIONS

Tom Godwin

He was not alone.

There was nothing to indicate that fact but the white hand of the tiny gauge on the board before him. The control room was empty but for himself; there was no sound other than the murmur of the drives—but the white hand had moved. It had been on zero when the little ship was launched from the *Stardust;* now, an hour later, it had crept up. There was something in the supplies closet across the room, it was saying, some kind of a body that radiated heat.

It could be but one kind of body—a living, human body.

He leaned back in the pilot's chair and drew a deep, slow breath, considering what he would have to do. He was an EDS pilot, inured to the sight of death, long since accustomed to it and to viewing the dying of another man with an objective lack of emotion, and he had no choice in what he must do. There could be no alternative—but it required a few moments of conditioning for even an EDS pilot to prepare himself to walk across the room and coldly, deliberately, take the life of a man he had yet to meet.

He would, of course, do it. It was the law, stated very bluntly and   *5* definitely in grim Paragraph L, Section 8, of Interstellar Regulations: *Any stowaway discovered in an EDS shall be jettisoned immediately following discovery.*

It was the law, and there could be no appeal.

It was a law not of men's choosing but made imperative by the circumstances of the space frontier. Galactic expansion had followed the development of the hyperspace drive and as men scattered wide across the frontier there had come the problem of contact with the isolated first-colonies and exploration parties. The huge hyperspace cruisers were the product of the combined genius and effort of Earth and were long and expensive in the building. They were not available in such numbers that small colonies could possess them. The cruisers carried the colonists to their new worlds and made periodic visits, running on tight schedules, but they could not stop and turn aside to visit colonies scheduled to be visited at another time; such a delay would destroy their schedule and produce a confusion and uncertainty that would wreck the complex interdependence between old Earth and new worlds of the frontier.

Some method of delivering supplies or assistance when an emergency occurred on a world not scheduled for a visit had been needed and the Emergency Dispatch Ships had been the answer. Small and collapsible, they occupied little room in the hold of the cruiser; made of light metal and plastics, they were driven by a small rocket drive that consumed relatively little fuel. Each cruiser carried four EDS's and when a call for aid was received the nearest cruiser would drop into normal space long enough to launch an EDS with the needed supplies or personnel, then vanish again as it continued on its course.

The cruisers, powered by nuclear converters, did not use the liquid rocket fuel but nuclear converters were far too large and complex to permit their installation in the EDS's. The cruisers were forced by necessity to carry a limited amount of bulky rocket fuel and the fuel was rationed with care; the cruiser's computers determining the exact amount of fuel each EDS would require for its mission. The computers considered the course coordinates, the mass of the EDS, the mass of pilot and cargo; they were very precise and accurate and omitted nothing from their calculations. They could not, however, foresee, and allow for, the added mass of a stowaway.

The *Stardust* had received the request from one of the exploration   *10* parties stationed on Woden; the six men of the party already being stricken with the fever carried by the green *kala* midges and their own

the equation= ship weight / fuel need / fuel taken

supply of serum destroyed by the tornado that had torn through their camp. The *Stardust* had gone through the usual procedure; dropping into normal space to launch the EDS with the fever serum, then vanishing again in hyperspace. Now, an hour later, the gauge was saying there was something more than the small carton of serum in the supplies closet.

He let his eyes rest on the narrow white door of the closet. There, just inside, another man lived and breathed and was beginning to feel assured that discovery of his presence would now be too late for the pilot to alter the situation. It *was* too late—for the man behind the door it was far later than he thought and in a way he would find terrible to believe.

There could be no alternative. Additional fuel would be used during the hours of deceleration to compensate for the added mass of the stowaway; infinitesimal increments of fuel that would not be missed until the ship had almost reached its destination. Then, at some distance above the ground that might be as near as a thousand feet or as far as tens of thousands of feet, depending upon the mass of ship and cargo and the preceding period of deceleration, the unmissed increments of fuel would make their absence known; the EDS would expend its last drops of fuel with a sputter and go into whistling free fall. Ship and pilot and stowaway would merge together upon impact as a wreckage of metal and plastic, flesh and blood, driven deep into the soil. The stowaway had signed his own death warrant when he concealed himself on the ship; he could not be permitted to take seven others with him.

He looked again at the telltale white hand, then rose to his feet. What he must do would be unpleasant for both of them; the sooner it was over, the better. He stepped across the control room, to stand by the white door.

"Come out!" His command was harsh and abrupt above the murmur of the drive.

It seemed he could hear the whisper of a furtive movement inside the   15
closet, then nothing. He visualized the stowaway cowering into one corner, suddenly worried by the possible consequences of his act and his self-assurance evaporating.

"I said *out!*"

He heard the stowaway move to obey and he waited with his eyes alert on the door and his hand near the blaster at his side.

The door opened and the stowaway stepped through it, smiling. "All right—I give up. Now what?"

It was a girl.

He stared without speaking, his hand dropping away from the blaster   20
and acceptance of what he saw coming like a heavy and unexpected physical blow. The stowaway was not a man—she was a girl in her teens, standing before him in little white gypsy sandals with the top of her brown, curly head hardly higher than his shoulder, with a faint, sweet scent of perfume coming from her and her smiling face tilted up so her

eyes could look unknowing and unafraid into his as she waited for his answer.

Now what? Had it been asked in the deep, defiant voice of a man he would have answered it with action, quick and efficient. He would have taken the stowaway's identification disk and ordered him into the air lock. Had the stowaway refused to obey, he would have used the blaster. It would not have taken long; within a minute the body would have been ejected into space—had the stowaway been a man.

He returned to the pilot's chair and motioned her to seat herself on the boxlike bulk of the drive-control units that set against the wall beside him. She obeyed, his silence making the smile fade into the meek and guilty expression of a pup that has been caught in mischief and knows it must be punished.

"You still haven't told me," she said. "I'm guilty, so what happens to me now? Do I pay a fine, or what?"

"What are you doing here?" he asked. "Why did you stow away on this EDS?"

"I wanted to see my brother. He's with the government survey crew   25 on Woden and I haven't seen him for ten years, not since he left Earth to go into government survey work."

"What was your destination on the *Stardust?*"

"Mimir. I have a position waiting for me there. My brother has been sending money home all the time to us—my father and mother and I—and he paid for a special course in linguistics I was taking. I graduated sooner than expected and I was offered this job on Mimir. I knew it would be almost a year before Gerry's job was done on Woden so he could come on to Mimir and that's why I hid in the closet there. There was plenty of room for me and I was willing to pay the fine. There were only the two of us kids—Gerry and I—and I haven't seen him for so long, and I didn't want to wait another year when I could see him now, even though I knew I would be breaking some kind of a regulation when I did it."

I knew I would be breaking some kind of a regulation—In a way, she could not be blamed for her ignorance of the law; she was of Earth and had not realized that the laws of the space frontier must, of necessity, be as hard and relentless as the environment that gave them birth.

Yet, to protect such as her from the results of their own ignorance of the frontier, there had been a sign over the door that led to the section of the *Stardust* that housed EDS's; a sign that was plain for all to see and heed:

UNAUTHORIZED PERSONNEL
KEEP OUT!

"Does your brother know that you took passage on the *Stardust* for   30 Mimir?"

"Oh, yes. I sent him a spacegram telling him about my graduation and about going to Mimir on the *Stardust* a month before I left Earth. I already knew Mimir was where he would be stationed in a little over a year. He gets a promotion then, and he'll be based on Mimir and not have to stay out a year at a time on field trips, like he does now."

There were two different survey groups on Woden, and he asked, "What is his name?"

"Cross—Gerry Cross. He's in Group Two—that was the way his address read. Do you know him?"

Group One had requested the serum; Group Two was eight thousand miles away, across the Western Sea.

"No, I've never met him," he said, then turned to the control board   *35* and cut the deceleration to a fraction of a gravity; knowing as he did so that it could not avert the ultimate end, yet doing the only thing he could do to prolong the ultimate end. The sensation was like that of the ship suddenly dropping and the girl's involuntary movement of surprise half lifted her from the seat.

"We're going faster now, aren't we?" she asked. "Why are we doing that?"

He told her the truth. "To save fuel for a little while."

"You mean, we don't have very much?"

He delayed the answer he must give her so soon to ask: "How did   you manage to stow away?"

"I just sort of walked in when no one was looking my way," she said.   *40* "I was practicing my Gelanese on the native girl who does the cleaning in the Ship's Supply office when someone came in with an order for supplies for the survey crew on Woden. I slipped into the closet there after the ship was ready to go and just before you came in. It was an impulse of the moment to stow away, so I could get to see Gerry—and from the way you keep looking at me so grim, I'm not sure it was a very wise impulse.

"But I'll be a model criminal—or do I mean prisoner?" She smiled at him again. "I intended to pay for my keep on top of paying the fine. I can cook and I can patch clothes for everyone and I know how to do all kinds of useful things, even a little bit about nursing."

There was one more question to ask:

"Did you know what the supplies were that the survey crew ordered?"

"Why, no. Equipment they needed in their work, I suppose."

Why couldn't she have been a man with some ulterior motive? A   *45* fugitive from justice, hoping to lose himself on a raw new world; an opportunist, seeking transportation to the new colonies where he might find golden fleece for the taking; a crackpot, with a mission—

Perhaps once in his lifetime an EDS pilot would find such a stowaway on his ship; warped men, mean and selfish men, brutal and dangerous men—but never, before, a smiling, blue-eyed girl who was willing to pay her fine and work for her keep that she might see her brother.

He turned to the board and turned the switch that would signal the *Stardust.* The call would be futile but he could not, until he had exhausted that one vain hope, seize her and thrust her into the air lock as he would an animal—or a man. The delay, in the meantime, would not be dangerous with the EDS decelerating at fractional gravity.

A voice spoke from the communicator. "*Stardust.* Identify yourself and proceed."

"Barton, EDS 34G11. Emergency. Give me Commander Delhart."

There was a faint confusion of noises as the request went through the proper channels. The girl was watching him, no longer smiling.   50

"Are you going to order them to come back after me?" she asked.

The communicator clicked and there was the sound of a distant voice saying, "Commander, the EDS requests—"

"Are they coming back after me?" she asked again. "Won't I get to see my brother, after all?"

"Barton?" The blunt, gruff voice of Commander Delhart came from the communicator. "What's this about an emergency?"

"A stowaway," he answered.   55

"A stowaway?" There was a slight surprise to the question. "That's rather unusual—but why the 'emergency' call? You discovered him in time so there should be no appreciable danger and I presume you've informed Ship's Records so his nearest relatives can be notified."

"That's why I had to call you, first. The stowaway is still aboard and the circumstances are so different—"

"Different?" the commander interrupted, impatience in his voice. "How can they be different? You know you have a limited supply of fuel; you also know the law, as well as I do: 'Any stowaway discovered in an EDS shall be jettisoned immediately following discovery.'"

There was the sound of a sharply indrawn breath from the girl. "*What does he mean?*"

"The stowaway is a girl."   60

"*What?*"

"She wanted to see her brother. She's only a kid and she didn't know what she was really doing."

"I see." All the curtness was gone from the commander's voice. "So you called me in the hope I could do something?" Without waiting for an answer he went on. "I'm sorry—I can do nothing. This cruiser must maintain its schedule; the life of not one person but the lives of many depend on it. I know how you feel but I'm powerless to help you. You'll have to go through with it. I'll have you connected with Ship's Records."

The communicator faded to a faint rustle of sound and he turned back to the girl. She was leaning forward on the bench, almost rigid, her eyes fixed wide and frightened.

"What did he mean, to go through with it? To jettison me . . . to go   65
through with it—what did he mean? Not the way it sounded . . . he couldn't have. What did he mean . . . what did he really mean?"

Her time was too short for the comfort of a lie to be more than a cruelly fleeting delusion.

"He meant it the way it sounded."

"*No!*" She recoiled from him as though he had struck her, one hand half upraised as though to fend him off and stark unwillingness to believe in her eyes.

"It will have to be."

"No! You're joking—you're insane! You can't mean it!"   70

"I'm sorry." He spoke slowly to her, gently. "I should have told you before—I should have, but I had to do what I could first; I had to call the *Stardust*. You heard what the commander said."

"But you can't—if you make me leave the ship, I'll *die*."

"I know."

She searched his face and the unwillingness to believe left her eyes, giving way slowly to a look of dazed terror.

"You—know?" She spoke the words far apart, numb and wonder-   75
ingly.

"I know. It has to be like that."

"You mean it—you really mean it." She sagged back against the wall, small and limp like a little rag doll and all the protesting and disbelief gone.

"You're going to do it—you're going to make me die?"

"I'm sorry," he said again. "You'll never know how sorry I am. It has to be that way and no human in the universe can change it."

"You're going to make me die and I didn't do anything to die for—   80
I didn't *do* anything—"

He sighed, deep and weary. "I know you didn't, child. I know you didn't—"

"EDS." The communicator rapped brisk and metallic. "This is Ship's Records. Give us all information on subject's identification disk."

He got out of his chair to stand over her. She clutched the edge of the seat, her upturned face white under the brown hair and the lipstick standing out like a blood-red cupid's bow.

"*Now?*"

"I want your identification disk," he said.   85

She released the edge of the seat and fumbled at the chain that suspended the plastic disk from her neck with fingers that were trembling and awkward. He reached down and unfastened the clasp for her, then returned with the disk to his chair.

"Here's your data, Records: Identification Number T837—"

"One moment," Records interrupted. "This is to be filed on the gray card, of course?"

"Yes."

"And the time of the execution?"   90

"I'll tell you later."

"Later? This is highly irregular; the time of the subject's death is required before—"

He kept the thickness out of his voice with an effort. "Then we'll do it in a highly irregular manner—you'll hear the disk read, first. The subject is a girl and she's listening to everything that's said. Are you capable of understanding that?"

There was a brief, almost shocked, silence, then Records said meekly: "Sorry. Go ahead."

He began to read the disk, reading it slowly to delay the inevitable   *95* for as long as possible, trying to help her by giving her what little time he could to recover from her first terror and let it resolve into the calm of acceptance and resignation.

"Number T8374 dash Y54. Name: Marilyn Lee Cross. Sex: Female. Born: July 7, 2160. *She was only eighteen.* Height: 5–3. Weight: 110. *Such a slight weight, yet enough to add fatally to the mass of the shell-thin bubble that was an EDS.* Hair: Brown. Eyes: Blue. Complexion: Light. Blood Type: O. *Irrelevant data.* Destination: Port City, Mimir. *Invalid data*—"

He finished and said, "I'll call you later," then turned once again to the girl. She was huddled back against the wall, watching him with a look of numb and wondering fascination.

"They're waiting for you to kill me, aren't they? They want me dead, don't they? You and everybody on the cruiser wants me dead, don't you?" Then the numbness broke and her voice was that of a frightened and bewildered child. "Everybody wants me dead and I didn't *do* anything. I didn't hurt anyone—I only wanted to see my brother."

"It's not the way you think—it isn't that way, at all," he said. "Nobody wants it this way; nobody would ever let it be this way if it was humanly possible to change it."

"Then why is it! I don't understand. Why is it?"   *100*

"This ship is carrying *kala* fever serum to Group One on Woden. Their own supply was destroyed by a tornado. Group Two—the crew your brother is in—is eight thousand miles away across the Western Sea and their helicopters can't cross it to help Group One. The fever is invariably fatal unless the serum can be had in time, and the six men in Group One will die unless this ship reaches them on schedule. These little ships are always given barely enough fuel to reach their destination and if you stay aboard your added weight will cause it to use up all its fuel before it reaches the ground. It will crash, then, and you and I will die and so will the six men waiting for the serum."

It was a full minute before she spoke, and as she considered his words the expression of numbness left her eyes.

"Is that it?" she asked at last. "Just that the ship doesn't have enough fuel?"

"Yes."

she searches for a way out in a panic

"I can go alone or I can take seven others with me—is that the way it is?"   *105*

"That's the way it is."

"And nobody wants me to have to die?"

"Nobody."

"Then maybe—Are you sure nothing can be done about it? Wouldn't people help me if they could?"

"Everyone would like to help you but there is nothing anyone can do. I did the only thing I could do when I called the *Stardust*."   *110*

"And it won't come back—but there might be other cruisers, mightn't there? Isn't there any hope at all that there might be someone, some-where, who could do something to help me?"

She was leaning forward a little in her eagerness as she waited for his answer.

"No."

The word was like the drop of a cold stone and she again leaned back against the wall, the hope and eagerness leaving her face. "You're sure— you *know* you're sure?"

"I'm sure. There are no other cruisers within forty light-years; there is nothing and no one to change things."   *115*

She dropped her gaze to her lap and began twisting a pleat of her skirt between her fingers, saying no more as her mind began to adapt itself to the grim knowledge.

It was better so; with the going of all hope would go the fear; with the going of all hope would come resignation. She needed time and she could have so little of it. How much?

The EDS's were not equipped with hull-cooling units: their speed had to be reduced to a moderate level before entering the atmosphere. They were decelerating at .10 gravity; approaching their destination at a far higher speed than the computers had calculated on. The *Stardust* had been quite near Woden when she launched the EDS; their present ve-locity was putting them nearer by the second. There would be a critical point, soon to be reached, when he would have to resume deceleration. When he did so the girl's weight would be multiplied by the gravities of deceleration, would become, suddenly, a factor of paramount impor-tance; the factor the computers had been ignorant of when they deter-mined the amount of fuel the EDS should have. She would have to go when deceleration began; it could be no other way. When would that be—how long could he let her stay?

"How long can I stay?"

He winced involuntarily from the words that were so like an echo of his own thoughts. How long? He didn't know; he would have to ask the ship's computers. Each EDS was given a meager surplus of fuel to com-pensate for unfavorable conditions within the atmosphere and relatively little fuel was being consumed for the time being. The memory banks of   *120* the computers would still contain all data pertaining to the course set for the EDS; such data would not be erased until the EDS reached its destination. He had only to give the computers the new data; the girl's weight and the exact time at which he had reduced the deceleration to .10.

"Barton." Commander Delhart's voice came abruptly from the communicator, as he opened his mouth to call the *Stardust*. "A check with Records shows me you haven't completed your report. Did you reduce the deceleration?"

So the commander knew what he was trying to do.

"I'm decelerating at point ten," he answered. "I cut the deceleration at seventeen fifty and the weight is a hundred and ten. I would like to stay at point ten as long as the computers say I can. Will you give them the question?"

It was contrary to regulations for an EDS pilot to make any changes in the course or degree of deceleration the computers had set for him but the commander made no mention of the violation, neither did he ask the reason for it. It was not necessary for him to ask; he had not become commander of an interstellar cruiser without both intelligence and an understanding of human nature. He said only: "I'll have that given the computers."

The communicator fell silent and he and the girl waited, neither of them speaking. They would not have to wait long; the computers would give the answer within moments of the asking. The new factors would be fed into the steel maw of the first bank and the electrical impulses would go through the complex circuits. Here and there a relay might click, a tiny cog turn over, but it would be essentially the electrical impulses that found the answer: formless, mindless, invisible, determining with utter precision how long the pale girl beside him might live. Then five little segments of metal in the second bank would trip in rapid succession against an inked ribbon and a second steel maw would spit out the slip of paper that bore the answer.

The chronometer on the instrument board read 18:10 when the commander spoke again.

"You will resume deceleration at nineteen ten."

She looked toward the chronometer, then quickly away from it. "Is that when . . . when I go?" she asked. He nodded and she dropped her eyes to her lap again.

"I'll have the course corrections given you," the commander said. "Ordinarily I would never permit anything like this but I understand your position. There is nothing I can do, other than what I've just done, and you will not deviate from these new instructions. You will complete your report at nineteen ten. Now—here are the course corrections."

The voice of some unknown technician read them to him and he wrote them down on the pad clipped to the edge of the control board. There would, he saw, be periods of deceleration when he neared the atmosphere when the deceleration would be five gravities—and at five gravities, one hundred ten pounds would become five hundred fifty pounds.

The technician finished and he terminated the contact with a brief acknowledgment. Then, hesitating a moment, he reached out and shut off the communicator. It was 18:13 and he would have nothing to report until 19:10. In the meantime, it somehow seemed indecent to permit others to hear what she might say in her last hour.

He began to check the instrument readings, going over them with unnecessary slowness. She would have to accept the circumstances and there was nothing he could do to help her into acceptance; words of sympathy would only delay it.

It was 18:20 when she stirred from her motionlessness and spoke.

"So that's the way it has to be with me?"

He swung around to face her. "You understand now, don't you? No   *135* one would ever let it be like this if it could be changed."

"I understand," she said. Some of the color had returned to her face and the lipstick no longer stood out so vividly red. "There isn't enough fuel for me to stay; when I hid on this ship I got into something I didn't know anything about and now I have to pay for it."

She had violated a man-made law that said KEEP OUT but the penalty was not of men's making or desire and it was a penalty men could not revoke. A physical law had decreed: *h amount of fuel will power an EDS with a mass of m safely to its destination;* and a second physical law had decreed: *h amount of fuel will not power an EDS with a mass of m plus x safely to its destination.*

EDS's obeyed only physical laws and no amount of human sympathy for her could alter the second law.

"But I'm afraid. I don't want to die—not now. I want to live and nobody is doing anything to help me; everybody is letting me go ahead and acting just like nothing was going to happen to me. I'm going to die and nobody *cares.*"

"We all do," he said. "I do and the commander does and the clerk   *140* in Ship's Records; we all care and each of us did what little he could to help you. It wasn't enough—it was almost nothing—but it was all we could do."

"Not enough fuel—I can understand that," she said, as though she had not heard his own words. "But to have to die for it. *Me,* alone—"

How hard it must be for her to accept the fact. She had never known danger of death: had never known the environments where the lives of men could be as fragile and fleeting as sea foam tossed against a rocky shore. She belonged on gentle Earth, in that secure and peaceful society where she could be young and gay and laughing with the others of her kind; where life was precious and well-guarded and there was always the assurance that tomorrow would come. She belonged in the world of soft winds and warm suns, music and moonlight and gracious manners and not on the hard, bleak frontier.

"How did it happen to me, so terribly quick? An hour ago I was on the *Stardust,* going to Mimir. Now the *Stardust* is going on without me and I'm going to die and I'll never see Gerry and Mama and Daddy again—I'll never see anything again."

He hesitated, wondering how he could explain it to her so she would really understand and not feel she had, somehow, been the victim of a reasonlessly cruel injustice. She did not know what the frontier was like; she thought in terms of safe-and-secure Earth. Pretty girls were not jettisoned on Earth; there was a law against it. On Earth her plight would have filled the newscasts and a fast black Patrol ship would have been racing to her rescue. Everyone, everywhere, would have known of Marilyn Lee Cross and no effort would have been spared to save her life. But this was not Earth and there were no Patrol ships; only the *Stardust* leaving them behind at many times the speed of light. There was no one to help her, there would be no Marilyn Lee Cross smiling from the newscasts tomorrow. Marilyn Lee Cross would be but a poignant memory for an EDS pilot and a name on a gray card in Ship's Records.

"It's different here; it's not like back on Earth," he said. "It isn't that   *145* no one cares; it's that no one can do anything to help. The frontier is big and here along its rim the colonies and exploration parties are scattered so thin and far between. On Woden, for example, there are only sixteen men—sixteen men on an entire world. The exploration parties, the survey crews, the little first-colonies—they're all fighting alien environments, trying to make a way for those who will follow after. The environments fight back and those who go first usually make mistakes only once. There is no margin of safety along the rim of the frontier; there can't be until the way is made for the others who will come later, until the new worlds are tamed and settled. Until then men will have to pay the penalty for making mistakes with no one to help them because there is no one *to* help them."

"I was going to Mimir," she said. "I didn't know about the frontier; I was only going to Mimir and *it's* safe."

"Mimir is safe but you left the cruiser that was taking you there."

She was silent for a little while. "It was all so wonderful at first; there was plenty of room for me on this ship and I would be seeing Gerry so soon . . . I didn't know about the fuel, didn't know what would happen to me—"

Her words trailed away and he turned his attention to the viewscreen, not wanting to stare at her as she fought her way through the black horror of fear toward the calm gray of acceptance.

Woden was a ball, enshrouded in the blue haze of its atmosphere,   *150* swimming in space against the background of star-sprinkled dead blackness. The great mass of Manning's Continent sprawled like a gigantic hourglass in the Eastern Sea with the western half of the Eastern Continent still visible. There was a thin line of shadow along the right-hand edge of the globe and the Eastern Continent was disappearing into it as the planet turned on its axis. An hour before the entire continent had been in view, now a thousand miles of it had gone into the edge of shadow and around to the night that lay on the other side of the world. The dark blue spot that was Lotus Lake was approaching the shadow. It was somewhere near the southern edge of the lake that Group Two had their camp. It would be night there, soon, and quick behind the coming of night the rotation of Woden on its axis would put Group Two beyond the reach of the ship's radio.

He would have to tell her before it was too late for her to talk to her brother. In a way, it would be better for both of them should they not do so but it was not for him to decide. To each of them the last words would be something to hold and cherish, something that would cut like the blade of a knife yet would be infinitely precious to remember, she for her own brief moments and he for the rest of his life.

He held down the button that would flash the grid lines on the viewscreen and used the known diameter of the planet to estimate the distance the southern tip of Lotus Lake had yet to go until it passed beyond radio range. It was approximately five hundred miles. Five hundred miles; thirty minutes—and the chronometer read 18:30. Allowing for error in estimating, it could not be later than 19:05 that the turning of Woden would cut off her brother's voice.

The first border of the Western Continent was already in sight along the left side of the world. Four thousand miles across it lay the shore of the Western Sea and the Camp of Group One. It had been in the Western Sea that the tornado had originated, to strike with such fury at the camp and destroy half their prefabricated buildings, including the one that housed the medical supplies. Two days before the tornado had not existed; it had been no more than great gentle masses of air out over the calm Western Sea. Group One had gone about their routine survey work, unaware of the meeting of the air masses out at sea, unaware of the force the union was spawning. It had struck their camp without warning; a thundering, roaring destruction that sought to annihilate all that lay before it. It had passed on, leaving the wreckage in its wake. It had destroyed the labor of months and had doomed six men to die and then, as though its task was accomplished, it once more began to resolve into gentle masses of air. But for all its deadliness, it had destroyed with neither malice nor intent. It had been a blind and mindless force, obeying the laws of nature, and it would have followed the same course with the same fury had men never existed.

Existence required Order and there was order; the laws of nature, irrevocable and immutable. Men could learn to use them but men could not change them. The circumference of a circle was always pi times the diameter and no science of Man would ever make it otherwise. The combination of chemical A with chemical B under condition C invariably produced reaction D. The law of gravitation was a rigid equation and it made no distinction between the fall of a leaf and the ponderous circling of a binary star system. The nuclear conversion process powered the cruisers that carried men to the stars; the same process in the form of a nova would destroy a world with equal efficiency. The laws *were,* and the universe moved in obedience to them. Along the frontier were arrayed all the forces of nature and sometimes they destroyed those who were fighting their way outward from Earth. The men of the frontier had long ago learned the bitter futility of cursing the forces that would destroy them for the forces were blind and deaf; the futility of looking to the heavens for mercy, for the stars of the galaxy swung in their long, long sweep of two hundred million years, as inexorably controlled as they by the laws that knew neither hatred nor compassion.

The men of the frontier knew—but how was a girl from Earth to   155
fully understand? *H amount of fuel will not power an EDS with a mass of m plus x safely to its destination.* To himself and her brother and parents she was a sweet-faced girl in her teens; to the laws of nature she was *x,* the unwanted factor in a cold equation.

She stirred again on the seat. "Could I write a letter? I want to write to Mama and Daddy and I'd like to talk to Gerry. Could you let me talk to him over your radio there?"

"I'll try to get him," he said.

He switched on the normal-space transmitter and pressed the signal button. Someone answered the buzzer almost immediately.

"Hello. How's it going with you fellows now—is the EDS on its way?"

"This isn't Group One; this is the EDS," he said. "Is Gerry Cross   160
there?"

"Gerry? He and two others went out in the helicopter this morning and aren't back yet. It's almost sundown, though, and he ought to be back right away—in less than an hour at the most."

"Can you connect me through to the radio in his 'copter?"

"Huh-uh. It's been out of commission for two months—some printed circuits went haywire and we can't get any more until the next cruiser stops by. Is it something important—bad news for him, or something?"

"Yes—it's very important. When he comes in get him to the transmitter as soon as you possibly can."

"I'll do that; I'll have one of the boys waiting at the field with a truck.   165
Is there anything else I can do?"

"No, I guess that's all. Get him there as soon as you can and signal me."

He turned the volume to an inaudible minimum, an act that would not affect the functioning of the signal buzzer, and unclipped the pad of paper from the control board. He tore off the sheet containing his flight instructions and handed the pad to her, together with pencil.

"I'd better write to Gerry, too," she said as she took them. "He might not get back to camp in time."

She began to write, her fingers still clumsy and uncertain in the way they handled the pencil and the top of it trembling a little as she poised it between words. He turned back to the viewscreen, to stare at it without seeing it.

She was a lonely little child, trying to say her good-by, and she would
lay out her heart to them. She would tell them how much she loved them and she would tell them not to feel badly about it, that it was only something that must happen eventually to everyone and she was not afraid. The last would be a lie and it would be there to read between the sprawling, uneven lines; a valiant little lie that would make the hurt all the greater for them.

Her brother was of the frontier and he would understand. He would not hate the EDS pilot for doing nothing to prevent her going; he would know there had been nothing the pilot could do. He would understand, though the understanding would not soften the shock and pain when he learned his sister was gone. But the others, her father and mother—they would not understand. They were of Earth and they would think in the manner of those who had never lived where the safety margin of life was a thin, thin line—and sometimes not at all. What would they think of the faceless, unknown pilot who had sent her to her death?

They would hate him with cold and terrible intensity but it really didn't matter. He would never see them, never know them. He would have only the memories to remind him; only the nights to fear, when a blue-eyed girl in gypsy sandals would come in his dreams to die again—

He scowled at the viewscreen and tried to force his thoughts into less emotional channels. There was nothing he could do to help her. She had unknowingly subjected herself to the penalty of a law that recognized neither innocence nor youth nor beauty, that was incapable of sympathy or leniency. Regret was illogical—and yet, could knowing it to be illogical ever keep it away?

She stopped occasionally, as though trying to find the right words to tell them what she wanted them to know, then the pencil would resume its whispering to the paper. It was 18:37 when she folded the letter in a square and wrote a name on it. She began writing another, twice looking up at the chronometer as though she feared the black hand might reach its rendezvous before she had finished. It was 18:45 when she folded it as she had done the first letter and wrote a name and address on it.

She held the letters out to him. "Will you take care of these and see
that they're enveloped and mailed?"

"Of course." He took them from her hand and placed them in a pocket of his gray uniform shirt.

"These can't be sent off until the next cruiser stops by and the *Stardust* will have long since told them about me, won't it?" she asked. He nodded

170

175

and she went on, "That makes the letters not important in one way but in another way they're very important—to me, and to them."

"I know. I understand, and I'll take care of them."

She glanced at the chronometer, then back to him. "It seems to move faster all the time, doesn't it?"

He said nothing, unable to think of anything to say, and she asked,   *180*
"Do you think Gerry will come back to camp in time?"

"I think so. They said he should be in right away."

She began to roll the pencil back and forth between her palms. "I hope he does. I feel sick and scared and I want to hear his voice again and maybe I won't feel so alone. I'm a coward and I can't help it."

"No," he said, "you're not a coward. You're afraid, but you're not a coward."

"Is there a difference?"

He nodded. "A lot of difference."   *185*

"I feel so alone. I never did feel like this before; like I was all by myself and there was nobody to care what happened to me. Always, before, there was Mama and Daddy there and my friends around me. I had lots of friends, and they had a going-away party for me the night before I left."

Friends and music and laughter for her to remember—and on the viewscreen Lotus Lake was going into the shadow.

"Is it the same with Gerry?" she asked. "I mean, if he should make a mistake, would he die for it, all alone and with no one to help him?"

"It's the same with all along the frontier; it will always be like that so long as there is a frontier."

"Gerry didn't tell us. He said the pay was good and he sent money   *190*
home all the time because Daddy's little shop just brought in a bare living but he didn't tell us it was like this."

"He didn't tell you his work was dangerous?"

"Well—yes. He mentioned that, but we didn't understand. I always thought danger along the frontier was something that was a lot of fun; an exciting adventure, like in the three-D shows." A wan smile touched her face for a moment. "Only it's not, is it? It's not the same at all, because when it's real you can't go home after the show is over."

"No," he said. "No, you can't."

Her glance flicked from the chronometer to the door of the air lock then down to the pad and pencil she still held. She shifted her position slightly to lay them on the bench beside, moving one foot out a little. For the first time he saw that she was not wearing Vegan gypsy sandals but only cheap imitations; the expensive Vegan leather was some kind of grained plastic, the silver buckle was gilded iron, the jewels were colored glass. *Daddy's little shop just brought in a bare living*—She must have left college in her second year, to take the course in linguistics that would enable her to make her own way and help her brother provide for her parents, earning what she could by part-time work after classes were over. Her personal possessions on the *Stardust* would be taken back to her parents—they would neither be of much value nor occupy much storage space on the return voyage.

"Isn't it—" She stopped, and he looked at her questioningly. "Isn't it   *195*
cold in here?" she asked, almost apologetically. "Doesn't it seem cold to you?"

"Why, yes," he said. He saw by the main temperature gauge that the room was at precisely normal temperature. "Yes, it's colder than it should be."

"I wish Gerry would get back before it's too late. Do you really think he will, and you didn't just say so to make me feel better?"

"I think he will—they said he would be in pretty soon." On the viewscreen Lotus Lake had gone into the shadow but for the thin blue line of its western edge and it was apparent he had overestimated the time she would have in which to talk to her brother. Reluctantly, he said to her, "His camp will be out of radio range in a few minutes; he's on that part of Woden that's in the shadow"—he indicated the viewscreen— "and the turning of Woden will put him beyond contact. There may not be much time left when he comes in—not much time to talk to him before he fades out. I wish I could do something about it—I would call him right now if I could."

"Not even as much time as I will have to stay?"

"I'm afraid not."   *200*

"Then—" She straightened and looked toward the air lock with pale resolution. "Then I'll go when Gerry passes beyond range. I won't wait any longer after that—I won't have anything to wait for."

Again there was nothing he could say.

"Maybe I shouldn't wait at all. Maybe I'm selfish—maybe it would be better for Gerry if you just told him about it afterward."

There was an unconscious pleading for denial in the way she spoke and he said, "He wouldn't want you to do that, to not wait for him."

"It's already coming dark where he is, isn't it? There will be all the   *205*
long night before him, and Mama and Daddy don't know yet that I won't ever be coming back like I promised them I would. I've caused everyone I love to be hurt, haven't I? I didn't want to—I didn't intend to."

"It wasn't your fault," he said. "It wasn't your fault at all. They'll know that. They'll understand."

"At first I was so afraid to die that I was a coward and thought only of myself. Now, I see how selfish I was. The terrible thing about dying like this is not that I'll be gone but that I'll never see them again; never be able to tell them that I didn't take them for granted; never be able to tell them I knew of the sacrifices they made to make my life happier, that I knew all the things they did for me and that I loved them so much more than I ever told them. I've never told them any of those things. You don't tell them such things when you're young and your life is all before you— you're afraid of sounding sentimental and silly.

"But it's so different when you have to die—you wish you had told them while you could and you wish you could tell them you're sorry for all the little mean things you ever did or said to them. You wish you could tell them that you didn't really mean to ever hurt their feelings and for them to only remember that you always loved them far more than you ever let them know."

"You don't have to tell them that," he said. "They will know—they've always known it."

"Are you sure?" she asked, "How can you be sure? My people are strangers to you."   *210*

"Wherever you go, human nature and human hearts are the same."

"And they will know what I want them to know—that I love them?"

"They've always known it, in a way far better than you could ever put in words for them."

"I keep remembering the things they did for me, and it's the little things they did that seem to be the most important to me, now. Like Gerry—he sent me a bracelet of fire-rubies on my sixteenth birthday. It was beautiful—it must have cost him a month's pay. Yet, I remember him more for what he did the night my kitten got run over in the street. I was only six years old and he held me in his arms and wiped away my tears and told me not to cry, that Flossy was gone for just a little while, for just long enough to get herself a new fur coat and she would be on the foot of my bed the very next morning. I believed him and quit crying and went to sleep dreaming about my kitten coming back. When I woke up the next morning, there was Flossy on the foot of my bed in a brand-new white fur coat, just like he had said she would be.

"It wasn't until a long time later that Mama told me Gerry had got the pet-shop owner out of bed at four in the morning and, when the man got mad about it, Gerry told him he was either going to go down and sell him the white kitten right then or he'd break his neck."   *215*

"It's always the little things you remember people by; all the little things they did because they wanted to do them for you. You've done the same for Gerry and your father and mother; all kinds of things that you've forgotten about but that they will never forget."

"I hope I have. I would like for them to remember me like that."

"They will."

"I wish—" She swallowed. "The way I'll die—I wish they wouldn't ever think of that. I've read how people look who die in space—their insides all ruptured and exploded and their lungs out between their teeth and then, a few seconds later, they're all dry and shapeless and horribly ugly. I don't want them to ever think of me as something dead and horrible, like that."

"You're their own, their child and their sister. They could never think of you other than the way you would want them to; the way you looked the last time they saw you."   *220*

"I'm still afraid," she said. "I can't help it, but I don't want Gerry to know it. If he gets back in time, I'm going to act like I'm not afraid at all and—"

The signal buzzer interrupted her, quick and imperative.

"Gerry!" She came to her feet. "It's Gerry, now!"

He spun the volume control knob and asked: "Gerry Cross?"

"Yes," her brother answered, an undertone of tenseness to his reply.   225
"The bad news—what is it?"

She answered for him, standing close behind him and leaning down a little toward the communicator, her hand resting small and cold on his shoulder.

"Hello, Gerry." There was only a faint quaver to betray the careful casualness of her voice. "I wanted to see you—"

"Marilyn!" There was sudden and terrible apprehension in the way he spoke her name. "What are you doing on that EDS?"

"I wanted to see you," she said again. "I wanted to see you, so I hid on this ship—"

"You *hid* on it?"   230

"I'm a stowaway . . . I didn't know what it would mean—"

"*Marilyn!*" It was the cry of a man who calls hopeless and desperate to someone already and forever gone from him. "What have you done?"

"I . . . it's not—" Then her own composure broke and the cold little hand gripped his shoulder convulsively. "Don't Gerry—I only wanted to see you; I didn't intend to hurt you. Please, Gerry, don't feel like that—"

Something warm and wet splashed on his wrist and he slid out of the chair, to help her into it and swing the microphone down to her own level.

"Don't feel like that— Don't let me go knowing you feel like that—"   235

The sob she had tried to hold back choked in her throat and her brother spoke to her. "Don't cry, Marilyn." His voice was suddenly deep and infinitely gentle, with all the pain held out of it. "Don't cry, Sis—you mustn't do that. It's all right, Honey—everything is all right."

"I—" Her lower lip quivered and she bit into it. "I didn't want you to feel that way—I just wanted us to say good-by because I have to go in a minute."

"Sure—sure. That's the way it will be, Sis. I didn't mean to sound the way I did." Then his voice changed to a tone of quick and urgent demand. "EDS—have you called the *Stardust?* Did you check with the computers?"

"I called the *Stardust* almost an hour ago. It can't turn back, there are no other cruisers within forty light-years, and there isn't enough fuel."

"Are you sure that the computers had the correct data—sure of   240
everything?"

"Yes—do you think I could ever let it happen if I wasn't sure? I did everything I could do. If there was anything at all I could do now, I would do it."

"He tried to help me, Gerry." Her lower lip was no longer trembling and the short sleeves of her blouse were wet where she had dried her tears. "No one can help me and I'm not going to cry any more and everything will be all right with you and Daddy and Mama, won't it?"

"Sure—sure it will. We'll make out fine."

Her brother's words were beginning to come in more faintly and he turned the volume control to maximum. "He's going out of range," he said to her. "He'll be gone within another minute."

"You're fading out, Gerry," she said. "You're going out of range. I wanted to tell you—but I can't, now. We must say good-by so soon—but maybe I'll see you again. Maybe I'll come to you in your dreams with my hair in braids and crying because the kitten in my arms is dead; maybe I'll be the touch of a breeze that whispers to you as it goes by; maybe I'll be one of those gold-winged larks you told me about, singing my silly head off to you; maybe, at times, I'll be nothing you can see but you will know I'm there beside you. Think of me like that, Gerry; always like that and not—the other way." 245

Dimmed to a whisper by the turning of Woden, the answer came back:

"Always like that, Marilyn—always like that and never any other way."

"Our time is up, Gerry—I have to go now. Good—" Her voice broke in mid-word and her mouth tried to twist into crying. She pressed her hand hard against it and when she spoke again the words came clear and true:

"Good-by, Gerry."

Faint and ineffably poignant and tender, the last words came from the cold metal of the communicator: 250

"Good-by, little sister—"

She sat motionless in the hush that followed, as though listening to the shadow-echoes of the words as they died away, then she turned away from the communicator, toward the air lock, and he pulled the black lever beside him. The inner door of the air lock slid swiftly open, to reveal the bare little cell that was waiting for her, and she walked to it.

She walked with her head up and the brown curls brushing her shoulders, with the white sandals stepping as sure and steady as the fractional gravity would permit and the gilded buckles twinkling with little lights of blue and red and crystal. He let her walk alone and made no move to help her, knowing she would not want it that way. She stepped into the air lock and turned to face him, only the pulse in her throat to betray the wild beating of her heart.

"I'm ready," she said.

He pushed the lever up and the door slid its quick barrier between them, enclosing her in black and utter darkness for her last moments of life. It clicked as it locked in place and he jerked down the red lever. There was a slight waver to the ship as the air gushed from the lock, a 255 vibration to the wall as though something had bumped the outer door in passing, then there was nothing and the ship was dropping true and steady again. He shoved the red lever back to close the door on the empty air lock and turned away, to walk to the pilot's chair with the slow steps of a man old and weary.

Back in the pilot's chair he pressed the signal button of the normal-space transmitter. There was no response; he had expected none. Her brother would have to wait through the night until the turning of Woden permitted contact through Group One.

It was not yet time to resume deceleration and he waited while the ship dropped endlessly downward with him and the drives purred softly. He saw that the white hand of the supplies closet temperature gauge was on zero. A cold equation had been balanced and he was alone on the ship. Something shapeless and ugly was hurrying ahead of him, going to Woden where its brother was waiting through the night, but the empty ship still lived for a little while with the presence of the girl who had not known about the forces that killed with neither hatred nor malice. It seemed, almost, that she still sat small and bewildered and frightened on the metal box beside him, her words echoing hauntingly clear in the void she had left behind her:

I didn't do anything to die for—I didn't do anything—

THE DEATH OF THE MOTH

Virginia Woolf

Moths that fly by day are not properly to be called moths; they do not excite that pleasant sense of dark autumn nights and ivy-blossom which the commonest yellow underwing asleep in the shadow of the curtain never fails to rouse in us. They are hybrid creatures, neither gay like butterflies nor sombre like their own species. Nevertheless the present specimen, with his narrow hay-coloured wings, fringed with a tassel of the same colour, seemed to be content with life. It was a pleasant morning, mid-September, mild, benignant, yet with a keener breath than that of the summer months. The plough was already scoring the field opposite the window, and where the share had been, the earth was pressed flat and gleamed with moisture. Such vigour came rolling in from the fields and the down beyond that it was difficult to keep the eyes strictly turned upon the book. The rooks too were keeping one of their annual festivities; soaring round the tree-tops until it looked as if a vast net with thousands of black knots in it has been cast up into the air; which, after a few moments sank slowly down upon the trees until every twig seemed to have a knot at the end of it. Then, suddenly, the net would be thrown into the air again in a wider circle this time, with the utmost clamour and vociferation, as though to be thrown into the air and settle slowly down upon the tree-tops were a tremendously exciting experience.

The same energy which inspired the rooks, the ploughmen, the horses, and even, it seemed, the lean bare-backed downs, sent the moth fluttering from side to side of his square of the window-pane. One could not help watching him. One was, indeed, conscious of a queer feeling of pity for him. The possibilities of pleasure seemed that morning so enormous and so various that to have only a moth's part in life, and a day moth's at that, appeared a hard fate, and his zest in enjoying his meagre opportunities to the full, pathetic. He flew vigorously to one corner of his compartment, and, after waiting there a second, flew across to the other. What remained for him but to fly to a third corner and then to a fourth? That was all he could do, in spite of the size of the downs, the width of the sky, the far-off smoke of houses, and the romantic voice, now and then, of a steamer out at sea. What he could do he did. Watching him, it seemed as if a fiber, very thin but pure, of the enormous energy of the world had been thrust into his frail and diminutive body. As often as he crossed the pane, I could fancy that a thread of vital light became visible. He was little or nothing but life.

Yet, because he was so small, and so simple a form of the energy that was rolling in at the open window and driving its way through so many narrow and intricate corridors in my own brain and in those of other human beings, there was something marvelous as well as pathetic about him. It was as if someone had taken a tiny bead of pure life and decking it as lightly as possible with down and feathers, had set it dancing and zigzagging to show us the true nature of life. Thus displayed one could not get over the strangeness of it. One is apt to forget all about life, seeing it humped and bossed and garnished and cumbered so that it has to move with the greatest circumspection and dignity. Again, the thought of all that life might have been had he been born in any other shape caused one to view his simple activities with a kind of pity.

After a time, tired by his dancing apparently, he settled on the window ledge in the sun, and the queer spectacle being at an end, I forgot about him. Then, looking up, my eye was caught by him. He was trying to resume his dancing, but seemed either so stiff or so awkward that he could only flutter to the bottom of the window-pane; and when he tried to fly across it he failed. Being intent on other matters I watched these futile attempts for a time without thinking, unconsciously waiting for him to resume his flight, as one waits for a machine, that has stopped momentarily, to start again without considering the reason for its failure. After perhaps a seventh attempt he slipped from the wooden ledge and fell, fluttering his wings, on to his back on the window-sill. The helplessness of his attitude roused me. It flashed upon me that he was in difficulties; he could no longer raise himself; his legs struggled vainly. But, as I stretched out a pencil, meaning to help him to right himself, it came over *death*

me that the failure and awkwardness were the approach of death. I laid the pencil down again.

The legs agitated themselves once more. I looked as if for the enemy   5
against which he struggled. I looked out of doors. What had happened there? Presumably it was midday, and work in the fields had stopped. Stillness and quiet had replaced the previous animation. The birds had taken themselves off to feed in the brooks. The horses stood still. Yet the power was there all the same, massed outside indifferent, impersonal, not attending to anything in particular. Somehow it was opposed to the little hay-coloured moth. It was useless to try to do anything. One could only watch the extraordinary efforts made by those tiny legs against an oncoming doom which could, had it chosen, have submerged an entire city, not merely a city, but masses of human beings; nothing, I knew, had any chance against death. Nevertheless after a pause of exhaustion the legs fluttered again. It was superb this last protest, and so frantic that he succeeded at last in righting himself. One's sympathies, of course, were all on the side of life. Also, when there was nobody to care or to know, this gigantic effort on the part of an insignificant little moth, against a power of such magnitude, to retain what no one else valued or desired to keep, moved one strangely. Again, somehow, one saw life, a pure bead. I lifted the pencil again, useless though I knew it to be. But even as I did so, the unmistakable tokens of death showed themselves. The body relaxed, and instantly grew stiff. The struggle was over. The insignificant little creature now knew death. As I looked at the dead moth, this minute wayside triumph of so great a force over so mean an antagonist filled me with wonder. Just as life had been strange a few minutes before, so death was now as strange. The moth having righted himself now lay most decently and uncomplainingly composed. O yes, he seemed to say, death is stronger than I am.

describes his death

DESIGN

Robert Frost

I found a dimpled spider, fat and white,
On a white heal-all,° holding up a moth
Like a white piece of rigid satin cloth—
Assorted characters of death and blight
Mixed ready to begin the morning right,   5
Like the ingredients of a witches' broth—
A snow-drop spider, a flower like a froth,
And dead wings carried like a paper kite.

---

2. *heal-all:* a plant said to have healing properties

What had that flower to do with being white,
The wayside blue and innocent heal-all?   *10*
What brought the kindred spider to that height,
Then steered the white moth thither in the night?
What but design of darkness to appall?—
If design govern in a thing so small. ·

Write a short statement answering each of the following questions. If you are working with a group, meet and compare your answers with those of the other group members. After discussion, write a collaborative answer to each of the questions. Compare your group's conclusions with those of other groups.

1. What do you think is the dominant idea of each selection?

2. Are there ways in which the dominant ideas of the three selections are similar to each other? Are there ways in which they are different?

3. If you see similarities among the dominant ideas of the selections, can you develop a comprehensive dominant idea of your own that pulls together the similar elements in the selections?

4. If you have created a comprehensive dominant idea, write a short statement showing how your experiences reflect that dominant idea.

5. Do you think Woolf tells you the whole truth? Do you think Frost and Godwin tell you lies?

6. Do you think it's necessary for Godwin and Frost to tell you the factual truth to speak to your experience with the issues they take up?

✒ *An Invitation to Write*

After reading the three selections, take what you consider to be the most important idea that links them and connect it to your own experience—things you've seen, heard about, and done. Write an account of an event that reflects the idea as you experienced and understand it. Feel free to write a poem, a story, or a short drama instead of an essay.

YOU ALREADY TALK AND WRITE GRAMMATICALLY

In writing, grammar is the set of rules by which you shape and arrange words to make your ideas and the relationships between them clear to other people. Through speech, you have been making yourself understood with strings of words since you were one or two years old. Much of what you did naturally in speech carried over later to your writing. You've been speaking and writing for some time, and you've been able to make yourself more or less understood along the way.

Like everyone else, you make most of your grammatical choices unconsciously. Talking and writing are so much a part of your life that you rarely think about your grammar. And in most cases, when you must make yourself understood through language, you make effective choices. The writer of the selection that opens this book made many excellent choices without thinking about them.

However, you can become aware of grammar not just as a pattern of relationships you have mastered without thinking much about them but as a set of tools you can consciously use to arrange your thoughts in various ways. A conscious awareness of grammatical relationships will help you discover the places in your writing where an unconscious choice did not work out as well as you had hoped, and you'll be able to think about ways to make your writing more effective. You'll also find yourself recognizing and admiring your successful choices, as well as those of other writers in your class and those of writers whose work appears in this book. Knowledge of the options lets you use them in other writing. Developing the ability to stand back from your and others' grammatical choices and to think about them will help you say what you mean to say more clearly and to understand where your preliminary writing might have gone wrong. That ability will also help you help other writers discover better ways of making themselves clear to their readers. This skill—to establish a distance between yourself and your work and to look at your choices as if they were another person's—is the mark of an effective writer, a person whose ability in grammar has become conscious. This conscious knowledge becomes a powerfully useful tool when it is applied to your own and others' writing.

YOU ALREADY USE RHETORIC

More than two thousand years ago Aristotle said that rhetoric is the discovery of the best available means of persuasion. According to that definition, you have been practicing rhetoric all your life.

Through nonverbal means, babies persuade their parents to do what they want. When you were a child, you were probably an expert at judging your audience and acting or speaking in such a way as to persuade that audience to do what you wanted. As you gained more experience and learned from the results of your choices, your talent grew. Through trial and error you learned which alternatives worked best and refined your talent. By this time, you are probably good at discovering effective means of persuasion in different situations.

Looking at the piece of student writing that begins this book, you can see that the writer made many effective rhetorical choices: the order in which he presented his material, the way he moved from general statements to specific examples, and the way he appealed to his readers' senses. Like this writer, you probably make most of your choices without consciously thinking a great deal about the alternatives. As you become conscious of the many choices available to you, you will become a better editor of your writing as well as of the writing of others.

THERE IS STRENGTH IN NUMBERS

The many readings—essays, short stories, poems, and short plays—in this book represent different approaches to organizing ideas and experiences, different voices, and different grammatical choices. Many of these readings will raise issues or questions in your mind and remind you of experiences in your own life. Many of these readings are accompanied by questions as well as by invitations to write about the issues these works raise as those issues collide with your experiences and your ideas.

You can respond to these questions in two ways: working alone or with a group. Circumstances or your instructor will probably determine which alternative you use. There is much to be said, however, for working with a group.

As writers work at shaping their writing, many find themselves growing too close to their words and ideas and too committed to the choices they've made. This commitment causes them to miss problems they have created for themselves, to forget that they are not the only readers of their work, or to overlook possibilities for conveying their ideas and attitudes more clearly. Groups help writers avoid these problems. A fresh reader can alert you to problems in your writing that you might miss if you read it yourself. Also, another person can suggest voices, ideas, examples, or ways of organizing and shaping your message that you had not thought of.

Your instructor may form your class into writing groups (four or fewer members is best), or you and some other students may decide to form a group on your own. Your group might meet weekly, once every two weeks, during each class for a specified amount of time, or some combination of these. Here are some ways of structuring the group's work that have proven effective.

Because the aim of a writing group is to work with each member's writing to point the writer toward ways of making his or her work stronger, it's important that each member of the group receive a copy of every member's draft well before the group meeting. It's impossible for one writer to help another unless the helper has had time to read and think about the writer's draft. Judgments off the top of one's head can sometimes do a great deal more harm than good. Arrange matters so that each member of the group gets a copy of every member's draft well ahead of the meeting time.

When you work in groups, you may be told, or you may decide, to concentrate on one group member's paper at each meeting. Another possibility is to look at a draft from each member at every meeting. Or you can compromise. The decision you make will probably depend on the time allotted for group meetings. In addition, because every group is unique, each group will establish a rhythm of its own. Some groups find it more comfortable to work slowly and methodically through one paper at a time, no matter how long it takes. Other groups find they work best by first moving quickly through the members' writings and then returning to each piece as many times as necessary. Discover your group's rhythm, and within the limits of the time available, follow it.

During your first meetings, concentrate on creating an atmosphere of mutual trust. Although some writers may not admit it, most invest a good deal of their egos in their writing; starting by pointing out what is wrong with a paper often creates resentment and defensiveness. Because a resentful or defensive person doesn't listen to others very well, these responses practically guarantee a group's failure.

Furthermore, at first you probably will not know the other members of your group. It's difficult to trust someone you don't know or to take his or her advice. During the first meetings, try pointing out to the other members of the group what you think is successful in their work. This approach allows group members to learn each other's strengths and to begin to understand each other's interests and ideas in an atmosphere of mutual trust and concern. There will be plenty of time to deal with the problems in members' papers. But those problems can be far more effectively confronted when every member of the group knows that all the other members are interested in helping his or her writing improve.

When you begin your group meetings, establish a set of steps that your group follows for each paper. Some steps that have worked for other writing groups follow, but they are certainly not the only way to run a writing group. Your teacher may have other preferences. Give this sequence a try, but don't feel bound by it. Your group might eliminate or modify some of the steps, change their order, or invent an entirely new stage in the process. Your group's only goal should be to establish a group process that helps each member become a better writer, reader, and helper.

WRITING GROUP PROCEDURES

1. *Each writer should read his or her paper out loud to the rest of the group.* While the writer is reading, the other group members should follow along silently on their copies, making quick, simple notes in the margins about issues they want to raise during the discussion that will follow.

Writing represents spoken language, and most of us hear the writing we read. Often a sentence or a phrase that seemed effective to the writer while he or she drafted the paper and to the readers while they read the paper silently does not work well when the readers—and the writer, too—hear it.

Making notes in the margins facilitates the real work of the group: discussion of the paper. Noting points you'd like to raise later ensures that you'll remember them.

2. *After the writer has read his or her paper aloud, the members of the group should read the paper silently.* During the silent reading, each group member can expand or add to the marginal notes to reflect other issues that may arise.

Listening to somebody read is a linear experience. You are carried along on the flow of the words, hearing what is effective, getting a sense of the paper as somebody's voice speaking to you. When you read silently, you can take your time, going back over certain parts to see how those parts mesh with other parts of the paper. Hearing a paper read aloud can sensitize you to the sound of a person's writing, but reading silently helps you sense the work's logic: how well the parts fit together, whether any of those parts seem to distract you from the writer's central idea or purpose as you understand it.

3. *After every member of the group is finished reading silently, the writer of the paper should comment on it,* pointing out those parts he or she is especially happy with, parts that seem to be effective. The writer should also point out those parts of the paper that seem to be less effective, that gave the writer problems that remain unsolved. In both cases, the writer should support his or her opinions by explaining why the successful parts are successful and why the less effective parts do not work as well as he or she hoped.

By evaluating your own work, you are training yourself to think critically about your writing. To make judgments about your writing, you have to stand back from it and think about the choices you made—how well they reflect your aims and your central idea. In other words, you have to try to evaluate your paper as if you were not its writer.

4. *Now each member of the group should respond to the writer's comments.* The members may find that the writer's sense of what is effective or ineffective about the paper is accurate, and they should acknowledge this. But it is equally possible that readers of the paper may disagree with the writer's assessment of what parts succeed and what parts cause problems. In either case, the following is especially important: If you agree with the writer that a part of his or her writing is especially effective, be sure to give reasons for your agreement. If you agree with the writer that a certain part of the draft causes problems, be ready to suggest solutions to those problems. If you disagree with the writer, be certain to give reasons for your disagreement. Again, if you are pointing out a problem, be ready to come up with possible solutions to it.

The writer should listen and take notes. He or she should speak only to answer questions from other members of the group.

This step reminds you that readers who don't know you well need extra help in order not to have to guess at what you mean. Hearing what other group members have to say about what you consider to be the strengths and weaknesses of your paper shows you how your writing comes across to them.

5. *Take time for free discussion of the draft.* Did some of the writer's ideas suggest further ideas to other members of the group? Did experiences that the writer used to make his or her ideas clear remind other group members of experiences of their own? Can members of the group suggest other approaches that might make the writer's draft more effective?

Free discussion is an important part of your group's work. Three or four people working on the same set of ideas and examples can feed one another's thinking and build on one another's suggestions. Although the writer of the draft may not choose to use the suggested ideas and approaches, other group members may find material in the discussion that leads them to revise their drafts or that suggests subjects for other papers.

2

The Qualities of Effective Writing

EFFECTIVE WRITING IS CLEAR WRITING

Many student writers believe that the purpose of writing is to make their readers agree with them. However, you have learned by now that there are many different answers to most questions that create a reason to write. Different people facing the same problem may have entirely different ideas as to how to solve it. Although you may write effectively enough to persuade your reader of the sincerity of your position, it is also possible that because your reader is a different person with different information and experiences, he or she may have found an entirely different solution to the problem you have taken on.

Although all your readers may not agree with the stance you take, your writing isn't wasted. You have accomplished a great deal if you make yourself clear. At the least, you have opened avenues of understanding with another person and invited new ideas in for yourself. You probably don't expect, or even want, the whole world to think as you do, but you would probably like people to understand you.

Your task as a writer is to make your position clear through the precise statement of your dominant idea, clear examples that make the basis of your idea plain, arrangement of your points so that they lead your reader along the path of your thoughts without confusion, and effective language that holds your reader's attention. If you have written effectively, your reader might not agree with you when he or she has finished, but there should be no doubt in your reader's mind as to what you mean.

⇜ Working with the Readings

Read the following pair of selections. Alone or in your group, answer the questions that follow them.

THE PASSIONATE SHEPHERD
TO HIS LOVE

Christopher Marlowe

Come live with me and be my love,
And we will all the pleasures prove°
That valleys, groves, hills, and fields,
Woods, or steepy mountain yields.

And we will sit upon the rocks,   5
Seeing the shepherds feed their flocks,
By shallow rivers to whose falls
Melodious birds sing madrigals.°

And I will make thee beds of roses
And a thousand fragrant posies,   10
A cap of flowers, and a kirtle°
Embroidered all with leaves of myrtle;

A gown made of the finest wool;
Which from our pretty lambs we pull;
Fair lined slippers for the cold,   15
With buckles of the purest gold;

A belt of straw and ivy buds,
With coral clasps and amber studs:
And if these pleasures may thee move,
Come live with me, and be my love.   20

The shepherd's swains° shall dance and sing
For thy delight each May morning:
If these delights thy mind may move,
Come live with me and be my love.

---

2. *prove:* test
8. *madrigals:* highly ornamented songs
11. *kirtle:* skirt
21. *swain:* lover

THE NYMPH'S REPLY TO THE SHEPHERD

Sir Walter Raleigh

If all the world and love were young,
And truth in every shepherd's tongue
These pretty pleasures might me move
To live with thee and be thy love.

Time drives the flocks from field to fold°   5
When rivers rage and rocks grow cold,
And Philomel° becometh dumb;
The rest complains of cares to come.

The flowers do fade, and wanton° fields
To wayward winter reckoning yields;   10
A honey tongue, a heart of gall
Is fancy's spring, but sorrow's fall.

Thy gowns, thy shoes, thy beds of roses,
Thy cap, thy kirtle, and thy posies
Soon break, soon wither, soon forgotten—   15
In folly ripe, in reason rotten.

The belt of straw and ivy buds,
The coral clasps and amber studs,
All these in me no means can move
To come to thee and be thy love.   20

But could youth last and love still breed,
Had joys no date° nor age no need,
Then these delights my mind might move
To live with thee and be thy love.

Individually or in your group, set a scene for Marlowe's poem by answering the following questions.

1. Who is talking to whom?

2. What point is the speaker trying to make?

3. What examples does the speaker use to make his case?

---

5. *fold:* enclosure
7. *Philomel:* Nightingale
9. *wanton:* having luxuriant growth
22. *date:* end

Now look at Raleigh's poem and compare each stanza with the corresponding stanza of Marlowe's poem.

1. Who is speaking to whom? What is *this* speaker's point?
2. What examples does *this* speaker use?
3. Are the two speakers seeing the same situation?
4. Do they see the situation in the same way?

Now compare the two poems.

1. What are the differences between the two speakers?
2. How do those differences lead to the different statements?
3. If you were the speaker of the first poem, would the second speaker's statement bring you to see the event in a different way? What would that way be?

➤ *An Invitation to Write*

Think about a situation in which you and a friend disagreed about an issue, an action, or a way of accomplishing a task that was equally important to both of you. Write a short statement of about three paragraphs in which you make your case. Then take the opposite position; write an equally strong statement supporting that position. Feel free to express your position in either poetry or prose.

EFFECTIVE WRITING SPRINGS FROM A REASON TO WRITE

You've probably done your best writing when you felt there was an important, troublesome situation that should be set right, a situation that gave you a reason to write. Few people write well without an emotional and intellectual investment in their subject. Think of the times when writing seemed effortless, when words seemed to flow in a direct current from your mind, down your arm, through the pen (or keyboard), and to the paper (or monitor). What was the relationship between you and your subject? Then consider those times when writing seemed no more than a pointless effort, when each word seemed to be a heavy weight you had to drag to the page. How did you feel about your subject or about the assignment then?

When you don't care about your subject, you probably won't care much about your writing. Your best writing happens when you meet a fascinating or disturbing person or when you see a place or event that interests you so much that you want to tell others about it. At other times, it may be prompted by your discovery of a difference between the way you think things ought to be and the way they are. Such a difference creates a disorder or disharmony troubling enough to make you want to take steps to make it right by telling people about it and, perhaps, recommending what they ought to do.

The student who wrote the paper that begins Chapter 1 did so in a hot, sunny classroom at about 2:30 p.m. on a warm spring day. In his piece, he creates a different time of day and a very different place and mood. Why do you think he did that?

Because your best writing begins with *your* response, the writing invitations in this book will never ask you to deal with predefined ideas. Instead, the questions that follow the readings ask you to discover issues that the readings raise and connect those issues with your experience. They invite you to identify your own reasons to write.

Another significant point: One person's reason to write is as important as any other person's. There is no such thing as an idea that is not "important" or one that is "too simple." If the subject and the approach you choose reflect your need to discover ways of making a disharmonious situation more pleasing or to show another person what you have seen, heard, tasted, felt, or smelled, and if you think and feel strongly enough about your discoveries to want to tell other people about them, you will write in such a way as to interest your audience.

Writing also helps you discover what you think. When you are having trouble solving a problem, perhaps you sit alone and think about it. Sometimes that approach works, but at other times it doesn't. You may just sink more and more deeply into the problem, with a solution becoming no more than a forlorn hope. Many people discover that talking to a friend or writing a letter clarifies the problem, and solutions seem to appear almost on their own.

This happens because words themselves represent ideas. When you put your ideas into words, connect those words to each other in sentences, and then connect those sentences with each other in chains of ideas, you separate yourself from your own thought processes. Your thoughts seem to exist independently of you. You create a distance from them that allows you to examine them. When you look at the structure of your own thoughts, you sometimes find ways of thinking about an issue that you had not considered before. Your words seem to take on a life of their own, presenting themselves and the ideas they represent in combinations you might not have thought of before you gave those ideas their own life in language.

No writer writes without a reason to write, a pressing need to confront a problem or express an idea or feeling through the distance that language creates. Writers often write because they want to find out just what it is they think and feel about a subject that is important to them. Most writers hope and expect to be surprised by their words as they appear on the page. E. M. Forster once asked, "How do I know what I think until I see what I've said?"

Here is an excellent example of what can happen when a person writes out a problem.

Dear Ann,

I'm a 26-year-old woman and I feel like a fool for asking you this question, but—should I marry the guy or not? Jerry is 30, but sometimes he acts like 14. We have gone together nearly a year. He was married for three years but never talks about it. My parents haven't said anything either for or against him, but I know deep down they don't like him much.

Jerry is a salesman and makes good money but he has lost his wallet three times since I've known him and I've had to help him make the payments on his car. The thing that bothers me most, I think, is that I have the feeling he doesn't trust me. After every date he telephones. He says it's to "say an extra goodnight" but I'm sure he is checking to see if I had a late date with someone else.

One night I was in the shower and didn't hear the phone. He came over and sat on the porch all night. I found him asleep on the swing when I went to get the paper the next morning at 6:30 a.m. I had a hard time convincing him I had been in the house the whole time.

Now on the plus side: Jerry is very good-looking and appeals to me physically. Well—that does it. I have been sitting here with this pen in my hand for 15 minutes trying to think of something else good to say about him and nothing comes to mind.

Don't bother to answer this. You have helped me more than you will ever know.

Eyes Opened

EFFECTIVE WRITING SERVES THE INTERESTS OF THE READER

Why do you choose to read a book, a magazine article, a story, or a poem? You probably choose to read a piece of writing because it has to do with a subject you are interested in, it speaks about an emotion or a situation that has meaning for you, or it is by a writer whose work has previously captured your interest.

People who read whatever and whenever they choose generally read for pleasure. It may be the pleasure of learning something new about a subject that interests them. It may be the pleasure of reading well-chosen words. In some cases, people read to "identify" with a person in a situation that strikes them as being like one they have faced, are facing, or would like to face. By living through that situation with another person, they learn about themselves.

In short, when people read voluntarily, they do so for a purpose that has to do with issues that are important to them as individuals or as members of a larger community. Reading is inevitably linked to learning about self and one's relation to one's inner world, outer world, or both.

Because readers read for their own purposes, to write effectively, you have to write with some knowledge of your readers—your audience—and their purposes for reading what you have to tell them. If you want your writing to be effective, you must connect your subject and your dominant idea with the concerns of your audience so that they may learn about their worlds and your world through what you have to say.

EFFECTIVE WRITING DOES JUSTICE TO THE DOMINANT IDEA

When you discover a dominant idea for your writing, you have established its theme—the center around which the rest of your ideas revolve. Your idea should be absolutely clear and familiar to you by the time you finish writing, but you cannot count on your audience having the same familiarity with that idea. In fact, if your readers were as familiar with your dominant idea as you are, why would you bother writing? You would be telling them what they already know.

Your audience may know the background for your dominant idea, or they may not. They may know some of the reasons you arrived at that idea, but they may not know all of them. Or your audience may know almost nothing about what you have discovered and what you consider important enough to communicate to them.

When you write effectively, you do justice to your dominant idea by thinking about it in terms of your readers and the knowledge you assume they have or need to have to understand your point. You do justice to your dominant idea by providing your audience with enough information to allow its members to understand what you have to say. You also do justice to your dominant idea by recognizing what your audience probably already knows and does not need to be reminded of.

EFFECTIVE WRITING IS APPROPRIATE TO THE SITUATION

You write in response to a situation that you feel is important enough to engage your reader's attention. Earlier, you learned that most people choose to write when they feel a need to make others aware of a condition or a situation that they believe is important. As they write, writers define for themselves as best they can the interests, attitudes, assumptions, and experiences of their audience. They then adjust the organization of their ideas, the examples they choose to make their ideas clear, and their language to make their writing appropriate to their audience.

Effective writing, then, is a complex, continuously changing, challenging balance of audience, ideas and responses, and language. To create an effective balance, you must think consciously about the choices you make. Do your words represent you and your subject in the most effective way? Is the voice you have created appropriate to the situation and your subject as well as to how you want your readers to feel about them? Have you chosen appropriate examples, neither talking down to your reader nor assuming too much about him or her? Have you made it clear to your reader why what you have to say is important and deserves attention? This book invites you to discover ways of answering these questions.

PUTTING THE ELEMENTS OF EFFECTIVE WRITING TOGETHER

Looking at the qualities of effective writing one by one does not do justice to the complexity of those elements and the way they combine to give your writing power. Each element influences—and is influenced by— all the others.

To visualize the interconnections between the elements of effective writing, look at the environment in which your writing occurs, as illustrated in Figure 2.1.

You (the writer) have chosen a topic to write about that reflects your purpose. That purpose reflects your experience in the world around you and often the conflict between what you see to be the case and what you think ought to be the case. Out of that conflict, you discover a subject and a dominant idea about your subject that fulfills your purposes.

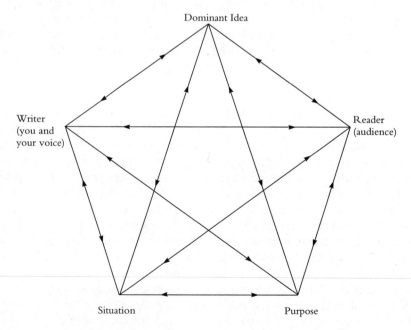

Figure 2.1 The Rhetorical Pentagon

Although your dominant idea is important to you, you cannot be sure that it is equally important to your reader. He or she may be ignorant both of what you've observed and of the dominant idea you've discovered as a result. Or your reader may have encountered the same facts as you have, but he or she may not understand the importance of those facts. Or your reader may have the same information available but might have derived an entirely different conclusion from it, possibly one that does not leave room for him or her to consider the conclusion you have reached.

To do justice to your dominant idea, you have to show your reader that considering your thoughts will serve his or her purposes. You have to adjust your message to your reader in such a way as to engage his or her interest in considering what you have to say.

In addition, writing is generally intended for a particular situation. Some writing will appear in a formal situation, perhaps as a paper published in a professional journal. Some writing is intended for a less formal situation, such as a popular magazine or the opinion–editorial pages of a newspaper. Some writing is quite informal—for example, a letter to a friend or a member of your family. Each situation presents you with a specific audience with certain expectations of how you will present your ideas: the language you will use, the voice you will create through your choice of words, the nature and amount of support you will give your ideas, and the way you will order those ideas.

To do justice to your dominant idea, you will find yourself thinking about all of these issues. Your aim in presenting your dominant idea is partly shaped by your awareness of your readers and their interests. You introduce your readers to your idea in the context of a specific situation. Your understanding of that situation will affect your perception of your readers, who are part of that situation, and your purpose, which is shaped by that situation. Moreover, all of these elements shape the language you choose to create your voice. And the voice you choose also affects all the other elements.

In short, a sort of ecology shapes writing. Every part depends on every other part, and a problem in any one element has consequences for every other element. If you do not think about your reader, you cannot fulfill the purpose of your writing—to clearly express your sense of a particular situation to another person. If you do not think about the situation that surrounds your writing, you can't think clearly about your reader and how to address him or her. Also, without a clear sense of how to do justice to your subject and your dominant idea through your language, you cannot effectively fulfill your purpose as a writer. Finally, the voice you choose to express your ideas—your choice of words, the length and rhythm of your sentences, whether or not you use figurative language and words that appeal to your readers' emotions—both reflects and helps you refine your sense of your situation, your purpose, and your audience.

3

How Writing Happens: An Overview of the Process

WRITING IS MESSY AND KEEPS TURNING BACK ON ITSELF

Because most written works move in a neat, logical, straight line from beginning to end, many people believe the act of writing is an equally neat process that moves in a straight line—from the idea to the completed piece. Every experienced writer knows that the reality of writing is very different.

The process of writing is recursive: it constantly turns back on itself. The four stages of writing—*invention* (thinking about possibilities for writing), *drafting* (getting the first version of your words on a page), *revising* (polishing your words to serve your interests, your reader, the situation, and your topic), and *editing and proofreading* (checking your writing for problems of usage, grammar, spelling, and punctuation)—seem to turn into each other. Even when a writer is at the final editing stage, he or she might discover the germ of an even better idea and return to revising, redrafting, or even reinventing his or her work.

The assumption that "good" writers find writing to be simple and linear can be demoralizing to students, who find themselves wrestling with each paragraph, each sentence, and sometimes even a single word. They compare their process to the way they think "real" writers write, and they come out losers. But the truth about writing is quite different. When those who study writing watch people as they write, it appears that writing is really four processes that both turn back on themselves and also often magically turn into each other. These processes also often appear to get out of the writer's control, telling him or her what the writing wants to be about.

Writing is a process that is sometimes easy, sometimes difficult, and almost always messy. But if you are interested in your material—if you have discovered a real reason to write—writing is never boring. Listen to what Annie Dillard, an accomplished writer, has to say about the process in *The Writing Life:*

I do not so much write a book as sit up with it, as with a dying friend. During visiting hours, I enter its room with dread and sympathy for its many disorders. I hold its hand and hope it will get better.

This tender relationship can change in a twinkling. If you skip a visit or two, a work in progress will turn on you.

A work in progress quickly becomes feral. It reverts to a wild state overnight. It is barely domesticated, a mustang on which you one day fastened a halter, but which now you cannot catch. It is a lion you cage in your study. As the work grows, it gets harder to control; it is a lion growing in strength. You must visit it every day and reassert your mastery over it. If you skip a day, you are, quite rightly, afraid to open the door to its room. You enter its room with bravura, holding a chair at the thing and shouting, "Simba!"

Any book like this one that tries to describe how writing happens sometimes makes the act appear very different than it is. Reading writing is linear. One word follows another. So do paragraphs. So do chapters. That fact is as true of this book as it is of any other. However, the act of writing is not linear just because its product is. Because books are linear, this one approaches writing as if it, too, were linear, showing you the different stages separately. But please remember this as you read: These stages rarely occur apart from each other. Even while you think about what to write, you consider what the end product might look like. While you shape the paper, a new idea might come to you and send you back to the beginning of the whole process.

THE STAGES OF THE WRITING PROCESS

An old recipe for rabbit stew begins, "First, catch a rabbit." If there were a recipe for writing, it might begin, "First, find something you want to say. Discover your reason to write." One of the most difficult stages of writing is discovering an idea that is important enough to you to make the effort of putting it on the page in the best possible way seem worthwhile.

Invention, or Prewriting

You are always inventing your world. Consider this: You receive tens of thousands of sensations every second. You're surrounded by sounds. Every square centimeter of your body responds to the varying touch of your clothes, the pressure of the chair you may be sitting on as you read this, the pressure of the ground against your feet, the currents of air in the room or outdoors where you're sitting right now. Few places in the world do not have a collection of smells. Your mouth carries the aftertaste of the meal you just ate or the mint you just crunched between your teeth. You are using your eyes to read this book, but your peripheral vision registers other things occurring around you.

With all these sensations in your world, it's a wonder that you're not overwhelmed by them. The reason you don't drown in them is that you *perceive* only a few of the sensations available to you. You select and connect only those sensations that are important to your purposes at the time. Some recede into the background; some seem to disappear entirely. For example, watch a cat when there is a bird in the neighborhood. The cat's concentration is absolute, and it seems to filter out every other sensation that is not relevant to its purposes: the possibility of a poultry dinner.

In every situation, you shape your perceptions by what is important to you at the time. When you attend a lecture in American history, you connect the words you hear with the ideas you already have in mind, and out of this mixture you project or predict other ideas that are the result of the linkages you've already made. When you drive, you focus your perceptions on the cars around you, your physical sensations of your car's behavior, the sounds your car is making, and possibly the sounds of the traffic around you. If you have your radio on or a tape playing, you find it fading into the background as the demands of traffic increase. At other times, events may happen around you that touch you in sensitive places—places where you keep memories of earlier experiences or past or present concerns arising from things you already know, fear, or hope for. Suddenly, your perceptions connect in a new way. You reshape the familiar world in a form that had not occurred to you before. Seeing your surroundings through the lens of new linkages between old events, you shape them into an idea and then search out other support for your idea or ways you might apply it to what you thought you already knew. Sometimes, your idea and the way it changes your familiar world seem important enough to tell others about, and sometimes those others are not right in front of you and you cannot speak to them. Then you must write. Then your perceptions, the new connections among them, and the ideas that grow from both of them become prewriting.

Drafting: Getting the First Words Down

The preliminary stage of actual writing is the first draft. At this point, you try to get ideas and examples on the page without worrying a great deal about what is correct, relevant, or appropriate. You can deal with these issues most effectively after—not before—you have material to work with, much as a sculptor cannot sculpt without clay.

When you decide to write, or when an assignment decides the issue for you, the first hurdle is often the blank page. For many writers, the sight of a page with nothing started, no words, produces anxiety. Reluctance to begin is often a sort of stage fright. The writer asks: Will my ideas be convincing? Will I make mistakes in organization? spelling? grammar? Will I have enough to say? Will what I have to say be "important" enough?

Of course, logic tells you that none of these questions makes any sense without actual material to apply it to. However, the fantasy many people share of how "real writers" write defeats this logic. "Real writers" make many false starts and find themselves wandering down blind alleys just like you. They don't sit down and spin out perfect writing. For the most part, they work as hard as you do. And they begin with a draft.

A draft is a way of getting words down on the page, if only to discover where those words take you. Writers often find that, at a certain point in their drafting, their writing begins to tell them what it wants to be about. Writers of fiction often speak of their characters taking over their stories, telling them what is going to happen next. Such magic happens when the writer begins by writing uncritically, thinking of the draft as a first exploration of his or her ideas and the way they fit together.

Of course, effective drafting isn't magic. It's an approach that is very simple to describe and, for some people, very difficult to practice. It is the process of getting words on the page while turning off your inner critic, who learned in third grade from Miss Fairweather that a noun is a person, place, or thing or that a comma introduces the second coordinate clause in a compound sentence or that *i* comes before *e* except after *c* or when sounded like *a* as in *neighbor* or *weigh*.

That inner critic—the voice of teachers past—can stop a draft dead in its tracks. The inner critic encourages the writer to go back and make sure that the last sentence or paragraph is "correct" or that the words following the last coordinating conjunction are really an independent clause. The writer who gives in to that voice often finds that the idea he or she is discovering or pursuing vanishes, never to be exactly recovered.

It is not that the rules covering correct grammar and spelling are not important. Issues of correctness are crucial in presenting your ideas to others in the most effective form, in "dressing" them appropriately to be seen in public. But these rules are not important when you are first finding your way through your experiences, your ideas, their support, and the dominant idea they suggest. The rules are not important when you are exploring your writing to find out what it has to say. The best way to begin to write is simply to cover the blankness of the first page—to begin to write and let the words take you where you and they want to go.

Drafting is only a first stage, and it is a private stage which nobody else has to see. Since there is often strength in numbers, however, it is a good idea to show your draft to a writing group and to try to see it through the other members' eyes. The key to working with a draft in a group is *not* to ask questions regarding organization or correctness, but to look at the draft for what it is—an exploration—and to ask questions about what the draft reveals. Here is a set of effective questions group members can use to review members' drafts. If you are not working with a group, you can ask yourself these questions about your own draft.

Questions for Reading First Drafts

1. Does the draft have a center: a single idea it returns to or concentrates on? Be aware that the writer might have approached his or her issue from many different directions or that the writer might have written around

the dominant idea without stating it directly. See if you can identify the central issue that the draft raises.

2. What—in one or two sentences—is the dominant issue of the draft? There may be as many different ideas about the dominant issue as there are people in the group. The writer shouldn't worry about that. Others might suggest ways of combining thoughts to make the overall idea more interesting, or they might suggest different ways of looking at the dominant idea.

With the comments of group members in mind, the writer should settle on one idea that reflects his or her concerns and interests best and report it to the group (or jot it down if he or she is working alone).

3. Now reread the draft, focusing on its clarity. Does the draft provide enough information to make the writer's dominant idea and the writer's attitude clear to you? Do you need more information or background? What else would you like to know? What ideas, terms, events, or processes seem unclear to you? What experiences or thoughts of your own might help the writer add to his or her idea?

Revision: Looking Again at What You've Done

Revision (literally, "re-seeing" or "seeing again") means looking at your paper from the point of view of the people who will read it. When you revise, you try to look at your draft from a distance, as if you were another person who does not know you well and who is not familiar with the way you connect ideas to each other or examples to ideas.

The questions for looking at first drafts invited you to search out the focus of the draft—its dominant idea—as well as ways of making the draft clearer to the reader.

When you revise, you look again at your draft, taking into account what you learned when you (and your group) answered the questions asked of your first draft. As you reread, look for ways of sharpening your focus—making certain that each idea leads logically to the next and that all the ideas point toward your dominant idea. Consider what your audience doesn't know and might need to know to understand what you have to say. Also look for information and ideas that your readers might not need to know. Although those pieces of information might be fascinating, they might also lead your readers away from your dominant idea.

Another important issue is the voice and character you have created for yourself. Do you come across in an effective way? Have you created a voice and an attitude that are appropriate to your subject and that your readers will want to listen to? Have you shown your readers that you know what you're writing about?

It's important to keep in mind the successes, or strengths, that you and your group (or you alone) discovered in the first draft. If you concentrate on making those strengths still stronger, many of the problems in your draft will begin to disappear.

Here are some useful questions for examining the results of your revision of your first draft. Remember, as you revise or discuss your second draft, you might discover a whole new slant on your idea or an even more interesting dominant idea. Be prepared for surprises. Drafting never really ends. Writers who look at their pieces of writing years later have discovered new possibilities for still better writing.

Questions for Reviewing Second Drafts

1. Is the dominant idea of this draft clear? Does it have only one dominant idea or is the writer trying to develop two ideas at the same time? If so, is there a way of combining those ideas into one single, larger idea? If not, which idea should be cut out to establish a single focus?

2. Is this draft clearly focused? That is, is it unified? Is all the information in this draft clearly related to the dominant idea, or does the reader have to guess what some of the information has to do with the writer's point? If you find problems in the focus, suggest ways of solving them.

3. Is this draft coherent? That is, are the connections between the ideas clear? As the reader, can you move easily from idea to idea or do you get lost between them? If you see problems, what solutions would you suggest?

4. Is there enough information in this draft to make the writer's point clear? Has the writer mistakenly assumed that what is clear to him or her is equally clear to you? If you need more information from the writer, what do you need and where do you need it?

5. Does the beginning of this draft do what beginnings should do? Does it catch your interest? Does it give you a clear idea of what the writer's concerns are? Does the writer give you enough background to understand what he or she is talking about and why what he or she has to say is important to you? If there are problems in this part of the draft, suggest solutions.

6. Does the conclusion of this draft do what conclusions should do? Does it complete the dominant idea? Does it lead you to understand how the writer's ideas might be important to you? Does it lead you to further ideas about the writer's topic? Does it give you the sense that the piece is over? What solutions do you have to problems you see in this area?

7. Now that you've finished reading the draft, do you feel you know something that you didn't know before? Or do you see the writer's subject in a way in which you had not seen it before? Has the writer made his or her ideas and attitudes important to *you?*

Editing and Proofreading: Respecting Your Reader and the Conventions

Many people confuse editing and proofreading. They are not the same process at all. When you edit, you reconsider your audience in more detail than you do when you revise, although as you edit, you may find yourself moving back to issues that are appropriate to revision.

When you revise your work or review another's revision, you look at its overall unity and coherence. You also ask whether the writer has kept his or her audience in mind or has made unwarranted assumptions about the audience. In a way, you take the large view of the piece of writing when you revise.

When you edit, you take a more microscopic view of the writing. You still pay attention to issues of form and structure and to whether the choices made are appropriate to the dominant idea. But in editing, you begin to look more closely at individual sentences and even choices of single words. You look to see if the sentences connect with each other in such a way that the reader does not have to guess how they fit together. You ask if the words the writer has chosen are precise and familiar enough not to confuse the reader or to convey an idea or attitude that is different from the one the writer intends.

Proofreading is a matter of seeing that the writing observes the conventions of standard American English or breaks those conventions intentionally when it serves the writer's purpose to do so. There are two very good reasons for observing these conventions.

The first is a matter of self-presentation. It's probably true that if you omit an apostrophe here or a comma there or incorrectly spell a word someplace else, your reader will have no trouble understanding what you mean. On the other hand, what will your reader think of you? If you create the impression of carelessness or ignorance, why should your reader be willing to take what you have to say seriously? And if you don't want to be taken seriously, why are you writing at all?

The second reason for following the conventions has to do with the function of punctuation marks. The purpose of most marks is to clarify relationships between ideas. A period at the end of a string of words tells you that the idea has come to a full stop. Another idea will follow. However, when you see a comma at the end of a string of words, it is an indication that the idea isn't over. There is more information to follow. When you put a comma down, you tell the reader to suspend his or her conclusion until the end of the idea comes along. If you use punctuation effectively, your reader will understand the structure of your ideas and the relationships between your ideas and examples. Look at the past few sentences to see how the marks work.

Working with your group or alone, use the following questions to focus your attention on the issues of editing and proofreading.

Questions for Editing

1. Do the paragraphs follow one another in a logical order? Do some paragraphs need to be reordered?

2. Are the connections between the paragraphs clear? Is a short paragraph needed to connect two larger paragraphs?

3. Do the sentences in each paragraph follow one another in a logical order? Are words or phrases needed to make the connections between sentences clear, or do some of the sentences in a paragraph need to be reordered?

4. Has the writer used effective words and avoided clichés? Are there too many abstract words that do not convey precisely the information the audience needs? Has the writer used wordy phrases where a single, precise word would do?

5. When you finished this paper, were you left with a clear dominant idea and the impression that *every* part of the paper contributed to that idea?

Questions for Proofreading

1. Are all the sentences *really* sentences? Is there a subject doing an action somewhere in each sentence? If the writer has written an incomplete sentence, does it work in its context?

2. Has the writer taken two separate sentences and combined them into one without any indication to the reader (by way of a semicolon) that there is a conceptual boundary between them?

3. Is the relationship between the subject of each sentence and the action it undertakes logical? Or has the writer created a situation in which the subject is doing something it could not possibly do?

4. Do commas show how one idea adds to another without closing off either of the ideas?

5. Has the writer capitalized all the words which should be capitalized? Are there capital letters where they should not be?

6. Has the writer misspelled any words?

7. Has the writer misused any words? (Pay special attention to words which sound alike, such as *affect* and *effect, accept* and *except,* or *its* and *it's.*)

A NOTE ABOUT WORD PROCESSORS

You've learned that as writers draft, revise, and edit their work, they circle through their work over and over again. They rewrite sentences and paragraphs, change the order of their paragraphs, add new material as it occurs to them, and reconsider and rewrite introductions and conclusions. Before computers and word processors were available, many writers avoided extensive rewriting or considered it an unavoidable chore, and with good reason. A writer limited to handwriting or a typewriter had to rewrite or retype the whole text with every revision.

Attempting to make one's writing more effective felt like a punishment. The more concerned the writer became with the effectiveness of his or her work, the more maddening the writing process became. Typing and retyping many of the same words and ideas over and over is boring. A bored writer is a careless writer, a writer who is tempted to cut as many corners as possible to get the job done.

The arrival of microcomputers and word processing programs has eliminated much of the drudgery from drafting, revision, and editing, leaving only the exciting parts. When you write with a word processor, you really write the whole paper only once. You can add revisions, try them out, change your mind, or change the sequence of your ideas by pressing a few keys. Parts that you cut can be held in the computer's memory; if you decide you want to return them to the paper, you can recall them. Using a word processing program makes writing what it should be: play and experimentation with ideas and words to see what works best. One student compared writing on a word processor to swimming in the text like a fish in water.

In addition, most word processing programs include a spelling checker, making much easier a job that gives many professional and student writers a great deal of difficulty. However, it is easy to rely too much on spelling checkers. These programs only flag misspelled words and guess at the correct words. They do not catch the incorrect use of homonyms—such as using *their* instead of *there* or *they're*, or *to* instead of *too* or *two*. After using a spelling checker, you still have to proofread for such errors.

For many people, learning a word processing program can seem overwhelming. There are so many commands and key combinations to learn that old-fashioned typing seems more and more attractive. If you're just learning a word processing program, don't try to learn the whole program at once. You will rarely use some commands, and you will never use others. Learn only what you need to know to do what you want to do: how to enter text, how to move around in the text, how to insert or delete material, and how to move blocks of your text around. Learn other commands only when you need to use them, and then you'll learn them well.

PART 2

Discovering Your Experiences and Your Ideas

4

Prewriting Strategies: Discovering What You Have to Say

SUBJECT AND STANCE

At the same time you discover a subject that is important to you, you also discover a stance you will take toward that subject. These two elements—subject and stance—are equally important but quite different. A piece of effective writing not only directs the reader's attention to the writer's subject, but it also takes a position with reference to that subject. It might assert something about a subject—a thesis, an idea, a proposition, or a position. Or it might present a dominant idea or impression. As you explore ways of discovering subjects for your writing, be alert for dominant impressions, ideas, or viewpoints that you might discover in those subjects. Your reason to write grows out of a need to make a difference, to suggest a change in the way your audience sees your subject, or to make a dominant impression or idea clear to your reader.

You might find a subject to write about before you begin to write. Some writers spend a lot of time thinking about their experiences and the questions they suggest before beginning to write. Others find that they need to write in order to discover what they intend to say. In either case, a good deal of the writer's time before writing is devoted to collecting information by observing, remembering, projecting from what he or she knows, and reading—and by connecting the results of all this mental activity.

For many writers, prewriting may stretch over hours, days, or months. Years of experience may suddenly fall into a pattern that leads to an idea. You might stumble over an idea while showering, waiting in a supermarket checkout line, or walking down the street. You might witness an event, hear a conversation, read a single line in a book. At that moment, days, months, or years of experience might suddenly come together and create a reason to write. That instant has been described by some writers as a "felt sense"—a physical sensation that a worthwhile idea is lurking somewhere close. As you work at discovery, be alert for the "felt sense." Trust it when you have it.

Even after you have discovered an idea, sharpening that idea and seeing its connections with other experiences and ideas—both yours and those of others—is essential. People have discovered and developed strategies for prying open their ideas and experiences and finding where they lead. These strategies are questions that will encourage you to ask further questions of your experiences, your thoughts, and of yourself.

Discovery is a personal affair. As you grow up, you develop a style of perceiving and of shaping your perceptions that works best for you. Because each discovery strategy is different, different persons will respond differently to each one. Some approaches work well for one person and not for another. Some may work well for you in one situation but not at all in another situation. Sometimes one angle or approach produces partial success, only to be completed by another approach. Try each of these approaches separately and in combination. When you discover the strategies that work best for you, make them a part of your writing tactics, especially when you get stuck.

Each of these approaches is a prompt to thinking about something—an object, a person, a process, an idea, an event you might have seen, heard about, or read about. However, thought is elusive. We have ideas all the time. Most of us promise ourselves to remember our good ideas. Most of us forget. It's nearly impossible to recall the crucial idea you had two days ago but didn't bother to record. You'll find it useful to record your ideas when you are working toward beginning a piece of writing. Try to develop the habit of jotting down ideas, thoughts, and memories as they occur to you. That way, you can retrieve the useful ones as you work toward your draft— and discard those that don't lead anywhere.

Furthermore, when a discovery strategy is working well, ideas come thick and fast. It's almost impossible to keep track of them all. As you keep notes, try not to order them or rewrite them. If you do, there's a good chance that you will lose the train of your ideas. Save ordering and shaping for later.

After you have finished any discovery process, you will most likely find yourself with a disorganized, messy, and generally unpromising mass of words, a diagram, or both. However, most of us would be shocked if we kept a written record of our thoughts while we were thinking them. We fool ourselves after we're finished thinking into believing our thoughts are orderly, but we confuse the result of thinking *about* our thinking with thinking itself. Thinking is random and associative, leaping from idea to idea. It is only when we try to communicate our thoughts to others or to arrange them for our own examination that we create a linear, logical, organized pattern from them. Your written record of your prewriting strategy is a moment-to-moment map of your thoughts. Have confidence in it.

Look at your jottings with the idea of finding a theme in them. Do your ideas circle around a single point? Is there a central attitude or issue from which they radiate? Look for repetition of an idea in different words, for facts or perceptions which seem to have the same focus or theme.

Remember a time when you had a problem on your mind, when a particular situation bothered you, or when you couldn't free yourself from a thought or the memory of an incident. You probably found yourself returning to it from different angles. This is what you look for when you examine the results of your prewriting. The important point is that these results reflect your concerns, attitudes, and ways of connecting your thoughts and experiences. *You* are the only person responsible for the words on the page. If *you* put those words there, then they must reflect something *you* want to express.

CLUSTERING: DREAMING AWAKE

Clustering is based on the idea that your brain has two hemispheres. Each hemisphere appears to process information differently. Your left hemisphere deals with one event or idea at a time. It is responsible for sequential, logical thought: straight–line thinking. Your left hemisphere also appears to be rule-bound. It draws on routines and codes for thinking or behaving that you learned earlier in life. Such systems as grammar, spelling, and arithmetic live in that hemisphere. This half of your brain is the reason you don't have to relearn language and grammar every time you write a sentence or relearn arithmetic every time you balance your checkbook. It is the reason that you can make reasonable guesses at the spelling of a word you have never seen before.

Your right hemisphere connects experiences and ideas. It sees incidents, objects, or ideas as parts of larger wholes connected with other moments, not as a collection of separate entities. It can combine incidents, objects, and ideas into entirely new patterns that you have never seen before. Because it is flexible in this way, the right hemisphere is especially good at coping with new situations that do not match the learned sequences you have stored in your left hemisphere.

Of course, your two hemispheres work together, exchanging information, confirming your conclusions, and testing new ideas. The discovery of the benzene ring provides a striking example of the cooperation of the two hemispheres. Friedrich August Kekule, a German chemist, had been trying to discover the chemical structure of organic compounds. Although the nature and behavior of these compounds had been recorded and classified for years, that information had apparently led nowhere.

At this point, let Kekule tell the story:

> . . . it did not go well; my spirit was with other things. I turned the chair to the fireplace and sank into a half sleep. The atoms flitted before my eyes. Long rows, variously, more closely, united; all in movement wriggling and turning like snakes. And see, what was that? One of the snakes seized its own tail and the image whirled scornfully before my

eyes. As though from a flash of lightning I awoke; I occupied the rest of the night in working out the consequences of the hypothesis. . . . Let us learn to dream. . . .

—quoted in W.I.B. BEVERIDGE, *The Art of Scientific Investigation*

Kekule's discovery of the circular structure of atoms in benzene revolutionized organic chemistry and made possible, for better or worse, all the different forms of plastic that surround us today. Kekule's experience shows you how the two hemispheres work together. The left collects and orders information; the right connects it in new ways and comes up with new answers. Then the left hemisphere tests the new connections for validity.

Clustering is a way of letting your right hemisphere help you discover ideas and relationships between them that you might not have imagined. Clustering leaves you with a map of your ideas and their relationships. Because you create the map, the cluster is yours alone; it reflects your experience, your ideas, and the connections that are important to you.

When you cluster, be prepared for surprises. If you are honest in your efforts and forget what is "important" enough for other people to see or what is "intelligent" enough for a paper, you'll find yourself making connections between ideas you might not have been aware of. Astonishing new ideas and combinations of ideas may present themselves as you map your thoughts, but only if you make an effort not to censor any idea because it is "too stupid" or "not important."

Clustering begins with an idea or event reduced to a word or a phrase. Your teacher may assign a word or phrase to you or encourage you to invent one that reflects your present concerns. Write the word or phrase at the center of a sheet of paper and draw a circle around it (Figure 4.1).

Now, without rejecting any idea or word that occurs to you, let the ideas, phrases, or memories of your experiences that the word or phrase in the center of the circle suggests come to you. As you think of them, write them down around the central idea, circle them, and draw lines from those circles to the central circle (Figure 4.2).

As you write these secondary ideas down, each will probably bring up further ideas. Write them down and circle them. Draw a line from each idea to the idea that suggested it or to other secondary ideas as the connections occur to you. These lines reflect the relationships you create between your ideas. At this point, more ideas will suggest themselves. You might find connections between one idea you've already noted and another. Connect them. These new combinations will suggest further ideas. Note, circle, and connect these (Figure 4.3).

When you finish, you'll probably have created a sprawling network of lines and circles. But if you look carefully, you'll find that you have a map of your experiences and thoughts and the associations between them. Looking still more carefully, you will find that there is probably an area which seems to have created more ideas and connections than the others. This area may have generated enough specific information to suggest a first draft to you.

Figure 4.1 Clustering: Starting with a Phrase

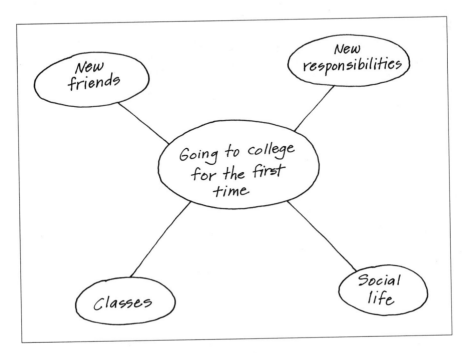

Figure 4.2 Clustering: Adding Secondary Ideas

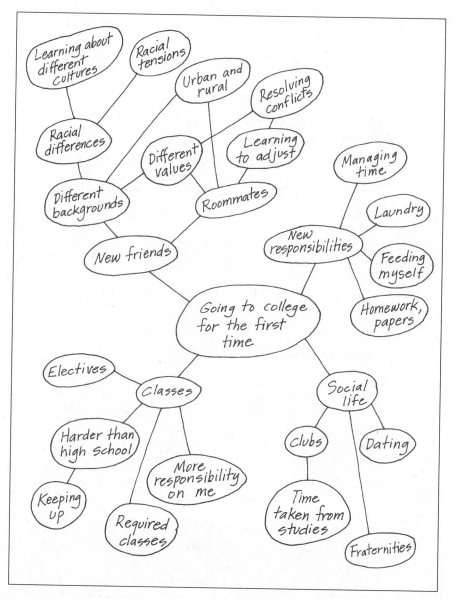

Figure 4.3 Clustering: Expanding and Making Connections

On the other hand, the result may look promising, but you might want to think about it some more. If that is the case, isolate that area and reduce it to a word or phrase, circle it, and cycle through another cluster with that as your center. You may have to work through the process a number of times, but eventually you will have a connected set of ideas and experiences that may suggest a reason to write.

 Working with the Readings

Read the three poems that follow. Choose the poem or combination of poems that speaks to your own experiences, that brings up reasons to write about the feelings and issues these poems raise. Condense your response into a single word or phrase that reflects it most clearly. If you have trouble finding an interesting word or phrase, use the questions that follow each poem to help you. Then experiment with clustering as explained on page 67 under "An Invitation to Write."

SADIE AND MAUD

Gwendolyn Brooks

Maud went to college
Sadie stayed at home.
Sadie scraped life
With a fine-tooth comb.

She didn't leave a tangle in. 5
Her comb found every strand.
Sadie was one of the livingest chits°
In all the land.

Sadie bore two babies
Under her maiden name. 10
Maud and Ma and Papa
Nearly died of shame.

When Sadie said her last so-long
Her girls struck out from home.
(Sadie had left as heritage 15
Her fine-tooth comb.)

---

7. *chit:* a bold girl

Maud, who went to college,
Is a thin brown mouse.
She is living all alone
In this old house.

20

---

1. Gwendolyn Brooks is an African American poet. Does this fact influence your reading of this poem? How?

2. What is a fine-tooth comb? What is it used for? Why is it important that Maud does not seem to have one?

3. What words would you use to define the differences between Sadie and Maud?

4. Do you think Brooks wants you to sympathize with Sadie? with Maud? Who do you sympathize with?

5. Do you think you are more like Sadie or Maud? Have you ever wanted to be the other way?

LYING IN A HAMMOCK AT WILLIAM DUFFY'S FARM IN PINE ISLAND, MINNESOTA

James Wright

Over my head, I see the bronze butterfly,
Asleep on the black trunk,
Blowing like a leaf in green shadow.
Down the ravine behind the empty house,
The cowbells follow one another
Into the distances of the afternoon.
To my right,
In a field of sunlight between two pines,
The droppings of last year's horses
Blaze up into golden stones.
I lean back, as the evening darkens and comes on.
A chicken hawk floats over, looking for home.
I have wasted my life.

5

10

---

1. People usually see this poem in one of two ways. Some think that the speaker feels he has wasted his life because he is lying in the ham-

mock; others, that he feels he has wasted his life because he has never lain in the hammock before. What do you think?

2. In this poem, the poet has the speaker mention four perceptions. What are they? Why does he mention these four out of all the others that might have been possible? Are they alike in any way?

3. What time of day is it? Why does the poet have the speaker tell you this?

4. Have you ever felt the way the speaker feels? When and where? What made you feel that way?

MR. FLOOD'S PARTY

Edwin Arlington Robinson

Old Eben Flood, climbing alone one night
Over the hill between the town below
And the forsaken upland hermitage
That held as much as he should ever know
On earth again of home, paused warily.   5
The road was his, and not a native near
And Eben, having leisure, said aloud,
For no man else in Tilbury Town to hear:

"Well, Mr. Flood, we have the harvest moon
Again, and we may not have many more;   10
The bird is on the wing, the poet says,
And you and I have said it here before.
Drink to the bird." He raised up to the light
The jug that he had gone so far to fill,
And answered huskily: "Well, Mr. Flood,   15
Since you propose it, I believe I will."

Alone, as if enduring to the end
A valiant armor of scarred hopes outworn
He stood there in the middle of the road
Like Roland's° ghost winding a silent horn.   20
Below him in the town among the trees,
Where friends of other days had honored him,
A phantom salutation of the dead
Rang thinly till old Eben's eyes were dim

---

20. *Roland:* the hero of a medieval French epic

Then, as a mother lays her sleeping child 25
Down tenderly, fearing it may awake
He set the jug down slowly at his feet
With trembling care, knowing that most things break;
And only when assured that on firm earth
It stood, as the uncertain lives of men 30
Assuredly did not, he paced away,
And with his hand extended paused again:

"Well, Mr. Flood, we have not met like this
In a long time; and many a change has come
To both of us, I fear, since last it was 35
We had a drop together. Welcome home!"
Convivially returning with himself,
Again he raised the jug up to the light;
And with an acquiescent quaver said:
"Well, Mr. Flood, if you insist, I might. 40

"Only a very little, Mr. Flood—
For auld lang syne. No more, sir; that will do."
So, for the time, apparently it did,
And Eben evidently thought so too;
For soon amid the silver loneliness 45
Of night he lifted up his voice and sang,
Secure, with only two moons listening,
Until the whole harmonious landscape rang—

"For auld lang syne." The weary throat gave out,
The last word wavered, and the song was done. 50
He raised again the jug regretfully
And shook his head, and was again alone.
There was not much that was ahead of him,
And there was nothing in the town below—
Where strangers would have shut the many doors 55
That many friends had opened long ago.

---

1. Do you think Eben Flood is a crazy old alcoholic who goes out alone and talks to himself because nobody will have anything to do with such a disreputable person? Does Robinson suggest other ways of seeing him?

2. What do you think Mr. Flood feels about the world? What would have led him to feel that way?

3. What time of day could it be? Do you think that the time of year has anything to do with the way Mr. Flood feels?

4. When you walk down the street, do you ever see people who behave like Mr. Flood? What did you think of them before you read this poem? What do you think of them now?

❧ *An Invitation to Write*

Using as the center the word or phrase that represents your response to one or more of the poems, do a cluster. Look at the resulting pattern of connections and isolate the one that seems to show the most activity. Reduce it to a word or phrase and do another cluster.

Cycle through the process again and again until you feel your response to the poem or poems you have chosen is clear to you, until you have a "felt sense" that you have found an idea that is important to you.

Now write a short draft. It may be an essay, a story, or a poem. Don't worry about spelling or grammar or perfect use of language. Just get the ideas and experiences that your cluster suggests to you on the page as quickly as you can.

If you are working in a group, give a copy of your writing to each member. At the meeting, members should discuss, one by one, how their experiences connected with the poem or poems they chose, where those connections led, and what reason to write they discovered as a result.

After each group member's statement, other members should respond by asking questions about connections that are not clear to them; suggesting other connections that they see in the writing; and volunteering experiences, ideas, and memories. Use the first-draft questions in Chapter 3 (page 49) as a starting point.

Take notes during the group meeting. Other people's questions, suggestions, or responses might suggest further ways of exploring your idea or writing another draft.

FREEWRITING: WRITING UNCONSCIOUSLY

Freewriting is another way of discovering what you know and what your writing wants to be about. In addition, through freewriting you often find your writing telling you how it wants to express your ideas. Sometimes freewriting will leave you with a workable first draft.

Freewriting is very simple. Take out a sheet of paper and begin to write whatever comes to mind. Or if you work at a computer, turn down the brightness control on the monitor until you can no longer see the characters on the screen; then begin to type. Once you have begun, do not stop, and above all, do not go back to edit or revise what you've written. Don't worry about grammar and spelling. If you can't think of anything to write, write "I can't think of anything to write" or some other phrase that seems appropriate until something different occurs to you. You will find your writing seeming to wander from topic to topic. Don't worry. Let the writing pursue its own direction. Don't deliberately try to stick to one idea. Usually, you'll discover that you are working with a single thought and that you are wandering through the associations that your thought has suggested. Your mind turns the idea over, looks at it from different angles, makes connections with other ideas.

Your instructor may specify a time period for freewriting or may tell you to continue until you feel it is time to stop. If you are freewriting on your own, be alert for the sense that you have run out of words or ideas. When you feel that you have run dry, give yourself five more minutes of freewriting time to discover if you really have exhausted your topic.

Remember the example of student freewriting at the beginning of Chapter 1 and how the ideas and language appeared to fit themselves to each other without the student's conscious effort. Some writing happens like that because writers often write their first ideas best when they write unconsciously, when they let the words flow directly from their minds through their fingers to the paper or to the computer keyboard without any intervention. Effective freewriting draws on your knowledge of grammar and rhetoric without your worrying about whether the language, grammar, or spelling is correct or appropriate. Not worrying about the conventions of grammar and spelling leaves you free to create writing that tells you what *it* wants to be about.

Perhaps the idea of your writing telling you what it wants to be about seems a little eerie, as if your writing could have a life of its own. But your writing, like your thoughts, does have its own life. When you work at a task of any kind—writing, listening to a lecture, preparing a meal—another part of your mind works away at other thoughts as well, taking the material in the foreground and letting it suggest other ideas or memories, weaving it with other thoughts, building and dismantling whole structures of ideas, sometimes creating new networks of ideas and experiences you had never considered before.

From time to time while writing a paper, you might have discovered what seemed to be unrelated ideas occurring to you as you worked at shaping your writing. You probably did your best to ignore those thoughts. After all, the paper was due; time was short. But it is important to realize that those "alien" ideas you resisted so strenuously were also yours and might have been suggested by the writing you were doing. Almost beyond your control, your words and ideas opened the door to other words and ideas, telling you more about your subject or connecting it to other thoughts. Freewriting is a way you can pull these "wild" relationships out of the background and examine them.

Another way of using freewriting is to begin with a focus—for example, an issue or idea that creates a reason to write for you but that you cannot yet develop into a dominant idea. Begin writing, keeping the topic in the back of your mind but letting the writing go where it wants to go. This technique works very well when you have been given a specific assignment that has you stuck.

With its emphasis upon discovering connections, freewriting looks like clustering, and in many ways it is clustering in prose. The major difference between the two is that in freewriting you have the potential of discovering, not only your ideas and the connections between them, but also effective ways you might organize those ideas and the language to dress them in. In effect, after you've finished freewriting, you have a draft to work with. Pay attention to your choice of words and phrases, and to the rhythms of your sentences. Often these "unconscious" choices suggest the most effective ways of clothing your ideas.

❧ *Working with the Readings*

Read these two poems and use the questions that follow each one to prompt your ideas, not to close off possibilities. Choose one of the poems—or both—and sit and think about it for a few minutes. Let the poem or poems speak to your experiences with the same situations and feelings. Then see the instructions for freewriting on page 71 under "An Invitation to Write."

BARBIE DOLL

Marge Piercy

This girlchild was born as usual
and presented dolls that did pee-pee
and miniature GE stoves and irons
and wee lipsticks the color of cherry candy.
Then in the magic of puberty, a classmate said: *5*
You have a great big nose and fat legs.

She was healthy, tested intelligent,
possessed strong arms and back,
abundant sexual drive and manual dexterity.
She went to and fro apologizing.   *10*
Everyone saw a fat nose on thick legs.

She was advised to play coy,
exhorted to come on hearty,
exercise, diet, smile and wheedle.
Her good nature wore out   *15*
like a fan belt.
So she cut off her nose and her legs
and offered them up.

In the casket displayed on satin she lay
with the undertaker's cosmetics painted on,   *20*

a turned-up putty nose,
dressed in a pink and white nightie.
Doesn't she look pretty? everyone said.
Consummation at last.
To every woman a happy ending.   *25*

---

1. What do you think the title of Piercy's poem has to do with the poem?
2. What makes a big nose and fat legs important?
3. What is the "happy ending"?
4. Can the idea of this poem be applied to a "manchild" with a change in the details? What would the changes have to be?
5. Have you known anyone who has searched for a "happy ending" like the girl's in the poem? How did you treat that person? What did you think of him or her?

THE VICTIMS

Sharon Olds

When Mother divorced you, we were glad. She took it and
took it in silence, all those years and then
kicked you out, suddenly, and her
kids loved it. Then you were fired, and we
grinned inside, the way people grinned when   *5*
Nixon's helicopter lifted off the South
Lawn for the last time. We were tickled
to think of your office taken away,
your secretaries taken away,
your lunches, with three double bourbons,   *10*
your pencils, your reams of paper. Would they take your
suits back, too, those dark
carcasses hung in your closet, and the black
noses of your shoes with their large pores?
She had taught us to take it, to hate you and take it   *15*
until we pricked with her for your
annihilation. Father. Now I
pass the bums in doorways, the white
slugs of their bodies gleaming through slits in their
suits of compressed silt, the stained   *20*
flippers of their hands, the underwater

fire of their eyes, ships gone down with the
lanterns lit and I wonder who took it and
took it from them in silence until they had
given it all away and had nothing   *25*
left but this.

---

1. Who are the victims?
2. What is the relationship between the mother and her children?
3. Is the speaker in the last third of the poem different from the speaker in the first two-thirds? What is the difference?
4. What does "take it" and "took it" mean in the poem? Does the meaning of the phrase change?
5. Do you think the poem would have been different if a man had written it? In what way?
6. There are two ways of seeing (two points of view) the father in this poem. What do they have to do with each other? Does the speaker's movement from one to the other make sense to you?

⚛ *An Invitation to Write*

Using your experiences with situations and feelings like those expressed in the poem or poems you chose, freewrite for the amount of time specified by your instructor or until you feel you have used up the ideas and experiences that have occurred to you. Then, freewrite for another five minutes. Remember: Don't go back to revise or edit. Just keep writing.

Look at the writing you've done. Does it suggest an essay? a short story? a poem?

If you're working with a group, give each member a copy of your freewriting to read. Using the first-draft questions in Chapter 3 (page 49) as your starting point, discuss the possibilities of making your writing an essay, a poem, or a short story.

Be certain to take notes as the group discusses your freewriting, to remind you of what members say or to record your own thoughts.

If your teacher asks you to do so, move on to a second draft and a finished piece of writing.

THE JOURNALIST'S QUESTIONS AND THE PENTAD: EXAMINING WHAT HAPPENED AND WHY IT HAPPENED

A reporter writing a story for a newspaper must answer six questions— Who? What? When? Where? Why? How?—if that writer intends to write an accurate account of an incident. In fact, these questions work very nicely as a discovery strategy for reporting an event.

Although the journalist's questions are effective up to a point, they can also lead to overhasty or too-simple conclusions. Kenneth Burke devised a variation on these questions which he called the Pentad.[1]

The Pentad is especially effective when you want to look beyond the surface of an incident, especially when that incident is tied up with people's conflicts, motives, and actions. Many events which touch you or those around you arise from the behavior and confrontation or cooperation of others, as well as from your actions. Many times it is not people's actions alone, but the reasons for the actions and how the actors' surroundings influenced them that are as important as the actions themselves. To completely understand what you have observed and to communicate that understanding, you have to examine such matters as what sorts of persons were involved in the event, the reasons they acted as they did, what they hoped to gain by their actions, how their surroundings affected their actions, and what means they used to accomplish their actions.

The Pentad is a set of five questions (and their possible combinations) which suggest possible explanations for the behavior and motives of persons involved in a conflict. These are the questions:

Act	What was done?
Scene	Where was the act done? What time?
Agent	Who did it?
Agency	How was the act done? What was used?
Purpose	Why was the act done?

You could answer these questions in the simplest way and make them behave like the journalist's questions. But if you do that, you misuse a very powerful tool, not unlike buying a computer to play a video game. To understand the possibilities built into these questions, it is important to look at them more closely and then to ask them in combination with each other.

Act: What Was Done?

Questions about acts focus on what an individual does by choice and for reasons. Blinking your eyes or breathing is simply a physical event, a reflex. However, if you go to see a violent or frightening movie and you close your eyes at what happens on the screen, you chose to do so. That is an *act*. An act never happens without an actor to do it, a means by which it is accomplished, a reason, or the surroundings in which it happens. When you consider an act, you must also consider the nature of the person who chose to act, the means by which the person carried out the act, the situation in which the act occurred, and the reasons why it occurred.

---

1. Kenneth Burke, *A Grammar of Motives* (Berkeley: U of California P, 1969).

Scene: Where and When Did It Happen?

Scene—the environment in which an act occurs—is the most elastic of all the elements of the Pentad. Consider the setting in which you are reading this book. Where are you? Are you in a room? If you are, what sort of room are you in? Is the room in a house? an apartment? a library? a dormitory? Maybe you're reading this book on your way to or from school. You could be on a bus or riding the subway. What is going on around you? When will you stop reading and do something else? Why will you stop? All these questions grow from the scene in which your act of reading this book happens.

But there is a still larger scene for reading this book that you might consider. That scene is most likely the course for which this book is one of the required textbooks. The course is being taught in a particular school. You are taking the course during a particular term—fall, winter, or spring— and that term may be a quarter or a semester in a certain year, in a certain century. Furthermore, your school is in or near a town or city in a particular state, in a particular country. Your presence in the school may be partly the result of its location.

Scene becomes still more elastic when you consider that the term does not have to mean something physical to be useful. The very existence of the school where you go to the class for which you're reading this book is the result of a political scene, an economic scene, and, certainly, a philosophical scene. Is your school a liberal arts school? a polytechnic school? a community college? You have placed yourself in this scene. Why this school and not another one? What does the scene of your family, its values, its finances have to do with your presence at this school and not at another?

As you can see, the apparently simple question of scene becomes a complex, fascinating web of interrelated questions—questions that often depend on your answers to the previous questions. The same act may suggest different relationships to different observers, leading to different definitions of the scene. Since you are the writer, you must exercise your own judgment as to how and where to limit the scene that interests you. It is up to you to decide which questions and answers are relevant.

Agent: Who Did It?

Agent is the term for the person who acts. To consider the character of the agent, you have to consider the act as well and the relation between the two. For example, there are many versions of the story of the woman whose child or husband was trapped under a car that had fallen off its jack. As the story goes, the woman raised the car with one hand while pulling her child or husband from beneath it with the other. At the time, that particular person (agent) was capable of that particular act—but not at other times. Often you'll find that the combination of the act and the agent leads you to the next question.

Agency: What Was Used?

You can think of *agency* as the means or method the actor uses to bring the act into being. The agency may be physical—for example, a hammer used to drive a nail. The agency can be mental; for example, you might use a logical argument to persuade someone to adopt your point of view. An agency can be emotional; for example, you can appeal to another person's emotions to get what you want. Or you might use a combination of these approaches.

Often the agency is at least partially created by the scene in which the event occurs. An event happening at a particular time and place contains certain agencies that a person might use. That same event at another time and in another place might offer different agencies.

If you talk a friend into going to a movie he or she does not want to see by reminding your friend that you went to a movie you did not want to see just the week before, your agency is an argument based on guilt, or at least on a sense of obligation. If that argument alone doesn't work, you might offer to pay for your friend's ticket. Then financial temptation becomes a part of your agency. Offering to drive your friend to the movie would be another addition to your agency. However, if your friend has a car and you do not, your agency might be offering to pay for gas in addition to everything else.

Purpose: Why Was It Done?

As you know from examining your behavior and the behavior of others, the reasons you or another person may give for doing something are not always the real, the only, or *all* the reasons that underlie the act. To discover the truth of an act, you have to discover the *purpose* behind it. When, for example, you complimented your mother on her new hairstyle, was it just because you wanted to make her feel good? Was it because you really liked it? Or did you need to borrow her car? Maybe it was for all three purposes. Motives are rarely as simple or straightforward as we and others pretend. Because we have to get on with our daily lives, we hardly ever stop to think about this question. However, when we come to examine our own or other people's actions, it is important to look more carefully and to probe more deeply into the purpose behind the act.

The Ratios of the Pentad

As you have seen, it is almost impossible to consider one element of the Pentad without weighing at least some of the others. However, you'll find the Pentad far more effective if you create and examine these combinations deliberately. When you do this, your questions become more complicated, but with this complexity comes more power.

The power comes from combining these questions systematically into what Kenneth Burke calls "ratios." That is, you can consider any one of the elements in relation to each of the other four. Doing so will create twenty questions, each of which may lead to discoveries. Remember, each event or action is different, and in different cases different ratios will be more productive than others.

For example, here are the ratios of *act:*

ACT–SCENE	What does the scene reveal about the act?
ACT–AGENT	What does the agent reveal about the act?
ACT–AGENCY	What does the agency reveal about the act?
ACT–PURPOSE	How does the purpose shape the act?

The other Pentad ratios follow the same principle.

✎ *Working with a Reading*

Read the following story and apply the Pentad and its ratios to one of the characters. As you use the Pentad on the story, remember that not every question will necessarily produce answers for you and that there is no "approved" order to the questions; one might lead you to any of the others. As you ask the questions, keep a record of the answers on a sheet of paper. Write quickly and don't censor yourself. Play with your ideas.

If you are working with a group, duplicate a copy of your responses for each member. As you read through the discoveries other members of your group have recorded, see what experiences or observations in your life you remember that help you understand more about this reading.

Now discuss how your reading of this story differs from those of other members of your group. But remember: You are not trying to discover who is "right" or "wrong" in this discussion. You are only attempting to see how different people can see the same event in different ways.

What you discover by using the Pentad may suggest a subject for an essay, poetry, prose fiction, or a drama. Your teacher might ask you to write a draft or to freewrite on the basis of your discoveries. If so, meet with your group afterward and apply the first-draft questions in Chapter 3 (page 49).

THE USE OF FORCE

William Carlos Williams

They were new patients to me, all I had was the name, Olson. Please come down as soon as you can, my daughter is very sick.

When I arrived I was met by the mother, a big startled looking woman, very clean and apologetic who merely said, Is this the doctor? and let me in. In the back, she added. You must excuse us, doctor, we have her in the kitchen where it is warm. It is very damp here sometimes.

The child was fully dressed and sitting on her father's lap near the kitchen table. He tried to get up, but I motioned for him not to bother, took off my overcoat and started to look things over. I could see that they were all very nervous, eyeing me up and down distrustfully. As often, in such cases, they weren't telling me more than they had to, it was up to me to tell them; that's why they were spending three dollars on me.

The child was fairly eating me up with her cold, steady eyes, and no expression to her face whatever. She did not move and seemed, inwardly, quiet; an unusually attractive little thing, and as strong as a heifer in appearance. But her face was flushed, she was breathing rapidly, and I realized that she had a high fever. She had magnificent blonde hair, in profusion. One of those picture children often reproduced in advertising leaflets and the photogravure sections of the Sunday papers.

She's had a fever for three days, began the father and we don't know what it comes from. My wife has given her things, you know, like people do, but it don't do no good. And there's been a lot of sickness around. So we tho't you'd better look her over and tell us what is the matter.

As doctors often do I took a trial shot at it as a point of departure. Has she had a sore throat?

Both parents answered me together, No . . . No, she says her throat don't hurt her.

Does your throat hurt you? added the mother to the child. But the little girl's expression didn't change nor did she move her eyes from my face.

Have you looked?

I tried to, said the mother, but I couldn't see.

As it happens we had been having a number of cases of diphtheria in the school to which this child went during that month and we were all, quite apparently, thinking of that, though no one had as yet spoken of the thing.

Well, I said, suppose we take a look at the throat first. I smiled in my best professional manner and asking for the child's first name I said, come on, Mathilda, open your mouth and let's take a look at your throat.

Nothing doing.

Aw, come on, I coaxed, just open your mouth wide and let me take a look. Look, I said opening both hands wide, I haven't anything in my hands. Just open up and let me see.

Such a nice man, put in the mother. Look how kind he is to you. Come on, do what he tells you to. He won't hurt you.

At that I ground my teeth in disgust. If only they wouldn't use the word "hurt" I might be able to get somewhere. But I did not allow myself to be hurried or disturbed but speaking quietly and slowly I approached the child again.

As I moved my chair a little nearer suddenly with one catlike movement both her hands clawed instinctively for my eyes and she almost reached them too. In fact she knocked my glasses flying and they fell, though unbroken, several feet away from me on the kitchen floor.

Both the mother and father almost turned themselves inside out in embarrassment and apology. You bad girl, said the mother, taking her and shaking her by one arm. Look what you've done. The nice man . . .

For heaven's sake, I broke in. Don't call me a nice man to her. I'm here to look at her throat on the chance that she might have diphtheria and possibly die of it. But that's nothing to her. Look here, I said to the child, we're going to look at your throat. You're old enough to understand what I'm saying. Will you open it now by yourself or shall we have to open it for you?

Not a move. Even her expression hadn't changed. Her breaths however were coming faster and faster. Then the battle began. I had to do it. I had to have a throat culture for her own protection. But first I told the parents that it was entirely up to them. I explained the danger but said that I would not insist on a throat examination so long as they would take the responsibility.

If you don't do what the doctor says you'll have to go to the hospital, the mother admonished her severely.

Oh yeah? I had to smile to myself. After all, I had already fallen in love with the savage brat, the parents were contemptible to me. In the ensuing struggle they grew more and more abject, crushed, exhausted while she surely rose to magnificent heights of insane fury of effort bred of her terror of me.

The father tried his best, and he was a big man but the fact that she was his daughter, his shame at her behavior and his dread of hurting her made him release her just at the critical moment several times when I had almost achieved success, till I wanted to kill him. But his dread also that she might have diphtheria made him tell me to go on, go on though he himself was almost fainting, while the mother moved back and forth behind us raising and lowering her hands in an agony of apprehension.

Put her in front of you on your lap, I ordered, and hold both her wrists.

But as soon as he did the child let out a scream. Don't, you're hurting me. Let go of my hands. Let them go I tell you. Then she shrieked terrifyingly, hysterically. Stop it! Stop it! You're killing me!

Do you think she can stand it, doctor! said the mother.

You get out, said the husband to his wife. Do you want her to die of diphtheria?

Come on now, hold her, I said.

Then I grasped the child's head with my left hand and tried to get the wooden tongue depressor between her teeth. She fought, with clenched teeth, desperately! But now I also had grown furious—at a child. I tried to hold myself down but I couldn't. I know how to expose a throat for inspection. And I did my best. When finally I got the wooden spatula behind the last teeth and just the point of it into the mouth cavity, she opened up for an instant but before I could see anything she came down again and gripping the wooden blade between her molars she reduced it to splinters before I could get it out again.

Aren't you ashamed, the mother yelled at her. Aren't you ashamed to act like that in front of the doctor?

Get me a smooth–handled spoon of some sort, I told the mother. We're going through with this. The child's mouth was already bleeding. Her tongue was cut and she was screaming in wild hysterical shrieks. Perhaps I should have desisted and come back in an hour or more. No doubt it would have been better. But I have seen at least two children lying dead in bed of neglect in such cases, and feeling that I must get a diagnosis now or never I went at it again. But the worst of it was that I too had got beyond reason. I could have torn the child apart in my own fury and enjoyed it. It was a pleasure to attack her. My face was burning with it.

The damned little brat must be protected against her own idiocy, one says to one's self at such times. Others must be protected against her. It is social necessity. And all these things are true. But a blind fury, a feeling of adult shame, bred of a longing for muscular release are the operatives. One goes on to the end.

In a final unreasoning assault I overpowered the child's neck and jaws. I forced the heavy silver spoon back of her teeth and down her throat till she gagged. And there it was—both tonsils covered with membrane. She had fought valiantly to keep me from knowing her secret. She had been hiding that sore throat for three days at least and lying to her parents in order to escape just such an outcome as this.

Now truly she *was* furious. She had been on the defensive before but now she attacked. Tried to get off her father's lap and fly at me while tears of defeat blinded her eyes.

KNOWING AND EXAMINING: CHANGING YOUR PERSPECTIVE [2]

Watch a very young child explore an unfamiliar object. The child will pick it up, look closely at it, turn it over to see it from different angles, bang it against another object, feel its texture, and even try to taste it. That child's behavior is a version of what we all do when we encounter something new. When we come across an interesting object, idea, or event that we have never seen before, we try to identify it in relation to what we already know

---

2. This approach has been adapted from Richard E. Young, Alton L. Becker, and Kenneth L. Pike, *Rhetoric: Discovery and Change* (New York: Harcourt, 1970).

and to examine its details to find out more about it. Many people in a town or city they have never visited before find themselves trying to discover ways it is like a place that is familiar to them—and, inevitably, they find ways that it is different. They might walk about, looking at the location from different angles. They sniff the air, look at how the light shines on various surfaces, eat the food, and listen and talk to people. They try to get the "feel" of the place.

You can make this exploring behavior into a discovery strategy that will open an event, object, or even an idea for you. This strategy contains four sets of questions. These question sets reflect the way you come to know events or objects and the way you examine them more closely. Taken together, the questions reflect and illuminate each other until you see the object in more depth. Using these questions is something like first seeing a black-and-white picture in two dimensions and then adding depth and color.

The knowing and examining questions are presented here in a specific order, and it's not a bad idea to follow that order the first few times you use them. As you become more experienced with them, and they begin to feel familiar to you, don't feel bound to ask them in the recommended sequence. Let your topic and how you respond to it determine the order.

How Is This Object or Event
Different From and Like Similar Objects or Events?

Which of its qualities make it like similar objects or events?

Which qualities are the most important in knowing this object or event?

Which of its qualities make it different from similar objects or events?

Do these important qualities reflect the object's or event's likeness or difference from similar objects?

How Does the Object or Event Change?

Does the object or event have only one name, or does it have different names?

Do the different names cause you to see the object or event in a different way?

With the passing of time, has the event or object changed? Have its names changed over time?

How do you expect this object or event to change in the future?

How much and what kind of future change would it take to make this object or event something other than what it is?

At what point in that change will this object or event become different?

How is the object or event changing right now?

What Are the Object's or Event's Parts?

What are the parts of the object or event?

How do these parts fit together to make the object or event?

Which of these parts are important in identifying the object or event?

Which of these parts can be changed without changing the object or event?

Where Does the Object or Event Fit In?

What caused the object or event?

What does the object or event cause?

What does the object or event look like from different angles?

What is the object or event most like?

What is the object or event least like?

In what ways is the object or event like the thing it is least like?

Here are two very different invitations to write. Look at both of them and choose one.

✎ An Invitation to Write

Take a familiar object that you can easily carry to class, one you have lived with and used so long that you never pay attention to it—for example, your toothbrush or your shoe. Apply the question sets to it, taking notes as you go. Keep in mind that one of the later questions might take you back to rethink an earlier one.

Look at your notes. Have you discovered something about your object that is surprising or strange? Your discovery might have something to do with the way you see the object itself, or it may reflect a connection between you and the object or the object's surroundings that you had not noticed before. Or you might have learned something new about your relationship to the object.

Put your discovery into a paragraph or two, a poem, or a story so that what you have seen and thought is clear to someone who might read your piece.

If you are working with a group, provide each member with a copy of your writing. Bring the object you've chosen to your group. Listen to each other's paragraphs. After each person has read, the other members of your group should answer the following questions:

1. What have you learned about the object that you had not realized before?

2. What ideas can you add to the writer's ideas about his or her object?

If your teacher asks you to, draft a piece of writing that makes your new idea about the object you have chosen clear to the reader and that shows how your new idea could be important to the reader.

 An Invitation to Write

Apply the knowing and examining question sets to yourself, taking notes as you do so. You might find this exercise much more difficult than the previous one, not because the questions are any different but because the answers are far more personal. You might find yourself seeing yourself in ways you had not expected. If you are preparing this exercise for your group, don't feel that you have to include everything that appears in your notes. But do choose one way of seeing yourself that you found to be new and surprising and put that discovery in a short piece of writing—essay, story, or poem—that makes your discovery clear to someone who might read your piece.

If you are working with a group, provide a copy of your paragraph(s) to each member. Listen to each other's paragraphs. After each person has read, the other group members should answer the following questions:

1. What has the writer's statement taught you about a different way of seeing yourself?
2. Can that idea be turned into an statement about yourself?

If your teacher asks you to, write a draft showing the differences between how you viewed yourself before you applied the questions to yourself and how you see yourself now. As you write this draft, don't assume that your reader knows anything about you.

Working with a Reading

Read the following essay. Then apply the knowing and examining questions to one of the characters, as explained in the instructions that follow the essay.

DISCOVERY OF A FATHER

Sherwood Anderson

You hear it said that fathers want their sons to be what they feel they cannot themselves be, but I tell you it also works the other way. A boy wants something very special from his father. I know that as a small boy I wanted my father to be a certain thing he was not. I wanted him to be a proud, silent, dignified father. When I was with other boys and he passed along the street, I wanted to feel a flow of pride: "There he is. That is my father."

But he wasn't such a one. He couldn't be. It seemed to me then that he was always showing off. Let's say someone in our town had got up a show. They were always doing it. The druggist would be in it, the shoe-store clerk, the horse doctor, and a lot of women and girls. My father would manage to get the chief comedy part. It was, let's say, a Civil War play and he was a comic Irish soldier. He had to do the most absurd things. They thought he was funny, but I didn't.

I thought he was terrible. I didn't see how mother could stand it. She even laughed with the others. Maybe I would have laughed if it hadn't been my father.

Or there was a parade, the Fourth of July or Decoration Day. He'd be in that, too, right at the front of it, as Grand Marshal or something, on a white horse hired from a livery stable.

He couldn't ride for shucks. He fell off the horse and everyone   5
hooted with laughter, but he didn't care. He even seemed to like it. I remember once when he had done something ridiculous, and right out on Main Street, too. I was with some other boys and they were laughing and shouting at him and he was shouting back and having as good a time as they were. I ran down an alley back of some stores and there in the Presbyterian Church sheds I had a good long cry.

Or I would be in bed at night and father would come home a little lit up and bring some men with him. He was a man who was never alone. Before he went broke, running a harness shop, there were always a lot of men loafing in the shop. He went broke, of course, because he gave too much credit. He couldn't refuse it and I thought he was a fool. I had got to hating him.

There'd be men I didn't think would want to be fooling around with him. There might even be the superintendent of our schools and a quiet man who ran the hardware store. Once I remember there was a white-haired man who was a cashier of the bank. It was a wonder to me they'd want to be seen with such a windbag. That's what I thought he was. I know now what it was that attracted them. It was because life in our town, as in all small towns, was at times pretty dull and he livened it up. He made them laugh. He could tell stories. He'd even get them to singing.

If they didn't come to our house they'd go off, say at night, to where there was a grassy place by a creek. They'd cook food there and drink beer and sit about listening to his stories.

He was always telling stories about himself. He'd say this or that wonderful thing had happened to him. It might be something that made him look like a fool. He didn't care.

If an Irishman came to our house, right away father would say he was   10
Irish. He'd tell what county in Ireland he was born in. He'd tell things that happened there when he was a boy. He'd make it seem so real that,

if I hadn't known he was born in southern Ohio, I'd have believed him myself.

If it was a Scotchman the same thing happened. He'd get a burr into his speech. Or he was a German or a Swede. He'd be anything the other man was. I think they all knew he was lying, but they seemed to like him just the same. As a boy that was what I couldn't understand.

And there was mother. How could she stand it? I wanted to ask but never did. She was not the kind you asked such questions.

I'd be upstairs in my bed, in my room above the porch, and father would be telling some of his tales. A lot of father's stories were about the Civil War. To hear him tell it he'd been in about every battle. He'd known Grant, Sherman, Sheridan and I don't know how many others. He'd been particularly intimate with General Grant so that when Grant went East, to take charge of all the armies, he took father along.

"I was an orderly at headquarters and Sim Grant said to me, 'Irve,' he said, 'I'm going to take you along with me.'"

It seems he and Grant used to slip off sometimes and have a quiet drink together. That's what my father said. He'd tell about the day Lee surrendered and how, when the great moment came, they couldn't find Grant.

"You know," my father said, "about General Grant's book, his memoirs. You've read of how he said he had a headache and how, when he got word that Lee was ready to call it quits, he was suddenly and miraculously cured.

"Huh," said father. "He was in the woods with me.

"I was in there with my back against a tree. I was pretty well corned. I had got hold of a bottle of pretty good stuff.

"They were looking for Grant. He had got off his horse and come into the woods. He found me. He was covered with mud.

"I had the bottle in my hand. What'd I care? The war was over. I knew we had them licked."

My father said that he was the one who told Grant about Lee. An orderly riding by had told him, because the orderly knew how thick he was with Grant. Grant was embarrassed.

"But, Irve, look at me. I'm all covered with mud," he said to father.

And then, my father said, he and Grant decided to have a drink together. They took a couple of shots and then, because he didn't want Grant to show up potted before the immaculate Lee, he smashed the bottle against the tree.

"Sim Grant's dead now and I wouldn't want it to get out on him," my father said.

That's just one of the kind of things he'd tell. Of course, the men knew he was lying, but they seemed to like it just the same.

When we got broke, down and out, do you think he ever brought anything home? Not he. If there wasn't anything to eat in the house, he'd go off visiting around at farmhouses. They all wanted him. Sometimes he'd stay away for weeks, mother working to keep us fed, and then home he'd come bringing, let's say, a ham. He'd got it from some farmer friend. He'd slap it on the table in the kitchen. "You bet I'm going to see that my kids have something to eat," he'd say, and mother would just stand smiling at him. She'd never say a word about all the weeks and months he'd been away, not leaving us a cent for food. Once I heard her speaking to a woman in our street. Maybe the woman had dared to sympathize with her. "Oh," she said, "it's all right. He isn't ever dull like most of the men in this street. Life is never dull when my man is about."

But often I was filled with bitterness, and sometimes I wished he wasn't my father. I'd even invent another man as my father. To protect my mother I'd make up stories of a secret marriage that for some strange reason never got known. As though some man, say the president of a railroad company or maybe a Congressman, had married my mother, thinking his wife was dead and then it turned out she wasn't.

So they had to hush it up but I got born just the same. I wasn't really the son of my father. Somewhere in the world there was a very dignified, quite wonderful man who was really my father. I even made myself half believe these fancies.

And then there came a certain night. He'd been off somewhere for two or three weeks. He found me alone in the house, reading by the kitchen table.

It had been raining and he was very wet. He sat and looked at me for 30 a long time, not saying a word. I was startled, for there was on his face the saddest look I had ever seen. He sat for a time, his clothes dripping. Then he got up.

"Come on with me," he said.

I got up and went with him out of the house. I was filled with wonder but I wasn't afraid. We went along a dirt road that led down into a valley, about a mile out of town, where there was a pond. We walked in silence. The man who was always talking had stopped his talking.

I didn't know what was up and had the queer feeling that I was with a stranger. I don't know whether my father intended it so. I don't think he did.

The pond was quite large. It was still raining hard and there were flashes of lightning followed by thunder. We were on a grassy bank at the pond's edge when my father spoke, and in the darkness and rain his voice sounded strange.

"Take off your clothes," he said. Still filled with wonder, I began to 35 undress. There was a flash of lightning and I saw that he was already naked.

Naked, we went into the pond. Taking my hand he pulled me in. It may be that I was too frightened, too full of a feeling of strangeness, to speak. Before that night my father had never seemed to pay any attention to me.

"And what is he up to now?" I kept asking myself. I did not swim very well, but he put my hand on his shoulder and struck out into the darkness.

He was a man with big shoulders, a powerful swimmer. In the darkness I could feel the movement of his muscles. We swam to the far edge of the pond and then back to where we had left our clothes. The rain continued and the wind blew. Sometimes my father swam on his back and when he did he took my hand in his large powerful one and moved it over so that it rested always on his shoulder. Sometimes there would be a flash of lightning and I could see his face quite clearly.

It was as it was earlier, in the kitchen, a face filled with sadness. There would be the momentary glimpse of his face and then again the darkness, the wind and the rain. In me there was a feeling I had never known before.

It was a feeling of closeness. It was something strange. It was as though there were only we two in the world. It was as though I had been jerked suddenly out of myself, out of my world of the schoolboy, out of a world in which I was ashamed of my father.   *40*

He had become blood of my blood; he the strong swimmer and I the boy clinging to him in the darkness. We swam in silence and in silence we dressed in our wet clothes, and went home.

There was a lamp lighted in the kitchen and when we came in, the water dripping from us, there was my mother. She smiled at us. I remember that she called us "boys."

"What have you boys been up to?" she asked, but my father did not answer. As he had begun the evening's experience with me in silence, so he ended it. He turned and looked at me. Then he went, I thought, with a new and strange dignity out of the room.

I climbed the stairs to my own room, undressed in the darkness and got into bed. I couldn't sleep and did not want to sleep. For the first time I knew that I was the son of my father. He was a story teller as I was to be. It may be that I even laughed a little softly there in the darkness. If I did, I laughed knowing that I would never again be wanting another father.

Concentrating on the father, the son, or the mother in Anderson's story, apply the knowing and examining questions to the character you have chosen, taking notes on your responses.

Using your notes as a focus, do about twenty minutes of freewriting about that character as he or she connects with your own experience of your or another person's parents.

If you are working with a group, duplicate enough copies of your freewriting for each member to have one to read. At the meeting, members should read their freewriting aloud one by one, and group members should answer the first-draft questions in Chapter 3 (page 49) as a starting point to discussing each piece.

Group members should also answer these questions:

1. What seems to be the writer's central idea about parents and their relationship to their children? That is, what idea does the writer seem to return to in different ways?

2. How does the writer's central idea (as you understand it) conflict with ideas you have about the relationship between a child and one of his or her parents?

3. Define and describe that conflict to the other members of the group.

If your teacher asks you to, write a draft of a story, a poem, or an essay that reflects a dominant idea you have discovered about parents and children. Allow that idea to grow from your experience and from what you think was the most important conflict between your ideas about parents and children and the other ideas that grew out of your group discussion.

Remember as you write this draft that your reader probably doesn't know you or your family.

———————————————

Your Subject and Your Dominant Idea

THE RELATIONSHIP BETWEEN YOUR SUBJECT AND YOUR DOMINANT IDEA

When you use one or more discovery strategies, you generate a lot of information. All of it reflects your interests, your concerns, and your responses to the focus of your attention. All of it is potentially a central point from which your writing can grow. However, before you begin to draft a piece of writing, you should think about what its central subject might be: the position or attitude that the results of your discovery strategy suggest you might take toward your subject and what parts of your first exploration of your ideas might be useful in making your idea clear to others.

Moving from a tentative sense of your subject to your dominant idea about your subject and beginning to create a relationship between them are two of the most important steps in making your writing effective. Exploring that relationship leads you to a clear, focused, successful piece of writing instead of one that is disorganized and wanders aimlessly from point to point.

Your subject is what your writing is about, the theme of the piece. Your dominant idea is the focus you put upon your subject. Your dominant idea reflects the conclusions you have reached about your subject or the attitude toward your subject that you want to share with your reader. Picture the dominant idea as a light that you focus on the topic; it highlights certain parts and throws others into shadow. Often, your dominant idea will be a declarative statement—an assertion—about the topic, although you may never make that statement directly to your reader. You might find yourself developing a statement *about* the topic that takes a position in relation to it. At other times, you might find yourself reflecting an attitude about your topic. Or you might discover that you are presenting your topic to your reader in a special way that you have discovered but which your reader might not have considered before.

Working with the Readings

Read the following pair of essays; then, either alone or in discussion with your group, answer the questions that follow the second essay.

WHO KILLED BENNY PARET?

Norman Cousins

Sometime about 1935 or 1936 I had an interview with Mike Jacobs, the prize-fight promoter. I was a fledgling newspaper reporter at that time; my beat was education, but during the vacation season I found myself on varied assignments, all the way from ship news to sports reporting. In this way I found myself sitting opposite the most powerful figure in the boxing world.

There was nothing spectacular in Mr. Jacobs's manner or appearance; but when he spoke about prize fights, he was no longer a bland little man but a colossus who sounded the way Napoleon must have sounded when he reviewed a battle. You knew you were listening to Number One. His saying something made it true.

We discussed what to him was the only important element in successful promoting—how to please the crowd. So far as he was concerned, there was no mystery to it. You put killers in the ring and the people filled your arena. You hire boxing artists—men who are adroit at feinting, parrying, weaving, jabbing, and dancing, but who don't pack dynamite in their fists—and you wind up counting your empty seats. So you searched for the killers and sluggers and maulers—fellows who could hit with the force of a baseball bat.

I asked Mr. Jacobs if he was speaking literally when he said people came out to see the killer.

"They don't come out to see a tea party," he said evenly. "They come out to see the knockout. They come out to see a man hurt. If they think anything else, they're kidding themselves." *5*

Recently a young man by the name of Benny Paret was killed in the ring. The killing was seen by millions; it was on television. In the twelfth round he was hit hard in the head several times, went down, was counted out, and never came out of the coma.

The Paret fight produced a flurry of investigation. Governor Rockefeller was shocked by what happened and appointed a committee to assess the responsibility. The New York State Boxing Commission decided to find out what was wrong. The District Attorney's office expressed its concern. One question that was solemnly studied in all three probes concerned the action of the referee. Did he act in time to stop the fight? Another question had to do with the role of the examining doctors who certified the physical fitness of the fighters before the bout. Still another question involved Mr. Paret's manager; did he rush his boy into the fight without adequate time to recuperate from the previous one?

In short, the investigators looked into every possible cause except the real one. Benny Paret was killed because the human fist delivers enough impact, when directed against the head, to produce a massive hemorrhage in the brain. The human brain is the most delicate and complex mechanism in all creation. It has a lacework of millions of highly fragile nerve connections. Nature attempts to protect this exquisitely intricate machinery by encasing it in a hard shell. Fortunately, the shell is thick enough to withstand a great deal of pounding. Nature, however, can protect man against everything except man himself. Not every blow to the head will kill a man—but there is always the risk of concussion and damage to the brain. A prize fighter may be able to survive even repeated brain concussions and go on fighting, but the damage to his brain may be permanent.

In any event, it is futile to investigate the referee's role and seek to determine whether he should have intervened to stop the fight earlier. This is not where the primary responsibility lies. The primary responsibility lies with the people who pay to see a man hurt. The referee who stops a fight too soon from the crowd's viewpoint can expect to be booed. The crowd wants the knockout; it wants to see a man stretched out on the canvas. This is the supreme moment in boxing. It is nonsense to talk about prize fighting as a test of boxing skills. No crowd was ever brought to its feet screaming and cheering at the sight of two men beautifully dodging and weaving out of each other's jabs. The time the crowd comes alive is when a man is hit hard over the heart or the head, when his mouthpiece flies out, when blood squirts out of his nose or eyes, when he wobbles under the attack and his pursuer continues to smash at him with poleax impact.

Don't blame it on the referee. Don't even blame it on the fight man- *10* agers. Put the blame where it belongs—on the prevailing mores that regard prize fighting as a perfectly proper enterprise and vehicle of entertainment. No one doubts that many people enjoy prize fighting and will miss it if it should be thrown out. And that is precisely the point.

THE DEATH OF BENNY PARET

Norman Mailer

Paret was a Cuban, a proud club fighter who had become welterweight champion because of his unusual ability to take a punch. His style of fighting was to take three punches to the head in order to give back two. At the end of ten rounds, he would still be bouncing, his opponent would have a headache. But in the last two years, over the fifteen–round fights, he had started to take some bad maulings.

This fight had its turns. Griffith won most of the early rounds, but Paret knocked Griffith down in the sixth. Griffith had trouble getting up, but made it, came alive and was dominating Paret again before the round was over. Then Paret began to wilt. In the middle of the eighth round, after a clubbing punch had turned his back to Griffith, Paret walked three disgusted steps away, showing his hindquarters. For a champion, he took much too long to turn back around. It was the first hint of weakness Paret had ever shown, and it must have inspired a particular shame, because he fought the rest of the fight as if he were seeking to demonstrate that he could take more punishment than any man alive. In the twelfth, Griffith caught him. Paret got trapped in a corner. Trying to duck away, his left arm and his head became tangled on the wrong side of the top rope. Griffith was in like a cat ready to rip the life out of a huge boxed rat. He hit him eighteen right hands in a row, an act which took perhaps three or four seconds, Griffith making a pent-up whimpering sound all the while he attacked, the right hand whipping like a piston rod which has broken through the crankcase, or like a baseball bat demolishing a pumpkin. I was sitting in the second row of that corner—they were not ten feet away from me, and like everybody else, I was hypnotized. I had never seen one man hit another so hard and so many times. Over the referee's face came a look of woe as if some spasm had passed its way through him, and then he leaped on Griffith to pull him away. It was the act of a brave man. Griffith was uncontrollable. His trainer leaped into the ring, his manger, his cut man, there were four people holding Griffith, but he was off on an orgy, he had left the Garden, he was back on a hoodlum's street. If he had been able to break loose from his handlers and the referee, he would have jumped Paret to the floor and whaled on him there.

And Paret? Paret died on his feet. As he took those eighteen punches something happened to everyone who was in psychic range of the event. Some part of his death reached out to us. One felt it hover in the air. He was still standing in the ropes, trapped as he had been before, he gave some little half-smile of regret, as if he were saying, "I didn't know I was going to die just yet," and then, his head leaning back but still erect, his death came to breathe about him. He began to pass away. As he passed, so his limbs descended beneath him, and he sank slowly to the floor. He went down more slowly than any fighter had ever gone down, he went down like a large ship which turns on end and slides second by second into its grave. As he went down, the sound of Griffith's punches echoed in the mind like a heavy ax in the distance chopping into a wet log.

---

1. These essays are not only about the same subject, but they are about the same event. What do you think Cousins's dominant idea is?

What is Mailer's? How do the two ideas differ from each other? Do they overlap at any point?

2. Each writer chooses to present the subject to you in a different way. What does Mailer choose to describe to you? What does Cousins describe? What do these choices have to do with each writer's dominant idea?

3. Each writer opens his piece with the description of a person. How does each writer use that description? How does each writer's opening reflect his dominant idea?

4. Each writer narrates the fight. What are the differences in the narrations? How do the differences reflect each writer's purpose?

5. Each writer uses language differently to present his dominant idea. Try to describe Mailer's and Cousins's voices. How does each writer's choice of language reflect his dominant idea?

❧ *An Invitation to Write*

Find a subject that you feel strongly about and that you can present to your reader through the narration of an incident. Write three or four paragraphs (fiction or nonfiction) or a poem that reflects your feelings about that subject.

Now write three or four paragraphs or a poem that reflects a different set of feelings about the same subject.

Provide each member of your group with a copy of both pieces of writing. Be prepared to discuss with your group or in class how the choices you made differed from the approach you took to the subject.

FINDING YOUR SUBJECT

You've learned that before you can discover your dominant idea, you must discover your subject. You've also learned to keep a record of your thoughts as you use discovery strategies. The thought–map you create helps you see possibilities for an idea or theme and forms the basis for writing a first draft. Your draft is a first exploration of your thoughts to see where they lead and what further information or ideas present themselves as you link your thoughts to each other in connected statements. If you have used freewriting as a discovery strategy, you already have a first draft in hand, but you can often learn a great deal about the possibilities of your ideas if you write a new draft from your freewriting.

Sometimes you'll find that writing your first draft has done a lot of your work for you and that the draft suggests a dominant idea as well as useful examples. At other times, your draft may boil with many possibilities.

Look, for example, at this piece of freewriting and all the possibilities that the writer discovered in his thinking on paper:

I learned in Chemistry today that the total worth of the human body in terms of its chemicals is about $2.50. That's not a lot. I think I value myself more than that. But that shows me that there is more than one way of looking at me or anybody else. It's interesting in my philosophy class we were talking about what a person is worth and how it is measured. I guess there are two types of measurement of people. I don't know why that makes me think about dating. Sometimes I ask a girl out because I like her as a person. Other times I ask a girl out because I like the way she looks. That seems like two different kinds of measurement. In the first situation I'm valuing the girl for what she is to me emotionally and for her mind. In the second situation I look at her almost like a chemist would. Not what she means to me but what her parts are worth to me, just the outside, how she looks. That makes me think about what I learned about the Nazis and the concentration camps in history class. They treated people like things. When they killed them, they even used their parts, like the gold fillings in their teeth and their hair. It scares me that I could be treating other people like that but that's the way it seems to me right now.

On first reading, this piece of writing may seem to wander from idea to idea without any consistent focus—from chemistry to philosophy to dating to modern history. On the other hand, if you look at the draft with the idea of discovering a theme, or repetitions, in it, you might see a number of promising possibilities. For example, the writer touches on the ways apparently unrelated pieces of information he meets in different courses speak to each other and to his life. The writer also speaks of dating and his attitudes toward girls he asks out. He also touches on how a human being is sometimes valued on the basis of what another person wants from him or her.

Looking for topics or repetition, this student found a number of possibilities. For example:

The ways apparently unrelated course material can lead to ideas we can apply to our lives.

The double standard in dating, *or* the different purposes for which people date other people.

The ways in which people are treated like objects.

You may see other possibilities in the draft, but no matter what you (or the writer) come up with, all you have so far is a grouping of potential subjects, general statements of what the writing might be about. Now the writer has to discover a dominant idea among the many possibilities contained in the freewritten draft. Of the possible subjects, the following looked to the writer like the best choices for developing a dominant idea. Remember, these ideas are only possibilities. Looking at the draft from the angle of your experience, you might discover entirely new approaches to both the topic and the dominant idea.

Subject 1

The ways apparently unrelated material from different courses leads to ideas I can apply to my life

Possible Dominant Ideas

- Although I sometimes think that what I learn in college seems disorganized and unrelated, I often find that there are connections I never thought of that teach me something about how to manage my life.
- Many students here think that the required courses outside of their majors are useless, but I have found that the information I get in one course adds to my understanding of the material I learn in courses more relevant to my major.
- College is not valuable simply for learning important material in my major. It also teaches me how to connect ideas from many different fields and apply them to my life.

Subject 2

The different reasons for which people date

Possible Dominant Ideas

- I have found that people date other people for different reasons. Sometimes they date simply for what they can get from the other person. At other times, they want to be with certain people for reasons other than immediate pleasure.
- It is wrong for one person to treat another person as an object intended just for his or her gratification, but I see this attitude in myself and my friends.
- It is perfectly acceptable for people to date each other only for the purposes of immediate pleasure as long as both persons understand the conditions of the relationship and agree to those conditions.

Subject 3

The ways in which people are treated like objects

Possible Dominant Ideas

- Because of the great number of people in our country, it is unfortunately the case that in order to maintain the services we depend on, we have to be treated as if we were objects, identified only by numbers and generalized characteristics.
- There are so many records kept by the various bureaucracies in our society that we have become numbers. As a result, we are rarely treated like individuals. If this goes on much longer, we will all be treated as objects to be used by the government.

❧ *Exercise*

Read the following examples of student freewriting and derive from each piece at least three possible subjects and then at least three possible dominant ideas from each topic.

If you are working with a group, negotiate with each other until you've narrowed your choices for subjects down to three and your choices for dominant ideas down to three for each subject. Report the choices your group has made to the other groups. (*Note:* For clarity, the grammar, punctuation, and spelling have been corrected in these selections.)

Example 1

My boyfriend likes horror movies and he drags me along with him to see them. It's not the gore that scares me about these movies. It's the reactions of the people who come to see them. During the most horrifying parts, I mean the parts that are the bloodiest, the people in the audience cheer for the villain or get excited about the different ways people can be stabbed, shot, chopped, or torn to pieces. I find myself wondering how these same people would react if they say somebody hurt on the street. In these movies, every time Freddy or Jason or whoever attacks another victim, people shout "right on" or "go get him" or they laugh or cheer. This reminds me of the stories I read in the paper of how one person gets angry at another on the freeway or someplace and pulls up next to him and shoots him, or follows him home and tries to beat him up. Or how people see another person in trouble and stand by and watch or try to ignore the situation.

Another part of these movies that scares me is who gets killed or maimed. In most of the ones I've seen, it's people my age who are the victims, and it's usually while they are hugging and kissing or undressing each other and hugging and kissing. I wonder why these people are the victims. I wonder what the message is in these movies or what type of person would write a script that makes these people die and not others.

I wonder why my boyfriend makes me go to these movies with him. I wonder why I go.

Example 2

I hate poetry. Why can't these writers say what they mean? Everything means something else when you read a poem. And the teacher doesn't make it any better. I mean, she stands up there and like magic she gets meaning from these poems that I never even dreamed of. And it's not just me. All the other people I talk to in the class feel the same way. When the teacher stands up there and pulls these incredible meanings out of a poem, I feel stupid. I'm really afraid she's going to call on me one of these days and I'll have to show her how little I know about what she's talking about.

So there I sit with the rest of the class listening to the teacher and wondering what's going on. What does she think? Could she possibly think that we're all getting it just because a few people in the class seem to know what questions to ask and what answers to give? She stands there and lectures. Every now and then she asks a question and some-body answers it and she seems satisfied. If she only knew how little we're getting and how little we care.

Example 3

When I was a kid, I was fat. That's no fun. Everybody made fun of me and I took it. In fact I went along with the fun. They called me "Man-Mountain," and I sort of liked it because at least people knew who I was. But I also hated it. It showed me what people thought of me and how I was known by them. Now that I'm not fat, I'm astounded by how much crap I took from people, and I laughed and let them make fun of me. I guess it was better than being ignored, and people liked me because I let them call me that name.

The only thing I had going for me was football, but that was some-thing important. Because I was so heavy, I was the largest player on a very small team. I mean I weighed 260 pounds, and with me on the line it averaged 200 pounds. But once I made the team, the very thing people made fun of me for became valuable. You hear it said that foot-ball players are dumb jocks, but I found that football made me smarter. My GPA moved from a C before I played football to an A − after I made the team. That led to other problems, though. In my school there were the jocks who hung out together and there were the people with high grades who took the "academic" courses. Because I played football, the "academic" people didn't want to have much to do with me. Because I took the "academic" courses and did well in them, the jocks didn't really trust me.

PLAYING DETECTIVE WITH YOUR THOUGHTS: CHOOSING AND LIMITING YOUR DOMINANT IDEA

When you have developed possibilities for your dominant idea, you will probably be faced with the problem of which one to begin to work with. When you discover which dominant idea suggests a conclusion or attitude you would like to present to an audience of readers, one that re-flects your most pressing reason to write, you have solved that problem. De-ciding which dominant idea is the most important is up to you. You are the best judge of what you want to write about. Earlier in this book you learned about the felt sense: the physical sensation or feeling of excite-ment when you discover an approach that is important to you. Be alert for this excitement as you examine your own ideas and as you listen to what others have to say about them.

In addition, you will almost certainly have greater success if you choose a subject that you know enough about to bring your experience or reading to it. Or you might choose a subject that you want to know more about badly enough to search for more information. Few experiences match the painful frustration of trying to write about a subject you know nothing about, have no interest in, and can find no information on.

Once you have discovered an interesting dominant idea and considered your knowledge of the material and the availability of useful information about that material, the size of the dominant idea is your next concern. How much territory your dominant idea covers is an important element in your writing's success.

When you state your dominant idea, you make a commitment to your reader to provide enough specific, supporting information to make your assumptions, feelings, and conclusions about the idea clear. The size of the commitment a dominant idea makes, then, determines whether it will fit nicely into a short paper, require a longer paper, or be more appropriate to a book. When space and time for making your idea clear are limited and your dominant idea is too large to fit in that space, you have two choices. You can pick a smaller dominant idea—a perfectly intelligent choice if another approach to your topic is more or less equally important to you—or you can work at limiting your idea.

To limit a dominant idea, begin by examining it for terms or phrases that are so broad that they commit you to cover more territory than you can include in the time and space available. It is a good idea to start by writing your dominant idea on paper. Pay special attention to the terms and phrases that have the widest meaning. Then break smaller, more precise, ideas out of them. Another approach is to see if the whole dominant idea contains a number of smaller ideas that are as interesting as, but more manageable than, the original statement.

As an example, review the provisional statement of the first dominant idea for the first example subject proposed on page 93:

> Although I sometimes think that what I learn in college seems disorganized and unrelated, I often find that there are connections I never thought of that teach me something about how to manage my life.

What follows is simply a model of what can happen when a writer works at limiting a dominant idea. The first important phrase in this writer's statement is "what I learn in college." As you know, students in college learn a great deal. Much of it seems irrelevant to their academic goals. Some people learn to take responsibility for the first time by doing their own laundry, shopping, and cooking. Others learn to live in close quarters with people other than family members.

One way the writer could decide which possibility he had in mind when he wrote this phrase is to return to his freewriting. Looking back at the draft on page 93, you might see that the writing seems to declare that it wants to be about the sort of learning that goes on in classes. The examples in the writing seem to cluster around this issue.

Second, the writer has stated in his dominant idea that what he learns in college seems "disorganized and unrelated." This phrase is not precise. The writer might mean that individual courses are badly taught and that the material in them is not clearly organized. It is also possible that he means that the mass of material presented by all the courses seems to be disconnected, although the courses themselves may be well taught. Again, examining the freewriting shows that it is the second idea that he seems to have in mind. However, it is difficult to believe that this judgment is meant to apply to all the courses the writer has taken. For example, chemistry, biology, and physics are closely related and share some concepts and approaches. The same might be said of courses in history, psychology, and sociology. On the basis of the examples the writer spontaneously developed in his freewriting, it seems that he is wondering about the relationship between areas of study that appear unrelated or only distantly related.

So far, then, the more limited dominant idea appears to be the relationship and relevance of courses that seem to the writer to be unrelated to each other or to his life and goals.

The second half of the dominant idea contains this statement: ". . . there are connections I never thought of that teach me something about how I manage my life." As you examine your dominant idea for the first time, you might find yourself making vague statements or using vague terms in relation to each other. "Connections" is not a precise, limited term, and it is difficult to know exactly what this writer means by "manage my life." Each depends on and seems to define the other. Finding relationships between the ideas often shows the writer what he or she means by a vague term or phrase. In this case, the meaning of "connections" might be clearer if the writer could define what he means by "manage my life."

"Manage" can mean almost any sort of control that a person tries to establish. Since the freewriting seems to focus on college, the meaning of "manage" becomes somewhat narrower. This writer seems to be trying to balance the demands of his life as a student: class attendance, homework, recreation, club activities, his social life, and sleeping and eating. Looking back at the freewriting, it seems that this student is especially concerned with a much narrower area. He writes about his relationships with female students and his behavior toward them, with special reference to dating. With this in mind, the meaning of "connections" becomes clearer.

This student's closer examination of his ideas helps him discover that his writing reflects his concern with how the material in his courses has extended his understanding of his behavior toward women and how that understanding resulted from material he never expected would have anything to do with his life.

The result of examining the terms of the first dominant idea and the relationships between them might be a statement something like this:

Although it appears that many of the courses I am required to take in college have nothing to do with my major or career, I have found that what I have learned in these courses gives me important ways of understanding and judging my actions that I had not seen before. For example, in history I learned that dominant groups of people treat other people as if they were objects that they could do with as they chose. When I watch myself and others date girls, or when I hear my friends talking about their girlfriends, I sometimes see the same sort of behavior that I learned about in history class.

The important point of this example is that the writer uncovers what he means by examining the results of his discovery strategy—in this case, freewriting—and working from the map of his ideas, interests, and experiences provided by that strategy. The writer takes his first statement of the dominant idea and he quizzes himself. He asks how the general terms and phrases reflect specific issues and experiences in his life. The answers to these questions help him to find a more manageable dominant idea.

➤ *Exercise*

Read each of the following first attempts at the statement of a dominant idea. Identify the words or phrases that cause trouble because they are too general or because they commit the writer to an idea that is too large for the paper he or she is writing. Assume that the writer has two to four typewritten pages to work with.

By reducing the general words to more specific words or phrases and by taking the commitment the writer makes and breaking smaller assertions out of larger ones if necessary, arrive at what you consider to be a manageable dominant idea for each of the five examples.

If you are working with a group, meet and discuss each member's statements of possible dominant ideas. If the dominant-idea statements derived from each example differ, compare the ways members arrived at their statements, decide which of the results is the most effective, and determine why it is the most effective.

Example 1

The speed limit on the residential street I live on is too high. If the city government does not do something about it, something bad will happen.

Example 2

There are too many students here who are not getting the classes they need in order to graduate. The people who budget the money for the university must take steps to assure that students graduate in a reasonable period of time.

Example 3

We humans have a difficult time sorting out the complications of our world without coming up with extreme or simple ideas. We try to define everything as either black or white, evil or good. We reject relativity; instead of examining our options from case to case, we assume that whatever works in one instance must naturally be the correct line of action for every situation. This is how we were trapped into composing the rigid rules that shape today's society and that have left so many people feeling limited and lacking an outlet for expression, resulting in protest and revolution.

Example 4

Throughout our childhood we are influenced by and controlled by others. Where we go and what we do is influenced by our parents and society. As we grow older and set out on our own, we find that having complete freedom means having complete responsibility.

Example 5

Is the phrase "all men are created equal" the same as stating that all men are created the same? Human genes cause humans to be different from one another. They were created this way to maintain individuality. Yet every being, willing or not, compromises a certain degree of his or her uniqueness to conform to the values of others in order to be accepted.

THE IMPORTANCE OF *ONE* DOMINANT IDEA

Look again at the original piece of freewriting (page 92) that led to the dominant idea you watched our hypothetical student work on. In arriving at his dominant idea, the writer excluded more of his original ideas than he included, notably the ideas regarding chemistry and those having to do with Nazi Germany and the concentration camps. The writer might have developed another, equally interesting dominant idea as well as an entirely different paper out of either one of those possibilities. However, he could not have included all of his material and created a single, unified piece of writing that kept his reader's attention directed at one idea.

To compose effectively, you have to begin with a single dominant idea. That idea might be an assertion of a position that you feel is important; it might be the exploration of a topic from the standpoint of a dominant impression that you want to communicate to others. Whatever your aim, you have to have a clear focal point in mind as you write.

Imagine hiking along a path in the woods, coming to a fork in the path, and trying to follow both trails at the same time. Now imagine presenting your reader with two unrelated or partially related, equally important ideas while trying to make yourself clear to that reader. You might find yourself presenting one idea and then the other. You might drift from one to the other in the middle of a paragraph. You might deal completely with one and then move on to the next, trying desperately to show some connection between the two. No matter which of these alternatives you choose, you will almost certainly confuse your reader.

⟶ *Working with a Reading: A Student Paper*

Here is an example of a student paper. As you read it, try to discover the dominant idea. See if you can define the problems this student created for herself in this paper and then propose solutions for those problems.

If you are meeting in a group, formulate a group statement of the problems in the paper as well as specific solutions your group devises for helping this student make her paper more effective. Report your group's conclusions to the rest of your class.

Stereotypes

If you were lost and needed to ask directions from one of two strangers, who would you ask: a scruffy-looking man wearing tight pink bell-bottom pants or a clean-cut man in a nice suit and tie? Most Americans would choose the man who's clean-cut and wearing a nice suit and tie because he'd seem to be the safer choice. This is because he's stereotyped. He'd be considered respectable and smart by most people because of the way he's dressed. There are many different stereotypes out there, and this is just one of many.

Many people dress the way they do because that is how they want to be stereotyped. If everyone dressed the same, then any form of personalization would be impossible by just looking at someone. I think it's important that everyone has his or her own tastes and styles because they can reveal much information about a person. When someone has a certain style, it can often be easy to tell what the person likes or is like. For example, someone who wears "surfer" clothes will usually either surf or like surfing. It is the same with many other styles. People also may not be associated with their stereotype but may dress that way to make other people believe that they are.

Of course, many of these concepts won't always be true. Some people dress a certain way because they have to. It may be for their career or because they just can't afford anything else. Or they may not like to be stereotyped, so they are always changing their look. Some play games so that no one can generalize about them by what they're wearing.

Almost all people stereotype others, whether they want to or not. It's just part of our society.

PART 3

Revising Your Work

6

Thinking about Your Audience

As you've already discovered, any piece of writing—be it a poem, a short story, a novel, an essay, or a drama—begins with the writer's reason to write. As the writer, your purpose is to take the dominant idea that lies at the center of your reason to write and to make it clear to your reader—your audience. You create clarity through the choices you make as you revise your writing.

When you use discovery strategies and as you write your first draft, you discover your subject and your dominant idea. Looking at these preliminary maps of your ideas and the relationships of those ideas to each other and to your experiences leads you to consider what supporting examples might help make your idea clearer to your audience. Other readers of your preliminary exploration of your thoughts, such as the members of your group, might suggest different approaches or additional examples. Eventually, you have to begin to make choices regarding the ways you can organize your material to focus your audience's attention on your dominant idea.

After you have written your first draft, you ask questions of it like those suggested in Chapter 3. The answers to those questions help you see what supporting examples might grow from your exploration of your topic and, if you are working in a group, what further ideas and examples readers of your draft might suggest. Then you have to begin to make choices regarding the ways you can make your theme clear and important to your audience. The process of considering those choices and using the tools available to you is called revision.

When you revise, keep in mind that the impact of your writing develops for your audience over the span of the whole work. The sequence of events or ideas you choose; the characters, if any, through whose actions and speech you represent your idea; the point of view you choose; and your use of language to create a voice for yourself are all part of the impression your writing creates. All reflect your choices. And the aim of your choices is to make your dominant idea as clear as possible to your audience: to present the reader with ideas or examples that define the dominant idea; to describe important objects, concepts, characters, or events; or to give the dominant idea support by connecting it with events or ideas that the reader may be familiar with. All the elements of an effective piece of writing work to make the dominant idea clear, interesting, and important to the reader.

 ### Working with a Reading

Read the following story. Then decide what you think its theme or subject might be, using the questions that follow it to help you focus your ideas.

GREASY LAKE

T. Coraghessan Boyle

> *It's about a mile down on the dark side of Route 88.*
>
> —BRUCE SPRINGSTEEN

There was a time when courtesy and winning ways went out of style, when it was good to be bad, when you cultivated decadence like a taste. We were all dangerous characters then. We wore torn-up leather jackets, slouched around with toothpicks in our mouths, sniffed glue and ether and what somebody claimed was cocaine. When we wheeled our parents' whining station wagons out into the street we left a patch of rubber half a block long. We drank gin and grape juice, Tango, Thunderbird, and Bali Hai. We were nineteen. We were bad. We read André Gide° and struck elaborate poses to show that we didn't give a shit about anything. At night, we went up to Greasy Lake.

Through the center of town, up the strip, past the housing developments and shopping malls, street lights giving way to the thin streaming illumination of the headlights, trees crowding the asphalt in a black unbroken wall: that was the way out to Greasy Lake. The Indians had called it Wakan, a reference to the clarity of its waters. Now it was fetid and murky, the mud banks glittering with broken glass and strewn with beer cans and the charred remains of bonfires. There was a single ravaged island a hundred yards from shore, so stripped of vegetation it looked as if the air force had strafed it. We went up to the lake because everyone went there, because we wanted to snuff the rich scent of possibility on the breeze, watch a girl take off her clothes and plunge into the festering

---

André Gide: French novelist and critic (1869–1951), whose work—much of it semi-autobiographical—examines the conflict between desire and discipline and shows individuals battling conventional morality.

murk, drink beer, smoke pot, howl at the stars, savor the incongruous full-throated roar of rock and roll against the primeval susurrus of frogs and crickets. This was nature.

I was there one night, late, in the company of two dangerous characters. Digby wore a gold star in his right ear and allowed his father to pay his tuition at Cornell; Jeff was thinking of quitting school to become a painter/musician/head-shop proprietor. They were both expert in the social graces, quick with a sneer, able to manage a Ford with lousy shocks over a rutted and gutted blacktop road at eighty-five while rolling a joint as compact as a Tootsie Roll Pop stick. They could lounge against a bank of booming speakers and trade "man"'s with the best of them or roll out across the dance floor as if their joints worked on bearings. They were slick and quick and they wore their mirror shades at breakfast and dinner, in the shower, in closets and caves. In short, they were bad.

I drove. Digby pounded the dashboard and shouted along with Toots & the Maytals while Jeff hung his head out the window and streaked the side of my mother's Bel Air with vomit. It was early June, the air soft as a hand on your cheek, the third night of summer vacation. The first two nights we'd been out till dawn, looking for something we never found. On this, the third night, we'd cruised the strip sixty-seven times, been in and out of every bar and club we could think of in a twenty-mile radius, stopped twice for bucket chicken and forty-cent hamburgers, debated going to a party at the house of a girl Jeff's sister knew, and chucked two dozen raw eggs at mailboxes and hitchhikers. It was 2:00 A.M.; the bars were closing. There was nothing to do but take a bottle of lemon-flavored gin up to Greasy Lake.

The taillights of a single car winked at us as we swung into the dirt   5
lot with its tufts of weed and washboard corrugations; '57 Chevy, mint, metallic blue. On the far side of the lot, like the exoskeleton of some gaunt chrome insect, a chopper leaned against its kickstand. And that was it for excitement: some junkie half-wit biker and a car freak pumping his girlfriend. Whatever it was we were looking for, we weren't about to find it at Greasy Lake. Not that night.

But then all of a sudden Digby was fighting for the wheel. "Hey, that's Tony Lovett's car! Hey!" he shouted, while I stabbed at the brake pedal and the Bel Air nosed up to the gleaming bumper of the parked Chevy. Digby leaned on the horn, laughing, and instructed me to put my brights on. I flicked on the brights. This was hilarious. A joke. Tony would experience premature withdrawal and expect to be confronted by grim-looking state troopers with flashlights. We hit the horn, strobed the lights, and then jumped out of the car to press our witty faces to Tony's windows; for all we knew we might even catch a glimpse of some little fox's tit, and then we could slap backs with red-faced Tony, roughhouse a little, and go on to new heights of adventure and daring.

The first mistake, the one that opened the whole floodgate, was losing my grip on the keys. In the excitement, leaping from the car with the gin in one hand and a roach clip in the other, I spilled them in the grass—in the dark, rank, mysterious nighttime grass of Greasy Lake. This was a tactical error, as damaging and irreversible in its way as Westmoreland's decision to dig in at Khe Sanh.° I felt it like a jab of intuition, and I stopped there by the open door, peering vaguely into the night that puddled up round my feet.

The second mistake—and this was inextricably bound up with the first—was identifying the car as Tony Lovett's. Even before the very bad character in greasy jeans and engineer boots ripped out of the driver's door, I began to realize that this chrome blue was much lighter than the robin's-egg of Tony's car, and that Tony's car didn't have rear-mounted speakers. Judging from their expressions, Digby and Jeff were privately groping toward the same inevitable and unsettling conclusion as I was.

In any case, there was no reasoning with this bad greasy character—clearly he was a man of action. The first lusty Rockette° kick of his steel-toed boot caught me under the chin, chipped my favorite tooth, and left me sprawled in the dirt. Like a fool, I'd gone down on one knee to comb the stiff hacked grass for the keys, my mind making connections in the most dragged-out, testudineous way, knowing that things had gone wrong, that I was in a lot of trouble, and that the lost ignition key was my grail and my salvation. The three or four succeeding blows were mainly absorbed by my right buttock and the tough piece of bone at the base of my spine.

Meanwhile, Digby vaulted the kissing bumpers and delivered a savage kung-fu blow to the greasy character's collarbone. Digby had just finished a course in martial arts for phys-ed credit and had spent the better part of the past two nights telling us apocryphal tales of Bruce Lee types and of the raw power invested in lightning blows shot from coiled wrists, ankles, and elbows. The greasy character was unimpressed. He merely backed off a step, his face like a Toltec mask, and laid Digby out with a single whistling roundhouse blow . . . but by now Jeff had got into the act, and I was beginning to extricate myself from the dirt, a tinny compound of shock, rage, and impotence wadded in my throat.

Jeff was on the guy's back, biting at his ear. Digby was on the ground, cursing. I went for the tire iron I kept under the driver's seat. I kept it there because bad characters always keep tire irons under the driver's seat, for just such an occasion as this. Never mind that I hadn't been involved in a fight since sixth grade, when a kid with a sleepy eye and two streams of mucus depending from his nostrils hit me in the knee with a Louisville

10

Khe Sanh: In late 1967 North Vietnamese and Viet Cong forces mounted a strong attack against American troops at Khe Sanh, thereby causing General William C. Westmoreland, commander of U.S. forces in Vietnam, to "dig in" to defend an area of relatively little tactical importance.
Rockette: famed dancing troupe at New York's Radio City Music Hall, noted for their precision and can-can-like high kicks

slugger,° never mind that I'd touched the tire iron exactly twice before, to change tires: it was there. And I went for it.

I was terrified. Blood was beating in my ears, my hands were shaking, my heart turning over like a dirtbike in the wrong gear. My antagonist was shirtless, and a single cord of muscle flashed across his chest as he bent forward to peel Jeff from his back like a wet overcoat. "Motherfucker," he spat, over and over, and I was aware in that instant that all four of us—Digby, Jeff, and myself included—were chanting "motherfucker, motherfucker," as if it were a battle cry. (What happened next? the detective asks the murderer from beneath the turned-down brim of his porkpie hat. I don't know, the murderer says, something came over me. Exactly.)

Digby poked the flat of his hand in the bad character's face and I came at him like a kamikaze, mindless, raging, stung with humiliation—the whole thing, from the initial boot in the chin to this murderous primal instant involving no more than sixty hyperventilating, gland-flooding seconds—I came at him and brought the tire iron down across his ear. The effect was instantaneous, astonishing. He was a stunt man and this was Hollywood, he was a big grimacing toothy balloon and I was a man with a straight pin. He collapsed. Wet his pants. Went loose in his boots.

A single second, big as a zeppelin, floated by. We were standing over him in a circle, gritting our teeth, jerking our necks, our limbs and hands and feet twitching with glandular discharges. No one said anything. We just stared down at the guy, the car freak, the lover, the bad greasy character laid low. Digby looked at me; so did Jeff. I was still holding the tire iron, a tuft of hair clinging to the crook like dandelion fluff, like down. Rattled, I dropped it in the dirt, already envisioning the headlines, the pitted faces of the police inquisitors, the gleam of handcuffs, clank of bars, the big black shadows rising from the back of the cell . . . when suddenly a raw torn shriek cut through me like all the juice in all the electric chairs in the country.

It was the fox. She was short, barefoot, dressed in panties and a man's 15 shirt. "Animals!" she screamed, running at us with her fists clenched and wisps of blow-dried hair in her face. There was a silver chain round her ankle, and her toenails flashed in the glare of the headlights. I think it was the toenails that did it. Sure, the gin and the cannabis and even the Kentucky Fried may have had a hand in it, but it was the sight of those flaming toes that set us off—the toad emerging from the loaf in *Virgin Spring,*° lipstick smeared on a child: she was already tainted. We were on her like Bergman's deranged brothers—see no evil, hear none, speak none—panting, wheezing, tearing at her clothes, grabbing for flesh. We were

---

Louisville slugger: a popular brand of baseball bat
Virgin Spring: film by Swedish director Ingmar Bergman

bad characters, and we were scared and hot and three steps over the line—anything could have happened.

It didn't.

Before we could pin her to the hood of the car, our eyes masked with lust and greed and the purest primal badness, a pair of headlights swung into the lot. There we were, dirty, bloody, guilty, dissociated from humanity and civilization, the first of the Ur-crimes behind us, the second in progress, shreds of nylon panty and spandex brassiere dangling from our fingers, our flies open, lips licked—there we were, caught in the spotlight. Nailed.

We bolted. First for the car, and then, realizing we had no way of starting it, for the woods. I thought nothing. I thought escape. The headlights came at me like accusing fingers. I was gone.

Ram-bam-bam, across the parking lot, past the chopper and into the feculent undergrowth at the lake's edge, insects flying up in my face, weeds whipping, frogs and snakes and red-eyed turtles splashing off into the night: I was already ankle-deep in muck and tepid water and still going strong. Behind me, the girl's screams rose in intensity, disconsolate, incriminating, the screams of the Sabine women,° the Christian martyrs, Anne Frank° dragged from the garret. I kept going, pursued by those cries, imagining cops and bloodhounds. The water was up to my knees when I realized what I was doing: I was going to swim for it. Swim the breadth of Greasy Lake and hide myself in the thick clot of woods on the far side. They'd never find me there.

I was breathing in sobs, in gasps. The water lapped at my waist as I   *20* looked out over the moon-burnished ripples, the mats of algae that clung to the surface like scabs. Digby and Jeff had vanished. I paused. Listened. The girl was quieter now, screams tapering to sobs, but there were male voices, angry, excited, and the high-pitched ticking of the second car's engine. I waded deeper, stealthy, hunted, the ooze sucking at my sneakers. As I was about to take the plunge—at the very instant I dropped my shoulder for the first slashing stroke—I blundered into something. Something unspeakable, obscene, something soft, wet, moss-grown. A patch of weed? A log? When I reached out to touch it, it gave like a rubber duck, it gave like flesh.

In one of those nasty little epiphanies for which we are prepared by films and TV and childhood visits to the funeral home to ponder the shrunken painted forms of dead grandparents, I understood what it was

---

Sabine women: according to legend, members of an ancient Italian tribe abducted by Romans who took them for wives

Anne Frank: German Jewish girl (1929–1945) whose family was forced to hide in an attic in Amsterdam during the Nazi occupation of the Netherlands. Frank, who along with her family was discovered by storm troopers and sent to die at the concentration camp at Belsen, is famous for her diary, which recounts her days in hiding.

that bobbed there so inadmissibly in the dark. Understood, and stumbled back in horror and revulsion, my mind yanked in six different directions (I was nineteen, a mere child, an infant, and here in the space of five minutes I'd struck down one greasy character and blundered into the water-logged carcass of a second), thinking, The keys, the keys, why did I have to go and lose the keys? I stumbled back, but the muck took hold of my feet—a sneaker snagged, balance lost—and suddenly I was pitching face forward into the buoyant black mass, throwing out my hands in desperation while simultaneously conjuring the image of reeking frogs and muskrats revolving in slicks of their own deliquescing juices. AAAAArrrgh! I shot from the water like a torpedo, the dead man rotating to expose a mossy beard and eyes cold as the moon. I must have shouted out, thrashing around in the weeds, because the voices behind me suddenly became animated.

"What was that?"

"It's them, it's them: they tried to, tried to . . . *rape* me!" Sobs.

A man's voice, flat Midwestern accent. "You sons a bitches, we'll kill you!"

Frogs, crickets.   25

Then another voice, harsh, *r*-less, Lower East Side: "Motherfucker!" I recognized the verbal virtuosity of the bad greasy character in the engineer boots. Tooth chipped, sneakers gone, coated in mud and slime and worse, crouching breathless in the weeds waiting to have my ass thoroughly and definitively kicked and fresh from the hideous stinking embrace of a three-days-dead-corpse, I suddenly felt a rush of joy and vindication: the son of a bitch was alive! Just as quickly, my bowels turned to ice. "Come on out of there, you pansy mothers!" the bad greasy character was screaming. He shouted curses till he was out of breath.

The crickets started up again, then the frogs. I held my breath. All at once there was a sound in the reeds, a swishing, a splash: thunk-a-thunk. They were throwing rocks. The frogs fell silent. I cradled my head. Swish, swish, thunk-a-thunk. A wedge of feldspar the size of a cue ball glanced off my knee. I bit my finger.

It was then that they turned to the car. I heard a door slam, a curse, and then the sound of the headlights shattering—almost a good-natured sound, celebratory, like corks popping from the necks of bottles. This was succeeded by the dull booming of the fenders, metal on metal, and then the icy crash of the windshield. I inched forward, elbows and knees, my belly pressed to the muck, thinking of guerrillas and commandos and *The Naked and the Dead.*° I parted the weeds and squinted the length of the parking lot.

The Naked and the Dead: a popular and critically successful 1948 novel by Norman Mailer, depicting U.S. Army life during World War II

The second car—it was a Trans-Am—was still running, its high beams washing the scene in a lurid stagy light. Tire iron flailing, the greasy bad character was laying into the side of my mother's Bel Air like an avenging demon, his shadow riding up the trunks of the trees. Whomp. Whomp. Whomp-whomp. The other two guys—blond types, in fraternity jackets—were helping out with tree branches and skull-sized boulders. One of them was gathering up bottles, rocks, muck, candy wrappers, used condoms, pop-tops, and other refuse and pitching it through the window on the driver's side. I could see the fox, a white bulb behind the windshield of the '57 Chevy. "Bobbie," she whined over the thumping, "come *on*." The greasy character paused a moment, took one good swipe at the left taillight, and then heaved the tire iron halfway across the lake. Then he fired up the '57 and was gone.

Blond head nodded at blond head. One said something to the other,   *30* too low for me to catch. They were no doubt thinking that in helping to annihilate my mother's car they'd committed a fairly rash act, and thinking too that there were three bad characters connected with that very car watching them from the woods. Perhaps other possibilities occurred to them as well—police, jail cells, justices of the peace, reparations, lawyers, irate parents, fraternal censure. Whatever they were thinking, they suddenly dropped branches, bottles, and rocks and sprang for their car in unison, as if they'd choreographed it. Five seconds. That's all it took. The engine shrieked, the tires squealed, a cloud of dust rose from the rutted lot and then settled back on darkness.

I don't know how long I lay there, the bad breath of decay all around me, my jacket heavy as a bear, the primordial ooze subtly reconstituting itself to accommodate my upper thighs and testicles. My jaws ached, my knee throbbed, my coccyx was on fire. I contemplated suicide, wondered if I'd need bridgework, scraped the recesses of my brain for some sort of excuse to give my parents—a tree had fallen on the car, I was blindsided by a bread truck, hit and run, vandals had got to it while we were playing chess at Digby's. Then I thought of the dead man. He was probably the only person on the planet worse off than I was. I thought about him, fog on the lake, insects chirring eerily, and felt the tug of fear, felt the darkness opening up inside me like a set of jaws. Who was he, I wondered, this victim of time and circumstance bobbing sorrowfully in the lake at my back. The owner of the chopper, no doubt, a bad older character come to this. Shot during a murky drug deal, drowned while drunkenly frolicking in the lake. Another headline. My car was wrecked; he was dead.

When the eastern half of the sky went from black to cobalt and the trees began to separate themselves from the shadows, I pushed myself up from the mud and stepped out into the open. By now the birds had begun to take over for the crickets, and dew lay slick on the leaves. There was a smell in the air, raw and sweet at the same time, the smell of the sun firing buds and opening blossoms. I contemplated the car. It lay there like a wreck along the highway, like a steel sculpture left over from a vanished civilization. Everything was still. This was nature.

I was circling the car, as dazed and bedraggled as the sole survivor of an air blitz, when Digby and Jeff emerged from the trees behind me. Digby's face was crosshatched with smears of dirt; Jeff's jacket was gone and his shirt was torn across the shoulder. They slouched across the lot, looking sheepish, and silently came up beside me to gape at the ravaged automobile. No one said a word. After a while Jeff swung open the driver's door and began to scoop the broken glass and garbage off the seat. I looked at Digby. He shrugged. "At least they didn't slash the tires," he said.

It was true: the tires were intact. There was no windshield, the headlights were staved in, and the body looked as if it had been sledgehammered for a quarter a shot at the county fair, but the tires were inflated to regulation pressure. The car was drivable. In silence, all three of us bent to scrape the mud and shattered glass from the interior. I said nothing about the biker. When we were finished, I reached in my pocket for the keys, experienced a nasty stab of recollection, cursed myself, and turned to search the grass. I spotted them almost immediately, no more than five feet from the open door, glinting like jewels in the first tapering shaft of sunlight. There was no reason to get philosophical about it: I eased into the seat and turned the engine over.

It was at that precise moment that the silver Mustang with the flame   *35* decals rumbled into the lot. All three of us froze; then Digby and Jeff slid into the car and slammed the door. We watched as the Mustang rocked and bobbed across the ruts and finally jerked to a halt beside the forlorn chopper at the far end of the lot. "Let's go," Digby said. I hesitated, the Bel Air wheezing beneath me.

Two girls emerged from the Mustang. Tight jeans, stiletto heels, hair like frozen fur. They bent over the motorcycle, paced back and forth aimlessly, glanced once or twice at us, and then ambled over to where the reeds sprang up in a green fence round the perimeter of the lake. One of them cupped her hands to her mouth. "Al," she called, "Hey, Al!"

"Come on," Digby hissed. "Let's get out of here."

But it was too late. The second girl was picking her way across the lot, unsteady on her heels, looking up at us and then away. She was older—twenty-five or -six—and as she came closer we could see there was something wrong with her: she was stoned or drunk, lurching now and waving her arms for balance. I gripped the steering wheel as if it were the ejection lever of a flaming jet, and Digby spat out my name, twice, terse and impatient.

"Hi," the girl said.

We looked at her like zombies, like war veterans, like deaf-and-dumb   *40* pencil peddlers.

She smiled, her lips cracked and dry. "Listen," she said, bending from the waist to look in the window, "you guys seen Al?" Her pupils were pinpoints, her eyes glass. She jerked her neck. "That's his bike over there—Al's. You seen him?"

Al. I didn't know what to say. I wanted to get out of the car and retch, I wanted to go home to my parents' house and crawl into bed. Digby poked me in the ribs. "We haven't seen anybody," I said.

The girl seemed to consider this, reaching out a slim veiny arm to brace herself against the car. "No matter," she said, slurring the *t*'s, "he'll turn up." And then, as if she'd just taken stock of the whole scene—the ravaged car and our battered faces, the desolation of the place—she said: "Hey, you guys look like some pretty bad characters—been fightin', huh?" We stared straight ahead, rigid as catatonics. She was fumbling in her pocket and muttering something. Finally she held out a handful of tablets in glassine wrappers: "Hey, you want to party, you want to do some of these with me and Sarah?"

I just looked at her. I thought I was going to cry. Digby broke the silence. "No, thanks," he said, leaning over me. "Some other time."

I put the car in gear and it inched forward with a groan, shaking off   *45* pellets of glass like an old dog shedding water after a bath, heaving over the ruts on its worn springs, creeping toward the highway. There was a sheen of sun on the lake. I looked back. The girl was still standing there, watching us, her shoulders slumped, hand outstretched.

---

1. Describe the setting that Boyle creates in "Greasy Lake." What does the setting suggest about his dominant idea?

2. What is the plot (the sequence of events) in Boyle's story? Does what happens seem expected or unexpected to you? How does the plot reflect what you think is the dominant idea?

3. What are the characters like in this story, especially the narrator, Digby, and Jeff? How do they see themselves? Does the way Boyle's narrator describe them support or conflict with their sense of themselves? How does the combination of what they say and how they act with what Boyle's narration says reflect what you take to be Boyle's dominant idea?

4. What do you think the lake and its surroundings—the contrast between what it used to be and what it is—and, especially, the corpse have to do with what you take to be Boyle's dominant idea?

5. Is there anything in this story that you think is irrelevant to what you believe to be Boyle's purpose? What is it? Why do you think it's irrelevant?

Now read the story again and see what elements in it—such as the events, the descriptions of the surroundings, how the characters speak to each other, what the narrator tells you about his feelings—work together to lead you to your conclusion about its theme or subject.

If you are working with a group, get together and compare your conclusions regarding the theme of the story. Listen to what other members have to say and what each noticed in the story that led to his or her conclusion.

❧ *An Invitation to Write*

Take what you have learned from your reading or from your group discussion and, using one of the discovery strategies, write a draft about an experience you have had that reflects a similar theme.

If you are working with a group, make a copy of your draft for each member. Discuss all the drafts, using the questions for reading first drafts in Chapter 3 (page 49). If you are working alone, work through your draft on your own.

Use the answers to the first-draft questions to lead you toward a second draft. With your group or individually, apply the second-draft questions (page 51) to your paper and see what problems they reveal. Keep a careful account of the solutions your group suggests.

As you've already learned, revision is a way of looking at your paper again from the point of view of the people who will read it. When you do this, you ask yourself some important questions to try to ensure that your audience will understand what you have to say.

Have I accounted for what my audience may not know?

Have I thought about how my audience might respond to issues or ideas that may be controversial? Is it important for me not to offend my readers?

Have I thought about what my audience's expectations are of me and of the form and language of my writing?

These questions encourage you to consider whether you have given your readers enough background to help them understand what you have to say, whether the sequence you have given your ideas makes sense for your audience as well as it does for you, whether you have worked out a way of making controversial or difficult material acceptable to your audience. Finally, they make you aware of what your audience's expectations might be.

The relationship you create between you and your ideas, the sequence you give those ideas, the examples you choose to make those ideas clear, and the language you choose to communicate those elements are all under your control. How you choose to exercise that control is a matter of the type of audience you have discovered for the purposes of your writing and how you hope to have them respond to your statement.

If you've concluded that your audience is the most important element in shaping your writing, you're correct. Writing takes place in a community. Writers usually write to be read by somebody else, and the best idea makes no difference without an audience. Except for those times when they write journals or diaries, most writers mean their work to become part of a community of readers and writers who speak to each other through pieces of writing. When you read or write, you enter that community. As you read and respond to your reading, you comment, question, agree, and find reasons to disagree with the author. When you read, you revise and rewrite the author's words. Then, when you write, much of the reading you have done up to that time influences your writing. Conscious or unconscious memories of what other writers have written, the words they used, and how they arranged their ideas suggest further possibilities to you. You read your own writing in terms of a much larger community of writers, and you shape your writing in terms of your experience as part of a larger community of readers.

What is true of you as a reader/writer is equally true of your audience. Therefore, all the elements of revision—specific examples; the shape of the work; imagery; all of the resources of language, rhythm, and sound—will be shaped by your subject and dominant idea and your relationship to it, by what you believe the nature and expectations of your audience to be, by the responses you hope to create in your audience, as well as by the concepts you intend to introduce them to and where you hope to take them.

IMAGINING YOUR AUDIENCE

A writer who is thinking about writing an article for a specific magazine will usually read enough issues of that magazine to learn about its audience—their interests, attitudes, and politics—as well as about the style of language that is common in the publication. Then, with an image of a typical member of that audience in mind, the writer composes his or her work. Although you need not do the research that a professional writer does, your challenge is somewhat the same. If you're writing for someone other than yourself, you have to have your audience in mind to write effectively.

It is here that the differences between speaking and writing become clearest. When you speak to another person or to a group of people, you can see your audience's responses and adjust your presentation accordingly. You can reinforce your points through tone of voice, speed, and gesture. You have none of these resources when you write. Instead, you have to make informed guesses about the people you are aiming your words at. You have to create an audience in your imagination and present your ideas to that audience using only written words.

Some audiences you know so well that you hardly have to think before writing for them. For example, in a letter to your parents or to a close friend, most of your decisions regarding your reader's knowledge, attitudes, and language will occur without much thought, and most of your choices will be so easy that you'll hardly have to think about them. However, when you write a piece that is "public"—that is, a piece that may be read by a reader or a community of readers with different interests—you have to solve the problem of audience.

Of course, you will rarely be able to investigate an audience in enough detail to "know" it. Instead, you can make some informed guesses about your audience. You can create a fictional audience based on the answers to questions you ask yourself while you play the role of the readers you have in mind. The answers you arrive at can guide you in the choices you make during revision.

THE AUDIENCE DIALOGUE: A DISCOVERY STRATEGY FOR IMAGINING AN AUDIENCE

One effective way to discover what sort of audience you intend to write to is to hold an imaginary dialogue with a "typical" member of that audience. Ask your hypothetical reader the following questions and record the answers as they occur to you. Depending on the nature of your dominant idea, not all of these questions may be relevant to your purpose. However, try them anyway. They might suggest new ways of approaching your topic, of presenting and shaping your dominant idea, or of developing and organizing the supporting material to further define and clarify your ideas. These questions work very much like the strategies you learned for discovering your subject and your dominant idea. Refer to the notes you record of your answers to these questions as you make choices during revision.

How old are you?

How does your age affect your point of view with regard to my dominant idea?

What is your economic condition? your social condition?

How do your economic and social conditions shape your attitude toward my dominant idea?

How well educated are you?

Because of your level or type of education, how much do you understand of my dominant idea and its support and how much do you need to have explained to you?

What is your political position?

How does your political position affect your response to my dominant idea and its support?

What are your religious beliefs?

How do your religious beliefs affect your response to my dominant idea and its support?

Of your religious beliefs, economic position, social position, or political position, which is most important to you? Which is least important?

Do you think the past is important for understanding the present?

Do you look to the past for your values?

Do you think the present is important to your values and choices?

Do you make your choices on the basis of what is happening in the present alone?

What hopes do you hold for the future?

What issues generally make you angry or defensive?

If I need to raise these issues, how can I help you consider them with a more open mind?

Are you more likely to respond to an emotional appeal, or are you impressed by logic?

In light of the questions I have asked, what expectations do you have for my writing in terms of language and organization?

Have I oversimplified you, forgetting that you may be one of a significant number of individuals who have views and expectations different from those of the majority?

Once you have discovered answers to these questions, you can review your preliminary writing from the point of view of your audience and begin to revise your paper effectively.

⌁ Exercise

Read the following three paragraphs. At the end of each one, you will find four possible audiences.

If you are working alone, choose one of the audiences for each paragraph and revise the paragraph with that audience in mind. If you are working with a group, the group should choose one of the paragraphs, and each member should choose a different audience and rewrite the paragraph for that audience. Then each member should read the revised paragraph to the group and define the changes he or she made for the audience he or she chose. Group members should suggest additional revisions to add to your revision if they come to mind.

Paragraph 1

Although the vigor and vitality of most young people are the envy of their elders, a significant range of serious health problems are present at ages 15–24, including venereal disease, alcoholism, and drug abuse. Moreover, a large number of adolescents and youth are making themselves vulnerable to future health problems through cigarette smoking, poor diet, and inadequate exercise (Institute of Medicine 1978). One of the most disturbing trends is the rising mortality among youth at a time when death rates at all other ages are declining rapidly. Male death rates at ages 15–19 and 20–24 were 12 percent higher in 1977 than in 1960, while mortality at other ages declined an average of 12 percent. A large differential in mortality trends by age is also evident for women. The deaths of young people take a tremendous toll and are also particularly costly because these men and women are at the threshold of productive lives during which they and society could realize a return on the investment that has been made in them.

A group of college students
A group of parents of college students
A group of legislators voting on funding a student health program
Your best friend, who drinks too much

Paragraph 2

It is never too late to give up our prejudices. No way of thinking or doing, however ancient, can be trusted without proof. What every body echoes or in silence passes by as true to-day may turn out to be falsehood to-morrow, mere smoke of opinion, which some had trusted for a cloud that would sprinkle fertilizing rain on their fields. What old people say you cannot do you try and find that you can. Old deeds for old people and new deeds for new. Old people did not know enough once, perchance, to fetch fresh fuel to keep the fire a-going; new people put a little dry wood under a pot, and are whirled round the globe, in a way to kill old people as the phrase is. Age is no better, hardly so well qualified for an instructor as youth, for it has not profited so much as it has lost. One may almost doubt if the wisest man has learned anything of absolute value by living. Practically, the old have no very important advice to give the young, their own experience has been so partial, and their lives have been such miserable failures, as they must believe; and it may be that they have some faith left which belies that experience, and they are only less young than they were. I have lived some thirty years on this planet, and I have yet to hear the first syllable of valuable or even earnest advice from my seniors. They have told me nothing and probably cannot tell me anything, to the purpose. Here is life, an experiment to a great extent untried by me; but it does not avail me that they have tried it. If I have any experience which I think valuable, I am sure to reflect that this my Mentors said nothing about.

A group of fellow students
A group of people over thirty
Your parents
Your professor

Paragraph 3

Where the N.R.A. [National Rifle Association] has always revealed its nature as a paranoid lobby, a political anachronism, is in its rigid ideological belief that *any* restriction on the private ownership of *any* kind

of hand-held gun leads inexorably to *total* abolition of *all* gun ownership—that if today the U.S. Government takes the Kalashnikov from
the hands of the maniac on the school playground, it will be coming
for my Winchester pump tomorrow. There is no evidence for this absurd belief, but it remains an article of faith. And it does so because the
faith is bad faith: the stand the N.R.A. takes is only nominally in behalf
of recreational hunters. The people it really serves are gun manufacturers and gun importers, whose sole interest is to sell as many deadly weapons of as many kinds to as many Americans as possible. The N.R.A.
never saw a weapon it didn't love. When American police officers
raised their voices against the sale of "cop-killer" bullets—Teflon-
coated projectiles whose sole purpose is to penetrate body armor—the
N.R.A. mounted a campaign to make people believe this ban would
infringe on the rights of deer hunters, as though the woods of America
were full of whitetails in Kevlar vests. Now that the pressure is on to
restrict public ownership of semiautomatic assault weapons, we hear
the same threadbare rhetoric about the rights of hunters. No serious
hunter goes after deer with an Uzi or an AK–47; those weapons are
not made for picking off an animal in the woods but for blowing people
to chopped meat at close-to-medium range, and anyone who needs a
banana clip with 30 shells in it to hit a buck should not be hunting at
all. These guns have only two uses: you can take them down to the
local range and spend a lot of money blasting off 500 rounds an afternoon at silhouette targets of the Ayatollah, or you can use them to off
your rivals and create lots of police widows. It depends on what kind
of guy you are. But the N.R.A. doesn't care—underneath its dumb
incantatory slogans ("Gun's don't kill people; people kill people"), it is
defending both guys. It helps ensure that cops are outgunned right
across America. It preaches hunters' rights in order to defend the distribution of weapons in what is, in effect, a drug-based civil war.

Your friend who believes in the right to bear arms
Your congressional representative, who has voted against gun control
Your father, who likes to spend his weekends at a shooting range
Your local law enforcement officer

❧ *Working with the Readings*

Read the following pair of essays. (The first, "Some Conditions of Obedience and Disobedience to Authority," was originally published in the
journal *Human Relations.* "The Perils of Obedience" is excerpted from Milgram's book *Obedience to Authority.*)

Using the audience-dialogue questions on page 115, try to define the
audience the author had in mind when he wrote each essay. Alone or with
your group, write a short definition of the audience Milgram had in mind
for each essay and describe the choices Milgram made for each audience.

SOME CONDITIONS OF OBEDIENCE AND DISOBEDIENCE TO AUTHORITY

Stanley Milgram

The situation in which one agent commands another to hurt a third turns up time and again as a significant theme in human relations.[1] It is powerfully expressed in the story of Abraham, who is commanded by God to kill his son. It is no accident that Kierkegaard, seeking to orient his thought to the central themes of human experience, chose Abraham's conflict as the springboard to his philosophy.

War too moves forward on the triad of an authority which commands a person to destroy the enemy, and perhaps all organized hostility may be viewed as a theme and variation on the three elements of authority, executant, and victim.[2] We describe an experimental program, recently concluded at Yale University, in which a particular expression of this conflict is studied by experimental means.

In its most general form the problem may be defined thus: if X tells Y to hurt Z, under what conditions will Y carry out the command of X and under what conditions will he refuse. In the more limited form possible in laboratory research, the question becomes: If an experimenter tells a subject to hurt another person, under what conditions will the subject go along with this instruction, and under what conditions will he refuse to obey. The laboratory problem is not so much a dilution of the general statement as one concrete expression of the many particular forms this question may assume.

One aim of the research was to study behavior in a strong situation of deep consequence to the participants, for the psychological forces operative in powerful and life-like forms of the conflict may not be brought into play under diluted conditions.

This approach meant, first, that we had a special obligation to protect the welfare and dignity of the persons who took part in the study; subjects were, of necessity, placed in a difficult predicament, and steps had to be taken to ensure their well-being before they were discharged from the laboratory. Toward this end, a careful, post-experimental treatment was devised and has been carried through for subjects in all conditions.[3]

Terminology

If Y follows the command of X we shall say that he has obeyed X; if he fails to carry out the command of X, we shall say that he has disobeyed X. The terms to *obey* and to *disobey,* as used here, refer to the subject's

5

overt action only, and carry no implication for the motive or experiential states accompanying the action.[4]

To be sure, the everyday use of the word *obedience* is not entirely free from complexities. It refers to action within widely varying situations, and connotes diverse motives within those situations: a child's obedience differs from a soldier's obedience, or the love, honor, and *obey* of the marriage vow. However, a consistent behavioral relationship is indicated in most uses of the term: in the act of obeying, a person does what another person tells him to do. Y obeys X if he carries out the prescription for action which X has addressed to him; the term suggests, moreover, that some form of dominance-subordination, or hierarchical element, is part of the situation in which the transaction between X and Y occurs.

A subject who complies with the entire series of experimental commands will be termed an *obedient* subject; one who at any point in the command series defies the experimenter will be called a *disobedient* or *defiant* subject. As used in this report the terms refer only to the subject's performance in the experiment, and do not necessarily imply a general personality disposition to submit to or reject authority.

Subject Population

The subjects used in all experimental conditions were male adults, residing in the greater New Haven and Bridgeport areas, aged 20 to 50 years, and engaged in a wide variety of occupations. Each experimental condition described in this report employed 40 fresh subjects and was carefully balanced for age and occupational types. The occupational composition for each experiment was: workers, skilled and unskilled: 40 percent; white collar, sales, business: 40 percent; professionals: 20 percent. The occupations were intersected with three age categories (subjects in 20's, 30's, and 40's, assigned to each condition in the proportions of 20, 40, and 40 percent, respectively).

The General Laboratory Procedure[5]

The focus of the study concerns the amount of electric shock a sub-   *10*
ject is willing to administer to another person when ordered by an experimenter to give the "victim" increasingly more severe punishment. The act of administering shock is set in the context of a learning experiment, ostensibly designed to study the effect of punishment on memory. Aside from the experimenter, one naïve subject and one accomplice perform in each session. On arrival each subject is paid $4.50. After a general talk by the experimenter, telling how little scientists know about the effect of punishment on memory, subjects are informed that one member of the pair will serve as teacher and one as learner. A rigged drawing is

held so that the naïve subject is always the teacher, and the accomplice becomes the learner. The learner is taken to an adjacent room and strapped into an "electric chair."

The naïve subject is told that it is his task to teach the learner a list of paired associates, to test him on the list, and to administer punishment whenever the learner errs in the test. Punishment takes the form of electric shock, delivered to the learner by means of a shock generator controlled by the naïve subject. The teacher is instructed to increase the intensity of electric shock one step on the generator on each error. The learner, according to plan, provides many wrong answers, so that before long the naïve subject must give him the strongest shock on the generator. Increases in shock level are met by increasingly insistent demands from the learner that the experiment be stopped because of the growing discomfort to him. However, in clear terms the experimenter orders the teacher to continue with the procedure in disregard of the learner's protests. *Thus, the naïve subject must resolve a conflict between two mutually incompatible demands from the social field. He may continue to follow the orders of the experimenter and shock the learner with increasing severity, or he may refuse to follow the orders of the experimenter and heed the learner's pleas. The experimenter's authority operates not in a free field, but against ever-mounting countervailing pressure from the person being punished.*

A few technical points need to be considered before the findings of the study are described. For the purpose of delivering shock, a simulated shock generator is used, with 30 clearly marked voltage levels that range from 15 to 450 volts. (Each level is activated by one of 30 individual lever switches set in a horizontal line.) The naïve subject is given a sample shock of 45 volts to convince him of the authenticity of the instrument. The generator bears verbal designations that range from "Slight Shock" to "Danger: Severe Shock."

The responses of the victim are standardized on tape, and each protest is coordinated to a particular voltage level on the shock generator. Starting with 75 volts the learner begins to grunt and moan. At 150 volts he demands to be let out of the experiment. At 180 volts he cries out that he can no longer stand the pain. At 300 volts he refuses to provide any more answers to the memory test, insisting that he is no longer a participant in the experiment and must be freed. In response to this last tactic, the experimenter instructs the naïve subject to treat the absence of an answer as equivalent to a wrong answer, and to follow the usual shock procedure. The experimenter reinforces his demand with the statement: "You have no other choice, you must go on!" (This imperative is used whenever the naïve subject tries to break off the experiment.) If the subject refuses to give the next higher level of shock, the experiment is considered at an end. A quantitative value is assigned to the subject's performance based on the maximum-intensity shock he administered before breaking off. Thus any subject's score may range from zero (for a subject unwilling to administer the first shock level) to 30 (for a subject who proceeds to the highest voltage level on the board). For any particular subject and for any particular experiment condition, the degree to which participants have followed the experimenter's orders may be specified with a numerical value, corresponding to the metric on the shock generator.

This laboratory situation gives us a framework in which to study the subject's reactions to the principal conflict of the experiment. Again, this conflict is between the experimenter's demands that he continue to administer the electric shock, and the learner's demands, which become increasingly more insistent, that the experiment be stopped. The crux of the study is to vary systematically the factors believed to alter the degree of obedience to the experimental commands, to learn under what conditions submission to authority is most probable and under what conditions defiance is brought to the fore.

Pilot Studies

Pilot studies for the present research were completed in the winter of   *15*
1960; they differed from the regular experiments in a few details: for one, the victim was placed behind a silvered glass, with the light balance on the glass such that the victim could be dimly perceived by the subject (Milgram, 1961).

Though essentially qualitative in treatment, these studies pointed to several significant features of the experimental situation. At first no vocal feedback was used from the victim. It was thought that the verbal and voltage designations on the control panel would create sufficient pressure to curtail the subject's obedience. However, this was not the case. In the absence of protests from the learner, virtually all subjects, once commanded, went blithely to the end of the board, seemingly indifferent to the verbal designations ("Extreme Shock" and "Danger: Severe Shock"). This deprived us of an adequate basis for scaling obedient tendencies. A force had to be introduced that would strengthen the subject's resistance to the experimenter's commands, and reveal individual differences in terms of a distribution of break-off points.

This force took the form of protests from the victim. Initially, mild protests were used, but proved inadequate. Subsequently, more vehement protests were inserted into the experimental procedure. To our consternation, even the strongest protests from the victim did not prevent all subjects from administering the harshest punishment ordered by the experimenter; but the protests did lower the mean maximum shock somewhat and created some spread in the subject's performance; therefore, the victim's cries were standardized on tape and incorporated into the regular experimental procedure.

The situation did more than highlight the technical difficulties of finding a workable experimental procedure: It indicated that subjects would obey authority to a greater extent than we had supposed. It also pointed to the importance of feedback from the victim in controlling the subject's behavior.

One further aspect of the pilot study was that subjects frequently averted their eyes from the person they were shocking, often turning their heads in an awkward and conspicuous manner. One subject explained: "I didn't want to see the consequences of what I had done." Observers wrote:

> . . . subjects showed a reluctance to look at the victim, whom they could see through the glass in front of them. When this fact was brought to their attention they indicated that it caused them discomfort to see the victim in agony. We note, however, that although the subject refuses to look at the victim, he continues to administer shocks.

This suggested that the salience of the victim may have, in some degree, regulated the subject's performance. If, in obeying the experimenter, the subject found it necessary to avoid scrutiny of the victim, would the converse be true? If the victim were rendered increasingly more salient to the subject, would obedience diminish? The first set of regular experiments was designed to answer this question.   *20*

Immediacy of the Victim

This series consisted of four experimental conditions. In each condition the victim was brought "psychologically" closer to the subject giving him shocks.

In the first condition (Remote Feedback) the victim was placed in another room and could not be heard or seen by the subject, except that, at 300 volts, he pounded on the wall in protest. After 315 volts he no longer answered or was heard from.

The second condition (Voice Feedback) was identical to the first except that voice protests were introduced. As in the first condition the victim was placed in an adjacent room, but his complaints could be heard clearly through a door left slightly ajar and through the walls of the laboratory.[6]

The third experimental condition (Proximity) was similar to the second, except that the victim was now placed in the same room as the subject, and 1½ feet from him. Thus he was visible as well as audible, and voice cues were provided.

The fourth, and final, condition of this series (Touch-Proximity) was   *25* identical to the third, with this exception: The victim received a shock only when his hand rested on a shockplate. At the 150-volt level the victim again demanded to be let free and, in this condition, refused to

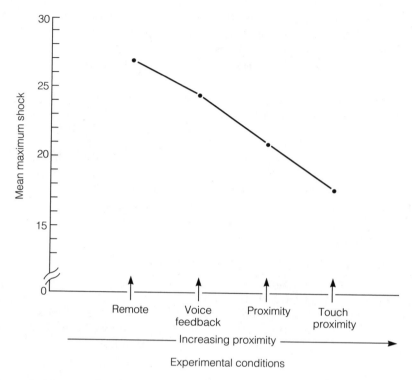

Figure 1 Mean maxima in proximity series.

place his hand on the shockplate. The experimenter ordered the naïve subject to force the victim's hand onto the plate. Thus obedience in this condition required that the subject have physical contact with the victim in order to give him punishment beyond the 150-volt level.

Forty adult subjects were studied in each condition. The data revealed that obedience was significantly reduced as the victim was rendered more immediate to the subject. The mean maximum shock for the conditions is shown in Figure 1.

Expressed in terms of the proportion of obedient to defiant subjects, the findings are that 34 percent of the subjects defied the experimenter in the Remote condition, 37.5 percent in Voice Feedback, 60 percent in Proximity, and 70 percent in Touch-Proximity.

How are we to account for this effect? A first conjecture might be that as the victim was brought closer the subject became more aware of the intensity of his suffering and regulated his behavior accordingly. This makes sense, but our evidence does not support the interpretation. There are no consistent differences in the attributed level of pain across the four conditions (i.e., the amount of pain experienced by the victim as estimated by the subject and expressed on a 14-point scale). But it is easy to speculate about alternative mechanisms:

Empathic Cues. In the Remote and to a lesser extent the Voice Feedback conditions, the victim's suffering possesses an abstract, remote quality for the subject. He is aware, but only in a conceptual sense, that his actions cause pain to another person; the fact is apprehended, but not felt. The phenomenon is common enough. The bombardier can reasonably suppose that his weapons will inflict suffering and death, yet this knowledge is divested of affect and does not move him to a felt, emotional response to the suffering resulting from his actions. Similar observations have been made in wartime. It is possible that the visual cues associated with the victim's suffering trigger empathic responses in the subject and provide him with a more complete grasp of the victim's experience. Or it is possible that the empathic responses are themselves unpleasant, possessing drive properties which cause the subject to terminate the arousal situation. Diminishing obedience, then, would be explained by the enrichment of empathic cues in the successive experimental conditions.

Denial and Narrowing of the Cognitive Field. The Remote condition allows a narrowing of the cognitive field so that the victim is put out of mind. The subject no longer considers the act of depressing a lever relevant to moral judgment, for it is no longer associated with the victim's suffering. When the victim is close it is more difficult to exclude him phenomenologically. He necessarily intrudes on the subject's awareness since he is continuously visible. In the Remote condition his existence and reactions are made known only after the shock has been administered. The auditory feedback is sporadic and discontinuous. In the Proximity conditions his inclusion in the immediate visual field renders him a continuously salient element for the subject. The mechanism of denial can no longer be brought into play. One subject in the Remote condition said: "It's funny how you really begin to forget that there's a guy out there, even though you can hear him. For a long time I just concentrated on pressing the switches and reading the words."

Reciprocal Fields. If in the Proximity condition the subject is in an improved position to observe the victim, the reverse is also true. The actions of the subject now come under proximal scrutiny by the victim. Possibly, it is easier to harm a person when he is unable to observe our actions than when he can see what we are doing. His surveillance of the action directed against him may give rise to shame, or guilt, which may then serve to curtail the action. Many expressions of language refer to the discomfort or inhibitions that arise in face-to-face confrontation. It is often said that it is easier to criticize a man "behind his back" than to "attack him to his face." If we are in the process of lying to a person it is reputedly difficult to "stare him in the eye." We "turn away from others in shame" or in "embarrassment" and this action serves to reduce our discomfort. The manifest function of allowing the victim of a firing squad to be blindfolded is to make the occasion less stressful for him, but it may also serve a latent function of reducing the stress of the executioner. In short, in the Proximity conditions, the subject may sense that he has become more salient in the victim's field of awareness. Possibly he becomes more self-conscious, embarrassed, and inhibited in his punishment of the victim.

Phenomenal Unity of Act. In the Remote condition it is more difficult for the subject to gain a sense of *relatedness* between his own actions and the consequence of these actions for the victim. There is a physical and spatial separation of the act and its consequences. The subject depresses a lever in one room, and protests and cries are heard from another. The two events are in correlation, yet they lack a compelling phenomenological unity. The structure of a meaningful act—*I am hurting a man*—breaks down because of the spatial arrangements in a manner somewhat analogous to the disappearance of phi phenomena when the blinking lights are spaced too far apart. The unity is more fully achieved in the Proximity condition as the victim is brought closer to the action that causes him pain. It is rendered complete in Touch-Proximity.

Incipient Group Formation. Placing the victim in another room not only takes him further from the subject, but the subject and the experimenter are drawn relatively closer. There is incipient group formation between the experimenter and the subject, from which the victim is excluded. The wall between the victim and the others deprives him of an intimacy which the experimenter and subject feel. In the Remote condition, the victim is truly an outsider, who stands alone, physically and psychologically.

When the victim is placed close to the subject, it becomes easier to form an alliance with him against the experimenter. Subjects no longer have to face the experimenter alone. They have an ally who is close at hand and eager to collaborate in a revolt against the experimenter. Thus, the changing set of spatial relations leads to a potentially shifting set of alliances over the several experimental conditions.

Acquired Behavior Dispositions. It is commonly observed that laboratory mice will rarely fight with their litter mates. Scott (1958) explains this in terms of passive inhibition. He writes: "By doing nothing under . . . circumstances [the animal] learns to do nothing, and this may be spoken of as passive inhibition . . . this principle has great importance in teaching an individual to be peaceful, for it means that he can learn not to fight simply by not fighting." Similarly, we may learn not to harm others simply by not harming them in everyday life. Yet this learning occurs in a context of proximal relations with others, and may not be generalized to that situation in which the person is physically removed from us. Or possibly, in the past, aggressive actions against others who were physically close resulted in retaliatory punishment which extinguished the original form of response. In contrast, aggression against others at a distance may have only sporadically led to retaliation. Thus the organism learns that it is safer to be aggressive toward others at a distance, and precarious to be so when the parties are within arm's reach. Through a pattern of rewards and punishments, he acquires a disposition to avoid aggression at close quarters, a disposition which does not extend to harming others at a distance. And this may account for experimental findings in the remote and proximal experiments.

Proximity as a variable in psychological research has received far less attention than it deserves. If men were sessile it would be easy to understand this neglect. But we move about; our spatial relations shift from one situation to the next, and the fact that we are near or remote may have a powerful effect on the psychological processes that mediate our behavior toward others. In the present situation, as the victim is brought closer to the subject ordered to give him shocks, increasing numbers of subjects break off the experiment, refusing to obey. The concrete, visible, and proximal presence of the victim acts in an important way to counteract the experimenter's power to generate disobedience.[7]

Closeness of Authority

If the spatial relationship of the subject and victim is relevant to the degree of obedience, would not the relationship of subject to experimenter also play a part? 30

There are reasons to feel that, on arrival, the subject is oriented primarily to the experimenter rather than to the victim. He has come to the laboratory to fit into the structure that the experimenter—not the victim—would provide. He has come less to understand his behavior than to *reveal* that behavior to a competent scientist, and he is willing to display himself as the scientist's purposes require. Most subjects seem quite concerned about the appearance they are making before the experimenter, and one could argue that this preoccupation in a relatively new and strange setting makes the subject somewhat insensitive to the triadic nature of the social situation. In other words, the subject is so concerned about the show he is putting on for the experimenter that influences from other parts of the social field do not receive as much weight as they ordinarily would. This overdetermined orientation to the experimenter would account for the relative insensitivity of the subject to the victim, and would also lead us to believe that alterations in the relationship between subject and experimenter would have important consequences for obedience.

In a series of experiments we varied the physical closeness and degree of surveillance of the experimenter. In one condition the experimenter sat just a few feet away from the subject. In a second condition, after giving initial instructions, the experimenter left the laboratory and gave his orders by telephone. In still a third condition the experimenter was never seen, providing instructions by means of a tape recording activated when the subjects entered the laboratory.

Obedience dropped sharply as the experimenter was physically removed from the laboratory. The number of obedient subjects in the first condition (Experimenter Present) was almost three times as great as in the second, where the experimenter gave his orders by telephone. Twenty-six subjects were fully obedient in the first condition, and only nine in the second (Chi square obedient *vs.* defiant in the two conditions, df = 14.7; $p < 0.001$). Subjects seemed able to take a far stronger stand against the experimenter when they did not have to encounter him face to face, and the experimenter's power over the subject was severely curtailed.[8]

Moreover, when the experimenter was absent, subjects displayed an interesting form of behavior that had not occurred under his surveillance. Though continuing with the experiment, several subjects administered lower shocks than were required and never informed the experimenter of their deviation from the correct procedure. (Unknown to the subjects, shock levels were automatically recorded by an Esterline-Angus event recorder wired directly into the shock generator; the instrument provided us with an objective record of the subjects' performance.) Indeed, in telephone conversations some subjects specifically assured the experimenter that they were raising the shock level according to instruction, whereas in fact they were repeatedly using the lowest shock on the board. This form of behavior is particularly interesting: although these subjects acted in a way that clearly undermined the avowed purposes of the experiment, they found it easier to handle the conflict in this manner than to precipitate an open break with authority.

Other conditions were completed in which the experimenter was absent during the first segment of the experiment, but reappeared at the point that the subject definitely refused to give higher shocks when commanded by telephone. Although he had exhausted his power via telephone, the experimenter could frequently force further obedience when he reappeared in the laboratory.

Experiments in this series show that the *physical presence* of an authority is an important force contributing to the subject's obedience or defiance. Taken together with the first experimental series on the proximity of the victim, it would appear that something akin to fields of force, diminishing in effectiveness with increasing psychological distance from their source, have a controlling effect on the subject's performance. As the victim is brought closer, the subject finds it harder to administer shocks to him. When the victim's position is held constant relative to the subject, and the authority is made more remote, the subject finds it easier to break off the experiment. This effect is substantial in both cases, but manipulation of the experimenter's position yielded the more powerful results. Obedience to destructive commands is highly dependent on the proximal relations between authority and subject.

Tensions

The description of final scores does not fully convey the character of the subjects' performance, and it would be useful to interrupt our reporting of quantitative relationships to remark on the subjects' general reaction to the situation.

One might suppose that a subject would simply break off or continue as his conscience and temperament dictated. Yet this is very far from what happened. There were powerful reactions of tension and emotional strain in a substantial proportion of the participants. Persons were observed to sweat, tremble, stutter, bite their lips, and groan as they found themselves increasingly implicated in the experimental conflict. Some sense of the subjects' mood can be found in a transcript of their remarks at break-off point. Here are the remarks of two defiant subjects:

Is he banging? . . . Is he hurt out there? Well, I don't want to be responsible for anything that happens to him. No, I can't go on with it. I don't know whether he's all right or not. I mean he may have a heart condition or something; I wouldn't feel right doing it. He's banging for help. He's evidently in trouble or he wouldn't bang . . . I don't see any sense to this—to knocking him out or something. I just can't see it.

[Subject refuses to administer shocks]   *[Subject 0108]*

The man is banging. He wants to get out . . . I'm sorry. If the man wants to get out I'd just as soon stop . . . I don't want to administer any more [extremely excited] . . . I will gladly refund the check, but I will not harm this man . . . I'm sorry, I will not give him any more if he obviously wants to get out. There is no money in the world that will make me hurt another individual.

[Subject 010X]

And here is a transcript from an obedient subject. He began the experiment calmly, but became increasingly tense as the experiment proceeded. After administering the 150-volt shock, he began to address the experimenter in agitated tones:

150 volts delivered. You want me to keep going?
165 volts delivered. That guy is hollering in there. There's a lot of them here. He's liable to have heart condition. You want me to go?
180 volts delivered. He can't stand it! I'm not going to kill that man in there! You hear him hollering? He's hollering. He can't stand it. What if something happens to him? . . . I'm not going to get that man sick in there. He's hollering in there. You know what I mean? I

mean I refuse to take responsibility. He's getting hurt in there. He's
in there hollering. Too many left here. Geez, if he gets them wrong.
There's too many of them left. I mean who is going to take responsibility if anything happens to that gentleman?
[*The experimenter accepts responsibility.*] All right.
195 volts delivered. You see he's hollering. Hear that. Gee, I
don't know.
[*The experimenter says: "The experiment requires that you go on."*]—I
know it does, sir, but I mean—hugh—he don't know what he's in
for. He's up to 195 volts.
210 volts delivered.
225 volts delivered.
240 volts delivered. Aw, no. You mean I've got to keep going up with
the scale? No sir. I'm not going to kill that man! I'm not going to
give him 450 volts!
[*The experimenter says: "The experiment requires that you go on."*]—I
know it does, but that man is hollering there, sir . . .

Despite his numerous, agitated objections, which were constant accom-
paniments to his actions, the subject unfailingly obeyed the experimenter,
proceeding to the highest shock level on the generator. He displayed a
curious dissociation between word and action. Although at the verbal
level he had resolved not to go on, his actions were fully in accord with
the experimenter's commands. This subject did not want to shock the
victim, and he found it an extremely disagreeable task, but he was unable
to invent a response that would free him from *E*'s authority. Many subjects cannot find the specific verbal formula that would enable them to
reject the role assigned to them by the experimenter. Perhaps our culture
does not provide adequate models for disobedience.

One puzzling sign of tension was the regular occurrence of nervous   40
laughing fits. In the first four conditions 71 of the 160 subjects showed
definite signs of nervous laughter and smiling. The laughter seemed entirely out of place, even bizarre. Full-blown, uncontrollable seizures were
observed for 15 of these subjects. On one occasion we observed a seizure
so violently convulsive that it was necessary to call a halt to the experiment. In the post-experimental interviews subjects took pains to point
out that they were not sadistic types and that the laughter did not mean
they enjoyed shocking the victim.

In the interview following the experiment subjects were asked to
indicate on a 14-point scale just how nervous or tense they felt at the
point of maximum tension (Figure 2). The scale ranged from "not at all
tense and nervous" to "extremely tense and nervous." Self-reports of this
sort are of limited precision and at best provide only a rough indication
of the subject's emotional response. Still, taking the reports for what they
are worth, it can be seen that the distribution of responses spans the entire
range of the scale, with the majority of subjects concentrated at the center

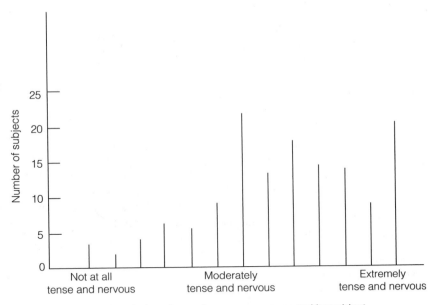

Figure 2 Level of tension and nervousness: the self-reports on "tension and nervousness" for 137 subjects in the Proximity experiments. Subjects were given a scale with 14 values ranging from "not at all tense and nervous" to "extremely tense and nervous." They were instructed: "Thinking back to that point in the experiment when you felt the most tense and nervous, indicate just how you felt by placing an X at the appropriate point on the scale." The results are shown in terms of midpoint values.

and upper extreme. A further breakdown showed that obedient subjects reported themselves as having been slightly more tense and nervous than the defiant subjects at the point of maximum tension.

How is the occurrence of tension to be interpreted? First, it points to the presence of conflict. If a tendency to comply with authority were the only psychological force operating in the situation, all subjects would have continued to the end and there would have been no tension. Tension, it is assumed, results from the simultaneous presence of two or more incompatible response tendencies (Miller, 1944). If sympathetic concern for the victim were the exclusive force, all subjects would have calmly defied the experimenter. Instead, there were both obedient and defiant outcomes, frequently accompanied by extreme tension. A conflict develops between the deeply ingrained disposition not to harm others and the equally compelling tendency to obey others who are in authority. The subject is quickly drawn into a dilemma of a deeply dynamic character, and the presence of high tension points to the considerable strength of each of the antagonistic vectors.

Moreover, tension defines the strength of the aversion state from which the subject is unable to escape through disobedience. When a person is uncomfortable, tense, or stressed, he tries to take some action that will allow him to terminate this unpleasant state. Thus tension may serve as a drive that leads to escape behavior. But in the present situation, even where tension is extreme, many subjects are unable to perform the response that will bring about relief. Therefore there must be a competing drive, tendency, or inhibition that precludes activation of the disobedient response. The strength of this inhibiting factor must be of greater magnitude than the stress experienced, or else the terminating act would occur. Every evidence of extreme tension is at the same time an indication of the strength of the forces that keep the subject in the situation.

Finally, tension may be taken as evidence of the reality of the situations for the subjects. Normal subjects do not tremble and sweat unless they are implicated in a deep and genuinely felt predicament.

Background Authority

In psychophysics, animal learning, and other branches of psychology, the fact that measures are obtained at one institution rather than another is irrelevant to the interpretation of the findings, so long as the technical facilities for measurement are adequate and the operations are carried out with competence. *45*

But it cannot be assumed that this holds true for the present study. The effectiveness of the experimenter's commands may depend in an important way on the larger institutional context in which they are issued. The experiments described thus far were conducted at Yale University, an organization which most subjects regarded with respect and sometimes awe. In post-experimental interviews several participants remarked that the locale and sponsorship of the study gave them confidence in the integrity, competence, and benign purposes of the personnel; many indicated that they would not have shocked the learner if the experiments had been done elsewhere.

This issue of background authority seemed to us important for an interpretation of the results that had been obtained thus far; moreover it is highly relevant to any comprehensive theory of human obedience. Consider, for example, how closely our compliance with the imperatives of others is tied to particular institutions and locales in our day-to-day activities. On request, we expose our throats to a man with a razor blade in the barber shop, but would not do so in a shoe store; in the latter setting we willingly follow the clerk's request to stand in our stockinged feet, but resist the command in a bank. In the laboratory of a great university, subjects may comply with a set of commands that would be resisted if given elsewhere. *One must always question the relationship of obedience to a person's sense of the context in which he is operating.*

To explore the problem we moved our apparatus to an office building in industrial Bridgeport and replicated experimental conditions, without any visible tie to the university.

Bridgeport subjects were invited to the experiment through a mail circular similar to the one used in the Yale study, with appropriate changes in letterhead, etc. As in the earlier study, subjects were paid $4.50 for coming to the laboratory. The same age and occupational distributions used at Yale and the identical personnel were employed.

The purpose in relocating in Bridgeport was to assure a complete 50 dissociation from Yale, and in this regard we were fully successful. On the surface, the study appeared to be conducted by Research Associates of Bridgeport, an organization of unknown character (the title had been concocted exclusively for use in this study).

The experiments were conducted in a three-room office suite in a somewhat run-down commercial building located in the downtown shopping area. The laboratory was sparsely furnished, though clean, and marginally respectable in appearance. When subjects inquired about professional affiliations, they were informed only that we were a private firm conducting research for industry.

Some subjects displayed skepticism concerning the motives of the Bridgeport experimenter. One gentleman gave us a written account of the thoughts he experienced at the control board:

> . . . Should I quit this damn test? Maybe he passed out? What dopes we were not to check up on this deal. How do we know that these guys are legit? No furniture, bare walls, no telephone. We could of called the Police up or the Better Business Bureau. I learned a lesson tonight. How do I know that Mr. Williams [the experimenter] is telling the truth . . . I wish I knew how many volts a person could take before lapsing into unconsciousness. [*Subject 2414*]

Another subject stated:

> I questioned on my arrival my own judgment [about coming]. I had doubts as to the legitimacy of the operation and the consequences of participation. I felt it was a heartless way to conduct memory or learning processes on human beings and certainly dangerous without the presence of a medical doctor. [*Subject 2440V*]

There was no noticeable reduction in tension for the Bridgeport subjects. And the subjects' estimation of the amount of pain felt by the victim was slightly, though not significantly, higher than in the Yale study.

A failure to obtain complete obedience in Bridgeport would indicate that the extreme compliance found in New Haven subjects was tied closely to the background authority of Yale University; if a large proportion of the subjects remained fully obedient, very different conclusions would be called for.

As it turned out, the level of obedience in Bridgeport, although   55
somewhat reduced, was not significantly lower than that obtained at Yale.
A large proportion of the Bridgeport subjects were fully obedient to the
experimenter's commands (48 percent of the Bridgeport subjects delivered the maximum shock versus 65 percent in the corresponding condition at Yale).

How are these findings to be interpreted? It is possible that if commands of a potentially harmful or destructive sort are to be perceived as
legitimate they must occur within some sort of institutional structure. But
it is clear from the study that it need not be a particularly reputable or
distinguished institution. The Bridgeport experiments were conducted
by an unimpressive firm lacking any credentials; the laboratory was set up
in a respectable office building with title listed in the building directory.
Beyond that, there was no evidence of benevolence or competence. It is
possible that the *category* of institution, judged according to its professed
function, rather than its qualitative position within that category, wins
our compliance. Persons deposit money in elegant, but also in seedy-
looking banks, without giving much thought to the differences in security they offer. Similarly, our subjects may consider one laboratory to be
as competent as another, so long as it is a scientific laboratory.

It would be valuable to study the subjects' performance in other contexts which go even further than the Bridgeport study in denying institutional support to the experimenter. It is possible that, beyond a certain
point, obedience disappears completely. But that point had not been
reached in the Bridgeport office: almost half the subjects obeyed the experimenter fully.

Further Experiments

We may mention briefly some additional experiments undertaken in
the Yale series. A considerable amount of obedience and defiance in everyday life occurs in connection with groups. And we had reason to feel
in light of the many group studies already done in psychology that group
forces would have a profound effect on reactions to authority. A series of
experiments was run to examine these effects. In all cases only one naïve
subject was studied per hour, but he performed in the midst of actors
who, unknown to him, were employed by the experimenter. In one experiment (Groups for Disobedience) two actors broke off in the middle
of the experiment. When this happened 90 percent of the subjects followed suit and defied the experimenter. In another condition the actors followed the orders obediently; this strengthened the experimenter's
power only slightly. In still a third experiment the job of pushing the
switch to shock the learner was given to one of the actors, while the naïve
subject performed a subsidiary act. We wanted to see how the teacher
would respond if he were involved in the situation but did not actually

give the shocks. In this situation only three subjects out of forty broke off. In a final group experiment the subjects themselves determined the shock level they were going to use. Two actors suggested higher and higher shock levels; some subjects insisted, despite group pressure, that the shock level be kept low; others followed along with the group.

Further experiments were completed using women as subjects, as well as a set dealing with the effects of dual, unsanctioned, and conflicting authority. A final experiment concerned the personal relationship between victim and subject. These will have to be described elsewhere, lest the present report be extended to monographic length.

It goes without saying that future research can proceed in many different directions. What kinds of response from the victim are most effective in causing disobedience in the subject? Perhaps passive resistance is more effective than vehement protest. What conditions of entry into an authority system lead to greater or lesser obedience? What is the effect of anonymity and masking on the subject's behavior? What conditions lead to the subject's perception of responsibility for his own actions? Each of these could be a major research topic in itself, and can readily be incorporated into the general experimental procedure described here.

60

Levels of Obedience and Defiance

One general finding that merits attention is the high level of obedience manifested in the experimental situation. Subjects often expressed deep disapproval of shocking a man in the face of his objections, and others denounced it as senseless and stupid. Yet many subjects complied even while they protested. The proportion of obedient subjects greatly exceeded the expectations of the experimenter and his colleagues. At the outset, we had conjectured that subjects would not, in general, go above the level of "Strong Shock." In practice, many subjects were willing to administer the most extreme shocks available when commanded by the experimenter. For some subjects the experiment provided an occasion for aggressive release. And for others it demonstrated the extent to which obedient dispositions are deeply ingrained and engaged, irrespective of their consequences for others. Yet this is not the whole story. Somehow, the subject becomes implicated in a situation from which he cannot disengage himself.

The departure of the experimental results from intelligent expectation, to some extent, has been formalized. The procedure was to describe the experimental situation in concrete detail to a group of competent persons, and to ask them to predict the performance of 100 hypothetical subjects. For purposes of indicating the distribution of break-off points, judges were provided with a diagram of the shock generator and recorded their predictions before being informed of the actual results. Judges typically underestimated the amount of obedience demonstrated by subjects.

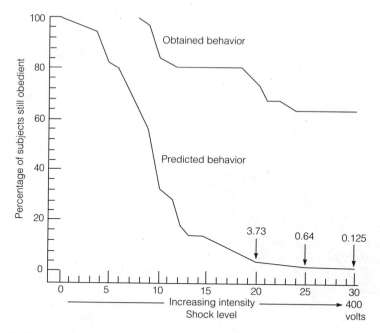

Figure 3 Predicted and obtained behavior in voice feedback.

In Figure 3, we compare the predictions of forty psychiatrists at a leading medical school with the actual performance of subjects in the experiment. The psychiatrists predicted that most subjects would not go beyond the tenth shock level (150 volts; at this point the victim makes his first explicit demand to be freed). They further predicted that by the twentieth shock level (300 volts; the victim refuses to answer) 3.73 percent of the subjects would still be obedient; and that only a little over one-tenth of one percent of the subjects would administer the highest shock on the board. But, as the graph indicates, the obtained behavior was very different. Sixty-two percent of the subjects obeyed the experimenter's commands fully. Between expectation and occurrence there is a whopping discrepancy.

Why did the psychiatrists underestimate the level of obedience? Possibly, because their predictions were based on an inadequate conception of the determinants of human action, a conception that focuses on motives in *vacuo*. This orientation may be entirely adequate for the repair of bruised impulses as revealed on the psychiatrist's couch, but as soon as our interest turns to action in larger settings, attention must be paid to the situations in which motives are expressed. A situation exerts an important press on the individual. It exercises constraints and may provide push. In certain circumstances it is not so much the kind of person a man is, as the kind of situation in which he is placed, that determines his actions.

Many people, not knowing much about the experiment, claim that *65* subjects who go to the end of the board are sadistic. Nothing could be more foolish than an overall characterization of these persons. It is like saying that a person thrown into a swift-flowing stream is necessarily a fast swimmer, or that he has great stamina because he moves so rapidly relative to the bank. The context of action must always be considered. The individual, upon entering the laboratory, becomes integrated into a situation that carries its own momentum. The subject's problem then is how to become disengaged from a situation which is moving in an altogether ugly direction.

The fact that disengagement is so difficult testifies to the potency of the forces that keep the subject at the control board. Are these forces to be conceptualized as individual motives and expressed in the language of personality dynamics, or are they to be seen as the effects of social structure and pressures arising from the situational field?

A full understanding of the subject's action will, I feel, require that both perspectives be adopted. The person brings to the laboratory enduring dispositions toward authority and aggression, and at the same time he becomes enmeshed in a social structure that is no less an objective fact of the case. From the standpoint of personality theory one may ask: What mechanisms of personality enable a person to transfer responsibility to authority? What are the motives underlying obedient and disobedient performance? Does orientation to authority lead to a short-circuiting of the shame-guilt system? What cognitive and emotional defenses are brought into play in the case of obedient and defiant subjects?

The present experiments are not, however, directed toward an exploration of the motives engaged when the subject obeys the experimenter's commands. Instead, they examine the situational variables responsible for the elicitation of obedience. Elsewhere, we have attempted to spell out some of the structural properties of the experimental situation that account for high obedience, and this analysis need not be repeated here (Milgram, 1963). The experimental variations themselves represent our attempt to probe that structure, by systematically changing it and noting the consequences for behavior. It is clear that some situations produce greater compliance with the experimenter's commands than others. However, this does not necessarily imply an increase or decrease in the strength of any single definable motive. Situations producing the greatest obedience could do so by triggering the most powerful, yet perhaps the most idiosyncratic, of motives in each subject confronted by the setting. Or they may simply recruit a greater number and variety of motives in their service. But whatever the motives involved—and it is far from certain that they can ever be known—action may be studied as a direct function of the situation in which it occurs. This has been the approach of the present study, where we sought to plot behavioral regularities against manipulated properties of the social field. Ultimately, social psychology would like to have a compelling *theory of situations* which will, first, present a language in terms of which situations can be defined; proceed to a typology of situations; and then point to the manner in which definable properties of situations are transformed into psychological forces in the individual.[9]

Postscript

Almost a thousand adults were individually studied in the obedience research, and there were many specific conclusions regarding the variables that control obedience and disobedience to authority. Some of these have been discussed briefly in the preceding sections, and more detailed reports will be released subsequently.

There are now some other generalizations I should like to make, 70 which do not derive in any strictly logical fashion from the experiments as carried out, but which, I feel, ought to be made. They are formulations of an intuitive sort that have been forced on me by observation of many subjects responding to the pressures of authority. The assertions represent a painful alteration in my own thinking; and since they were acquired only under the repeated impact of direct observation, I have no illusion that they will be generally accepted by persons who have not had the same experience.

With numbing regularity good people were seen to knuckle under the demands of authority and perform actions that were callous and severe. Men who are in everyday life responsible and decent were seduced by the trappings of authority, by the control of their perceptions, and by the uncritical acceptance of the experimenter's definition of the situation, into performing harsh acts.

What is the limit of such obedience? At many points we attempted to establish a boundary. Cries from the victim were inserted; not good enough. The victim claimed heart trouble; subjects still shocked him on command. The victim pleaded that he be let free, and his answers no longer registered on the signal box; subjects continued to shock him. At the outset we had not conceived that such drastic procedures would be needed to generate disobedience, and each step was added only as the ineffectiveness of the earlier techniques became clear. The final effort to establish a limit was the Touch-Proximity condition. But the very first subject in this condition subdued the victim on command, and proceeded to the highest shock level. A quarter of the subjects in this condition performed similarly.

The results, as seen and felt in the laboratory, are to this author disturbing. They raise the possibility that human nature or, more specifically, the kind of character produced in American democratic society cannot be counted on to insulate its citizens from brutality and inhumane treatment at the direction of malevolent authority. A substantial proportion of people do what they are told to do, irrespective of the content of the act and without limitations of conscience, so long as they perceive that the command comes from a legitimate authority. If in this study an anonymous experimenter could successfully command adults to subdue a fifty-year-old man and force on him painful electric shocks against his protests, one can only wonder what government, with its vastly greater authority and prestige, can command of its subjects. There is, of course, the extremely important question of whether malevolent political institutions could or would arise in American society. The present research contributes nothing to this issue.

In an article titled "The Danger of Obedience," Harold J. Laski wrote:

> . . . civilization means, above all, an unwillingness to inflict unnecessary pain. Within the ambit of that definition, those of us who heedlessly accept the commands of authority cannot yet claim to be civilized men.
>
> . . . Our business, if we desire to live a life, not utterly devoid of meaning and significance, is to accept nothing which contradicts our basic experience merely because it comes to us from tradition or convention or authority. It may well be that we shall be wrong; but our self-expression is thwarted at the root unless the certainties we are asked to accept coincide with the certainties we experience. That is why the condition of freedom in any state is always a widespread and consistent skepticism of the canons upon which power insists.

NOTES

1. This research was supported by two grants from the National Science Foundation: NSF G-17916 and NSF G-24152. Exploratory studies carried out in 1960 were financed by a grant from the Higgins Funds of Yale University. I am grateful to John T. Williams, James J. McDonough, and Emil Elges for the important part they played in the project. Thanks are due also to Alan Elms, James Miller, Taketo Murata, and Stephen Stier for their aid as graduate assistants. My wife, Sasha, performed many valuable services. Finally, I owe a profound debt to the many persons in New Haven and Bridgeport who served as subjects.

2. Consider, for example, J. P. Scott's analysis of war in his monograph on aggression:
   "... while the actions of key individuals in a war may be explained in terms of direct stimulation to aggression, vast numbers of other people are involved simply by being part of an organized society.
   ... For example, at the beginning of World War I an Austrian archduke was assassinated in Sarajevo. A few days later soldiers from all over Europe were marching toward each other, not because they were stimulated by the archduke's misfortune, but because they had been trained to obey orders." (Slightly rearranged from Scott [1958], *Aggression,* p. 103.)

3. It consisted of an extended discussion with the experimenter and, of equal importance, a friendly reconciliation with the victim. It is made clear that the victim did *not* receive

painful electric shocks. After the completion of the experimental series, subjects were sent a detailed report of the results and full purposes of the experimental program. A formal assessment of this procedure points to its overall effectiveness. Of the subjects, 83.7 percent indicated that they were glad to have taken part in the study; 15.1 percent reported neutral feelings; and 1.3 percent stated that they were sorry to have participated. A large number of subjects spontaneously requested that they be used in further experimentation. Four-fifths of the subjects felt that more experiments of this sort should be carried out, and 74 percent indicated that they had learned something of personal importance as a result of being in the study. Furthermore, a university psychiatrist, experienced in outpatient treatment, interviewed a sample of experimental subjects with the aim of uncovering possible injurious effects resulting from participation. No such effects were in evidence. Indeed, subjects typically felt that their participation was instructive and enriching. A more detailed discussion of this question can be found in Milgram (1964).

4. To *obey* and to *disobey* are not the only terms one could use in describing the critical action of Y. One could say that Y is cooperating with X, or displays conformity with regard to X's commands. However, *cooperation* suggests that X agrees with Y's ends, and understands the relationship between his own behavior and the attainment of those ends. (But the experimental procedure, and, in particular, the experimenter's command that the subject shock the victim even in the absence of a response from the victim, preclude such understanding.) Moreover, cooperation implies status parity for the co-acting agents, and neglects the asymmetrical, dominance-subordination element prominent in the laboratory relationship between experimenter and subject. *Conformity* has been used in other important contexts in social psychology, and most frequently refers to imitating the judgments or actions of others when no explicit requirement for imitation has been made. Furthermore, in the present study there are two sources of social pressure; pressure from the experimenter issuing the commands, and pressure from the victim to stop the punishment. It is the pitting of a common man (the victim) against an authority (the experimenter) that is the distinctive feature of the conflict. At a point in the experiment the victim demands that he be let free. The experimenter insists that the subject continue to administer shocks. Which act of the subject can be interpreted as conformity? The subject may conform to the wishes of his peer or to the wishes of the experimenter, and conformity in one direction means the absence of conformity in the other. Thus the word has no useful reference in this setting, for the dual and conflicting social pressures cancel out its meaning.

   In the final analysis, the linguistic symbol representing the subject's action must take its meaning from the concrete context in which that action occurs; and there is probably no word in everyday language that covers the experimental situation exactly, without omissions or irrelevant connotations. It is partly for convenience, therefore, that the terms *obey* and *disobey* are used to describe the subject's actions. At the same time, our use of the words is highly congruent with dictionary meaning.

5. A more detailed account of the laboratory procedure can be found in Milgram (1963). A similar and independently evolved experimental procedure, employing a shock generator, victim, and learning task, was reported by Buss (1961). Buss used the technique for studying aggression, not obedience, and did not make use of the fundamental measure employed in the present study: break-off points.

6. It is difficult to convey on the printed page the full tenor of the victim's responses, for we have no adequate notation for vocal intensity, timing, and general qualities of delivery. Yet these features are crucial to producing the effect of an increasingly severe reaction to mounting voltage levels. (They can be communicated fully only by sending

interested parties the recorded tapes.) In general terms, however, the victim indicates no discomfort until the 75-volt shock is administered, at which time there is a light grunt in response to the punishment. Similar reactions follow the 90- and 105-volt shocks, and at 120 volts the victim shouts to the experimenter that the shocks are becoming painful. Painful groans are heard on administration of the 135-volt shock, and at 150 volts the victim cries out, "Experimenter, get me out of here! I won't be in the experiment any more! I refuse to go on!" Cries of this type continue with generally rising intensity, so that at 180 volts the victim cries out, "I can't stand the pain," and by 270 volts his response to the shock is definitely an agonized scream. Throughout, he insists that he be let out of the experiment. At 300 volts the victim shouts in desperation that he will no longer provide answers to the memory test; and at 315 volts, after a violent scream, he reaffirms with vehemence that he is no longer a participant. From this point on, he provides no answers, but shrieks in agony whenever a shock is administered; this continues through 450 volts. Of course, many subjects will have broken off before this point.

A revised and stronger set of protests was used in all experiments outside the Proximity series. Naturally, new baseline measures were established for all comparisons using the new set of protests.

There is overwhelming evidence that the great majority of subjects, both obedient and defiant, accepted the victims' reactions as genuine. The evidence takes the form of: (a) tension created in the subjects (see discussion of tension); (b) scores on "estimated-pain" scales filled out by the subjects immediately after the experiment; (c) subjects' accounts of their feelings in post-experimental interviews; and (d) quantifiable responses to questionnaires distributed to subjects several months after their participation in the experiments. This matter will be treated fully in a forthcoming monograph.

(The procedure in all experimental conditions was to have the naïve subject announce the voltage level before administering each shock, so that—independently of the victim's responses—he was continually reminded of delivering punishment of ever-increasing severity.)

7. Admittedly, the terms *proximity, immediacy, closeness,* and *salience-of-the-victim* are used in a loose sense, and the experiments themselves represent a very coarse treatment of the variable. Further experiments are needed to refine the notion and tease out such diverse factors as spatial distance, visibility, audibility, barrier interposition, etc.

   The Proximity and Touch-Proximity experiments were the only conditions where we were unable to use taped feedback from the victim. Instead, the victim was trained to respond in these conditions as he had in Experiment 2 (which employed taped feedback). Some improvement is possible here, for it should be technically feasible to do a proximity series using taped feedback.

8. The third condition also led to significantly lower obedience than this first situation in which the experimenter was present, but it contains technical difficulties that require extensive discussion.

9. My thanks to Professor Howard Leventhal of Yale for strengthening the writing in this paragraph.

REFERENCES

Buss, Arnold. 1961. *The Psychology of Aggression.* New York and London: John Wiley.

Kierkegaard, S. 1843. *Fear and Trembling.* English edition, Princeton: Princeton University Press, 1941.

Laski, Harold J. 1929. "The dangers of obedience." *Harper's Monthly Magazine,* 15 June 1–10.

Milgram, S. 1961. "Dynamics of obedience: experiments in social psychology." Mimeographed report, *National Science Foundation,* January 25.

——. 1963. "Behavioral study of obedience." *J. Abnorm. Soc. Psychol.* 67, 371–378.

——. 1964. "Issues in the study of obedience: a reply to Baumrind." *Amer. Psychol.* 1, 848–852.

Miller, N. E. 1944. "Experimental studies of conflict." In J. McV. Hunt (ed.), *Personality and the Behavior Disorders.* New York: Ronald Press.

Scott, J. P. 1958. *Aggression.* Chicago: University of Chicago Press.

THE PERILS OF OBEDIENCE

Stanley Milgram

Obedience is as basic an element in the structure of social life as one can point to. Some system of authority is a requirement of all communal living, and it is only the person dwelling in isolation who is not forced to respond, with defiance or submission, to the commands of others. For many people, obedience is a deeply ingrained behavior tendency, indeed a potent impulse overriding training in ethics, sympathy, and moral conduct.

The dilemma inherent in submission to authority is ancient, as old as the story of Abraham, and the question of whether one should obey when commands conflict with conscience has been argued by Plato, dramatized in *Antigone,* and treated to philosophic analysis in almost every historical epoch. Conservative philosophers argue that the very fabric of society is threatened by disobedience, while humanists stress the primacy of the individual conscience.

The legal and philosophic aspects of obedience are of enormous import, but they say very little about how most people behave in concrete situations. I set up a simple experiment at Yale University to test how much pain an ordinary citizen would inflict on another person simply because he was ordered to by an experimental scientist. Stark authority was pitted against the subjects' strongest moral imperatives against hurting others, and, with the subjects' ears ringing with the screams of the victims, authority won more often than not. The extreme willingness of adults to go to almost any lengths on the command of an authority constitutes the chief finding of the study and the fact most urgently demanding explanation.

In the basic experimental design, two people come to a psychology laboratory to take part in a study of memory and learning. One of them is designated as a "teacher" and the other a "learner." The experimenter explains that the study is concerned with the effects of punishment on learning. The learner is conducted into a room, seated in a kind of miniature electric chair; his arms are strapped to prevent excessive movement, and an electrode is attached to his wrist. He is told that he will be read lists of simple word pairs, and that he will then be tested on his ability to remember the second word of a pair when he hears the first one again. Whenever he makes an error, he will receive electric shocks of increasing intensity.

The real focus of the experiment is the teacher. After watching the learner being strapped into place, he is seated before an impressive shock generator. The instrument panel consists of thirty lever switches set in a horizontal line. Each switch is clearly labeled with a voltage designation ranging from 15 to 450 volts. The following designations are clearly indicated for groups of four switches, going from left to right: Slight Shock, Moderate Shock, Strong Shock, Very Strong Shock, Intense Shock, Extreme Intensity Shock, Danger: Severe Shock. (Two switches after this last designation are simply marked XXX.)

When a switch is depressed, a pilot light corresponding to each switch is illuminated in bright red; an electric buzzing is heard; a blue light, labeled "voltage energizer," flashes; the dial on the voltage meter swings to the right; and various relay clicks sound off.

The upper left–hand corner of the generator is labeled SHOCK GENERATOR, TYPE ZLB, DYSON INSTRUMENT COMPANY, WALTHAM, MASS. OUTPUT 15 VOLTS—450 VOLTS.

Each subject is given a sample 45-volt shock from the generator before his run as teacher, and the jolt strengthens his belief in the authenticity of the machine.

The teacher is a genuinely naïve subject who has come to the laboratory for the experiment. The learner, or victim, is actually an actor who receives no shock at all. The point of the experiment is to see how far a person will proceed in a concrete and measurable situation in which he is ordered to inflict increasing pain on a protesting victim.

Conflict arises when the man receiving the shock begins to show that he is experiencing discomfort. At 75 volts, he grunts; at 120 volts, he complains loudly; at 150, he demands to be released from the experiment. As the voltage increases, his protests become more vehement and emotional. At 285 volts, his response can be described only as an agonized scream. Soon thereafter, he makes no sound at all.

For the teacher, the situation quickly becomes one of gripping tension. It is not a game for him; conflict is intense and obvious. The manifest suffering of the learner presses him to quit; but each time he hesitates to administer a shock, the experimenter orders him to continue. To extricate himself from this plight, the subject must make a clear break with authority.[1]

---

1. The ethical problems of carrying out an experiment of this sort are too complex to be dealt with here, but they receive extended treatment in the book from which this article is adapted.

The subject, Gretchen Brandt,[2] is an attractive thirty-one-year-old medical technician who works at the Yale Medical School. She had emigrated from Germany five years before.

On several occasions when the learner complains, she turns to the experimenter coolly and inquires, "Shall I continue?" She promptly returns to her task when the experimenter asks her to do so. At the administration of 210 volts, she turns to the experimenter, remarking firmly, "Well, I'm sorry, I don't think we should continue."

> EXPERIMENTER: The experiment requires that you go on until he has learned all the word pairs correctly.
> BRANDT: He has a heart condition, I'm sorry. He told you that before.   *15*
> EXPERIMENTER: The shocks may be painful but they are not dangerous.
> BRANDT: Well, I'm sorry, I think when shocks continue like this, they *are* dangerous. You ask him if he wants to get out. It's his free will.
> EXPERIMENTER: It is absolutely essential that we continue. . . .
> BRANDT: I'd like you to ask him. We came here of our free will. If he wants to continue I'll go ahead. He told you he had a heart condition. I'm sorry. I don't want to be responsible for anything happening to him. I wouldn't like it for me either.
> EXPERIMENTER: You have no other choice.   *20*
> BRANDT: I think we are here on our own free will. I don't want to be responsible if anything happens to him. Please understand that.

She refuses to go further and the experiment is terminated.

The woman is firm and resolute throughout. She indicates in the interview that she was in no way tense or nervous, and this corresponds to her controlled appearance during the experiment. She feels that the last shock she administered to the learner was extremely painful and reiterates that she "did not want to be responsible for any harm to him."

The woman's straightforward, courteous behavior in the experiment, lack of tension, and total control of her own action seem to make disobedience a simple and rational deed. Her behavior is the very embodiment of what I envisioned would be true for almost all subjects.

An Unexpected Outcome

Before the experiments, I sought predictions about the outcome from   *25* various kinds of people—psychiatrists, college sophomores, middle-class adults, graduate students and faculty in the behavioral sciences. With remarkable similarity, they predicted that virtually all subjects would refuse to obey the experimenter. The psychiatrists, specifically, predicted that

---

2. Names of subjects described in this piece have been changed.

most subjects would not go beyond 150 volts, when the victim makes his first explicit demand to be freed. They expected that only 4 percent would reach 300 volts, and that only a pathological fringe of about one in a thousand would administer the highest shock on the board.

These predictions were unequivocally wrong. Of the forty subjects in the first experiment, twenty-five obeyed the orders of the experimenter to the end, punishing the victim until they reached the most potent shock available on the generator. After 450 volts were administered three times, the experimenter called a halt to the session. Many obedient subjects then heaved sighs of relief, mopped their brows, rubbed their fingers over their eyes, or nervously fumbled cigarettes. Others displayed only minimal signs of tension from beginning to end.

When the very first experiments were carried out, Yale undergraduates were used as subjects, and about 60 percent of them were fully obedient. A colleague of mine immediately dismissed these findings as having no relevance to "ordinary" people, asserting that Yale undergraduates are a highly aggressive, competitive bunch who step on each other's necks on the slightest provocation. He assured me that when "ordinary" people were tested, the results would be quite different. As we moved from the pilot studies to the regular experimental series, people drawn from every stratum of New Haven life came to be employed in the experiment: professionals, white-collar workers, unemployed persons, and industrial workers. *The experiment's total outcome was the same as we had observed among the students.*

Moreover, when the experiments were repeated in Princeton, Munich, Rome, South Africa, and Australia, the level of obedience was invariably somewhat *higher* than found in the investigation reported in this article. Thus one scientist in Munich found 85 percent of his subjects to be obedient.

Fred Prozi's reactions, if more dramatic than most, illuminate the conflicts experienced by others in less visible form. About fifty years old and unemployed at the time of the experiment, he has a good-natured, if slightly dissolute, appearance, and he strikes people as a rather ordinary fellow. He begins the session calmly but becomes tense as it proceeds. After delivering the 180-volt shock, he pivots around in his chair and, shaking his head, addresses the experimenter in agitated tones:

> PROZI: I can't stand it. I'm not going to kill that man in there. You *30*
>   hear him hollering?
> EXPERIMENTER: As I told you before, the shocks may be painful,
>   but . . .
> PROZI: But he's hollering. He can't stand it. What's going to happen
>   to him?
> EXPERIMENTER (*his voice is patient, matter-of-fact*): The experiment requires that you continue, Teacher.

PROZI: Aaah, but, unh, I'm not going to get that man sick in there—know what I mean?

EXPERIMENTER: Whether the learner likes it or not, we must go on, through all the word pairs.   *35*

PROZI: I refuse to take the responsibility. He's in there hollering!

EXPERIMENTER: It's absolutely essential that you continue, Prozi.

PROZI (*indicating the unused questions*): There's too many left here, I mean, Jeez, if he gets them wrong, there's too many of them left. I mean, who's going to take the responsibility if anything happens to that gentleman?

EXPERIMENTER: I'm responsible for anything that happens to him. Continue, please.

PROZI: All right. (*Consults list of words.*) The next one's "Slow—walk, truck, dance, music." Answer, please. (*A buzzing sound indicates the learner has signaled his answer.*) Wrong. A hundred and ninety-five volts. "Dance." (*Zzumph!*)   *40*

LEARNER (*yelling*): Let me out of here! My heart's bothering me! (*Teacher looks at experimenter.*)

EXPERIMENTER: Continue, please.

LEARNER (*screaming*): Let me out of here! You have no right to keep me here! Let me out of here, my heart's bothering me, let me out!

PROZI (*shakes head, pats the table nervously*): You see, he's hollering. Hear that? Gee, I don't know.

EXPERIMENTER: The experiment requires . . .   *45*

PROZI (*interrupting*): I know it does, sir, but I mean—hunh! He don't know what he's getting in for. He's up to 195 volts! (*Experiment continues, through 210 volts, 225 volts, 240 volts, 255 volts, 270 volts, at which point Prozi, with evident relief, runs out of word-pair questions.*)

EXPERIMENTER: You'll have to go back to the beginning of that page and go through them again until he's learned them all correctly.

PROZI: Aw, no. I'm not going to kill that man. You mean I've got to keep going up with the scale? No sir. He's hollering in there. I'm not going to give him 450 volts.

EXPERIMENTER: The experiment requires that you go on.

LEARNER: Ohhh. I absolutely refuse to answer anymore. (*Shouting urgently now.*) Let me out of here! You can't hold me here! Get me out. Get-me-out-of-here!   *50*

EXPERIMENTER: Continue. The next word is "Green," please.

PROZI: "Green—grass, hat, ink, apple." (*Nothing happens. No answering buzz. Just gloomy silence.*)

PROZI: I don't think he is going to answer.

EXPERIMENTER: If the learner doesn't answer in a reasonable time, about four or five seconds, consider the answer wrong. And follow the same procedures you have been doing for wrong answers.

Say, "Wrong," tell him the number of volts, give him the punishment, read him the correct answer. Continue, please.

PROZI: "Green—grass, hat, ink, apple." Answer, please. (*More silence. Subject just sits there.*)

EXPERIMENTER: Go on with the procedure, please.

PROZI: Three hundred and fifteen volts. The answer is "ink." (*Zzumph!*)

LEARNER: Ohh. Ooohh.

PROZI (*relieved to hear response*): Next one . . .

LEARNER: I absolutely refuse to answer.

PROZI: You got to. You get a shock if you don't answer. (*Experiment continues with learner refusing to answer, and, finally, failing even to grunt or groan. At 375 volts, the subject stands up.*)

PROZI: I think something's happened to that fellow in there. I don't get no answer. He was hollering at less voltage. Can't you check in and see if he's all right, please?

EXPERIMENTER (*with same detached calm*): Not once we've started. Please continue, Teacher.

PROZI (*sits down, sighs deeply*): "Cool—day, shade, water, paint." Answer, please. Are you all right in there? Are you all right?

EXPERIMENTER: Please continue, Teacher. Continue, please. (*Subject pushes lever. Zzumph!*)

PROZI (*swiveling around in his chair*): Something's happened to that man in there. (*Swiveling back.*) Next one. "Low—dollar, necklace, moon, paint." (*Turning around again.*) Something's happened to that man in there. You better check in on him, sir. He won't answer or nothing.

EXPERIMENTER: Continue. Go on, please.

PROZI: You accept all responsibility?

EXPERIMENTER: The responsibility is mine. Correct. Please go on. (*Subject returns to his list, starts running through words as rapidly as he can read them, works through to 450 volts.*)

PROZI: That's that.

EXPERIMENTER: Continue using the 450 switch for each wrong answer. Continue, please.

PROZI: But I don't get anything!

EXPERIMENTER: Please continue. The next word is "white."

PROZI: Don't you think you should look in on him, please?

EXPERIMENTER: Not once we've started the experiment.

PROZI: What if he's dead in there? (*Gestures toward the room with the electric chair.*) I mean, he told me he can't stand the shock, sir. I don't mean to be rude, but I think you should look in on him. All you have to do is look in on him. All you have to do is look in the door. I don't get no answer, no noise. Something might have happened to the gentleman in there, sir.

EXPERIMENTER: We must continue. Go on, please.

PROZI: You mean keep giving him what? Four-hundred-fifty volts, what he's got now?

EXPERIMENTER: That's correct. Continue. The next word is "white."

PROZI (*now at a furious pace*): "White—cloud, horse, rock, house."   80
Answer, please. The answer is "horse." Four hundred and fifty volts. (*Zzumph!*) Next word, "Bag—paint, music, clown, girl." The answer is "paint." Four hundred and fifty volts. (*Zzumph!*) Next word is "Short—sentence, movie . . ."

EXPERIMENTER: Excuse me, Teacher. We'll have to discontinue the experiment.

Peculiar Reactions

Morris Braverman, another subject, is a thirty-nine-year-old social worker. He looks older than his years because of his bald head and serious demeanor. His brow is furrowed, as if all the world's burdens were carried on his face. He appears intelligent and concerned.

When the learner refuses to answer and the experimenter instructs Braverman to treat the absence of an answer as equivalent to a wrong answer, he takes his instruction to heart. Before administering 300 volts he asserts officiously to the victim, "Mr. Wallace, your silence has to be considered as a wrong answer." Then he administers the shock. He offers halfheartedly to change places with the learner, then asks the experimenter, "Do I have to follow these instructions literally?" He is satisfied with the experimenter's answer that he does. His very refined and authoritative manner of speaking is increasingly broken up by wheezing laughter.

The experimenter's notes on Mr. Braverman at the last few shocks are:

Almost breaking up now each time gives shock. Rubbing face to hide laughter. Squinting, trying to hide face with hand, still laughing. Cannot control his laughter at this point no matter what he does. Clenching fist, pushing in onto table.

In an interview after the session, Mr. Braverman summarizes the ex-   85
periment with impressive fluency and intelligence. He feels the experiment may have been designed also to "test the effects on the teacher of being in an essentially sadistic role, as well as the reactions of a student to a learning situation that was authoritative and punitive." When asked how painful the last few shocks administered to the learner were, he indicates that the most extreme category on the scale is not adequate (it read EXTREMELY PAINFUL) and places his mark at the edge of the scale with an arrow carrying it beyond the scale.

It is almost impossible to convey the greatly relaxed, sedate quality of his conversation in the interview. In the most relaxed terms, he speaks about his severe inner tension.

EXPERIMENTER: At what point were you most tense or nervous?

MR. BRAVERMAN: Well, when he first began to cry out in pain, and I realized this was hurting him. This got worse when he just blocked and refused to answer. There was I. I'm a nice person, I think, hurting somebody, and caught up in what seemed a mad situation . . . and in the interest of science, one goes through with it.

When the interviewer pursues the general question of tension, Mr. Braverman spontaneously mentions his laughter.

"My reactions were awfully peculiar. I don't know if you were 90 watching me, but my reactions were giggly, and trying to stifle laughter. This isn't the way I usually am. This was a sheer reaction to a totally impossible situation. And my reaction was to the situation of having to hurt somebody. And being totally helpless and caught up in a set of circumstances where I just couldn't deviate and I couldn't try to help. This is what got me."

Mr. Braverman, like all subjects, was told the actual nature and purpose of the experiment, and a year later he affirmed in a questionnaire that he had learned something of personal importance: "What appalled me was that I could possess this capacity for obedience and compliance to a central idea, i.e., the value of a memory experiment, even after it became clear that continued adherence to this value was at the expense of violation of another value, i.e., don't hurt someone who is helpless and not hurting you. As my wife said, 'You can call yourself Eichmann.'[3] I hope I deal more effectively with any future conflicts of values I encounter."

The Etiquette of Submission

One theoretical interpretation of this behavior holds that all people harbor deeply aggressive instincts continually pressing for expression, and that the experiment provides institutional justification for the release of these impulses. According to this view, if a person is placed in a situation in which he has complete power over another individual, whom he may punish as much as he likes, all that is sadistic and bestial in man comes to the fore. The impulse to shock the victim is seen to flow from the potent aggressive tendencies, which are part of the motivational life of the individual, and the experiment, because it provides social legitimacy, simply opens the door to their expression.

---

3. *Adolf Eichmann:* The Nazi official (1906–1962) responsible for implementing Hitler's "Final Solution" to exterminate the Jews; escaped to Argentina after World War II. In 1960, Israeli agents captured Eichmann and brought him to Israel, where he was tried as a war criminal and sentenced to death. At his trial, Eichmann maintained that he was merely following orders in arranging the murders of his victims.

It becomes vital, therefore, to compare the subject's performance when he is under orders and when he is allowed to choose the shock level.

The procedure was identical to our standard experiment, except that the teacher was told that he was free to select any shock level on any of the trials. (The experimenter took pains to point out that the teacher could use the highest levels on the generator, the lowest, any in between, or any combination of levels.) Each subject proceeded for thirty critical trials. The learner's protests were coordinated to standard shock levels, his first grunt coming at 75 volts, his first vehement protest at 150 volts.

The average shock used during the thirty critical trials was less than 60 volts—lower than the point at which the victim showed the first signs of discomfort. Three of the forty subjects did not go beyond the very lowest level on the board, twenty-eight went no higher than 75 volts, and thirty-eight did not go beyond the first loud protest at 150 volts. Two subjects provided the exception, administering up to 325 and 450 volts, but the overall result was that the great majority of people delivered very low, usually painless, shocks when the choice was explicitly up to them. 95

This condition of the experiment undermines another commonly offered explanation of the subjects' behavior—that those who shocked the victim at the most severe levels came only from the sadistic fringe of society. If one considers that almost two-thirds of the participants fall into the category of "obedient" subjects, and that they represented ordinary people drawn from working, managerial, and professional classes, the argument becomes very shaky. Indeed, it is highly reminiscent of the issue that arose in connection with Hannah Arendt's 1963 book, *Eichmann in Jerusalem*. Arendt contended that the prosecution's effort to depict Eichmann as a sadistic monster was fundamentally wrong, that he came closer to being an uninspired bureaucrat who simply sat at his desk and did his job. For asserting her views, Arendt became the object of considerable scorn, even calumny. Somehow, it was felt that the monstrous deeds carried out by Eichmann required a brutal, twisted personality, evil incarnate. After witnessing hundreds of ordinary persons submit to the authority in our own experiments, I must conclude that Arendt's conception of the banality of evil comes closer to the truth than one might dare imagine. The ordinary person who shocked the victim did so out of a sense of obligation—an impression of his duties as a subject—and not from any peculiarly aggressive tendencies.

This is, perhaps, the most fundamental lesson of our study: ordinary people, simply doing their jobs, and without any particular hostility on their part, can become agents in a terrible destructive process. Moreover, even when the destructive effects of their work become patently clear, and they are asked to carry out actions incompatible with fundamental standards of morality, relatively few people have the resources needed to resist authority.

Many of the people were in some sense against what they did to the learner, and many protested even while they obeyed. Some were totally convinced of the wrongness of their actions but could not bring themselves to make an open break with authority. They often derived satisfaction from their thoughts and felt that—within themselves, at least—they had been on the side of the angels. They tried to reduce strain by obeying the experimenter but "only slightly," encouraging the learner, touching the generator switches gingerly. When interviewed, such a subject would stress that he had "asserted my humanity" by administering the briefest shock possible. Handling the conflict in this manner was easier than defiance.

The situation is constructed so that there is no way the subject can stop shocking the learner without violating the experimenter's definitions of his own competence. The subject fears that he will appear arrogant, untoward, and rude if he breaks off. Although these inhibiting emotions appear small in scope alongside the violence being done to the learner, they suffuse the mind and feelings of the subject, who is miserable at the prospect of having to repudiate the authority to his face. (When the experiment was altered so that the experimenter gave his instructions by telephone instead of in person, only a third as many people were fully obedient through 450 volts.) It is a curious thing that a measure of compassion on the part of the subject—an unwillingness to "hurt" the experimenter's feelings—is part of those binding forces inhibiting his disobedience. The withdrawal of such deference may be as painful to the subject as to the authority he defies.

Duty without Conflict

The subjects do not derive satisfaction from inflicting pain, but they often like the feeling they get from pleasing the experimenter. They are proud of doing a good job, obeying the experimenter under difficult circumstances. While the subjects administered only mild shocks on their own initiative, one experimental variation showed that, under orders, 30 percent of them were willing to deliver 450 volts even when they had to forcibly push the learner's hand down on the electrode.

100

Bruno Batta is a thirty-seven-year-old welder who took part in the variation requiring the use of force. He was born in New Haven, his parents in Italy. He has a rough-hewn face that conveys a conspicuous lack of alertness. He has some difficulty in mastering the experimental procedure and needs to be corrected by the experimenter several times. He shows appreciation for the help and willingness to do what is required. After the 150-volt level, Batta has to force the learner's hand down on the shock plate, since the learner himself refuses to touch it.

When the learner first complains, Mr. Batta pays no attention to him. His face remains impassive, as if to dissociate himself from the learner's disruptive behavior. When the experimenter instructs him to force the learner's hand down, he adopts a rigid, mechanical procedure. He tests the generator switch. When it fails to function, he immediately forces the learner's hand onto the shock plate. All the while he maintains the same rigid mask. The learner, seated alongside him, begs him to stop, but with robotic impassivity he continues the procedure.

What is extraordinary is his apparent total indifference to the learner; he hardly takes cognizance of him as a human being. Meanwhile, he relates to the experimenter in a submissive and courteous fashion.

At the 330-volt level, the learner refuses not only to touch the shock plate but also to provide any answers. Annoyed, Batta turns to him, and chastises him: "You better answer and get it over with. We can't stay here all night." These are the only words he directs to the learner in the course of an hour. Never again does he speak to him. The scene is brutal and depressing, his hard, impassive face showing total indifference as he subdues the screaming learner and gives him shocks. He seems to derive no pleasure from the act itself, only quiet satisfaction at doing his job properly.

When he administers 450 volts, he turns to the experimenter and asks, "Where do we go from here, Professor?" His tone is deferential and expresses his willingness to be a cooperative subject, in contrast to the learner's obstinacy. *105*

At the end of the session he tells the experimenter how honored he has been to help him, and in a moment of contrition, remarks, "Sir, sorry it couldn't have been a full experiment."

He has done his honest best. It is only the deficient behavior of the learner that has denied the experimenter full satisfaction.

The essence of obedience is that a person comes to view himself as the instrument for carrying out another person's wishes, and he therefore no longer regards himself as responsible for his actions. Once this critical shift of viewpoint has occurred, all of the essential features of obedience follow. The most far-reaching consequence is that the person feels responsible *to* the authority directing him but feels no responsibility *for* the content of the actions that the authority prescribes. Morality does not disappear—it acquires a radically different focus: the subordinate person feels shame or pride depending on how adequately he has performed the actions called for by authority.

Language provides numerous terms to pinpoint this type of morality: *loyalty, duty, discipline* all are terms heavily saturated with moral meaning and refer to the degree to which a person fulfills his obligations to authority. They refer not to the "goodness" of the person per se but to the adequacy with which a subordinate fulfills his socially defined role. The most frequent defense of the individual who has performed a heinous act under command of authority is that he has simply done his duty. In asserting this defense, the individual is not introducing an alibi concocted for the moment but is reporting honestly on the psychological attitude induced by submission to authority.

For a person to feel responsible for his actions, he must sense that the behavior has flowed from "the self." In the situation we have studied, subjects have precisely the opposite view of their actions—namely, they see them as originating in the motives of some other person. Subjects in the experiment frequently said, "If it were up to me, I would not have administered shocks to the learner." *110*

Once authority has been isolated as the cause of the subject's behavior, it is legitimate to inquire into the necessary elements of authority and how it must be perceived in order to gain his compliance. We conducted some investigations into the kinds of changes that would cause the experimenter to lose his power and to be disobeyed by the subject. Some of the variations revealed that:

- *The experimenter's physical presence has a marked impact on his authority.* As cited earlier, obedience dropped off sharply when orders were given by telephone. The experimenter could often induce a disobedient subject to go on by returning to the laboratory.

- *Conflicting authority severely paralyzes action.* When two experimenters of equal status, both seated at the command desk, gave incompatible orders, no shocks were delivered past the point of their disagreement.

- *The rebellious action of others severely undermines authority.* In one variation, three teachers (two actors and a real subject) administered a test and shocks. When the two actors disobeyed the experimenter and refused to go beyond a certain shock level, thirty-six of forty subjects joined their disobedient peers and refused as well.

Although the experimenter's authority was fragile in some respects, it is also true that he had almost none of the tools used in ordinary command structures. For example, the experimenter did not threaten the subjects with punishment—such as loss of income, community ostracism, or jail—for failure to obey. Neither could he offer incentives. Indeed, we should expect the experimenter's authority to be much less than that of someone like a general, since the experimenter has no power to enforce his imperatives, and since participation in a psychological experiment scarcely evokes the sense of urgency and dedication found in warfare. Despite these limitations, he still managed to command a dismaying degree of obedience.

I will cite one final variation of the experiment that depicts a dilemma that is more common in everyday life. The subject was not ordered to pull the lever that shocked the victim, but merely to perform a subsidiary task (administering the word-pair test) while another person administered the shock. In this situation, thirty-seven of forty adults continued to the highest level on the shock generator. Predictably, they excused their behavior by saying that the responsibility belonged to the man who actually pulled the switch. This may illustrate a dangerously typical arrangement in a complex society: it is easy to ignore responsibility when one is only an intermediate link in a chain of action.

The problem of obedience is not wholly psychological. The form and shape of society and the way it is developing have much to do with it. There was a time, perhaps, when people were able to give a fully human response to any situation because they were fully absorbed in it as human beings. But as soon as there was a division of labor things changed. Beyond a certain point, the breaking up of society into people carrying out narrow and very special jobs takes away from the human quality of work and life. A person does not get to see the whole situation but only a small part of it, and is thus unable to act without some kind of overall direction. He yields to authority but in doing so is alienated from his own actions.

Even Eichmann was sickened when he toured the concentration camps, but he had only to sit at a desk and shuffle papers. At the same time the man in the camp who actually dropped Cyclon-b into the gas chambers was able to justify *his* behavior on the ground that he was only following orders from above. Thus there is a fragmentation of the total human act; no one is confronted with the consequences of his decision to carry out the evil act. The person who assumes responsibility has evaporated. Perhaps this is the most common characteristic of socially organized evil in modern society.

115

➤ *An Invitation to Write*

Consider how the issues Milgram raises in these writings speak to your experience. Think of a time when you acted in a way that contradicted your principles of behavior or when you saw another person act in such a way. Draw a conclusion or express an attitude with regard to that experience. As you write, choose an audience for your piece of writing and adjust your work to that audience. Don't think that you have to write an essay. You might find that a story, a poem, or a short play serves your purposes better.

Bring your draft to your group with a copy for each member and work through the first-draft questions (Chapter 3). If your teacher asks you to do so, revise the piece of writing and, with your group, apply the second-draft questions to it. Revise it again and edit and proofread the piece with your group.

7

Focusing Your
Reader's Attention

GENERAL AND SPECIFIC

The difference between a general and a specific word, phrase, or idea has to do with the amount of territory the word, phrase, or idea covers. An idea or a word that includes a lot of smaller ideas is *general*. The narrower a word or concept is—the fewer ideas that can fit under its umbrella—the more *specific* it is. There is nothing wrong with presenting a general idea or using a general word or phrase, especially when you introduce a concept, a response, or an event. However, when you use general terms to draw the boundaries around your area of interest, you need to help your reader understand their meaning by making these terms more precise. Usually your ideas and terms become more definite—more "visible" to your audience—as you add more information to them. Look at this arrangement:

Object
Living Object
Living Animate Object
Living Animate Human
Living Animate Human Student
Living Animate Fourteen-Year-Old Human Student in Jeans
and a Red T-Shirt

With each level of detail, you get a clearer picture of the "object" under discussion and can better distinguish it from the mass of all the other possible objects. With the addition of each piece of information, the scope of the term *object* becomes narrower; it includes fewer possibilities. Conversely, the further up the list you go, the more territory the statement covers. No other term except *thing* includes as many possibilities as *object*.

A term is called "general" because it carries a lot of information. That fact is both the strength and the weakness of a generality. A general term

155

does a great deal of work very quickly *if* everyone in the audience under-stands what the term means. However, if the members of an audience don't share the same understanding of a general word or statement, then confusion results. For example, *great* is a word so overused that usually no reader can be certain what it means. Literally, *great* means unusually large in size. But if a person tells you that he or she had a "great" time over the weekend or saw a "great" movie, you really have no precise idea what this person means. What might have been "great" for him or her might be unimportant or even distasteful to you. Until you know the events or feelings that define a term like *great* for the person using it, you cannot have a clear sense of what the person has in mind.

Other words or phrases may penetrate so deeply into the experiences or values of audience members that their meanings vary for each individual. You must define such terms for your audience before you can use them with any hope of being understood. If you choose to use words like *love, religion, good,* or *evil,* you need to give them a background and to support them with specific examples so that each person in your audience can separate the words from his or her assumptions and experience and understand exactly what you mean.

Still other words and phrases may be common to a particular field of study or group with a specialized area of interest. Such words are called "jargon." They refer to activities or concepts that are common and therefore familiar to people who share the same field or interest. For example, a com-puter programmer will know what a *kludge* or a *bug* is, but few others will know. Because it conveys a great deal of information in very little space, jargon is a very efficient tool when you can count on your audience's know-ing the meaning of the words and phrases. But if you can't count on that, either define the term the first time you use it or find a way to convey your information in common language.

Here is a selection from a computer review published in *PC World,* a magazine intended for people who are familiar with computers but who are not computer scientists or engineers. The words and phrases that might give an average reader trouble are underlined:

We examined a $1695 model with a 25MHz 486SX CPU, 8MB of RAM, a 160MB hard drive, and a 14-inch SVGA color monitor. The system unit was ruggedly built; its metal case should survive the day-to-day rigors without cramping anyone's style or office. The device re-quires about a square foot of desk space, or about half as much space as a desk blotter occupies. This is one of the most compact systems in its price range, according to [the manufacturer]. In cramped quarters, you can stand [this computer] vertically.

To keep the system petite, [the manufacturer] had to make some sacrifices. The product comes with only one expansion slot, which you'll most likely use for a network card. The [computer] also includes a VL bus . . . Windows accelerator integrated into the motherboard with 1MB of VRAM (the VRAM cannot be expanded). The chip displays up to 16.8 million colors at a resolution of 800 by 600 and provides a maximum noninterlaced resolution of 1024 by 768 with 256 colors.

In this selection, the writer writes to readers who share the same interests and concepts as he does. In addition, his audience is used to the sort of terms that are specific to computers, their nature, and their use. However, imagine the effect of this language on a group of average individuals who are planning to buy their first computer.

❧ *An Invitation to Write*

Find a piece of writing in a book or magazine that has to do with a field in which you have a good deal of experience and interest. It could be a hobby, a sport, or your major. Make certain that the piece is filled with the sort of terms that are special to that field or activity and that cover a good deal of territory. These terms should be familiar to others who are interested in the field but not to people whose interests and experience lie outside it.

Now choose a paragraph or two that in your judgment would give the reader unfamiliar with the subject the most trouble. Rewrite the selection, adding material where you think it is necessary to let the reader in on the meaning of special terms, phrases, or concepts or substitute simple, more specific language at those points. In doing so, you might find yourself writing a whole new paragraph or two.

If you are working with a group, bring both the original piece of writing and your revision to the group meeting with enough copies for every member. Each member should point out spots where he or she is still confused, if there are any, as well as show you spots where your revision seems especially effective compared with the original.

Because they create many of the same problems as generalizations, terms or phrases that reflect a set of controversial values or beliefs should be defined with specific material. Of course, you might present a dominant idea to an audience that holds the same values as you do. But if that were the case, why would you bother to confirm what your audience already believes? More often, when you use terms, ideas, or phrases that reflect a set of values, you cannot assume that your audience holds the same values in quite the same way as you do. In that case, you have to make your position clear by giving your audience specific references or examples through which they can understand your assumptions.

Look, for example, at the following reading to see how one author approaches a very personal relationship.

Working with a Reading

Read the following poem and answer the questions that follow it.

THOSE WINTER SUNDAYS
Robert Hayden

Sundays too my father got up early
and put his clothes on in the blueblack cold,
then with cracked hands that ached
from labor in the weekday weather made
banked fires blaze. No one ever thanked him.   5

I'd wake and hear the cold splintering, breaking.
When the rooms were warm, he'd call,
and slowly I would rise and dress,
fearing the chronic angers of that house,

Speaking indifferently to him,   10
who had driven out the cold
and polished my good shoes as well.
What did I know, what did I know
of love's austere and lonely offices?

1. What relationship does Hayden present to you?
2. Define the nature of the relationship as specifically as you can. What
   have you learned about the feelings of each person for the other?
3. What specific information does Hayden give you to lead you to your
   conclusions about that relationship?

An Invitation to Write

Choose a relationship of your own that is as complex and important to
you as this one was to Hayden. Using the ways Hayden employs to make
the relationship clear, write an essay, a poem, or a short story that shows
your reader what you mean.

If you are working in a group, bring copies of your piece to the group
and work through the first-draft procedures. If your teacher wants you to
do so, write a second draft and work through the revision procedures.

ORGANIZING YOUR SPECIFIC INFORMATION

Generally, you make yourself clear by adding information to your dominant idea until you are as certain as possible that the audience you have in mind will understand what you mean. Or you might begin with specific information and add to it until you feel you have provided enough material to allow your audience to understand your dominant idea—whether you have stated it directly or are allowing the accumulated material to suggest it. When you command the information that you add to a dominant idea or use to build toward a dominant idea, you have control over one of the most basic patterns of writing. Every statement you make should directly support, suggest, or add to your dominant idea until you are as certain as possible that the audience you have in mind will understand it. In this approach, you make yourself clear by adding information.

 Working with a Reading

Notice how the author of the following short essay uses concrete information to make his point clear to his audience.

DARKNESS AT NOON

Harold Krents

Blind from birth, I have never had the opportunity to see myself and have been completely dependent on the image I create in the eye of the observer. To date it has not been narcissistic.

There are those who assume that since I can't see, I obviously also cannot hear. Very often people will converse with me at the top of their lungs, enunciating each word very carefully. Conversely, people will also often whisper, assuming that since my eyes don't work, my ears don't either.

For example, when I go to the airport and ask the ticket agent for assistance to the plane, he or she will invariably pick up the phone, call a ground hostess and whisper: "Hi, Jane, we've got a 76 here." I have concluded that the word "blind" is not used for one of two reasons: Either they fear that if the dread word is spoken, the ticket agent's retina will immediately detach, or they are reluctant to inform me of my condition, of which I may not have been previously aware.

On the other hand, others know that of course I can hear, but believe I can't talk. Often, therefore, when my wife and I go out to dinner, a waiter or waitress will ask Kit if "he would like a drink" to which I respond that "indeed he would."

This point was graphically driven home to me while we were in En-   *5*
gland. I had been given a year's leave of absence from my Washington law
firm to study for a diploma in law degree at Oxford University. During
the year I became ill and was hospitalized. Immediately after admission, I
was wheeled down to the X-ray room. Just at the door sat an elderly
woman—elderly I would judge from the sound of her voice. "What is
his name?" the woman asked the orderly who had been wheeling me.

"What's your name?" the orderly repeated to me.

"Harold Krents," I replied.

"Harold Krents," he repeated.

"When was he born?"

"When were you born?"   *10*

"November 5, 1944," I responded.

"November 5, 1944," the orderly intoned.

This procedure continued for approximately five minutes at which
point even my saint-like disposition deserted me. "Look," I finally blurted
out, "this is absolutely ridiculous. Okay, granted I can't see, but it's got to
have become pretty clear to both of you that I don't need an interpreter."

"He says he doesn't need an interpreter," the orderly reported to the
woman.

The toughest misconception of all is the view that because I can't   *15*
see, I can't work. I was turned down by over forty law firms because
of my blindness, even though my qualifications included a cum laude
degree from Harvard College and a good ranking in my Harvard law
school class.

The attempt to find employment, the continuous frustration of being
told it was impossible for a blind person to practice law, the rejection
letters, not based on my lack of ability but rather on my disability, will
always remain one of the most disillusioning experiences of my life.

I therefore look forward to the day, with the expectation that it is
certain to come, when employers will view their handicapped workers as
a little child did me years ago when my family still lived in Scarsdale.

I was playing basketball with my father in our backyard according to
procedures we had developed. My father would stand beneath the hoop,
shout, and I would shoot over his head at the basket attached to the garage. Our next-door neighbor, aged five, wandered over into our yard
with a playmate. "He's blind," our neighbor whispered to her friend in
a voice that could be heard distinctly by Dad and me. Dad shot and
missed; I did the same. Dad hit the rim; I missed entirely; Dad shot and
missed the garage entirely. "Which one is blind?" whispered back the
little friend.

I would hope that in the near future when a plant manager is touring
the factory with the foreman and comes upon a handicapped and non-
handicapped person working together, his comment after watching them
work will be, "Which one is disabled?"

Write down what you consider to be the dominant idea of "Darkness at Noon." Then look at each of the specific examples Krents uses and show how each one makes his dominant idea clearer to the reader.

If you are working in a group, present your version of Krents's dominant idea to the other members and show how his concrete examples work to effectively make that idea clear to the audience. Listen to other members' interpretations as well.

An Extra Question: Most of us do not consider a disability to be a subject of humor. However, most of Krents's examples are humorous. Why does he choose examples like these? Are all the examples funny? If Krents changes his tone anywhere in this essay, why do you think he chooses to do so?

An Invitation to Write

Imagine being blind or having another disability to cope with. Better yet, see if you can create for yourself something of the experience of that disability. For example, spend a couple of hours blindfolded; see if you can borrow a wheelchair from the disabled student services office at your campus; maybe a friend of yours has an old pair of crutches. Draft a paper that accumulates specific examples as a way of reflecting your experience to a reader without the same disability. Keep in mind the tone of many of Krents's examples. You might want to experiment with it.

If you are working with a group, provide members with a copy of your draft. Use the first-draft questions to work with each member's draft, revise, and then work with the second-draft questions.

Working with a Reading

Read the following story and then, individually or in your group, examine the questions that follow it.

MY FIRST GOOSE

Isaac Babel

Savitsky, Commander of the VI Division, rose when he saw me, and I wondered at the beauty of his giant's body. He rose, the purple of his riding breeches and the crimson of his little tilted cap and the decorations stuck on his chest cleaving the hut as a standard cleaves the sky. A smell of scent and the sickly sweet freshness of soap emanated from him. His long legs were like girls sheathed to the neck in shining riding boots.

He smiled at me, struck his riding whip on the table, and drew toward him an order that the Chief of Staff had just finished dictating. It was an order for Ivan Chesnokov to advance on Chugunov-Dobryvodka with the regiment entrusted to him, to make contact with the enemy and destroy the same.

"For which destruction," the Commander began to write, smearing the whole sheet, "I make this same Chesnokov entirely responsible, up to and including the supreme penalty, and will if necessary strike him down on the spot; which you, Chesnokov, who have been working with me at the front for some months now, cannot doubt."

The Commander signed the order with a flourish, tossed it to his orderlies and turned upon me gray eyes that danced with merriment.

I handed him a paper with my appointment to the Staff of the   5
Division.

"Put it down in the Order of the Day," said the Commander. "Put him down for every satisfaction save the front one. Can you read and write?"

"Yes, I can read and write," I replied, envying the flower and iron of that youthfulness. "I graduated in law from St. Petersburg University."

"Oh, are you one of those grinds?" he laughed. "Specs on your nose, too! What a nasty little object! They've sent you along without making any enquiries; and this is a hot place for specs. Think you'll get on with us?"

"I'll get on all right," I answered, and went off to the village with the quartermaster to find a billet for the night.

The quartermaster carried my trunk on his shoulder. Before us   10
stretched the village street. The dying sun, round and yellow as a pumpkin, was giving up its roseate ghost to the skies.

We went up to a hut painted over with garlands. The quartermaster stopped, and said suddenly, with a guilty smile:

"Nuisance with specs. Can't do anything to stop it, either. Not a life for the brainy type here. But you go and mess up a lady, and a good lady too, and you'll have the boys patting you on the back."

He hesitated, my little trunk on his shoulder; then he came quite close to me, only to dart away again despairingly and run to the nearest yard. Cossacks were sitting there, shaving one another.

"Here, you soldiers," said the quartermaster, setting my little trunk down on the ground. "Comrade Savitsky's orders are that you're to take this chap in your billets, so no nonsense about it, because the chap's been through a lot in the learning line."

The quartermaster, purple in the face, left us without looking back.   15
I raised my hand to my cap and saluted the Cossacks. A lad with long straight flaxen hair and the handsome face of the Ryazan Cossacks went over to my little trunk and tossed it out at the gate. Then he turned

his back on me and with remarkable skill emitted a series of shameful noises.

"To your guns—number double-zero!" an older Cossack shouted at him, and burst out laughing. "Running fire!"

His guileless art exhausted, the lad made off. Then, crawling over the ground, I began to gather together the manuscript and tattered garments that had fallen out of the trunk. I gathered them up and carried them to the other end of the yard. Near the hut, on a brick stove, stood a cauldron in which pork was cooking. The steam that rose from it was like the far-off smoke of home in the village, and it mingled hunger with desperate loneliness in my head. Then I covered my little broken trunk with hay, turning it into a pillow, and lay down on the ground to read in *Pravda* Lenin's speech at the Second Congress of the Comintern. The sun fell upon me from behind the toothed hillocks, the Cossacks trod on my feet, the lad made fun of me untiringly, the beloved lines came toward me along a thorny path and could not reach me. Then I put aside the paper and went out to the landlady, who was spinning on the porch.

"Landlady," I said, "I've got to eat."

The old woman raised to me the diffused whites of her purblind eyes and lowered them again.

"Comrade," she said, after a pause, "what with all this going on, I   20 want to go and hang myself."

"Christ!" I muttered, and pushed the old woman in the chest with my fist. "You don't suppose I'm going to go into explanations with you, do you?"

And turning around I saw somebody's sword lying within reach. A severe-looking goose was waddling about the yard, inoffensively preening its feathers. I overtook it and pressed it to the ground. Its head cracked beneath my boot, cracked and emptied itself. The white neck lay stretched out in the dung, the wings twitched.

"Christ!" I said, digging into the goose with my sword. "Go and cook it for me, landlady."

Her blind eyes and glasses glistening, the old woman picked up the slaughtered bird, wrapped it in her apron, and started to bear it off toward the kitchen.

"Comrade," she said to me, after a while, "I want to go and hang   25 myself." And she closed the door behind her.

The Cossacks in the yard were already sitting around their cauldron. They sat motionless, stiff as heathen priests at a sacrifice, and had not looked at the goose.

"The lad's all right," one of them said, winking and scooping up the cabbage soup with his spoon.

The Cossacks commenced their supper with all the elegance and restraint of peasants who respect one another. And I wiped the sword with sand, went out at the gate, and came in again, depressed. Already the moon hung above the yard like a cheap earring.

"Hey, you," suddenly said Surovkov, an older Cossack. "Sit down and feed with us till your goose is done."

He produced a spare spoon from his boot and handed it to me. We   30
supped up the cabbage soup they had made and ate the pork.

"What's in the newspaper?" asked the flaxen-haired lad, making room for me.

"Lenin writes in the paper," I said, pulling out *Pravda*. "Lenin writes that there's a shortage of everything."

And loudly, like a triumphant man hard of hearing, I read Lenin's speech out to the Cossacks.

Evening wrapped about me the quickening moisture of its twilight sheets; evening laid a mother's hand upon my burning forehead. I read on and rejoiced, spying out exultingly the secret curve of Lenin's straight line.

"Truth tickles everyone's nostrils," said Surovkov, when I had come   35
to the end. "The question is, how's it to be pulled from the heap. But he goes and strikes at it straight off like a hen pecking at a grain!"

This remark about Lenin was made by Surovkov, platoon commander of the Staff Squadron; after which we lay down to sleep in the hayloft. We slept, all six of us, beneath a wooden roof that let in the stars, warming one another, our legs intermingled. I dreamed: and in my dreams saw women. But my heart, stained with bloodshed, grated and brimmed over.

----

1. Babel's story is built around a single incident in which there is an "I" at the center. What specific information does Babel give you to establish what kind of a person "I" is? what his background is? what his goals are? How does "I" feel about the situation he finds himself in?

2. What do you discover about the Cossacks through Babel's examples? What kind of people are they? How do they feel about "I"?

3. Taking what you have learned about "I" and about the Cossacks, how do you account for "I's" behavior in the story.

4. How does "I" feel about the choices he has made? What specific information does Babel give you to lead you to your conclusion?

5. Note that the title of the story implies that there will be other geese following this "first" one. What do you think Babel means by that?

6. Taking all the examples together, what do you think Babel's dominant idea is? What is his purpose in offering you this story?

⇜ *An Invitation to Write*

Consider an experience you have had in which you acted in some of the same ways that the narrator of "My First Goose" acted or that made you feel the way the narrator felt. Or perhaps you have seen another person act this way. Write a draft of an essay, a poem, a story, or a short play in which you communicate the experience and its feelings to the reader using a set of examples and a reflection of your feelings to make your point. See how many examples or images that work in the way Babel's examples or images work you can include in your piece.

If you are working with a group, provide a copy of your draft to each member. If your teacher asks you to do so, apply the first- and second-draft questions to each member's writing.

 Working with a Reading

Read the following essay and then, individually or with your group, answer the questions that follow it.

THE JUDGMENT OF THE BIRDS
Loren Eiseley

It is a commonplace of all religious thought, even the most primitive, that the man seeking visions and insight must go apart from his fellows and live for a time in the wilderness. If he is of the proper sort, he will return with a message. It may not be a message from the god he set out to seek, but even if he has failed in that particular, he will have had a vision or seen a marvel, and these are always worth listening to and thinking about.

The world, I have come to believe, is a very queer place, but we have been part of this queerness for so long that we tend to take it for granted. We rush to and fro like Mad Hatters upon our peculiar errands, all the time imagining our surroundings to be dull and ourselves quite ordinary creatures. Actually, there is nothing in the world to encourage this idea, but such is the mind of man, and this is why he finds it necessary from time to time to send emissaries into the wilderness in the hope of learning of great events, or plans in store for him, that will resuscitate his waning taste for life. His great news services, his world-wide radio network, he knows with a last remnant of healthy distrust will be of no use to him in this matter. No miracle can withstand a radio broadcast, and it is certain that it would be no miracle if it could. One must seek, then, what only the solitary approach can give—a natural revelation.

Let it be understood that I am not the sort of man to whom is entrusted direct knowledge of great events or prophecies. A naturalist, however, spends much of his life alone, and my life is no exception. Even in New York City there are patches of wilderness, and a man by himself is bound to undergo certain experiences falling into the class of which I speak. I set mine down, therefore: a matter of pigeons, a flight of chemicals, and a judgment of birds, in the hope that they will come to the eye of those who have retained a true taste for the marvelous, and who are capable of discerning in the flow of ordinary events the point at which the mundane world gives way to quite another dimension.

New York is not, on the whole, the best place to enjoy the downright miraculous nature of the planet. There are, I do not doubt, many remarkable stories to be heard there and many strange sights to be seen, but to grasp a marvel fully it must be savored from all aspects. This cannot be done while one is being jostled and hustled along a crowded street. Nevertheless, in any city there are true wildernesses where a man can be alone. It can happen in a hotel room, or on the high roofs at dawn.

One night on the twentieth floor of a midtown hotel I awoke in the 5 dark and grew restless. On an impulse I climbed upon the broad old-fashioned window sill, opened the curtains and peered out. It was the hour just before dawn. . . . I leaned out sleepily through the open window. I had expected depths, but not the sight I saw.

I found I was looking down from that great height into a series of curious cupolas or lofts that I could just barely make out in the darkness. As I looked, the outlines of these lofts became more distinct because the light was being reflected from the wings of pigeons who, in utter silence, were beginning to float outward upon the city. In and out through the open slits in the cupolas passed the white-winged birds on their mysterious errands. At this hour the city was theirs, and quietly, without the brush of a single wing tip against stone in that high, eerie place, they were taking over the spires of Manhattan. They were pouring upward in a light that was not yet perceptible to human eyes, while far down in the blackness of the alleys it was still midnight.

As I crouched half asleep across the sill, I had a moment's illusion that the world had changed in the night, as in some immense snowfall, and that if I were to leave, it would have to be as these other inhabitants were doing, by the window. I should have to launch out into that great bottomless void with the simple confidence of young birds reared high up there among the familiar chimney pots and interposed horrors of the abyss.

I leaned farther out. To and fro went the white wings, to and fro. There were no sounds from any of them. They knew man was asleep and this light for a little while was theirs. . . .

Around and around went the wings. It needed only a little courage, only a little shove from the window ledge to enter that city of light. The muscles of my hands were already making little premonitory lunges. I wanted to enter that city and go away over the roofs in the first dawn. I wanted to enter it so badly that I drew back carefully into the room and opened the hall door. I found my coat on the chair, and it slowly became clear to me that there was a way down through the floors, that I was, after all, only a man.

I dressed then and went back to my own kind, and I have been rather   *10*
more than usually careful ever since not to look into the city of light. I
had seen, just once, man's greatest creation from a strange inverted angle,
and it was not really his at all. I will never forget how those wings went
round and round, and how, by the merest pressure of the fingers and a
feeling for air, one might go away over the roofs. It is a knowledge, however, that is better kept to oneself. I think of it sometimes in such a way
that the wings, beginning far down in the black depths of the mind, begin
to rise and whirl till all the mind is lit by their spinning, and there is a
sense of things passing away, but lightly, as a wing might veer over an
obstacle.

To see from an inverted angle, however, is not a gift allotted merely
to the human imagination. I have come to suspect that within their degree it is sensed by animals, though perhaps as rarely as among men. The
time has to be right; one has to be, by chance or intention, upon the
border of two worlds. And sometimes these two borders may shift or
interpenetrate and one sees the miraculous.

I once saw this happen to a crow.

This crow lives near my home, and though I have never injured him,
he takes good care to stay up in the very highest trees and, in general, to
avoid humanity. His world begins at about the limit of my eyesight.

On the particular morning when this episode occurred, the whole
countryside was buried in one of the thickest fogs in years. The ceiling
was absolutely zero. All planes were grounded, and even a pedestrian
could hardly see his outstretched hand before him.

I was groping across a field in the general direction of the railroad   *15*
station, following a dimly outlined path. Suddenly out of the fog, at about
the level of my eyes, and so closely that I flinched, there flashed a pair of
immense black wings and a huge beak. The whole bird rushed over my
head with a frantic cawing outcry of such hideous terror as I have never
heard in a crow's voice before, and never expect to hear again.

He was lost and startled, I thought, as I recovered my poise. He ought
not to have flown out in this fog. He'd knock his silly brains out.

All afternoon that great awkward cry rang in my head. Merely being
lost in a fog seemed scarcely to account for it—especially in a tough,
intelligent old bandit such as I knew that particular crow to be. I even
looked once in the mirror to see what it might be about me that had so
revolted him that he had cried out in protest to the very stones.

Finally, as I worked my way homeward along the path, the solution
came to me. It should have been clear before. The borders of our worlds
had shifted. It was the fog that had done it. That crow, and I knew him
well, never under normal circumstances flew low near men. He had been
lost all right, but it was more than that. He had thought he was high
up, and when he encountered me looming gigantically through the fog,
he had perceived a ghastly and, to the crow mind, unnatural sight. He
had seen a man walking on air, desecrating the very heart of the crow

kingdom, a harbinger of the most profound evil a crow mind could conceive of—air-walking men. The encounter, he must have thought, had taken place a hundred feet over the roofs.

He caws now when he sees me leaving for the station in the morning, and I fancy that in that note I catch the uncertainty of a mind that has come to know things are not always what they seem. He has seen a marvel in his heights of air and is no longer as other crows. He has experienced the human world from an unlikely perspective. He and I share a viewpoint in common: our worlds have interpenetrated, and we both have faith in the miraculous.

It is a faith that in my own case has been augmented by two remarkable sights. As I have hinted previously, I once saw some very odd chemicals fly across a waste so dead it might have been upon the moon, and once, by an even more fantastic piece of luck, I was present when a group of birds passed a judgment upon life. 20

On the maps of the old voyageurs it is called *Mauvaises Terres,* the evil lands, and, slurred a little with the passage through many minds, it has come down to us anglicized as the Badlands. The soft shuffle of moccasins has passed through its canyons on the grim business of war and flight, but the last of those slight disturbances of immemorial silences died out almost a century ago. The land, if one can call it a land, is a waste as lifeless as that valley in which lie the kings of Egypt. Like the Valley of the Kings, it is a mausoleum, a place of dry bones in what once was a place of life. Now it has silences as deep as those in the moon's airless chasms.

Nothing grows among its pinnacles; there is no shade except under great toadstools of sandstone whose bases have been eaten to the shape of wine glasses by the wind. Everything is flaking, cracking, disintegrating, wearing away in the long, imperceptible weather of time. The ash of ancient volcanic outbursts still sterilizes its soil, and its colors in that waste are the colors that flame in the lonely sunsets on dead planets. Men come there but rarely, and for one purpose only, the collection of bones.

It was a late hour on a cold, wind-bitten autumn day when I climbed a great hill spined like a dinosaur's back and tried to take my bearings. The tumbled waste fell away in waves in all directions. Blue air was darkening into purple along the bases of the hills. I shifted my knapsack, heavy with the petrified bones of long-vanished creatures, and studied my compass. I wanted to be out of there by nightfall, and already the sun was going sullenly down in the west.

It was then that I saw the flight coming on. It was moving like a little close-knit body of black specks that danced and darted and closed again. It was pouring from the north and heading toward me with the undeviating relentlessness of a compass needle. It streamed through the shadows rising out of monstrous gorges. It rushed over towering pinnacles in the red light of the sun, or momentarily sank from sight within their shade. Across that desert of eroding clay and wind-worn stone they came with a faint wild twittering that filled all the air about me as those tiny living bullets hurtled past into the night.

It may not strike you as a marvel. It would not, perhaps, unless you stood in the middle of a dead world at sunset, but that was where I stood. Fifty million years lay under my feet, fifty million years of bellowing monsters moving in a green world now gone so utterly that its very light was travelling on the farther edge of space. The chemicals of all that vanished age lay about me in the ground. Around me still lay the shearing molars of dead titanotheres, the delicate sabers of soft-stepping cats, the hollow sockets that had held the eyes of many a strange, out-moded beast. Those eyes had looked out upon a world as real as ours; dark, savage brains had roamed and roared their challenges into the steaming night.

Now they were still here, or, put it as you will, the chemicals that made them were here about me in the ground. The carbon that had driven them ran blackly in the eroding stone. The stain of iron was in the clays. The iron did not remember the blood it had once moved within, the phosphorus had forgot the savage brain. The little individual moment had ebbed from all those strange combinations of chemicals as it would ebb from our living bodies into the sinks and runnels of oncoming time.

I had lifted up a fistful of that ground. I held it while that wild flight of south-bound warblers hurtled over me into the oncoming dark. There went phosphorus, there went iron, there went carbon, there beat the calcium in those hurrying wings. Alone on a dead planet I watched that incredible miracle speeding past. It ran by some true compass over field and waste land. It cried its individual ecstasies into the air until the gullies rang. It swerved like a single body, it knew itself and, lonely, it bunched close in the racing darkness, its individual entities feeling about them the rising night. And so, crying to each other their identity, they passed away out of my view.

I dropped my fistful of earth. I heard it roll inanimate back into the gully at the base of the hill: iron, carbon, the chemicals of life. Like men from those wild tribes who had haunted these hills before me seeking visions, I made my sign to the great darkness. It was not a mocking sign, and I was not mocked. As I walked into my camp late that night, one man, rousing from his blankets beside the fire, asked sleepily, "What did you see?"

"I think, a miracle," I said softly, but I said it to myself. Behind me that vast waste began to glow under the rising moon.

I have said that I saw a judgment upon life, and that it was not passed by men. Those who stare at birds in cages or who test minds by their closeness to our own may not care for it. It comes from far away out of my past, in a place of pouring waters and green leaves. I shall never see an episode like it again if I live to be a hundred, nor do I think that one man in a million has ever seen it, because man is an intruder into such silences.

The light must be right, and the observer must remain unseen. No man sets up such an experiment. What he sees, he sees by chance.

You may put it that I had come over a mountain, that I had slogged through fern and pine needles for half a long day, and that on the edge of a little glade with one long, crooked branch extending across it, I had sat down to rest with my back against a stump. Through accident I was concealed from the glade, although I could see into it perfectly.

The sun was warm there, and the murmurs of forest life blurred softly away into my sleep. When I awoke, dimly aware of some commotion and outcry in the clearing, the light was slanting down through the pines in such a way that the glade was lit like some vast cathedral. I could see the dust motes of wood pollen in the long shaft of light, and there on the extended branch sat an enormous raven with a red and squirming nestling in his beak.

The sound that awoke me was the outraged cries of the nestling's parents, who flew helplessly in circles about the clearing. The sleek black monster was indifferent to them. He gulped, whetted his beak on the dead branch a moment and sat still. Up to that point the little tragedy had followed the usual pattern. But suddenly, out of all that area of woodland, a soft sound of complaint began to rise. Into the glade fluttered small birds of half a dozen varieties drawn by the anguished outcries of the tiny parents.

No one dared to attack the raven. But they cried there in some instinctive common misery, the bereaved and the unbereaved. The glade filled with their soft rustling and their cries. They fluttered as though to point their wings at the murderer. There was a dim intangible ethic he had violated, that they knew. He was a bird of death.

And he, the murderer, the black bird at the heart of life, sat on there, *35* glistening in the common light, formidable, unmoving, unperturbed, untouchable.

The sighing died. It was then I saw the judgment. It was the judgment of life against death. I will never see it again so forcefully presented. I will never hear it again in notes so tragically prolonged. For in the midst of protest, they forgot the violence. There, in that clearing, the crystal note of a song sparrow lifted hesitantly in the hush. And finally, after painful fluttering, another took the song, and then another, the song passing from one bird to another, doubtfully at first, as though some evil thing were being slowly forgotten. Till suddenly they took heart and sang from many throats joyously together as birds are known to sing. They sang because life is sweet and sunlight beautiful. They sang under the brooding shadow of the raven. In simple truth they had forgotten the raven, for they were the singers of life, and not of death.

I was not of that airy company. My limbs were the heavy limbs of an earthbound creature who could climb mountains, even the mountains of the mind, only by a great effort of will. I knew I had seen a marvel and observed a judgment, but the mind which was my human endowment was sure to question it and to be at me day by day with its heresies until I grew to doubt the meaning of what I had seen. Eventually darkness and subtleties would ring me round once more.

And so it proved until, on the top of a stepladder, I made one more observation upon life. It was cold that autumn evening, and, standing under a suburban street light in a spate of leaves and beginning snow, I was suddenly conscious of some huge and hairy shadows dancing over the pavement. They seemed attached to an odd, globular shape that was magnified above me. There was no mistaking it. I was standing under the shadow of an orb-weaving spider. Gigantically projected against the street, she was about her spinning when everything was going underground. Even her cables were magnified upon the sidewalk and already I was half-entangled in their shadows.

"Good Lord," I thought, "she has found herself a kind of minor sun and is going to upset the course of nature."

I procured a ladder from my yard and climbed up to inspect the situation. There she was, the universe running down around her, warmly arranged among her guy ropes attached to the lamp supports—a great black and yellow embodiment of the life force, not giving up to either frost or stepladders. She ignored me and went on tightening and improving her web.

I stood over her on the ladder, a faint snow touching my cheeks, and surveyed her universe. There were a couple of iridescent green beetle cases turning slowly on a loose strand of web, a fragment of luminescent eye from a moth's wing and a large indeterminable object, perhaps a cicada, that had struggled and been wrapped in silk. There were also little bits and slivers, little red and blue flashes from the scales of anonymous wings that had crashed there.

Some days, I thought, they will be dull and gray and the shine will be out of them; then the dew will polish them again and drops hang on the silk until everything is gleaming and turning in the light. It is like a mind, really, where everything changes but remains, and in the end you have these eaten-out bits of experience like beetle wings.

I stood over her a moment longer, comprehending somewhat reluctantly that her adventure against the great blind forces of winter, her seizure of this warming globe of light, would come to nothing and was hopeless. Nevertheless it brought the birds back into my mind, and that faraway song which had traveled with growing strength around a forest clearing years ago—a kind of heroism, a world where even a spider refuses to lie down and die if a rope can still be spun on to a star. Maybe man himself will fight like this in the end, I thought, slowly realizing that the web and its threatening yellow occupant had been added to some luminous store of experience, shining for a moment in the fogbound reaches of my brain.

The mind, it came to me as I slowly descended the ladder, is a very remarkable thing; it has gotten itself a kind of courage by looking at a spider in a street lamp. Here was something that ought to be passed on to those who will fight our final freezing battle with the void. I thought of setting it down carefully as a message to the future: *In the days of the frost seek a minor sun.*

But as I hesitated, it became plain that something was wrong. The marvel was escaping—a sense of bigness beyond man's power to grasp, the essence of life in its great dealings with the universe. It was better, I decided, for the emissaries returning from the wilderness, even if they were merely descending from a stepladder, to record their marvel, not to define its meaning. In that way it would go echoing on through the minds of men, each grasping at that beyond out of which the miracles emerge, and which, once defined, ceases to satisfy the human need for symbols.

In the end I merely made a mental note: One specimen of Epeira observed building a web in a street light. Late autumn and cold for spiders. Cold for men, too. I shivered and left the lamp glowing there in my mind. The last I saw of Epeira she was hauling steadily on a cable. I stepped carefully over her shadow as I walked away.

---

1. List the extended examples that Eiseley uses. Can you find any dominant idea that pulls them together?

2. How do the scenes Eiseley chooses in each example suit what you see to be his overall purpose?

3. As his audience, do you think Eiseley's examples are effective? If you think so, see if you can define what makes them effective. If you think they are not forceful, try to define the reason they do not work for you. Can you suggest more effective examples or better ways Eiseley might present his material?

4. Returning to your list of examples, play with their order. Can you come up with a better order, or is Eiseley's the best for his purpose? If you came up with an order you think is better, what makes it better? If you think Eiseley's is the best, what makes it so?

5. "Voice" is an idea that we have not yet taken up specifically, but generally, the term means the type of character the author creates for him- or herself through the language he or she chooses. What kind of voice does Eiseley create in "The Judgment of the Birds"? How does his voice affect your relationship to him and to his ideas? Find some examples of how he creates the voice you hear in your reading.

❧ An Invitation to Write

Remember how you responded to Eiseley's essay, how it made you feel about the examples he presented and the central idea that those examples defined. Write a draft of an essay, a story, or a poem that responds to what you see to be Eiseley's idea—supporting it, extending it, or arguing with it—and use your own observations to make your position clear. If you decided that Eiseley's examples were effective, see if you can duplicate that effectiveness. If you thought that there might have been a better way for Eiseley to make his point, try it out in your writing.

If you are working with a group, provide each member with a copy of your draft. If your teacher asks you to do so, apply first- and second-draft procedures to each member's writing.

Specific material and its arrangement is just as important for the writer of fiction, poetry, or drama as it is for the writer of the essay. "Creative" writers usually make their points clear by giving them life and weight in characters, situations, and reflections of feelings. These writers create those elements so carefully that while you read the work, you believe in their reality. However, for the writer of fiction, poetry, or drama, the incidents, setting, and characters may be imaginary, whereas the writer of nonfiction makes a bargain with the audience that what he or she reports really did happen and could have been observed by any reader who might have been there. The concern of all writers is the precision and concreteness of their language and the degree to which they can involve the reader in the reality of their fiction or observations and the ideas that give it life.

FOREGROUND AND BACKGROUND

Read this paragraph and try to answer the following questions:

Where do the events in this account take place?
In what field of music does Dr. P. teach?
How old is Dr. P?
What symptoms of diabetes did Dr. P. first notice?
Is Dr. P. married?
Does Dr. P. have children?

Dr. P. was a musician of distinction, well-known for many years as a singer, and then, at the local School of Music, as a teacher. It was here, in relation to his students, that certain strange problems were first observed. Sometimes a student would present himself, and Dr. P. would not recognize him; or, more specifically, would not recognize his face. The moment that student spoke, he would be recognized by his voice. Such incidents multiplied, causing embarrassment, perplexity, fear— and, sometimes, comedy. Not only did Dr. P. increasingly fail to see faces, but he saw faces when there were no faces to see: genially, Magoo-like, when in the street, he might pat the heads of water-hydrants and parking-meters, taking these to be the heads of children; he would amiably address carved knobs on the furniture, and be astounded when they did not reply. At first these odd mistakes were laughed off as jokes, not least by Dr. P. himself. Had he not always had a quirky sense of humor, and been given to Zen-like paradoxes and jests? His musical powers were as dazzling as ever; he did not feel ill—he had never felt better; and the mistakes were so ludicrous—and so ingenious—that they could hardly be serious or betoken anything serious. The notion of there being "something the matter" did not emerge until three years later, when diabetes developed. Well aware that diabetes could affect his eyes, Dr. P. consulted an ophthalmologist, who took a careful history and examined his eyes closely. "There's nothing wrong with your eyes," the doctor concluded. "But there is trouble with the visual parts of your brain. You don't need my help, you must see a neurologist." And so, as a result of this referral, Dr. P. came to me.

—OLIVER SACKS, "The Man Who Mistook His Wife for a Hat"

You won't find the answers to the earlier questions in the paragraph. In fact, few of the questions are answered in the whole essay. Most likely, the questions seem stupid to you because they don't seem relevant to the paragraph. Writers do not tell you everything. Instead, they show you only what they think you ought to see, hear, or even taste, smell, or feel to understand their point. Writers emphasize certain ideas, objects, and events; mention others; and ignore still others. They use a principle of selection that depends upon their purpose in writing and their guesses about their audience.

When you look at a scene, you rarely look at all of it. Instead, you select what to look at based on what you need to see. Depending on your purpose, certain objects leap into the foreground, others recede into the background to set off the foregrounded objects, and still others disappear entirely. When you drive, you look at the other cars on the road, the exit signs, street signs, traffic control signs, traffic lights. It is dangerous to drive and to admire the scenery. People who are driven along a route they usually drive alone often find themselves astounded at how much they see that they never noticed when they were driving.

Look, for example, at Figure 7.1. Either you can see a wine glass, or you can see two profiles facing each other. Which picture you see depends upon which picture you *choose* to see. When you make your choice, certain details leap out at you while others, belonging to the other possibility, recede into the background and outline your choice.

The example in Figure 7.2 is somewhat different. At first, you probably see a confusing mass of spots and blobs. If you look carefully, and you might need some help, you'll begin to make out the figure of a dalmatian walking through the shadows of leaves on the ground. In this case, your mind, searching to make a pattern out of the shapes, finally discovers a relationship between the foreground and the background that makes sense.

When you revise, the results of your dialogue with your audience combined with your knowledge of your subject and your commitment to your dominant idea should guide you toward effective choices. As you examine your material, you may decide to add some information at one point—allow

Figure 7.1 What Do You See?

it to come to the foreground—because you think your audience needs this information to understand your point clearly. At another point, you may decide that a certain piece of information, even a whole paragraph or more, does not add anything to your idea. In fact, it may direct your audience's attention away from your central concept. And so you decide to cut it entirely. At still another point, you may decide that the details contained in a particular paragraph are important as background but that you have emphasized them too much. In that case, you might consider keeping that material but devoting less space to it, perhaps combining it with other information.

Look upon writing a paper as if you are taking your reader on a trip. Before you begin, you might draw a map, telling him or her what the high points of the trip will be. Along the way, you direct your reader's attention to what you consider to be the important landmarks while making certain that he or she does not wander off the important track of the journey onto other paths. If you are a good guide, both you and your reader will finish the journey where you expected to. For the space of time a person reads your work, you are responsible for everything he or she encounters. You are in control of what he or she perceives.

UNITY AND COHERENCE: KEEPING YOUR READER ON THE PATH

If you have kept your dominant idea in mind and if you have made sure that all of the specific material you have added really makes your dominant idea, its background, and the steps by which you arrived at it clear to your reader, you are well on the way to establishing both unity and coherence in your writing.

[Photograph by R. C. James; Carraher and Thurston 1966; reprinted by permission of Van Nostrand Reinhold.]

Figure 7.2 What Is Happening Here?

Coherence means that you've created a clear relationship both between your ideas themselves and between your ideas and the specific material that you've chosen to bring those ideas to the foreground. For your reader, there should be something like a bridge that carries him or her from one idea to the next, not a yawning chasm into which he or she could disappear. Unity means that everything you put in your paper is clearly related to your dominant idea and that nothing leads your reader away from the central focus.

One way of visualizing unity, coherence, and the relationship between them is to see them as if they were the hub, spokes, and rim of a wheel. At the center of the wheel you'll find the hub. All of the spokes of the wheel radiate from the hub, or they all lead toward the hub. The rim of the wheel connects the spokes with each other. Without a hub, the spokes have no logical focal point. Without a rim, there's nothing to hold the spokes together. If your piece of writing is a wheel, then its hub is your dominant idea. Your examples and supporting ideas—your specific material—lead like spokes from (or to) your dominant idea. Finally, the means by which you connect the pieces of specific material to each other so that the reader can see their relationship is the rim of the wheel. As a whole, the relationship between unity and coherence in your writing looks something like the illustration in Figure 7.3.

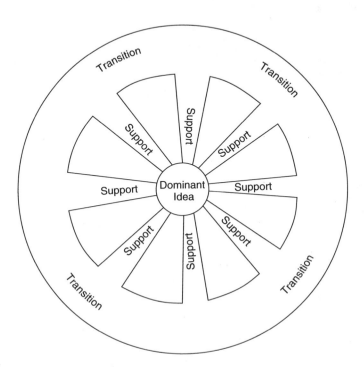

Figure 7.3 Writing and the Wheel Analogy

Coherence

Often, the order in which you present your ideas and examples is almost enough to make the connections between them clear to your reader. Chronological order, the arrangement of objects in space, or arrangement by degree of importance is sometimes enough to keep your reader headed in the direction you want. For example, if you arrange a paragraph or a paper according to a sequence of events, then your reader will be able to understand the relationships between the parts of your writing from their chronology. If, in a different case, you need to describe a location, your reader will follow you if you move logically from place to place. If you present objects, events, or ideas in terms of their logical relation to each other and to your dominant idea, ending with the conclusion, your reader will follow you toward that conclusion.

✎ Exercise

Read the following paragraphs. The first is arranged chronologically; the second, spatially. Working on your own or in your group, note the ways the writers have organized the ideas and events they write about to create unity and coherence in their writing.

> From the very beginning of school we make books and reading a constant source of possible failure and public humiliation. When children are little we make them read aloud, before the teacher and other children, so that we can be sure they "know" all the words they are reading. This means that when they don't know a word, they are going to make a mistake, right in front of everyone. Instantly they are made to realize that they have done something wrong. Perhaps some of the other children will begin to wave their hands and say, "Ooooh! O-o-o-oh!" Perhaps the teacher will say, "Are you sure?" or ask someone else what he thinks. Or perhaps, if the teacher is kindly, she will just smile a sweet, sad smile—often one of the most painful punishments a child can suffer in school. In any case, the child who has made the mistake knows he has made it, and feels foolish, stupid, and ashamed, just as any of us would in his shoes.
>
> —JOHN HOLT, "How Teachers Make Children Hate Reading"

I stopped very gently and sat upon the Time Machine, looking round. The sky was no longer blue. North-eastward it was inky black, and out of the blackness shone brightly and steadily the pale white stars. Overhead it was a deep Indian red and starless, and south-eastward it grew brighter to a glowing scarlet where, cut by the horizon, lay the huge hull of the sun, red and motionless. The rocks about me were of a harsh reddish colour, and all the trace of life that I could see at first was the intensely green vegetation that covered every projecting point on their south-eastern face. It was the same rich green that one sees on forest moss or on the lichen in caves: plants like these which grow in a perpetual twilight.

—H. G. WELLS, *The Time Machine*

✒ An Invitation to Write

On your own or as a group project, write a description of your classroom. First decide what is the most important aspect of your classroom. It might be the mood the classroom creates for you, or what the decor of the classroom implies about the nature of the education you're receiving, or how the way the classroom is arranged reflects the sort of class that is held in it, or any other approach that occurs to you.

As an alternate assignment, you might describe the five or ten minutes in your classroom *before* class begins.

Once you've settled on the idea, write the description. Have a member of your group read it aloud and compare its organization with the other arrangements discovered by the other groups.

Often there will be times in your writing and revision when your ideas are not closely related to a description of an event or a location. In those cases you have to figure out how to make the direction of your thoughts clear to your reader. You can keep your reader on the track by reminding him or her of the central idea of your paragraph or piece through words or phrases which signal the relationship between ideas. It is often useful to show your reader how one paragraph or sentence connects to those that came before it or anticipates what comes next.

There are many words or phrases you can use to signal the way one paragraph or sentence responds to the previous one or anticipates the following one. Here are some useful examples arranged according to their purposes.

Consequence
thus, therefore, accordingly, as a result, since

Likeness
likewise, in the same way, similarly

Difference
although, but, however, on the other hand, yet, nevertheless

Continuing the idea
and, furthermore, also, too, in addition, perhaps, then

Restatement of the idea
that is, in other words, to put it differently; you can also refer to a previous idea or object by using a pronoun or a synonym for it or by repeating the word or idea itself

Example

for instance, for example

Sequence

first (second, third, etc.), finally, later, earlier, formerly, subsequently, at the same time, so far, until now

Location

elsewhere, here, there, above, below, farther on

Summary or conclusion

in conclusion, to summarize, finally

Look at how the writer of this paragraph uses words or phrases (underlined) to establish coherence:

> This half-minute commercial for a laundry detergent called Wisk appears fairly frequently on daytime and evening television. In a recent version, a young woman and a young man are shown being led down the corridor of a hotel by a bellman who is carrying suitcases. The hotel seems to be an attractive one—not very elegant but definitely not an ordinary motel. Similarly, the young man and woman are attractive, but with nothing either glamorous or working class about their appearance. Perhaps he is a junior executive. And she is probably his wife, though there is nothing so far that says the two people are married. Since the framework of the drama is a commercial, the assumption is that they are married. On the other hand, against the familiar framework of similar modern movie scenes, there is no such assumption; possibly it is the beginning of an adventure. Then, suddenly, the bellman drops one of the suitcases in the corridor; some of the contents spill out. The bellman crouches down on the corridor carpet to put the items back in. He notices one of the man's shirts and holds it up. "Ring around the collar!" he says accusingly; these words are then taken up in the kind of singsong chant that has become a feature of these ads. . . .

Unity

Your paragraph or paper is unified when everything in it is related directly or indirectly to your dominant idea. If you do not pay attention to unity in your writing, you will lose your reader, leaving him or her confused as to what you are saying, what relationship your ideas have to each other, and where they all lead.

It's easier to create unity in your writing when you are certain of your dominant idea. When you don't have a clear idea of your central concept, you cannot make intelligent choices as to what should be kept, what should be cut, and what connections between your ideas make the most sense.

Often, lack of unity is accompanied by coherence problems. If you are not sure what your writing is about, you can't make clear connections between your ideas. On the other hand, you may be perfectly certain of your idea, but it is easy to forget that your reader does not think like you. Connections between ideas that may be perfectly clear to you may not be at all clear to your reader.

Here is an example of an opening paragraph that shows serious problems in unity as well as coherence. This writer's problems resulted from his not knowing what he wanted to write about and what he wanted to say about it.

> Many women think that men are all dishonest jerks. There are relationships where the male does what he pleases behind the back of his girlfriend. Too many men are just out to manipulate the opposite sex. This is why many women accuse men of only wanting "one thing." All men are not out for this "one thing." Although many are, the men that are looking for a serious relationship are at a disadvantage. Many women I know stereotype men as all wanting nothing but sex, and they do not give each a chance to express himself as an individual.

❧ *An Invitation to Write*

Alone or in your group, see if you can reduce the previous paragraph to a manageable central idea. That is, guess at what the author really wanted to assert as a dominant idea. Once you have decided on the idea, revise the paragraph so that it is unified and coherent. Feel free to add, cut, reorder, and reword.

Now read the following paragraphs and analyze the ways the writers have given their writing unity and coherence.

Example 1

The single-minded pursuit of sports fame and fortune is today approaching an institutionalized triple tragedy in Black society: the tragedy of thousands and thousands of Black youths in obsessive pursuit of sports goals foredoomed to elude the vast and overwhelming majority of them; the tragedy of the personal and cultural underdevelopment that afflicts so many among both successful and unsuccessful Black sports aspirants; and the tragedy of cultural and institutional underdevelopment in Black society overall, partially as a consequence of the talent drain toward sports and away from other critically vital areas of occupational and career emphasis (medicine, law, economics, politics, education, the technical fields, etc.).

Example 2

Students these days are, in general, nice. I choose the word carefully. They are not particularly moral or noble. Such niceness is a facet of democratic character when times are good. Neither war nor tyranny nor want has hardened them or made demands on them. The wounds and rivalries caused by class distinction have disappeared along with any strong sense of class (as it once existed in universities in America and as it still does, poisonously, in England). Students are free of most constraints, and their families make sacrifices for them without asking for much in the way of obedience or respect. Religion and national origin have almost no noticeable effect on their social life or their career prospects. Although few really believe in "the system," they do not have any burning sentiment that injustice is being done to them. The drugs and sex once thought to be forbidden are available in the quantities required for sensible use. A few radical feminists still feel the old-time religion, but most of the women are comfortably assured that not much stands in the way of their careers. There is an atmosphere of easy familiarity with their elders, and even of the kind of respect of free young people for them that Tocqueville asserted equality encourages. Above all, there are none of the longings, romantic or otherwise, that used to make bourgeois society, or society in general, repugnant to the young. The impossible dreams of the sixties proved to be quite possible within the loosened fabric of American life. Students these days are pleasant, friendly and, if not great-souled, at least not particularly mean-spirited. Their primary preoccupation is themselves, understood in the narrowest sense.

Example 3

This seems to be the era of gratuitous inventions and negative improvements. Consider the beer can. It was beautiful—as beautiful as the clothespin, as inevitable as the wine bottle, as dignified and reassuring as the fire hydrant. A tranquil cylinder of delightfully resonant metal, it could be opened in an instant, requiring only the application of a handy gadget freely dispensed by every grocer. Who can forget the small, symmetrical thrill of those two triangular punctures, the dainty *pffff,* the little crest of suds that foamed eagerly in the exultation of release? Now we are given, instead, a top beetling with an ugly, shmoo–shaped "tab," which, after fiercely resisting the tugging, bleeding fingers of the thirsty man, threatens his lips with a dangerous and hideous hole. However, we have discovered a way to thwart Progress, usually so un–thwartable. *Turn the beer can upside down and open the bottom.* The bottom is still the way the top used to be. True, this operation gives the beer an unsettling jolt, and the sight of a consistently inverted beer can might make people edgy, not to say queasy. But the latter difficulty could be eliminated if manufacturers would design cans that looked the same whichever end was up, like playing cards. What we need is Progress with an escape hatch.

❧ *Working with a Reading*

Read the following poem and then, alone or with your group, answer the questions that follow it.

THE COLLEGE COLONEL

Herman Melville

He rides at their head;
   A crutch by his saddle just slants in view,
One slung arm is in splints, you see,
   Yet he guides his strong steed—how coldly too.

He brings his regiment home—   5
   Not as they filed two years before,
But a remnant half-tattered, and battered, and worn,
Like castaway sailors, who—stunned
     By the surf's loud roar,
   Their mates dragged back and seen no more—   10
Again and again breast the surge,
   And at last crawl, spent, to shore.

A still rigidity and pale—
   An Indian aloofness lones his brow;
He has lived a thousand years   15
Compressed in battles pains and prayers,
   Marches and watches slow.
There are welcoming shouts, and flags;
   Old men off hat to the Boy,
Wreaths from gay balconies fall at his feet,   20
   But to *him* there comes alloy.°

It is not that a leg is lost,
   It is not that an arm is maimed,
It is not that a fever has racked—
   Self he has long disclaimed.   25

But all through the Seven Days' Fight
   And deep in the Wilderness grim,
And in the field-hospital tent,
   And Petersburg crater,° and dim
Lean brooding in Libby,° there came—   30
   Ah heaven!—what *truth* to him.

21. *alloy:* adulteration, mixture
27, 29. *the Wilderness* and *Petersburg crater:* The Battle of the Wilderness and the Battle of the
Crater at Petersburg were events in the American Civil War.
30. *Libby:* a Confederate prison camp at Richmond, Virginia

1. What do you think Melville is telling you through this poem? In other words, what is Melville's dominant idea?

2. With Melville's dominant idea in mind, read the poem carefully again and list those parts that reflect that idea.

3. Write quick notes to yourself about how each of the elements you listed expresses the dominant idea.

4. Referring to your list, see if you can define how each of the elements connect with each other.

If you are working with a group, bring your answers to these questions to a group meeting and compare your answers with those of the other members. Try to arrive at a group statement that reflects your answers to these questions. If there are disagreements, make the differences part of your statement. Report your conclusions to the other groups in your class.

An Invitation to Write

Think of a situation in which you or another person learned something essential about a situation that other people evaluated differently. Write a paper, a story, or a poem that reflects the differing assumptions about that situation.

8

Openings and Closings

Beginning and ending a piece of writing gives many writers trouble. Most want to begin by making a forceful impression on their audience and to close leaving a similar impression.

When you begin an interview for a job, you probably want your prospective employer to know that you are qualified for the job, that you are interested in the job, and that you are a trustworthy individual. And you want your prospective employer to be interested in you. When you create a piece of writing, your situation is the same in many ways. Your reader wants to have a clear idea of your subject and a sense of how you intend to approach it. Your reader probably wants a reason to read your writing; what will he or she gain by taking this time with you and your ideas? Finally, your reader may be skeptical about you. After all, he or she usually does not know you. Your reader might wonder whether you know what you're writing about and whether you are honest.

At the end of a job interview, you try to leave the potential employer with a favorable dominant impression. You might end the interview by telling your interviewer how interested you are in working for his or her company. Or you might spell out the important ways you believe you're qualified for the position. In doing this, you essentially summarize and repeat the material you covered in your interview so as to reinforce what you hope is the favorable impression you have already created.

When you close your piece of writing, you might remind your reader of the theme (or subject) or the dominant idea that you and your reader have been examining. Or you might want to leave your reader with the attitude or emotion you've worked toward through your piece of writing. Another approach is to leave your reader with a renewed sense of the importance of your subject and your dominant idea.

However, the crucial difference between interviewing for a job or giving a speech and writing is this: When you speak or interview, you don't have a second chance to make a good first impression. Although your reader will get only one chance to read your piece for the first time, you can revise it and review it as many times as you feel necessary before your reader sees it. Your ability to revise gives you power. You control the way you present your ideas in writing.

OPENINGS

There are no magic rules for introducing your ideas. However, unless you are writing to an intimate friend or a family member, you cannot assume that the members of your audience care about what you have to say, have any idea why it is important to you and to them, or know anything of the events that constitute the background of your idea and your writing. You have to address these elements before you begin to develop your dominant idea.

The two most important considerations that shape an introduction are what occurs in the rest of your work and the audience for whom your work is intended. In introducing your ideas and observations, you should let the members of your audience know what is to come and engage their interest by giving them a sense of what they will gain by reading what is to follow. That is, your introduction should answer questions like these for your readers: What will they learn? How does it fit into their experience? Why is what you have to say important to them?

How much attention you devote to each of these issues depends on your evaluation of your audience. What do you think the members of your audience already know? How might they respond to the issues you intend to raise or the support you intend to provide for those issues? Do the issues have intrinsic interest? Do you have to convince your audience of the importance of what you have to say? The audience discovery strategy in Chapter 6 (page 115) provides suggestions for discovering the answers to those questions.

Most important, your introduction should inform your readers with as much background as you feel is necessary for them to enter your writing with their interest, attention, and sympathy engaged.

Here is an example of how one writer engages her audience's interest in an unpromising subject:

> New Yorkers are a provincial lot. They wear their city's accomplishments like blue ribbons. To anyone who will listen they boast of leading the world in everything from Mafia murders to porno moviehouses. They can also boast that their city produces more garbage than any other city in the world. In fact, it produces more than most countries.
> In its 1970–71 garbage season—a boffo season if there ever was one—New York City produced an average of 28,900 tons per day, as against a mere 4,800 tons per day for Los Angeles and a paltry 2,000 tons per day for San Francisco. But it is not only in quantity that New York excels. Fully 20 percent of the city's garbage consists of quality paper:

canceled checks, rough drafts of Broadway hits, executive memos, IBM punch cards, and so on. On Mondays alone seven million pounds of the Sunday *New York Times* are donated to New York garbage cans.

—KATIE KELLY, "Garbage"

And here is an introduction that deals with a controversial, potentially unpopular idea:

Rape is an outrage that cannot be tolerated in civilized society. Yet feminism, which has waged a crusade for rape to be taken more seriously, has put young women in danger by hiding the truth about sex from them.

In dramatizing the pervasiveness of rape, feminists have told young women that before they have sex with a man, they must give consent as explicit as a legal contract's. In this way, young women have been convinced that they have been the victims of rape. On elite campuses in the Northeast and on the West Coast, they have held consciousness-raising sessions, petitioned administrations, demanded inquests. At Brown University, outraged, panicky "victims" have scrawled the names of alleged attackers on the walls of women's rest rooms. What marital rape was to the '70's, "date rape" is to the '90's.

The incidence and seriousness of rape do not require this kind of exaggeration. Real acquaintance rape is nothing new. It has been a horrible problem for women for all of recorded history. Once, father and brothers protected women from rape. Once, the penalty for rape was death. I come from a fierce Italian tradition where, not so long ago in the motherland, a rapist would end up knifed, castrated, and hung out to dry.

But the old clans and small rural communities have broken down. In our cities, on our campuses far from home, young women are vulnerable and defenseless. Feminism has not prepared them for this. Feminism keeps saying the sexes are the same. It keeps telling women they can do anything, go anywhere, say anything, wear anything. No, they can't. Women will always be in sexual danger.

—CAMILLE PAGLIA, "Rape: A Bigger Danger Than Feminists Know"

Introductions also engage your reader's attention and sometimes position him or her in a particular place or situation. Many writers choose to begin with a striking example of the idea, event, or circumstance they want to bring to their readers' notice. Writers choosing such an introduction usually let it lead their readers to the dominant idea. Some arrange their examples in a way that allows them to save the dominant idea for the end of their writing. They lead their readers through a sequence of examples and smaller ideas to the discovery of the dominant idea.

Your introduction is also a commitment to your reader. In it, you present your reader with both the ideas you intend to cover and the approach you intend to take. In doing so, you make a commitment—a promise—to your reader that the issues you raise at the beginning of your piece are what you will keep your and your reader's attention focused on throughout your writing. In addition, your introduction probably implies one dominant way of organizing your material. Once you have led your reader to expect a particular approach, not following through with it will more than likely leave your reader confused and lost. When you have confused your reader or left your reader adrift, he or she will not be inclined to read what you have to say or to take it or you seriously.

Remember, drafting your piece of writing is rarely sequential or linear because it doesn't have to be. Only you and your peers see it. Many inexperienced writers make the mistake of believing that because the introduction opens their writing, they must write it first when they begin their drafts. When you draft and revise, you give yourself the power to shape your writing any way you choose. In many cases it makes a lot more sense for you to wait to write your introduction until you have finished most of your drafting. At that point you have a much better idea of what you intend to introduce and where you want to aim your readers.

CLOSINGS

Eventually, your writing will come to an end. At that point you are faced with the question of the dominant impression you want to leave in your reader's mind. You will already have made part of that decision through how you have visualized your audience and what you have written as a result. Your closing paragraphs should leave your readers with a primary attitude toward the subject you have chosen and should remind them of your dominant idea and its importance to them. In addition, there will be times when engaging your audience's emotions is an effective part of your plan. In other cases, you might want to leave your audience with some questions that grow out of your dominant idea. You have a number of choices and combinations of choices available to you to establish an effective closing.

- *The Summary:* Closing your writing with a summary means repeating your major ideas. This approach is most useful when the ideas you have covered are complex or unfamiliar to your audience. However, unless you are certain that your material is challenging, you risk boring your audience or insulting their intelligence. If you choose to summarize, try not to repeat your ideas in the same language you have already used.

- *The Appeal:* If your goal is to move your audience to take a position or an action in response to a particular situation, merely summarizing what you have said is probably not enough. You may want to invite your readers to take that position or action. You might have to appeal directly or indirectly to their reason as well as to their emotion to remind them that your ideas speak to issues in their lives.

There are a number of effective ways to invite your audience to further thought and possible action. One of the strongest is the final, striking example that sticks with them after they have finished reading. Another is the direct call for action. No matter which approach you take, the appeal must be clearly and honestly connected to the material that has come before. If it is not, your audience will probably feel either manipulated or confused—and there is a good chance they will resent you and reject your ideas.

- *The Question:* You can often strengthen the appeal of your position if your audience can reach the conclusion you had in mind on their own—and can even apply that conclusion to other cases. A thoughtful, guiding question growing out of the information you have presented invites the members of your audience to reach a conclusion based on their own thoughts. If you choose this approach, be certain that your information, the way you have arranged it, and the question you pose can lead to no other conclusion than the one you have in mind.

Here are the concluding paragraphs of the essays whose openings appear in the previous section. First, here is the close of the essay dealing with New York City's garbage:

> Opened in 1948, Fresh Kills is already almost full to the brim, for New York City, like every other city in this country, has more garbage than it can cope with. The city is, in fact, due to run out of landfill space—preferably swampland or a sandpit or gully—in 1985. The solution: Pile it higher. But even here there are limits. As one city official put it, "We have to leave some room between the sea gulls and the planes."
>
> "It sure has changed out here," one worker, who has been at Fresh Kills for years, told me. "Why, there used to be fresh natural springs over there." He gestured out over the hundreds of acres of garbage. Natural crab beds once flourished in the area. Now they, too, are gone, buried under tons of garbage.

Here is the conclusion of the essay on rape:

> The only solution to date rape is female self-awareness and self-control. A woman's number-one line of defense against rape is herself. When a real rape occurs, she should report it to the police. Complaining to college committees because the courts "take too long" is ridiculous. College administrations are not a branch of the judiciary. They are not equipped or trained for legal inquiry. Colleges must alert incoming students to the problems and dangers of adulthood. Then colleges must stand back and get out of the sex game.

❧ Working with a Reading

Read the following selection and, alone or with your group, answer the questions that follow it.

ON NATURAL DEATH
Lewis Thomas

There are so many new books about dying that there are now special shelves set aside for them in bookshops, along with the health-diet and home-repair paperbacks and the sex manuals. Some of them are so packed with detailed information and step-by-step instructions for performing the function that you'd think this was a new sort of skill which all of us are now required to learn. The strongest impression the casual reader gets, leafing through, is that proper dying has become an extraordinary, even an exotic experience, something only the specially trained get to do.

Also, you could be led to believe that we are the only creatures capable of the awareness of death, that when all the rest of nature is being cycled through dying, one generation after another, it is a different kind of process, done automatically and trivially, more "natural," as we say.

An elm in our backyard caught the blight this summer and dropped stone dead, leafless, almost overnight. One weekend it was a normal-looking elm, maybe a little bare in spots but nothing alarming, and the next weekend it was gone, passed over, departed, taken. Taken is right, for the tree surgeon came by yesterday with his crew of young helpers and their cherry picker, and took it down branch by branch and carted it off in the back of a red truck, everyone singing.

The dying of a field mouse, at the jaws of an amiable household cat, is a spectacle I have beheld many times. It used to make me wince. Early in life I gave up throwing sticks at the cat to make him drop the mouse, because the dropped mouse regularly went ahead and died anyway, but I always shouted unaffections at the cat to let him know the sort of animal he had become. Nature, I thought, was an abomination.

Recently I've done some thinking about that mouse, and I wonder if his dying is necessarily all that different from the passing of our elm. The main difference, if there is one, would be in the matter of pain. I do not believe that an elm tree has pain receptors, and even so, the blight seems to me a relatively painless way to go even if there were nerve endings in a tree, which there are not. But the mouse dangling tail-down from the teeth of a gray cat is something else again, with pain beyond bearing, you'd think, all over his small body.

There are now some plausible reasons for thinking it is not like that at all, and you can make up an entirely different story about the mouse and his dying if you like. At the instant of being trapped and penetrated by teeth, peptide hormones are released by cells in the hypothalamus and the pituitary gland; instantly these substances, called endorphins, are

5

attached to the surface of other cells responsible for pain perception; the hormones have the pharmacologic properties of opium; there is no pain. Thus it is that the mouse seems always to dangle so languidly from the jaws, lies there so quietly when dropped, dies of his injuries without a struggle. If a mouse could shrug, he'd shrug.

I do not know if this is true or not, nor do I know how to prove it if it is true. Maybe if you could get in there quickly enough and administer naloxone, a specific morphine antagonist, you could turn off the endorphins and observe the restoration of pain, but this is not something I would care to do or see. I think I will leave it there, as a good guess about the dying of a cat-chewed mouse, perhaps about dying in general.

Montaigne had a hunch about dying, based on his own close call in a riding accident. He was so badly injured as to be believed dead by his companions, and was carried home with lamentations, "all bloody, stained all over with the blood I had thrown up." He remembers the entire episode, despite having been "dead, for two full hours," with wonderment:

> It seemed to me that my life was hanging only by the tip of my lips. I closed my eyes in order, it seemed to me, to help push it out, and took pleasure in growing languid and letting myself go. It was an idea that was only floating on the surface of my soul, as delicate and feeble as all the rest, but in truth not only free from distress but mingled with that sweet feeling that people have who have let themselves slide into sleep. I believe that this is the same state in which people find themselves whom we see fainting in the agony of death, and I maintain that we pity them without cause. . . . In order to get used to the idea of death, I find there is nothing like coming close to it.

Later, in another essay, Montaigne returns to it:

> If you know not how to die, never trouble yourself; Nature will in a moment fully and sufficiently instruct you; she will exactly do that business for you; take you no care for it.

The worst accident I've ever seen was in Okinawa, in the early days of the invasion, when a jeep ran into a troop carrier and was crushed nearly flat. Inside were two young MPs, trapped in bent steel, both mortally hurt, with only their heads and shoulders visible. We had a conversation while people with the right tools were prying them free. Sorry about the accident, they said. No, they said, they felt fine. Is everyone else okay, one of them said. Well, the other one said, no hurry now. And then they died.

Pain is useful for avoidance, for getting away when there's time to get away, but when it is end game, and no way back, pain is likely to be turned off, and the mechanisms for this are wonderfully precise and quick. If I had to design an ecosystem in which creatures had to live off each other and in which dying was an indispensable part of living, I could not think of a better way to manage.

---

1. How does Thomas use his introduction for you? Consider such issues as how he engages your interest, what important themes he introduces, and how he focuses your attention on his dominant idea.

2. How does the material Thomas introduces you to in his introduction link the examples that he gives you in the essay?

3. How does Thomas use his conclusion? Where does it take you from the body of the essay? What does it leave you with?

A FINAL WORD ABOUT REVISION

As you revise, be prepared for surprises. You may find, in adding more concrete information to make your idea clearer, that the material you have chosen to expand becomes an independent idea that seems more exciting than the idea you began with. Or you may discover, as you reorder your ideas to make their relationships clearer, that the new order suggests a new direction for your writing. Or as you prepare your introduction or conclusion, a more interesting version of your original dominant idea may declare itself. If you work in a group, you may find that one of the members discovers an idea or approach in your piece that suggests an entirely new way to present your idea.

When you begin to revise, discovery and thinking don't stop. As you revise, you experiment with different approaches to expressing your ideas. This means that while you review your writing, you also examine different strategies for thinking about your ideas. With this type of thinking going on, it would be strange if other schemes and whole new structures of ideas did not suggest themselves. Be prepared for better ideas or for new directions for ideas you already have on paper to make themselves known. Be open to the possibility that these intruders may create a greater reason to write than the approaches and ideas you started with.

Annie Dillard is one of the better contemporary writers. Her published work is polished; it looks effortless. In the following excerpt from *The Writing Life,* Dillard speaks to her readers about revision:

It is the beginning of a work that a writer throws away.
A painting covers its tracks. Painters work from the ground up. The latest version of a painting overlays earlier versions, and obliterates them. Writers, on the other hand, work from left to right. The discardable chapters are on the left. The latest version of a literary work begins somewhere in the work's middle, and hardens toward the end. The earlier version remains lumpishly on the left; the work's beginning

greets the reader with the wrong hand. In those early pages and chapters anyone may find bold leaps to nowhere, read the brave beginnings of dropped themes, hear a tone since abandoned, discover blind alleys, track red herrings, and laboriously learn a setting now false.

Several delusions weaken the writer's resolve to throw away work. If he has read his pages too often, those pages will have a necessary quality, the ring of the inevitable, like poetry known by heart; they will perfectly answer their own familiar rhythms. He will retain them. He may retain those pages if they possess some virtues, such as power in themselves, though they lack the cardinal virtue, which is pertinence to, and unity with, the book's thrust. Sometimes the writer leaves his early chapters in place from gratitude; he cannot contemplate them or read them without feeling again the blessed relief that exalted him when the words first appeared—relief that he was writing anything at all. That beginning served to get him where he was going, after all; surely the reader needs it, too, as groundwork. But no.

Every year the aspiring photographer brought a stack of his best prints to an old, honored photographer, seeking his judgment. Every year the old man studied the prints and painstakingly ordered them into two piles, bad and good. Every year the old man moved a certain landscape print into the bad stack. At length he turned to the young man: "You submit this same landscape every year, and every year I put it on the bad stack. Why do you like it so much?" The young photographer said, "Because I had to climb a mountain to get it."

A cabdriver sang his songs to me, in New York. Some we sang together. He had turned the meter off; he drove around midtown, singing. One long song he sang twice. I said, "You already sang that one; let's sing something else." And he said, "You don't know how long it took me to get that one together."

How many books do we read from which the writer lacked the courage to tie off the umbilical cord? How many gifts do we open from which the writer neglected to remove the price tag? Is it pertinent, is it courteous, for us to learn what it cost the writer personally?

Chapter 9
#204

Style, Voice, and Language

STYLE

Nobody uses the materials available for living life in exactly the same way as anyone else. Every person has a specific "style," or way of doing things, in every area of his or her life. For example, you have your own way of getting to sleep—many people have habitual things they do in more or less the same order almost every night. You have your own way of eating—do you cut all your meat before you eat it or as you eat it? Do you cut your pasta? You even have your own way of getting dressed—Do you dress bottom up or top down? Which leg of your pants do you put on first? Without question, you have your own way of using words.

Your style of behaving is a matter of what you've learned. Because style is characteristic or habitual, you cannot have a style of doing something that you have not done before. Your style is based on your previous experience. When you write or speak, the words and ways of arranging them that you grew up with—what you've read; what your family, your peer group, the people in charge expected of you—have helped create your style. Much of your style has been shaped by the influence of your parents, your teachers, and other important persons in your life whom you found worthy of imitation. Nevertheless, you have made these examples of living—be they dress, music, cooking, or words—distinctively your own.

To someone who knows you, your style could not possibly be mistaken for any other person's style, nor would any friend's style be a mystery to you. When a close friend calls you on the telephone, you rarely have to ask who it is. That person's language, way of using language, and tone of voice are usually all you need to hear.

Your style in writing is the way you take your raw materials—words, their order, the combinations and rhythms that are available to you—and use them to make your dominant idea clear and to keep your audience's intellect and emotion engaged with that idea. Style is a set of resources—

including vocabulary, imagery, figurative language, tone, dialogue, patterns of sound and rhythm, and point of view—that are available to you when you write.

VOCABULARY: YOUR RAW MATERIAL

Although there is a broad range of expression where people's vocabularies overlap, each person has been exposed to different words, different combinations of words, or different meanings of the same words. Each person has a different vocabulary. In addition, each person has read different books, has different interests, has had different experiences. Also, different people's experiences teach them to weight the same word differently. For example, *spider* will cause some people to shiver with revulsion whereas others may hardly respond to the word other than to identify it with an arachnid. Entomologists may respond to the word with interest and excitement.

Each person also uses a different vocabulary for different situations. You would not consider choosing the same words in a formal situation—a job interview or a speech to a professional organization—as you would when speaking with members of your family (and you probably talk to your siblings in a different way than you talk to your parents). Most likely, you use a different selection of words with your friends than you do with your mother and father. Furthermore, the situations in which you find yourself as well as the persons you address shape your choices. If you were to find yourself in a formal public debate with a close friend, you would probably find yourself choosing different language from that you might use after the debate in speaking with the same friend.

As you grow up, you learn to make many of these choices almost without thinking, usually as the result of a number of embarrassing mistakes, reprimands, and rewarding experiences as well as through others' examples. Nonetheless, each of us makes these choices in our own way. None of us has exactly the same language. None of us uses the same words in exactly the same way. Each of us chooses and arranges words differently to cope with different situations.

⌁ *An Invitation to Write*

Working alone or with your group, make a case for eliminating grading at your school. Select one of these audiences to make your case to: your professor, the administration of your school, your parents, the general public, or your fellow students. Pay special attention to the language you use to make your case; your examples and organization will likely depend on the audience you choose. When you are finished, compare your results with those of others who chose a different audience.

Using Words Precisely

A great deal of the time, you use words to communicate your ideas, feelings, and desires. In most cases, you don't have to place many demands on your vocabulary to do so. When you speak with good friends or with your family, one or two general words can often do the work of many, more precise words. This is so because the people you speak with are familiar with you and to you and share so many of the same experiences and assumptions with you that a single word—with, perhaps, an intonation or a gesture— can speak a sentence or even a paragraph.

In most writing situations, making yourself clear is not that simple. Consider how many resources you *don't* have when you write. You don't have gestures; you don't have tone of voice; you don't have facial expressions or posture. Most of the time you don't know your audience, and they don't know you. Finally, you don't have the immediate feedback of an audience's response to tell you how well or badly you're doing. The impersonal writing situation places much greater demands on your vocabulary than does speaking or writing a letter to a friend or family member.

One of the greatest of these demands is precision and specificity: the use of exact language to make general ideas clear to your audience. Confusion is frustrating under the best of circumstances; unless your reader is very charitable, he or she will not put up with very much vagueness before abandoning the attempt to understand what you have to say. Consider the following dialogue. You are sitting at a table in the library studying. The other person is sitting across from you.

OTHER PERSON: Say, could you get that book for me?
YOU: Which book?
OTHER: The one over there.
YOU: Where?
OTHER: To the right.
YOU: To the right of what?
OTHER: To the right of the room.
YOU: [*Getting up and walking to the right side of the room*]
   OK, here I am. Which book?
OTHER: The one on the shelf.
YOU: [*Barely controlling yourself*]
   Which shelf?
OTHER: The bottom shelf.
YOU: [*Kneeling at the shelf, shaking with barely suppressed rage*]
   Here I am. Which book?
OTHER: The blue one.
YOU: *Which* of the five blue ones?

By now you have the idea. At this point, many people in your position would probably have taken all five blue books on the bottom shelf and thrown them at the other person. On the other hand, if the other person had said, "Say, if you look on the left-hand side of the bottom shelf on the right side of the room, you'll find a copy of *Zen and the Art of Motorcycle Maintenance*. It's got a blue cover. Could you get it for me?" you might have gladly done the favor. The more precise and concrete the language, the less chance there is of confusing and frustrating your audience.

Specific, concrete language paints a picture and communicates attitudes and responses. The selections that follow show how writers use language to support their dominant idea.

 ## Working with the Readings

Read the three selections that follow: a poem, an essay, and a short story. Alone or with your group, answer the questions as you complete each piece.

MY PAPA'S WALTZ

Theodore Roethke

The whiskey on your breath
Could make a small boy dizzy;
But I hung on like death:
Such waltzing was not easy.

We romped until the pans   5
Slid from the kitchen shelf;
My mother's countenance
Could not unfrown itself.

The hand that held my wrist
Was battered on one knuckle;   10
At every step you missed
My right ear scraped a buckle.

You beat time on my head
With a palm caked hard by dirt,
Then waltzed me off to bed   15
Still clinging to your shirt.

---

1. This poem is full of specific language. However, Roethke does not describe everything in the kitchen or everything about the father. Look at the specific elements he has chosen to direct your attention to. What do these choices tell you about the narrator, the father, and the mother?

2. What do you think Roethke wants you to think and feel about the relationships in this poem? How does the father feel about the son?

The son about the father? How does the mother figure in the relationship? Do you think the place where the father and son waltz and the dance's effects on that place tell you more about these relationships? What does the idea of a dance—and, especially, a waltz—suggest to you?

MY FATHER'S TRIBAL RULE

Mark Mathabane

One night our dingy shack, which had been leaning precipitously on the edge of a *donga,°* collapsed. Luckily no one was hurt, but we were forced to move to another one, similarly built. This new shack, like the old one, had two rooms and measured something like fifteen by fifteen feet, and overlooked the same unlit, unpaved, potholed street. It had an interior flaked with old whitewash, a leaky ceiling of rusted zinc propped up by a thin wall of crumbling adobe bricks, two tiny windows made of cardboard and pieces of glass, a creaky, termite-eaten door too low for a person of average height to pass through without bending double, and a floor made of patches of cement and earth. It was similar to the dozen or so shacks strewn irregularly, like lumps on a leper, upon the cracked greenless piece of ground named yard number thirty-five.

In this new shack my brother, George, was weaned. It was amusing to witness my mother do it. The first day she began the process she secretly smeared her breasts with red pepper and then invited my brother to suckle. Unsuspecting, George energetically attacked my mother's breast only to let go of it instantly and start hollering because of the hot pepper. This continued throughout the day whenever he wanted to suckle. Finally, after a few days, he began to dread the sight of my mother's breast, and each time she teased him with it he would turn his face. He was now weaned. My father bought a small white chicken, my mother brewed beer, a few relatives were invited, and a small celebration was held to mark George's passage from infancy to childhood. He was almost two years old. He now had to sleep with Florah and me in the kitchen.

Soon after George was weaned my father began teaching him, as he had been teaching me, tribal ways of life. My father belonged to a loosely knit group of black families in the neighbourhood to whom tribal traditions were a way of life, and who sought to bring up their offspring

---

donga: a gully or ravine

according to its laws. He believed that feeding us a steady diet of tribal beliefs, values and rituals was one way of ensuring our normal growth, so that in the event of our returning to the tribal reserve, something he insistently believed would happen soon, we would blend in perfectly. This diet he administered religiously, seemingly bent on moulding George and me in his image. At first I had tried to resist the diet, but my father's severe looks frightened me.

A short, gaunt figure, with a smooth, tight, black-as-coal skin, large prominent jaws, thin, uneven lips whose sole function seemed to be the production of sneers, a broad nose with slightly flaring nostrils, small, bloodshot eyes which never cried, small, close-set ears, and a wide, prominent forehead—such were my father's fearsome features.

Born and bred in a tribal reserve and nearly twice my mother's age,   5
my father existed under the illusion, formed as much by a strange innate pride as by a blindness to everything but his own will, that someday all white people would disappear from South Africa, and black people would revert to their old ways of living. To prepare for this eventuality, he ruled the house strictly according to tribal law, tolerating no deviance, particularly from his children. At the same time that he was force-feeding us tribalism we were learning other ways of life, modern ways, from mingling with children whose parents had shed their tribal cloth and embraced Western culture.

My father's tribal rule had as its fulcrum the constant performing of rituals spanning the range of day-to-day living. There were rituals to protect the house from evildoers, to ward off starvation, to prevent us from becoming sick, to safeguard his job, to keep the police away, to bring us good luck, to make him earn more money and many others which my young mind could not understand. Somehow they did not make sense to me; they simply awed, confused and embarrassed me, and the only reason I participated in them night after night was because my father made certain that I did, by using, among other things, the whip, and the threat of the retributive powers of my ancestral spirits, whose favour the rituals were designed to curry. Along with the rituals, there were also tribal laws governing manners.

One day I intentionally broke one of these laws: I talked while eating.

"That's never done in my house," my father screamed at me as he rose from the table where he had been sitting alone, presiding over our meal. I was eating *pap 'n vleis*° out of the same bowl with George and Florah. We were sitting on the floor, about the brazier, and my mother was in the bedroom doing something.

"You don't have two mouths to afford you such luxury!" he fumed, advancing threateningly toward me, a cold sneer on his thin-lipped, cankerous mouth. He seemed ten feet tall.

---

pap 'n vleis: meat porridge

Terrified, I deserted the *pap 'n vleis* and fled to Mother.   10

"Bring him back here, woman!" my father called through the door as he unbuckled his rawhide belt. "He needs to be taught how to eat properly."

I began bawling, sensing I was about to be whipped.

My mother led me into the kitchen and pleaded for me. "He won't do it again. He's only a child, and you know how forgetful children are." At this point George and Florah stopped eating and watched with petrified eyes. "Don't give me that," snarled my father. "He's old enough to remember how to eat properly." He tore me away from my mother and lashed me. She tried to intervene, but my father shoved her aside and promised her the same. I never finished my meal; sobbing, I slunk off to bed, my limbs afire with pain where the rawhide had raised welts. The next day, as I nursed my wounds, while my father was at work, I told my mother that I hated him and promised her I would kill him when I grew up.

"Don't say that!" my mother reprimanded me.

"I will," I said stoutly, "if he won't leave me alone."   15

"He's your father, you know."

"He's not my father."

"Shut that bad mouth of yours!" My mother threatened to smack me.

"Why does he beat me, then?" I protested. "Other fathers don't beat their children." My friends always boasted that their fathers never laid a hand on them.

"He's trying to discipline you. He wants you to grow up to be   20 like him."

"What! Me! Never!" I shook with indignation. "I'm never going to be like him! Why should I?"

"Well, in the tribes sons grow up to be like their fathers."

"But we're not living in the tribes."

"But we're still of the tribes."

"I'm not," I said. Trying to focus the conversation on rituals, my   25 nemesis, I said, after a thoughtful pause, "Is that why Papa insists that we do rituals?"

"Yes."

"But other people don't."

"Everybody does rituals, Mr. Mathabane," my mother said. "You just don't notice it because they do theirs differently. Even white people do rituals."

"Why do people do rituals, Mama?"

"People do rituals because they were born in the tribes. And in the   30 tribes rituals are done every day. They are a way of life."

"But we don't live in the tribes," I countered. "Papa should stop doing rituals."

My mother laughed. "Well, it's not as simple as that. Your father grew up in the tribes, as you know. He didn't come to the city until he was quite old. It's hard to stop doing things when you're old. I, too, do rituals because I was raised in the tribes. Their meaning, child, will become clear as you grow up. Have patience."

But I had no patience with rituals, and I continued hating them.

Participation in my father's rituals sometimes led to the most appalling scenes, which invariably made me the laughingstock of my friends, who thought that my father, in his ritual garb, was the most hilarious thing they had ever seen since natives in Tarzan movies. Whenever they laughed at me I would feel embarrassed and would cry. I began seeking ways of distancing myself from my father's rituals. I found one: I decided I would no longer, in the presence of my friends, speak Venda, my father's tribal language. I began speaking Zulu, Sotho and Tsonga, the languages of my friends. It worked. I was no longer an object of mockery. My masquerade continued until my father got wind of it.

"My boy," he began. "Who is ruler of this house?"   *35*

"You are, Papa," I said with a trembling voice.

"Whose son are you?"

"Yours and Mama's."

"Whose?"

"Yours."   *40*

"That's better. Now tell me, which language do I speak?"

"Venda."

"Which does your mama speak?"

"Venda."

"Which should you speak?"

"Venda."

"Then why do I hear you're speaking other tongues; are you a prophet?" Before I could reply he grabbed me and lashed me thoroughly. Afterward he threatened to cut out my tongue if he ever again heard I wasn't speaking Venda. As further punishment, he increased the number of rituals I had to participate in. I hated him more for it.

---

1. What do you think Mathabane's dominant idea is?

2. At the beginning of the essay, there is a lot of concrete, specific description of the setting. How does this description contribute to Mathabane's purpose?

3. How does Mathabane use the people's own words through dialogue to make his dominant idea clear?

4. Is there a hero in this essay? A villain? Who are they? What is it that makes each person fill one of these roles?

5. What do you make of the conclusion? What idea or attitude does it leave you with? How does it contribute to what you see to be Mathabane's dominant idea?

FATHER AND I

Pär Lagerkvist

I remember one Sunday afternoon when I was about ten years old, Daddy took my hand and we went for a walk in the woods to hear the birds sing. We waved good-bye to mother, who was staying at home to prepare supper, and so couldn't go with us. The sun was bright and warm as we set out briskly on our way. We didn't take this bird-singing too seriously, as though it was something special or unusual. We were sensible people, Daddy and I. We were used to the woods and the creatures in them, so we didn't make any fuss about it. It was just because it was Sunday afternoon and Daddy was free. We went along the railway line where other people aren't allowed to go, but Daddy belonged to the railway and had a right to. And in this way we came direct into the woods and did not need to take a roundabout way. Then the bird song and all the rest began at once. They chirped in the bushes; hedge-sparrows, thrushes, and warblers; and we heard all the noises of the little creatures as we came into the woods. The ground was thick with anemones, the birches were dressed in their new leaves, and the pines had young, green shoots. There was such a pleasant smell everywhere. The mossy ground was steaming a little, because the sun was shining upon it. Everywhere there was life and noise; bumble-bees flew out of their holes, midges circled where it was damp. The birds shot out of the bushes to catch them and then dived back again. All of a sudden a train came rushing along and we had to go down the embankment. Daddy hailed the driver with two fingers to his Sunday hat: the driver saluted and waved his hand. Everything seemed on the move. As we went on our way along the sleepers° which lay and oozed tar in the sunshine, there was a smell of everything, machine oil and almond blossom, tar and heather, all mixed. We took big steps from sleeper to sleeper so as not to step among the stones, which were rough to walk on, and wore your shoes out. The rails shone in the sunshine. On both sides of the line stood the telephone poles that sang as we went by them. Yes! That was a fine day! The sky was absolutely clear. There wasn't a single cloud to be seen: there just couldn't be any on a day like this, according to what Daddy said. After a while we came to a field of oats on the right side of the line, where a farmer, whom we knew, had a clearing. The oats had grown thick and even; Daddy looked at it knowingly, and I could feel that he was satisfied. I didn't understand that sort of thing much, because I was born in town. Then we came to the bridge over the

---

sleeper: railroad tie

brook that mostly hadn't much water in it, but now there was plenty. We took hands so that we shouldn't fall down between the sleepers. From there it wasn't far to the railway gate-keeper's little place, which was quite buried in green. There were apple trees and gooseberry bushes right close to the house. We went in there, to pay a visit, and they offered us milk. We looked at the pigs, the hens, and the fruit trees, which were in full blossom, and then we went on again. We wanted to go to the river, because there it was prettier than anywhere else. There was something special about the river, because higher up stream it flowed past Daddy's old home. We never liked going back before we got to it, and, as usual, this time we got there after a fair walk. It wasn't far to the next station, but we didn't go on there. Daddy just looked to see whether the signals were right. He thought of everything. We stopped by the river, where it flowed broad and friendly in the sunshine, and the thick leafy trees on the banks mirrored themselves in the calm water. It was all so fresh and bright. A breeze came from the little lakes higher up. We climbed down the bank, went a little way along the very edge. Daddy showed me the fishing spots. When he was a boy he used to sit there on the stones and wait for perch all day long. Often he didn't get a single bite, but it was a delightful way to spend the day. Now he never had time. We played about for some time by the side of the river, and threw in pieces of bark that the current carried away, and we threw stones to see who could throw farthest. We were, by nature, very merry and cheerful, Daddy and I. After a while we felt a bit tired. We thought we had played enough, so we started off home again.

Then it began to get dark. The woods were changed. It wasn't quite dark yet, but almost. We made haste. Maybe mother was getting anxious, and waiting supper. She was always afraid that something might happen, though nothing had. This had been a splendid day. Everything had been just as it should, and we were satisfied with it all. It was getting darker and darker, and the trees were so queer. They stood and listened for the sound of our footsteps, as though they didn't know who we were. There was a glow-worm under one of them. It lay down there in the dark and stared at us. I held Daddy's hand tight, but he didn't seem to notice the strange light: he just went on. It was quite dark when we came to the bridge over the stream. It was roaring down underneath us as if it wanted to swallow us up, as the ground seemed to open under us. We went along the sleepers carefully, holding hands tight so that we shouldn't fall in. I thought Daddy would carry me over, but he didn't say anything about it. I suppose he wanted me to be like him, and not think anything of it. We went on. Daddy was so calm in the darkness, walking with even steps without speaking. He was thinking his own thoughts. I couldn't understand how he could be so calm when everything was so ghostly. I looked round scared. It was nothing but darkness everywhere. I hardly dared to breathe deeply, because then the darkness comes into one, and that was dangerous, I thought. One must die soon. I remember quite well thinking so then. The railway embankment was very steep. It finished in black night. The telephone posts stood up ghostlike against the sky, mumbling deep inside as though someone were speaking, way down in the earth. The white china hats sat there scared, cowering with fear, listening. It was all so creepy. Nothing was real, nothing was natural, all seemed a mystery. I went closer to Daddy, and whispered: "Why is it so creepy when it's dark?"

"No child, it isn't creepy," he said, and took my hand.

"Oh, yes, but it is, Daddy."

"No, you mustn't think that. We know there is a God don't we?" I felt so lonely, so abandoned. It was queer that it was only me that was frightened, and not Daddy. It was queer that we didn't feel the same about it. And it was queerer still that what he said didn't help, didn't stop me being frightened. Not even what he said about God helped. The thought of God made one feel creepy too. It was creepy to think that He was everywhere here in the darkness, down there under the trees, and in the telephone posts that mumbled so—probably that was Him everywhere. But all the same one could never see Him.

We went along silently, each of us thinking his own thoughts. My heart felt cramped as though the darkness had come in and was squeezing it.

Then, when we were in a bend, we suddenly heard a great noise behind us. We were startled out of our thoughts. Daddy pulled me down the embankment and held me tight, and a train rushed by; a black train. The lights were out in all the carriages, as it whizzed past us. What could it be? There shouldn't be any train now. We looked at it, frightened. The furnace roared in the big engine, where they shovelled in coal, and the sparks flew out into the night. It was terrible. The driver stood so pale and immovable, with such a stony look in the glare. Daddy didn't recognize him—didn't know who he was. He was just looking ahead as though he was driving straight into darkness, far into darkness, which had no end.

Startled and panting with fear I looked after the wild thing. It was swallowed up in the night. Daddy helped me up on to the line, and we hurried home. He said, "That was strange! What train was that I wonder? And I didn't know the driver either." Then he didn't say any more.

I was shaking all over. That had been for me—for my sake. I guessed what it meant. It was all the fear which would come to me, all the unknown; all that Daddy didn't know about, and couldn't save me from. That was how the world would be for me, and the strange life I should live; not like Daddy's, where everyone was known and sure. It wasn't a real world, or a real life—it just rushed burning into the darkness which had no end.

---

1. In this story, Lagerkvist does not create a narrator that steps away from the action and explains it for you. How does Lagerkvist lead you to a dominant idea?

2. How would you characterize the boy's father? What information does Lagerkvist give you to lead you to that characterization?

3. How old do you think the boy is? How does Lagerkvist lead you to that conclusion?

4. How would you define the relationship between the father and the son. How does Lagerkvist make that clear to you?

5. What elements of the setting does Lagerkvist describe for you? Why do you think he chose those elements out of all the possible things he might have described? How do they support what you take to be Lagerkvist's dominant idea?

6. How does the last paragraph function as a conclusion to everything that has come before? What idea or attitude does that paragraph leave you with.

❦ *An Invitation to Write*

Each of these selections deals with the relationship between father and son or perhaps parent and child. Do you think these selections would be the same if they told you about mothers and daughters? Fathers and daughters? Mothers and sons?

Try writing a short sketch—a poem, a short story, a short paper—in which you suggest the way parents and children relate to each other. Using precise language, make both the action and the setting create your dominant idea.

Developing a Vocabulary

Your world swarms with words. You deal with words all the time. You attend classes or use words to do your job; you watch television; listen to the radio; or you read books, newspapers, and magazines. Even during thought, most people subvocalize—that is, they put their thoughts into words which they speak silently to themselves.

Vocabulary is a resource you draw on when you want to make yourself clear, move your audience to action, suggest a feeling, or describe a scene or a situation. Therefore, the more words you have under your control and the more certain you are of the meanings of the words you use and the appropriate place to use them, the more powerful your writing will be. The larger your working vocabulary, the more tools you will have available to you when you write.

There are a number of effective ways to add to your vocabulary. The first, and most important, of these is to read everything you can. When you read, you actively work with words, combining them to gain meaning from them. It really doesn't matter what you read, as long as you keep reading, as long as you take words in and make meaning out of them. Reading can also give you good ideas for using words in your own writing. Some people copy into a notebook pieces of writing that they find especially effective, saving them for a time they might want to imitate the writers' use of words or just because they like them. Imitating another person's good writing is not dishonest. Most excellent writers imitate other writers as part of learning the sound of their own writing.

✎ An Invitation to Write

Find a piece of writing, no more than a paragraph or two, that you especially like. Using your own subject matter, imitate the writer's use of words, rhythms, organization.

If you're working with a group, provide a copy of your writing and the piece you've imitated to each member. Explain how the choices you made regarding what you used of the other writer's techniques suited your purpose as well as how your topic invited you to modify the writer's approach.

The dictionary is an especially good vocabulary resource, not only for looking up the definitions of words you don't understand, but also for seeing how words themselves are put together. Learning the ways words are put together helps you tease the meaning out of words you've never seen before. In most good dictionaries, each word has not only a definition but also an etymology, if there is one available. For example, here is a definition from the *Random House Dictionary of the English Language*:

> **et-y-mol-o-gy** n., pl. **gies** 1. The study of historical linguistic change, esp. as applied to individual words. 2. an account of the history of a particular word. 3. the derivation of a word. [<L *etymologia* <Gk= *etymolog(os)* studying words (see ETYMON, LOGOS)] —**et-y-mo-log-i-cal,** adj. —**et-y-mo-log-i-cal-ly,** adv. —**et-y-mol-o-gist,** n.

As you can see, a definition often refers you to other words. If you look up *etymon* (the next word in most dictionaries), you'll find that it has as its stem *etymos,* from the Greek for "true," "actual," or "real." If you look up *logos,* you'll find that it is derived from the Greek for "a word, saying, principle, speech, discourse, thought, proportion, ratio, reckoning." So *etymology* means "the real (or true) word." But look at what else you've just learned. Knowing that "logos" becomes "(o)-logy," you suddenly have access to the meanings of other words. For example, *biology:* "the word of life"; *anthropology:* "the word of humanity"; or *astrology:* "the word of the stars." You might also guess that "word" probably does not have a literal meaning in the definitions of these words, but comes closer to meaning "the study of." Knowing how the parts of words work together gives you access to still more words.

Another resource that is available to you is a thesaurus. Because a thesaurus is a list of words and their synonyms, it is an invaluable tool, but you must also use it with a good deal of caution. Although synonyms generally express the same concept, each one carries slightly different meanings or associations. Going to a thesaurus and choosing any of the synonyms for a word because you have been told not to repeat a word too often or because you think the synonym "sounds better" is often not an effective approach to strong writing. First, you have to be sure of the meaning of the word you choose as well as what the word suggests. If you do not investigate the meaning of a synonym, you can find your writing saying something you did not intend it to—something that can affect your readers in ways you did not have in mind. In short, you can embarrass yourself. For example, a student writes a paper having to do with love as an emotion that makes people act in ways that make them better persons. While revising the paper, this writer shows it to a friend, who suggests that the word *love* is repeated too often. In the thesaurus, the writer finds a number of synonyms for *love,* among them, *venery.* She decides that *venery* "sounds good" and puts it in her paper here and there in place of *love.* Had she looked up *venery* in a dictionary, she would have discovered that its meaning (*venereal* has the same stem) is entirely inappropriate for her paper. Given the thrust of her paper, the writer probably would not want to use *venery* as one of her synonyms for *love.* Thus, you can easily misuse the power of a thesaurus and make yourself look silly along the way by choosing a synonym whose definition you are unsure of and by not confirming your choices with a dictionary.

An Experiment with the Thesaurus

Alone or in your group, choose a word that you have read recently, one whose meaning you don't know or at least are not entirely certain of. Look up that word in a *hardcover* dictionary and list the stem(s) of the word. Use those stems to find other words with the same source. Then go to a thesaurus and list three synonyms for the word you selected. Look up those synonyms in a dictionary. Report to your group how the synonyms differ in meaning from the word you began with.

VOICE

Voice is style and more. It is the choices you make in your writing that give it a human sound. Voice is the way you, as one human being, reflect your relationship to your idea and communicate your human responses to other human beings. Because your voice is the flesh-and-blood element of your writing, it is also the way you can create and focus your audience's response to what you have to tell them—your dominant idea and your support.

You have many resources for expressing voice that you've used almost without conscious decision in your writing and your talk. Listen to a person's words and sentences when he or she is angry and see how they reflect that person's tone: his or her feelings. You will probably find that angry people rarely speak in long, involved sentences, nor are their angry words many-syllabled and abstract. On the other hand, in a formal situation, especially when a person has to make a presentation of some sort, his or her tone tends to reflect the circumstance. The person's sentences become longer and more complex, and the language becomes more formal and impersonal. That person takes on a "formal" voice. In addition, the images a person chooses, the examples he or she uses to illustrate his or her point, even the person's choice of patterns of sound often reinforce that person's writing or speaking voice.

It is important to control your voice and to make it appropriate to your subject because the choices you make regarding the emotions your writing reveals have an important, direct effect on your audience's response to your ideas. Many writers have been defeated by their inability to control voice, by choices which do not reflect, or which even contradict, the attitude they want their readers to take. Successful writers control voice in such a way as to intentionally create a desired effect in their audience.

 ### Working with the Readings

Alone or in your group, read the following poems and answer the questions that follow the second one.

RINGING THE BELLS

Anne Sexton

> And this is the way they ring
> the bells in Bedlam
> and this is the bell–lady
> who comes each Tuesday morning
> to give us a music lesson   5
> and because the attendants make you go
> and because we mind by instinct,
> like bees caught in the wrong hive,
> we are the circle of the crazy ladies
> who sit in the lounge of the mental house   10
> and smile at the smiling woman
> who passes us each a bell,
> who points to the bell in my hand
> that holds my bell, E flat,
> and this is the gray dress next to me   15

who grumbles as if it were special
to be old, to be old,
and this is the small hunched squirrel girl
on the other side of me
who picks at the hairs over her lip,   20
who picks at the hairs over her lip all day,
and this is how the bells really sound,
as untroubled and clean
as a workable kitchen,
and this is always my bell responding   25
to my hand that responds to the lady
who points at me, E flat;
and although we are no better for it,
they tell you to go. And you do.

THE UNKNOWN CITIZEN

W. H. Auden

*(To JS/07/m/378 This Marble Monument is Erected
by the State)*

He was found by the Bureau of Statistics to be
One against whom there was no official complaint,
And all the reports on his conduct agree
That, in the modern sense of an old-fashioned word, he was a saint,
For in everything he did he served the Greater Community.   5
Except for the War till the day he retired
He worked in a factory and never got fired
But satisfied his employers, Fudge Motors Inc.
Yet he wasn't a scab or odd in his views,
For his Union reports that he paid his dues,   10
(Our report on his Union shows it was sound)
And our Social Psychology workers found
That he was popular with his mates and liked a drink.
The Press are convinced that he bought a paper every day
And that his reactions to advertisements were normal in every way. 15
Policies taken out in his name prove that he was fully insured,
And his Health-card shows that he was in hospital once but left it cured.
Both Producers Research and High-Grade Living declare
He was fully sensible to the advantages of the installment plan
And had everything necessary to the Modern Man,   20

A phonograph, a radio, a car, and a frigidaire.
Our researchers into Public Opinion are content
That he held the proper opinions for the time of year;
When there was peace, he was for peace; when there was war,
  he went.
He was married and added five children to the population,   25
Which our Eugenist says was the right number for a parent of his
  generation.
And our teachers report that he never interfered with their education.
Was he free? Was he happy? The question is absurd:
Had anything been wrong, we should certainly have heard.

———————

1. Compare the dominant ideas of the two poems. How are they the same? How are they different?

2. Compare the voices of the two poems. Try to describe the two voices. How does Sexton create the voice of her poem? How does Auden create the voice of his poem?

3. How does the voice of each poem react with the subject of the poem? How does the combination of the two affect your attitude toward both the speaker and the dominant idea?

———————

DENOTATION AND CONNOTATION

A writer who knows the difference between connotation and denotation has mastered one of the most important ways of controlling tone and voice. The *denotation* of a word is its literal meaning––the one you find in a dictionary. The *connotation* of a word is the baggage of values, associations, feelings, and judgments that a word carries with it. For example, a person walking down the street can

amble
hike
promenade
saunter
stagger
stamp
stride
stroll

down the street. Each word implies a slightly different attitude toward the person on the part of the writer or a slightly different state of mind or condition on the person's part. In a similar manner, consider the ways to say a person died:

X died.
X has expired.
X is deceased.
X passed on.
X went to his (her) reward.
X was terminated.
X kicked the bucket.
X bit the dirt.
X is pushing up daisies.
X is with the angels.

Working with the Readings

Read the following pieces of writing and, alone or in your group, answer the questions that follow each of them.

MY ABORTION

Deborah Salazar

The procedure itself was the easiest part. A friend had told me to close my eyes and think about anything, think about Donald Duck—sweet and useless advice, I thought at the time—but when I heard the machine come on and the doctor say, "The cervix is slanted at a right angle, this could be a problem; okay, honey, *relax,*" I thought, Donald Duck, Donald Duck, Donald Duck, Donald Duck. I will never be able to watch another Donald Duck cartoon without thinking about my abortion, but I went through the experience feeling pretty calm and entitled. Twenty-seven years old and pregnant for the first time in my life. God bless America, I thought, I sure as hell want a cheap, legal, safe abortion.

After I learned that I was pregnant, I started practicing a necessary detachment. The Supreme Court was due to hand down its *Webster* decision any day, and the usual mobs of protesters around women's clinics were doubling in size. I got up before dawn on the fifteenth of June and packed a paper bag with a sweater and socks (because the receptionist said it would be cold inside the clinic) and maxi pads. I wanted to get there as soon as the doors opened, before most of the cross-waving, sign-carrying, chanting, singing protesters showed up. When I pulled into the clinic parking lot with my friend Beth, I saw only two people standing on the curb: a woman, dressed all in black, and a man. As we got closer, I saw that the woman was about my age, with straight black hair and pale eyes turned skyward. She was moaning the words, "Don't kill me, Mommy, don't kill me."

The man and the woman followed our car until it stopped at the door. I stepped out, and the man stood in front of me. He was tall, wearing a suit and tie and singing, "Jesus loves the little children." I laughed in his face. Strange. Three years ago I had worked as a volunteer escort at this very clinic, and I'd always been so solemn with these people. I never would've expected to laugh today. The man obviously hadn't expected me to laugh either. He got angry. "Lesbian!" he called after me as I walked into the clinic. "You're a lesbian. That's why you hate babies!" A tall young man wearing an official clinic-escort T-shirt was standing at the threshold. "Sorry about this," he muttered as I passed by. I was still laughing. "I wish I were a lesbian," I said a little hysterically. "I wouldn't be pregnant." And then I was inside the clinic.

I knew the routine. I took my forms and my plastic cup. I went directly to the bathroom. I could hear the protesters while I was in the bathroom. I could hear them the whole time I was in the clinic. The chanting was discontinuous, but it was louder every time it started up. "Murderers! Murderers!" I could hear them in the dressing room, in the weigh-in room, in counseling, in recovery, although I don't remember if I heard them in the procedure room itself. I was told later that my encounter with the protesters had been relatively undramatic: one escort said that these days he was seeing protesters trying to hold car doors shut while women fought to get out.

After I turned in my urine cup, I sat back in the waiting room and   5
started filling out forms. One of them was a personal questionnaire and included the question, "What method of birth control were you using at the time you got pregnant?" I thought about lying for a second before I checked the box beside "none." One of the protesters outside had started playing a tape of a baby crying. I signed my name over and over. Yes, I understand the risks involved, yes, I understand that the alternatives to abortion are birth and adoption. I wanted to do more—I wanted to fill out a page or so explaining why I had chosen to do this. I wanted to explain to someone that I was a responsible person; you see, ladies and gentlemen, I never had sex without condoms unless I was having my period; I got pregnant during my period, isn't there something I could sign swearing to that? I had a three-day affair with a friend, I'm broke and unemployed, I can't give up a baby for adoption, I can't afford to be pregnant while I look for a job.

In counseling, I was asked why I'd gone off the pill, and I didn't hesitate to respond, "I can get rid of an accidental pregnancy. I can't get rid of cancer." In the lounge room where I sat in my dressing gown before going in to see the doctor, there was a tiny television (Pee-wee Herman was on) and a table with magazines (*Cosmopolitan, Vogue, American Baby*). The room was already filled to capacity, all twelve chairs taken, when the little bowhead came in. She couldn't have been more than seventeen, wearing only her gown and a very big white satin bow in her hair. She was a beauty. She looked like she belonged on a homecoming float. She had been crying. "I hate them," she announced, dropping her shopping bag of clothes on the floor. "They don't have to say the things they say. Makes me want to go out there and shoot them with a gun."

"You can't hear them that well in here, honey," one of the older women said. "You can watch the cartoons."

"You know what one of them called my mama?" the beauty said. "Called her a slut, an unchristian woman. My mama yelled back that I got raped by a priest, that's how come I'm here." Stares. The bowhead picked up her shopping bag and leaned against the wall. She spoke again in a quieter voice. "I didn't really get raped by a priest. My mama just said that."

The doctor was late that morning. Outside, the chants were getting louder, competing with Pee-wee Herman, who was on full blast. The protesters were singing a hymn when my name was called. I walked down a short hallway in my bare feet, and then liquid Valium injected directly into my left arm made everything after that feel like it was taking place on another planet. I remember that the doctor was wearing a dark red surgical outfit and that it looked pretty gruesome—I wished he'd worn the traditional pale blue or green. I remember that the Valium made me want to laugh and I didn't want to laugh because I was afraid I'd wiggle, and I'd been warned *not* to wiggle unless I wanted my uterus perforated. I'd been at the clinic six hours already, preparing for this little operation that would take only five minutes. I remember that after the machine came on, it seemed like less than five minutes. I remember that it hurt and that I was amazed at how empty, relieved, and not pregnant I felt as soon as it was over. The cramps that followed were painful but not terribly so; I could feel my uterus contracting, trying to collapse back to its former size. I was led by a nurse into a dark room, where I sat on a soft mat in a soft chair and bled for a while. I closed my eyes. The woman in the next seat was sobbing softly. I knew it was the blond with the white bow in her hair. I reached over and took her hand in mine. The Valium made me feel as though we were both wearing gloves. Her hand was so still I wondered if she knew I was there, but the sobbing grew softer and softer and eventually it just stopped.

---

1. What do you think is the voice of Salazar's essay? What elements of the writing lead you to your conclusion?

2. If you went through the same experience as Salazar, what would your emotions be?

3. Do you think Salazar's voice is appropriate to her subject? Why? How did her tone affect you in relation to her subject?

4. Can you think of other voices Salazar might have created? What would their effect on you be?

HOLY SONNET 14

John Donne

Batter my heart, three-personed God, for you
As yet but knock, breathe, shine, and seek to mend;
That I may rise and stand, o'erthrow me; and bend
Your force to break, blow, burn, and make me new.
I, like an usurped town, to another due,   5
Labor to admit you, but oh, to no end;
Reason, your viceroy° in me, me should defend,
But is captived, and proves weak or untrue.
Yet dearly I love you and would be loved fain,°
But am betrothed unto your enemy;   10
Divorce me, untie or break that knot again,
Take me to you, imprison me, for I
Except you enthrall me, never shall be free,
Nor ever chaste, except you ravish me.

---

1. Who is the speaker in this poem speaking to? What does he want?

2. Just as it is possible for a person's mood to change, it is equally possible for the voice to change in a piece of writing. Is there more than one tone in this poem? Name the voice or voices you see in Donne's piece.

3. How does the speaker communicate his voice(s) in the poem? Is it simply a matter of denotative words, or has he used some connotations that communicate a voice?

4. How does the voice(s) the writer chooses for his speaker define the relationship he has and wishes to have with the being he speaks to?

5. Does the combination of the voice(s) the speaker communicates, the metaphors he uses, and the speaker's audience define the problem the speaker is trying to solve? What is the problem?

---

7. *viceroy:* a person appointed to rule
9. *fain:* gladly

POPULAR MECHANICS

Raymond Carver

Early that day the weather turned and the snow was melting into dirty water. Streaks of it ran down from the little shoulder-high window that faced the backyard. Cars slushed by on the street outside, where it was getting dark. But it was getting dark on the inside too.

He was in the bedroom pushing clothes into a suitcase when she came to the door.

I'm glad you're leaving! I'm glad you're leaving! she said. Do you hear?

He kept on putting his things into the suitcase.

Son of a bitch! I'm so glad you're leaving! She began to cry. You can't   5
even look me in the face, can you?

Then she noticed the baby's picture on the bed and picked it up.

He looked at her and she wiped her eyes and stared at him before turning and going back to the living room.

Bring that back, he said.

Just get your things and get out, she said.

He did not answer. He fastened the suitcase, put on his coat, looked   10
around the bedroom before turning off the light. Then he went out to the living room.

She stood in the doorway of the little kitchen, holding the baby.

I want the baby, he said.

Are you crazy?

No, but I want the baby. I'll get someone to come by for his things.

You're not touching this baby, she said.   15

The baby had begun to cry and she uncovered the blanket from around his head.

Oh, oh, she said, looking at the baby.

He moved toward her.

For God's sake! she said. She took a step back into the kitchen.

I want the baby.   20

Get out of here!

She turned and tried to hold the baby over in a corner behind the stove.

But he came up. He reached across the stove and tightened his hands on the baby.

Let go of him, he said.

Get away, get away! she cried.   25

The baby was red-faced and screaming. In the scuffle they knocked down a flowerpot that hung behind the stove.

He crowded her into the wall then, trying to break her grip. He held on to the baby and pushed with all his weight.

Let go of him, he said.

Don't, she said. You're hurting the baby, she said.

I'm not hurting the baby, he said.   30

The kitchen window gave no light. In the near-dark he worked on her fisted fingers with one hand and with the other hand he gripped the screaming baby up under an arm near the shoulder.

She felt her fingers being forced open. She felt the baby going from her.

No! she screamed just as her hands came loose.

She would have it, this baby. She grabbed for the baby's other arm. She caught the baby around the wrist and leaned back.

But he would not let go. He felt the baby slipping out of his hands   35 and he pulled back very hard.

In this manner, the issue was decided.

---

1. How does Carver use description in this story? Does it create a voice that affects your response to the events that follow?

2. What is the dominant point of view in this story? How does Carver use it to set the voice?

3. How do you understand the title of this story? How does it function in relation to the story?

4. The narrator speaks directly to the audience only once, but when he does, it's clear that he is in control of everything you see and hear. How does what he selects to show you help create the voice in the story? What voice does the last sentence convey to you? Does it seem appropriate to the events? Why do you think so?

❧ *An Invitation to Write*

Write a short essay, a poem, or a story in which you consciously choose a voice and use imagery, metaphor (if you want), and denotation to communicate that voice to your audience.

IRONY

Although *irony* is challenging to use well, its power can add immeasurably to the effect of your writing by inviting your reader to step away from the ideas you express or the actions you describe and making him or her look at them more critically. This is so because irony depends on difference and distance. It works through a contrast between what the writer or a character in the writing itself believes is so and expresses in his or her writing or speech, actions, or thoughts and what the audience knows to be true. Once the reader sees the difference, he or she must step back and put some distance between him- or herself and the words to examine and understand that difference. The writer uses the contrast and creates the distance to speak ironically.

Sarcasm, a form of *verbal irony* that you create by saying the opposite of what you mean, is familiar to most people. For example, one day you sleep through the alarm, rush to get dressed and miss breakfast, arrive at your job five minutes late anyway, have nothing go right at your job, and run out of gas on the way home because in your rush that morning you forgot to stop at the gas station. Dragging yourself through your front door, you hear the phone ringing. When you pick it up, your friend asks you how your day was.

"Just great," you answer.

Now, the difference between how your day really was and what you say to your friend creates the verbal irony called sarcasm. Of course, in this situation, you would have had tone of voice to create the irony. But although tone of voice is impossible to convey directly in writing, a writer creating verbal irony will give you enough information about the events surrounding the ironic statement to make the irony clear. In other words, the author makes his or her intent clear by presenting you with enough relevant facts through exposition, action, or previous dialogue to allow you to understand his or her point.

Working with a Reading

Alone or in your group, read the following poem and answer the questions that follow it.

HE PREACHED UPON BREADTH

Emily Dickinson

> He preached upon "Breadth" till it argued him narrow—
> The Broad are too broad to define
> And of "Truth" until it proclaimed him a Liar—
> The Truth never flaunted a Sign—
>
> Simplicity fled from his counterfeit presence   5
> As Gold the Pyrites° would shun—
> What confusion would cover the innocent Jesus
> To meet so enabled a Man!

---

6. *Pyrites:* iron pyrite, known as fool's gold

---

1. Note the examples of irony in this poem and define how they work.
2. Who is the victim of Dickinson's irony in this poem? What type of a person is he?
3. What dominant idea does Dickinson communicate to her audience through her use of irony?

Dramatic irony depends on the difference between what a character says or intends and what the reader knows to be the case. A situation in which a friend tells you of his or her expectations while you know of facts that will make those goals impossible to achieve is a good example of dramatic irony. As in the case of verbal irony, in dramatic irony the writer has to present you with enough facts about both the people and the situation that surrounds them so that the difference becomes clear. When the author defines the difference that creates dramatic irony, he or she helps you to understand the situation.

 Working with a Reading

Read the following story and, alone or in your group, answer the questions that follow it.

THE REAL THING

Henry James

I

When the porter's wife, who used to answer the house-bell, announced "A gentleman and a lady, sir," I had, as I often had in those days—the wish being father to the thought—an immediate vision of sitters. Sitters my visitors in this case proved to be; but not in the sense I should have preferred. There was nothing at first however to indicate that they mightn't have come for a portrait. The gentleman, a man of fifty, very high and very straight, with a moustache slightly grizzled and a dark grey walking-coat admirably fitted, both of which I noted professionally—I don't mean as a barber or yet as a tailor—would have struck me as a celebrity if celebrities often were striking. It was a truth of which I had for some time been conscious that a figure with a good deal of frontage°

---

frontage: impressive appearance

was, as one might say, almost never a public institution. A glance at the lady helped to remind me of this paradoxical law: she also looked too distinguished to be a "personality." Moreover one would scarcely come across two variations together.

Neither of the pair immediately spoke—they only prolonged the preliminary gaze suggesting that each wished to give the other a chance. They were visibly shy; they stood there letting me take them in—which, as I afterwards perceived, was the most practical thing they could have done. In this way their embarrassment served their cause. I had seen people painfully reluctant to mention that they desired anything so gross as to be represented on canvas; but the scruples of my new friends appeared almost insurmountable. Yet the gentleman might have said "I should like a portrait of my wife," and the lady might have said "I should like a portrait of my husband." Perhaps they were n't husband and wife—this naturally would make the matter more delicate. Perhaps they wished to be done together—in which case they ought to have brought a third person to break the news.

"We come from Mr. Rivet," the lady finally said with a dim smile that had the effect of a moist sponge passed over a "sunk"° piece of painting, as well as of a vague allusion to vanished beauty. She was as tall and straight, in her degree, as her companion, and with ten years less to carry. She looked as sad as a woman could look whose face was not charged with expression; that is her tinted oval mask showed waste as an exposed surface shows friction. The hand of time had played over her freely, but to an effect of elimination. She was slim and stiff, and so well-dressed, in dark blue cloth, with lappets° and pockets and buttons, that it was clear she employed the same tailor as her husband. The couple had an indefinable air of prosperous thrift—they evidently got a good deal of luxury for their money. If I was to be one of their luxuries it would behove me to consider my terms.

"Ah Claude Rivet recommended me?" I echoed; and I added that it was very kind of him, though I could reflect that, as he only painted landscape, this was n't a sacrifice.

The lady looked very hard at the gentleman, and the gentleman 5 looked round the room. Then staring at the floor a moment and stroking his moustache, he rested his pleasant eyes on me with the remark: "He said you were the right one."

"I try to be, when people want to sit."

"Yes, we should like to," said the lady anxiously.

"Do you mean together?"

My visitors exchanged a glance. "If you could do anything with *me* I suppose it would be double," the gentleman stammered.

---

sunk: faded
lappets: folds, flaps

"Oh yes, there's naturally a higher charge for two figures than   10
for one."

"We should like to make it pay," the husband confessed.

"That's very good of you," I returned, appreciating so unwonted a
sympathy—for I supposed he meant pay the artist.

A sense of strangeness seemed to dawn on the lady. "We mean for
the illustrations—Mr. Rivet said you might put one in."

"Put in—an illustration?" I was equally confused.

"Sketch her off, you know," said the gentleman, colouring.   15

It was only then that I understood the service Claude Rivet had rendered me; he had told them how I worked in black-and-white, for magazines, for storybooks, for sketches of contemporary life, and consequently
had copious employment for models. These things were true, but it was
not less true—I may confess it now; whether because the aspiration was
to lead to everything or to nothing I leave the reader to guess—that I
could n't get the honours, to say nothing of the emoluments, of a great
painter of portraits out of my head. My "illustrations" were my pot-
boilers; I looked to a different branch of art—far and away the most interesting it had always seemed to me—to perpetuate my fame. There
was no shame in looking to it also to make my fortune; but that fortune
was by so much further from being made from the moment my visitors
wished to be "done" for nothing. I was disappointed; for in the pictorial
sense I had immediately *seen* them. I had seized their type—I had already
settled what I would do with it. Something that would n't absolutely have
pleased them, I afterwards reflected.

"Ah you're—you're—a—?" I began as soon as I had mastered my
surprise. I could n't bring out the dingy word "models": it seemed so
little to fit the case.

"We have n't had much practice," said the lady.

"We've got to *do* something, and we've thought that an artist in your
line might perhaps make something of us," her husband threw off. He
further mentioned that they did n't know many artists and that they had
gone first, on the off-chance—he painted views of course, but sometimes
put in figures; perhaps I remembered—to Mr. Rivet, whom they had
met a few years before at a place in Norfolk where he was sketching.

"We used to sketch a little ourselves," the lady hinted.   20

"It's very awkward, but we absolutely *must* do something," her husband went on.

"Of course we're not so *very* young," she admitted with a wan smile.

With the remark that I might as well know something more about
them the husband had handed me a card extracted from a neat new
pocket-book—their appurtenances were all of the freshest—and in-
scribed with the words "Major Monarch." Impressive as these words
were they did n't carry my knowledge much further; but my visitor presently added: "I've left the army and we've had the misfortune to lose our
money. In fact our means are dreadfully small."

"It's awfully trying—a regular strain," said Mrs. Monarch.

They evidently wished to be discreet—to take care not to swagger because they were gentlefolk. I felt them willing to recognise this as something of a drawback, at the same time that I guessed at an underlying sense—their consolation in adversity—that they *had* their points. They certainly had; but these advantages struck me as preponderantly social; such for instance as would help to make a drawing-room look well. However, a drawing-room was always, or ought to be, a picture.

In consequence of his wife's allusion to their age Major Monarch   25 observed: "Naturally it's more for the figure that we thought of going in. We can still hold ourselves up." On the instant I saw that the figure was indeed their strong point. His "naturally" did n't sound vain, but it lighted up the question. "*She* has the best one," he continued, nodding at his wife with a pleasant after-dinner absence of circumlocution. I could only reply, as if we were in fact sitting over our wine, that this did n't prevent his own from being very good; which led him in turn to make answer: "We thought that if you ever have to do people like us we might be something like it. *She* particularly—for a lady in a book, you know."

I was so amused by them that, to get more of it, I did my best to take their point of view; and though it was an embarrassment to find myself appraising physically, as if they were animals on hire or useful blacks, a pair of whom I should have expected to meet only in one of the relations in which criticism is tacit, I looked at Mrs. Monarch judicially enough to be able to exclaim after a moment with conviction: "Oh yes, a lady in a book!" She was singularly like a bad illustration.

"We'll stand up, if you like," said the Major; and he raised himself before me with a really grand air.

I could take his measure at a glance—he was six feet two and a perfect gentleman. It would have paid any club in process of formation and in want of a stamp to engage him at a salary to stand in the principal window. What struck me at once was that in coming to me they had rather missed their vocation; they could surely have been turned to better account for advertising purposes. I could n't of course see the thing in detail, but I could see them make somebody's fortune—I don't mean their own. There was something in them for a waistcoat-maker, an hotel-keeper or a soap–vendor. I could imagine "We always use it" pinned on their bosoms with the greatest effect; I had a vision of the brilliancy with which they would launch a table d'hôte.°

Mrs. Monarch sat still, not from pride but from shyness, and presently her husband said to her: "Get up, my dear, and show how smart you are." She obeyed, but she had no need to get up to show it. She walked to the end of the studio and then came back blushing, her fluttered eyes on the

---

table d'hôte: a restaurant

partner of her appeal. I was reminded of an incident I had accidentally had a glimpse of in Paris—being with a friend there, a dramatist about to produce a play, when an actress came to him to ask to be entrusted with a part. She went through her paces before him, walked up and down as Mrs. Monarch was doing. Mrs. Monarch did it quite as well, but I abstained from applauding. It was very odd to see such people apply for such poor pay. She looked as if she had ten thousand a year. Her husband had used the word that described her: she was in the London current jargon essentially and typically "smart." Her figure was, in the same order of ideas, conspicuously and irreproachably "good." For a woman of her age her waist was surprisingly small; her elbow moreover had the orthodox crook. She held her head at the conventional angle, but why did she come to *me?* She ought to have tried on jackets at a big shop. I feared my visitors were not only destitute but "artistic"—which would be a great complication. When she sat down again I thanked her, observing that what a draughtsman most valued in his model was the faculty of keeping quiet.

"Oh *she* can keep quiet," said Major Monarch. Then he added jo-   30
cosely: "I've always kept her quiet."

"I'm not a nasty fidget, am I?" It was going to wring tears from me, I felt, the way she hid her head, ostrich-like, in the other broad bosom.

The owner of this expanse addressed his answer to me. "Perhaps it is n't out of place to mention—because we ought to be quite business-like, ought n't we?—that when I married her she was known as the Beautiful Statue."

"Oh dear!" said Mrs. Monarch ruefully.

"Of course I should want a certain amount of expression," I rejoined.

"Of *course!*"—and I had never heard such unanimity.   35

"And then I suppose you know that you'll get awfully tired."

"Oh, we *never* get tired!" they eagerly cried.

"Have you had any kind of practice?"

They hesitated—they looked at each other. "We've been photo-graphed—*immensely,*" said Mrs. Monarch.

"She means the fellows have asked us themselves," added the Major.   40

"I see—because you're so good-looking."

"I don't know what they thought, but they were always after us."

"We always got our photographs for nothing," smiled Mrs. Monarch.

"We might have brought some, my dear," her husband remarked.

"I'm not sure we have any left. We've given quantities away," she   45
explained to me.

"With our autographs and that sort of thing," said the Major.

"Are they to be got in the shops?" I enquired as a harmless pleasantry.

"Oh yes, *hers*—they used to be."

"Not now," said Mrs. Monarch with her eyes on the floor.

II

I could fancy the "sort of thing" they put on the presentation copies   *50*
of their photographs, and I was sure they wrote a beautiful hand. It was
odd how quickly I was sure of everything that concerned them. If they
were now so poor as to have to earn shillings and pence they could never
have had much of a margin. Their good looks had been their capital, and
they had good-humouredly made the most of the career that this resource
marked out for them. It was in their faces, the blankness, the deep intellectual repose of the twenty years of country-house visiting that had
given them pleasant intonations. I could see the sunny drawing-rooms,
sprinkled with periodicals she did n't read, in which Mrs. Monarch had
continuously sat; I could see the wet shrubberies in which she had
walked, equipped to admiration for either exercise. I could see the rich
covers° the Major had helped to shoot and the wonderful garments in
which, late at night, he repaired to the smoking-room to talk about them.
I could imagine their leggings and waterproofs, their knowing tweeds and
rugs, their rolls of sticks and cases of tackle and neat umbrellas; and I could
evoke the exact appearance of their servants and the compact variety of
their luggage on the platforms of country stations.

They gave small tips, but they were liked; they did n't do anything
themselves, but they were welcome. They looked so well everywhere;
they gratified the general relish for stature, complexion and "form." They
knew it without fatuity or vulgarity, and they respected themselves in
consequence. They were n't superficial; they were thorough and kept
themselves up—it had been their line. People with such a taste for activity had to have some line. I could feel how even in a dull house they
could have been counted on for the joy of life. At present something had
happened—it didn't matter what, their little income had grown less, it
had grown least—and they had to do something for pocket-money.
Their friends could like them, I made out, without liking to support
them. There was something about them that represented credit—their
clothes, their manners, their type; but if credit is a large empty pocket in
which an occasional chink reverberates, the chink at least must be audible. What they wanted of me was to help to make it so. Fortunately
they had no children—I soon divined that. They would also perhaps wish
our relations to be kept secret: this was why it was "for the figure"—the
reproduction of the face would betray them.

I liked them—I felt, quite as their friends must have done—they
were so simple; and I had no objection to them if they would suit. But
somehow with all their perfections I did n't easily believe in them. After
all they were amateurs, and the ruling passion of my life was the detestation

---

covers: woods and thickets from which game is driven for hunters

of the amateur. Combined with this was another perversity—an innate preference for the represented subject over the real one: the defect of the real one was so apt to be a lack of representation. I liked things that appeared; then one was sure. Whether they *were* or not was a subordinate and almost always a profitless question. There were other considerations, the first of which was that I already had two or three recruits in use, notably a young person with big feet, in alpaca, from Kilburn, who for a couple of years had come to me regularly for my illustrations and with whom I was still—perhaps ignobly—satisfied. I frankly explained to my visitors how the case stood, but they had taken more precautions than I supposed. They had reasoned out their opportunity, for Claude Rivet had told them of the projected *édition de luxe* of one of the writers of our day—the rarest of the novelists—who, long neglected by the multitudinous vulgar and dearly prized by the attentive (need I mention Philip Vincent?) had had the happy fortune of seeing, late in life, the dawn and then the full light of a higher criticism; an estimate in which on the part of the public there was something really of expiation. The edition preparing, planned by a publisher of taste, was practically an act of high reparation; the wood-cuts with which it was to be enriched were the homage of English art to one of the most independent representations of English letters. Major and Mrs. Monarch confessed to me they had hoped I might be able to work *them* into my branch of the enterprise. They knew I was to do the first of the books, "Rutland Ramsay," but I had to make clear to them that my participation in the rest of the affair—this first book was to be a test—must depend on the satisfaction I should give. If this should be limited my employers would drop me with scarce common forms. It was therefore a crisis for me, and naturally I was making special preparations, looking about for new people, should they be necessary, and securing the best types. I admitted however that I should like to settle down to two or three good models who would do for everything.

"Should we have often to—a—put on special clothes?" Mrs. Monarch timidly demanded.

"Dear yes—that's half the business."

"And should we be expected to supply our own costumes?"   55

"Oh no; I've got a lot of things. A painter's models put on—or put off—anything he likes."

"And you mean—a—the same?"

"The same?"

Mrs. Monarch looked at her husband again.

"Oh she was just wondering," he explained, "if the costumes are in   60 *general* use." I had to confess that they were, and I mentioned further that some of them—I had a lot of genuine greasy last-century things—had served their time, a hundred years ago, on living world-stained men and women; on figures not perhaps so far removed, in that vanished world, from *their* type, the Monarchs', *quoi!°* of a breeched and bewigged age. "We'll put on anything that *fits,*" said the Major.

"Oh I arrange that—they fit in the pictures."

"I'm afraid I should do better for the modern books. I'd come as you like," said Mrs. Monarch.

"She has got a lot of clothes at home: they might do for contemporary life," her husband continued.

"Oh I can fancy scenes in which you'd be quite natural." And indeed I could see the slipshod rearrangements of stale properties—the stories I tried to produce pictures for without the exasperation of reading them—whose sandy tracts the good lady might help to people. But I had to return to the fact that for this sort of work—the daily mechanical grind—I was already equipped: the people I was working with were fully adequate.

"We only thought we might be more like *some* characters," said Mrs.   *65* Monarch mildly, getting up.

Her husband also rose; he stood looking at me with a dim wistfulness that was touching in so fine a man. "Would n't it be rather a pull sometimes to have—a—to have—?" He hung fire; he wanted me to help him by phrasing what he meant. But I could n't—I did n't know. So he brought it out awkwardly: "The *real* thing; a gentleman, you know, or a lady." I was quite ready to give a general assent—I admitted that there was a great deal in that. This encouraged Major Monarch to say, following up his appeal with an unacted gulp: "It's awfully hard—we've tried everything." The gulp was communicative; it proved too much for his wife. Before I knew it Mrs. Monarch had dropped again upon a divan and burst into tears. Her husband sat down beside her, holding one of her hands; whereupon she quickly dried her eyes with the other, while I felt embarrassed as she looked up at me. "There is n't a confounded job I have n't applied for—waited for—prayed for. You can fancy we'd be pretty bad first. Secretaryships and that sort of thing? You might as well ask for a peerage. I'd be *anything*—I'm strong; a messenger or a coal-heaver. I'd put on a gold-laced cap and open carriage-doors in front of the haberdasher's; I'd hang about a station to carry portmanteaux;° I'd be a postman. But they won't *look* at you; there are thousands as good as yourself already on the ground. *Gentlemen,* poor beggars, who've drunk their wine, who've kept their hunters!"

I was as reassuring as I knew how to be, and my visitors were presently on their feet again while, for the experiment, we agreed on an hour. We were discussing it when the door opened and Miss Churm came in with a wet umbrella. Miss Churm had to take the omnibus to Maida Vale

---

quoi: French for "what!"
portmanteaux: large suitcases

and then walk half a mile. She looked a trifle blowsy and slightly splashed. I scarcely ever saw her come in without thinking afresh how odd it was that, being so little in herself, she should yet be so much in others. She was a meagre little Miss Churm, but was such an ample heroine of romance. She was only a freckled cockney, but she could represent everything, from a fine lady to a shepherdess; she had the faculty as she might have had a fine voice or long hair. She could n't spell and she loved beer, but she had two or three "points," and practice, and a knack, and mother-wit, and a whimsical sensibility, and love of the theatre, and seven sisters, and not an ounce of respect, especially for the *h*. The first thing my visitors saw was that her umbrella was wet, and in their spotless perfection they visibly winced at it. The rain had come on since their arrival.

"I'm all in a soak; there *was* a mess of people in the 'bus. I wish you lived near a stytion," said Miss Churm. I requested her to get ready as quickly as possible, and she passed into the room in which she always changed her dress. But before going out she asked me what she was to get into this time.

"It's the Russian princess, don't you know?" I answered; "the one with the 'golden eyes,' in black velvet, for the long thing in the *Cheapside.*" °

"Golden eyes? I *say!*" cried Miss Churm, while my companions   70
watched her with intensity as she withdrew. She always arranged herself, when she was late, before I could turn round; and I kept my visitors a little on purpose, so that they might get an idea, from seeing her, what would be expected of themselves. I mentioned that she was quite my notion of an excellent model—she was really very clever.

"Do you think she looks like a Russian princess?" Major Monarch asked with lurking alarm.

"When I make her, yes."

"Oh if you have to *make* her—!" he reasoned, not without point.

"That's the most you can ask. There are so many who are not makeable."

"Well now, *here's* a lady"—and with a persuasive smile he passed his   75
arm into his wife's—"who's already made!"

"Oh I'm not a Russian princess," Mrs. Monarch protested a little coldly. I could see she had known some and did n't like them. There at once was a complication of a kind I never had to fear with Miss Churm.

This young lady came back in black velvet—the gown was rather rusty and very low on her lean shoulders—and with a Japanese fan in her red hands. I reminded her that in the scene I was doing she had to look over some one's head. "I forget whose it is; but it does n't matter. Just look over a head."

Cheapside: a magazine named for a commercial street in London

"I'd rather look over a stove," said Miss Churm; and she took her station near the fire. She fell into position, settled herself into a tall attitude, gave a certain backward inclination to her head and a certain forward droop to her fan, and looked, at least to my prejudiced sense, distinguished and charming, foreign and dangerous. We left her looking so while I went downstairs with Major and Mrs. Monarch.

"I believe I could come about as near as that," said Mrs. Monarch.

"Oh you think she's shabby, but you must allow for the alchemy   80
of art."

However, they went off with an evident increase of comfort founded on their demonstrable advantage in being the real thing. I could fancy them shuddering over Miss Churm. She was very droll about them when I went back, for I told her what they wanted.

"Well, if *she* can sit I'll tyke to bookkeeping," said my model.

"She's very ladylike," I replied as an innocent form of aggravation.

"So much the worse for *you*. That means she can't turn round."

"She'll do for the fashionable novels."   85

"Oh yes, she'll *do* for them!" my model humorously declared. "Ain't they bad enough without her?" I had often sociably denounced them to Miss Churm.

III

It was for the elucidation of a mystery in one of these works that I first tried Mrs. Monarch. Her husband came with her, to be useful if necessary—it was sufficiently clear that as a general thing he would prefer to come with her. At first I wondered if this were for "propriety's" sake—if he were going to be jealous and meddling. The idea was too tiresome, and if it had been confirmed it would speedily have brought our acquaintance to a close. But I soon saw there was nothing in it and that if he accompanied Mrs. Monarch it was—in addition to the chance of being wanted—simply because he had nothing else to do. When they were separate his occupation was gone and they never *had* been separate. I judged rightly that in their awkward situation their close union was their main comfort and that this union had no weak spot. It was a real marriage, an encouragement to the hesitating, a nut for pessimists to crack. Their address was humble—I remember afterwards thinking it had been the only thing about them that was really professional—and I could fancy the lamentable lodgings in which the Major would have been left alone. He could sit there more or less grimly with his wife—he couldn't sit there anyhow without her.

He had too much tact to try and make himself agreeable when he couldn't be useful; so when I was too absorbed in my work to talk he simply sat and waited. But I liked to hear him talk—it made my work, when not interrupting it, less mechanical, less special. To listen to him was to combine the excitement of going out with the economy of staying at home. There was only one hindrance—that I seemed not to know any of the people this brilliant couple had known. I think he wondered extremely, during the term of our intercourse, whom the deuce I *did* know. He had n't a stray sixpence of an idea to fumble for, so we did n't spin it very fine; we confined ourselves to questions of leather and even of liquor—saddlers and breeches-makers and how to get excellent claret cheap—and matters like "good trains" and the habits of small game. His lore on these last subjects was astonishing—he managed to interweave the stationmaster with the ornithologist. When he could n't talk about greater things he could talk cheerfully about smaller, and since I could n't accompany him into reminiscences of the fashionable world he could lower the conversation without a visible effort to my level.

So earnest a desire to please was touching in a man who could so easily have knocked one down. He looked after the fire and had an opinion on the draught of the stove without my asking him, and I could see that he thought many of my arrangements not half knowing. I remember telling him that if I were only rich I'd offer him a salary to come and teach me how to live. Sometimes he gave a random sigh of which the essence might have been: "Give me even such a bare old barrack as *this,* and I'd do something with it!" When I wanted to use him he came alone; which was an illustration of the superior courage of women. His wife could bear her solitary second floor, and she was in general more discreet; showing by various small reserves that she was alive to the propriety of keeping our relations markedly professional—not letting them slide into sociability. She wished it to remain clear that she and the Major were employed, not cultivated, and if she approved of me as a superior, who could be kept in his place, she never thought me quite good enough for an equal.

She sat with great intensity, giving the whole of her mind to it, and was capable of remaining for an hour almost as motionless as before a photographer's lens. I could see she had been photographed often, but somehow the very habit that made her good for that purpose unfitted her for mine. At first I was extremely pleased with her ladylike air, and it was a satisfaction, on coming to follow her lines, to see how good they were and how far they could lead the pencil. But after a little skirmishing I began to find her too insurmountably stiff; do what I would with it my drawing looked like a photograph or a copy of a photograph. Her figure had no variety of expression—she herself had no sense of variety. You may say that this was my business and was only a question of placing her. Yet I placed her in every conceivable position and she managed to obliterate their differences. She was always a lady certainly, and into the bargain was always the same lady. She was the real thing, but always the same thing. There were moments when I rather writhed under the serenity of her confidence that she *was* the real thing. All her dealings with me and all her husband's were an implication that this was lucky for *me*. Mean-

90

while I found myself trying to invent types that approached her own, instead of making her own transform itself—in the clever way that was not impossible for instance to poor Miss Churm. Arrange as I would and take the precautions I would, she always came out, in my pictures, too tall—landing me in the dilemma of having represented a fascinating woman as seven feet high, which (out of respect perhaps to my own very much scantier inches) was far from my idea of such a personage.

The case was worse with the Major—nothing I could do would keep *him* down, so that he became useful only for the representation of brawny giants. I adored variety and range, I cherished human accidents, the illustrative note; I wanted to characterise closely, and the thing in the world I most hated was the danger of being ridden by a type. I had quarrelled with some of my friends about it; I had parted company with them for maintaining that one *had* to be, and that if the type was beautiful—witness Raphael and Leonardo°—the servitude was only a gain. I was neither Leonardo nor Raphael—I might only be a presumptuous young modern searcher; but I held that everything was to be sacrificed sooner than character. When they claimed that the obsessional form could easily *be* character I retorted, perhaps superficially, "Whose?" It could n't be everybody's—it might end in being nobody's.

After I had drawn Mrs. Monarch a dozen times I felt surer even than before that the value of such a model as Miss Churm resided precisely in the fact that she had no positive stamp, combined of course with the other fact that what she did have was a curious and inexplicable talent for imitation. Her usual appearance was like a curtain which she could draw up at request for a capital performance. This performance was simply suggestive; but it was a word to the wise—it was vivid and pretty. Sometimes even I thought it, though she was plain herself, too insipidly pretty; I made it a reproach to her that the figures drawn from her were monotonously (*bêtement,*° as we used to say) graceful. Nothing made her more angry: it was so much her pride to feel she could sit for characters that had nothing in common with each other. She would accuse me at such moments of taking away her "reputytion."

It suffered a certain shrinkage, this queer quantity, from the repeated visits of my new friends. Miss Churm was greatly in demand, never in want of employment, so I had no scruple in putting her off occasionally, to try them more at my ease. It was certainly amusing at first to do the real thing—it was amusing to do Major Monarch's trousers. They *were* the real thing, even if he did come out colossal. It was amusing to do his wife's back hair—it was so mathematically neat—and the particular "smart" tension of her tight stays. She lent herself especially to positions

---

Raphael and Leonardo: Raphael Sanzio (1483–1520) and Leonardo da Vinci (1452–1519), Italian painters
bêtement: French for "stupidly"

in which the face was somewhat averted or blurred; she abounded in
ladylike back views and *profils perdus.*° When she stood erect she took
naturally one of the attitudes in which court-painters represent queens
and princesses; so that I found myself wondering whether, to draw out
this accomplishment, I could n't get the editor of the *Cheapside* to publish
a really royal romance, "A Tale of Buckingham Palace." Sometimes however the real thing and the make-believe came into contact; by which I
mean that Miss Churm, keeping an appointment or coming to make one
on days when I had much work in hand, encountered her invidious rivals.
The encounter was not on their part, for they noticed her no more than
if she had been the housemaid; not from intentional loftiness, but simply
because as yet, professionally, they did n't know how to fraternise, as I
could imagine they would have liked—or at least that the Major would.
They could n't talk about the omnibus—they always walked; and they
did n't know what else to try—she was n't interested in good trains
or cheap claret. Besides, they must have felt—in the air—that she was
amused at them, secretly derisive of their ever knowing how. She wasn't
a person to conceal the limits of her faith if she had had a chance to show
them. On the other hand Mrs. Monarch did n't think her tidy; for why
else did she take pains to say to me—it was going out of the way, for
Mrs. Monarch—that she did n't like dirty women?

One day when my young lady happened to be present with my other
sitters—she even dropped in, when it was convenient, for a chat—I
asked her to be so good as to lend a hand in getting tea, a service with
which she was familiar and which was one of a class that, living as I did
in a small way, with slender domestic resources, I often appealed to my
models to render. They liked to lay hands on my property, to break the
sitting, and sometimes the china—it made them feel Bohemian. The
next time I saw Miss Churm after this incident she surprised me greatly
by making a scene about it—she accused me of having wished to humiliate her. She had n't resented the outrage at the time, but had seemed
obliging and amused, enjoying the comedy of asking Mrs. Monarch, who
sat vague and silent, whether she would have cream and sugar, and putting an exaggerated simper into the question. She had tried intonations—as if she too wished to pass for the real thing—till I was afraid my
other visitors would take offence.

Oh they were determined not to do this, and their touching patience   95
was the measure of their great need. They would sit by the hour, uncom-
plaining, till I was ready to use them; they would come back on the
chance of being wanted and would walk away cheerfully if it failed. I used
to go to the door with them to see in what magnificent order they retreated. I tried to find other employment for them—I introduced them

---

profils perdus: French for "lost profiles," poses that show the back of the head more than the
profile

to several artists. But they didn't "take," for reasons I could appreciate, and I became rather anxiously aware that after such disappointments they fell back upon me with a heavier weight. They did me the honour to think me most *their* form. They were n't romantic enough for the paint-ers, and in those days there were few serious workers in black-and-white. Besides, they had an eye to the great job I had mentioned to them—they had secretly set their hearts on supplying the right essence for my pictorial vindication of our fine novelist. They knew that for this undertaking I should want no costume-effects, none of the frippery of past ages—that it was a case in which everything would be contemporary and satirical and presumably genteel. If I could work them into it their future would be assured, for the labour would of course be long and the occupation steady.

One day Mrs. Monarch came without her husband—she explained his absence by his having had to go to the City.° While she sat there in her usual relaxed majesty there came at the door a knock which I im-mediately recognised as the subdued appeal of a model out of work. It was followed by the entrance of a young man whom I at once saw to be a foreigner and who proved in fact an Italian acquainted with no English word but my name, which he uttered in a way that made it seem to include all others. I had n't then visited his country, nor was I proficient in his tongue; but as he was not so meanly constituted—what Italian is?—as to depend only on that member of expression he conveyed to me, in familiar but graceful mimicry, that he was in search of exactly the em-ployment in which the lady before me was engaged. I was not struck with him at first, and while I continued to draw I dropped few signs of interest or encouragement. He stood his ground however—not importunately, but with a dumb dog-like fidelity in his eyes that amounted to innocent impudence, the manner of a devoted servant—he might have been in the house for years—unjustly suspected. Suddenly it struck me that this very attitude and expression made a picture; whereupon I told him to sit down and wait till I should be free. There was another picture in the way he obeyed me, and I observed as I worked that there were others still in the way he looked wonderingly, with his head thrown back, about the high studio. He might have been crossing himself in Saint Peter's. Before I finished I said to myself "The fellow's a bankrupt orange-monger, but a treasure."

When Mrs. Monarch withdrew he passed across the room like a flash to open the door for her, standing there with the rapt pure gaze of the young Dante spellbound by the young Beatrice.° As I never insisted, in such situations, on the blankness of the British domestic, I reflected that

---

City: London's financial and commercial center
Beatrice: Beatrice Portinari (1266–1290), Florentine woman said to be the ideal and the in-spiration of the poet Dante, who first saw her when he was nine

he had the making of a servant—and I needed one, but could n't pay him to be only that—as well as of a model; in short I resolved to adopt my bright adventurer if he would agree to officiate in the double capacity. He jumped at my offer, and in the event my rashness—for I had really known nothing about him—wasn't brought home to me. He proved a sympathetic though a desultory ministrant, and had in a wonderful degree the *sentiment de la pose.*° It was uncultivated, instinctive, a part of the happy instinct that had guided him to my door and helped him to spell out my name on the card nailed to it. He had had no other introduction to me than a guess, from the shape of my high north window, seen outside, that my place was a studio and that as a studio it would contain an artist. He had wandered to England in search of fortune, like other itinerants, and had embarked, with a partner and a small green hand-cart, on the sale of penny ices. The ices had melted away and the partner had dissolved in their train. My young man wore tight yellow trousers with reddish stripes and his name was Oronte. He was sallow but fair, and when I put him into some old clothes of my own he looked like an Englishman. He was as good as Miss Churm, who could look, when requested, like an Italian.

IV

I thought Mrs. Monarch's face slightly convulsed when, on her coming back with her husband, she found Oronte installed. It was strange to have to recognise in a scrap of lazzarone° a competitor to her magnificent Major. It was she who scented danger first, for the Major was anecdotically unconscious. But Oronte gave us tea, with a hundred eager confusions—he had never been concerned in so queer a process—and I think she thought better of me for having at last an "establishment." They saw a couple of drawings that I had made of the establishment, and Mrs. Monarch hinted that it never would have struck her he had sat for them. "Now the drawings you make from *us,* they look exactly like us," she reminded me, smiling in triumph; and I recognised that this was indeed just their defect. When I drew the Monarchs I could n't anyhow get away from them—get into the character I wanted to represent; and I hadn't the least desire my model should be discoverable in my picture. Miss Churm never was, and Mrs. Monarch thought I hid her, very properly, because she was vulgar; whereas if she was lost it was only as the dead who go to heaven are lost—in the gain of an angel the more.

By this time I had got a certain start with "Rutland Ramsay," the first novel in the great projected series; that is I had produced a dozen draw-

---

sentiment de la pose: French for "instinct for posing"
lazzarone: Italian for "beggar"

ings, several with the help of the Major and his wife, and I had sent them in for approval. My understanding with the publishers, as I have already hinted, had been that I was to be left to do my work, in this particular case, as I liked, with the whole book committed to me; but my connexion with the rest of the series was only contingent. There were moments when, frankly, it *was* a comfort to have the real thing under one's hand; for there were characters in "Rutland Ramsay" that were very much like it. There were people presumably as erect as the Major and women of as good a fashion as Mrs. Monarch. There was a great deal of countryhouse life—treated, it is true, in a fine fanciful ironical generalised way—and there was a considerable implication of knickerbockers° and kilts. There were certain things I had to settle at the outset; such things for instance as the exact appearance of the hero and the particular bloom and figure of the heroine. The author of course gave me a lead, but there was a margin for interpretation. I took the Monarchs into my confidence, I told them frankly what I was about, I mentioned my embarrassments and alternatives. "Oh take *him!*" Mrs. Monarch murmured sweetly, looking at her husband; and "What could you want better than my wife?" the Major enquired with the comfortable candour that now prevailed between us.

I was n't obliged to answer these remarks—I was only obliged to   *100*
place my sitters. I was n't easy in mind, and I postponed a little timidly perhaps the solving of my question. The book was a large canvas, the other figures were numerous, and I worked off at first some of the episodes in which the hero and the heroine were not concerned. When once I had set *them* up I should have to stick to them—I could n't make my young man seven feet high in one place and five feet nine in another. I inclined on the whole to the latter measurement, though the Major more than once reminded me that *he* looked about as young as any one. It was indeed quite possible to arrange him, for the figure, so that it would have been difficult to detect his age. After the spontaneous Oronte had been with me a month, and after I had given him to understand several times over that his native exuberance would presently constitute an insurmountable barrier to our further intercourse, I waked to a sense of his heroic capacity. He was only five feet seven, but the remaining inches were latent. I tried him almost secretly at first, for I was really rather afraid of the judgment my other models would pass on such a choice. If they regarded Miss Churm as little better than a snare what would they think of the representation by a person so little the real thing as an Italian street-vendor of a protagonist formed by a public school?

If I went a little in fear of them it was n't because they bullied me, because they had got an oppressive foothold, but because in their really pathetic decorum and mysteriously permanent newness they counted on

---

knickerbockers: trousers gathered at the knee, knickers

me so intensely. I was therefore very glad when Jack Hawley came home: he was always of such good counsel. He painted badly himself, but there was no one like him for putting his finger on the place. He had been absent from England for a year; he had been somewhere—I don't remember where—to get a fresh eye. I was in a good deal of dread of any such organ, but we were old friends; he had been away for months and a sense of emptiness was creeping into my life. I had n't dodged a missile for a year.

He came back with a fresh eye, but with the same old black velvet blouse, and the first evening he spent in my studio we smoked cigarettes till the small hours. He had done no work himself, he had only got the eye; so the field was clear for the production of my little things. He wanted to see what I had produced for the *Cheapside,* but he was disappointed in the exhibition. That at least seemed the meaning of two or three comprehensive groans which, as he lounged on my big divan, his leg folded under him, looking at my latest drawings, issued from his lips with the smoke of the cigarette.

"What's the matter with you?" I asked.

"What's the matter with *you?*"

"Nothing save that I'm mystified."   *105*

"You are indeed. You're quite off the hinge. What's the meaning of this new fad?" And he tossed me, with visible irreverence, a drawing in which I happened to have depicted both my elegant models. I asked if he did n't think it good, and he replied that it struck him as execrable, given the sort of thing I had always represented myself to him as wishing to arrive at; but I let that pass—I was so anxious to see exactly what he meant. The two figures in the picture looked colossal, but I supposed this was *not* what he meant, inasmuch as, for aught he knew to the contrary, I might have been trying for some such effect. I maintained that I was working exactly in the same way as when he last had done me the honour to tell me I might do something some day. "Well, there's a screw loose somewhere," he answered; "wait a bit and I'll discover it." I depended upon him to do so: where else was the fresh eye? But he produced at last nothing more luminous than "I don't know—I don't like your types." This was lame for a critic who had never consented to discuss with me anything but the question of execution, the direction of strokes and the mystery of values.

"In the drawings you've been looking at I think my types are very handsome."

"Oh, they won't do!"

"I've been working with new models."

"I see you have. *They* won't do."   *110*

"Are you very sure of that?"

"Absolutely—they're stupid."

"You mean *I* am—for I ought to get around that."

"You *can't*—with such people. Who are they?"

I told him, so far as was necessary, and he concluded heartlessly: *"Ce* 115
sont des gens qu'il faut mettre à la porte."°

"You've never seen them; they're awfully good"—I flew to their
defence.

"Not seen them? Why all this recent work of yours drops to pieces
with them. It's all I want to see of them."

"No one else has said anything against it—the *Cheapside* people are
pleased."

"Every one else is an ass, and the *Cheapside* people the biggest asses
of all. Come, don't pretend at this time of day to have pretty illusions
about the public, especially about publishers and editors. It's not for *such*
animals you work—it's for those who know, *coloro che sanno,"*° so keep
straight for *me* if you can't keep straight for yourself. There was a certain
sort of thing you used to try for—and a very good thing it was. But this
twaddle is n't *in* it." When I talked with Hawley later about "Rutland
Ramsay" and its possible successors he declared that I must get back into
my boat again or I should go to the bottom. His voice in short was the
voice of warning.

I noted the warning, but I did n't turn my friends out of doors. They   120
bored me a good deal; but the very fact that they bored me admonished
me not to sacrifice them—if there was anything to be done with
them—simply to irritation. As I look back at this phase they seem to me
to have pervaded my life not a little. I have a vision of them as most of
the time in my studio, seated against the wall on an old velvet bench to
be out of the way, and resembling the while a pair of patient courtiers in
a royal ante-chamber. I'm convinced that during the coldest weeks of the
winter they held their ground because it saved them fire. Their newness
was losing its gloss, and it was impossible not to feel them objects of charity. Whenever Miss Churm arrived they went away, and after I was fairly
launched in "Rutland Ramsay" Miss Churm arrived pretty often. They
managed to express to me tacitly that they supposed I wanted her for the
low life of the book, and I let them suppose it, since they had attempted
to study the work—it was lying about the studio—without discovering
that it dealt only with the highest circles. They had dipped into the most
brilliant of our novelists without deciphering many passages. I still took
an hour from them, now and again, in spite of Jack Hawley's warning; it
would be time enough to dismiss them, if dismissal should be necessary,
when the rigour of the season was over. Hawley had made their acquaintance—he had met them at my fireside—and thought them a ridiculous
pair. Learning that he was a painter they tried to approach him, to show
him too that they were the real thing; but he looked at them, across the

---

Ce sont des gens qu'il faut mettre à la porte: French for "They are people one must show to the
door," i.e., get rid of
coloro che sanno: Italian for "those who know"

big room, as if they were miles away; they were a compendium of everything he most objected to in the social system of his country. Such people
as that, all convention and patent-leather, with ejaculations that stopped
conversation, had no business in a studio. A studio was a place to learn to
see, and how could you see through a pair of feather-beds?

The main inconvenience I suffered at their hands was that at first I
was shy of letting it break upon them that my artful little servant had
begun to sit to me for "Rutland Ramsay." They knew I had been odd
enough—they were prepared by this time to allow oddity to artists—to
pick a foreign vagabond out of the streets when I might have had a person
with whiskers and credentials; but it was some time before they learned
how high I rated his accomplishments. They found him in an attitude
more than once, but they never doubted I was doing him as an organ-
grinder. There were several things they never guessed, and one of them
was that for a striking scene in the novel, in which a footman briefly
figured, it occurred to me to make use of Major Monarch as the menial.
I kept putting this off, I did n't like to ask him to don the livery—beside
the difficulty of finding a livery to fit him. At last, one day late in the
winter, when I was at work on the despised Oronte, who caught one's
idea on the wing, and was in the glow of feeling myself go very straight,
they came in, the Major and his wife, with their society laugh about
nothing (there was less and less to laugh at); came in like country-
callers—they always reminded me of that—who have walked across the
park after church and are presently persuaded to stay to luncheon. Luncheon was over, but they could stay to tea—I knew they wanted it. The
fit was on me, however, and I could n't let my ardour cool and my work
wait, with the fading daylight, while my model prepared it. So I asked
Mrs. Monarch if she would mind laying it out—a request which for an
instant brought all the blood to her face. Her eyes were on her husband's
for a second, and some mute telegraphy passed between them. Their folly
was over the next instant; his cheerful shrewdness put an end to it. So far
from pitying their wounded pride, I must add, I was moved to give it as
complete a lesson as I could. They bustled about together and got out the
cups and saucers and made the kettle boil. I know they felt as if they were
waiting on my servant, and when the tea was prepared I said: "He'll have
a cup, please—he's tired." Mrs. Monarch brought him one where he
stood, and he took it from her as if he had been a gentleman at a party
squeezing a crush-hat with an elbow.

Then it came over me that she had made a great effort for me—made
it with a kind of nobleness—and that I owed her a compensation. Each
time I saw her after this I wondered what the compensation could be. I
could n't go on doing the wrong thing to oblige them. Oh it *was* the
wrong thing, the stamp of the work for which they sat—Hawley was not
the only person to say it now. I sent in a large number of the drawings I
had made for "Rutland Ramsay," and I received a warning that was more

to the point than Hawley's. The artistic adviser of the house for which I was working was of the opinion that many of my illustrations were not what had been looked for. Most of these illustrations were the subjects in which the Monarchs had figured. Without giving into the question of what *had* been looked for, I had to face the fact that at this rate I should n't get the other books to do. I hurled myself in despair on Miss Churm—I put her through all her paces. I not only adopted Oronte publicly as my hero, but one morning when the Major looked in to see if I did n't require him to finish a *Cheapside* figure for which he had begun to sit the week before, I told him I had changed my mind—I'd do the drawing from my man. At this my visitor turned pale and stood looking at me. "Is *he* your idea of an English gentleman?" he asked.

I was disappointed, I was nervous, I wanted to get on with my work; so I replied with irritation: "Oh my dear Major—I can't be ruined for *you!*"

It was a horrid speech, but he stood another moment—after which, without a word, he quitted the studio. I drew a long breath, for I said to myself that I should n't see him again. I had n't told him definitely that I was in danger of having my work rejected, but I was vexed at his not having felt the catastrophe in the air, read with me the moral of our fruitless collaboration, the lesson that in the deceptive atmosphere of art even the highest respectability may fail of being plastic.

I did n't owe my friends money, but I did see them again. They reappeared together three days later, and, given all the other facts, there was something tragic in that one. It was a clear proof they could find nothing else in life to do. They had threshed the matter out in a dismal conference—they had digested the bad news that they were not in for the series. If they were n't useful to me even for the *Cheapside* their function seemed difficult to determine, and I could only judge at first that they had come, forgivingly, decorously, to take a last leave. This made me rejoice in secret that I had little leisure for a scene; for I had placed both my other models in position together and I was pegging away at a drawing from which I hoped to derive glory. It had been suggested by the passage in which Rutland Ramsay, drawing up a chair to Artemisia's piano-stool, says extraordinary things to her while she ostensibly fingers out a difficult piece of music. I had done Miss Churm at the piano before—it was an attitude in which she knew how to take on an absolutely poetic grace. I wished the two figures to "compose" together with intensity, and my little Italian had entered perfectly into my conception. The pair were vividly before me, the piano had been pulled out; it was a charming show of blended youth and murmured love, which I had only to catch and keep. My visitors stood and looked at it, and I was friendly to them over my shoulder.

They made no response, but I was used to silent company and went on with my work, only a little disconcerted—even though exhilarated by the sense that *this* was at least the ideal thing—at not having got rid of

125

them after all. Presently I heard Mrs. Monarch's sweet voice beside or rather above me: "I wish her hair were a little better done." I looked up and she was staring with a strange fixedness at Miss Churm, whose back was turned to her. "Do you mind my just touching it?" she went on—a question which made me spring up for an instant as with the instinctive fear that she might do the young lady a harm. But she quieted me with a glance I shall never forget—I confess I should like to have been able to paint *that*—and went for a moment to my model. She spoke to her softly, laying a hand on her shoulder and bending over her; and as the girl, understanding, gratefully assented, she disposed her rough curls, with a few quick passes, in such a way as to make Miss Churm's head twice as charming. It was one of the most heroic personal services I've ever seen rendered. Then Mrs. Monarch turned away with a low sigh and, looking about her as if for something to do, stooped to the floor with a noble humility and picked up a dirty rag that had dropped out of my paint-box.

The Major meanwhile had also been looking for something to do, and, wandering to the other end of the studio, saw before him my breakfast-things neglected, unremoved. "I say, can't I be useful here?" he called out to me with an irrepressible quaver. I assented with a laugh that I fear was awkward, and for the next ten minutes, while I worked, I heard the light clatter of china and the tinkle of spoons and glass. Mrs. Monarch assisted her husband—they washed up my crockery, they put it away. They wandered off into my little scullery, and I afterwards found that they had cleaned my knives and that my slender stock of plate had an unprecedented surface. When it came over me, the latent eloquence of what they were doing, I confess that my drawing was blurred for a moment—the picture swam. They had accepted their failure, but they could n't accept their fate. They had bowed their heads in bewilderment to the perverse and cruel law in virtue of which the real thing could be so much less precious than the unreal; but they did n't want to starve. If my servants were my models, then my models might be my servants. They would reverse the parts—the others would sit for the ladies and gentlemen and *they* would do the work. They would still be in the studio—it was an intense dumb appeal to me not to turn them out. "Take us on," they wanted to say—"we'll do *anything*."

My pencil dropped from my hand; my sitting was spoiled and I got rid of my sitters, who were also evidently rather mystified and awestruck. Then, alone with the Major and his wife I had a most uncomfortable moment. He put their prayer into a single sentence: "I say, you know— just let *us* do for you, can't you?" I could n't—it was dreadful to see them emptying my slops, but I pretended I could, to oblige them, for about a week. Then I gave them a sum of money to go away, and I never saw them again. I obtained the remaining books, but my friend Hawley repeats that Major and Mrs. Monarch did me a permanent harm, got me into false ways. If it be true I'm content to have paid the price—for the memory.

1. Through whose eyes is this story told?

2. What do you learn about the narrator of this story? What type of person do you think he is? What are his values? his goals?

3. What do you learn about the Monarchs? What is their situation? What do they hope to accomplish?

4. Does the narrator see the Monarchs in the same way you do? How do you account for the way in which he sees them?

5. How does the way the narrator sees the Monarchs affect the way he treats them? How does the way he sees them control the way he draws them?

6. Account for the ease with which the narrator is able to control his drawings of Miss Churm and Oronte and his difficulty with the Monarchs.

7. Why do the Monarchs "lower" themselves to become the narrator's servants? Why does their behavior cause the narrator such difficulty?

8. Does your understanding of the Monarchs differ from that of the narrator? Would you call that difference dramatic irony? Why?

9. What do you think is James's dominant idea in this story? What devices does he use to support that idea?

REPETITION, SOUND, AND RHYTHM

In writing, we represent sound with the symbols we call "letters." People combine sounds to make words and words to make meaning. It is important not to forget that writing represents the spoken word—the *sound* of the word. Long before there was writing or before the written word and literacy became common with the invention of movable type, people still kept up with the news of the day, learned their countries' histories, and expressed their ideas and emotions through the spoken and sung word.

Effective writing remembers its sources in sound. Furthermore, when you read or when your readers read your writing, you and they hear the written word. Knowing this, writers use patterns of sound and rhythm to create voice—to add emotional weight to their work—as well as to reflect the nature of their subject.

Alliteration and Assonance

Alliteration is the repetition of the same or similar consonant sounds—usually, but not always, at the beginning of words. *Assonance* is the repetition of the same or similar vowel sounds. A writer often uses alliteration and assonance to reflect the sense of words—to draw a picture with sounds—or to create greater emotional weight in his or her language. Alliteration and assonance are not devices invented by writers. They are common in everyday language. Listen to your or to another person's voice under the influence of a strong emotion—anger, for example.

Here is a paragraph from Fred Reed's essay "A Veteran Writes" (reprinted in its entirety in Chapter 17) about fighting in Viet Nam:

> [I] remember the shuddering flight of a helicopter high over glowing green jungle that spread beneath us like a frozen sea. [I] made the low runs a foot above treetops along paths that led like rivers through branches that clawed at the skids, never peered down into murky clearings and bubbling swamps of sucking snake-ridden muck. [I] remember monsoon mornings in the highlands where dragons of mist twisted in the valleys, coiling lazily on themselves, puffing up and swallowing whole villages in their dank breath. [I] remember driving before dawn to Red Beach, when the headlights in the blackness caught ghostly shapes, maybe VC, thin yellow men mushroom-headed in the night, bicycling along the alien roads.

Practically any sentence in this paragraph shows both alliteration and assonance, but this one is an especially good example of these devices:

> [I] made the low runs a foot above treetops along paths that led like rivers through branches that clawed at the skids, never peered down into murky clearings and bubbling swamps of sucking snake-ridden muck.

Assonance: *runs, foot, above, murky, bubbling, sucking, muck*

Alliteration: *low, led like*
skids, swamps of sucking snake-ridden
made, murky, muck

To get an idea of the effect of Reed's use of sound patterns and their effect upon voice, see what happens when the words that make those patterns are changed to synonyms which create neither alliteration nor assonance but which keep the imagery:

> [I] made the low runs a foot over treetops along paths that turned like rivers through branches that clawed at the skids, never looked down into obscure clearings and bubbling marshes of gluey snake-ridden mud.

❧ Working with a Reading

Alone or in your group, read this poem and answer the questions that follow it.

PIED BEAUTY°

Gerard Manley Hopkins

Glory be to God for dappled things—
    For skies of couple-color as a brinded cow;
        For rose-moles all in stipple upon trout that swim;
Fresh-firecoal chestnut-falls; finches' wings;
    Landscape plotted and pieced—fold, fallow, and plow;   *5*
        And all trades, their gear and tackle and trim.
All things counter, original, spare, strange;
    Whatever is fickle, freckled (who knows how?)
        With swift, slow; sweet sour; adazzle, dim;
He fathers-forth whose beauty is past change: *10*
    Praise him.

---

1. What does Hopkins praise God for?
2. How does the pattern of sounds in this poem reflect Hopkins's subject? Identify at least three examples of sound patterns that reflect his subject.
3. Does it seem strange to you that God should be praised for something that seems so unimportant? How does Hopkins make his subject important to you?

Rhythm and Meter

Your lives are driven and surrounded by regular rhythms. Some are outside of you: the ticking of clocks, the beat of a song, the purring of your cat, or a dog's repetitive barking in the middle of the night. Others are internal: your heartbeat, your breathing. There are still others that you create for yourself. You probably parcel your day into more or less regular segments, at least between Monday and Friday. Many people find regular patterns comforting, at least in some areas of their lives. We take pleasure in the rhythms of music; we listen to the rhythms as well as to the sounds and the words of others' speech to discover what emotions lie behind those words.

Often we choose the most effective rhythms for our statements without realizing it. For example, it is difficult to communicate intense emotion with long, meandering sentences. It is equally difficult to create the impres-

---

Title. *pied:* multicolored

sion of calm, mature thought with short, abrupt sentences. A writer can also suggest the rhythms of action with the rhythms of his or her words and sentences. In the reading that follows, Ernest Hemingway describes the shooting of a lion using the length and rhythm of his sentences to reflect the action he describes.

✎ *Exercise*

After you have read this selection, answer the questions that follow it alone or with your group.

Macomber stepped out of the curved opening at the side of the front seat, onto the step and down onto the ground. The lion still stood looking majestically and coolly toward this object that his eyes only showed in silhouette, bulking like some super-rhino. There was no man smell carried toward him and he watched the object, moving his great head a little from side to side. Then watching the object, not afraid, but hesitating before going down to the bank to drink with such a thing opposite him, he saw a man figure detach itself from it and he turned his heavy head and swung away toward the cover of the trees as he heard a cracking crash and felt the slam of a .30-06 220-grain solid bullet that bit his flank and ripped in sudden hot scalding nausea through his stomach. He trotted, heavy, big-footed, swinging wounded full-bellied, through the trees toward the tall grass and cover, and the crash came again to go past him ripping the air apart. Then it crashed again and he felt the blow as it hit his lower ribs and ripped on through, blood sudden hot and frothy in his mouth, and he galloped toward the high grass where he could crouch and not be seen and make them bring the crashing thing close enough so he could make a rush and get the man that held it.

—ERNEST HEMINGWAY, from "The Short, Happy Life of Francis Macomber"

1. Compare what you know about correct punctuation with the choices Hemingway makes in using periods and commas. How do those choices measure up with what you've been taught to regard as correct grammar and punctuation? How do they affect the length and rhythm of his sentences? Can you explain his choices?

2. Why does Hemingway begin and end his sentences where he does? How are these choices influenced by the action he describes?

3. How many points of view do you find in this paragraph? How do you know which one is which? Do the language, the rhythm of the words, and the grammatical choices help place you in each point of view?

In some cases, artists use repetition to lend power to their work. If you have never listened to "Bolero" by Maurice Ravel, give it a try. Abraham Lincoln also knew the power of repetition when he wrote in "The Gettysburg Address":

But, in a larger sense, we can not dedicate—we can not consecrate—
we can not hallow—this ground. The brave men, living and dead,
who struggled here, have consecrated it, far above our poor power to
add or detract. The world will little note nor long remember what we
say here, but it can never forget what they did here. It is for us the
living, rather, to be dedicated here to the unfinished work which they
who fought here have thus far so nobly advanced. It is rather for us to
be here dedicated to the great task remaining before us—that from
these honored dead we take increased devotion to that cause for which
they gave the last full measure of devotion—that we here highly resolve that these dead shall not have died in vain—that this nation,
under God, shall have a new birth of freedom—and that government
of the people, by the people, for the people, shall not perish from the
earth.

Before the invention of movable type permitted the wide availability of
printed material and increasing literacy, history and news was a poetic art,
kept in the minds of bards (poets who sang of history) and balladeers (singers
of legends and of the current news). For them the regular repetition of
sound and beat was an aid to memory, and it pleased the audience's ear, as
well. Here is a modern version of a ballad:

Ballad of Birmingham

(On the bombing of a church in Birmingham, Alabama, 1963)

"Mother dear, may I go downtown
Instead of out to play,
And march the streets of Birmingham
In a Freedom March today?"

"No, baby, no, you may not go,   *5*
For the dogs are fierce and wild,
And clubs and hoses, guns and jails
Aren't good for a little child."

"But, mother, I won't be alone.
Other children will go with me,   *10*
And march the streets of Birmingham
To make our country free."

No, baby, no, you may not go,
For I fear those guns will fire.
But you may go to church instead   *15*
And sing in the children's choir."

She has combed and brushed her night-dark hair,
And bathed rose-petal sweet,
And drawn white gloves on her small brown hands,
And white shoes on her feet.   *20*

The mother smiled to know her child
Was in the sacred place,
But that smile was the last smile
to come upon her face.

For when she heard the explosion,   25
Her eyes grew wet and wild.
She raced through the streets of Birmingham
Calling for her child.

She clawed through bits of glass and brick,
Then lifted out a shoe.   30
"O, here's the shoe my baby wore,
But, baby, where are you?"

—Dudley Randall

Regular repetition of sound and rhythm is no longer a defining characteristic of poetry. However, some modern poetry and most older poetry reflect the need for regular patterns on the part of both the authors and the audience. In addition, poets use regular patterns of rhythm and sound and variations of them to help create a voice to contain the dominant ideas in their poetry. This uniform repetition is called meter and rhyme. *Meter* is a regular pattern of accented and unaccented syllables in a line. *Rhyme* is a regular pattern of similar sounds, usually, but not always, occurring at the end of a line. Although rhyme is rarely an important element in prose and regular rhythmic patterns are often difficult to recognize in prose, they are tools that poets use to give their writing more impact and to add to the meaning of their words.

As you gain experience in "hearing" words as you read, you will begin to notice the rhythm of an author's words almost without thinking about it. Rhythm may even find its way into your writing. But to begin, it helps to know how to analyze a line or more of poetry to discover the rhythmic pattern the author has chosen. Learning to do this—to "hear" the rhythm of words in your mind's ear—will help you become sensitive to the effect of the rhythm of words and sentences in your own and other people's writing.

When you read the words in poetry to discover their rhythms, you are *scanning* the words. When you scan poetry, you can remind yourself of the rhythms by marking the stressed (heavily accented) syllables with this mark— / —and the unstressed (lightly accented) syllables with this mark— ◡. Scanning is that simple; all it takes is listening. For example, take the familiar word *dictionary* and scan it:

DICTIONARY

You can scan any collection of words for their arrangement of stressed and unstressed syllables. For example:

YOU CĂN SCĂN ĂNY COLLECTION OF WORDS

FOR THEIR ARRĂNGEMENT

When a writer creates patterns of light and heavy beats (or stresses) and consciously arranges them for effect, he or she uses *meter*. Meter has four primary patterns in English poetry:

Iambic (˘ ´):	The most commonly used meter in English, iambic is a two–syllable pattern in which an unstressed syllable is followed by a stressed syllable (an iamb). For example:

because

Trochaic (´ ˘):	The other two–syllable pattern in English poetry, the trochaic is the opposite of the iambic. In it, a stressed syllable is followed by an unstressed syllable (a trochee). For example:

morning

Anapestic (˘ ˘ ´):	In the anapestic pattern, one of the two three-syllable patterns common to English poetry, two unstressed syllables are followed by a stressed syllable (an anapest). For example:

nonetheless

Dactylic (´ ˘ ˘):	The other three–syllable pattern in English poetry, the dactylic is essentially a mirror-image of the anapestic meter in that a stressed syllable is followed by two unstressed syllables. For example:

Benjamin Robinson

Each unit of stressed and unstressed syllable patterns is called a *foot*. The number of feet in combination with the type of foot being used identifies the meter. For example:

Monometer	one foot
Dimeter	two feet
Trimeter	three feet
Tetrameter	four feet

Pentameter	five feet
Hexameter	six feet
Heptameter	seven feet
Octameter	eight feet

However, the meter of a poem is hardly ever regular. If it were, the poem would become monotonous. Instead, the writer uses rhythm as a tool, keeping to a predominant meter, but varying it to reflect the tone of the words or the nature of the events they describe.

Notice how the writers use rhythm in the four examples that follow.

IAMBIC

Her Face

Her face
So faier
first bent
myne eye

Myne eye
to lyke
her face
doth lead

Her face
with beames
doth blynd
myne eye

Myne eye
with lyfe
her face
doth feede

O face
with frownes
wronge not
myne eye

This eye
shall Joye
her face

Her Tongue

Her tongue
So sweete
then drewe
myne eare

Myne eare
to learne
her tongue
doth teache

Her tongue
with sounde
doth charm
myne eare

myne eare
with hope
her tongue
doth feaste

O tongue
with cheeks
vex not
myne eare

This eare
shall yeald
her tongue

Her Wytt[1]

Her wytt
So sharpe
then hitt
my harte

My harte   5
to love
her wytt
doth move

Her wytt
with arte   10
doth knitt
my harte

My harte
with skill
her witt   15
doth fyll

O wytt
with smarte
wounde not
my harte   20

This harte
shall swear
her witt

—ARTHUR GORGES

———

1. There's a trick to this poem. Try reading down each column as well as across each complete line.

ANAPESTIC

The Reverie of Poor Susan

At the corner of wood Street, when daylight appears
Hangs a thrush that sings loud, it has sung for three years;
Poor Susan has passed by the spot, and has heard
In the silence of morning the song of the bird.

'Tis a note of enchantment; what ails her? She sees   *5*
A mountain ascending, a vision of trees;
Bright volumes of vapor through Lothbury glide,
And a river flows on through the vale of Cheapside.

Green pastures she views in the midst of the dale,
Down which she so often tripped with her pail;   *10*
And a single small cottage, a nest like a dove's,
The one only dwelling on earth that she loves.

She looks, and her heart is in heaven; but they fade,
The mist and the river, the hill and the shade;
The stream will not flow, and the hill will not rise,   *15*
And the colors have all passed away from her eyes.

—WILLIAM WORDSWORTH

TROCHAIC

From "The Raven"

Once upon a midnight dreary, while I pondered, weak and weary
Over many a quaint and curious volume of forgotten lore—
While I nodded, nearly napping, suddenly there came a tapping,
As of someone gently rapping, rapping at my chamber door,
"'Tis some visiter," I muttered, "tapping at my chamber door— *5*
          Only this and nothing more."

Ah, distinctly I remember it was in the bleak December;
And each separate dying ember wrought its ghost upon the floor.
Eagerly I wished the morrow;—vainly I had sought to borrow
From my books surcease of sorrow—sorrow for the lost Lenore—   *10*
For the rare and radiant maiden whom the angels named Lenore—
          Nameless *here* for evermore.

—EDGAR ALLAN POE

DACTYLIC The dactylic meter is very difficult to keep up over a long stretch of words. First, words in English seem to have a pattern of accents that fight against the one-heavy/two-light pattern of the dactylic meter. Second, a lot of successive dactylic feet tend to become monotonous (you might have found the anapestic meter to have the same effect). Here is an excerpt from "Evangeline" by Henry Wadsworth Longfellow that demonstrates both a predominantly dactylic meter as well as the reasons it is used so rarely:

This is the forest primeval. The murmuring pines and the hemlocks,
Bearded with moss, and in garments green, indistinct in the twilight,
Stand like the Druids of eld, with voices sad and prophetic,
Stand like harpers hoar, with beards that rest on their bosoms.
Loud from its rocky caverns, the deep-voiced neighboring ocean
Speaks, and in accents disconsolate answers the wail of the forest.

BLANK VERSE Blank verse is a form of verse written in regular meter—usually iambic pentameter—but without rhyme. Shakespeare's plays
are written predominantly in blank verse. Regular patterns of accent without rhyme allow a poet to use rhythm to help his or her poetry reflect its
dominant idea while allowing it to maintain the vitality of spoken language.
Here is an excerpt from Shakespeare's *Macbeth* that can stand by itself as a
poem in blank verse. Try reading it aloud to yourself and notice how the
accent pattern helps the poet create his meaning while allowing you to read
the poem as if you were speaking.

Tomorrow, and tomorrow, and tomorrow
Creeps in this petty pace from day to day
To the last syllable of recorded time.
And all our yesterdays have lighted fools
The way to dusty death. Out, out, brief candle—
Life's but a walking shadow, a poor player
That struts and frets his hour upon the stage
And then is heard no more. It is a tale
Told by an idiot, full of sound and fury,
Signifying nothing.

FREE VERSE Other poems are written without consideration for regularity of meter. These are called *free verse,* although such poetry is hardly free
in the sense that anything goes. More often, writers of this type of verse
decide on the length of its lines and its patterns of rhythm to complement
the sense and sound of its words. Poets writing free verse think in terms of
the weight of repetition. Often they regulate the length of the line according
to the rise and fall of the speaking voice. Because the end of a line creates a
pause in the reader's voice, the last word in a line of free verse is often emphasized. The grammatical structure of the sentences and clauses in the
words the writer chooses sometimes creates the line length as well. Look at
how Walt Whitman uses all of these devices in the following poem:

The Dalliance° of the Eagles

Skirting the river road, (my forenoon walk, my rest,)
Skyward in air a sudden muffled sound, the dalliance of the eagles,

---

Title. *dalliance:* lovemaking

The rushing amorous contact high in space together,
The clinching interlocking claws, a living, fierce, gyrating wheel,
Four beating wings, two beaks, a swirling mass tight grappling,   5
In tumbling turning clustering loops, straight downward falling,
Till o'er the river poised, the twain yet one, a moment's lull,
A motionless still balance in the air, then parting, talons loosing,
Upward again on slow-firm pinions° slanting, their separate diverse
    flight,
She hers, he his pursuing.   10

                        —Walt Whitman

    There is still freer free verse that uses the shape of the poem on the page
to help create the meaning of the poem. Here is a poem by e.e. cummings
that defies grammar as well as the sense of the words to give the poem its
own shape on the page:

            l (a

            le
            af
            fa

            ll

            s)
            one
            l

            iness

Rhyme

    You've seen how prose writers sometimes use regular, repeated rhythms
to accent their ideas and help create a voice. However, the regular pattern
of rhyme is restricted entirely to poetry and to some dramas written in poetic
form. *Rhyme* is the more or less regular arrangement of identical or similar
sounds, usually at the ends of lines. Marking rhyme for analysis is very
simple. You assign the letter A to the first end-sound in a poem. All end-
sounds like it are also A. The next end-sound and all sounds like it are B,
and so forth. Here is a poem with the rhymes marked for you:

To the Virgins to Make Much of Time

Gather ye Rosebuds while ye may,   A
    Old time is still a-flying: B
And this same flower that smiles today,   A
    Tomorrow will be dying.   B

---

9. *pinions:* wings

The glorious lamp of heaven, the sun	C	5
The higher he's a getting,	D	
The sooner will his race be run,	C	
And nearer he's to setting.	D	
That age is best which is the first,	E	
When youth and blood are warmer;	F	10
But being spent, the worse and worst	E	
Times still succeed the former.	F	
Then be not coy, but use your time,	G	
And while ye may, go marry;	H	
For having lost but once your prime,	G	15
You may forever tarry.	H	

—ROBERT HERRICK

Regularly occurring *end rhyme,* like that used in the example, is the sort of rhyme most people associate with poetry. Poets sometimes use *off rhyme* —rhyme which employs sounds that are similar, but not the same. Variation often lends variety and vitality to a poem. Here is a poem that uses both types of rhyme. The rhymes have been marked to indicate both the regular and the off rhymes:

Futility

Move him into the sun—	A	
Gently its touch awoke him once,	B	
At home, whispering of fields unsown.	A′	
Always it woke him, even in France,	B′	
Until this morning and this snow.	C	5
If anything might rouse him now	C′	
The kind old sun will know.	C	
Think how it wakes the seeds,—	D	
Woke, once, the clays of a cold star.	E	
Are limbs so dear-achieved, are sides,	D′	10
Full-nerved—still warm—too hard to stir?	E′	
Was it for this the clay grew tall?	F	
—O what made fatuous sunbeams toil	F′	
To break earth's sleep at all?	F	

—WILFRED OWEN

✎ *An Invitation to Write*

Try writing a poem. Use rhythm and rhyme to support the ideas or events you write about. Or try free verse and use the length of the lines or the rhythms of speech to reflect the subject and your dominant idea.

PART 4

Strategies for Organizing Your Ideas

WHEN YOU WRITE with the aim of presenting a dominant idea or impression, you commit yourself to making your idea clear to an audience. Fulfilling that commitment well takes time and effort. If you're willing to put that time and effort into your idea, it follows that you must consider the idea important enough to your audience to be worth their time as well. As you give your idea its shape and dress it in appropriate language, you will find yourself using supporting examples from your and others' words, observations, and experiences. Such examples may help convince your audience that what you say has happened really has occurred. Or your examples may help to clarify a concept for members of your audience who are unfamiliar with it. In addition, your larger ideas often find their support in a series of smaller ideas that leads the reader toward your dominant idea.

Each of the elements of support you discover as you draft your writing has to be put in a clear relationship to the other elements. As you revise your paper, you give it a form. That form will lead your readers from the beginning of the work, where you supply them with the necessary background to help them understand your dominant idea; through the supporting examples, quotations, facts, and ideas; to the conclusion. Along the way, your ideas and examples fall into patterns—or organizational schemes—that connect the separate stages of your thought with each other and with your dominant idea.

There is nothing mysterious in what you do when you look for an effective arrangement for your ideas. You already know effective organizational strategies. Everyone uses these approaches to present his or her thoughts. These resources are available to you, as well. When you were ten or eleven and asked your parents for a new bike, you might have told

251

them that your best friend had just gotten one—thereby comparing yourself to your friend. Or you might have told them that if you had a new bike, you would be able to complete your paper route more quickly—and so you used a cause-and-effect strategy. In another case, perhaps you wanted to convince the rest of your family that you should all go to Yosemite for vacation—and so you described the park to show them how beautiful it would be.

Because you already know these strategies, making decisions about the most effective organizational scheme for your ideas boils down to making yourself conscious of the organizational resources you have available for arranging your ideas. Conscious consideration of the options prepares you to choose the most effective approach for presenting your dominant idea and its support to your reader.

One useful approach to defining and describing the organizational schemes that are available to you gives each form of organization a name, such as "comparison and contrast" or "cause and effect." To help you understand the potential value of each approach in making your dominant idea clear, each is discussed separately. However, it's important to keep in mind that any one strategy rarely exists in isolation from any of the others. Each one draws on a number of others to do its work. As you work with each one, you'll see ways in which others contribute to its effectiveness.

Furthermore, these strategies for organizing your ideas are *means* that you discover *when* you revise with the aim of making your dominant idea clear to your audience. They are not *ends* that you aim at *before* you write your paper. Nobody in a real writing situation decides, "I think I'll organize my thoughts along the lines of comparison and contrast today. It's that sort of day." Instead, these strategies are more useful when you view them as additional discovery strategies that open potential ways of expanding and developing your dominant idea for your readers. Since the aim of writing is to make your idea as clear as possible, look at these organizational schemes as ways of discovering the best means of clarifying your thoughts.

Because these strategies are useful as a means of discovering effective ways to arrange your ideas, the time to consider them is after you have a draft of your writing. Your draft will often suggest one or more organizational approaches to you. More realistically, because you've written the draft, you have already thought about a way of arranging your ideas. The important skill in revision is to look at your draft and the dominant idea it suggests through the lens of as many of these approaches as seem useful to you. By thinking about your writing in this way, you take the innate organizational skill you have and make it a matter of conscious choices.

When you visualize what your paper might look like in terms of these strategies, you run a "thought experiment," trying out each approach in your mind and judging which seems to be the most effective.

Remember, also, that although your piece of writing may reflect an overall organizational strategy, along the way you may find yourself using others to good effect. As you've learned, almost every paragraph is a unit containing a dominant idea and its support. In the general scheme of your paper, each supporting element might suggest its own most effective way of presenting its information and making its contribution to your whole work. Each of your paragraphs, other than some paragraphs which help your reader make a transition from one idea to the next, has its own dominant organizational scheme.

Description: Using Imagery to Put Your Audience in the Place

Description is a way of using *imagery*—concrete language that speaks to your audience's senses—to paint a picture of a place, an object, or a living thing. Some would say that everything humans know begins with our senses. If that is true, every approach to arranging information depends on careful observation leading to effective description.

When you explain an idea to another person and you have the feeling that he or she doesn't really understand what you are saying, you might find yourself searching for some examples to make your thought clearer, to show that person the innards of your idea—where it comes from and what it means. When you want to put your reader in a situation or location to show him or her what you mean, you rely on concrete imagery.

Through imagery, you show your readers what you mean instead of simply telling them. Imagery is built with language that appeals directly to your readers' experiences and that communicates your or another person's experience to your readers. It is the engine that drives all effective writing. Without imagery, you cannot make your idea live in your readers' minds. Without images, you give your readers no way to be certain of what you mean or to connect your ideas to their worlds.

Furthermore, you can use images and examples to clarify not only what you see and what you want your audience to see, but also to suggest feelings and attitudes toward your subject.

❧ Working with a Reading

Here is a poem that lives through its concrete imagery. When you've finished reading it, answer the questions that follow it, alone or in your group.

UPON JULIA'S CLOTHES

Robert Herrick

> Whenas in silks my Julia goes,
> Then, then, methinks how sweetly flows
> That liquefaction of her clothes.
>
> Next, when I cast mine eyes and see
> That brave vibration each way free,   5
> O, how that glittering taketh me!

To see the effect of the images, read this modified version:

Whenas in robes my Julia goes,
Then, then, methinks how subtly shows
The benediction of her clothes.

Next, when I turn my eyes and see
That revelation barely free,   5
O, how that swaying pleaseth me!

1. What does the first version reveal about how the speaker sees Julia?
   How does he feel about her?

2. Do Julia and the writer's attitude toward her appear to be different in
   the second version?

3. Take either of these descriptions and reduce it to a general, nonde-
   scriptive statement. What, if anything, is gained by doing this? What
   is lost?

Here is another example of powerful imagery, this time in nonfiction
prose, from Annie Dillard's *Pilgrim at Tinker Creek*:

Where Tinker Creek flows under the sycamore log bridge to the tear-
shaped island, it is slow and shallow, fringed thinly in cattail marsh. At
this point an astonishing bloom of life supports vast breeding popula-
tions of insects, fish, reptiles, birds, and mammals. On windless summer evenings I stalk along the creek bank or straddle the sycamore log
in absolute stillness, watching for muskrats. The night I stayed too late
I was hunched on the log staring spellbound at spreading, reflected
stains of lilac on the water. A cloud in the sky suddenly lighted as if
turned on by a switch; its reflection just as suddenly materialized on
the water upstream, flat and floating, so that I couldn't see the creek
bottom, or life in the water under the cloud. Downstream, away from

the cloud on the water, water turtles smooth as beans were gliding down with the current in a series of easy, weightless push-offs, as men bound on the moon. I didn't know whether to trace the progress of one turtle I was sure of, risking sticking my face in one of the bridge's spider webs made invisible by the gathering dusk, or take a chance on seeing the carp, or scan the mudbank in hope of seeing a muskrat, or follow the last of the swallows who caught at my heart and trailed it after them like streamers as they appeared from directly below, under the log, flying upstream with their tails forked, so fast.

Look what happens when the imagery and the examples are removed and the approximate meaning remains:

Where Tinker Creek flows under a bridge, I go to watch the animals on summer evenings. One night I stayed too late, and the light from the sunset kept me from seeing animals in the water upstream. But downstream I saw so many animals I didn't know what to look at first.

ᕯ *An Invitation to Write*

Read the following poem. Using it as a pattern, write a poem or a prose description from the point of view of a person on a day as cold as the day suggested in this poem is hot. Use imagery to make your reader see how cold the day is and what you hope will happen as the weather changes.

Heat

O wind, rend open the heat,
cut apart the heat,
rend it to tatters

Fruit cannot drop
through this thick air— 5
fruit cannot fall into heat
that presses up and blunts
the points of pears
and rounds the grapes.

Cut the heat— 10
plough through it,
turning it on either side
of your path.

—H. D. (Hilda Doolittle)

DECIDING WHAT TO DESCRIBE

What to describe and how much to describe are two of the most important decisions you must make when you write a description. You can answer these questions by asking yourself what your reader needs to know to understand your dominant idea and its background. The opposite question is equally important: What doesn't your reader need to know? That is, what material have you left in your draft that might lead your reader away from your dominant idea, that does not clarify your point?

Often in your first draft you will have written far more description than you need to make your dominant idea clear to your reader. There are two reasons that this might happen. First, writing a first draft, or freewriting, encourages you to put down as many of your observations, your experiences, and your thoughts as possible on the theory that you cannot know what is important to your dominant idea until you see what ideas and experiences are available to you. Second, if you have discovered a subject that creates a strong "felt sense" that you have found material that is important to you, both ideas and experiences will flow through your pen or your fingers before your critical eye can control or censor them. That is as it should be when you use a discovery strategy or when you draft. Most of us tend to speak freely and enthusiastically about what is important to us.

Often, as you revise, you or the members of your group will find descriptive material that you have to cut out. Effective and well-written as it might be, the material simply does not add to your reader's view of your subject in terms of your dominant idea. Be merciless. Cut those parts out of your draft. But don't throw them away. Later drafts of your writing might make them useful again. Or you may find them suggesting another piece of writing to you. They may even become the core of an entirely new poem, story, or essay.

YOUR RELATION TO YOUR DESCRIPTION

When you write a description, you can write yourself into that description—that is, you can write a *subjective description*. Or you can aim for a description that is a detached, impersonal observation: an *objective description*. Neither approach is better than the other. However, one may be more appropriate than the other for your audience and its expectations. If your dominant idea directly reflects your experience or your judgment of a situation and your audience does not require you to create the illusion of being objective, then the subjective description is probably appropriate. However, if the description you have chosen to present is the result of another's experience or if your audience expects an impersonal approach to an issue—for example, in reporting the results of an experiment or in journalistic reporting—the objective description is usually more effective.

Here is an example of a subjective description:

> I was a timid child. For all that, I am sure I was also obstinate, as children are. I am sure that Mother spoilt me too, but I cannot believe

I was particularly difficult to manage; I cannot believe that a kindly word, a quiet taking of me by the hand, a friendly look, could not have got me to do anything that was wanted of me. Now you are after all at bottom a kindly and soft hearted person (what follows will not be in contradiction to this, I am speaking only of the impression you made on the child), but not every child has the endurance and fearlessness to go on searching until it comes to the kindliness that lies beneath the surface. You can only treat a child in the way you yourself are constituted, with vigor, noise, and a hot temper. . . .

There is only one episode in the early years of which I have a direct memory. You may remember it, too. Once in the night I kept on whimpering for water, not, I am certain, because I was thirsty, but probably partly to be annoying, partly to amuse myself. After several vigorous threats had failed to have any effect, you took me out of bed, carried me out onto the balcony and left me there alone for awhile in my nightshirt, outside the shut door. I am not going to say that this was wrong—perhaps at that time there was really no other way of getting peace and quiet that night—but I mention it as typical of your methods of bringing up a child and their effect on me. I dare say I was quite obedient afterwards at that period, but it did me inner harm. What was for me a matter of course, that senseless asking for water, and the extraordinary terror of being carried outside were two things that I, my nature being what it is, could never properly connect with each other. Even years afterwards I suffered from the tormenting fancy that the huge man, my father, the ultimate authority, would come almost for no reason at all and take me out of bed in the night and carry me out onto the balcony, and that therefore I was such a mere nothing for him.

—FRANZ KAFKA, "Letter to His Father"

✎ An Invitation to Write

Together with your group or on your own, rewrite the preceding paragraph so that it is an impersonal description, without losing any of the details. Then examine the objective version in light of these questions: How has the description changed for you? What sort of audience would be interested in this version of the description?

Here is an example of objective description. In this excerpt from an article in the *New York Times,* the author uses language as neutrally as he possibly can without revealing his feelings:

In one of the biggest computer errors in banking history, Chemical Bank mistakenly deducted about $15 million from more than 100,000 customers' accounts on Tuesday night, causing consternation around the New York area.

The problem stemmed from a single line in an updated computer program installed by Chemical on Tuesday in its Somerset, N.J. computer center that caused the bank to process every withdrawal and transfer at its automated teller machines twice. Thus a person who took $100 from a cash machine had $200 deducted, although the receipt only indicated a withdrawal of $100.

—SAUL HANSELL, "Cash Machines Getting Greedy at a Big Bank"

⤙ *An Invitation to Write*

With your group or on your own, rewrite the previous description to make it subjective. You might make yourself one of the people who use Chemical Bank's teller machines, you might take the role of the unfortunate computer programmer or the president of Chemical Bank, or you might make yourself another observer of the scene. Then examine the subjective description in light of these questions: How have the changes you've made altered the effect of the description on you? Would an audience respond differently to this version than to the original version?

Although it is possible that a piece of writing could be almost exclusively description, that organizational strategy rarely occurs independently. More usually, a writer uses description to reinforce or develop his or her point. However, it is possible for a writer to arrange the elements of the description so carefully that the description itself suggests an idea to the audience.

⤙ *Working with the Readings*

Read the two selections that follow and, alone or with your group, answer the questions at the end of each one.

FILLING STATION

Elizabeth Bishop

Oh, but it is dirty!
—this little filling station,
oil-soaked, oil permeated
to a disturbing over-all
black translucency.
Be careful with that match!

5

Father wears a dirty,
oil–soaked monkey suit°
that cuts him under the arms,
and several quick and saucy   10
and greasy sons assist him
(it's a family filling station),
all quite thoroughly dirty.

Do they live in the station?
It has a cement porch   15
behind the pumps, and on it
a set of crushed and grease-
impregnated wickerwork;
on the wicker sofa
a dirty dog, quite comfy.   20

Some comic books provide
the only note of color—
of certain color. They lie
upon a big dim doily
draping a taboret°   25
(part of the set), beside
a big hirsute° begonia.

Why the extraneous plant?
Why the taboret?
Why, oh why, the doily?   30
(Embroidered in daisy stitch
with marguerites, I think,
and heavy with grey crochet.)
Somebody embroidered the doily.
Somebody waters the plant,   35
or oils it, maybe. Somebody
arranges the rows of cans
so that they softly say:
ESSO—SO—SO—SO
To high-strung automobiles.   40
Somebody loves us all.

---

1. Is this a subjective or an objective description? What makes you
   think so? What would the effect of the other kind of description be?

---

8. *monkey suit:* jump suit
25. *taboret:* stool
27. *hirsute:* hairy

2. In this description, what elements are emphasized (brought into the foreground)? What other objects that are completely left out could you imagine in this description? Why do you think they were left out? What do you think would be the effect of including them?

3. There is "somebody" missing from this description. How does Bishop make you aware of this omission? Who do you think this person is? What makes you think so? Why is this person omitted from the description? Is this person really absent?

4. How do you think this person's "absence" and "presence" conflict with each other? How does this conflict serve Bishop's purposes as you understand them?

SPRING, FROM WALDEN

Henry David Thoreau

The opening of large tracts by the ice–cutters commonly causes a pond to break up earlier; for the water, agitated by the wind, even in cold weather, wears away the surrounding ice. But such was not the effect on Walden that year, for she had soon got a thick new garment to take the place of the old. This pond never breaks up so soon as the others in this neighborhood, on account both of its greater depth and its having no stream passing through it to melt or wear away the ice. I never knew it to open in the course of a winter, not excepting that of '52–3, which gave the ponds so severe a trial. It commonly opens about the first of April, a week or ten days later than Flint's Pond and Fair–Haven, beginning to melt on the north side and in the shallower parts where it began to freeze. It indicates better than any water hereabouts the absolute progress of the season, being least affected by transient changes of temperature. A severe cold of a few days' duration in March may very much retard the opening of the former ponds, while the temperature of Walden increases almost uninterruptedly. A thermometer thrust into the middle of Walden on the 6th of March, 1847, stood at 32°, or freezing point; near the shore at 33°; in the middle of Flint's Pond, the same day, at 32½°; at a dozen rods from the shore, in shallow water, under ice a foot thick, at 36°. This difference of three and a half degrees between the temperature of the deep water and the shallow in the latter pond, and the fact that a great proportion of it is comparatively shallow, show why it should break up so much sooner than Walden. The ice in the shallowest part was at this time several inches thinner than in the middle. In mid–winter the middle had been the warmest and the ice thinnest there. So, also, every one who has waded about the shores of a pond in summer must have perceived how much warmer the water is close to the shore, where only three or four inches deep, than a little distance out, and on the surface where it is deep, than near the bottom. In spring the sun not only exerts an influence through the increased temperature of the air and earth, but its heat passes through ice a foot or more thick, and is reflected from the bottom in shallow water, and so also warms the water and melts the under side of the ice, at the same time that it is melting it more directly above, making it uneven, and causing the air bubbles which it contains to extend themselves upward and downward until it is completely honeycombed, and at last disappears suddenly in a single spring rain. Ice has its grain as well as wood, and when a cake begins to rot or "comb," that is, assume the appearance of honeycomb, whatever may be its position, the air cells are at right angles with what was the water surface. Where there is a rock or a log rising near to the surface the ice over it is much thinner, and is frequently quite dissolved by this reflected heat; and I have been told that in the experiment at Cambridge to freeze water in a shallow wooden pond, though the cold air circulated underneath, and so had access to both sides, the reflection of the sun from the bottom more than counterbalanced this advantage. When a warm rain in the middle of the winter melts off the snow-ice from Walden, and leaves a hard dark or transparent ice on the middle, there will be a strip of rotten though thicker white ice, a rod or more wide, about the shores, created by this reflected heat. Also, as I have said, the bubbles themselves within the ice operate as burning glasses to melt the ice beneath.

The phenomena of the year take place every day in a pond on a small scale. Every morning, generally speaking, the shallow water is being warmed more rapidly than the deep, though it may not be made so warm after all, and every evening it is being cooled more rapidly until the morning. The day is an epitome of the year. The night is the winter, the morning and evening are the spring and fall, and the noon is the summer. The cracking and booming of the ice indicate a change of temperature. One pleasant morning after a cold night, February 24th, 1850, having gone to Flint's Pond to spend the day, I noticed with surprise, that when I struck the ice with the head of my axe, it resounded like a gong for many rods around, or as if I had struck on a tight drum-head. The pond began to boom about an hour after sunrise, when it felt the influence of the sun's rays slanted upon it from over the hills; it stretched itself and yawned like a waking man with a gradually increasing tumult, which was kept up three or four hours. It took a short siesta at noon, and boomed once more toward night, as the sun was withdrawing his influence. In the right state of the weather a pond fires its evening gun with great regularity. But in the middle of the day, being full of cracks, and the air also being less elastic, it had completely lost its resonance, and probably fishes and muskrats could not then have been stunned by a blow on it. The fishermen say that the "thundering of the pond" scares the fishes and prevents their biting. The pond does not thunder every evening, and I cannot tell surely when to expect its thundering; but though I may perceive no difference in the weather, it does. Who would have suspected so large and cold and thick-skinned a thing to be so sensitive? Yet it has its law to which it thunders obedience when it should as surely as the buds expand in the spring. The earth is all alive and covered with papillæ. The largest pond is as sensitive to atmospheric changes as the globule of mercury in its tube.

One attraction in coming to the woods to live was that I should have leisure and opportunity to see the spring come in. The ice in the pond at length begins to be honey-combed, and I can set my heel in it as I walk. Fogs and rains and warmer suns are gradually melting the snow; the days have grown sensibly longer; and I see how I shall get through the winter without adding to my wood-pile, for large fires are no longer necessary. I am on the alert for the first signs of spring, to hear the chance note of some arriving bird, or the striped squirrel's chirp, for his stores must be now nearly exhausted, or see the woodchuck venture out of his winter quarters. On the 13th of March, after I had heard the bluebird, song-sparrow, and red-wing, the ice was still nearly a foot thick. As the weather grew warmer, it was not sensibly worn away by the water, nor broken up and floated off as in rivers, but, though it was completely melted for half a rod in width about the shore, the middle was merely honey-combed and saturated with water, so that you could put your foot through it when six inches thick; but by the next day evening, perhaps, after a warm rain followed by fog, it would have wholly disappeared, all gone off with the fog, spirited away. One year I went across the middle only five days before it disappeared entirely. In 1845 Walden was first completely open on the 1st of April; in '46, the 25th of March; in '47, the 8th of April; in '51, the 28th of March; in '52, the 18th of April, in '53, the 23d of March; in '54, about the 7th of April.

Every incident connected with the breaking up of the rivers and ponds and the settling of the weather is particularly interesting to us who live in a climate of so great extremes. When the warmer days come, they who dwell near the river hear the ice crack at night with a startling whoop as loud as artillery, as if its icy fetters were rent from end to end, and within a few days see it rapidly going out. So the alligator comes out of the mud with quakings of the earth. One old man, who has been a close observer of Nature, and seems as thoroughly wise in regard to all her operations as if she had been put upon the stocks when he was a boy, and he had helped to lay her keel,—who has come to his growth, and can hardly acquire more of natural lore if he should live to the age of Methuselah,°—told me, and I was surprised to hear him express wonder at any of Nature's operations, for I thought that there were no secrets

---

Methuselah: said to have lived 969 years (Genesis 5:27)

between them, that one spring day he took his gun and boat, and thought that he would have a little sport with the ducks. There was ice still on the meadows, but it was all gone out of the river, and he dropped down without obstruction from Sudbury, where he lived, to Fair-Haven Pond, which he found, unexpectedly, covered for the most part with a firm field of ice. It was a warm day, and he was surprised to see so great a body of ice remaining. Not seeing any ducks, he hid his boat on the north or back side of an island in the pond, and then concealed himself in the bushes on the south side, to await them. The ice was melted for three or four rods from the shore, and there was a smooth and warm sheet of water, with a muddy bottom, such as the ducks love, within, and he thought it likely that some would be along pretty soon. After he had lain still there about an hour he heard a low and seemingly very distant sound, but singularly grand and impressive, unlike any thing he had ever heard, gradually swelling and increasing as if it would have a universal and memorable ending, a sullen rush and roar, which seemed to him all at once like the sound of a vast body of fowl coming in to settle there, and, seizing his gun, he started up in haste and excited; but he found, to his surprise, that the whole body of the ice had started while he lay there, and drifted in to the shore, and the sound he had heard was made by its edge grating on the shore,—at first gently nibbled and crumbled off, but at length heaving up and scattering its wrecks along the island to a considerable height before it came to a stand still.

At length the sun's rays have attained the right angle, and warm winds   5
blow up mist and rain and melt the snow banks, and the sun dispersing the mist smiles on a checkered landscape of russet and white smoking with incense, through which the traveller picks his way from islet to islet, cheered by the music of a thousand tinkling rills and rivulets whose veins are filled with the blood of winter which they are bearing off.

Few phenomena gave me more delight than to observe the forms which thawing sand and clay assume in flowing down the sides of a deep cut on the railroad through which I passed on my way to the village, a phenomenon not very common on so large a scale, though the number of freshly exposed banks of the right material must have been greatly multiplied since railroads were invented. The material was sand of every degree of fineness and of various rich colors, commonly mixed with a little clay. When the frost comes out in the spring, and even in a thawing day in the winter, the sand begins to flow down the slopes like lava, sometimes bursting out through the snow and overflowing it where no sand was to be seen before. Innumerable little streams overlap and interlace one with another, exhibiting a sort of hybrid product, which obeys half way the law of currents, and half way that of vegetation. As it flows it takes the forms of sappy leaves or vines, making heaps of pulpy sprays a foot or more in depth, and resembling, as you look down on them, the laciniated lobed and imbricated thalluses of some lichens; or you are reminded of coral, of leopards' paws or birds' feet, of brains or lungs or bowels, and excrements of all kinds. It is a truly *grotesque* vegetation, whose forms and color we see imitated in bronze, a sort of architectural foliage more ancient and typical than acanthus, chiccory, ivy, vine, or any vegetable leaves; destined perhaps, under some circumstances, to become a puzzle to future geologists. The whole cut impressed me as if it were a cave with its stalactites laid open to the light. The various shades of the sand are singularly rich and agreeable, embracing the different iron colors, brown, gray, yellowish, and reddish. When the flowing mass reaches the drain at the foot of the bank it spreads out flatter into *strands,* the separate streams losing their semi-cylindrical form and gradually becoming more flat and broad, running together as they are more moist, till they form an almost flat *sand,* still variously and beautifully shaded, but in which you can trace the original forms of vegetation; till at length, in the water itself, they are converted into *banks,* like those formed off the mouths of rivers, and the forms of vegetation are lost in the ripple marks on the bottom.

The whole bank, which is from twenty to forty feet high, is sometimes overlaid with a mass of this kind of foliage, or sandy rupture, for a quarter of a mile on one or both sides, the produce of one spring day. What makes this sand foliage remarkable is its springing into existence thus suddenly. When I see on the one side the inert bank,—for the sun acts on one side first,—and on the other this luxuriant foliage, the creation of an hour, I am affected as if in a peculiar sense I stood in the laboratory of the Artist who made the world and me,—had come to where he was still at work, sporting on this bank, and with excess of energy strewing his fresh designs about. I feel as if I were nearer to the vitals of the globe, for this sandy overflow is something such a foliaceous mass as the vitals of the animal body. You find thus in the very sands an anticipation of the vegetable leaf. No wonder that the earth expresses itself outwardly in leaves, it so labors with the idea inwardly. The atoms have already learned this law, and are pregnant by it. The overhanging leaf sees here its prototype. *Internally,* whether in the globe or animal body, it is a moist thick *lobe,* a word especially applicable to the liver and lungs and the *leaves* of fat, ($\lambda\epsilon\acute{\iota}\beta\omega$, *labor, lapsus,* to flow or slip downward, a lapsing; $\lambda o\beta o\varsigma$, *globus,* lobe, globe; also lap, flap, and many other words,) *externally* a dry thin *leaf,* even as the *f* and *v* are a pressed and dried *b.* The radicals of lobe are *lb,* the soft mass of the *b* (single lobed, or B, double lobed,) with a liquid *l* behind it pressing it forward. In globe, *glb,* the guttural *g* adds to the meaning the capacity of the throat. The feathers and wings of birds are still drier and thinner leaves. Thus, also, you pass from the lumpish grub in the earth to the airy and fluttering butterfly. The very globe continually transcends and translates itself, and becomes winged in its orbit. Even ice begins with delicate crystal leaves, as if it had flowed into moulds which the fronds of water plants have impressed on the watery mirror. The whole tree itself is but one leaf, and rivers are still vaster leaves whose pulp is intervening earth, and towns and cities are the ova of insects in their axils.

When the sun withdraws the sand ceases to flow, but in the morning the streams will start once more and branch and branch again into a myriad of others. You here see perchance how blood vessels are formed. If you look closely you observe that first there pushes forward from the thawing mass a stream of softened sand with a drop-like point, like the ball of the finger, feeling its way slowly and blindly downward, until at last with more heat and moisture, as the sun gets higher, the most fluid portion, in its effort to obey the law to which the most inert also yields, separates from the latter and forms for itself a meandering channel or artery within that, in which is seen a little silvery stream glancing like lightning from one stage of pulpy leaves or branches to another, and ever and anon swallowed up in the sand. It is wonderful how rapidly yet perfectly the sand organizes itself as it flows, using the best material its mass affords to form the sharp edges of its channel. Such are the sources of rivers. In the silicious matter which the water deposits is perhaps the bony system, and in the still finer soil and organic matter the fleshy fibre or cellular tissue. What is man but a mass of thawing clay? The ball of the human finger is but a drop congealed. The fingers and toes flow to their extent from the thawing mass of the body. Who knows what the human body would expand and flow out to under a more genial heaven? Is not the hand a spreading *palm* leaf with its lobes and veins? The ear may be regarded, fancifully, as a lichen, *umbilicaria,* on the side of the head, with its lobe or drop. The lip (*labium* from *labor* (?)) laps or lapses from the sides of the cavernous mouth. The nose is a manifest congealed drop or stalactite. The chin is a still larger drop, the confluent dripping of the face. The cheeks are a slide from the brows into the valley of the face, opposed and diffused by the cheek bones. Each rounded lobe of the vegetable leaf, too, is a thick and now loitering drop, larger or smaller; the lobes are the fingers of the leaf; and as many lobes as it has, in so many directions it tends to flow, and more heat or other genial influences would have caused it to flow yet farther.

Thus it seemed that this one hillside illustrated the principle of all the operations of Nature. The Maker of this earth but patented a leaf. What Champollion° will decipher this hieroglyphic for us, that we may turn over a new leaf at last? This phenomenon is more exhilarating to me than the luxuriance and fertility of vineyards. True, it is somewhat excrementitious in its character, and there is no end to the heaps of liver lights and bowels, as if the globe were turned wrong side outward; but this suggests at least that Nature has some bowels, and there again is mother of humanity. This is the frost coming out of the ground; this is Spring. It precedes the green and flowery spring, as mythology precedes regular poetry. I know of nothing more purgative of winter fumes and indigestions. It

---

Champollion: Jean François Champollion, the person who translated the hieroglyphics on the Rosetta Stone and so opened ancient Egyptian civilization to modern thought.

convinces me that Earth is still in her swaddling clothes, and stretches forth baby fingers on every side. Fresh curls spring from the baldest brow. There is nothing inorganic. These foliaceous heaps lie along the bank like the slag of a furnace, showing that Nature is "in full blast" within. The earth is not a mere fragment of dead history, stratum upon stratum like the leaves of a book, to be studied by geologists and antiquaries chiefly, but living poetry like the leaves of a tree, which precede flowers and fruit,—not a fossil earth, but a living earth; compared with whose great central life all animal and vegetable life is merely parasitic. Its throes will heave our exuviæ° from their graves. You may melt your metals and cast them into the most beautiful moulds you can; they will never excite me like the forms which this molten earth flows out into. And not only it, but the institutions upon it, are plastic like clay in the hands of the potter.

Ere long, not only these banks, but on every hill and plain and in every hollow, the frost comes out of the ground like a dormant quadruped from its burrow, and seeks the sea with music, or migrates to other climes in clouds. Thaw with his gentle persuasion is more powerful than Thor° with his hammer. The one melts, the other but breaks in pieces. 10

When the ground was partially bare of snow, and a few warm days had dried its surface somewhat, it was pleasant to compare the first tender signs of the infant year just peeping forth with stately beauty of the withered vegetation which had withstood the winter,—life-everlasting, golden-rods, pinweeds, and graceful wild grasses, more obvious and interesting frequently than in summer even, as if their beauty was not ripe till then; even cotton-grass, cat-tails, mulleins, johnswort, hard-hack, meadow-sweet, and other strong stemmed plants, those unexhausted granaries which entertain the earliest birds,—decent weeds, at least, which widowed Nature wears. I am particularly attracted by the arching and sheaf-like top of the wool-grass; it brings back the summer to our winter memories, and is among the forms which art loves to copy, and which, in the vegetable kingdom, have the same relation to types already in the mind of man that astronomy has. It is an antique style older than Greek or Egyptian. Many of the phenomena of Winter are suggestive of an inexpressible tenderness and fragile delicacy. We are accustomed to hear this king described as a rude and boisterous tyrant; but with the gentleness of a lover he adorns the tresses of Summer.

At the approach of spring the red-squirrels got under my house, two at a time, directly under my feet as I sat reading or writing, and kept up the queerest chuckling and chirruping and vocal pirouetting and gurgling sounds that ever were heard; and when I stamped they only chirruped

---

exuviæ: cast-off skins or shells of animals
Thor: Norse god of thunder

the louder, as if past all fear and respect in their mad pranks, defying humanity to stop them. No you don't—chickaree—chickaree. They were wholly deaf to my arguments, or failed to perceive their force, and fell into a strain of invective that was irresistible.

The first sparrow of spring! The year beginning with younger hope than ever! The faint silvery warblings heard over the partially bare and moist fields from the blue-bird, the song-sparrow, and the red-wing, as if the last flakes of winter tinkled as they fell! What at such a time are histories, chronologies, traditions, and all written revelations? The brooks sing carols and glees to the spring. The marsh-hawk sailing low over the meadow is already seeking the first slimy life that awakes. The sinking sound of melting snow is heard in all dells, and the ice dissolves apace in the ponds. The grass flames up on the hillsides like a spring fire,—"et primitus oritur herba imbribus primoribus evocata,"°—as if the earth sent forth an inward heat to greet the returning sun; not yellow but green is the color of its flame;—the symbol of perpetual youth, the grass-blade, like a long green ribbon, streams from the sod into the summer, checked indeed by the frost, but anon pushing on again, lifting its spear of last year's hay with the fresh life below. It grows as steadily as the rill oozes out of the ground. It is almost identical with that, for in the growing days of June, when the rills are dry, the grass blades are their channels, and from year to year the herds drink at this perennial green stream, and the mower draws from it betimes their winter supply. So our human life but dies down to its root, and still puts forth its green blade to eternity.

Walden is melting apace. There is a canal two rods wide along the northerly and westerly sides, and wider still at the east end. A great field of ice has cracked off from the main body. I hear a song-sparrow singing from the bushes on the shore,—*olit, olit, olit,*—*chip, chip, chip, che char,*—*che wiss, wiss, wiss.* He too is helping to crack it. How handsome the great sweeping curves in the edge of the ice, answering somewhat to those of the shore, but more regular! It is unusually hard, owing to the recent severe but transient cold, and all watered or waved like a palace floor. But the wind slides eastward over its opaque surface in vain, till it reaches the living surface beyond. It is glorious to behold this ribbon of water sparkling in the sun, the bare face of the pond full of glee and youth, as if it spoke the joy of the fishes within it, and of the sands on its shore,—a silvery sheen as from the scales of a *leuciscus,*° as it were all one active fish. Such is the contrast between winter and spring. Walden was dead and is alive again. But this spring it broke up more steadily, as I have said.

The change from storm and winter to serene and mild weather, from dark and sluggish hours to bright and elastic ones, is a memorable crisis

15

---

et . . . evocata: Latin: "and summoned by the early rains, the grass starts to grow."
leuciscus: a freshwater fish

which all things proclaim. It is seemingly instantaneous at last. Suddenly an influx of light filled my house, though the evening was at hand, and the clouds of winter still overhung it, and the eaves were dripping with sleety rain. I looked out the window, and lo! where yesterday was cold gray ice there lay the transparent pond already calm and full of hope as on a summer evening, reflecting a summer evening sky in its bosom, though none was visible overhead, as if it had intelligence with some remote horizon. I heard a robin in the distance, the first I had heard for many a thousand years, methought, whose note I shall not forget for many a thousand more,—the same sweet and powerful song of yore. O the evening robin, at the end of a New England summer day! If I could ever find the twig he sits upon! I mean *he;* I mean *the twig.* This at least is not the *Turdus migratorius.°* The pitch-pines and shrub-oaks about my house, which had so long drooped, suddenly resumed their several characters, looked brighter, greener, and more erect and alive, as if effectually cleansed and restored by the rain. I knew that it would not rain any more. You may tell by looking at any twig of the forest, ay, at your very wood-pile, whether its winter is past or not. As it grew darker, I was startled by the *honking* of geese flying low over the woods, like weary travellers getting in late from southern lakes, and indulging at last in unrestrained complaint and mutual consolation. Standing at my door, I could hear the rush of their wings; when, driving toward my house, they suddenly spied my light, and with hushed clamor wheeled and settled in the pond. So I came in, and shut the door, and passed my first spring night in the woods.

In the morning I watched the geese from the door through the mist, sailing in the middle of the pond, fifty rods off, so large and tumultuous that Walden appeared like an artificial pond for their amusement. But when I stood on the shore they at once rose up with a great flapping of wings at the signal of their commander, and when they had got into rank circled about over my head, twenty-nine of them, and then steered straight to Canada, with a regular *honk* from the leader at intervals, trusting to break their fast in muddier pools. A "plump"° of ducks rose at the same time and took the route to the north in the wake of their noisier cousins.

For a week I heard the circling groping clangor of some solitary goose in the foggy mornings, seeking its companion, and still peopling the woods with the sound of a larger life than they could sustain. In April the pigeons were seen again flying express in small flocks, and in due time I heard the martins twittering over my clearing, though it had not seemed that the township contained so many that it could afford me any, and I fancied that they were peculiarly of the ancient race that dwelt in hollow trees ere white men came. In almost all climes the tortoise and the frog

---

Turdus migratorius: American Robin
plump: flock

are among the precursors and heralds of this season, and birds fly with song and glancing plumage, and plants spring and bloom, and winds blow, to correct this slight oscillation of the poles and preserve the equilibrium of Nature.

As every season seems best to us in its turn, so the coming in of spring is like the creation of Cosmos out of Chaos and the realization of the Golden Age.——

> "Eurus ad Auroram, Nabathæaque regna recessit,
> Persidaque, et radiis juga subdita matutinis."

> "The East-Wind withdrew to Aurora and the Nabathæan kingdom,
> And the Persian, and the ridges placed under the morning rays.
>
> *   *   *
>
> Man was born. Whether that Artificer of things,
> The origin of a better world, made him from the divine seed;
> Or the earth being recent and lately sundered from the high
> Ether, retained some seeds of cognate heaven."°

A single gentle rain makes the grass many shades greener. So our prospects brighten on the influx of better thoughts. We should be blessed if we lived in the present always, and took advantage of every accident that befell us, like the grass which confesses the influence of the slightest dew that falls on it; and did not spend our time in atoning for the neglect of past opportunities, which we call doing our duty. We loiter in winter while it is already spring. In a pleasant spring morning all men's sins are forgiven. Such a day is a truce to vice. While such a sun holds out to burn, the vilest sinner may return. Through our own recovered innocence we discern the innocence of our neighbors. You may have known your neighbor yesterday for a thief, a drunkard, or a sensualist, and merely pitied or despised him, and despaired of the world; but the sun shines bright and warm this first spring morning, re-creating the world, and you meet him at some serene work, and see how his exhausted and debauched veins expand with still joy and bless the new day, feel the spring influence with the innocence of infancy, and all his faults are forgotten. There is not only an atmosphere of good will about him, but even a savor of holiness groping for expression, blindly and ineffectually perhaps, like a new-born instinct, and for a short hour the south hill-side echoes to no vulgar jest. You see some innocent fair shoots preparing to burst from his gnarled rind and try another year's life, tender and fresh as the youngest plant. Even he has entered into the joy of his Lord. Why the jailer does not leave open his prison doors,—why the judge does not dismiss his case,—why the preacher does not dismiss his congregation! It is because they do not obey the hint which God gives them, nor accept the pardon which he freely offers to all.

"The . . . heaven": from Ovid's *Metamorphosis*, Book I

"A return to goodness produced each day in the tranquil and benefi-   20
cent breath of the morning, causes that in respect to the love of virtue
and the hatred of vice, one approaches a little the primitive nature of man,
as the sprouts of the forest which has been felled. In like manner the evil
which one does in the interval of a day prevents the germs of virtues
which began to spring up again from developing themselves and destroys them.

"After the germs of virtue have thus been prevented many times from
developing themselves, then the beneficent breath of evening does not
suffice to preserve them. As soon as the breath of evening does not suffice
longer to preserve them, then the nature of man does not differ much
from that of the brute. Men seeing the nature of this man like that of the
brute, think that he has never possessed the innate faculty of reason. Are
those the true and natural sentiments of man?"

> "The Golden Age was first created, which without any avenger
> Spontaneously without law cherished fidelity and rectitude.
> Punishment and fear were not; nor were threatening words read
> On suspended brass; nor did the suppliant crowd fear
> The words of their judge; but were safe without an avenger.
> Not yet the pine felled on its mountains had descended
> To the liquid waves that it might see a foreign world,
> And mortals knew no shores but their own.
> *   *   *   *   *   *   *   *   *   *   *   *
> There was eternal spring, and placid zephyrs with warm
> Blasts soothed the flowers born without seed." °

On the 29th of April, as I was fishing from the bank of the river near
the Nine-Acre-Corner bridge, standing on the quaking grass and willow
roots, where the muskrats lurk, I heard a singular rattling sound, somewhat like that of the sticks which boys play with their fingers, when,
looking up, I observed a very slight and graceful hawk, like a night-hawk,
alternately soaring like a ripple and tumbling a rod or two over and over,
showing the underside of its wings, which gleamed like a satin ribbon in
the sun, or like the pearly inside of a shell. This sight reminded me of
falconry and what nobleness and poetry are associated with that sport.
The Merlin it seemed to me it might be called: but I care not for its name.
It was the most ethereal flight I had ever witnessed. It did not simply
flutter like a butterfly, nor soar like the larger hawks, but it sported with
proud reliance in the fields of air; mounting again and again with its
strange chuckle, it repeated its free and beautiful fall, turning over and
over like a kite, and then recovering from its lofty tumbling, as if it had
never set its foot on *terra firma*. It appeared to have no companion in the
universe,—sporting there alone,—and to need none but the morning

---

"*The Golden . . . seed*": from Ovid's *Metamorphosis*, Book I and the ether with which it played. It was not lonely, but made all the earth lonely beneath it. Where was the parent which hatched it, its kindred, and its father in the heavens? The tenant of the air, it seemed related to the earth but by an egg hatched some time in the crevice of a crag; —or was its native nest made in the angle of a cloud, woven of the rainbow's trimmings and the sunset sky, and lined with some soft midsummer haze caught up from earth? Its eyry° now some cliffy cloud.

Beside this I got a rare mess of golden and silver and bright cupreous fishes, which looked like a string of jewels. Ah! I have penetrated to those meadows on the morning of many a first spring day, jumping from hummock to hummock, from willow root to willow root, when the wild river valley and the woods were bathed in so pure and bright a light as would have waked the dead, if they had been slumbering in their graves, as some suppose. There needs no stronger proof of immortality. All things must live in such a light. O Death, where was thy sting? O Grave, where was thy victory, then?

Our village life would stagnate if it were not for the unexplored forests and meadows which surround it. We need the tonic of wildness,—to wade sometimes in marshes where the bittern and the meadow-hen lurk, and hear the booming of the snipe; to smell the whispering sedge where only some wilder and more solitary fowl builds her nest, and the mink crawls with its belly close to the ground. At the same time that we are earnest to explore and learn all things, we require that all things be mysterious and unexplorable, that land and sea be infinitely wild, unsurveyed and unfathomed by us because unfathomable. We can never have enough of Nature. We must be refreshed by the sight of inexhaustible vigor, vast and Titanic features, the sea-coast with its wrecks, the wilderness with its living and its decaying trees, the thunder cloud, and the rain which lasts three weeks and produces freshets. We need to witness our own limits transgressed, and some life pasturing freely where we never wander. We are cheered when we observe the vulture feeding on the carrion which disgusts and disheartens us and deriving health and strength from the repast. There was a dead horse in the hollow by the path to my house, which compelled me sometimes to go out of my way, especially in the night when the air was heavy, but the assurance it gave me of the strong appetite and inviolable health of Nature was my compensation for this. I love to see that Nature is so rife with life that myriads can be afforded to be sacrificed and suffered to prey on one another; that tender organizations can be so serenely squashed out of existence like pulp,—tadpoles which herons gobble up, and tortoises and toads run over in the road; and that sometimes it has rained flesh and blood! With the liability to accident, we must see how little account is to be made of it. The impression made on a wise man is that of universal innocence. Poison is not poisonous after all,

---

eyry: bird's nest

nor are any wounds fatal. Compassion is a very untenable ground. It must be expeditious. Its pleadings will not bear to be stereotyped.

Early in May, the oaks, hickories, maples, and other trees, just putting out amidst the pine woods around the pond, imparted a brightness like sunshine to the landscape, especially in cloudy days, as if the sun were breaking through mists and shining faintly on the hill-sides here and there. On the third or fourth of May I saw a loon in the pond, and during the first week of the month I heard the whippoorwill, the brown-thrasher, the veery, the wood-pewee, the chewink, and other birds. I had heard the wood-thrush long before. The phoebe had already come once more and looked in at my door and window, to see if my house was cavern-like enough for her, sustaining herself on humming wings with clinched talons, as if she held by the air, while she surveyed the premises. The sulphur-like pollen of the pitch-pine soon covered the pond and the stones and rotten wood along the shore, so that you could have collected a barrel-ful. This is the "sulphur showers" we hear of. Even in Calidas' drama of Sacontala,° we read of "rills dyed yellow with the golden dust of the lotus." And so the seasons went rolling on into summer, as one rambles into higher and higher grass.

Thus was my first year's life in the woods completed; and the second year was similar to it. I finally left Walden September 6th, 1847.

---

1. This essay tells a story, and so it is narrative (see Chapter 11), but much of the essay is descriptive. Look especially at the extended descriptions. Do they help you toward what you see to be the dominant idea of the essay?

2. Thoreau writes a lot about changing shapes in his physical surroundings. Why do you think he wants to call your attention to these sights?

3. Thoreau writes a lot about dead things seeming alive in this selection. Why do you think he wants to call your attention to this issue?

4. Can you find other consistent patterns of images that Thoreau uses?

5. When you put all the image patterns together, what do they suggest?

✑ An Invitation to Write

rite a short description or a poem that uses the setting—not the people—to present a dominant idea about the people who live or work in that setting.

On your own or working in your group, apply the first-draft questions to your writing. Then rewrite your draft based on your answers or following

---

Sacontala: Fifth-century Sanskrit drama by Kalidasa

group members' suggestions that you find useful. Then apply the second-draft questions to your writing. Write a third draft incorporating useful suggestions your group has made or your own observations.

 A Student Paper

The student paper that follows uses a descriptive organizational approach. When you have read it, answer the questions that follow it, alone or with your group.

I WAS THIRTEEN

Scott Davis

I was thirteen that day. I'd only lived eleven years and a few months, but that day I was thirteen. At least that's what I told everybody. I wanted to be able to see the movie before touring the museum, and since viewers had to be thirteen, I said I was.

Sitting with my parents and my fifteen-year-old brother, Mike, in the second row of the small theater, I waited for the short movie to begin. A solemn atmosphere permeated the theater. Some people on the tour who had been to Poland before knew what they were about to see. Others had chosen not to view the movie, but I was curious. When the tour guide came in and was seated, the movie began.

I watched the black and white film's introduction. Because I had been told that I had to be "old enough to handle it," I was interested to see what the movie was all about. Before my eyes unfolded the story of Auschwitz, a place that seemed inconceivable to me.

Auschwitz was the Nazis' brainchild and, being very proud of it, they had meticulously captured every aspect of the death camp on film. The movie began with the overview and plans of the camp and pictures of Himmler, Hitler, and SS commandants touring the facility, followed by footage of long lines of Jews walking from the train station to the gates of Auschwitz, where a big band playing joyous music merrily greeted them. At a table one man pointed: go to the left, or go to the right. The movie showed the barracks where Jews slept four to a bunk. It showed them as slaves working around the camp. This only bothered me a little as I did not really know much about the concentration camps.

Then the film turned its focus to the death machine that Auschwitz   5 was. I saw the gas chambers, the crematorium, and the cartloads of dead bodies being thrown into a mass grave to be buried by surviving Jews in tattered prison clothing. The film showed Jewish prisoners' extracted gold teeth that would be melted down for German use, the piles of eyeglasses, the prosthetic legs and arms, and crutches. I felt horror at the sight of these personal items, knowing that their owners had been exterminated. Now I knew why I had to be thirteen that day. I stared at the screen in amazement. One child my age was punished for something ridiculous like being late to roll call and was sentenced to stand barefoot in the snow all day. He lost both his feet to frostbite in the cold Polish snow.

Finally the movie approached the end. The last part was footage taken by the Allies as they liberated the camp. The Nazis tried to eliminate the evidence, but ran out of time. Allied footage showed the discovery of the piles of hair, suitcases, jewelry, dishes, clothing, and other personal items robbed from the Jews and stockpiled for shipment to Germany. The film showed the Allied doctors treating the malnourished walking skeletons—all that remained of the Jewish prisoners. As I viewed the liberation of Auschwitz, I sat silently cheering the Allies for winning the war and wishing that they could have done it sooner.

The movie drew to an end with a plea to humanity to learn from Auschwitz and to ensure that attempted genocide never be allowed to happen again. As it finished, the room that had once held a steady murmur of voices was dead silent. Except for an occasional sniff from someone wiping away tears, there were no sounds. None at all. Tears were in my eyes too.

The guide broke the silence with a soft voice as she ushered us out of the theater to the walking tour of the camp. It was a cold, overcast day. As I looked at the ground blanketed by pristine white snow, I thought of the child in the film who had been forced to stand barefoot; yet I still could not picture the thousands of prisoners who had walked here forty years ago. I could not picture the ash-filled smoke coming out of the chimneys of the crematorium. I could not imagine the sounds of gunfire and whips. Auschwitz looked too peaceful and picturesque. But then we came to the front entrance. "*ARBEIT MACHT FREI*," the sign read: German for a false promise to the Jews that "Work makes freedom." But it was not true for the more than five million Jews who were brutally murdered here. We walked next to the fence that once was electrified. Many Jews killed themselves by flinging their bodies onto this fence because it was a quicker way to die than to be gassed or shot. Some SS guards displayed the bodies as a warning to other Jews.

We walked on to the museum, which houses rooms and rooms filled with belongings that had been stripped from the prisoners. Buildings housing mounds of suitcases, glasses, clothes, pots and pans, shoes, kitchen utensils, pictures, the prosthetic legs and arms as well as crutches, and most horrifying to me, the mountain of human hair that had been cut from the prisoners as they entered, hair that after forty years was still in perfect braids, curls, and whose color was as bright red, blonde, brown, and gray as it had been the day it was cut. Mom told me that Dad's relatives probably donated some of their fine red hair to these or other such piles. Seeing these rooms made Auschwitz real for me. Some of my family might have been here. Seeing the cell blocks, the barracks, the crematorium, and the gas chambers all made me think that this happened for five years. On the walls of the buildings were the pictures of children my age and younger dressed in black–and–white striped jail suits. Their crime was only that they had been Jewish. Their sentence had been death. If it had been me or my family, we'd all be gone. Mom is handicapped, Dad is of Jewish heritage, and children (considered useless to the Nazis) usually were among the first to be gassed.

The final stop on the tour was the execution wall, where one man had   10
shot thousands of people. The wall was ringed with flowers at the base, as well as pictures, and Stars of David as tributes to lost loved ones. There was only the sound of weeping and tears from within the group. I spent a lot of time looking at the ground, trying to comprehend all that I had seen.

We left Auschwitz to board the bus. The tour guide offered to drive us over to Birkenau, the sister camp where more women had been housed and where soup bowls were also the toilets, but we had all seen enough. No one got off the bus.

Being "thirteen" that day didn't make me any more prepared for the horror at hand than if I had been thirty. As the bus pulled away from Birkenau and off to lunch (for which few were in the mood), I reflected on what I had seen. Auschwitz had been a human destruction factory, a place where there were no names, just numbers and faces, faces of people who were not much different than me or Mike, or Mom, or Dad.

I returned home from the tour, the only fifth grader in my school to know what Auschwitz was and what it meant. Asked by teachers to give presentations in the local elementary schools, I went from class to class showing slides of my tour. I found it difficult to convey the importance, significance, and horror of Auschwitz to other elementary school kids. I think having the personal experience of viewing Auschwitz and seeing the film made by the Nazis themselves was essential to my knowledge and belief that it existed. The film made a plea to humanity to prevent ethnic cleansing like this from happening again and my continuing prayer is that people will learn about it and put an end to what is happening now in Bosnia. I pray that we never allow genocide again. I don't want any future child to have to be "thirteen" to view a similar film of another holocaust because of any humans' forgetting the lessons of the past.

---

1. What do you see to be the writer's dominant idea in this paper?

2. How does that dominant idea control the writer's selection of scenes and objects in his description?

3. Do you think the writer's choice to describe his experience through his eyes instead of objectively was an effective choice?

4. If the writer were a member of your group or if you were editing this paper for him, what suggestions would you have for him to help him make his paper better? Why do you think your suggestions are good ones?

FURTHER READINGS

On the following pages you will find readings that use description as their primary organizational strategy. If your instructor assigns some or all of these readings or if you are inclined to read them on your own, pay attention to the ways the writers use description to support their dominant ideas. Also, note how the writers use voice and style to engage your feelings, your interest, and your intellect.

Remember, these writers are writing to you—a fellow human being. They have chosen to tell you something about coping with the effort of being human in their worlds. See how their examples and ideas speak to your experience. See how the combination of your experiences and those the writers offer you might lead you to your own ideas about your world.

REBECCA

Oliver Sacks

Rebecca was no child when she was referred to our clinic. She was nineteen, but, as her grandmother said, "just like a child in some ways." She could not find her way around the block, she could not confidently open a door with a key (she could never "see" how the key went, and never seemed to learn). She had left/right confusion, she sometimes put on her clothes the wrong way—inside out, back-to-front, without appearing to notice, or, if she noticed, without being able to get them right. She might spend hours jamming a hand or foot into the wrong glove or shoe—she seemed, as her grandmother said, to have "no sense of space." She was clumsy and ill-coordinated in all her movements—a "klutz," one report said, a "motor moron" another (although when she danced, all her clumsiness disappeared).

Rebecca had a partial cleft palate, which caused a whistling in her speech; short, stumpy fingers, with blunt, deformed nails; and a high, degenerative myopia requiring very thick spectacles—all stigmata of the same congenital condition which had caused her cerebral and mental defects. She was painfully shy and withdrawn, feeling that she was, and had always been, a "figure of fun."

But she was capable of warm, deep, even passionate attachments. She had a deep love for her grandmother, who had brought her up since she was three (when she was orphaned by the death of both parents). She was very fond of nature, and, if she was taken to the city parks and botanic gardens, spent many happy hours there. She was very fond too of stories, though she never learned to read (despite assiduous, and even frantic, attempts), and would implore her grandmother or others to read to her. "She has a hunger for stories," her grandmother said; and fortunately her grandmother loved reading stories and had a fine reading voice which kept Rebecca entranced. And not just stories—poetry too. This seemed a deep need or hunger in Rebecca—a necessary form of nourishment, of reality, for her mind. Nature was beautiful, but mute. It was not enough. She needed the world represented to her in verbal images, in language, and seemed to have little difficulty following the metaphors and symbols of even quite deep poems, in striking contrast to her incapacity with simple propositions and instructions. The language of feeling, of the concrete, of image and symbol formed a world she loved and, to a remarkable extent, could enter. Though conceptually (and "propositionally") inept, she was at home with poetic language, and was herself, in a stumbling, touching way, a sort of "primitive," natural poet. Metaphors, figures of speech, rather striking similitudes, would come naturally to her, though unpredictably, as sudden poetic ejaculations or allusions. Her grandmother was devout, in a quiet way, and this also was true of Rebecca: she loved the lighting of the Shabbath candles,° the benisons and orisons° which thread the Jewish day; she loved going to the synagogue, where she too was loved (and seen as a child of God, a sort of innocent, a holy fool); and she fully understood the liturgy, the chants, the prayers, rites and symbols of which the Orthodox service consists. All this was possible for her, accessible to her, loved by her, despite gross perceptual and spatio-temporal problems, and gross impairments in every schematic capacity—she could not count change, the simplest calculations defeated her, she could never learn to read or write, and she would average 60 or less in IQ tests (though doing notably better on the verbal than the performance parts of the test).

Thus she was a "moron," a "fool," a "booby," or had so appeared, and so been called, throughout her whole life, but one with an unexpected, strangely moving, poetic power. Superficially she *was* a mass of handicaps and incapacities, with the intense frustrations and anxieties attendant on these; at this level she was, and felt herself to be, a mental cripple—beneath the effortless skills, the happy capacities, of others; but at some deeper level there was no sense of handicap or incapacity, but a feeling of calm and completeness, of being fully alive, of being a soul, deep and high, and equal to all others. Intellectually, then, Rebecca felt a cripple; spiritually she felt herself a full and complete being.

When I first saw her—clumsy, uncouth, all-of-a-fumble—I saw her 5 merely, or wholly, as a casualty, a broken creature, whose neurological impairments I could pick out and dissect with precision: a multitude of apraxias

---

Shabbath candles: Among Sephardic Jews and in the State of Israel, Shabbath (also Shabbat and Shabat) is the Sabbath, the day of holiness and rest observed from sunset on Friday to nightfall of the following day. In Jewish homes, the woman of the house lights white Sabbath candles before sunset on Friday evening.
benisons and orisons: blessings and prayers

and agnosias,° a mass of sensorimotor impairments and breakdowns, limitations of intellectual schemata and concepts similar (by Piaget's° criteria) to those of a child of eight. A poor thing, I said to myself, with perhaps a "splinter skill," a freak gift, of speech; a mere mosaic of higher cortical functions, Piagetian schemata—most impaired.

The next time I saw her, it was all very different. I didn't have her in a test situation, "evaluating" her in a clinic. I wandered outside, it was a lovely spring day, with a few minutes in hand before the clinic started, and there I saw Rebecca sitting on a bench, gazing at the April foliage quietly, with obvious delight. Her posture had none of the clumsiness which had so impressed me before. Sitting there, in a light dress, her face calm and slightly smiling, she suddenly brought to mind one of Chekov's° young women— Irene, Anya, Sonya, Nina—seen against the backdrop of a Chekovian cherry orchard. She could have been any young woman enjoying a beautiful spring day. This was my human, as opposed to my neurological, vision.

As I approached, she heard my footsteps and turned, gave me a broad smile, and wordlessly gestured. "Look at the world," she seemed to say. "How beautiful it is." And then there came out, in Jacksonian spurts,° odd, sudden, poetic ejaculations: "spring," "birth," "growing," "stirring," "coming to life," "seasons," "everything in its time." I found myself thinking of Ecclesiastes: "To everything there is a season, and a time to every purpose under the heaven. A time to be born, and a time to die; a time to plant, and a time. . . ." This was what Rebecca, in her disjointed fashion, was ejaculating—a vision of seasons, of times, like that of the Preacher. "She is an idiot Ecclesiastes," I said to myself. And in this phrase, my two visions of her—as idiot and as symbolist—met, collided and fused. She had done appallingly in the testing—which, in a sense, was designed, like all neurological and psychological testing, not merely to uncover, to bring out deficits, but to decompose her into functions and deficits. She had come apart, horribly, in formal testing, but now she was mysteriously "together" and composed.

Why was she so decomposed before, how could she be so recomposed now? I had the strongest feeling of two wholly different modes of thought, or of organization, or of being. The first schematic—pattern-seeing, problem-solving—this is what had been tested, and where she had been found so defective, so disastrously wanting. But the tests had given no inkling of anything *but* the deficits, anything, so to speak, *beyond* her deficits.

They had given me no hint of her positive powers, her ability to perceive the real world—the world of nature, and perhaps of the imagina-

---

apraxias and agnosias: terms describing inabilities to recognize familiar objects
Jean Piaget: Swiss psychologist (1896–1980) and pioneer student of cognitive development through childhood
Anton Pavlovich Chekov: Russian playwright (1860–1904) and short-story writer
Jacksonian spurts: The spurts are "words or phrases uttered under stress of emotion when they cannot be spoken voluntarily."

tion—as a coherent, intelligible, poetic whole: her ability to see this, think this, and (when she could) live this; they had given me no intimation of her inner world, which clearly *was* composed and coherent, and approached as something other than a set of problems or tasks.

But what was the composing principle which could allow her compo-   *10* sure (clearly it was something other than schematic)? I found myself thinking of her fondness for tales, for narrative composition and coherence. Is it possible, I wondered, that this being before me—at once a charming girl, and a moron, a cognitive mishap—can *use* a narrative (or dramatic) mode to compose and integrate a coherent world, in place of the schematic mode, which, in her, is so defective that it simply doesn't work? And as I thought, I remembered her dancing, and how this could organize her otherwise ill-knit and clumsy movements.

Our tests, our approaches, I thought, as I watched her on the bench—enjoying not just a simple but a sacred view of nature—our approach, our "evaluations," are ridiculously inadequate. They only show us deficits, they do not show us powers; they only show us puzzles and schemata, when we need to see music, narrative, play, a being conducting itself spontaneously in its own natural way.

Rebecca, I felt, was complete and intact as "narrative" being, in conditions which allowed her to organize herself in a narrative way; and this was something very important to know, for it allowed one to see her, and her potential, in a quite different fashion from that imposed by the schematic mode.

It was perhaps fortunate that I chanced to see Rebecca in her so-different modes—so damaged and incorrigible in the one, so full of promise and potential in the other—and that she was one of the first patients I saw in our clinic. For what I saw in her, what she showed me, I now saw in them all.

As I continued to see her, she seemed to deepen. Or perhaps she revealed, or I came to respect, her depths more and more. They were not wholly happy depths—no depths ever are—but they were predominantly happy for the greater part of the year.

Then, in November, her grandmother died, and the light, the joy, she   *15* had expressed in April now turned into the deepest grief and darkness. She was devastated, but conducted herself with great dignity. Dignity, ethical depth, was added at this time, to form a grave and lasting counterpoint to the light, lyrical self I had especially seen before.

I called on her as soon as I heard the news, and she received me, with great dignity, but frozen with grief, in her small room in the now empty house. Her speech was again ejaculated, "Jacksonian," in brief utterances of grief and lamentation. "Why did she have to go?" she cried; and added, "I'm crying for me, not for her." Then, after an interval, "Grannie's all right. She's gone to her Long Home." Long Home! Was this her own symbol, or an unconscious memory of, or allusion to, Ecclesiastes? "I'm so cold," she cried, huddling into herself. "It's not outside, it's winter inside. Cold as death," she added. "She was a part of me. Part of me died with her."

She was complete in her mourning—tragic and complete—there was absolutely no sense of her being then a "mental defective." After half an hour, she unfroze, regained some of her warmth and animation, said: "It is winter. I feel dead. But I know the spring will come again."

The work of grief was slow, but successful, as Rebecca, even when most stricken, anticipated. It was greatly helped by a sympathetic and supportive great aunt, a sister of her Grannie, who now moved into the house. It was greatly helped by the synagogue, and the religious community, above all by the rites of "sitting shiva,"° and the special status accorded her as the bereaved one, the chief mourner. It was helped too perhaps by her speaking freely to me. And it was helped also, interestingly, by *dreams,* which she related with animation, and which clearly marked *stages* in the grief-work.

As I remember her, like Nina, in the April sun, so I remember her, etched with tragic clearness, in the dark November of that year, standing in a bleak cemetery in Queens, saying the Kaddish° over her grandmother's grave. Prayers and Bible stories had always appealed to her, going with the happy, the lyrical, the "blessing" side of her life. Now, in the funeral prayers, in the 103rd Psalm, and above all in the Kaddish, she found the right and only words for her comfort and lamentation.

During the intervening months (between my first seeing her, in April, and her grandmother's death that November) Rebecca—like all our "clients" (an odious word then becoming fashionable, supposedly less degrading than "patients"), was pressed into a variety of workshops and classes, as part of our Developmental and Cognitive Drive (these too were "in" terms at the time).

It didn't work with Rebecca, it didn't work with most of them. It was not, I came to think, the right thing to do, because what we did was to drive them full-tilt upon their limitations, as had already been done, futilely, and often to the point of cruelty, throughout their lives.

We paid far too much attention to the defects of our patients, as Rebecca was the first to tell me, and far too little to what was intact or preserved. To use another piece of jargon, we were far too concerned with "defectology," and far too little with "narratology," the neglected and needed science of the concrete.

Rebecca made clear, by concrete illustrations, by her own self, the two wholly different, wholly separate, forms of thought and mind, "paradigmatic" and "narrative" (in Bruner's° terminology). And though equally natural and native to the expanding human mind, the narrative comes first,

20

---

sitting shiva: The Jewish tradition of sitting on chairs of less than normal height (or even sitting on the floor or ground) during the seven days of mourning (shiva) following the burial of a near relative

Kaddish: a prayer praising God, recited by mourners after the death of a near relative

Jerome Bruner (1915–90): American psychologist and educator

has spiritual priority. Very young children love and demand stories, and can understand complex matters presented as stories, when their powers of comprehending general concepts, paradigms, are almost nonexistent. It is this narrative or symbolic power which gives *a sense of the world*—a concrete reality in the imaginative form of symbol and story—when abstract thought can provide nothing at all. A child follows the Bible before he follows Euclid.° Not because the Bible is simpler (the reverse might be said), but because it is cast in a symbolic and narrative mode.

And in this way, Rebecca, at nineteen, was still, as her grandmother said, "just like a child." Like a child, but not a child, because she was adult. (The term "retarded" suggests a persisting child, the term "mentally defective" a defective adult; both terms, both concepts, combine deep truth and falsity.)

With Rebecca—and with other defectives allowed, or encouraged in, a personal development—the emotional and narrative and symbolic powers can develop strongly and exuberantly, and may produce . . . a sort of natural artist—while the paradigmatic or conceptual powers, manifestly feeble from the start, grind very slowly and painfully along, and are only capable of very limited and stunted development. 25

Rebecca realized this fully—as she had shown it to me so clearly, right from the very first day I saw her, when she spoke of her clumsiness, and of how her ill-composed and ill-organized movements became well-organized, composed and fluent, with music; and when she *showed* me how she herself was composed by a natural scene, a scene with an organic, aesthetic and dramatic unity and sense.

Rather suddenly, after her grandmother's death, she became clear and decisive. "I want no more classes, no more workshops," she said. "They do nothing for me. They do nothing to bring me together." And then, with that power for the apt model or metaphor I so admired, and which was so well developed in her despite her low IQ, she looked down at the office carpet and said:

"I'm like a sort of living carpet. I need a pattern, a design, like you have on that carpet. I come apart, I unravel, unless there's a design." I looked down at the carpet, as Rebecca said this, and found myself thinking of Sherrington's° famous image, comparing the brain/mind to an "enchanted loom," weaving patterns ever-dissolving, but always with meaning. I thought: can one have a raw carpet without a design? Could one have the design without the carpet (but this seemed like the smile without the Cheshire cat°)? A "living" carpet, as Rebecca was, had to have both—and she especially, with her lack of schematic structure (the warp and woof, the

---

Euclid: Greek mathematician (fl 300 B.C.), who lived and taught at Alexandria. His *Elements* in thirteen books became the basis of modern geometry.
Sir Charles Scott Sherrington: English physiologist (1857–1952)
Cheshire cat: in Lewis Carroll's *Alice's Adventures in Wonderland* (1865), a creature that has the ability to vanish at will, its grin being the last thing to go

knit, of the carpet, so to speak), might indeed unravel without a design (the scenic or narrative structure of the carpet).

"I must have meaning," she went on. "The classes, the odd jobs have no meaning. . . . What I really love," she added wistfully, "is the theater."

We removed Rebecca from the workshop she hated, and managed to enroll her in a special theater group. She loved this—it composed her; she did amazingly well: she became a complete person, poised, fluent, with style, in each role. And now if one sees Rebecca on stage, for theater and the theater group soon became her life, one would never even guess that she was mentally defective.

30

Postscript

The power of music, narrative and drama is of the greatest practical and theoretical importance. One may see this even in the case of idiots, with IQs below 20 and the extremest motor incompetence and bewilderment. Their uncouth movements may disappear in a moment with music and dancing—suddenly, with music, they know how to move. We see how the retarded, unable to perform fairly simple tasks involving perhaps four or five movements or procedures in sequence, can do these perfectly if they work to music—the sequence of movements they cannot hold as schemes being perfectly holdable as music, i.e., embedded in music. The same may be seen, very dramatically, in patients with severe frontal lobe damage and apraxia— an inability to *do* things, to retain the simplest motor sequences and programs, even to walk, despite perfectly preserved intelligence in all other ways. This procedural defect, or motor idiocy, as one might call it, which completely defeats any ordinary system of rehabilitative instruction, vanishes at once if music is the instructor. All this, no doubt, is the rationale, or one of the rationales, of work songs.

What we see, fundamentally, is the power of music to organize—and to do this efficaciously (as well as joyfully!), when abstract or schematic forms of organizations fail. Indeed, it is especially dramatic, as one would expect, precisely when no other form of organization will work. Thus music, or any other form of narrative, is essential when working with the retarded or apraxic—schooling or therapy for them must be centred on music or something equivalent. And in drama there is still more—there is the power of *rôle* to give organization, to confer, while it lasts, an entire personality. The capacity to perform, to play, to *be,* seems to be a "given" in human life, in a way which has nothing to do with intellectual differences. One sees this with infants, one sees it with the senile, and one sees it, most poignantly, with the Rebeccas of this world.

FROM McTEAGUE

Frank Norris

The day was very hot, and the silence of high noon lay close and thick between the steep slopes of the cañons like an invisible, muffling fluid. At intervals the drone of an insect bored the air and trailed slowly to silence again. Everywhere were pungent, aromatic smells. The vast, moveless heat seemed to distil countless odors from the brush—odors of warm sap, of pine needles, and of tarweed, and above all the medicinal odor of witch hazel. As far as one could look, uncounted multitudes of trees and manzanita bushes were quietly and motionlessly growing, growing, growing. A tremendous, immeasurable Life pushed steadily heavenward without a sound, without a motion. At turns of the road, on the higher points, cañons disclosed themselves far away, gigantic grooves in the landscape, deep blue in the distance, opening one into another, ocean–deep, silent, huge, and suggestive of colossal primeval forces held in reserve. At their bottoms they were solid, massive; on their crests they broke delicately into fine serrated edges where the pines and redwoods outlined their million of tops against the high white horizon. Here and there the mountains lifted themselves out of the narrow river beds in groups like giant lions rearing their heads after drinking. The entire region was untamed. In some places east of the Mississippi nature is cosey, intimate, small, and homelike, like a good–natured housewife. In Placer County, California, she is a vast, unconquered brute of the Pliocene epoch, savage, sullen, and magnificently indifferent to man.

But there were men in these mountains, like lice on mammoths' hides, fighting them stubbornly, now with hydraulic "monitors," now with drill and dynamite, boring into the vitals of them, or tearing away great yellow gravelly scars in the flanks of them, sucking their blood, extracting gold.

Here and there at long distances upon the cañon sides rose the headgear of a mine, surrounded with its few unpainted houses, and topped by its never–failing feather of black smoke. On near approach one heard the prolonged thunder of the stamp–mill, the crusher, the insatiable monster, gnashing the rocks to powder with its long iron teeth, vomiting them out again in a thin stream of wet gray mud. Its enormous maw, fed night and day with the car–boy's loads, gorged itself with gravel, and spat out the gold, grinding the rocks between its jaws, glutted, as it were, with the very entrails of the earth, and growling over its endless meal, like some savage animal, some legendary dragon, some fabulous beast, symbol of inordinate and monstrous gluttony.

THE FALL OF THE HOUSE OF USHER

Edgar Allan Poe

Son cœur est un luth suspendu;
Sitôt qu'on le touche il résonne.°

—DE BÉRANGER

During the whole of a dull, dark, and soundless day in the autumn of
the year, when the clouds hung oppressively low in the heavens, I had been
passing alone, on horseback, through a singularly dreary tract of country;
and at length found myself, as the shades of the evening drew on, within
view of the melancholy House of Usher. I know not how it was—but, with
the first glimpse of the building, a sense of insufferable gloom pervaded my
spirit. I say insufferable; for the feeling was unrelieved by any of that half-
pleasurable, because poetic, sentiment, with which the mind usually receives
even the sternest natural images of the desolate or terrible. I looked upon
the scene before me—upon the mere house, and the simple landscape features of the domain—upon the bleak walls—upon the vacant eye-like windows—upon a few rank sedges—and upon a few white trunks of decayed
trees—with an utter depression of soul which I can compare to no earthly
sensation more properly than to the after-dream of the reveller upon
opium—the bitter lapse into everyday life—the hideous dropping off of the
veil. There was an iciness, a sinking, a sickening of the heart—an unre-
deemed dreariness of thought which no goading of the imagination could
torture into aught of the sublime. What was it—I paused to think—what
was it that so unnerved me in the contemplation of the House of Usher? It
was a mystery all insoluble; nor could I grapple with the shadowy fancies
that crowded upon me as I pondered. I was forced to fall back upon the
unsatisfactory conclusion, that while, beyond doubt, there *are* combinations
of very simple natural objects which have the power of thus affecting us, still
the analysis of this power lies among considerations beyond our depth. It
was possible, I reflected, that a mere different arrangement of the particulars
of the scene, of the details of the picture, would be sufficient to modify, or
perhaps to annihilate its capacity for sorrowful impression; and, acting upon
this idea, I reined my horse to the precipitous brink of a black and lurid tarn
that lay in unruffled lustre by the dwelling, and gazed down—but with
a shudder even more thrilling than before—upon the remodelled and inverted images of the gray sedge, and the ghastly tree-stems, and the vacant
and eye-like windows.

Epigraph. *Son . . . résonne:* French for "His heart is a suspended lute; / Whenever it is
touched, it resounds."

Nevertheless, in this mansion of gloom I now proposed to myself a sojourn of some weeks. Its proprietor, Roderick Usher, had been one of my boon companions in boyhood; but many years had elapsed since our last meeting. A letter, however, had lately reached me in a distant part of the country—a letter from him—which, in its wildly importunate nature, had admitted of no other than a personal reply. The MS. gave evidence of nervous agitation. The writer spoke of acute bodily illness—of a mental disorder which oppressed him—and of an earnest desire to see me, as his best, and indeed his only personal friend, with a view of attempting, by the cheerfulness of my society, some alleviation of his malady. It was the manner in which all this, and much more, was said—it was the apparent *heart* that went with his request—which allowed me no room for hesitation; and I accordingly obeyed forthwith what I still considered a very singular summons.

Although, as boys, we had been even intimate associates, yet I really knew little of my friend. His reserve had been always excessive and habitual. I was aware, however, that his very ancient family had been noted, time out of mind, for a peculiar sensibility of temperament, displaying itself, through long ages, in many works of exalted art, and manifested, of late, in repeated deeds of munificent yet unobtrusive charity, as well as in a passionate devotion to the intricacies, perhaps even more than to the orthodox and easily recognisable beauties, of musical science. I had learned, too, the very remarkable fact, that the stem of the Usher race, all time-honoured as it was, had put forth, at no period, any enduring branch; in other words, that the entire family lay in the direct line of descent, and had always, with very trifling and very temporary variation, so lain. It was this deficiency, I considered, while running over in thought the perfect keeping of the character of the premises with the accredited character of the people, and while speculating upon the possible influence which the one, in the long lapse of centuries, might have exercised upon the other—it was this deficiency, perhaps, of collateral issue, and the consequent undeviating transmission, from sire to son, of the patrimony with the name, which had, at length, so identified the two as to merge the original title of the estate in the quaint and equivocal appellation of the "House of Usher"—an appellation which seemed to include, in the minds of the peasantry who used it, both the family and the family mansion.

I have said that the sole effect of my somewhat childish experiment—that of looking down within the tarn—had been to deepen the first singular impression. There can be no doubt that the consciousness of the rapid increase of my superstition—for why should I not so term it?—served mainly to accelerate the increase itself. Such, I have long known, is the paradoxical law of all sentiments having terror as a basis. And it might have been for this reason only, that, when I again uplifted my eyes to the house itself, from its image in the pool, there grew in my mind a strange fancy—a fancy so ridiculous, indeed, that I but mention it to show the vivid force of the sensations which oppressed me. I had so worked upon my imagination as really to believe that about the whole mansion and domain there hung an atmosphere peculiar to themselves and their immediate vicinity—an atmosphere which had no affinity with the air of heaven, but which had reeked up from the decayed trees, and the gray wall, and the silent tarn—a pestilent and mystic vapour, dull, sluggish, faintly discernible, and leaden-hued.

Shaking off from my spirit what *must* have been a dream, I scanned   5
more narrowly the real aspect of the building. Its principal feature seemed to be that of an excessive antiquity. The discoloration of ages had been great. Minute fungi overspread the whole exterior, hanging in a fine tangled web-work from the eaves. Yet all this was apart from any extraordinary dilapidation. No portion of the masonry had fallen; and there appeared to be a wild inconsistency between its still perfect adaptation of parts, and the crumbling condition of the individual stones. In this there was much that reminded me of the specious totality of old wood-work which has rotted for long years in some neglected vault, with no disturbance from the breath of the external air. Beyond this indication of extensive decay, however, the fabric gave little token of instability. Perhaps the eye of a scrutinising observer might have discovered a barely perceptible fissure, which, extending from the roof of the building in front, made its way down the wall in a zigzag direction, until it became lost in the sullen waters of the tarn.

Noticing these things, I rode over a short causeway to the house. A servant in waiting took my horse, and I entered the Gothic archway of the hall. A valet, of stealthy step, thence conducted me, in silence, through many dark and intricate passages in my progress to the *studio* of his master. Much that I encountered on the way contributed, I know not how, to heighten the vague sentiments of which I have already spoken. While the objects around me—while the carvings of the ceilings, the sombre tapestries of the walls, the ebon blackness of the floors, and the phantasmagoric armorial trophies which rattled as I strode, were but matters to which, or to such as which, I had been accustomed from my infancy—while I hesitated not to acknowledge how familiar was all this—I still wondered to find how unfamiliar were the fancies which ordinary images were stirring up. On one of the staircases, I met the physician of the family. His countenance, I thought, wore a mingled expression of low cunning and perplexity. He accosted me with trepidation and passed on. The valet now threw open a door and ushered me into the presence of his master.

The room in which I found myself was very large and lofty. The windows were long, narrow, and pointed, and at so vast a distance from the black oaken floor as to be altogether inaccessible from within. Feeble gleams of encrimsoned light made their way through the trellised panes, and served to render sufficiently distinct the more prominent objects around; the eye, however, struggled in vain to reach the remoter angles of the chamber, or the recesses of the vaulted and fretted ceiling. Dark draperies hung upon the walls. The general furniture was profuse, comfortless, antique, and tattered. Many books and musical instruments lay scattered about, but failed to give any vitality to the scene. I felt that I breathed an atmosphere of sorrow. An air of stern, deep, and irredeemable gloom hung over and pervaded all.

Upon my entrance, Usher arose from a sofa on which he had been lying at full length, and greeted me with a vivacious warmth which had much in it, I at first thought, of an overdone cordiality—of the constrained effort of the *ennuyé*° man of the world. A glance, however, at his countenance, convinced me of his perfect sincerity. We sat down; and for some moments, while he spoke not, I gazed upon him with a feeling half of pity, half of awe. Surely, man had never before so terribly altered, in so brief a period, as had Roderick Usher! It was with difficulty that I could bring myself to admit the identity of the wan being before me with the companion of my early boyhood. Yet the character of his face had been at all times remarkable. A cadaverousness of complexion; an eye large, liquid, and luminous beyond comparison; lips somewhat thin and very pallid, but of a surpassingly beautiful curve; a nose of delicate Hebrew model, but with a breadth of nostril unusual in similar formations; a finely moulded chin, speaking, in its want of prominence, of a want of moral energy; hair of a more than web-like softness and tenuity; these features, with an inordinate expansion above the regions of the temple, made up altogether a countenance not easily to be forgotten. And now in the mere exaggeration of the prevailing character of these features, and of the expression they were wont to convey, lay so much of change that I doubted to whom I spoke. The now ghastly pallor of the skin, and the now miraculous lustre of the eye, above all things startled and even awed me. The silken hair, too, had been suffered to grow all unheeded, and as, in its wild gossamer texture, it floated rather than fell about the face, I could not, even with effort, connect its Arabesque expression with any idea of simple humanity.

In the manner of my friend I was at once struck with an incoherence—an inconsistency; and I soon found this to arise from a series of feeble and futile struggles to overcome an habitual trepidancy—an excessive nervous agitation. For something of this nature I had indeed been prepared, no less by his letter, than by reminiscences of certain boyish traits, and by conclusions deduced from his peculiar physical conformation and temperament. His action was alternately vivacious and sullen. His voice varied rapidly from a tremulous indecision (when the animal spirits seemed utterly in abeyance) to that species of energetic concision—that abrupt, weighty, unhurried, and hollow-sounding enunciation—that leaden, self-balanced and perfectly modulated guttural utterance, which may be observed in the lost drunkard, or the irreclaimable eater of opium, during the periods of his most intense excitement.

It was thus that he spoke of the object of my visit, of his earnest desire to see me, and of the solace he expected me to afford him. He entered, at some length, into what he conceived to be the nature of his malady. It was, he said, a constitutional and a family evil, and one for which he despaired to find a remedy—a mere nervous affection, he immediately added, which

10

---

ennuyé: sophisticated

would undoubtedly soon pass off. It displayed itself in a host of unnatural sensations. Some of these, as he detailed them, interested and bewildered me; although, perhaps, the terms, and the general manner of the narration had their weight. He suffered much from a morbid acuteness of the senses; the most insipid food was alone endurable; he could wear only garments of certain texture; the odours of all flowers were oppressive; his eyes were tortured by even a faint light; and there were but peculiar sounds, and these from stringed instruments, which did not inspire him with horror.

To an anomalous species of terror I found him a bounden slave. "I shall perish," said he, "I *must* perish in this deplorable folly. Thus, thus, and not otherwise, shall I be lost. I dread the events of the future, not in themselves, but in their results. I shudder at the thought of any, even the most trivial, incident, which may operate upon this intolerable agitation of soul. I have, indeed, no abhorrence of danger, except in its absolute effect—in terror. In this unnerved—in this pitiable condition—I feel that the period will sooner or later arrive when I must abandon life and reason together, in some struggle with the grim phantasm, FEAR."

I learned, moreover, at intervals, and through broken and equivocal hints, another singular feature of his mental condition. He was enchained by certain superstitious impressions in regard to the dwelling which he tenanted, and whence, for many years, he had never ventured forth—in regard to an influence whose superstitious force was conveyed in terms too shadowy here to be re-stated—an influence which some peculiarities in the mere form and substance of his family mansion, had, by dint of long sufferance, he said, obtained over his spirit—an effect which the *physique* of the gray walls and turrets, and of the dim tarn into which they all looked down, had, at length, brought about upon the *morale* of his existence.

He admitted, however, although with hesitation, that much of the peculiar gloom which thus afflicted him could be traced to a more natural and far more palpable origin—to the severe and long-continued illness—indeed to the evidently approaching dissolution—of a tenderly beloved sister—his sole companion for long years—his last and only relative on earth. "Her decease," he said, with a bitterness which I can never forget, "would leave him (him the hopeless and the frail) the last of the ancient race of the Ushers." While he spoke, the lady Madeline (for so was she called) passed slowly through a remote portion of the apartment, and, without having noticed my presence, disappeared. I regarded her with an utter astonishment not unmingled with dread—and yet I found it impossible to account for such feelings. A sensation of stupor oppressed me, as my eyes followed her retreating steps. When a door, at length, closed upon her, my glance sought instinctively and eagerly the countenance of the brother—but he had buried his face in his hands, and I could only perceive that a far more than ordinary wanness had overspread the emaciated fingers through which trickled many passionate tears.

The disease of the lady Madeline had long baffled the skill of her physicians. A settled apathy, a gradual wasting away of the person, and frequent although transient affections of a partially cataleptical character, were the unusual diagnosis. Hitherto she had steadily borne up against the pressure of her malady, and had not betaken herself finally to bed; but, on the closing in of the evening of my arrival at the house, she succumbed (as her brother told me at night with inexpressible agitation) to the prostrating power of the destroyer; and I learned that the glimpse I had obtained of her person would thus probably be the last I should obtain—that the lady, at least while living, would be seen by me no more.

For several days ensuing, her name was unmentioned by either Usher   15 or myself: and during this period I was busied in earnest endeavours to alleviate the melancholy of my friend. We painted and read together; or I listened, as if in a dream, to the wild improvisations of his speaking guitar. And thus, as a closer and still closer intimacy admitted me more unreservedly into the recesses of his spirit, the more bitterly did I perceive the futility of all attempt at cheering a mind from which darkness, as if an inherent positive quality, poured forth upon all objects of the moral and physical universe, in one unceasing radiation of gloom.

I shall ever bear about me a memory of the many solemn hours I thus spent alone with the master of the House of Usher. Yet I should fail in any attempt to convey an idea of the exact character of the studies, or of the occupations, in which he involved me, or led me the way. An excited and highly distempered ideality threw a sulphureous lustre over all. His long improvised dirges will ring forever in my ears. Among other things, I hold painfully in mind a certain singular perversion and amplification of the wild air of the last waltz of Von Weber.° From the paintings over which his elaborate fancy brooded, and which grew, touch by touch, into vaguenesses at which I shuddered the more thrillingly, because I shuddered knowing not why;—from these paintings (vivid as their images now are before me) I would in vain endeavour to educe more than a small portion which should lie within the compass of merely written words. By the utter simplicity, by the nakedness of his designs, he arrested and overawed attention. If ever mortal painted an idea, that mortal was Roderick Usher. For me at least—in the circumstances then surrounding me—there arose out of the pure abstractions which the hypochondriac contrived to throw upon his canvas, an intensity of intolerable awe, no shadow of which felt I ever yet in the contemplation of the certainly glowing yet too concrete reveries of Fuseli.°

One of the phantasmagoric conceptions of my friend, partaking not so rigidly of the spirit of abstraction, may be shadowed forth, although feebly, in words. A small picture presented the interior of an immensely long and rectangular vault or tunnel, with low walls, smooth, white, and without interruption or device. Certain accessory points of the design served well to convey the idea that this excavation lay at an exceeding depth below the

---

Von Weber: Karl Maria von Weber (1786–1878), German composer, conductor, and pianist
Fuseli: John Henry Fuseli (1741–1825), Swiss-born English painter and essayist

surface of the earth. No outlet was observed in any portion of its vast extent, and no torch, or other artificial source of light was discernible; yet a flood of intense rays rolled throughout, and bathed the whole in a ghastly and inappropriate splendour.

I have just spoken of that morbid condition of the auditory nerve which rendered all music intolerable to the sufferer, with the exception of certain effects of stringed instruments. It was, perhaps, the narrow limits to which he thus confined himself upon the guitar, which gave birth, in great measure, to the fantastic character of his performances. But the fervid *facility* of his *impromptus* could not be so accounted for. They must have been, and were, in the notes, as well as in the words of his wild fantasias (for he not unfrequently accompanied himself with rhymed verbal improvisations), the result of that intense mental collectedness and concentration to which I have previously alluded as observable only in particular moments of the highest artificial excitement. The words of one of these rhapsodies I have easily remembered. I was, perhaps, the more forcibly impressed with it, as he gave it, because, in the under or mystic current of its meaning, I fancied that I perceived, and for the first time, a full consciousness on the part of Usher, of the tottering of his lofty reason upon her throne. The verses, which were entitled "The Haunted Palace," ran very nearly, if not accurately, thus:

In the greenest of our valleys,
    By good angels tenanted,
Once a fair and stately palace—
    Radiant palace—reared its head.
In the monarch Thought's dominion—
    It stood there!
Never seraph spread a pinion
    Over fabric half so fair.

Banners yellow, glorious, golden,
    On its roof did float and flow;
(This—all this—was in the olden
    Time long ago)
And every gentle air that dallied,
    In that sweet day,
Along the ramparts plumed and pallid,
    A winged odour went away.

Wanderers in that happy valley
    Through two luminous windows saw
Spirits moving musically
    To a lute's well-tunèd law,
Round about a throne, where sitting
    (Porphyrogene!)
In state his glory well befitting,
    The ruler of the realm was seen.

And all with pearl and ruby glowing
　　Was the fair palace door,
Through which came flowing, flowing, flowing
　　And sparkling evermore,
A troop of Echoes whose sweet duty
　　Was but to sing,
In voices of surpassing beauty,
　　The wit and wisdom of their king.

But evil things, in robes of sorrow,
　　Assailed the monarch's high estate;
(Ah, let us mourn, for never morrow
　　Shall dawn upon him, desolate!)
And, round about his home, the glory
　　That blushed and bloomed
Is but a dim-remembered story
　　Of the old time entombed.

And travellers now within that valley,
　　Through the red-litten windows, see
Vast forms that move fantastically
　　To a discordant melody;
While, like a rapid ghastly river,
　　Through the pale door,
A hideous throng rush out forever,
　　And laugh—but smile no more.

I well remember that suggestions arising from this ballad, led us into a train of thought wherein there became manifest an opinion of Usher's · which I mention not so much on account of its novelty, (for other men[1] have thought thus,) as on account of the pertinacity with which he maintained it. This opinion, in its general form, was that of the sentience of all vegetable things. But, in his disordered fancy, the idea had assumed a more daring character, and trespassed, under certain conditions, upon the kingdom of inorganization. I lack words to express the full extent, or the earnest *abandon* of his persuasion. The belief, however, was connected (as I have previously hinted) with the gray stones of the home of his forefathers. The conditions of the sentience had been here, he imagined, fulfilled in the method of collocation of these stones—in the order of their arrangement, as well as in that of the many *fungi* which overspread them, and of the decayed trees which stood around—above all, in the long undisturbed endurance of this arrangement, and in its reduplication in the still waters of the tarn. Its evidence—the evidence of the sentience—was to be seen, he said,

---

1.　*Watson, Dr. Percival, Spallanzani, and especially the Bishop of Landaff.—See* Chemical Essays, *vol. v.* [E.A.P.]

(and I here started as he spoke,) in the gradual yet certain condensation of an atmosphere of their own about the waters and the walls. The result was discoverable, he added, in that silent, yet importunate and terrible influence which for centuries had moulded the destinies of his family, and which made *him* what I now saw him—what he was. Such opinions need no comment, and I will make none.

Our books—the books which, for years, had formed no small portion   20
of the mental existence of the invalid—were, as might be supposed, in strict keeping with this character of phantasm. We pored together over such works as the *Ververt et Chartreuse* of Gresset; the *Belphegor* of Machiavelli; the *Heaven and Hell* of Swedenborg; the *Subterranean Voyage of Nicholas Klimm* by Holberg; the *Chiromancy* of Robert Flud, of Jean D'Indaginé, and of De la Chambre; the *Journey into the Blue Distance of Tieck;* and the *City of the Sun* of Campanella. One favourite volume was a small octavo edition of the *Directorium Inquisitorum,* by the Dominican Eymeric de Gironne; and there were passages in Pomponius Mela, about the old African Satyrs and Ægipans, over which Usher would sit dreaming for hours. His chief delight, however, was found in the perusal of an exceedingly rare and curious book in quarto Gothic—the manual of a forgotten church—the *Vigiliæ Mortuorum secundum Chorum Ecclesiæ Maguntinæ.*

I could not help thinking of the wild ritual of this work, and of its probable influence upon the hypochondriac, when, one evening, having informed me abruptly that the lady Madeline was no more, he stated his intention of preserving her corpse for a fortnight, (previously to its final interment,) in one of the numerous vaults within the main walls of the building. The worldly reason, however, assigned for this singular proceeding, was one which I did not feel at liberty to dispute. The brother had been led to his resolution (so he told me) by consideration of the unusual character of the malady of the deceased, of certain obtrusive and eager inquiries on the part of her medical men, and of the remote and exposed situation of the burial-ground of the family. I will not deny that when I called to mind the sinister countenance of the person whom I met upon the staircase, on the day of my arrival at the house, I had no desire to oppose what I regarded as at best but a harmless, and by no means an unnatural, precaution.

At the request of Usher, I personally aided him in the arrangements for the temporary entombment. The body having been encoffined, we two alone bore it to its rest. The vault in which we placed it (and which had been so long unopened that our torches, half smothered in its oppressive atmosphere, gave us little opportunity for investigation) was small, damp, and entirely without means of admission for light; lying, at great depth, immediately beneath that portion of the building in which was my own sleeping apartment. It had been used, apparently, in remote feudal times, for the worst purposes of a donjon-keep, and, in later days, as a place of deposit for powder, or some other highly combustible substance, as a portion of its floor, and the whole interior of a long archway through which we reached it, were carefully sheathed with copper. The door, of massive iron, had been, also, similarly protected. Its immense weight caused an unusually sharp grating sound, as it moved upon its hinges.

Having deposited our mournful burden upon tressels within this region of horror, we partially turned aside the yet unscrewed lid of the coffin, and looked upon the face of the tenant. A striking similitude between the brother and sister now first arrested my attention; and Usher, divining, perhaps, my thoughts, murmured out some few words from which I learned that the deceased and himself had been twins, and that sympathies of a scarcely intelligible nature had always existed between them. Our glances, however, rested not long upon the dead—for we could not regard her unawed. The disease which had thus entombed the lady in the maturity of youth, had left, as usual in all maladies of a strictly cataleptical character, the mockery of a faint blush upon the bosom and the face, and that suspiciously lingering smile upon the lip which is so terrible in death. We replaced and screwed down the lid, and, having secured the door of iron, made our way, with toil, into the scarcely less gloomy apartments of the upper portion of the house.

And now, some days of bitter grief having elapsed, an observable change came over the features of the mental disorder of my friend. His ordinary manner had vanished. His ordinary occupations were neglected or forgotten. He roamed from chamber to chamber with hurried, unequal, and objectless step. The pallor of his countenance had assumed, if possible, a more ghastly hue—but the luminousness of his eye had utterly gone out. The once occasional huskiness of his tone was heard no more; and a tremulous quaver, as if of extreme terror, habitually characterized his utterance. There were times, indeed, when I thought his unceasingly agitated mind was labouring with some oppressive secret, to divulge which he struggled for the necessary courage. At times, again, I was obliged to resolve all into the mere inexplicable vagaries of madness, for I beheld him gazing upon vacancy for long hours, in an attitude of the profoundest attention, as if listening to some imaginary sound. It was no wonder that his condition terrified—that it infected me. I felt creeping upon me, by slow yet certain degrees, the wild influences of his own fantastic yet impressive superstitions.

It was, especially, upon retiring to bed late in the night of the seventh or eighth day after the placing of the lady Madeline within the donjon, that I experienced the full power of such feelings. Sleep came not near my couch—while the hours waned and waned away. I struggled to reason off the nervousness which had dominion over me. I endeavoured to believe that much, if not all of what I felt, was due to the bewildering influence of the gloomy furniture of the room—of the dark and tattered draperies, which, tortured into motion by the breath of a rising tempest, swayed fitfully to and fro upon the walls, and rustled uneasily about the decorations of the bed. But my efforts were fruitless. An irrepressible tremour gradually pervaded my frame; and, at length, there sat upon my very heart an incubus of utterly causeless alarm. Shaking this off with a gasp and a struggle, I uplifted myself upon the pillows, and, peering earnestly within the intense darkness of the chamber, hearkened—I know not why, except that an instinctive spirit prompted me—to certain low and indefinite sounds which came, through the pauses of the storm, at long intervals, I knew not whence. Overpowered by an intense sentiment of horror, unaccountable yet unendurable, I threw on my clothes with haste (for I felt that I should sleep no more during the night), and endeavoured to arouse myself from the pitiable condition into which I had fallen, by pacing rapidly to and fro through the apartment.

I had taken but few turns in this manner, when a light step on an adjoining staircase arrested my attention. I presently recognized it as that of Usher. In an instant afterward he rapped, with a gentle touch, at my door, and entered, bearing a lamp. His countenance was, as usual, cadaverously wan—but, moreover, there was a species of mad hilarity in his eyes—an evidently restrained *hysteria* in his whole demeanour. His air appalled me—but anything was preferable to the solitude which I had so long endured, and I even welcomed his presence as a relief.

"And you have not seen it?" he said abruptly, after having stared about him for some moments in silence—"you have not then seen it?—but, stay! you shall." Thus speaking, and having carefully shaded his lamp, he hurried to one of the casements, and threw it freely open to the storm.

The impetuous fury of the entering gust nearly lifted us from our feet. It was, indeed, a tempestuous yet sternly beautiful night, and one wildly singular in its terror and its beauty. A whirlwind had apparently collected its force in our vicinity; for there were frequent and violent alterations in the direction of the wind; and the exceeding density of the clouds (which hung so low as to press upon the turrets of the house) did not prevent our perceiving the life-like velocity with which they flew careering from all points against each other, without passing away into the distance. I say that even their exceeding density did not prevent our perceiving this—yet we had no glimpse of the moon or stars—nor was there any flashing forth of the lightning. But the under surfaces of the huge masses of agitated vapour, as well as all terrestrial objects immediately around us, were glowing in the unnatural light of a faintly luminous and distinctly visible gaseous exhalation which hung about and enshrouded the mansion.

"You must not—you shall not behold this!" said I, shudderingly, to Usher, as I led him, with a gentle violence, from the window to a seat. "These appearances, which bewilder you, are merely electrical phenomena not uncommon—or it may be that they have their ghastly origin in the rank miasma of the tarn. Let us close this casement; the air is chilling and dangerous to your frame. Here is one of your favourite romances. I will read, and you shall listen; and so we will pass away this terrible night together."

The antique volume which I had taken up was the *Mad Trist* of Sir   30
Launcelot Canning; but I had called it a favourite of Usher's more in sad jest than in earnest; for, in truth, there is little in its uncouth and unimaginative prolixity which could have had interest for the lofty and spiritual ideality of my friend. It was, however, the only book immediately at hand; and I indulged a vague hope that the excitement which now agitated the hypo-

chondriac, might find relief (for the history of mental disorder is full of similar anomalies) even in the extremeness of the folly which I should read. Could I have judged, indeed, by the wild overstrained air of vivacity with which he hearkened, or apparently hearkened, to the words of the tale, I might well have congratulated myself upon the success of my design.

I had arrived at that well-known portion of the story where Ethelred, the hero of the Trist, having sought in vain for peaceable admission into the dwelling of the hermit, proceeds to make good an entrance by force. Here, it will be remembered, the words of the narrative run thus:

"And Ethelred, who was by nature of a doughty heart, and who was now mighty withal, on account of the powerfulness of the wine which he had drunken, waited no longer to hold parley with the hermit, who, in sooth, was of an obstinate and maliceful turn, but, feeling the rain upon his shoulders, and fearing the rising of the tempest, uplifted his mace outright, and, with blows, made quickly room in the plankings of the door for his gauntleted hand; and now pulling therewith sturdily, he so cracked, and ripped, and tore all asunder, that the noise of the dry and hollow-sounding wood alarumed and reverberated throughout the forest."

At the termination of this sentence I started, and for a moment, paused; for it appeared to me (although I at once concluded that my excited fancy had deceived me)—it appeared to me that, from some very remote portion of the mansion, there came, indistinctly, to my ears, what might have been, in its exact similarity of character, the echo (but a stifled and dull one certainly) of the very cracking and ripping sound which Sir Launcelot had so particularly described. It was, beyond doubt, the coincidence alone which had arrested my attention; for, amid the rattling of the sashes of the casements, and the ordinary commingled noises of the still increasing storm, the sound, in itself, had nothing, surely, which would have interested or disturbed me. I continued the story:

"But the good champion Ethelred, now entering within the door, was sore enraged and amazed to perceive no signal of the maliceful hermit; but, in the stead thereof, a dragon of a scaly and prodigious demeanour, and of a fiery tongue, which sate in guard before a palace of gold, with a floor of silver; and upon the wall there hung a shield of shining brass with this legend enwritten—

Who entereth herein, a conqueror hath bin;
Who slayeth the dragon, the shield he shall win.

And Ethelred uplifted his mace, and struck upon the head of the dragon, which fell before him, and gave up his pesty breath, with a shriek so horrid and harsh, and withal so piercing, that Ethelred had fain to close his ears with his hands against the dreadful noise of it, the like whereof was never before heard."

Here again I paused abruptly, and now with a feeling of wild amazement—for there could be no doubt whatever that, in this instance, I did actually hear (although from what direction it proceeded I found it impossible to say) a low and apparently distant, but harsh, protracted, and most unusual screaming or grating sound—the exact counterpart of what my fancy had already conjured up for the dragon's unnatural shriek as described by the romancer.

Oppressed, as I certainly was, upon the occurrence of the second and most extraordinary coincidence, by a thousand conflicting sensations, in which wonder and extreme terror were predominant, I still retained sufficient presence of mind to avoid exciting, by any observation, the sensitive nervousness of my companion. I was by no means certain that he had noticed the sounds in question; although, assuredly, a strange alteration had, during the last few minutes, taken place in his demeanour. From a position fronting my own, he had gradually brought round his chair, so as to sit with his face to the door of the chamber; and thus I could but partially perceive his features, although I saw that his lips trembled as if he were murmuring inaudibly. His head had dropped upon his breast—yet I knew that he was not asleep, from the wide and rigid opening of the eye as I caught a glance of it in profile. The motion of his body, too, was at variance with this idea—for he rocked from side to side with a gentle yet constant and uniform sway. Having rapidly taken notice of all this, I resumed the narrative of Sir Launcelot, which thus proceeded:

"And now, the champion, having escaped from the terrible fury of the dragon, bethinking himself of the brazen shield, and of the breaking up of the enchantment which was upon it, removed the carcass from out of the way before him, and approached valorously over the silver pavement of the castle to where the shield was upon the wall; which in sooth tarried not for his full coming, but fell down at his feet upon the silver floor, with a mighty great and terrible ringing sound."

No sooner had these syllables passed my lips, than—as if a shield of brass had indeed, at the moment, fallen heavily upon a floor of silver—I became aware of a distinct, hollow, metallic, and clangorous, yet apparently muffled reverberation. Completely unnerved, I leaped to my feet; but the measured rocking movement of Usher was undisturbed. I rushed to the chair in which he sat. His eyes were bent fixedly before him, and throughout his whole countenance there reigned a stony rigidity. But, as I placed my hand upon his shoulder, there came a strong shudder over his whole person; a sickly smile quivered about his lips; and I saw that he spoke in a low, hurried, and gibbering murmur, as if unconscious of my presence. Bending closely over him, I at length drank in the hideous import of his words.

"Not hear it?—yes, I hear it, and *have* heard it. Long—long—long— many minutes, many hours, many days, have I heard it—yet I dared not— oh, pity me, miserable wretch that I am!—I dared not—I *dared* not speak! *We have put her living in the tomb!* Said I not that my senses were acute? I *now* tell you that I heard her first feeble movements in the hollow coffin. I heard them—many, many days ago—yet I dared not—*I dared not speak!* And now—to-night—Ethelred—ha! ha! the breaking of the hermit's door, and the death-cry of the dragon, and the clangour of the shield!—say, rather, the rending of her coffin, and the grating of the iron hinges of her prison, and her struggles within the coppered archway of the vault! Oh whither shall I fly? Will she not be here anon? Is she not hurrying to upbraid me for my haste? Have I not heard her footstep on the stair? Do I not distinguish that heavy and horrible beating of her heart? MADMAN!" here he sprang furiously to his feet, and shrieked out his syllables, as if in the effort he were giving up his soul—"MADMAN! I TELL YOU THAT SHE NOW STANDS WITHOUT THE DOOR!"

As if in the superhuman energy of his utterance there had been found the potency of a spell—the huge antique panels to which the speaker pointed, threw slowly back, upon the instant, their ponderous and ebony jaws. It was the work of the rushing gust—but then without those doors there DID stand the lofty and enshrouded figure of the lady Madeline of Usher. There was blood upon her white robes, and the evidence of some bitter struggle upon every portion of her emaciated frame. For a moment she remained trembling and reeling to and fro upon the threshold, then, with a low moaning cry, fell heavily inward upon the person of her brother, and in her violent and now final death-agonies, bore him to the floor a corpse, and a victim to the terrors he had anticipated.

From that chamber, and from that mansion, I fled aghast. The storm was still abroad in all its wrath as I found myself crossing the old causeway. Suddenly there shot along the path a wild light, and I turned to see whence a gleam so unusual could have issued; for the vast house and its shadows were alone behind me. The radiance was that of the full, setting, and blood-red moon which now shone vividly through that once barely-discernible fissure of which I have before spoken as extending from the roof of the building, in a zigzag direction, to the base. While I gazed, this fissure rapidly widened—there came a fierce breath of the whirlwind—the entire orb of the satellite burst at once upon my sight—my brain reeled as I saw the mighty walls rushing asunder—there was a long tumultuous shouting sound like the voice of a thousand waters—and the deep and dank tarn at my feet closed sullenly and silently over the fragments of the "HOUSE OF USHER."

ROOT CELLAR

Theodore Roethke

Nothing would sleep in that cellar, dank as a ditch,
Bulbs broke out of boxes hunting for chinks in the dark,
Shoots dangled and drooped,
Lolling obscenely from mildewed crates,
Hung down long yellow evil necks, like tropical snakes.
And what a congress of stinks!—

Roots ripe as old bait,
Pulpy stems, rank, silo-rich,
Leaf-mold, manure, lime, piled against slippery planks.
Nothing would give up life: 10
Even the dirt kept breathing a small breath.

THE SNOW-STORM

Ralph Waldo Emerson

Announced by all the trumpets of the sky,
Arrives the snow, and, driving o'er the fields
Seems nowhere to alight: the whited air
Hides hills and woods, the river, and the heaven,
And veils the farm-house at the garden's end.   5
The sled and traveller stopped, the courier's feet
Delayed, all friends shut out, the housemates sit
Around the radiant fireplace, enclosed
In a tumultuous privacy of storm.

Come see the north wind's masonry.   10
Out of an unseen quarry evermore
Furnished with tile, the fierce artificer
Curves his white bastions with projected roof
Round every windward stake, or tree, or door.
Speeding, the myriad-handed, his wild work   15
So fanciful, so savage, nought cares he
For number or proportion. Mockingly,
On coop or kennel he hangs Parian wreaths;
A swan-like form invests the hidden thorn;
Fills up the farmer's lane from wall to wall,   20
Maugre the farmer's sighs; and at the gate
A tapering turret overtops the work.
And when his hours are numbered, and the world
Is all his own, retiring, as he were not,
Leaves, when the sun appears, astonished Art   25
To mimic in slow structures, stone by stone,
Built in an age, the mad wind's night-work,
The frolic architecture of the snow.

MUSÉE DES BEAUX ARTS

W. H. Auden

About suffering they were never wrong,
The Old Masters: how well they understood
Its human position; how it takes place
While someone else is eating or opening a window or just walking dully
    along;
How, when the aged are reverently, passionately waiting   *5*
For the miraculous birth, there always must be
Children who did not specially want it to happen, skating
On a pond at the edge of the wood:
They never forgot
That even the dreadful martyrdom must run its course   *10*
Anyhow in a corner, some untidy spot
Where the dogs go on with their doggy life and the torturer's horse
Scratches its innocent behind on a tree.

In Brueghel's *Icarus,* for instance: how everything turns away
Quite leisurely from the disaster; the ploughman may   *15*
Have heard the splash, the forsaken cry,
But for him it was not an important failure; the sun shone
As it had to on the white legs disappearing into the green
Water; and the expensive delicate ship that must have seen
Something amazing, a boy falling out of the sky,   *20*
Had somewhere to get to and sailed calmly on.

11

Narration, Plot, and Character: Involving Your Reader in Time and Conflict

Suppose you had a really terrible day. On your way to your job as a waiter or waitress, your car ran out of gas. You had to walk half a mile to a gas station to borrow a gallon container full of gas, which you had to lug back to your car because nobody would stop to give you a lift. Finally, you got your car started and used your last five dollars to buy gas. When you finally arrived late at your job, you had to explain your tardiness to your supervisor, who did not seem very sympathetic. The customers you waited on were demanding and stingy with their tips. Because you had arrived late, you stayed a little later than normal to compensate. As a result, you walked into your class five minutes late and found that your teacher was giving a pop quiz and that there were only five minutes left to complete it. Finally arriving home, you snarl at your roommate, who asks you what he or she has done to deserve that kind of treatment.

"I had a really awful day," you begin. "Let me tell you what happened." When you tell your roommate what happened to you, you use *narration*—the arrangement of significant events over a span of time—to explain your behavior as well as to define what you mean by "really awful." You make your experiences into a sequence—a *plot*—to support your assertion.

PLOT

Because narration is shaped by time passing, it reflects a sequence of events. If an event involves beings of some sort—usually people—it also usually involves a clash of goals. Conflict gives most plots their shape. The conflict may be between two people, a person and the environment, or a person and a group of people, or the conflict may be between two aims in a single person. Somebody wants something to happen or not to happen, but persons or events get in the way of that person's goals. Finally, there is some resolution of the conflict, which brings the event to a point of rest, at least for a moment.

Each story of a conflict has a plot, a sequence of events driven by the conflict. These incidents are related to each other by a chain of cause and effect. The events don't have to be physical. They may be a set of emotions or thoughts or a combination of the two that may or may not include or lead to physical action. In any combination, these events normally arrange themselves in a connected sequence.

Plot, People, and Conflict   Protagonist –hero
antagonist – The obstacle

When we talk about people caught in a sequence of events, we use two important terms to identify them. The person who is the "hero" or "heroine" is called the *protagonist*. The name for the person, people, or forces that stand in the way of the protagonist and his or her goals is the *antagonist*. Although in short pieces of writing there is rarely more than one protagonist, it is possible for there to be more than one antagonist. However, if there is more than one person or force in opposition to the protagonist, they are most often related in terms of their qualities or their aims.

 Working with a Reading

Read the following poem and, alone or in your group, answer the questions that follow it.

INCIDENT

Countee Cullen

(For Eric Waldrond)

Once riding in old Baltimore,
　　Heart-filled, head-filled with glee,
I saw a Baltimorean
　　Keep looking straight at me.

Now I was eight and very small,　　　　　　　　　　　　　5
　　And he was no whit bigger,
And so I smiled, but he poked out
　　His tongue, and called me, "Nigger."

I saw the whole of Baltimore
　　From May until December;　　　　　　　　　　　　　10
Of all the things that happened there
　　That's all that I remember.

1. What do you learn about the protagonist in this poem? How are we told he feels at the beginning of this narration? Do you think it is important that we know this?

2. What or who is the antagonist in the poem? Is there only one? More than one? If there is more than one, what connects them? What are the antagonist's characteristics? What actions by the antagonist define him for you? Do you think it is important that you know his age? Why is that so important? How does the antagonist stand in the way of the protagonist's goals?

3. Is there a resolution to this narration? What is the point at which the story rests? Why do you think the writer wants you to know what he remembers as the conclusion to the plot?

4. Can you find a dominant idea in this narration? If you can, what do you think it is? How do the facts the writer chooses to give you lead you to this dominant idea?

5. You probably noticed that there is no description of the surroundings in this poem. Why did Cullen leave it out?

~➔ *An Invitation to Write*

Think of an incident in which a single action by an insignificant person created a situation that was antagonistic for you in much the same way as the situation in Cullen's poem was for the speaker. Write an account of that situation that reflects the effect the moment had upon you. Feel free to write an essay, a short story, a short play, or a poem.

Plot and Exposition

As you know from experience, every chain of events has its beginning in a situation. Imagine watching two people whom you don't know having an argument. Imagine trying to understand what they are arguing about and why they are having the argument in the first place. The task is almost impossible unless you know some background about the two. To help their readers understand the conflict that drives the plot of a story, writers usually provide an *exposition*. Using exposition, writers "put forward" the facts, feelings, and thoughts that their readers need to understand the situation and the motivation of the individuals caught up in the conflict. In understanding a conflict between a protagonist and an antagonist, parts of their pasts, their present attitudes, and the locations they occupy may all be important. The questions of the Pentad (Chapter 4) work particularly well in helping you address these elements.

As you read a poem, an essay, a story, or a drama, notice how the writer selects from all the possible facts about the individuals, their pasts, and the setting in which they are placed only as much information as he or she thinks is necessary to help you understand the conflict. An effective writer rarely, if ever, presents his or her readers with any information that sends their attention in directions that do not contribute to the writer's purpose. What was true in description (Chapter 10) is equally true in narration. Only what is relevant to the writer's idea should be a part of the foreground or the background.

 Working with a Reading

Read the following story and, alone or with your group, answer the questions that follow it.

THE STORY OF AN HOUR

Kate Chopin

Knowing that Mrs. Mallard was afflicted with a heart trouble, great care was taken to break to her as gently as possible the news of her husband's death.

It was her sister Josephine who told her, in broken sentences, veiled hints that revealed in half concealing. Her husband's friend Richards was there, too, near her. It was he who had been in the newspaper office when intelligence of the railroad disaster was received, with Brently Mallard's name leading the list of "killed." He had only taken the time to assure himself of its truth by a second telegram, and had hastened to forestall any less careful, less tender friend in bearing the sad message.

She did not hear the story as many women have heard the same, with a paralyzed inability to accept its significance. She wept at once, with sudden, wild abandonment, in her sister's arms. When the storm of grief had spent itself she went away to her room alone. She would have no one follow her.

There stood, facing the open window, a comfortable, roomy armchair. Into this she sank, pressed down by a physical exhaustion that haunted her body and seemed to reach into her soul.

She could see in the open square before her house the tops of trees that were all aquiver with the new spring life. The delicious breath of rain that was in the air. In the street below a peddler was crying his wares. The notes of a distant song which some one was singing reached her faintly, and countless sparrows were twittering in the eaves.

There were patches of blue sky showing here and there through the clouds that had met and piled one above the other in the west facing her window.

She sat with her head thrown back upon the cushion of the chair quite motionless, except when a sob came up into her throat and shook her, as a child who has cried itself to sleep continues to sob in its dreams.

She was young, with a fair, calm face, whose lines bespoke repression and even a certain strength. But now there was a dull stare in her eyes, whose gaze was fixed away off yonder on one of those patches of blue sky. It was not a glance of reflection, but rather indicated a suspension of intelligent thought.

There was something coming to her and she was waiting for it, fearfully. What was it? She did not know; it was too subtle and elusive to name. But she felt it, creeping out of the sky, reaching toward her through the sounds, the scents, the color that filled the air.

Now her bosom rose and fell tumultuously. She was beginning to   *10* recognize this thing that was approaching to possess her, and she was striving to beat it back with her will—as powerless as her two white slender hands would have been.

When she abandoned herself a little whispered word escaped her slightly parted lips. She said it over and over under her breath: "Free, free, free!" The vacant stare and look of terror that had followed it went from her eyes. They stayed keen and bright. Her pulses beat fast, and the coursing blood warmed and relaxed every inch of her body.

She did not stop to ask if it were not a monstrous joy that held her. A clear and exalted perception enabled her to dismiss the suggestion as trivial.

She knew that she would weep again when she saw the kind, tender hands folded in death; the face that had never looked save with love upon her, fixed and gray and dead. But she saw beyond that bitter moment a long procession of years to come that would belong to her absolutely. And she opened and spread her arms out to them in welcome.

There would be no one to live for her during those coming years; she would live for herself. There would be no powerful will bending her in that blind persistence with which men and women believe they have a right to impose a private will upon a fellow creature. A kind intention or a cruel intention made the act seem no less a crime as she looked upon it in that brief moment of illumination.

And yet she had loved him—sometimes. Often she had not. What   *15* did it matter! What could love, the unsolved mystery, count for in face of this possession of self-assertion which she suddenly recognized as the strongest impulse of her being.

"Free! Body and soul free!" she kept whispering.

Josephine was kneeling before the closed door with her lips to the keyhole, imploring for admission. "Louise, open the door! I beg; open the door—you will make yourself ill. What are you doing, Louise? For heaven's sake open the door."

"Go away. I am not making myself ill." No; she was drinking in a very elixir of life through that open window.

Her fancy was running riot along those days ahead of her. Spring days, and summer days, and all sorts of days that would be her own. She breathed a quick prayer that life might be long. It was only yesterday she had thought with a shudder that life might be long.

She arose at length and opened the door to her sister's importunities.   *20* There was a feverish triumph in her eyes, and she carried herself unwittingly like a goddess of Victory. She clasped her sister's waist, and together they descended the stairs. Richards stood waiting for them at the bottom.

Some one was opening the front door with a latchkey. It was Brently Mallard who entered, a little travel-stained, composedly carrying his gripsack and umbrella. He had been far from the scene of accident, and did not even know there had been one. He stood amazed at Josephine's piercing cry; at Richards' quick motion to screen him from the view of his wife.

But Richards was too late.

When the doctors came they said she had died of heart disease—of joy that kills.

---

1. What exposition does Chopin give you to help you understand the situation? Where does it occur in the story?

2. Do you think Mrs. Mallard is a selfish person? What information do you find in the story that makes you think so?

3. Do you feel sympathy with Mrs. Mallard? What information do you find in the story that makes you feel the way you do?

4. Are you undecided as to how to feel about Mrs. Mallard? What do you find in the story that puts you in the middle?

5. What do you think is the dominant idea of this story? Remember: A dominant idea can reflect confusion between two points of view or present two sides of an issue without resolving them.

ᕗᔑ *An Invitation to Write*

Think of a situation that you found yourself in or that you witnessed that was as full of reversals and misunderstandings as the one Chopin presents. Write an essay, a short story, a short play, or a poem that through its narration puts the reader in the position of understanding the differences between what people assume and what the truth is.

Plot Movement

The movement of a plot is often divided into three parts. First there is the *rising action*. During the rising action, the writer presents you with the necessary background through exposition and begins the action. Then the conflict develops and increases in intensity. The rising action often becomes more and more complex as the characters' actions, thoughts, or emotions—separately or in combination—lead to further events. The rising action finally builds to a *climax*. In the climax, the writer shows you the outcome of the conflict between the protagonist and the antagonist. The characters adjust themselves to a new situation that grows out of the clash of wills or the clash of an individual's desires against his or her surroundings. Usually, at least for a moment, disorder becomes order. Often a *denouement* (French for "untying a knot") follows the climax. The denouement straightens out the tangles and snarls of the conflict. Just as the exposition leads you into the narrative, the denouement does the equivalent job, leading you out of it.

exposition > THE author's explanation   conclusion

❧ Working with a Reading

Read the following essay and then, alone or in your group, answer the questions that follow it.

❧

MR. JONES' ORDEAL

Jessica Mitford

Embalming is indeed a most extraordinary procedure, and one must wonder at the docility of Americans who each year pay hundreds of millions of dollars for its perpetuation, blissfully ignorant of what it is all about, what is done, how it is done. Not one in ten thousand has any idea of what actually takes place. Books on the subject are extremely hard to come by. They are not to be found in most libraries or bookshops.

In an era when huge television audiences watch surgical operations in the comfort of their living rooms, when, thanks to the animated cartoon, the geography of the digestive system has become familiar territory even to the nursery school set, in a land where the satisfaction of curiosity about almost all matters is a national pastime, the secrecy surrounding embalming can, surely, hardly be attributed to the inherent gruesomeness of the subject. Custom in this regard has within this century suffered a complete reversal. In the early days of American embalming, when it was performed in the home of the deceased, it was almost mandatory for some relative to stay by the embalmer's side and witness the procedure. Today, family members who might wish to be in attendance would certainly be dissuaded by the funeral director. All others, except apprentices, are excluded by law from the preparation room.

A close look at what does actually take place may explain in large measure the undertaker's intractable reticence concerning a procedure that has become his major *raison d'être*. Is it possible he fears that public information about embalming might lead patrons to wonder if they really want this service? If the funeral men are loath to discuss the subject outside the trade, the reader may, understandably, be equally loath to go on reading at this point. For those who have the stomach for it, let us part the formaldehyde curtain. . . .

The body is first laid out in the undertaker's morgue—or rather, Mr. Jones is reposing in the preparation room—to be readied to bid the world farewell.

The preparation room in any of the better funeral establishments has   5
the tiled and sterile look of a surgery, and indeed the embalmer-restorative artist who does his chores there is beginning to adopt the term "dermasurgeon" (appropriately corrupted by some mortician-writers as "demisurgeon") to describe his calling. His equipment, consisting of scalpels, scissors, augers, forceps, clamps, needles, pumps, tubes, bowls and basins, is crudely imitative of the surgeon's, as is his technique, acquired in a nine- or twelve-month post-high-school course in an embalming school. He is supplied by an advanced chemical industry with a bewildering array of fluids, sprays, pastes, oils, powders, creams, to fix or soften tissue, shrink or distend it as needed, dry it here, restore the moisture there. There are cosmetics, waxes and paints to fill and cover features, even plaster of Paris to replace entire limbs. There are ingenious aids to prop and stabilize the cadaver: A Vari-Pose Head Rest, the Edwards Arm and Hand Positioner, the Repose Block (to support the shoulders during the embalming), and the Throop Foot Positioner, which resembles an old-fashioned stocks.

Mr. John H. Eckels, president of the Eckels College of Mortuary Science, thus describes the first part of the embalming procedure: "In the hands of a skilled practitioner, this work may be done in a comparatively short time and without mutilating the body other than by slight incision—so slight that it scarcely would cause serious inconvenience if made upon a living person. It is necessary to remove the blood, and doing this not only helps in the disinfecting, but removes the principal cause of disfigurements due to discoloration."

Another textbook discusses the all-important time element: "The earlier this is done, the better, for every hour that elapses between death and embalming will add to the problems and complications encountered. . . ." Just how soon should one get going on the embalming? The author tells us, "On the basis of such scanty information made available to this profession through its rudimentary and haphazard system of technical research, we must conclude that the best results are to be obtained if the subject is embalmed before life is completely extinct—that is, before cellular death has occurred. In the average case, this would mean within an hour after somatic death." For those who feel that there is something a little rudimentary, not to say haphazard, about this advice, a comforting thought is offered by another writer. Speaking of fears entertained in early days of premature burial, he points out, "One of the effects of embalming by chemical injection, however, has been to dispel fears of live burial." How true; once the blood is removed, chances of live burial are indeed remote.

To return to Mr. Jones, the blood is drained out through the veins and replaced by embalming fluid pumped in through the arteries. As noted in *The Principles and Practices of Embalming,* "every operator has a favorite injection and drainage point—a fact which becomes a handicap only if he fails or refuses to forsake his favorites when conditions demand it." Typical favorites are the carotid artery, femoral artery, jugular vein, subclavian vein. There are various choices of embalming fluid. If Flextone is used, it will produce a "mild, flexible rigidity. The skin retains a velvety softness, the tissues are rubbery and pliable. Ideal for women and children." It may be blended with B. and G. Products Company's Lyf-Lyk tint, which is guaranteed to reproduce "nature's own skin texture . . . the velvety appearance of living tissue." Suntone comes in three separate tints: Suntan; Special Cosmetic Tint, a pink shade "especially indicated for young female subjects"; and Regular Cosmetic Tint, moderately pink.

About three to six gallons of a dyed and perfumed solution of formaldehyde, glycerin, borax, phenol, alcohol and water is soon circulating through Mr. Jones, whose mouth has been sewn together with a "needle directed upward between the upper lip and gum and brought out through the left nostril," with the corners raised slightly "for a more pleasant expression." If he should be bucktoothed, his teeth are cleaned with Bon Ami and coated with colorless nail polish. His eyes, meanwhile, are closed with flesh-tinted eye caps and eye cement.

The next step is to have at Mr. Jones with a thing called a trocar. This *10* is a long, hollow needle attached to a tube. It is jabbed into the abdomen, poked around the entrails and chest cavity, the contents of which are pumped out and replaced with "cavity fluid." This done, and the hole in the abdomen sewn up, Mr. Jones's face is heavily creamed (to protect the skin from burns which may be caused by leakage of the chemicals), and he is covered with a sheet and left unmolested for a while. But not for long—there is more, much more, in store for him. He has been embalmed, but not yet restored, and the best time to start the restorative work is eight to ten hours after embalming, when the tissues have become firm and dry.

The object of all this attention to the corpse, it must be remembered, is to make it presentable for viewing in an attitude of healthy repose. "Our customs require the presentation of our dead in the semblance of normality . . . unmarred by the ravages of illness, disease or mutilation," says Mr. J. Sheridan Mayer in his *Restorative Art.* This is rather a large order since few people die in the full bloom of health, unravaged by ill-ness and unmarked by some disfigurement. The funeral industry is equal to the challenge: "In some cases the gruesome appearance of a mutilated or disease–ridden subject may be quite discouraging. The task of restora-tion may seem impossible and shake the confidence of the embalmer. This is the time for intestinal fortitude and determination. Once the for-mative work is begun and affected tissues are cleaned or removed, all doubts of success vanish. It is surprising and gratifying to discover the results which may be obtained."

The embalmer, having allowed an appropriate interval to elapse, returns to the attack, but now he brings into play the skill and equip-ment of sculptor and cosmetician. Is a hand missing? Casting one in plaster of Paris is a simple matter. "For replacement purposes, only a cast of the back of the hand is necessary; this is within the ability of the average operator and is quite adequate." If a lip or two, a nose or an ear should be missing, the embalmer has at hand a variety of restor-ative waxes with which to model replacements. Pores and skin texture are simulated by stippling with a little brush, and over this cosmetics are laid on. Head off? Decapitation cases are rather routinely handled. Ragged edges are trimmed, and head joined to torso with a series of splints, wires and sutures. It is a good idea to have a little something at the neck—a scarf or a high collar—when time for viewing comes. Swollen mouth: Cut out tissue as needed from inside the lips. If too much is removed, the surface contour can easily be restored by padding with cotton. Swollen necks and cheeks are reduced by removing tissue through vertical incisions made down each side of the neck. "When the deceased is casketed, the pillow will hide the suture incisions . . . as an extra precaution against leakage, the suture may be painted with liquid sealer."

The opposite condition is more likely to present itself—that of ema-ciation. His hypodermic syringe now loaded with massage cream, the embalmer seeks out and fills the hollowed and sunken areas by injection. In this procedure the backs of the hands and fingers and the under–chin area should not be neglected.

Positioning the lips is a problem that recurrently challenges the in-genuity of the embalmer. Closed too tightly, they tend to give a stern, even disapproving expression. Ideally, embalmers feel, the lips should give the impression of being ever so slightly parted, the upper lip protruding slightly for a more youthful appearance. This takes some engineering, however, as the lips tend to drift apart. Lip drift can sometimes be reme-died by pushing one or two straight pins through the inner margin of the lower lip and then inserting them between the two front upper teeth. If Mr. Jones happens to have no teeth, the pins can just as easily be anchored in his Armstrong Face Former and Denture Replacer. Another method to maintain lip closure is to dislocate the lower jaw, which is then held in its new position by a wire run through holes which have been drilled through the upper and lower jaws at the midline. As the French are fond of saying, *il faut souffrir pour être belle.*°

If Mr. Jones has died of jaundice, the embalming fluid will very likely   15
turn him green. Does this deter the embalmer? Not if he has intestinal fortitude. Masking pastes and cosmetics are heavily laid on, burial garments and casket interiors are color-correlated with particular care, and Jones is displayed beneath rose-colored lights. Friends will say "How *well* he looks." Death by carbon monoxide, on the other hand, can be rather a good thing from the embalmer's viewpoint: "One advantage is the fact that this type of discoloration is an exaggerated form of a natural pink coloration." This is nice because the healthy glow is already present and needs but little attention.

The patching and filling completed, Mr. Jones is now shaved, washed and dressed. Cream-based cosmetic, available in pink, flesh, suntan, brunette and blond, is applied to his hands and face, his hair is shampooed and combed (and, in the case of Mrs. Jones, set), his hands manicured. For the horny-handed son of toil special care must be taken; cream should be applied to remove ingrained grime, and the nails cleaned. "If he were not in the habit of having them manicured in life, trimming and shaping is advised for better appearance—never questioned by kin."

Jones is now ready for casketing (this is the present participle of the verb "to casket"). In this operation his right shoulder should be depressed slightly "to turn the body a bit to the right and soften the appearance of lying flat on the back." Positioning the hands is a matter of importance, and special rubber positioning blocks may be used. The hands should be cupped slightly for a more lifelike, relaxed appearance. Proper placement of the body requires a delicate sense of balance. It should lie as high as possible in the casket, yet not so high that the lid, when lowered, will hit the nose. On the other hand, we are cautioned, placing the body too low "creates the impression that the body is in a box."

Jones is next wheeled into the appointed slumber room where a few last touches may be added—his favorite pipe placed in his hand or, if he was a great reader, a book propped into position. (In the case of little Master Jones a Teddy bear may be clutched.) Here he will hold open house for a few days, visiting hours 10 A.M. to 9 P.M.

All now being in readiness, the funeral director calls a staff conference to make sure that each assistant knows his precise duties. Mr. Wilber Kriege writes: "This makes your staff feel that they are a part of the team, with a definite assignment that must be properly carried out if the whole plan is to succeed. You never heard of a football coach who failed to talk to his entire team before they go on the field. They have drilled on the plays they are to execute for hours and days, and yet the successful coach

---

il faut souffrir pour être belle: French for "one must suffer to be beautiful"

knows the importance of making even the bench-warming third-string substitute feel that he is important if the game is to be won." The winning of *this* game is predicated upon glass-smooth handling of the logistics. The funeral director has notified the pallbearers whose names were furnished by the family, has arranged for the presence of clergyman, organist, and soloist, has provided transportation for everybody, has organized and listed the flowers sent by friends. In *Psychology of Funeral Service*, Mr. Edward A. Martin points out: "He may not always do as much as the family thinks he is doing, but it is his helpful guidance that they appreciate in knowing they are proceeding as they should. . . . The important thing is how well his services can be used to make the family believe they are giving unlimited expression to their own sentiment."

The religious service may be held in a church or in the chapel of the   20 funeral home; the funeral director vastly prefers the latter arrangement, for not only is it more convenient for him but it affords him the opportunity to show off his beautiful facilities to the gathered mourners. After the clergyman has had his say, the mourners queue up to file past the casket for a last look at the deceased. The family is *never* asked whether they want an open-casket ceremony; in the absence of their instruction to the contrary, this is taken for granted. Consequently, well over 90 percent of all American funerals feature the open casket—a custom unknown in other parts of the world. Foreigners are astonished by it. An English woman living in San Francisco described her reaction in a letter to the writer:

> I myself have attended only one funeral here—that of an elderly fellow worker of mine. After the service I could not understand why everyone was walking towards the coffin (sorry, I mean casket), but thought I had better follow the crowd. It shook me rigid to get there and find the casket open and poor old Oscar lying there in his brown tweed suit, wearing a suntan makeup and just the wrong shade of lipstick. If I had not been extremely fond of the old boy, I have a horrible feeling that I might have giggled. Then and there I decided that I could never face another American funeral—even dead.

The casket (which has been resting throughout the service on a Classic Beauty Ultra Metal Casket Bier) is now transferred by a hydraulically operated device called Porto-Lift to a balloon-tired, Glide Easy casket carriage which will wheel it to yet another conveyance, the Cadillac Funeral Coach. This may be lavender, cream, light green—anything but black. Interiors, of course, are color-correlated, "for the man who cannot stop short of perfection."

At graveside, the casket is lowered into the earth. This office, once the prerogative of friends of the deceased, is now performed by a patented mechanical lowering device. A "Lifetime Green" artificial grass mat is at the ready to conceal the sere earth, and overhead, to conceal the sky, is a portable Steril Chapel Tent ("resists the intense heat and humidity of summer and the terrific storms of winter . . . available in Silver Grey, Rose or Evergreen"). Now is the time for the ritual scattering of earth over the coffin, as the solemn words "earth to earth, ashes to ashes, dust to dust" are pronounced by the officiating cleric. This can today be accomplished "with a mere flick of the wrist with the Gordon Leak-Proof Earth Dispenser. No grasping of a handful of dirt, no soiled fingers. Simple, dignified, beautiful, reverent! The modern way!" The Gordon Earth Dispenser (at $5) is of nickel-plated brass construction. It is not only "attractive to the eye and long wearing"; it is also "one of the 'tools' for building better public relations" if presented as "an appropriate non-commercial gift" to the clergyman. It is shaped something like a saltshaker.

Untouched by human hand, the coffin and the earth are now united.

It is in the function of directing the participants through this maze of gadgetry that the funeral director has assigned to himself his relatively new role of "grief therapist." He has relieved the family of every detail, he has revamped the corpse to look like a living doll, he has arranged for it to nap for a few days in a slumber room, he has put on a well-oiled performance in which the concept of *death* has played no part whatsoever—unless it was inconsiderately mentioned by the clergyman who conducted the religious service. He has done everything in his power to make the funeral a real pleasure for everybody concerned. He and his team have given their all to score an upset victory over death.

---

1. Although this selection is an essay, it tells a story, that is, it uses a plot—a series of events—to make its points. What does Mitford use as an exposition to set the background for her story?

2. Does Mitford's exposition invite you to take a certain attitude toward the story she tells? What is that attitude, and how does she arrange her information to control the way you see the events and to create that attitude? Does this technique stop with her exposition or do you find her using it throughout her essay?

3. Is there rising action in the story Mitford tells you? Is it based upon conflict? What is the conflict? Who is the protagonist? Who is the antagonist?

4. In this conflict, how do you know who is the protagonist and who is the antagonist? Who are your sympathies with? What does Mitford do to control your sympathies?

5. If there is conflict in the narration, what is its climax? Does the protagonist or the antagonist come out ahead?

6. Does this story have a denouement? What is it? How does the denouement leave you feeling?

✒ *An Invitation to Write*

Compare Chopin's story (page 305) and Mitford's essay. How do you know that one is fiction and the other is not fiction? Could Chopin's story have really happened? Do you think Mitford tells the whole truth? For example, if you were a mortician, what would you have to say about whether Mitford tells all the truth or whether she tells that truth truthfully?

Both of these pieces take on a cherished institution in our society and present it to us in ways that we might not have considered before. Write a draft that does the same thing. Consider a custom, habit, or ritual that you know well and present it so as to make your reader see it in a way that he or she had not thought of before. You might write a story that sounds like a factual narration, an essay that is based on a narrated event or set of events, or a poem that tells that sort of story.

Plot and Poetry

When you read poetry, you often have to think about plot a little differently than when you read prose. Nevertheless, if plot is a sequence of events, then many poems have plots because they have a sequence of events driven by a conflict that gives them shape. Often poetry looks more directly inward at feelings and thoughts than does narrative prose or drama, which presents you with actions. The result of this inwardness is that the plot may be the sequence of the states of mind or the feelings of a single person in the middle of a series of external events which produce conflict within that person. There are poems that narrate outside events, and there are poems that describe events as if you and the writer were observing them together, but most poetry has to do with connected states of mind and feeling as they follow each other in response to an event, the memory of an event, or the anticipation of an event. Or the event may be the thoughts and feelings themselves—their sequence and their relationship.

Because of poetry's inward nature, the conflict—and thus, the significant events of the plot—often lie within the speaker whom the writer has chosen to speak for him or her. The protagonist and the antagonist in a poem may each be a different voice in the mind of the speaker, making the speaker both protagonist and antagonist. If that idea seems difficult, think of a time when you felt two ways about a choice you had to make or an event or action you witnessed. If you remember one of those arguments you had with yourself, then you can see the possibility of a person being both protagonist and antagonist.

However, if the poet wants you to follow the plot, he or she is committed to some of the same responsibilities as the writer of prose fiction or an essay. The poet will suggest or directly provide a context in which you can understand the situation that drives the poem. In other words, the poet will use the equivalent of exposition to give his or her words a background.

Working with a Reading

Read the following poem and, alone or with your group, answer the questions that follow it.

CHERRYLOG ROAD

James Dickey

Off Highway 106
At Cherrylog Road I entered
The '34 Ford without wheels
Smothered in kudzu°
With a seat pulled out to run
Corn whiskey down from the hills,   5

And then from the other side
Crept into an Essex
With a rumble seat of red leather
And then out again, aboard
A blue Chevrolet, releasing   10
The rust from its other color,

Reared up on three building blocks.
None had the same body heat;
I changed with them inward, toward
The weedy heart of the junkyard,   15
For I knew that Doris Holbrook
Would escape from her father at noon

And would come from the farm
To seek parts owned by the sun
Among the abandoned chassis,   20
Sitting in each in turn
As I did, leaning forward
As in a wild stock car race

In the parking lot of the dead.
Time after time, I climbed in   25
And out the other side, like
An envoy or a movie star
Met at the station by crickets.
A radiator cap raised its head,   30

---

kudzu: a weed that grows along the roads in Georgia

Become a real toad or a kingsnake
As I neared the hub of the yard,
Passing through many states,
Many lives, to reach
Some grandmother's long Pierce-Arrow   35
Sending platters of blindness forth

From its nickel hubcaps
And spilling its tender upholstery
On sleepy roaches,
The glass panel in between   40
Lady and colored driver
Not all the way broken out,

The back-seat phone
Still on its hook.
I got in as though to exclaim,   45
"Let us go to the orphan asylum,
John; I have some old toys
For children who say their prayers."

I popped with sweat as I thought
I heard Doris Holbrook scrape   50
Like a mouse in the southern-state sun
That was eating the paint in blisters
From a hundred car tops and hoods.
She was tapping like code,

Loosening the screws,   55
Carrying off headlights,
Sparkplugs, bumpers,
Cracked mirrors and gear-knobs,
Getting ready, already,
To go back with something to show   60

Other than her lips' new trembling
I would hold to me soon, soon,
Where I sat in the ripped back seat
Talking over the interphone,
Praying for Doris Holbrook   65
To come from her father's farm

And to get back there
With no trace of me on her face
To be seen by her red-haired father
Who would change, in the squalling barn,   70
Her back's pale skin with a strop,
Then lay for me

In a bootlegger's roasting car
With a string-triggered 12-gauge shotgun
To blast the breath from the air.
Not cut by the jagged windshields,   75
Through the acres of wrecks she came
With a wrench in her hand,

Through the dust where the blacksnake dies
Of boredom, and the beetle knows   80
The compost has no more life.
Someone outside would have seen
The oldest car's door inexplicably
Close from within:

I held her and held her and held her,   85
Convoyed at terrible speed
By the stalled, dreaming traffic around us,
So the blacksnake, stiff
With inaction, curved back
Into life, and hunted the mouse   90

With deadly overexcitement,
The beetles reclaimed their field
As we clung, glued together,
With the hooks of the seat springs
Working through to catch us red-handed   95
Amidst the gray breathless batting

That burst from the seat at our backs.
We left by separate doors
Into the changed, other bodies
Of cars, she down Cherrylog Road   100
And I to my motorcycle
Parked like the soul of the junkyard

Restored, a bicycle fleshed
With power, and tore off
Up Highway 106, continually   105
Drunk on the wind in my mouth,
Wringing the handlebar for speed,
Wild to be wreckage forever.

---

1. Where does the story told in this poem take place? What do you
   think the location has to do with the events?

2. What information does Dickey give you to locate you in the situation? That is, what serves as exposition in this poem?
   ⟶ information
   needed to
   understand the
   story.

3. Of all the objects he could describe, what does Dickey choose to bring to the foreground? What is the background? What do Dickey's choice of foreground and background have to do with what you see to be his dominant idea?

4. What can you tell about the narrator from the exposition?

5. What senses does Dickey appeal to? How does he do it? Why do you think he chose these senses primarily and not others?

6. What is the situation that the writer tells you about?

7. How does the exposition of setting and sensation tell you about how the speaker feels about the situation?

8. What is the rising action, the climax, and the denouement? ⟶ *falling action* -

9. Who is the protagonist in this story? Who or what is the antagonist(s) in this story? Try to take your answer beyond the literal response.

10. What is the conflict that drives this narration? Is it just between the narrator and his imagination of what Doris Holbrook's father might be like? Do you think it's important that we only know what the narrator imagines Doris's father to be but that her father never appears?

11. What kind of "wreckage" do you think the narrator sees himself to be at the end? What has he wrecked? How does he feel about it? How do you account for this feeling?

12. What do you think the dominant idea of this poem is? What do the exposition of setting and situation and the nature of the antagonist and protagonist have to do with the dominant idea? For example, if these events took place on a cool night in a warm house, would the dominant idea of the narration be different? Would you respond to it differently?

An Invitation to Write

Have you found yourself in a situation that reflects a conflict like the one in "Cherrylog Road," a situation that leaves some kind of "wreckage" behind? Try writing a draft—poetry or prose—that makes clear to your audience the conflict, the resolution, and the nature of the wreckage you left behind.

Plot and Drama

In drama, plot behaves in many of the same ways it does in other writing. It is still a sequence of events, but playwrights often divide the sequence into units called *acts*. Acts are the main divisions of the play, each containing a logically, thematically connected group of events. Often, the dramatist uses the first act to provide the exposition you would normally find at the beginning of a piece of prose fiction. The next acts contain the rising action and conflict leading to the climax. The climax may occur in the final act or at the end of the middle section of a play, but the last act almost always contains the equivalent of the denouement.

Acts are often sub-divided into *scenes*. Each scene is a single unit of action taking place in a single location in a single span of time. Taken together, the scenes create an act, and each act serves to advance the plot of the play, leading it to its conclusion.

One way to look at the structure of a play is to approach the play as a whole—as a piece of writing that presents a dominant idea. From this standpoint, every act serves as a single element that supports the dominant idea. Each act is the author's way of establishing concrete subordinate material to bring you to see his or her assertion. Every scene, then, represents a unified idea.

A technique that you might find in drama, as well as in longer pieces of prose fiction, is the use of *subplot*. The subplot tells a secondary story that reinforces the writer's dominant idea through similarity or contrast. Usually the characters in the subplot and the central plot meet and interact with each other so that the similarity or difference between the two stories clarifies the writer's dominant idea. In this way, the subplot comments upon the main plot, is subordinate to the main plot, and sometimes adds necessary detail to the main plot. The author often uses the subplot to comment ironically on the main plot.

 Working with a Reading

Read the following play and, alone or with your group, answer the questions that follow it.

TRIFLES

Susan Glaspell

CHARACTERS

GEORGE HENDERSON, *County Attorney*
HENRY PETERS, *Sheriff*
LEWIS HALE, *A Neighboring Farmer*
MRS. PETERS
MRS. HALE

SCENE

The kitchen in the now abandoned farmhouse of JOHN WRIGHT, *a gloomy kitchen, and left without having been put in order—unwashed pans under the sink, a loaf of bread outside the breadbox, a dish towel on the table—other signs of incomplete work. At the rear the outer door opens and the* SHERIFF *comes in followed by the* COUNTY ATTORNEY *and* HALE. *The* SHERIFF *and* HALE *are men in middle life, the* COUNTY ATTORNEY *is a young man; all are much bundled up and go at once to the stove. They are followed by two women—the* SHERIFF's *wife first; she is a slight wiry woman, a thin nervous face.* MRS. HALE *is larger and would ordinarily be called more comfortable looking, but she is disturbed now and looks fearfully about as she enters. The women have come in slowly, and stand close together near the door.*

COUNTY ATTORNEY (*rubbing his hands*) This feels good. Come up to the fire, ladies.

MRS. PETERS (*after taking a step forward*) I'm not—cold.

SHERIFF (*unbuttoning his overcoat and stepping away from the stove as if to mark the beginning of official business*) Now, Mr. Hale, before we move things about, you explain to Mr. Henderson just what you saw when you came here yesterday morning.

COUNTY ATTORNEY By the way, has anything been moved? Are things just as you left them yesterday?

SHERIFF (*looking ahead*) It's just the same. When it dropped below zero last night I thought I'd better send Frank out this morning to make a fire for us—no use getting pneumonia with a big case on, but I told him not to touch anything except the stove—and you know Frank.

COUNTY ATTORNEY Somebody should have been left here yesterday.

SHERIFF Oh—yesterday. When I had to send Frank to Morris Center for that man who went crazy—I want you to know I had my hands full yesterday, I knew you could get back from Omaha by today and as long as I went over everything here myself—

COUNTY ATTORNEY Well, Mr. Hale, tell just what happened when you came here yesterday morning.

HALE Harry and I had started to town with a load of potatoes. We came along the road from my place and as I got here I said, "I'm going to see if I can't get John Wright to go in with me on a party telephone." I spoke to Wright about it once before and he put me off, saying folks talked too much anyway, and all he asked was peace and quiet—I guess you know about how much he talked himself; but I thought maybe if I went to the house and talked about it before his wife, though I said to Harry that I didn't know as what his wife wanted made much difference to John—

COUNTY ATTORNEY Let's talk about that later, Mr. Hale. I do want to talk about that, but tell now just what happened when you got to the house.

HALE I didn't hear or see anything; I knocked at the door, and still it was all quiet inside. I knew they must be up, it was past eight o'clock. So I knocked again, and I thought I heard somebody say, "Come in." I wasn't sure, I'm not sure yet, but I opened the door—this door (*Indicating the door by which the two women are still standing*) and there in that rocker—(*Pointing to it.*) sat Mrs. Wright.

(*They all look at the rocker.*)

COUNTY ATTORNEY What—was she doing?

HALE She was rockin' back and forth. She had her apron in her hand and was kind of—pleating it.

COUNTY ATTORNEY And how did she—look?

HALE Well, she looked queer.

COUNTY ATTORNEY How do you mean—queer?

HALE Well, as if she didn't know what she was going to do next. And kind of done up.

COUNTY ATTORNEY How did she seem to feel about your coming?

HALE Why, I don't think she minded—one way or other. She didn't pay much attention. I said, "How do, Mrs. Wright, it's cold, ain't it?" And she said, "Is it?"—and went on kind of pleating at her apron. Well, I was surprised; she didn't ask me to come up to the stove, or to set down, but just sat there, not even looking at me, so I said, "I want to see John." And then she—laughed. I guess you would call it a laugh. I thought of Harry and the team outside, so I said a little sharp: "Can't I see John?" "No," she says, kind o' dull like. "Ain't he home?" says I. "Yes," says she, "he's home." "Then why can't I see him?" I asked her, out of patience. "'Cause he's dead," says she. "*Dead?*" says I. She just nodded her head, not getting a bit excited, but rockin' back and forth. "Why—where is he?" says I, not knowing what to say. She just pointed upstairs—like that (*Himself pointing to the room above*). I got up, with the idea of going up there. I walked from there to here—then I says, "Why, what did he die of?" "He died of a rope around his neck," says she, and just went on pleatin' at her apron. Well, I went out and called Harry. I thought I might—need help. We went upstairs and there he was lyin'—

COUNTY ATTORNEY I think I'd rather have you go into that upstairs, where you can point it all out. Just go on now with the rest of the story.

HALE Well, my first thought was to get that rope off. It looked . . . (*Stops, his face twitches.*) . . . but Harry, he went up to him, and he said, "No, he's dead all right, and we'd better not touch anything." So we went back down stairs. She was still sitting that same way. "Has anybody been notified?" I asked. "No," says she, unconcerned. "Who did this, Mrs. Wright?" said Harry. He said it businesslike—and she stopped pleatin' of her apron. "I don't know," she says. "You don't *know?*" says

Harry. "No," says she. "Weren't you sleepin' in the bed with him?" says Harry. "Yes," says she, "but I was on the inside." "Somebody slipped a rope round his neck and strangled him and you didn't wake up?" says Harry. "I didn't wake up," she said after him. We must 'a looked as if we didn't see how that could be, for after a minute she said, "I sleep sound." Harry was going to ask her more questions but I said maybe we ought to let her tell her story first to the coroner, or the sheriff, so Harry went fast as he could to Rivers' place, where there's a telephone.

COUNTY ATTORNEY And what did Mrs. Wright do when she knew that you had gone for the coroner?

HALE She moved from that chair to this one over here (*Pointing to a small chair in the corner.*) and just sat there with her hands held together and looking down. I got a feeling that I ought to make some conversation, so I said I had come in to see if John wanted to put in a telephone, and at that she started to laugh, and then she stopped and looked at me—scared. (*The* COUNTY ATTORNEY, *who has had his notebook out, makes a note.*) I dunno, maybe it wasn't scared. I wouldn't like to say it was. Soon Harry got back, and then Dr. Lloyd came, and you, Mr. Peters, and so I guess that's all I know that you don't.

COUNTY ATTORNEY (*looking around*) I guess we'll go upstairs first—and then out to the barn and around there. (*to the* SHERIFF) You're convinced that there was nothing important here—nothing that would point to any motive.

SHERIFF Nothing here but kitchen things.

(*The* COUNTY ATTORNEY, *after again looking around the kitchen, opens the door of a cupboard closet. He gets up on a chair and looks on a shelf. Pulls his hand away, sticky.*)

COUNTY ATTORNEY Here's a nice mess.

(*The women draw nearer.*)

MRS. PETERS (*to the other woman*) Oh, her fruit; it did freeze. (*To the* COUNTY ATTORNEY) She worried about that when it turned so cold. She said the fire'd go out and her jars would break.

SHERIFF Well, can you beat the woman! Held for murder and worryin' about her preserves.

COUNTY ATTORNEY I guess before we're through she may have something more serious than preserves to worry about.

HALE Well, women are used to worrying over trifles.

(*The two women move a little closer together.*)

COUNTY ATTORNEY (*with the gallantry of a young politician*) And yet, for all their worries, what would we do without the ladies? (*The women do not unbend. He goes to the sink, takes a dipperful of water from the pail and pouring it into a basin, washes his hands. Starts to wipe them on the roller towel, turns it for a cleaner place.*) Dirty towels! (*Kicks his foot against the pans under the sink.*) Not much of a housekeeper, would you say, ladies?

MRS. HALE (*stiffly*) There's a great deal of work to be done on a farm.

COUNTY ATTORNEY To be sure. And yet (*With a little bow to her*) I know there are some Dickson county farmhouses which do not have such roller towels.

(*He gives it a pull to expose its full length again.*)

MRS. HALE Those towels get dirty awful quick. Men's hands aren't always as clean as they might be.

COUNTY ATTORNEY Ah,' loyal to your sex, I see. But you and Mrs. Wright were neighbors. I suppose you were friends, too.

MRS. HALE (*shaking her head*) I've not seen much of her of late years. I've not been in this house—it's more than a year.

COUNTY ATTORNEY And why was that? You didn't like her?

MRS. HALE I liked her all well enough. Farmers' wives have their hands full, Mr. Henderson. And then—

COUNTY ATTORNEY Yes—?

MRS. HALE (*looking about*) It never seemed a very cheerful place.

COUNTY ATTORNEY No—it's not cheerful. I shouldn't say she had the homemaking instinct.

MRS. HALE Well, I don't know as Wright had, either.

COUNTY ATTORNEY You mean that they didn't get on very well?

MRS. HALE No, I don't mean anything. But I don't think a place'd be any cheerfuller for John Wright's being in it.

COUNTY ATTORNEY I'd like to talk more of that a little later. I want to get the lay of things upstairs now.

(*He goes to the left, where three steps lead to a stair door.*)

SHERIFF I suppose anything Mrs. Peters does'll be all right. She was to take in some clothes for her, you know, and a few little things. We left in such a hurry yesterday.

COUNTY ATTORNEY Yes, but I would like to see what you take, Mrs. Peters, and keep an eye out for anything that might be of use to us.

MRS. PETERS Yes, Mr. Henderson.

(*The women listen to the men's steps on the stairs, then look about the kitchen.*)

MRS. HALE I'd hate to have men coming into my kitchen, snooping around and criticising.

(*She arranges the pans under sink which the* COUNTY ATTORNEY *had shoved out of place.*)

MRS. PETERS Of course it's no more than their duty.

MRS. HALE Duty's all right, but I guess that deputy sheriff that came out to make the fire might have got a little of this on. (*Gives the roller towel a pull.*) Wish I'd thought of that sooner. Seems mean to talk about her for not having things slicked up when she had to come away in such a hurry.

Mrs. Peters (*Who has gone to a small table in the left rear corner of the room, and lifted one end of a towel that covers a pan*) She had bread set.

(*Stands still.*)

Mrs. Hale (*eyes fixed on a loaf of bread beside the breadbox, which is on a low shelf at the other side of the room. Moves slowly toward it*) She was going to put this in there. (*Picks up loaf, then abruptly drops it. In a manner of returning to familiar things.*) It's a shame about her fruit. I wonder if it's all gone. (*Gets up on the chair and looks.*) I think there's some here that's all right, Mrs. Peters. Yes—here; (*Holding it toward the window.*) this is cherries, too. (*Looking again.*) I declare I believe that's the only one. (*Gets down, bottle in her hand. Goes to the sink and wipes it off on the outside.*) She'll feel awful bad after all her hard work in the hot weather. I remember the afternoon I put up my cherries last summer.

(*She puts the bottle on the big kitchen table, center of the room. With a sigh, is about to sit down in the rocking-chair. Before she is seated realizes what chair it is; with a slow look at it, steps back. The chair which she has touched rocks back and forth.*)

Mrs. Peters Well, I must get those things from the front room closet. (*She goes to the door at the right, but after looking into the other room, steps back.*) You coming with me, Mrs. Hale? You could help me carry them.

(*They go in the other room; reappear, Mrs. Peters carrying a dress and skirt, Mrs. Hale following with a pair of shoes.*)

Mrs. Peters My, it's cold in there.

(*She puts the clothes on the big table, and hurries to the stove.*)

Mrs. Hale (*examining her skirt*) Wright was close. I think maybe that's why she kept so much to herself. She didn't even belong to the Ladies Aid. I suppose she felt she couldn't do her part, and then you don't enjoy things when you feel shabby. She used to wear pretty clothes and be lively, when she was Minnie Foster, one of the town girls singing in the choir. But that—oh, that was thirty years ago. This all you was to take in?

Mrs. Peters She said she wanted an apron. Funny thing to want, for there isn't much to get you dirty in jail, goodness knows. But I suppose just to make her feel more natural. She said they was in the top drawer in this cupboard. Yes, here. And then her little shawl that always hung behind the door. (*Opens stair door and looks.*) Yes, here it is.

(*Quickly shuts door leading upstairs.*)

Mrs. Hale (*abruptly moving toward her*) Mrs. Peters?

Mrs. Peters Yes, Mrs. Hale?

MRS. HALE Do you think she did it?

MRS. PETERS (*in a frightened voice*) Oh, I don't know.

MRS. HALE Well, I don't think she did. Asking for an apron and her little shawl. Worrying about her fruit.

MRS. PETERS (*starts to speak, glances up, where footsteps are heard in the room above. In a low voice*) Mr. Peters says it looks bad for her. Mr. Henderson is awful sarcastic in a speech and he'll make fun of her sayin' she didn't wake up.

MRS. HALE Well, I guess John Wright didn't wake when they was slipping that rope under his neck.

MRS. PETERS No, it's strange. It must have been done awful crafty and still. They say it was such a—funny way to kill a man, rigging it all up like that.

MRS. HALE That's just what Mr. Hale said. There was a gun in the house. He says that's what he can't understand.

MRS. PETERS Mr. Henderson said coming out that what was needed for the case was a motive; something to show anger, or—sudden feeling.

MRS. HALE (*who is standing by the table*) Well, I don't see any signs of anger around here. (*She puts her hand on the dish towel which lies on the table, stands looking down at table, one half of which is clean, the other half messy.*) It's wiped to here. (*Makes a move as if to finish work, then turns and looks at loaf of bread outside the breadbox. Drops towel. In that voice of coming back to familiar things.*) Wonder how they are finding things upstairs. I hope she had it a little more red-up up there. You know, it seems kind of *sneaking*. Locking her up in town and then coming out here and trying to get her own house to turn against her!

MRS. PETERS But Mrs. Hale, the law is the law.

MRS. HALE I s'pose 'tis. (*Unbuttoning her coat.*) Better loosen up your things, Mrs. Peters. You won't feel them when you go out.

(MRS. PETERS *takes off her fur tippet, goes to hang it on hook at back of room, stands looking at the under part of the small corner table.*)

MRS. PETERS She was piecing a quilt.

(*She brings the large sewing basket and they look at the bright pieces.*)

MRS. HALE It's log cabin pattern. Pretty, isn't it? I wonder if she was goin' to quilt it or just knot it?

(*Footsteps have been heard coming down the stairs. The* SHERIFF *enters followed by* HALE *and the* COUNTY ATTORNEY.)

SHERIFF They wonder if she was going to quilt it or just knot it!

(*The men laugh; the women look abashed.*)

COUNTY ATTORNEY (*rubbing his hands over the stove*) Frank's fire didn't do much up there, did it? Well, let's go out to the barn and get that cleared up.

(*The men go outside.*)

MRS. HALE (*resentfully*) I don't know as there's anything so strange, our takin' up our time with little things while we're waiting for them to get the evidence. (*She sits down at the big table smoothing out a block with decision.*) I don't see as it's anything to laugh about.

MRS. PETERS (*apologetically*) Of course they've got awful important things on their minds.

(*Pulls up a chair and joins* MRS. HALE *at the table.*)

MRS. HALE (*examining another block*) Mrs. Peters, look at this one. Here, this is the one she was working on, and look at the sewing! All the rest of it has been so nice and even. And look at this! It's all over the place! Why, it looks as if she didn't know what she was about!

(*After she has said this they look at each other, then start to glance back at the door. After an instant* MRS. HALE *has pulled at a knot and ripped the sewing.*)

MRS. PETERS Oh, what are you doing, Mrs. Hale?

MRS. HALE (*mildly*) Just pulling out a stitch or two that's not sewed very good. (*Threading a needle.*) Bad sewing always made me fidgety.

MRS. PETERS (*nervously*) I don't think we ought to touch things.

MRS. HALE I'll just finish up this end. (*Suddenly stopping and leaning forward.*) Mrs. Peters?

MRS. PETERS Yes, Mrs. Hale?

MRS. HALE What do you suppose she was so nervous about?

MRS. PETERS Oh—I don't know. I don't know as she was nervous. I sometimes sew awful queer when I'm just tired. (*Mrs.* HALE *starts to say something, looks at* MRS. PETERS*, then goes on sewing.*) Well, I must get these things wrapped up. They may be through sooner than we think. (*Putting apron and other things together.*) I wonder where I can find a piece of paper, and string.

MRS. HALE In that cupboard, maybe.

MRS. PETERS (*looking in cupboard*) Why, here's a birdcage. (*Holds it up.*) Did she have a bird, Mrs. Hale?

MRS. HALE Why, I don't know whether she did or not—I've not been here for so long. There was a man around last year selling canaries cheap, but I don't know as she took one; maybe she did. She used to sing real pretty herself.

MRS. PETERS (*glancing around*) Seems funny to think of a bird here. But she must have had one, or why would she have a cage? I wonder what happened to it.

MRS. HALE I s'pose maybe the cat got it.

MRS. PETERS No, she didn't have a cat. She's got that feeling some people have about cats—being afraid of them. My cat got in her room and she was real upset and asked me to take it out.

MRS. HALE My sister Bessie was like that. Queer, ain't it?

MRS. PETERS (*examining the cage*) Why, look at this door. It's broke. One hinge is pulled apart.

MRS. HALE (*looking too*) Looks as if someone must have been rough with it.

MRS. PETERS Why, yes.

(*She brings the cage forward and puts it on the table.*)

MRS. HALE I wish if they're going to find any evidence they'd be about it. I don't like this place.

MRS. PETERS But I'm awful glad you came with me, Mrs. Hale. It would be lonesome for me sitting here alone.

MRS. HALE It would, wouldn't it? (*Dropping her sewing.*) But I tell you what I do wish, Mrs. Peters. I wish I had come over sometimes when *she* was here. I—(*Looking around the room.*)—wish I had.

MRS. PETERS But of course you were awful busy, Mrs. Hale—your house and your children.

MRS. HALE I could've come. I stayed away because it weren't cheerful—and that's why I ought to have come. I—I've never liked this place. Maybe because it's down in a hollow and you don't see the road. I dunno what it is but it's a lonesome place and always was. I wish I had come over to see Minnie Foster sometimes. I can see now—

(*Shakes her head.*)

MRS. PETERS Well, you mustn't reproach yourself, Mrs. Hale. Somehow we just don't see how it is with other folks until—something comes up.

MRS. HALE Not having children makes less work—but it makes a quiet house, and Wright out to work all day, and no company when he did come in. Did you know John Wright, Mrs. Peters?

MRS. PETERS Not to know him; I've seen him in town. They say he was a good man.

MRS. HALE Yes—good; he didn't drink, and kept his word as well as most, I guess, and paid his debts. But he was a hard man, Mrs. Peters. Just to pass the time of day with him—(*Shivers.*) Like a raw wind that gets to the bone. (*Pauses, her eye falling on the cage.*) I should think she would 'a wanted a bird. But what do you suppose went with it?

MRS. PETERS I don't know, unless it got sick and died.

(*She reaches over and swings the broken door, swings it again.*
Both women watch it.)

MRS. HALE You weren't raised round here, were you? (MRS. PETERS *shakes her head.*) You didn't know—her?

MRS. PETERS Not till they brought her yesterday.

MRS. HALE She—come to think of it, she was kind of like a bird herself—real sweet and pretty, but kind of timid and—fluttery. How—she—did—change. (*Silence; then as if struck by a happy thought and relieved to get back to every day things.*) Tell you what, Mrs. Peters, why don't you take the quilt in with you? It might take up her mind.

MRS. PETERS Why, I think that's a real nice idea, Mrs. Hale. There couldn't possibly be any objection to it, could there? Now, just what would I take? I wonder if her patches are in here—and her things.

(*They look in the sewing basket.*)

MRS. HALE Here's some red. I expect this has got sewing things in it. (*Brings out a fancy box.*) What a pretty box. Looks like something somebody would give you. Maybe her scissors are in here. (*Opens box. Suddenly puts her hand to her nose.*) Why—(MRS. PETERS *bends nearer, then turns her face away.*) There's something wrapped up in this piece of silk.

MRS. PETERS Why, this isn't her scissors.

MRS. HALE (*lifting the silk*) Oh, Mrs. Peters—it's—

MRS. PETERS It's the bird.

MRS. HALE (*jumping up*) But, Mrs. Peters—look at it! Its neck! Look at its neck! It's all—other side *to.*

MRS. PETERS Somebody—wrung—its—neck.

(*Their eyes meet. A look of growing comprehension, of horror. Steps are heard outside.* MRS. HALE *slips box under quilt pieces, and sinks into her chair. Enter* SHERIFF *and* COUNTY ATTORNEY. MRS. PETERS *rises.*)

COUNTY ATTORNEY (*as one turning from serious things to little pleasantries*) Well, ladies, have you decided whether she was going to quilt it or knot it?

MRS. PETERS We think she was going to—knot it.

COUNTY ATTORNEY Well, that's interesting. I'm sure. (*Seeing the birdcage.*) Has the bird flown?

MRS. HALE (*putting more quilt pieces over the box*) We think the—cat got it.

COUNTY ATTORNEY (*Preoccupied*) Is there a cat?

(MRS. HALE *glances in a quick covert way at* MRS. PETERS.)

MRS. PETERS Well, not *now.* They're superstitious, you know. They leave.

COUNTY ATTORNEY (*to* SHERIFF PETERS, *continuing an interrupted conversation*) No sign at all of anyone having come from the outside. Their own rope. Now let's go up again and go over it piece by piece. (*They start upstairs.*) It would have to have been someone who knew just the—

(MRS. PETERS *sits down. The two women sit there not looking at one another, but as if peering into something and at the same time holding back. When they talk now it is in the manner of feeling their way over strange ground, as if afraid of what they are saying, but as if they can not help saying it.*)

MRS. HALE She liked the bird. She was going to bury it in that pretty box.

MRS. PETERS (*in a whisper*) When I was a girl—my kitten—there was a boy took a hatchet, and before my eyes—and before I could get there—(*Covers her face an instant.*) If they hadn't held me back I would have—(*Catches herself, looks upstairs where steps are heard, falters weakly.*)—hurt him.

MRS. HALE (*with a slow look around her*) I wonder how it would seem never to have had any children around. (*Pause.*) No, Wright wouldn't like the bird—a thing that sang. She used to sing. He killed that, too.

MRS. PETERS (*moving uneasily*) We don't know who killed the bird.

MRS. HALE I knew John Wright.

MRS. PETERS It was an awful thing was done in this house that night, Mrs. Hale. Killing a man while he slept, slipping a rope around his neck that choked the life out of him.

MRS. HALE His neck. Choked the life out of him.

(*Her hand goes out and rests on the birdcage.*)

MRS. PETERS (*with rising voice*) We don't know who killed him. We don't *know.*

MRS. HALE (*her own feeling not interrupted*) If there'd been years and years of nothing, then a bird to sing to you, it would be awful—still, after the bird was still.

MRS. PETERS (*something within her speaking*) I know what stillness is. When we homesteaded in Dakota, and my first baby died—after he was two years old, and me with no other then—

MRS. HALE (*moving*) How soon do you suppose they'll be through, looking for the evidence?

MRS. PETERS I know what stillness is. (*Pulling herself back.*) The law has got to punish crime, Mrs. Hale.

MRS. HALE (*not as if answering that*) I wish you'd seen Minnie Foster when she wore a white dress with blue ribbons and stood up there in the choir and sang. (*A look around the room.*) Oh, I *wish* I'd come over here once in a while! That was a crime! That was a crime! Who's going to punish that?

MRS. PETERS (*looking upstairs*) We mustn't—take on.

MRS. HALE I might have known she needed help! I know how things can be—for women. I tell you, it's queer, Mrs. Peters. We live close together and we live far apart. We all go through the same things—it's all just a different kind of the same thing. (*Brushes her eyes; noticing the bottle of fruit, reaches out for it.*) If I was you I wouldn't tell her her fruit was gone. Tell her it *ain't.* Tell her it's all right. Take this in to prove it to her. She—she may never know whether it was broke or not.

MRS. PETERS (*takes the bottle, looks about for something to wrap it in; takes petticoat from the clothes brought from the other room, very nervously begins winding this around the bottle. In a false voice*) My, it's a good thing the men couldn't hear us. Wouldn't they just laugh! Getting all stirred up over a little thing like a—dead canary. As if that could have anything to do with—with—wouldn't they *laugh!*

(*The men are heard coming down stairs.*)

MRS. HALE (*under her breath*) Maybe they would—maybe they wouldn't.

COUNTY ATTORNEY No, Peters, it's all perfectly clear except a reason for doing it. But you know juries when it comes to women. If there was some definite thing. Something to show—something to make a story about—a thing that would connect up with this strange way of doing it—

(*The women's eyes meet for an instant. Enter* HALE *from outer door.*)

HALE Well, I've got the team around. Pretty cold out there.

COUNTY ATTORNEY I'm going to stay here a while by myself. (*To the* SHERIFF.) You can send Frank out for me, can't you? I want to go over everything. I'm not satisfied that we can't do better.

SHERIFF Do you want to see what Mrs. Peters is going to take in?

(*The* COUNTY ATTORNEY *goes to the table, picks up the apron, laughs.*)

COUNTY ATTORNEY Oh, I guess they're not very dangerous things the ladies have picked out. (*Moves a few things about, disturbing the quilt pieces which cover the box. Steps back.*) No, Mrs. Peters doesn't need supervising. For that matter, a sheriff's wife is married to the law. Ever think of it that way, Mrs. Peters?

MRS. PETERS Not—just that way.

SHERIFF (*Chuckling*) Married to the law. (*Moves toward the other room.*) I just want you to come in here a minute, George. We ought to take a look at these windows.

COUNTY ATTORNEY (*scoffingly*) Oh, windows!

SHERIFF We'll be right out, Mr. Hale.

(HALE *goes outside. The* SHERIFF *follows the* COUNTY ATTORNEY *into the other room. Then* MRS. HALE *rises, hands tight together, looking intensely at* MRS. PETERS, *whose eyes make a slow turn, finally meeting* MRS. HALE'S. *A moment* MRS. HALE *holds her, then her own eyes point the way to where the box is concealed. Suddenly* MRS. PETERS *throws back quilt pieces and tries to put the box in the bag she is wearing. It is too big. She opens box, starts to take bird out, cannot touch it, goes to pieces, stands there helpless. Sound of a knob turning in the other room.* MRS. HALE *snatches the box and puts it in the pocket of her big coat. Enter* COUNTY ATTORNEY *and* SHERIFF.)

COUNTY ATTORNEY (*facetiously*) Well, Henry, at least we found out that she was not going to quilt it. She was going to—what is it you call it, ladies?

MRS. HALE (*her hand against her pocket*) We call it—knot it, Mr. Henderson.

Curtain

1. Although technically this short play is not divided into separate scenes, it does split into three separate parts: first, when the men and women are together in Mrs. Wright's kitchen; second, when Mrs. Peters and Mrs. Hale are alone together; third, when the men return to the kitchen. What is the function of each of these "scenes"? What is the relation between them in terms of what they reveal to you?

2. What would you say is the plot of this play? Where do you find it? Is there a subplot as well? What is the relationship between the two?

3. The stage directions work like a description of the surroundings. What does Glaspell choose to emphasize, to call your attention to? What do these elements have to do with the narration?

4. Who is the protagonist(s)? Who is the antagonist(s)? How does Glaspell let you know which is which?

5. Describe the conflict that distinguishes the protagonist(s) from the antagonist(s).

6. Is there exposition, rising action, climax, and denouement in this play? Describe each.

7. What do you think is Glaspell's dominant idea?

CHARACTER

Since plot is a sequence of events that is set in motion and maintains its movement through conflict, in most cases, it is the interaction between the characters in the account of an event or in the telling of a story that creates the plot.

Writers define and develop their characters through *characterization*. They portray their characters through the characters' actions and through their reactions to situations as well as to other characters and their actions. Characters also grow through their physical appearance and gestures, through their speech, and sometimes through their names.

Writers use two ways to develop their characters. A writer can tell you about a character by stepping between you and the character and interpreting the character's actions for you. The writer can tell you what a character is doing or thinking, what the character's past experiences have been, what the character looks like, even what clothes the character wears. Sometimes, the writer can evaluate the character's behavior as well, telling you what to think about what the character has done or is doing or what the character has thought or is thinking.

The second way a writer can develop and define a character is by revealing that character through the character's actions. A writer may simply describe what a character is doing in a given situation and, by controlling the setting and by emphasizing certain actions while allowing others to fade into the background, suggest to you what the character is like. The character's speech often tells you a lot. A writer can use dialogue to reveal character to you. What the character says to other characters or about the situation surrounding him or her often defines the protagonist or antagonist.

Some characters are "round" characters. These characters are well developed, having many traits that are significant to the action and to the dominant idea. Other characters are "flat." They remain in the background. Often their function is to further define the central characters through the way the central characters respond to them.

Along the same lines, a character may be static or dynamic. A dynamic character changes through the movement of the plot. He or she may learn something that leads to change or reveal more and more of himself or herself as the plot advances. Often change reveals a great deal about a character. In other cases, the fact that a character is static in a situation where, as the reader, you believe change is necessary reveals the character to you.

When you choose to use characters and their actions to support your dominant idea, remember, you don't have to tell everything about a character or to pay equal attention to all the characters you use. Let your dominant idea suggest what it is important to reveal (what should be in the foreground of your reader's experience), what elements of the character should fade into the background, and what the reader does not need to know at all.

ᕦᕤ *Working with the Readings*

Read the following pieces of writing and, alone or with your group, answer the questions that follow each one.

A VIEW FROM THE BRIDGE

Cherokee Paul McDonald

I was coming up on the little bridge in the Rio Vista neighborhood of Fort Lauderdale, deepening my stride and my breathing to negotiate the slight incline without altering my pace. And then, as I neared the crest, I saw the kid.

He was a lumpy little guy with baggy shorts, a faded T-shirt and heavy sweat socks falling down over old sneakers.

Partially covering his shaggy blond hair was one of those blue baseball caps with gold braid on the bill and a sailfish patch sewn onto the peak. Covering his eyes and part of his face was a pair of those stupid-looking '50s-style wrap-around sunglasses.

He was fumbling with a beat-up rod and reel, and he had a little bait
bucket by his feet. I puffed on by, glancing down into the empty bucket
as I passed.

"Hey, mister! Would you help me, please?"   5

The shrill voice penetrated my jogger's concentration, and I was determined to ignore it. But for some reason, I stopped.

With my hands on my hips and the sweat dripping from my nose I
asked, "What do you want, kid?"

"Would you please help me find my shrimp? It's my last one and I've
been getting bites and I know I can catch a fish if can just find that shrimp.
He jumped outta my hand as I was getting him from the bucket."

Exasperated, I walked slowly back to the kid, and pointed.

"There's the damn shrimp by your left foot. You stopped me for   10
that?"

As I said it, the kid reached down and trapped the shrimp.

"Thanks a lot, mister," he said.

I watched as the kid dropped the baited hook down into the canal.
Then I turned to start back down the bridge.

That's when the kid let out a "Hey! Hey!" and the prettiest tarpon
I'd ever seen came almost six feet out of the water, twisting and turning
as he fell through the air.

"I got one!" the kid yelled as the fish hit the water with a loud splash   15
and took off down the canal.

I watched the line being burned off the reel at an alarming rate. The
kid's left hand held the crank while the extended fingers felt for the drag
setting.

"No, kid!" I shouted. "Leave the drag alone . . . just keep that damn
rod tip up!"

Then I glanced at the reel and saw there were just a few loops of line
left on the spool.

"Why don't you get yourself some decent equipment?" I said, but
before the kid could answer I saw the line go slack.

"Ohhh, I lost him," the kid said. I saw the flash of silver as the fish   20
turned.

"Crank, kid, crank! You didn't lose him. He's coming back toward
you. Bring in the slack!"

The kid cranked like mad, and a beautiful grin spread across his face.

"He's heading in for the pilings," I said. "Keep him out of those
pilings!"

The kid played it perfectly. When the fish made its play for the pilings, he kept just enough pressure on to force the fish out. When the
water exploded and the silver missile hurled into the air, the kid kept the
rod tip up and the line tight.

As the fish came to the surface and began a slow circle in the middle   25
of the canal, I said, "Whooee, is that a nice fish or what?"

The kid didn't say anything, so I said, "Okay, move to the edge of the bridge and I'll climb down to the seawall and pull him out."

When I reached the seawall I pulled in the leader, leaving the fish lying on its side in the water.

"How's that?" I said.

"Hey, mister, tell me what it looks like."

"Look down here and check him out," I said, "He's beautiful." 30

But then I looked up into those stupid-looking sunglasses and it hit me. The kid was blind.

"Could you tell me what he looks like, mister?" he said again.

"Well, he's just under three, uh, he's about as long as one of your arms," I said. "I'd guess he goes about 15, 20 pounds. He's mostly silver, but the silver is somehow made up of *all* the colors, if you know what I mean." I stopped. "Do you know what I mean by colors?"

The kid nodded.

"Okay. He has all these big scales, like armor all over his body. 35 They're silver too, and when he moves they sparkle. He has a strong body and a large powerful tail. He has big round eyes, bigger than a quarter, and a lower jaw that sticks out past the upper one and is very tough. His belly is almost white and his back is a gunmetal gray. When he jumped he came out of the water about six feet, and his scales caught the sun and flashed it all over the place."

By now the fish had righted itself, and I could see the bright-red gills as the gill plates opened and closed. I explained this to the kid, and then said, more to myself, "He's a beauty."

"Can you get him off the hook?" the kid asked. "I don't want to kill him."

I watched as the tarpon began to slowly swim away, tired but still alive.

By the time I got back up to the top of the bridge the kid had his line secured and his bait bucket in one hand.

He grinned and said, "Just in time. My mom drops me off here, and 40 she'll be back to pick me up any minute."

He used the back of one hand to wipe his nose.

"Thanks for helping me catch that tarpon," he said, "and for helping me to see it."

I looked at him, shook my head, and said, "No, my friend, thank you for letting *me* see that fish."

I took off, but before I got far the kid yelled again.

"Hey, mister!" 45

I stopped.

"Someday I'm gonna catch a sailfish and a blue marlin and a giant tuna and *all* those big sportfish!"

As I looked into those sunglasses I knew he probably would. I wished I could be there when it happened.

1. What is the plot of this essay? Is it simply about a kid catching a fish or is there more going on here?

2. What are the characters involved in the plot like? How does McDonald reveal these characters?

3. Is there a protagonist and an antagonist in the essay? Who or what are they? What makes you think so?

4. What do you see as the dominant idea of this essay? How does McDonald support that idea?

TWO FAWNS THAT DIDN'T SEE THE LIGHT THIS SPRING

Gary Snyder

A friend in a tipi in the
Northern Rockies went out
hunting white tail with a
.22 and creeped up on a few
day–bedded, sleeping, shot   5
what he thought was a buck.
"It was a doe, and she was
carrying a fawn."
He cured the meat without
salt; sliced it following the   10
grain.

A friend in the Northern Sierra
hit a doe with her car. It
walked out calmly in the lights,
"And when we butchered her   15
there was a fawn—about so long—
so tiny—but all formed and right.
It had spots. And the little
hooves were soft and white."

1. Snyder tells you two stories in two stanzas. How are they alike? How are they different?

2. Although there are two stories, are there two plots?

3. In each story, there is a character. Each character speaks. What does the speech of each character reveal about that person? Do the two

speeches taken together create a dialogue that defines each character in terms of the other?

4. What do you think the dominant idea of this poem is? How do the parts of the poem lead you to that idea?

THE MAGIC BARREL

Bernard Malamud

Not long ago there lived in uptown New York, in a small, almost meager room, though crowded with books, Leo Finkle, a rabbinical student in the Yeshivah University. Finkle, after six years of study, was to be ordained in June and had been advised by an acquaintance that he might find it easier to win himself a congregation if he were married. Since he had no present prospects of marriage, after two tormented days of turning it over in his mind, he called in Pinye Salzman, a marriage broker whose two-line advertisement he had read in the *Forward*.°

The matchmaker appeared one night out of the dark fourth-floor hallway of the graystone rooming house where Finkle lived, grasping a black, strapped portfolio that had been worn with use. Salzman, who had been long in the business, was of slight but dignified build, wearing an old hat, and an overcoat too short and tight for him. He smelled frankly of fish, which he loved to eat, and although he was missing a few teeth, his presence was not displeasing, because of an amiable manner curiously contrasted with mournful eyes. His voice, his lips, his wisp of beard, his bony fingers were animated, but give him a moment of repose and his mild blue eyes revealed a depth of sadness, a characteristic that put Leo a little at ease although the situation, for him, was inherently tense.

He at once informed Salzman why he had asked him to come, explaining that his home was in Cleveland, and that but for his parents, who had married comparatively late in life, he was alone in the world. He had for six years devoted himself almost entirely to his studies, as a result of which, understandably, he had found himself without time for a social life and the company of young women. Therefore he thought it the better part of trial and error—of embarrassing fumbling—to call in an experienced person to advise him on these matters. He remarked in passing that the function of the marriage broker was ancient and honorable, highly approved in the Jewish community, because it made practical the necessary without hindering joy. Moreover, his own parents had been brought

---

The Jewish Daily Forward: Yiddish newspaper in New York City

together by a matchmaker. They had made, if not a financially profitable marriage—since neither had possessed any worldly goods to speak of—at least a successful one in the sense of their everlasting devotion to each other. Salzman listened in embarrassed surprise, sensing a sort of apology. Later, however, he experienced a glow of pride in his work, an emotion that had left him years ago, and he heartily approved of Finkle.

The two went to their business. Leo had led Salzman to the only clear place in the room, a table near a window that overlooked the lamp-lit city. He seated himself at the matchmaker's side but facing him, attempting by an act of will to suppress the unpleasant tickle in his throat. Salzman eagerly unstrapped his portfolio and removed a loose rubber band from a thin packet of much-handled cards. As he flipped through them, a gesture and sound that physically hurt Leo, the student pretended not to see and gazed steadfastly out the window. Although it was still February, winter was on its last legs, signs of which he had for the first time in years begun to notice. He now observed the round white moon, moving high in the sky through a cloud menagerie, and watched with half-open mouth as it penetrated a huge hen, and dropped out of her like an egg laying itself. Salzman, though pretending through eyeglasses he had just slipped on, to be engaged in scanning the writing on the cards, stole occasional glances at the young man's distinguished face, noting with pleasure the long, severe scholar's nose, brown eyes heavy with learning, sensitive yet ascetic lips, and a certain, almost hollow quality of the dark cheeks. He gazed around at shelves upon shelves of books and let out a soft, contented sigh.

When Leo's eyes fell upon the cards, he counted six spread out in   5
Salzman's hand.

"So few?" he asked in disappointment.

"You wouldn't believe me how much cards I got in my office," Salzman replied. "The drawers are already filled to the top, so I keep them now in a barrel, but is every girl good for a new rabbi?"

Leo blushed at this, regretting all he had revealed of himself in a curriculum vitae he had sent to Salzman. He had thought it best to acquaint him with his strict standards and specifications, but in having done so, he felt he had told the marriage broker more than was absolutely necessary.

He hesitantly inquired, "Do you keep photographs of your clients on file?"

"First comes family, amount of dowry, also what kind promises,"   10
Salzman replied, unbuttoning his tight coat and settling himself in the chair. "After comes pictures, rabbi."

"Call me Mr. Finkle. I'm not yet a rabbi."

Salzman said he would, but instead called him doctor, which he changed to rabbi when Leo was not listening too attentively.

Salzman adjusted his horn-rimmed spectacles, gently cleared his throat and read in an eager voice the contents of the top card:

"Sophie P. Twenty four years. Widow one year. No children. Educated high school and two years college. Father promises eight thousand dollars. Has wonderful wholesale business. Also real estate. On the mother's side comes teachers, also one actor. Well known on Second Avenue."

Leo gazed up in surprise. "Did you say a widow?"

"A widow don't mean spoiled, rabbi. She lived with her husband maybe four months. He was a sick boy she made a mistake to marry him."

"Marrying a widow has never entered my mind."

"This is because you have no experience. A widow, especially if she is young and healthy like this girl, is a wonderful person to marry. She will be thankful to you the rest of her life. Believe me, if I was looking now for a bride, I would marry a widow."

Leo reflected, then shook his head.

Salzman hunched his shoulders in an almost imperceptible gesture of disappointment. He placed the card down on the wooden table and began to read another:

"Lily H. High school teacher. Regular. Not a substitute. Has savings and new Dodge car. Lived in Paris one year. Father is successful dentist thirty-five years. Interested in professional man. Well Americanized family. Wonderful opportunity."

"I knew her personally," said Salzman. "I wish you could see this girl. She is a doll. Also very intelligent. All day you could talk to her about books and theyater and what not. She also knows current events."

"I don't believe you mentioned her age?"

"Her age?" Salzman said, raising his brows. "Her age is thirty-two years."

Leo said after a while, "I'm afraid that seems a little too old."

Salzman let out a laugh. "So how old are you, rabbi?"

"Twenty-seven."

"So what is the difference, tell me, between twenty-seven and thirty-two? My own wife is seven years older than me. So what did I suffer?—Nothing. If Rothschild's daughter wants to marry you, would you say on account her age, no?"

"Yes," Leo said dryly.

Salzman shook off the no in the yes. "Five years don't mean a thing. I give you my word that when you will live with her for one week you will forget her age. What does it mean five years—that she lived more and knows more than somebody who is younger? On this girl, God bless her, years are not wasted. Each one that it comes makes better the bargain."

"What subject does she teach in high school?"

"Languages. If you heard the way she speaks French, you will think it is music. I am in the business twenty-five years, and I recommend her with my whole heart. Believe me, I know what I'm talking, rabbi."

"What's on the next card?" Leo said abruptly.

Salzman reluctantly turned up the third card.

"Ruth K. Nineteen years. Honor student. Father offers thirteen   *35*
thousand cash to the right bridegroom. He is a medical doctor. Stomach
specialist with marvelous practice. Brother in law owns own garment
business. Particular people."

Salzman looked as if he had read his trump card.

"Did you say nineteen?" Leo asked with interest.

"On the dot."

"Is she attractive?" He blushed. "Pretty?"

Salzman kissed his finger tips. "A little doll. On this I give my word.   *40*
Let me call the father tonight and you will see what means pretty."

But Leo was troubled. "You're sure she's that young?"

"This I am positive. The father will show you the birth certificate."

"Are you positive there isn't something wrong with her?" Leo
insisted.

"Who says there is wrong?"

"I don't understand why an American girl her age should go to a   *45*
marriage broker."

A smile spread over Salzman's face.

"So for the same reason you went, she comes."

Leo flushed. "I am pressed for time."

Salzman, realizing he had been tactless, quickly explained. "The father came, not her. He wants she should have the best, so he looks around
himself. When we will locate the right boy he will introduce him and
encourage. This makes a better marriage than if a young girl without
experience takes for herself. I don't have to tell you this."

"But don't you think this young girl believes in love?" Leo spoke   *50*
uneasily.

Salzman was about to guffaw but caught himself and said soberly,
"Love comes with the right person, not before."

Leo parted dry lips but did not speak. Noticing that Salzman had
snatched a glance at the next card, he cleverly asked, "How is her health?"

"Perfect," Salzman said, breathing with difficulty. "Of course, she is
a little lame on her right foot from an auto accident that it happened to
her when she was twelve years, but nobody notices on account she is so
brilliant and also beautiful."

Leo got up heavily and went to the window. He felt curiously bitter
and upbraided himself for having called in the marriage broker. Finally,
he shook his head.

"Why not?" Salzman persisted, the pitch of his voice rising.   *55*

"Because I detest stomach specialists."

"So what do you care what is his business? After you marry her do
you need him? Who says he must come every Friday night in your
house?"

Ashamed of the way the talk was going, Leo dismissed Salzman, who
went home with heavy, melancholy eyes.

Though he had felt only relief at the marriage broker's departure, Leo was in low spirits the next day. He explained it as arising from Salzman's failure to produce a suitable bride for him. He did not care for his type of clientele. But when Leo found himself hesitating whether to seek out another matchmaker, one more polished than Pinye, he wondered if it could be—his protestations to the contrary, and although he honored his father and mother—that he did not, in essence, care for the match-making institution? This thought he quickly put out of mind yet found himself still upset. All day he ran around in the woods—missed an important appointment, forgot to give out his laundry, walked out of a Broadway cafeteria without paying and had to run back with the ticket in his hand; had even not recognized his landlady in the street when she passed with a friend and courteously called out, "A good evening to you, Doctor Finkle." By nightfall, however, he had regained sufficient calm to sink his nose into a book and there found peace from his thoughts.

Almost at once there came a knock on the door. Before Leo could say enter, Salzman, commercial cupid, was standing in the room. His face was gray and meager, his expression hungry, and he looked as if he would expire on his feet. Yet the marriage broker managed, by some trick of the muscles, to display a broad smile.

"So good evening. I am invited?"

Leo nodded, disturbed to see him again, yet unwilling to ask the man to leave.

Beaming still, Salzman laid his portfolio on the table. "Rabbi, I got for you tonight good news."

"I've asked you not to call me rabbi. I'm still a student."

"Your worries are finished. I have for you a first-class bride."

"Leave me in peace concerning this subject." Leo pretended lack of interest.

"The world will dance at your wedding."

"Please, Mr. Salzman, no more."

"But first must come back my strength," Salzman said weakly. He fumbled with the portfolio straps and took out of the leather case an oily paper bag, from which he extracted a hard, seeded roll and a small, smoked white fish. With a quick motion of his hand he stripped the fish out of its skin and began ravenously to chew. "All day in a rush," he muttered.

Leo watched him eat.

"A sliced tomato you have maybe?" Salzman hesitantly inquired.

"No."

The marriage broker shut his eyes and ate. When he had finished he carefully cleaned up the crumbs and rolled up the remains of the fish, in the paper bag. His spectacled eyes roamed the room until he discovered, amid some piles of books, a one-burner gas stove. Lifting his hat he humbly asked, "A glass tea you got, rabbi?"

60

65

70

Conscience-stricken, Leo rose and brewed the tea. He served it with a chunk of lemon and two cubes of lump sugar, delighting Salzman.

After he had drunk his tea, Salzman's strength and good spirits were restored.

"So tell me, rabbi," he said amiably, "you considered some more the three clients I mentioned yesterday?"

"There was no need to consider."

"Why not?"

"None of them suits me."

"What then suits you?"

Leo let it pass because he could give only a confused answer.

Without waiting for a reply, Salzman asked, "You remember this girl I talked to you—the high school teacher?"

"Age thirty-two?"

But, surprisingly, Salzman's face lit in a smile. "Age twenty-nine."

Leo shot him a look. "Reduced from thirty-two?"

"A mistake," Salzman avowed, "I talked today with the dentist. He took me to his safety deposit box and showed me the birth certificate. She was twenty-nine years last August. They made her a party in the mountains where she went for her vacation. When her father spoke to me the first time I forgot to write the age and I told you thirty-two, but now I remember this was a different client, a widow."

"The same one you told me about? I thought she was twenty-four?"

"A different. Am I responsible that the world is filled with widows?"

"No, but I'm not interested in them, nor for that matter, in school teachers."

Salzman pulled his clasped hands to his breast. Looking at the ceiling he devoutly exclaimed, "Yiddishe kinder:° what can I say to somebody that he is not interested in high school teachers? So what then you are interested?"

Leo flushed but controlled himself.

"In what else will you be interested," Salzman went on, "if you not interested in this fine girl that she speaks four languages and has personally in the bank ten thousand dollars? Also her father guarantees further twelve thousand. Also she has a new car, wonderful clothes, talks on all subjects, and she will give you a first-class home and children. How near do we come in our life to paradise?"

"If she's so wonderful, why wasn't she married ten years ago?"

"Why?" said Salzman with a heavy laugh. "—Why? Because she is *partikiler*. This is why. She wants the *best*."

Leo was silent, amused at how he had entangled himself. But Salzman had aroused his interest in Lily H., and he began seriously to consider

Yiddishe kinder: Yiddish for "Yiddish children"

calling on her. When the marriage broker observed how intently Leo's mind was at work on the facts he had supplied, he felt certain they would soon come to an agreement.

Late Saturday afternoon, conscious of Salzman, Leo Finkle walked with Lily Hirschorn along Riverside Drive. He walked briskly and erectly, wearing with distinction the black fedora that he had that morning taken with trepidation out of the dusty hat box on his closet shelf, and the heavy black Saturday coat he had thoroughly whisked clean. Leo also owned a walking stick, a present from a distant relative, but quickly put temptation aside and did not use it. Lily, petite and not unpretty, had on something signifying the approach of spring. She was au courant,° animatedly, with all sorts of subjects, and he weighed her words and found her surprisingly sound—score another for Salzman, whom he uneasily sensed to be somewhere around, hiding perhaps high in a tree along the street, flashing the lady signals with a pocket mirror; or perhaps a cloven-hoofed Pan, piping nuptial ditties as he danced his invisible way before them, strewing wild buds on the walk and purple grapes in their path, symbolizing fruit of a union, though there was of course still none.

Lily startled Leo by remarking, "I was thinking of Mr. Salzman, a curious figure, wouldn't you say?"

Not certain what to answer, he nodded.

She bravely went on, blushing, "I for one am grateful for his introducing us. Aren't you?"

He courteously replied, "I am."   *100*

"I mean," she said with a little laugh—and it was all in good taste, or at least gave the effect of being not in bad—"do you mind that we came together so?"

He was not displeased with her honesty, recognizing that she meant to set the relationship aright, and understanding that it took a certain amount of experience in life, and courage, to want to do it quite that way. One had to have some sort of past to make that kind of beginning.

He said that he did not mind. Salzman's function was traditional and honorable—valuable for what it might achieve, which, he pointed out, was frequently nothing.

Lily agreed with a sigh. They walked on for a while and she said after a long silence, again with a nervous laugh, "Would you mind if I asked you something a little bit personal? Frankly, I find the subject fascinating." Although Leo shrugged, she went on half embarrassedly, "How was it that you came to your calling? I mean was it a sudden passionate inspiration?"

Leo, after a time, slowly replied, "I was always interested in the Law."   *105*

---

au courant: French for "informed, up-to-date"

"You saw revealed in it the presence of the Highest?"

He nodded and changed the subject. "I understand that you spent a little time in Paris, Miss Hirschorn?"

"Oh, did Mr. Salzman tell you, Rabbi Finkle?" Leo winced but she went on, "It was ages ago and almost forgotten. I remember I had to return for my sister's wedding."

And Lily would not be put off. "When," she asked in a trembly voice, "did you become enamored of God?"

He stared at her. Then it came to him that she was talking not about Leo Finkle, but of a total stranger, some mystical figure, perhaps even passionate prophet that Salzman had dreamed up for her—no relation to the living or dead. Leo trembled with rage and weakness. The trickster had obviously sold her a bill of goods, just as he had him, who'd expected to become acquainted with a young lady of twenty-nine, only to behold, the moment he laid eyes upon her strained and anxious face, a woman past thirty-five and aging rapidly. Only his self control had kept him this long in her presence. *110*

"I am not," he said gravely, "a talented religious person," and in seeking words to go on, found himself possessed by shame and fear. "I think," he said in a strained manner, "that I came to God not because I loved Him, but because I did not."

This confession he spoke harshly because its unexpectedness shook him.

Lily wilted. Leo saw a profusion of loaves of bread go flying like ducks high over his head, not unlike the winged loaves by which he had counted himself to sleep last night. Mercifully, then, it snowed, which he would not put past Salzman's machinations.

He was infuriated with the marriage broker and swore he would throw him out of the room the minute he reappeared. But Salzman did not come that night, and when Leo's anger had subsided, an unaccountable despair grew in its place. At first he thought this was caused by his disappointment in Lily, but before long it became evident that he had involved himself with Salzman without a true knowledge of his own intent. He gradually realized—with an emptiness that seized him with six hands—that he had called in the broker to find him a bride because he was incapable of doing it himself. This terrifying insight he had derived as a result of his meeting and conversation with Lily Hirschorn. Her probing questions had somehow irritated him into revealing—to himself more than her—the true nature of his relationship to God, and from that it had come upon him, with shocking force, that apart from his parents, he had never loved anyone. Or perhaps it went the other way, that he did not love God so well as he might, because he had not loved man. It seemed to Leo that his whole life stood starkly revealed and he saw himself for the first time as he truly was—unloved and loveless. This bitter but somehow not fully unexpected revelation brought him to a point of panic controlled only by extraordinary effort. He covered his face with his hands and cried.

The week that followed was the worst of his life. He did not eat and 115 lost weight. His beard darkened and grew ragged. He stopped attending seminars and almost never opened a book. He seriously considered leaving the Yeshivah, although he was deeply troubled at the thought of the loss of all his years of study—saw them like pages torn from a book, strewn over the city—and at the devastating effect of this decision upon his parents. But he had lived without knowledge of himself, and never in the Five Books and all the Commentaries—mea culpa°—had the truth been revealed to him. He did not know where to turn, and in all this desolating loneliness there was no *to whom,* although he often thought of Lily but not once could bring himself to go downstairs and make the call. He became touchy and irritable, especially with his landlady, who asked him all manner of personal questions; on the other hand, sensing his own disagreeableness, he waylaid her on the stairs and apologized abjectly, until mortified, she ran from him. Out of this, however, he drew the consolation that he was a Jew and that a Jew suffered. But gradually, as the long and terrible week drew to a close, he regained his composure and some idea of purpose in life: to go on as planned. Although he was imperfect, the ideal was not. As for his quest of a bride, the thought of continuing afflicted him with anxiety and heartburn, yet perhaps with this new knowledge of himself he would be more successful than in the past. Perhaps love would now come to him and a bride to that love. And for this sanctified seeking who needed a Salzman?

The marriage broker, a skeleton with haunted eyes, returned that very night. He looked, withal, the picture of frustrated expectancy—as if he had steadfastly waited the week at Miss Lily Hirschorn's side for a telephone call that never came.

Casually coughing, Salzman came immediately to the point: "So how did you like her?"

Leo's anger rose and he could not refrain from chiding the matchmaker: "Why did you lie to me, Salzman?"

Salzman's pale face went dead white, the world had snowed on him.

"Did you not state that she was twenty-nine?" Leo insisted. 120

"I gave you my word—"

"She was thirty-five, if a day. *At least* thirty-five."

"Of this don't be too sure. Her father told me—"

"Never mind. The worst of it was that you lied to her."

"How did I lie to her, tell me?" 125

"You told her things about me that weren't true. You made me out to be more, consequently less than I am. She had in mind a totally different person, a sort of semimystical Wonder Rabbi."

---

mea culpa: Latin for "my fault," a ritual phrase spoken by sinners

"All I said, you was a religious man."

"I can imagine."

Salzman sighed. "This is my weakness that I have," he confessed. "My wife says to me I shouldn't be a salesman, but when I have two fine people that they would be wonderful to be married, I am so happy that I talk too much." He smiled wanly. "This is why Salzman is a poor man."

Leo's anger left him. "Well, Salzman, I'm afraid that's all."   130

The marriage broker fastened hungry eyes on him.

"You don't want any more a bride?"

"I do," said Leo, "but I have decided to seek her in a different way. I am no longer interested in an arranged marriage. To be frank, I now admit the necessity of premarital love. That is, I want to be in love with the one I marry."

"Love?" said Salzman, astounded. After a moment he remarked "For us, our love is our life, not for the ladies. In the ghetto they——"

"I know, I know," said Leo. "I've thought of it often. Love, I have   135
said to myself, should be a by-product of living and worship rather than its own end. Yet for myself I find it necessary to establish the level of my need and fulfill it."

Salzman shrugged but answered, "Listen, rabbi, if you want love, this I can find for you also. I have such beautiful clients that you will love them the minute your eyes will see them."

Leo smiled unhappily. "I'm afraid you don't understand."

But Salzman hastily unstrapped his portfolio and withdrew a manila packet from it.

"Pictures," he said, quickly laying the envelope on the table.

Leo called after him to take the pictures away, but as if on the wings   140
of the wind, Salzman had disappeared.

March came. Leo had returned to his regular routine. Although he felt not quite himself yet—lacked energy—he was making plans for a more active social life. Of course it would cost something, but he was an expert in cutting corners; and when there were no corners left he would make circles rounder. All the while Salzman's pictures had lain on the table, gathering dust. Occasionally as Leo sat studying, or enjoying a cup of tea, his eyes fell on the manila envelope, but he never opened it.

The days went by and no social life to speak of developed with a member of the opposite sex—it was difficult, given the circumstances of his situation. One morning Leo toiled up the stairs to his room and stared out the window at the city. Although the day was bright his view of it was dark. For some time he watched the people in the street below hurrying along and then turned with a heavy heart to his little room. On the table was the packet. With a sudden relentless gesture he tore it open. For a half-hour he stood by the table in a state of excitement, examining the photographs of the ladies Salzman had included. Finally, with a deep sigh he put them down. There were six, of varying degrees of attractiveness, but look at them long enough and they all became Lily Hirschorn; all past their prime, all starved behind bright smiles, not a true personality in the lot. Life, despite their frantic yoohooings, had passed them by; they were pictures in a brief case that stunk of fish. After a while, however, as Leo attempted to return the photographs into the envelope, he found in it another, a snapshot of the type taken by a machine for a quarter. He gazed at it a moment and let out a cry.

Her face deeply moved him. Why, he could at first not say. It gave him the impression of youth—spring flowers, yet age—a sense of having been used to the bone, wasted; this came from the eyes, which were hauntingly familiar, yet absolutely strange. He had a vivid impression that he had met her before, but try as he might he could not place her although he could almost recall her name, as if he had read it in her own handwriting. No, this couldn't be; he would have remembered her. It was not, he affirmed, that she had an extraordinary beauty—no, though her face was attractive enough; it was that *something* about her moved him. Feature for feature, even some of the ladies of the photographs could do better; but she leaped forth to his heart—had *lived,* or wanted to—more than just wanted, perhaps regretted how she had lived—had somehow deeply suffered: it could be seen in the depths of those reluctant eyes, and from the way the light enclosed and shone from her, and within her, opening realms of possibility: this was her own. Her he desired. His head ached and eyes narrowed with the intensity of his gazing, then as if an obscure fog had blown up in the mind, he experienced fear of her and was aware that he had received an impression, somehow, of evil. He shuddered, saying softly, it is thus with us all. Leo brewed some tea in a small pot and sat sipping it without sugar, to calm himself. But before he had finished drinking, again with excitement he examined the face and found it good: good for Leo Finkle. Only such a one could understand him and help him seek whatever he was seeking. She might, perhaps, love him. How she had happened to be among the discards in Salzman's barrel he could never guess, but he knew he must urgently go find her.

Leo rushed downstairs, grabbed up the Bronx telephone book, and searched for Salzman's home address. He was not listed, nor was his office. Neither was he in the Manhattan book. But Leo remembered having written down the address on a slip of paper after he had read Salzman's advertisement in the "personals" column of the *Forward.* He ran up to his room and tore through his papers, without luck. It was exasperating. Just when he needed the matchmaker he was nowhere to be found. Fortunately Leo remembered to look in his wallet. There on a card he found his name written and a Bronx address. No phone number was listed, the reason—Leo now recalled—he had originally communicated with Salzman by letter. He got on his coat, put a hat on over his skull cap and hurried to the subway station. All the way to the far end of the Bronx he sat on the edge of his seat. He was more than once tempted to take out the picture and see if the girl's face was as he remembered it, but he refrained, allowing the snapshot to remain in his coat pocket, content to have her so close. When the train pulled into the station he was waiting at the door and bolted out. He quickly located the street Salzman had advertised.

The building he sought was less than a block from the subway, but it was not an office building, nor even a loft, nor a store in which one could rent office space. It was a very old tenement house. Leo found Salzman's name in pencil on a soiled tag under the bell and climbed three dark flights to his apartment. When he knocked, the door was opened by a thin, asthmatic, gray-haired woman, in felt slippers. 145

"Yes?" she said, expecting nothing. She listened without listening. He could have sworn he had seen her, too, before but knew it was an illusion.

"Salzman—does he live here? Pinye Salzman," he said, "the matchmaker?"

She stared at him a long minute. "Of course."

He felt embarrassed. "Is he in?"

"No." Her mouth, though left open, offered nothing more. 150

"The matter is urgent. Can you tell me where his office is?

"In the air." She pointed upward.

"You mean he has no office?" Leo asked.

"In his socks."

He peered into the apartment. It was sunless and dingy, one large room divided by a half-open curtain, beyond which he could see a sagging metal bed. The near side of a room was crowded with rickety chairs, old bureaus, a three-legged table, racks of cooking utensils, and all the apparatus of a kitchen. But there was no sign of Salzman or his magic barrel, probably also a figment of the imagination. An odor of frying fish made Leo weak to the knees. 155

"Where is he?" he insisted. "I've got to see your husband."

At length she answered. "So who knows where he is? Every time he thinks a new thought he runs to a different place. Go home, he will find you."

"Tell him Leo Finkle."

She gave no sign she had heard.

He walked downstairs, depressed. 160

But Salzman, breathless, stood waiting at his door.

Leo was astounded and overjoyed. "How did you get here before me?"

"I rushed."

"Come inside."

They entered. Leo fixed tea, and a sardine sandwich for Salzman. As they were drinking he reached behind him for the packet of pictures and handed them to the marriage broker. 165

Salzman put down his glass and said expectantly, "You found somebody you like?"

"Not among these."

The marriage broker turned away.

"Here is the one I want." Leo held forth the snapshot.

Salzman slipped on his glasses and took the picture into his trembling   *170*
hand. He turned ghastly and let out a groan.

"What's the matter?" cried Leo.

"Excuse me. Was an accident this picture. She isn't for you."

Salzman frantically shoved the manila packet into his portfolio. He
thrust the snapshot into his pocket and fled down the stairs.

Leo, after momentary paralysis, gave chase and cornered the marriage
broker in the vestibule. The landlady made hysterical outcries but neither
of them listened.

"Give me back the picture, Salzman."   *175*

"No." The pain in his eyes was terrible.

"Tell me who she is then."

"This I can't tell you. Excuse me."

He made to depart, but Leo, forgetting himself, seized the matchmaker by his tight coat and shook him frenziedly.

"Please," sighed Salzman. "*Please.*"   *180*

Leo ashamedly let him go. "Tell me who she is," he begged. "It's
very important for me to know."

"She is not for you. She is a wild one—wild, without shame. This is
not a bride for a rabbi."

"What do you mean wild?"

"Like an animal. Like a dog. For her to be poor was a sin. This is
why to me she is dead now."

"In God's name, what do you mean?"   *185*

"Her I can't introduce to you," Salzman cried.

"Why are you so excited?"

"Why, he asks," Salzman said, bursting into tears. "This is my baby,
my Stella, she should burn in hell."

Leo hurried up to bed and hid under the covers. Under the covers he
thought his life through. Although he soon fell asleep he could not sleep
her out of his mind. He woke, beating his breast. Though he prayed to
be rid of her, his prayers went unanswered. Through days of torment he
endlessly struggled not to love her; fearing success, he escaped it. He then
concluded to convert her to goodness, himself to God. The idea alternately nauseated and exalted him.

He perhaps did not know that he had come to a final decision until   *190*
he encountered Salzman in a Broadway cafeteria. He was sitting alone at
a rear table, sucking the bony remains of a fish. The marriage broker
appeared haggard, and transparent to the point of vanishing.

Salzman looked up at first without recognizing him. Leo had grown
a pointed beard and his eyes were weighted with wisdom.

"Salzman," he said, "love has at last come to my heart."

"Who can love from a picture?" mocked the marriage broker.

"It is not impossible."

"If you can love her, then you can love anybody. Let me show you   *195*
some new clients that they just sent me their photographs. One is a little
doll."

"Just her I want," Leo murmured.

"Don't be a fool, doctor. Don't bother with her."

"Put me in touch with her, Salzman," Leo said humbly. "Perhaps I
can be of service."

Salzman had stopped eating and Leo understood with emotion that
it was now arranged.

Leaving the cafeteria, he was, however, afflicted by a tormenting sus-   *200*
picion that Salzman had planned it all to happen this way.

Leo was informed by letter that she would meet him on a certain
corner, and she was there one spring night, waiting under a street lamp.
He appeared, carrying a small bouquet of violets and rosebuds. Stella
stood by the lamp post, smoking. She wore white with red shoes, which
fitted his expectations, although in a troubled moment he had imagined the dress red, and only the shoes white. She waited uneasily and
shyly. From afar he saw that her eyes—clearly her father's—were filled
with desperate innocence. He pictured, in her, his own redemption.
Violins and lit candles revolved in the sky. Leo ran forward with flowers
outthrust.

Around the corner, Salzman, leaning against a wall, chanted prayers
for the dead.

---

1. Who is the protagonist in this story? Who is the antagonist(s)? What
   makes you say so?

2. How does the setting Malamud provides for this story help describe
   Leo Finkle?

3. What resources does Malamud use to define Finkle's character? How
   do they work together? Would you say Finkle is a round or a flat
   character? Is he static or dynamic?

4. What is the conflict that drives this plot?

5. Do you find the resolution and denouement surprising? How do you
   account for Finkle's falling in love with Stella? Who is (are) the dead
   for whom Salzman chants?

Narration is more often the dominant element of a piece of writing than
description is. It is also useful as a primary means of support for your dominant idea. Often a well-told, focused sequence of events that the reader can
grasp through detailed, concrete imagery represents your idea effectively and
strongly, if the details that you bring to the foreground reflect the idea.
Burke's Pentad (Chapter 4) is an especially effective way of sorting out the

most important elements of a conflict and arranging them into a narration
that focuses your audience's attention and supports your dominant idea.

Working with the Readings

Read the following pieces of writing and, alone or in your group, answer the questions that follow the second one.

HURT HAWKS

Robinson Jeffers

I

The broken pillar of the wing jags from the clotted shoulder,
The wing trails like a banner in defeat,
No more to use the sky forever but live with famine
And pain a few days; cat nor coyote
Will shorten the week of waiting for death, there is game   5
    without talons.
He stands under the oak-bush and waits
The lame feet of salvation; at night he remembers freedom
And flies in a dream, the dawns ruin it.
He is strong and pain is worse to the strong, incapacity is worse.
The curs of the day come and torment him   10
At distance, no one but death the redeemer will humble that head,
The intrepid readiness, the terrible eyes.
The wild God of the world is sometimes merciful to those
That ask mercy, not often to the arrogant.
You do not know him, you communal people, or you have forgotten   15
    him;
Intemperate and savage, the hawk remembers him;
Beautiful and wild, the hawks, and men that are dying, remember him.

II

I'd sooner, except the penalties, kill a man than a hawk; but the great
    redtail
Had nothing left but unable misery
From the bones too shattered for mending, the wing that trailed under   20
    his talons when he moved.
We had fed him six weeks, I gave him freedom,
He wandered over the foreland hill and returned in the evening, asking
    for death.

Not like a beggar, still eyed with the old
Implacable arrogance. I gave him the lead gift in the twilight. What fell   25
    was relaxed,
Owl–downy, soft feminine feathers; but what
Soared: the fierce rush: the night-herons by the flooded river cried fear
    at its rising
Before it was quite unsheathed from reality.

SHOOTING AN ELEPHANT

George Orwell

    In Moulmein, in Lower Burma, I was hated by large numbers of people—the only time in my life that I have been important enough for this to happen to me. I was sub–divisional police officer of the town, and in an aimless, petty kind of way anti-European feeling was very bitter. No one had the guts to raise a riot, but if a European woman went through the bazaars alone somebody would probably spit betel juice over her dress. As a police officer I was an obvious target and was baited whenever it seemed safe to do so. When a nimble Burman tripped me up on the football field and the referee (another Burman) looked the other way, the crowd yelled with hideous laughter. This happened more than once. In the end the sneering yellow faces of young men that met me everywhere, the insults hooted after me when I was at a safe distance, got badly on my nerves. The young Buddhist priests were the worst of all. There were several thousands of them in the town and none of them seemed to have anything to do except stand on street corners and jeer at Europeans.

    All this was perplexing and upsetting. For at that time I had already made up my mind that imperialism was an evil thing and the sooner I chucked up my job and got out of it the better. Theoretically—and secretly, of course—I was all for the Burmese and all against their oppressors, the British. As for the job I was doing, I hated it more bitterly than I can perhaps make clear. In a job like that you see the dirty work of Empire at close quarters. The wretched prisoners huddling in the stinking cages of the lock-ups, the grey, cowed faces of the long-term convicts, the scarred buttocks of the men who had been flogged with bamboos—all these oppressed me with an intolerable sense of guilt. But I could get nothing into perspective. I was young and ill-educated and I had had to think out my problems in the utter silence that is imposed on every Englishman in the East. I did not even know that the British Empire is dying, still less did I know that it is a great deal better than the younger empires that are going to supplant it. All I knew was that I was stuck between my hatred of the empire I served and my rage against the evil-spirited little beasts who tried to make my job impossible. With one part of my mind I thought of the British Raj as an unbreakable tyranny, as something clamped down, in *saecula saeculorum*,° upon the will of prostrate peoples; with another part I thought that the greatest joy in the world would be to drive a bayonet into a Buddhist priest's guts. Feelings like these are the normal by-products of imperialism; ask any Anglo-Indian official, if you can catch him off duty.

One day something happened which in a roundabout way was enlightening. It was a tiny incident in itself, but it gave me a better glimpse than I had had before of the real nature of imperialism—the real motives for which despotic governments act. Early one morning the sub-inspector at a police station the other end of the town rang me up on the 'phone and said that an elephant was ravaging the bazaar. Would I please come and do something about it? I did not know what I could do, but I wanted to see what was happening and I got on to a pony and started out. I took my rifle, an old .44 Winchester and much too small to kill an elephant, but I thought the noise might be useful *in terrorem*. Various Burmans stopped me on the way and told me about the elephant's doings. It was not, of course, a wild elephant, but a tame one which had gone "must." It had been chained up, as tame elephants always are when their attack of "must" is due, but on the previous night it had broken its chain and escaped. Its mahout, the only person who could manage it when it was in that state, had set out in pursuit, but had taken the wrong direction and was now twelve hours' journey away, and in the morning the elephant had suddenly reappeared in the town. The Burmese population had no weapons and were quite helpless against it. It had already destroyed somebody's bamboo hut, killed a cow and raided some fruit-stalls and devoured the stock; also it had met the municipal rubbish van and, when the driver jumped out and took to his heels, had turned the van over and inflicted violences upon it.

The Burmese sub-inspector and some Indian constables were waiting for me in the quarter where the elephant had been seen. It was a very poor quarter, a labyrinth of squalid bamboo huts, thatched with palm-leaf, winding all over a steep hillside. I remember that it was a cloudy, stuffy morning at the beginning of the rains. We began questioning the people as to where the elephant had gone and, as usual, failed to get any definite information. That is invariably the case in the East; a story always sounds clear enough at a distance, but the nearer you get to the scene of events the vaguer it becomes. Some of the people said that the elephant had gone in one direction, some said that he had gone in another, some professed not even to have heard of any elephant. I had almost made up my mind that the whole story was a pack of lies, when we heard yells a little distance away. There was a loud, scandalized cry of "Go away, child!

---

saecula saeculorum: Latin for "forever and ever"

Go away this instant!" and an old woman with a switch in her hand came round the corner of a hut, violently shooing away a crowd of naked children. Some more women followed, clicking their tongues and exclaiming: evidently there was something that the children ought not to have seen. I rounded the hut and saw a man's dead body sprawling in the mud. He was an Indian, a black Dravidian coolie, almost naked, and he could not have been dead many minutes. The people said that the elephant had come suddenly upon him round the corner of the hut, caught him with its trunk, put its foot on his back and ground him into the earth. This was the rainy season and the ground was soft, and his face had scored a trench a foot deep and a couple of yards long. He was lying on his belly with arms crucified and head sharply twisted to one side. His face was coated with mud, the eyes wide open, the teeth bared and grinning with an expression of unendurable agony. (Never tell me, by the way, that the dead look peaceful. Most of the corpses I have seen looked devilish.) The friction of the great beast's foot had stripped the skin from his back as neatly as one skins a rabbit. As soon as I saw the dead man I sent an orderly to a friend's house nearby to borrow an elephant rifle. I had already sent back the pony, not wanting it to go mad with fright and throw me if it smelt the elephant.

The orderly came back in a few minutes with a rifle and five car-   5
tridges, and meanwhile some Burmans had arrived and told us that the elephant was in the paddy fields below, only a few hundred yards away. As I started forward practically the whole population of the quarter flocked out of the houses and followed me. They had seen the rifle and were all shouting excitedly that I was going to shoot the elephant. They had not shown much interest in the elephant when he was merely ravaging their homes, but it was different now that he was going to be shot. It was a bit of fun to them, as it would be to an English crowd; besides they wanted the meat. It made me vaguely uneasy. I had no intention of shooting the elephant—I had merely sent for the rifle to defend myself if necessary—and it is always unnerving to have a crowd following you. I marched down the hill, looking and feeling a fool, with the rifle over my shoulder and an ever-growing army of people jostling at my heels. At the bottom, when you got away from the huts, there was a metalled road and beyond that a miry waste of paddy fields a thousand yards across, not yet ploughed but soggy from the first rains and dotted with coarse grass. The elephant was standing eight yards from the road, his left side towards us. He took not the slightest notice of the crowd's approach. He was tearing up bunches of grass, beating them against his knees to clean them and stuffing them into his mouth.

I had halted on the road. As soon as I saw the elephant I knew with perfect certainty that I ought not to shoot him. It is a serious matter to shoot a working elephant—it is comparable to destroying a huge and costly piece of machinery—and obviously one ought not to do it if it can possibly be avoided. And at that distance, peacefully eating, the elephant looked no more dangerous than a cow. I thought then and I think now that his attack of "must" was already passing off; in which case he would merely wander harmlessly about until the mahout came back and caught him. Moreover, I did not in the least want to shoot him. I decided that I would watch him for a little while to make sure that he did not turn savage again, and then go home.

But at that moment I glanced round at the crowd that had followed me. It was an immense crowd, two thousand at the least and growing every minute. It blocked the road for a long distance on either side. I looked at the sea of yellow faces above the garish clothes—faces all happy and excited over this bit of fun, all certain that the elephant was going to be shot. They were watching me as they would watch a conjurer about to perform a trick. They did not like me, but with the magical rifle in my hands I was momentarily worth watching. And suddenly I realized that I should have to shoot the elephant after all. The people expected it of me and I had got to do it; I could feel their two thousand wills pressing me forward, irresistibly. And it was at this moment, as I stood there with the rifle in my hands, that I first grasped the hollowness, the futility of the white man's dominion in the East. Here was I, the white man with his gun, standing in front of the unarmed native crowd—seemingly the leading actor of the piece; but in reality I was only an absurd puppet pushed to and fro by the will of those yellow faces behind. I perceived in this moment that when the white man turns tyrant it is his own freedom that he destroys. He becomes a sort of hollow, posing dummy, the conventionalized figure of a sahib. For it is the condition of his rule that he shall spend his life in trying to impress the "natives," and so in every crisis he has got to do what the "natives" expect of him. He wears a mask, and his face grows to fit it. I had got to shoot the elephant. I had committed myself to doing it when I sent for the rifle. A sahib has got to act like a sahib; he has got to appear resolute, to know his own mind and do definite things. To come all that way, rifle in hand, with two thousand people marching at my heels, and then to trail feebly away, having done nothing—no, that was impossible. The crowd would laugh at me. And my whole life, every white man's life in the East, was one long struggle not to be laughed at.

But I did not want to shoot the elephant. I watched him beating his bunch of grass against his knees, with that preoccupied grandmotherly air that elephants have. It seemed to me that it would be murder to shoot him. At that age I was not squeamish about killing animals, but I had never shot an elephant and never wanted to. (Somehow it always seems worse to kill a *large* animal.) Besides, there was the beast's owner to be considered. Alive, the elephant was worth at least a hundred pounds; dead, he would only be worth the value of his tusks, five pounds, possibly. But I had got to act quickly. I turned to some experienced-looking Burmans who had been there when we arrived, and asked them how the elephant had been behaving. They all said the same thing: he took no notice of you if you left him alone, but he might charge if you went too close to him.

It was perfectly clear to me what I ought to do. I ought to walk up to within, say, twenty-five yards of the elephant and test his behavior. If he charged, I could shoot; if he took no notice of me, it would be safe to leave him until the mahout came back. But also I knew that I was going to do no such thing. I was a poor shot with a rifle and the ground was soft mud into which one would sink at every step. If the elephant charged and I missed him, I should have about as much chance as a toad under a steam-roller. But even then I was not thinking particularly of my own skin, only of the watchful yellow faces behind. For at that moment, with the crowd watching me, I was not afraid in the ordinary sense, as I would have been if I had been alone. A white man mustn't be frightened in front of "natives"; and so, in general, he isn't frightened. The sole thought in my mind was that if anything went wrong those two thousand Burmans would see me pursued, caught, trampled on and reduced to a grinning corpse like that Indian up the hill. And if that happened it was quite probable that some of them would laugh. That would never do. There was only one alternative. I shoved the cartridges into the magazine and lay down on the road to get a better aim.

The crowd grew very still, and a deep, low, happy sigh, as of people who see the theatre curtain go up at last, breathed from innumerable throats. They were going to have their bit of fun after all. The rifle was a beautiful German thing with cross-hair sights. I did not then know that in shooting an elephant one would shoot to cut an imaginary bar running from ear-hole to ear-hole. I ought, therefore, as the elephant was side-ways on, to have aimed straight at his ear-hole; actually I aimed several inches in front of this, thinking the brain would be further forward.

When I pulled the trigger I did not hear the bang or feel the kick—one never does when a shot goes home—but I heard the devilish roar of glee that went up from the crowd. In that instant, in too short a time, one would have thought, even for the bullet to get there, a myste-rious, terrible change had come over the elephant. He neither stirred nor fell, but every line of his body had altered. He looked suddenly stricken, shrunken, immensely old, as though the frightful impact of the bullet had paralysed him without knocking him down. At last, after what seemed a long time—it might have been five seconds, I dare say—he sagged flab-bily to his knees. His mouth slobbered. An enormous senility seemed to have settled upon him. One could have imagined him thousands of years old. I fired again into the same spot. At the second shot he did not col-lapse but climbed with desperate slowness to his feet and stood weakly upright, with legs sagging and head drooping. I fired a third time. That was the shot that did for him. You could see the agony of it jolt his whole body and knock the last remnant of strength from his legs. But in falling he seemed for a moment to rise, for as his hind legs collapsed beneath him he seemed to tower upward like a huge rock toppling, his trunk

10

reaching skywards like a tree. He trumpeted, for the first and only time. And then down he came, his belly towards me, with a crash that seemed to shake the ground even where I lay.

I got up. The Burmans were already racing past me across the mud. It was obvious that the elephant would never rise again, but he was not dead. He was breathing very rhythmically with long rattling gasps, his great mound of a side painfully rising and falling. His mouth was wide open—I could see far down into caverns of pale pink throat. I waited a long time for him to die, but his breathing did not weaken. Finally I fired my two remaining shots into the spot where I thought his heart must be. The thick blood welled out of him like red velvet, but still he did not die. His body did not even jerk when the shots hit him, the tortured breathing continued without a pause. He was dying, very slowly and in great agony, but in some world remote from me where not even a bullet could damage him further. I felt that I had got to put an end to that dreadful noise. It seemed dreadful to see the great beast lying there, powerless to move and yet powerless to die, and not even to be able to finish him. I sent back for my small rifle and poured shot after shot into his heart and down his throat. They seemed to make no impression. The tortured gasps continued as steadily as the ticking of a clock.

In the end I could not stand it any longer and went away. I heard later that it took him half an hour to die. Burmans were bringing dahs and baskets even before I left, and I was told they had stripped his body almost to the bones by the afternoon.

Afterwards, of course, there were endless discussions about the shooting of the elephant. The owner was furious, but he was only an Indian and could do nothing. Besides, legally I had done the right thing, for a mad elephant has to be killed, like a mad dog, if its owner fails to control it. Among the Europeans opinion was divided. The older men said I was right, the younger men said it was a damn shame to shoot an elephant for killing a coolie, because an elephant was worth more than any damn Coringhee coolie. And afterwards I was very glad that the coolie had been killed; it put me legally in the right and it gave me a sufficient pretext for shooting the elephant. I often wondered whether any of the others grasped that I had done it solely to avoid looking a fool.

---

1. How are the events, characters, and settings of these two pieces of writing alike? How are they different?

2. Compare the dominant idea of each of these pieces of writing. What likenesses can you find between them? What differences can you find?

3. What information does each writer give you at the beginning of his piece about the situation and his attitudes that helps you understand his dominant idea?

4. What parts of the setting does each writer emphasize to focus your attention on what you think is the dominant idea?

5. How do the conclusions of the two pieces of writing differ from each other? How does each conclusion emphasize the writer's dominant idea?

✑ An Invitation to Write

Write a draft that shows you or another person in a situation in which the issues are the same as in one of these pieces of writing. (You need not have had to shoot an animal. It is the situation that is important, not the action.) Using narration, description, and characterization in an essay, a story, or a poem, reflect your dominant idea regarding your choice of action in the situation you have chosen to tell your reader about.

NARRATION AND POINT OF VIEW

Commonly, *point of view* means what a person thinks about an issue. If you were to ask a friend, "What's your point of view on legalizing abortion?" you would probably mean, "What do you think about this issue?" In writing, however, point of view means the angle of vision through which the writer presents his or her material—whose eyes the writer causes the reader to look through. As a writer, you have four points of view to choose from.

The Omniscient ("All-Seeing") Point of View

The *omniscient* point of view speaks in the third person ("he" or "she"). As the writer, you are not limited by time and space. In an essay, a story, or a poem, for example, you can open the feelings and thoughts of any of the characters at any time and in any location to the reader. In addition, as the writer, you can speak directly to your audience whenever you think it's important to do so. You can interpret your characters' behavior, comment upon your characters and what they do, or even question your audience.

You might find the omniscient point of view particularly useful when you describe a conflict between individuals. This point of view allows you to show different opinions and feelings and to discuss them or interpret them for your audience. Of course, in the case of nonfiction, the events and the responses and actions of the characters are based on fact, whereas in poetry and prose fiction you are free to create any type of person or location you choose. One strength of the omniscient point of view is that it allows you to become part of the dominant idea you present and to engage your audience directly with your ideas.

Here are some examples of the omniscient point of view.

 Working with the Readings

Read the following selections and, alone or in your group, answer the questions that follow each one.

NOT WAVING BUT DROWNING

Stevie Smith

Nobody heard him, the dead man,
But still he lay moaning:
I was much further out than you thought
And not waving but drowning.

Poor chap, he always loved larking°   5
And now he's dead
It must have been too cold for him his heart gave way,
They said.

Oh, no no no, it was too cold always
(Still the dead one lay moaning)   10
I was much too far out all my life
And not waving but drowning.

---

1. Do you think that the poet means you to interpret the word *drowning* literally? If not, then try *drowning* out as a metaphor. What does it suggest to you?

2. How many points of view does the poet give you access to?

3. What are the differences between those points of view? What do those differences suggest to you?

4. Can you see ways in which those differences suggest your own experiences with other people to you?

---

5. *larking:* playing

THE OPEN BOAT: A TALE INTENDED TO BE AFTER THE FACT: BEING THE EXPERIENCE OF FOUR MEN FROM THE SUNK STEAMER COMMODORE.

Stephen Crane

I

None of them knew the color of the sky. Their eyes glanced level, and were fastened upon the waves that swept toward them. These waves were of the hue of slate, save for the tops, which were of foaming white, and all of the men knew the colors of the sea. The horizon narrowed and widened, and dipped and rose, and at all times its edge was jagged with waves that seemed thrust up in points like rocks.

Many a man ought to have a bath-tub larger than the boat which here rode upon the sea. These waves were most wrongfully and barbarously abrupt and tall, and each froth-top was a problem in small-boat navigation.

The cook squatted in the bottom, and looked with both eyes at the six inches of gunwale which separated him from the ocean. His sleeves were rolled over his fat forearms, and the two flaps of his unbuttoned vest dangled as he bent to bail out the boat. Often he said, "Gawd! that was a narrow clip." As he remarked it he invariably gazed eastward over the broken sea.

The oiler, steering with one of the two oars in the boat, sometimes raised himself suddenly to keep clear of water that swirled in over the stern. It was a thin little oar, and it seemed often ready to snap.

The correspondent, pulling at the other oar, watched the waves and wondered why he was there. 5

The injured captain, lying in the bow, was at this time buried in that profound dejection and indifference which comes, temporarily at least, to even the bravest and most enduring when, willy-nilly, the firm fails, the army loses, the ship goes down. The mind of the master of a vessel is rooted deep in the timbers of her, though he command for a day or a decade; and this captain had on him the stern impression of a scene in the grays of dawn of seven turned faces, and later a stump of a topmast with a white ball on it, that slashed to and fro at the waves, went low and lower, and down. Thereafter there was something strange in his voice. Although steady, it was deep with mourning, and of a quality beyond oration or tears.

"Keep 'er a little more south, Billie," said he.

"A little more south, sir," said the oiler in the stern.

A seat in this boat was not unlike a seat upon a bucking broncho, and, by the same token, a broncho is not much smaller. The craft pranced and reared and plunged like an animal. As each wave came, and she rose for it, she seemed like a horse making at a fence outrageously high. The manner of her scramble over these walls of water is a mystic thing, and, moreover, at the top of them were ordinarily these problems in white water, the foam racing down from the summit of each wave, requiring a new leap, and a leap from the air. Then, after scornfully bumping a crest, she would slide and race and splash down a long incline, and arrive bobbing and nodding in front of the next menace.

A singular disadvantage of the sea lies in the fact that, after successfully   *10*
surmounting one wave, you discover that there is another behind it, just as important and just as nervously anxious to do something effective in the way of swamping boats. In a ten-foot dinghy one can get an idea of the resources of the sea in the line of waves that is not probable to the average experience, which is never at sea in a dinghy. As each slaty wall of water approached, it shut all else from the view of the men in the boat, and it was not difficult to imagine that this particular wave was the final outburst of the ocean, the last effort of the grim water. There was a terrible grace in the move of the waves and they came in silence, save for the snarling of the crests.

In the wan light the faces of the men must have been gray. Their eyes must have glinted in strange ways as they gazed steadily astern. Viewed from a balcony, the whole thing would, doubtless, have been weirdly picturesque. But the men in the boat had no time to see it, and if they had had leisure, there were other things to occupy their minds. The sun swung steadily up the sky, and they knew it was broad day because the color of the sea changed from slate to emerald-green streaked with amber lights, and the foam was like tumbling snow. The process of the breaking day was unknown to them. They were aware only of this effect upon the color of the waves that rolled toward them.

In disjointed sentences the cook and the correspondent argued as to the difference between a life-saving station and a house of refuge. The cook had said: "There's a house of refuge just north of the Mosquito Inlet Light, and as soon as they see us they'll come off in their boat and pick us up."

"As soon as who see us?" said the correspondent.

"The crew," said the cook.

"Houses of refuge don't have crews," said the correspondent. "As I   *15*
understand them, they are only places where clothes and grub are stored for the benefit of shipwrecked people. They don't carry crews."

"Oh, yes, they do," said the cook.

"No, they don't," said the correspondent.

"Well, we're not there yet, anyhow," said the oiler in the stern.

"Well," said the cook, "perhaps it's not a house of refuge that I'm thinking of as being near Mosquito Inlet Light; perhaps it's a life-saving station."

"We're not there yet," said the oiler in the stern.   20

II

As the boat bounced from the top of each wave the wind tore through the hair of the hatless men, and as the craft plopped her stern down again the spray slashed past them. The crest of each of these waves was a hill, from the top of which the men surveyed for a moment a broad, tumultuous expanse, shining and wind-riven. It was probably splendid, it was probably glorious, this play of the free sea, wild with lights of emerald and white and amber.

"Bully good thing it's an on-shore wind," said the cook. "If not, where would we be? Wouldn't have a show."

"That's right," said the correspondent.

The busy oiler nodded his assent.

Then the captain, in the bow, chuckled in a way that expressed hu-   25
mor, contempt, tragedy, all in one. "Do you think we've got much of a show now, boys?" said he.

Whereupon the three were silent, save for a trifle of hemming and hawing. To express any particular optimism at this time they felt to be childish and stupid, but they all doubtless possessed this sense of the situation in their minds. A young man thinks doggedly at such times. On the other hand, the ethics of their condition was decidedly against any open suggestion of hopelessness. So they were silent.

"Oh, well," said the captain, soothing his children, "we'll get ashore all right."

But there was that in his tone which made them think; so the oiler quoth, "Yes! if this wind holds."

The cook was bailing. "Yes! if we don't catch hell in the surf."

Canton-flannel gulls flew near and far. Sometimes they sat down on   30
the sea, near patches of brown seaweed that rolled over the waves with a movement like carpets on a line in a gale. The birds sat comfortably in groups, and they were envied by some in the dinghy, for the wrath of the sea was no more to them than it was to a covey of prairie-chickens a thousand miles inland. Often they came very close and stared at the men with black, bead-like eyes. At these times they were uncanny and sinister in their unblinking scrutiny, and the men hooted angrily at them, telling them to be gone. One came, and evidently decided to alight on the top of the captain's head. The bird flew parallel to the boat, and did not circle, but made short sidelong jumps in the air in chicken fashion. His black eyes were wistfully fixed upon the captain's head. "Ugly brute," said the oiler to the bird. "You look as if you were made with a jack-knife." The

cook and the correspondent swore darkly at the creature. The captain naturally wished to knock it away with the end of the heavy painter, but he did not dare do it, because anything resembling an emphatic gesture would have capsized this freighted boat; and so, with his open hand, the captain gently and carefully waved the gull away. After it had been discouraged from the pursuit the captain breathed easier on account of his hair, and others breathed easier because the bird struck their minds at this time as being somehow gruesome and ominous.

In the meantime the oiler and the correspondent rowed; and also they rowed. They sat together in the same seat, and each rowed an oar. Then the oiler took both oars; then the correspondent. They rowed and they rowed. The very ticklish part of the business was when the time came for the reclining one in the stern to take his turn at the oars. By the very last star of truth, it is easier to steal eggs from under a hen than it was to change seats in the dinghy. First the man in the stern slid his hand along the thwart and moved with care, as if he were of Sèvres. Then the man in the rowing-seat slid his hand along the other thwart. It was all done with the most extraordinary care. As the two sidled past each other, the whole party kept watchful eyes on the coming wave, and the captain cried: "Look out, now! Steady, there!"

The brown mats of seaweed that appeared from time to time were like islands, bits of earth. They were traveling, apparently, neither one way nor the other. They were, to all intents, stationary. They informed the men in the boat that it was making progress slowly toward the land.

The captain, rearing cautiously in the bow after the dinghy soared on a great swell, said that he had seen the lighthouse at Mosquito Inlet. Presently the cook remarked that he had seen it. The correspondent was at the oars then, and for some reason he too wished to look at the lighthouse; but his back was toward the far shore, and the waves were important, and for some time he could not seize an opportunity to turn his head. But at last there came a wave more gentle than the others, and when at the crest of it he swiftly scoured the western horizon.

"See it?" said the captain.

"No," said the correspondent, slowly; "I didn't see anything." 35

"Look again," said the captain. He pointed. "It's exactly in that direction."

At the top of another wave the correspondent did as he was bid, and this time his eyes chanced on a small, still thing on the edge of the swaying horizon. It was precisely like the point of a pin. It took an anxious eye to find a lighthouse so tiny.

"Think we'll make it, Captain?"

"If this wind holds and the boat don't swamp, we can't do much else," said the captain.

The little boat, lifted by each towering sea and splashed viciously by 40
the crests, made progress that in the absence of seaweed was not apparent

to those in her. She seemed just a wee thing wallowing miraculously, top up, at the mercy of five oceans. Occasionally a great spread of water, like white flames, swarmed into her.

"Bail her, cook," said the captain, serenely.

"All right, Captain," said the cheerful cook.

III

It would be difficult to describe the subtle brotherhood of men that was here established on the seas. No one said that it was so. No one mentioned it. But it dwelt in the boat, and each man felt it warm him. They were a captain, an oiler, a cook, and a correspondent, and they were friends—friends in a more curiously iron-bound degree than may be common. The hurt captain, lying against the water-jar in the bow, spoke always in a low voice and calmly; but he could never command a more ready and swiftly obedient crew than the motley three of the dinghy. It was more than a mere recognition of what was best for the common safety. There was surely in it a quality that was personal and heartfelt. And after this devotion to the commander of the boat, there was this comradeship, that the correspondent, for instance, who had been taught to be cynical of men, knew even at the time was the best experience of his life. But no one said that it was so. No one mentioned it.

"I wish we had a sail," remarked the captain. "We might try my overcoat on the end of an oar, and give you two boys a chance to rest." So the cook and the correspondent held the mast and spread wide the overcoat; the oiler steered; and the little boat made good way with her new rig. Sometimes the oiler had to scull sharply to keep a sea from breaking into the boat, but otherwise sailing was a success.

Meanwhile the lighthouse had been growing slowly larger. It had now almost assumed color, and appeared like a little gray shadow on the sky. The man at the oars could not be prevented from turning his head rather often to try for a glimpse of this little gray shadow.

45

At last, from the top of each wave, the men in the tossing boat could see land. Even as the lighthouse was an upright shadow on the sky, this land seemed but a long black shadow on the sea. It certainly was thinner than paper. "We must be about opposite New Smyrna," said the cook, who had coasted this shore often in schooners. "Captain, by the way, I believe they abandoned that life-saving station there about a year ago."

"Did they?" said the captain.

The wind slowly died away. The cook and the correspondent were not now obliged to slave in order to hold high the oar; but the waves continued their old impetuous swooping at the dinghy, and the little craft, no longer under way, struggled woundily over them. The oiler or the correspondent took the oars again.

Shipwrecks are *apropos* of nothing. If men could only train for them and have them occur when the men had reached pink condition, there would be less drowning at sea. Of the four in the dinghy none had slept any time worth mentioning for two days and two nights previous to embarking in the dinghy, and in the excitement of clambering about the deck of a foundering ship they had also forgotten to eat heartily.

For these reasons, and for others, neither the oiler nor the correspon- *50* dent was fond of rowing at this time. The correspondent wondered ingenuously how in the name of all that was sane could there be people who thought it amusing to row a boat. It was not an amusement; it was a diabolical punishment, and even a genius of mental aberrations could never conclude that it was anything but a horror to the muscles and a crime against the back. He mentioned to the boat in general how the amusement of rowing struck him, and the weary-faced oiler smiled in full sympathy. Previously to the foundering, by the way, the oiler had worked double watch in the engine-room of the ship.

"Take her easy now, boys," said the captain. "Don't spend yourselves. If we have to run a surf you'll need all your strength, because we'll sure have to swim for it. Take your time."

Slowly the land arose from the sea. From a black line it became a line of black and a line of white—trees and sand. Finally the captain said that he could make out a house on the shore. "That's the house of refuge, sure," said the cook. "They'll see us before long, and come out after us."

The distant lighthouse reared high. "The keeper ought to be able to make us out now, if he's looking through a glass," said the captain. "He'll notify the life-saving people."

"None of those other boats could have got ashore to give word of the wreck," said the oiler, in a low voice, "else the lifeboat would be out hunting us."

Slowly and beautifully the land loomed out of the sea. The wind *55* came again. It had veered from the northeast to the southeast. Finally a new sound struck the ears of the men in the boat. It was the low thunder of the surf on the shore. "We'll never be able to make the lighthouse now," said the captain. "Swing her head a little more north, Billie."

"A little more north, sir," said the oiler.

Whereupon the little boat turned her nose once more down the wind, and all but the oarsman watched the shore grow. Under the influence of this expansion doubt and direful apprehension were leaving the minds of the men. The management of the boat was still most absorbing, but it could not prevent a quiet cheerfulness. In an hour, perhaps, they would be ashore.

Their backbones had become thoroughly used to balancing in the boat, and they now rode this wild colt of a dinghy like circus men. The correspondent thought that he had been drenched to the skin, but happening to feel in the top pocket of his coat, he found therein eight cigars. Four of them were soaked with sea-water; four were perfectly scatheless.

After a search, somebody produced three dry matches; and thereupon the four waifs rode in their little boat and, with an assurance of an impending rescue shining in their eyes, puffed at the big cigars, and judged well and ill of all men. Everybody took a drink of water.

IV

"Cook," remarked the captain, "there don't seem to be any signs of life about your house of refuge."

"No," replied the cook. "Funny they don't see us!"   60

A broad stretch of lowly coast lay before the eyes of the men. It was of low dunes topped with dark vegetation. The roar of the surf was plain, and sometimes they could see the white lip of a wave as it spun up the beach. A tiny house was blocked out black upon the sky. Southward, the slim lighthouse lifted its little gray length.

Tide, wind, and waves were swinging the dinghy northward. "Funny they don't see us," said the men.

The surf's roar was here dulled, but its tone was nevertheless thunderous and mighty. As the boat swam over the great rollers the men sat listening to this roar. "We'll swamp sure," said everybody.

It is fair to say here that there was not a life-saving station within twenty miles in either direction; but the men did not know this fact, and in consequence they made dark and approbrious remarks concerning the eyesight of the nation's life-savers. Four scowling men sat in the dinghy, and surpassed records in the invention of epithets.

"Funny they don't see us."   65

The light-heartedness of a former time had completely faded. To their sharpened minds it was easy to conjure pictures of all kinds of incompetency and blindness and, indeed, cowardice. There was the shore of the populous land, and it was bitter and bitter to them that from it came no sign.

"Well," said the captain, ultimately, "I suppose we'll have to make a try for ourselves. If we stay out here too long, we'll none of us have strength left to swim after the boat swamps."

And so the oiler, who was at the oars, turned the boat straight for the shore. There was a sudden tightening of muscles. There was some thinking.

"If we don't all get ashore," said the captain—"if we don't all get ashore, I suppose you fellows know where to send news of my finish?"

They then briefly exchanged some addresses and admonitions. As for   70
the reflections of the men, there was a great deal of rage in them. Perchance they might be formulated thus: "If I am going to be drowned—if I am going to be drowned—if I am going to be drowned, why, in the name of the seven mad gods who rule the sea, was I allowed to come thus far and contemplate sand and trees? Was I brought here merely to have

my nose dragged away as I was about to nibble the sacred cheese of life? It is preposterous! If this old ninny-woman, Fate, cannot do better than this, she should be deprived of the management of men's fortunes. She is an old hen who knows not her intention. If she has decided to drown me, why did she not do it in the beginning, and save me all this trouble? The whole affair is absurd. . . . But no; she cannot mean to drown me. She dare not drown me. She cannot drown me. Not after all this work!" Afterward the man might have had an impulse to shake his fist at the clouds. "Just you drown me, now, and then hear what I call you!"

The billows that came at this time were more formidable. They seemed always just about to break and roll over the little boat in a turmoil of foam. There was a preparatory and long growl in the speech of them. No mind unused to the sea would have concluded that the dinghy could ascend these sheer heights in time. The shore was still afar. The oiler was a wily surfman. "Boys," he said swiftly, "she won't live three minutes more, and we're too far out to swim. Shall I take her to sea again, Captain?"

"Yes; go ahead!" said the captain.

This oiler, by a series of quick miracles and fast and steady oarsmanship, turned the boat in the middle of the surf and took her safely to sea again.

There was a considerable silence as the boat bumped over the furrowed sea to deeper water. Then somebody in gloom spoke: "Well, anyhow, they must have seen us from the shore by now."

The gulls went in slanting flight up the wind toward the gray, desolate 75 east. A squall, marked by dingy clouds, and clouds brick-red, like smoke from a burning building, appeared from the southeast.

"What do you think of those life-saving people? Ain't they peaches?"

"Funny they haven't seen us."

"Maybe they think we're out here for sport! Maybe they think we're fishin'. Maybe they think we're damned fools."

It was a long afternoon. A changed tide tried to force them southward, but wind and wave said northward. Far ahead, where coast-line, sea, and sky formed their mighty angle, there were little dots which seemed to indicate a city on the shore.

"St. Augustine?" 80

The captain shook his head. "Too near Mosquito Inlet."

And the oiler rowed, and then the correspondent rowed; then the oiler rowed. It was a weary business. The human back can become the seat of more aches and pains than are registered in books for the composite anatomy of a regiment. It is a limited area, but it can become the theater of innumerable muscular conflicts, tangles, wrenches, knots, and other comforts.

"Did you ever like to row, Billie?" asked the correspondent.

"No," said the oiler; "hang it!"

When one exchanged the rowing-seat for a place in the bottom of 85 the boat, he suffered a bodily depression that caused him to be careless of everything save an obligation to wiggle one finger. There was cold sea-water swashing to and fro in the boat, and he lay in it. His head, pillowed on a thwart, was within an inch of the swirl of a wave-crest, and sometimes a particularly obstreperous sea came inboard and drenched him once more. But these matters did not annoy him. It is almost certain that if the boat had capsized he would have tumbled comfortably out upon the ocean as if he felt sure that it was a great, soft mattress.

"Look! There's a man on the shore!"

"Where?"

"There! See 'im? See 'im?"

"Yes, sure! He's walking along."

"Now he's stopped. Look! He's facing us!"   90

"He's waving at us!"

"So he is! By thunder!"

"Ah, now we're all right! Now we're all right! There'll be a boat out here for us in half an hour."

"He's going on. He's running. He's going up to that house there."

The remote beach seemed lower than the sea, and it required a   95
searching glance to discern the little black figure. The captain saw a floating stick, and they rowed to it. A bath towel was by some weird chance in the boat, and tying this on the stick, the captain waved it. The oarsman did not dare turn his head, so he was obliged to ask questions.

"What's he doing now?"

"He's standing still again. He's looking. I think. . . . There he goes again—toward the house. . . . Now he's stopped again."

"Is he waving at us?"

"No, not now; he was, though."

"Look! There comes another man!"   100

"He's running."

"Look at him go, would you!"

"Why, he's on a bicycle. Now he's met the other man. They're both waving at us. Look!"

"There comes something up the beach."

"What the devil is that thing?"   105

"Why, it looks like a boat."

"Why, certainly, it's a boat."

"No; it's on wheels."

"Yes, so it is. Well, that must be the life-boat. They drag them along shore on a wagon."

"That's the life-boat, sure."   110

"No, by——, it's—it's an omnibus."

"I tell you it's a life-boat."

"It is not! It's an omnibus. I can see it plain. See? One of these big hotel omnibuses."

"By thunder, you're right. It's an omnibus, sure as fate. What do you suppose they are doing with an omnibus? Maybe they are going around collecting the life-crew, hey?"

"That's it, likely. Look! There's a fellow waving a little black flag.   *115*
He's standing on the steps of the omnibus. There come those other two
fellows. Now they're all talking together. Look at the fellow with the flag.
Maybe he ain't waving it!"

"That ain't a flag, is it? That's his coat. Why, certainly that's his coat."

"So it is; it's his coat. He's taken it off and is waving it around his
head. But would you look at him swing it!"

"Oh, say, there isn't any life-saving station there. That's just a winter-
resort hotel omnibus that has brought over some of the boarders to see us
drown."

"What's that idiot with the coat mean? What's he signaling,
anyhow?"

"It looks as if he were trying to tell us to go north. There must be a   *120*
life-saving station up there."

"No; he thinks we're fishing. Just giving us a merry hand. See? Ah,
there, Willie!"

"Well, I wish I could make something out of those signals. What do
you suppose he means?"

"He don't mean anything; he's just playing."

"Well, if he'd just signal us to try the surf again, or to go to sea and
wait, or go north, or go south, or go to hell, there would be some reason
in it. But look at him! He just stands there and keeps his coat revolving
like a wheel. The ass!"

"There come more people."   *125*

"Now there's quite a mob. Look! Isn't that a boat?"

"Where? Oh, I see where you mean. No, that's no boat."

"That fellow is still waving his coat."

"He must think we like to see him do that. Why don't he quit it? It
don't mean anything."

"I don't know. I think he is trying to make us go north. It must be   *130*
that there's a life-saving station there somewhere."

"Say, he ain't tired yet. Look at 'im wave!"

"Wonder how long he can keep that up. He's been revolving his coat
ever since he caught sight of us. He's an idiot. Why aren't they getting
men to bring a boat out? A fishing-boat—one of those big yawls—could
come out here all right. Why don't he do something?"

"Oh, it's all right now."

"They'll have a boat out here for us in less than no time, now that
they've seen us."

A faint yellow tone came into the sky over the low land. The shadows   *135*
on the sea slowly deepened. The wind bore coldness with it, and the men
began to shiver.

"Holy smoke!" said one, allowing his voice to express his impious
mood, "if we keep on monkeying out here! If we've got to flounder out
here all night!"

"Oh, we'll never have to stay here all night! Don't you worry.

They've seen us now, and it won't be long before they'll come chasing out after us."

The shore grew dusky. The man waving a coat blended gradually into this gloom, and it swallowed in the same manner the omnibus and the group of people. The spray, when it dashed uproariously over the side, made the voyagers shrink and swear like men who were being branded.

"I'd like to catch the chump who waved the coat. I feel like soaking him one, just for luck."

"Why? What did he do?"   140

"Oh, nothing, but then he seemed so damned cheerful."

In the meantime the oiler rowed, and then the correspondent rowed, and then the oiler rowed. Gray-faced and bowed forward, they mechanically, turn by turn, plied the leaden oars. The form of the lighthouse had vanished from the southern horizon, but finally a pale star appeared, just lifting from the sea. The streaked saffron in the west passed before the all-merging darkness, and the sea to the east was black. The land had vanished, and was expressed only by the low and drear thunder of the surf.

"If I am going to be drowned—if I am going to be drowned—if I am going to be drowned, why, in the name of the seven mad gods who rule the sea, was I allowed to come thus far and contemplate sand and trees? Was I brought here merely to have my nose dragged away as I was about to nibble the sacred cheese of life?"

The patient captain, drooped over the water-jar, was sometimes obliged to speak to the oarsman.

"Keep her head up! Keep her head up!"   145

"Keep her head up, sir." The voices were weary and low.

This was surely a quiet evening. All save the oarsman lay heavily and listlessly in the boat's bottom. As for him, his eyes were just capable of noting the tall black waves that swept forward in a most sinister silence, save for an occasional subdued growl of a crest.

The cook's head was on a thwart, and he looked without interest at the water under his nose. He was deep in other scenes. Finally he spoke. "Billie," he murmured dreamfully, "what kind of pie do you like best?"

V

"Pie!" said the oiler and the correspondent, agitatedly. "Don't talk about those things, blast you!"

"Well," said the cook, "I was just thinking about ham sandwiches,   150 and—"

A night on the sea in an open boat is a long night. As darkness settled finally, the shine of the light, lifting from the sea in the south, changed to full gold. On the northern horizon a new light appeared, a small bluish gleam on the edge of the waters. These two lights were the furniture of the world. Otherwise there was nothing but waves.

Two men huddled in the stern, and distances were so magnificent in the dinghy that the rower was enabled to keep his feet partly warm by thrusting them under his companions. Their legs indeed extended far under the rowing-seat until they touched the feet of the captain forward. Sometimes, despite the efforts of the tired oarsman, a wave came piling into the boat, an icy wave of the night, and the chilling water soaked them anew. They would twist their bodies for a moment and groan, and sleep the dead sleep once more, while the water in the boat gurgled about them as the craft rocked.

The plan of the oiler and the correspondent was for one to row until he lost the ability, and then arouse the other from his sea-water couch in the bottom of the boat.

The oiler plied the oars until his head drooped forward and the overpowering sleep blinded him; and he rowed yet afterward. Then he touched a man in the bottom of the boat, and called his name. "Will you spell me for a little while?" he said meekly.

"Sure, Billie," said the correspondent, awaking and dragging himself 155 to a sitting position. They exchanged places carefully, and the oiler, cuddling down in the sea-water at the cook's side, seemed to go to sleep instantly.

The particular violence of the sea had ceased. The waves came without snarling. The obligation of the man at the oars was to keep the boat headed so that the tilt of the rollers would not capsize her, and to preserve her from filling when the crests rushed past. The black waves were silent and hard to be seen in the darkness. Often one was almost upon the boat before the oarsman was aware.

In a low voice the correspondent addressed the captain. He was not sure that the captain was awake, although this iron man seemed to be always awake. "Captain, shall I keep her making for that light north, sir?"

The same steady voice answered him. "Yes. Keep it about two points off the port bow."

The cook had tied a life-belt around himself in order to get even the warmth which this clumsy cork contrivance could donate, and he seemed almost stove-like when a rower, whose teeth invariably chattered wildly as soon as he ceased his labor, dropped down to sleep.

The correspondent, as he rowed, looked down at the two men sleep- 160 ing under foot. The cook's arm was around the oiler's shoulders, and, with their fragmentary clothing and haggard faces, they were the babes of the sea—a grotesque rendering of the old babes in the wood.

Later he must have grown stupid at his work, for suddenly there was a growling of water, and a crest came with a roar and a swash into the boat, and it was a wonder that it did not set the cook afloat in his life-belt. The cook continued to sleep, but the oiler sat up, blinking his eyes and shaking with the new cold.

"Oh, I'm awful sorry, Billie," said the correspondent, contritely.

"That's all right, old boy," said the oiler, and lay down again and was asleep.

Presently it seemed that even the captain dozed, and the correspondent thought that he was the one man afloat on all the oceans. The wind had a voice as it came over the waves, and it was sadder than the end.

There was a long, loud swishing astern of the boat, and a gleaming   *165* trail of phosphorescence, like blue flame, was furrowed on the black waters. It might have been made by a monstrous knife.

Then there came a stillness, while the correspondent breathed with the open mouth and looked at the sea.

Suddenly there was another swish and another long flash of bluish light, and this time it was alongside the boat, and might almost have been reached with an oar. The correspondent saw an enormous fin speed like a shadow through the water, hurling the crystalline spray and leaving the long glowing trail.

The correspondent looked over his shoulder at the captain. His face was hidden, and he seemed to be asleep. He looked at the babes of the sea. They certainly were asleep. So, being bereft of sympathy, he leaned a little way to one side and swore softly into the sea.

But the thing did not then leave the vicinity of the boat. Ahead or astern, on one side or the other, at intervals long or short, fled the long sparkling streak, and there was to be heard the whiroo of the dark fin. The speed and power of the thing was greatly to be admired. It cut the water like a gigantic and keen projectile.

The presence of this biding thing did not affect the man with the   *170* same horror that it would if he had been a picnicker. He simply looked at the sea dully and swore in an undertone.

Nevertheless, it is true that he did not wish to be alone with the thing. He wished one of his companions to awake by chance and keep him company with it. But the captain hung motionless over the water-jar, and the oiler and the cook in the bottom of the boat were plunged in slumber.

VI

"If I am going to be drowned—if I am going to be drowned—if I am going to be drowned, why, in the name of the seven mad gods who rule the sea, was I allowed to come thus far and contemplate sand and trees?"

During this dismal night, it may be remarked that a man would conclude that it was really the intention of the seven mad gods to drown him, despite the abominable injustice of it. For it was certainly an abominable injustice to drown a man who had worked so hard, so hard. The man felt it would be a crime most unnatural. Other people had drowned at sea since galleys swarmed with painted sails, but still—

When it occurs to a man that nature does not regard him as important, and that she feels she would not maim the universe by disposing of him, he at first wishes to throw bricks at the temple, and he hates deeply the fact that there are no bricks and no temples. Any visible expression of nature would surely be pelleted with his jeers.

Then, if there be no tangible thing to hoot, he feels, perhaps, the desire to confront a personification and indulge in pleas, bowed to one knee, and with hands supplicant, saying, "Yes, but I love myself." 175

A high cold star on a winter's night is the word he feels that she says to him. Thereafter he knows the pathos of his situation.

The men in the dinghy had not discussed these matters, but each had, no doubt, reflected upon them in silence and according to his mind. There was seldom any expression upon their faces save the general one of complete weariness. Speech was devoted to the business of the boat.

To chime the notes of his emotion, a verse mysteriously entered the correspondent's head. He had even forgotten that he had forgotten this verse, but it suddenly was in his mind.

> A soldier of the Legion lay dying in Algiers;
> There was lack of woman's nursing, there was dearth of woman's
> tears;
> But a comrade stood beside him, and he took that comrade's hand,
> And he said, "I never more shall see my own, my native land."

In his childhood the correspondent had been made acquainted with the fact that a soldier of the Legion lay dying in Algiers, but he had never regarded it as important. Myriads of his school-fellows had informed him of the soldier's plight, but the dinning had naturally ended by making him perfectly indifferent. He had never considered it his affair that a soldier of the Legion lay dying in Algiers, nor had it appeared to him as a matter for sorrow. It was less to him than breaking of a pencil's point.

Now, however, it quaintly came to him as a human, living thing. It 180 was no longer merely a picture of a few throes in the breast of a poet, meanwhile drinking tea and warming his feet at the grate; it was an actuality—stern, mournful, and fine.

The correspondent plainly saw the soldier. He lay on the sand with his feet out straight and still. While his pale left hand was upon his chest in an attempt to thwart the going of his life, the blood came between his fingers. In the far Algerian distance, a city of low square forms was set against a sky that was faint with the last sunset hues. The correspondent, plying the oars and dreaming of the slow and slower movements of the lips of the soldier, was moved by a profound and perfectly impersonal comprehension. He was sorry for the soldier of the Legion who lay dying in Algiers.

The thing which had followed the boat and waited had evidently grown bored at the delay. There was no longer to be heard the slash of the cutwater, and there was no longer the flame of the long trail. The light in the north still glimmered, but it was apparently no nearer to the boat. Sometimes the boom of the surf rang in the correspondent's ears, and he turned the craft seaward then and rowed harder. Southward, some one had evidently built a watch-fire on the beach. It was too low and too far to be seen, but it made a shimmering, roseate reflection upon the bluff back of it, and this could be discerned from the boat. The wind came stronger, and sometimes a wave suddenly raged out like a mountain-cat, and there was to be seen the sheen and sparkle of a broken crest.

The captain, in the bow, moved on his water-jar and sat erect. "Pretty long night," he observed to the correspondent. He looked at the shore. "Those life-saving people take their time."

"Did you see that shark playing around?"

"Yes, I saw him. He was a big fellow, all right."   *185*

"Wish I had known you were awake."

Later the correspondent spoke into the bottom of the boat.

"Billie!" There was a slow and gradual disentanglement. "Billie, will you spell me?"

"Sure," said the oiler.

As soon as the correspondent touched the cold, comfortable sea-   *190*
water in the bottom of the boat and had huddled close to the cook's life-belt he was deep in sleep, despite the fact that his teeth played all the popular airs. This sleep was so good to him that it was but a moment before he heard a voice call his name in a tone that demonstrated the last stages of exhaustion. "Will you spell me?"

"Sure, Billie."

The light in the north had mysteriously vanished, but the correspondent took his course from the wide-awake captain.

Later in the night they took the boat farther out to sea, and the captain directed the cook to take one oar at the stern and keep the boat facing the seas. He was to call out if he should hear the thunder of the surf. This plan enabled the oiler and the correspondent to get respite together. "We'll give those boys a chance to get into shape again," said the captain. They curled down and, after a few preliminary chatterings and trembles, slept once more the dead sleep. Neither knew they had bequeathed to the cook the company of another shark, or perhaps the same shark.

As the boat caroused on the waves, spray occasionally bumped over the side and gave them a fresh soaking, but this had no power to break their repose. The ominous slash of the wind and the water affected them as it would have affected mummies.

"Boys," said the cook, with the notes of every reluctance in his voice,   *195*
"she's drifted in pretty close. I guess one of you had better take her to sea again." The correspondent, aroused, heard the crash of the toppled crests.

As he was rowing, the captain gave him some whisky and water, and this steadied the chills out of him. "If I ever get ashore and anybody shows me even a photograph of an oar—"

At last there was a short conversation.

"Billie! . . . Billie, will you spell me?"

"Sure," said the oiler.

VII

When the correspondent again opened his eyes, the sea and the sky were each of the gray hue of the dawning. Later, carmine and gold was painted upon the waters. The morning appeared finally, in its splendor, with a sky of pure blue, and the sunlight flamed on the tips of the waves. *200*

On the distant dunes were set many little black cottages, and a tall white windmill reared above them. No man, nor dog, nor bicycle appeared on the beach. The cottages might have formed a deserted village.

The voyagers scanned the shore. A conference was held in the boat. "Well," said the captain, "if no help is coming, we might better try a run through the surf right away. If we stay out here much longer we will be too weak to do anything for ourselves at all." The others silently acquiesced in this reasoning. The boat was headed for the beach. The correspondent wondered if none ever ascended the tall wind-tower, and if then they never looked seaward. This tower was a giant, standing with its back to the plight of the ants. It represented in a degree, to the correspondent, the serenity of nature amid the struggles of the individual—nature in the wind, and nature in the vision of men. She did not seem cruel to him then, nor beneficent, nor treacherous, nor wise. But she was indifferent, flatly indifferent. It is, perhaps, plausible that a man in this situation, impressed with the unconcern of the universe, should see the innumerable flaws of his life and have them taste wickedly in his mind and wish for another chance. A distinction between right and wrong seems absurdly clear to him, then, in this new ignorance of the grave-edge, and he understands that if he were given another opportunity he would mend his conduct and his words, and be better and brighter during an introduction or at a tea.

"Now, boys," said the captain, "she is going to swamp sure. All we can do is to work her in as far as possible, and then when she swamps, pile out and scramble for the beach. Keep cool now, and don't jump until she swamps sure."

The oiler took the oars. Over his shoulder he scanned the surf. "Captain," he said, "I think I'd better bring her about, and keep her head-on to the seas, and back her in."

"All right, Billie," said the captain. "Back her in." The oiler swung the boat then, and, seated in the stern, the cook and the correspondent *205* were obliged to look over their shoulders to contemplate the lonely and indifferent shore.

The monstrous inshore rollers heaved the boat high until the men were again enabled to see the white sheets of water scudding up the slanted beach. "We won't get in very close," said the captain. Each time a man could wrest his attention from the rollers, he turned his glance toward the shore, and in the expression of the eyes during this contemplation there was a singular quality. The correspondent, observing the others, knew that they were not afraid, but the full meaning of their glances was shrouded.

As for himself, he was too tired to grapple fundamentally with the fact. He tried to coerce his mind into thinking of it, but the mind was dominated at this time by the muscles, and the muscles said they did not care. It merely occurred to him that if he should drown it would be a shame.

There were no hurried words, no pallor, no plain agitation. The men simply looked at the shore. "Now, remember to get well clear of the boat when you jump," said the captain.

Seaward the crest of a roller suddenly fell with a thunderous crash, and the long white comber came roaring down upon the boat.

"Steady now," said the captain. The men were silent. They turned their eyes from the shore to the comber and waited. The boat slid up the incline, leaped at the furious top, bounced over it, and swung down the long back of the wave. Some water had been shipped, and the cook bailed it out.   *210*

But the next crest crashed also. The tumbling, boiling flood of white water caught the boat and whirled it almost perpendicular. Water swarmed in from all sides. The correspondent had his hands on the gunwale at this time, and when the water entered at that place he swiftly withdrew his fingers, as if he objected to wetting them.

The little boat, drunken with this weight of water, reeled and snuggled deeper into the sea.

"Bail her out, cook! Bail her out!" said the captain.

"All right, Captain," said the cook.

"Now, boys, the next one will do for us sure," said the oiler. "Mind to jump clear of the boat."   *215*

The third wave moved forward, huge, furious, implacable. It fairly swallowed the dinghy, and almost simultaneously the men tumbled into the sea. A piece of life-belt had lain in the bottom of the boat, and as the correspondent went overboard he held this to his chest with his left hand.

The January water was icy, and he reflected immediately that it was colder than he had expected to find it off the coast of Florida. This appeared to his dazed mind as a fact important enough to be noted at the time. The coldness of the water was sad; it was tragic. This fact was somehow mixed and confused with his opinion of his own situation so that it seemed almost a proper reason for tears. The water was cold.

When he came to the surface he was conscious of little but the noisy water. Afterward he saw his companions in the sea. The oiler was ahead in the race. He was swimming strongly and rapidly. Off to the correspondent's left, the cook's great white and corked back bulged out of the water; and in the rear the captain was hanging with his one good hand to the keel of the overturned dinghy.

There is a certain immovable quality to a shore, and the correspondent wondered at it amid the confusion of the sea.

It seemed also very attractive; but the correspondent knew that it was   *220* a long journey, and he paddled leisurely. The piece of life-preserver lay under him, and sometimes he whirled down the incline of a wave as if he were on a hand-sled.

But finally he arrived at a place in the sea where travel was beset with difficulty. He did not pause swimming to inquire what manner of current had caught him, but there his progress ceased. The shore was set before him like a bit of scenery on a stage, and he looked at it, and understood with his eyes each detail of it.

As the cook passed, much farther to the left, the captain was calling to him, "Turn over on your back, cook! Turn over on your back and use the oar."

"All right, sir." The cook turned on his back, and, paddling with an oar, went ahead as if he were a canoe.

Presently the boat also passed to the left of the correspondent, with the captain clinging with one hand to the keel. He would have appeared like a man raising himself to look over a board fence if it were not for the extraordinary gymnastics of the boat. The correspondent marveled that the captain could still hold to it.

They passed on nearer to shore,—the oiler, the cook, the captain,—   *225* and following them went the water-jar, bouncing gaily over the seas.

The correspondent remained in the grip of this strange new enemy, a current. The shore, with its white slope of sand and its green bluff, topped with little silent cottages, was spread like a picture before him. It was very near to him then, but he was impressed as one who, in a gallery, looks at a scene from Brittany or Algiers.

He thought: "I am going to drown? Can it be possible? Can it be possible? Can it be possible?" Perhaps an individual must consider his own death to be the final phenomenon of nature.

But later a wave perhaps whirled him out of this small deadly current, for he found suddenly that he could again make progress toward the shore. Later still he was aware that the captain, clinging with one hand to the keel of the dinghy, had his face turned away from the shore and toward him, and was calling his name. "Come to the boat! Come to the boat!"

In his struggle to reach the captain and the boat, he reflected that when one gets properly wearied drowning must really be a comfortable arrangement—a cessation of hostilities accompanied by a large degree of relief; and he was glad of it, for the main thing in his mind for some moments had been horror of the temporary agony; he did not wish to be hurt.

Presently he saw a man running along the shore. He was undressing   *230* with most remarkable speed. Coat, trousers, shirt, everything flew magically off him.

"Come to the boat!" called the captain.

"All right, Captain." As the correspondent paddled, he saw the captain let himself down to bottom and leave the boat. Then the correspondent performed his one little marvel of the voyage. A large wave caught him and flung him with ease and supreme speed completely over the boat and far beyond it. It struck him even then as an event in gymnastics and a true miracle of the sea. An overturned boat in the surf is not a plaything to a swimming man.

The correspondent arrived in water that reached only to his waist, but his condition did not enable him to stand for more than a moment. Each wave knocked him into a heap, and the undertow pulled at him.

Then he saw the man who had been running and undressing, and undressing and running, come bounding into the water. He dragged ashore the cook, and then waded toward the captain; but the captain waved him away and sent him to the correspondent. He was naked—naked as a tree in winter; but a halo was about his head, and he shone like a saint. He gave a strong pull, and a long drag, and a bully heave at the correspondent's hand. The correspondent, schooled in the minor formulæ, said, "Thanks, old man." But suddenly the man cried, "What's that?" He pointed a swift finger. The correspondent said, "Go."

In the shallows, face downward, lay the oiler. His forehead touched   *235* sand that was periodically, between each wave, clear of the sea.

The correspondent did not know all that transpired afterward. When he achieved safe ground he fell, striking the sand with each particular part of his body. It was as if he had dropped from a roof, but the thud was grateful to him.

It seems that instantly the beach was populated with men with blankets, clothes, and flasks, and women with coffee-pots and all the remedies sacred to their minds. The welcome of the land to the men from the sea was warm and generous; but a still and dripping shape was carried slowly up the beach, and the land's welcome for it could only be the different and sinister hospitality of the grave.

When it came night, the white waves paced to and fro in the moonlight, and the wind brought the sound of the great sea's voice to the men on shore, and they felt that they could then be interpreters.

---

1. How many points of view do you find in this story? Name them, keeping in mind that there may be points of view that exist outside the characters and the situation.

2. How does Crane use the differences and the relationships between these points of view and the situation to suggest a dominant idea to you?

3. There is a great deal of description in this story. How does it fit into Crane's purpose in telling the story?

4. In the last sentence of the story, the narrator characterizes the survivors as having become interpreters. What does the term mean to you? What is it that they can interpret? What does the act of interpretation have to do with their points of view?

An Invitation to Write

Try writing a short story, an essay, or a poem in which you use the omniscient point of view to show how differing assumptions on the parts of the characters (and possibly your reader's assumptions as well) create a conflict.

The Limited Omniscient Point of View

If you choose the *limited omniscient* point of view, you also use the third person ("he" or "she"), but you and your audience are limited to the viewpoint of a single character. You show your audience the events through that character's eyes. You can tell your audience what the character sees, hears, feels, tastes, smells, and thinks, but you can go no further than that. As with the omniscient point of view, you can step in and interpret the protagonist's behavior, and you can show your reader how your protagonist responds to other characters' behavior. But you cannot show what other characters think or feel. Your readers are only as aware of actions, thoughts, and feelings as is the character through whose eyes they are seeing the events.

This approach is effective when you want to narrate a series of actions or events in which a single character is engaged. It allows you to step between the audience and the character and interpret the character's actions as a way of strengthening and defining your dominant idea.

Working with the Readings

Read the following pieces of writing and, alone or with your group, answer the questions that follow each one.

THE JUST-RIGHT WIFE

Ellen Goodman

The upper-middle-class men of Arabia are looking for just the right kind of wife. Arabia's merchant class, reports the Associated Press, finds the women of Libya too backward, and the women of Lebanon too forward, and have therefore gone shopping for brides in Egypt.

Egyptian women are being married off at the rate of thirty a day—an astonishing increase, according to the Egyptian marriage bureau. It doesn't know whether to be pleased or alarmed at the popularity of its women. According to one recent Saudi Arabian groom, the Egyptian women are "just right."

"The Egyptian woman is the happy medium," says Aly Abdul el-Korrary of his bride, Wafaa Ibrahiv (the happy medium herself was not questioned). "She is not too inhibited as they are in conservative Moslem societies, and not too liberal like many Lebanese."

Is this beginning to sound familiar? Well, the upper-middle-class, middle-aged, merchant-professional-class man of America also wants a "happy medium" wife. He is confused. He, too, has a problem and he would like us to be more understanding.

If it is no longer chic for a sheik to marry a veiled woman, it is some-   *5* how no longer "modern" for a successful member of the liberal establishment to be married to what he used to call a "housewife" and what he now hears called a "household drudge."

As his father once wanted a wife who had at least started college, now he would like a wife who has a mind, and even a job, of her own. The younger men in the office these days wear their wives' occupations on their sleeves. He thinks he, too, would like a wife—especially for social occasions—whose status would be his status symbol. A lady lawyer would be nice.

These men, you understand, now say (at least in private to younger working women in their office) that they are bored with women who "don't do anything." No matter how much some of them conspired in keeping them at home Back Then, many are now saying, in the best Moslem style, "I divorce thee." They are replacing them with more up-to-date models. A Ph.D. candidate would be nice.

The upper-middle-class, middle-aged man of today wants a wife who won't make him feel guilty. He doesn't want to worry if she's happy. He doesn't want to hear her complain about her dusty American history degree. He doesn't want to know if she's crying at the psychiatrist's office. He most definitely doesn't want to be blamed. He wants her to fulfill herself already! He doesn't mean that maliciously.

On the other hand, Lord knows, he doesn't want a wife who is too forward. The Saudi Arabian merchant believes that the Egyptian woman adapts more easily to his moods and needs. The American merchant also wants a woman who adapts herself to his moods and needs—his need for an independent woman and a traditional wife.

He doesn't want to live with a "household drudge," but it would be   10
nice to have an orderly home and well-scrubbed children. Certainly he wouldn't want a wife who got high on folding socks—he is not a Neanderthal—but it would be nice if she arranged for these things to get done. Without talking about marriage contracts.

He wants a wife who agreed that "marriage is a matter of give and take, not a business deal and 50–50 chores." It would help if she had just enough conflict herself (for not being her mother) to feel more than half the guilt for a full ashtray.

Of course, he sincerely would like her to be involved in her own work and life. But on the other hand, he doesn't want it to siphon away her energy for him. He needs to be taken care of, nurtured. He would like her to enjoy her job, but be ready to move for his, if necessary (after, of course, a long discussion in which he feels awful about asking and she ends up comforting him and packing).

He wants a wife who is a sexually responsive and satisfied woman, and he would even be pleased if she initiated sex with him. Sometimes. Not too often, however, because then he would get anxious.

He is confused, but he does, in all sincerity (status symbols aside), want a happy marriage to a happy wife. A happy medium. He is not sure exactly what he means, but he, too, would like a wife who is "just right."

The difference is that when the upper-middle-class, middle-aged   15
man of Arabia wants his wife he goes out and buys one. His American "brother" can only offer himself as the prize.

---

1. Whose point of view is the primary one in this essay? Define that person.

2. What is the attitude of the point-of-view person in this essay? What is that person looking for?

3. By the end of the essay, do you know what Goodman thinks? What *does* she think?

4. Notice that Goodman never refers to herself in this essay. How does she make her attitude clear?

5. Does this essay have a dominant idea? Decide what it is and express it in a sentence or two. Where does Goodman directly state the dominant idea—that is, is there a topic paragraph? How does she make her dominant idea clear to you?

THE MOST OF IT

Robert Frost

He thought he kept the universe alone;
For all the voice in answer he could wake
Was but the mocking echo of his own
From some tree-hidden cliff across the lake.
Some morning from the boulder-broken beach   5
He would cry out on life, that what it wants
Is not its own love back in copy-speech,
But counter-love, original response.
And nothing ever came of what he cried
Unless it was the embodiment that crashed   10
In the cliff's talus on the other side,
And then in the far distant water splashed.
But after a time allowed for it to swim,
Instead of proving human when it neared
And someone else additional to him,
As a great buck it powerfully appeared,   15
Pushing the crumpled water up ahead,
And landed pouring like a waterfall,
And stumbled through the rocks with horny tread,
And forced the underbrush—and that was all.   20

1. What does the narrator tell you about the attitude and expectations of the point-of-view character ("he")? What does "he" want and what does "he" want it from?

2. As opposed to what "he" wants, what does "he" get? What is the difference between the two?

3. Does the difference between "his" expectations and the results lead you to a dominant idea for this poem?

4. The poem is arranged so that "his" point of view is contained in the first eight lines. The remaining lines are given to the narrator's description of what happened. What effect does this arrangement have on the presentation of what you see to be the dominant idea? Experiment with other ways of arranging this poem. Is the effect different?

5. There is a lot of description in this poem. What does the narrator choose to describe? How does the description support and add to the dominant idea?

... *Y NO SE LO TRAGÓ LA TIERRA*°

Tomás Rivera

The first time he felt hate and anger was when he saw his mother cry for his uncle and for his aunt. They had both gotten tuberculosis and each of them had been sent to different sanitoriums. The children had then been parceled out among their aunts and uncles and they had taken care of them as best they could. His aunt had later died and shortly afterward his uncle had been brought home from the sanitorium, but he was already spitting blood every time he coughed. It was then that he saw his mother crying all the time. He had become angry because he couldn't strike back at anyone. He felt the same way now. But this time it was on account of his father.

"You should have left right away, son. Couldn't you see that your father was sick? All of you knew very well that he had been sun-struck before. Why didn't you come home?"

"Well, I don't know. Since the rest of us were soaking wet with sweat we didn't realize it was so hot, but I guess when one has been sunstruck it's different. Anyway, I told him to sit under the tree that's at the end of the rows but he didn't want to. It was then that he started to vomit. Then we saw that he couldn't hoe and we had to drag him to get him under the tree. He didn't struggle anymore. He simply let us take him. He didn't put up a fuss or anything."

"Poor man, my poor husband. He hardly slept last night. Didn't you hear him outside the house? He was twisting and turning all night; it must be painful. God, how I pray he gets well. I've been giving him cool lemonade all day but his eyes are still glassy. If I had been in the field yesterday I assure you that he would not have had a sunstroke. Poor man, he'll have spasms all over his body for at least three days and three nights. Now all of you take care of yourselves. If it gets too hot, rest. Don't overwork yourselves. Don't pay attention to the boss if he hurries you. Since he is not the one breaking his back, he thinks it's easy."

He became angrier when he heard his father moan outside the shack. His father didn't stay inside because he said that he was overcome with anxiety whenever he did. He had to be outside where he could get fresh air. There he could stretch out on the grass and roll around when the spasms hit him. Then he thought about whether his father was going to die from the sunstroke. From time to time he would hear his father pray and ask

---

... *Y no se lo tragó la tierra:* Spanish for "... and the earth did not devour him"

God for help. At first he had hoped that he would get well soon but the following day he felt his anger increase. And he felt it increase more when his mother or his father clamored for the mercy of God. And their father's moans had awakened them that night and also at dawn and their mother had gotten up and had taken off his scapularies° from around his neck and had washed them for him. She had then lighted some small candles. But to no avail. It was the same as with his uncle and his aunt.

"What do you gain by doing that, mother? Don't tell me that you believe that sort of thing helped my uncle and my aunt? Why is it that we are here on earth as though buried alive? Either the germs eat us from the inside or the sun from the outside. Always some illness. And work, work, day in and day out. And for what? Poor father, he works just as hard as the rest of us, perhaps harder. He was born working, as he says. Barely five years old and he was already out there planting corn with his father. After feeding the earth and the sun for such a long time, . . . one day unexpectedly he is felled by the sun. And powerless to do anything. And to top it off, praying to God. God doesn't even remember us. . . . There must not be a God. . . . No, better not to say it, what if father should worsen? Poor man, at least that must give him some hope."

His mother noticed how furious he was and in the morning she told him to calm down, that everything was in the hands of God and that his father would get well with God's help.

"Come now, do you really believe that? God, I am sure, doesn't give a damn about us. Look, can you tell me if father is mean or without love? You tell me if he has ever hurt anyone?"

"Well, no."

"There you are. See? And my uncle and my aunt? You tell me. And now their poor children not knowing their parents. Why did He have to take them? So you see, God doesn't give a damn about us poor people. Look, why do we have to live under these conditions? Are we hurting anybody? You're such a good person and yet you have to suffer so much. Can't you see? Tell me!"

"Oh, son, don't talk like that. Don't question the will of God. The ground might open up and devour you for talking like that. One must resign oneself to the will of God. Please don't talk like that, son. You frighten me. It seems that already the devil is in your very blood."

"Well, perhaps. At least that way I could release my anger. I'm tired of asking, why? Why you? Why father? Why my uncle? Why my aunt? Why their children? Can you tell me why? Why should we always be tied to the dirt, half buried in the earth like animals

---

scapularies: two small pieces of cloth worn over the shoulders as a token of religious devotion

without any hope of any kind? You know that the only thing we can look forward to is coming over here every year. And as you yourself say, one does not rest until one dies. I guess that is the way my uncle and my aunt felt, and that's the way father will eventually feel!"

"That's the way it is, son. Only death can bring us rest."

"But, why us?"

"Well, it is said that . . ."

"Don't say it! Don't tell me anything! I know what you're going to tell me!—that the poor will go to heaven."

The day started out cloudy and he felt the cool morning breeze brush his eyelashes as he and his brothers and sisters started to work. His mother had had to stay at home to take care of her husband. Thus he felt responsible for encouraging his brothers and sisters. In the morning, at least during the early hours, they were able to withstand the sun, but by tenthirty the sun had suddenly completely cleared the sky and penetrated everything and everyone. They worked much slower because they would feel weakness and suffocation overcome them if they worked at a hurried pace. They then had to wipe the sweat from their eyes every few minutes because their eyes would become blurry.

"When you kids see blurry, stop working or slow down. When we get to the end of the rows we'll rest awhile to regain our strength. It's going to be hot today. I wish it would remain cloudy, as it was this morning. No one would complain then. But no, once the sun bears down not even a tiny cloud dares show itself out of sheer fright. The hell of it is, we'll be finished here by two and then we have to go to that field that is nothing but hills. It's ok on the top of the hill but when we're in the low parts it's suffocating. Now even the slightest breeze blows through there. Air almost doesn't enter. Remember?"

"Yes."

"That's where we'll spend the hottest part of the day. Just drink a lot of water every few minutes even if the boss gets angry. If not you'll get sick. And if you can't take it any longer, tell me right away, ok? We'll go home. You saw what happened to father for holding out. The sun can suck the life out of you."

Just as they had thought, they had had to move to the other field by early afternoon. By three o'clock they were already sopping wet with sweat. Not a single part of their clothing remained dry. Every few minutes they stopped. Sometimes they gasped for breath, then everything became blurred and the fear of sunstroke creeped into them, but they continued.

"How do you feel?"

"Man, it's hot! But we have to keep going. At least until six. Only thing is that the water we have is no longer good for our thirst. How I wish I had a glass of cool water, real cold, just pulled up from the well, or an icy coke."

"You're crazy, you'd sure get sunstroke that way. Just don't work too fast. Let's see if we can hold up until six. Can you take it?"

At four o'clock the youngest became sick. He was only nine years old but since he was paid as an adult he tried to keep up with the others. He started to vomit and sat down, then he lay down. Fear stricken they all rushed over to him. He appeared to have fainted and when they opened his eyelids they found his eyes turned around. The one next to him in age started to cry but he told him immediately to shut up and help take him home. Spasms were moving over his small body. He then threw him on his back and carried him by himself. Once again he began asking why?

"Why my father, and now my little brother? He is barely nine years old. Why? He has to work like an animal, tied to the ground. Father, Mother, and he, my little brother, how could they possibly be guilty of anything?"

Each step that he took toward the house brought forth the echo of the question "why?" Half way down the road he became furious and then he started to cry out of despair. His other brothers and sisters didn't know what to do and they also started to cry, but out of fear. He then began to swear. And he didn't know when, but what he said he had been wanting to say for a long time. He cursed God. Upon doing it he felt the fear instilled in him by time and by his parents. For a split second he saw the earth open up to devour him. But, although he didn't look down, he then felt himself walking on very solid ground; *it was harder than he had ever felt it.* Anger swelled up in him again and he released it by cursing God. Then he noticed that his little brother no longer appeared quite so ill. He didn't know if his other little brothers and sisters realized how serious his curse had been.

That evening he didn't go to sleep until very late. He was experiencing a peace that he had never known before. It seemed to him that he had completely detached himself from everything. He was no longer worried about his father nor about his brother. All that he looked forward to was the new day, the coolness of the morning. By dawn his father was better. He was on his way to recovery. His little brother was also almost completely free of spasms. Time after time he felt surprised at what he had done the previous afternoon. He had cursed God and the earth had not parted. He was going to tell his mother but he decided to keep it a secret. He only told her that the earth didn't devour anyone, and that the sun didn't destroy anyone either.

He left for work and he was faced with a very cool morning. There were clouds and for the first time he felt himself capable of doing and undoing whatever he chose. He looked toward the ground and he kicked it and said to it,

"Not yet, you can't eat me yet. Someday. But I won't know."

1. How does Rivera use the limited omniscient point of view in this story? Is that the only voice in the story?

2. Rivera pays very little attention to the setting in the story. Why do you think he chooses to keep it in the background?

3. Is there a protagonist in this story? An antagonist(s)? Who or what are they?

4. What does the title have to do with the story?

5. What do you think Rivera's dominant idea is? How do the parts of this story lead you to that idea?

An Invitation to Write

These selections seem to focus upon the difference between what a person expects and what that person discovers when he or she looks more closely at the situation. Write an essay, a short story, or a poem from the limited omniscient point of view that reflects the difference between expectation and reality. Use the combination of the protagonist you choose and your ability to comment on his or her actions to lead your reader to a dominant idea about the character and his or her situation.

The First-Person Point of View

If you choose the *first-person* point of view, your readers see and hear everything from the standpoint of the character who tells the story in his or her words ("I"). If you choose to write from this point of view, you cannot step back and interpret the actions or feelings of the first-person narrator or of others for your readers. You can only give them what the narrator is aware of and what he or she thinks and feels about the surrounding events. However, as the writer, you are still responsible for everything that appears in your writing; it is still you making the choices. Using the first-person point of view, you create a *persona*—a mask—for yourself through which you've chosen to speak. Often the reader can find the dominant idea shaping a poem, an essay, or a piece of fiction told from this point of view in the difference between what the narrator believes to be true and what the reader discovers to be true.

Working with the Readings

Read the following selections and, alone or with your group, answer the questions that follow each one.

THE DISCUS THROWER

Richard Selzer

I spy on my patients. Ought not a doctor to observe his patients by any means and from any stance, that he might the more fully assemble evidence? So I stand in the doorways of hospital rooms and gaze. Oh, it is not all that furtive an act. Those in bed need only look up to discover me. But they never do.

From the doorway of Room 542 the man in the bed seems deeply tanned. Blue eyes and close-cropped white hair give him the appearance of vigor and good health. But I know that his skin is not brown from the sun. It is rusted, rather, in the last stage of containing the vile repose within. And the blue eyes are frosted, looking inward like the windows of a snowbound cottage. This man is blind. This man is also legless—the right leg missing from midthigh down, the left from just below the knee. It gives him the look of a bonsai, roots and branches pruned into the dwarfed facsimile of a great tree.

Propped on pillows, he cups his right thigh in both hands. Now and then he shakes his head as though acknowledging the intensity of his suffering. In all of this he makes no sound. Is he mute as well as blind?

The room in which he dwells is empty of all possessions—no get-well cards, small, private caches of food, day-old flowers, slippers, all the usual kickshaws of the sickroom. There is only the bed, a chair, a night-stand, and a tray on wheels that can be swung across his lap for meals.

"What time is it?" he asks.   5
"Three o'clock."
"Morning or afternoon?"
"Afternoon."
He is silent. There is nothing else he wants to know.
"How are you?" I say.   10
"Who is it?" he asks.
"It's the doctor. How do you feel?"
He does not answer right away.
"Feel?" he says.
"I hope you feel better," I say.   15
I press the button at the side of the bed.
"Down you go," I say.
"Yes, down," he says.

He falls back upon the bed awkwardly. His stumps, unweighted by legs and feet, rise in the air, presenting themselves. I unwrap the bandages from the stumps, and begin to cut away the black scabs and the dead, glazed fat with scissors and forceps. A shard of white bone comes loose. I pick it away. I wash the wounds with disinfectant and redress the stumps. All this while, he does not speak. What is he thinking behind those lids that do not blink? Is he remembering a time when he was whole? Does he dream of feet? Of when his body was not a rotting log?

He lies solid and inert. In spite of everything, he remains impressive, *20* as though he were a sailor standing athwart a slanting deck.

"Anything more I can do for you?" I ask.

For a long moment he is silent.

"Yes," he says at last and without the least irony. "You can bring me a pair of shoes."

In the corridor, the head nurse is waiting for me.

"We have to do something about him," she says. "Every morning he *25* orders scrambled eggs for breakfast, and, instead of eating them, he picks up the plate and throws it against the wall."

"Throws his plate?"

"Nasty. That's what he is. No wonder his family doesn't come to visit. They probably can't stand him any more than we can."

She is waiting for me to do something.

"Well?"

"We'll see," I say. *30*

The next morning I am waiting in the corridor when the kitchen delivers his breakfast. I watch the aide place the tray on the stand and swing it across his lap. She presses the button to raise the head of the bed. Then she leaves.

In time the man reaches to find the rim of the tray, then on to find the dome of the covered dish. He lifts off the cover and places it on the stand. He fingers across the plate until he probes the eggs. He lifts the plate in both hands, sets it on the palm of his right hand, centers it, balances it. He hefts it up and down slightly, getting the feel of it. Abruptly, he draws back his right arm as far as he can.

There is the crack of the plate breaking against the wall at the foot of his bed and the small wet sound of the scrambled eggs dropping to the floor.

And then he laughs. It is a sound you have never heard. It is something new under the sun. It could cure cancer.

Out in the corridor, the eyes of the head nurse narrow. *35*

"Laughed, did he?"

She writes something down on her clipboard.

A second aide arrives, brings a second breakfast tray, puts it on the nightstand, out of his reach. She looks over at me shaking her head and making her mouth go. I see that we are to be accomplices.

"I've got to feed you," she says to the man.

"Oh, no you don't," the man says. *40*

"Oh, yes I do," the aide says, "after the way you just did. Nurse says so."

"Get me my shoes," the man says.

"Here's oatmeal," the aide says. "Open." And she touches the spoon to his lower lip.

"I ordered scrambled eggs," says the man.

"That's right," the aide says.   *45*

I step forward.

"Is there anything I can do?" I say.

"Who are you?" the man asks.

In the evening I go once more to that ward to make my rounds. The head nurse reports to me that Room 542 is deceased. She has discovered this quite by accident, she says. No, there had been no sound. Nothing. It's a blessing, she says.

I go into his room, a spy looking for secrets. He is still there in his   *50* bed. His face is relaxed, grave, dignified. After a while, I turn to leave. My gaze sweeps the wall at the foot of the bed, and I see the place where it has been repeatedly washed, where the wall looks very clean and very white.

---

1. What do you learn about the narrator from reading this essay: his profession, his attitude toward his profession, his attitude toward the person he observes?

2. Why does the narrator place himself in the doorway of the room instead of in the room itself at the beginning of the essay?

3. In this essay, the narrator compares the person he observes with other objects. What do these comparisons tell you about the narrator?

4. How does the tone of the narrator's voice (your sense of his emotions) seem to change at the point in the essay where the narrator cleans the patient's wound? Define the difference between the two voices. Why does the voice change?

5. Aside from the obvious difference between the narrator and the patient, what other differences between the two does the author make clear to you? Why do you think he wants you to be especially aware of these differences?

6. Do you think the narrator is aware of these differences? What makes you think so?

7. Aside from the narrator and the patient, there is another character—the nurse—in this essay. What type of person is she? How does the writer use her in the essay?

8. The narrator, as you have seen, is a doctor. What do you think of the point of view he presents you with? Is he able to maintain that point of view or do you find him slipping into another one? Which

of the points of view do you sympathize with the most? Which of
them do you think is most useful to the narrator?

MY LAST DUCHESS

Robert Browning

Ferrara°

That's my last duchess painted on the wall,
Looking as if she were alive. I call
That piece a wonder, now: Frà Pandolf's° hands
Worked busily a day, and there she stands.
Will't please you sit and look at her? I said   5
"Frà Pandolf" by design, for never read
Strangers like you that pictured countenance,
The depth and passion of its earnest glance,
But to myself they turned (since none puts by
The curtain I have drawn for you, but I)   10
And seemed as they would ask me, if they durst,
How such a glance came there; so, not the first
Are you to turn and ask thus. Sir, 'twas not
Her husband's presence only, called that spot
Of joy into the Duchess' cheek: perhaps   15
Frà Pandolf chanced to say "Her mantle laps
Over my lady's wrist too much," or "Paint
Must never hope to reproduce the faint
Half-flush that dies along her throat": such stuff
Was courtesy, she thought, and cause enough   20
For calling up that spot of joy. She had
A heart—how shall I say?—too soon made glad,
Too easily impressed; she liked whate'er
She looked on, and her looks went everywhere.
Sir, 'twas all one! My favor at her breast,   25
The dropping of the daylight in the West,
The bough of cherries some officious fool
Broke in the orchard for her, the white mule
She rode with round the terrace—all and each

Ferrara: a center of culture during the Italian Renaissance
Frà Pandolf: An imaginary artist. "Frà" ("brother") was the title given to monks and friars.

Would draw from her alike the approving speech,   30
Or blush, at least. She thanked men—good! but thanked
Somehow—I know not how—as if she ranked
My gift of a nine-hundred-years-old name
With anybody's gift. Who'd stoop to blame
This sort of trifling? Even had you skill   35
In speech—which I have not—to make your will
Quite clear to such an one, and say, "Just this
Or that in you disgusts me; here you miss,
Or there exceed the mark"—and if she let
Herself be lessened so, nor plainly set   40
Her wits to yours, forsooth, and made excuse,
—E'en then would be some stooping; and I choose
Never to stoop. Oh sir, she smiled, no doubt,
Whene'er I passed her; but who passed without
Much the same smile? This grew; I gave commands;   45
Then all smiles stopped together. There she stands
As if alive. Will 't please you rise? We'll meet
The company below, then. I repeat,
The Count your master's known munificence
Is ample warrant that no just pretense   50
Of mine for dowry will be disallowed;
Though his fair daughter's self, as I avowed
At starting, is my object. Nay, we'll go
Together down, sir. Notice Neptune, though,
Taming a sea-horse, thought a rarity,   55
Which Claus of Innsbruck cast in bronze for me!

---

1. What is the scene of this monologue? (A monologue is a speech by a single speaker.)

2. Who is the speaker speaking to?

3. What is the situation that surrounds this monologue? How does the writer make you aware of this situation?

4. What are the events the speaker describes?

5. How does the speaker act toward his wife? Why does the speaker act as he does?

6. What does the speaker think of himself?

7. What do you think of the speaker?

8. If there are differences between your judgment of the speaker and his opinion of himself, what does Browning do to create those differences?

9. What conclusion or dominant idea does Browning's control of the point of view lead you to?

10. What attitude toward the speaker has Browning led you to? Do you
think that attitude is reasonable under the circumstances? Have you
felt this way about someone you know?

I STAND HERE IRONING

Tillie Olsen

I stand here ironing, and what you asked me moves tormented back
and forth with the iron.

"I wish you would manage the time to come in and talk with me
about your daughter. I'm sure you can help me understand her. She's a
youngster who needs help and whom I'm deeply interested in helping."

"Who needs help." . . . Even if I came, what good would it do? You
think because I am her mother I have a key, or that in some way you
could use me as a key? She has lived for nineteen years. There is all that
life that has happened outside of me, beyond me.

And when is there time to remember, to sift, to weigh, to estimate,
to total? I will start and there will be an interruption and I will have to
gather it all together again. Or I will become engulfed with all I did or
did not do, with what should have been and what cannot be helped.

She was a beautiful baby. The first and only one of our five that was   5
beautiful at birth. You do not guess how new and uneasy her tenancy in
her now-loveliness. You did not know her all those years she was thought
homely, or see her poring over her baby pictures, making me tell her over
and over how beautiful she had been—and would be, I would tell
her—and was now, to the seeing eye. But the seeing eyes were few or
nonexistent. Including mine.

I nursed her. They feel that's important nowadays. I nursed all the
children, but with her, with all the fierce rigidity of first motherhood, I
did like the books then said. Though her cries battered me to trembling
and my breasts ached with swollenness, I waited till the clock decreed.

Why do I put that first? I do not even know if it matters, or if it
explains anything.

She was a beautiful baby. She blew shining bubbles of sound. She
loved motion, loved light, loved color and music and textures. She would
lie on the floor in her blue overalls patting the surface so hard in ecstasy
her hands and feet would blur. She was a miracle to me, but when she
was eight months old I had to leave her daytimes with the woman downstairs to whom she was no miracle at all, for I worked or looked for work
and for Emily's father, who "could no longer endure" (he wrote in his
good-bye note) "sharing want with us."

I was nineteen. It was the pre-relief, pre-WPA world of the depression. I would start running as soon as I got off the streetcar, running up the stairs, the place smelling sour, and awake or asleep to startle awake, when she saw me she would break into a clogged weeping that could not be comforted, a weeping I can hear yet.

After a while I found a job hashing at night so I could be with her   10
days, and it was better. But it came to where I had to bring her to his family and leave her.

It took a long time to raise the money for her fare back. Then she got chicken pox and I had to wait longer. When she finally came, I hardly knew her, walking quick and nervous like her father, looking like her father, thin, and dressed in a shoddy red that yellowed her skin and glared at the pockmarks. All the baby loveliness gone.

She was two. Old enough for nursery school they said, and I did not know then what I know now—the fatigue of the long day, and the lacerations of group life in the kinds of nurseries that are only parking places for children.

Except that it would have made no difference if I had known. It was the only place there was. It was the only way we could be together, the only way I could hold a job.

And even without knowing, I knew. I knew the teacher that was evil because all these years it has curdled into my memory, the little boy hunched in the corner, her rasp, "why aren't you outside, because Alvin hits you? that's no reason, go out, scaredy." I knew Emily hated it even if she did not clutch and implore "don't go Mommy" like the other children, mornings.

She always had a reason why we should stay home. Momma, you   15
look sick. Momma, I feel sick. Momma, the teachers aren't there today, they're sick. Momma, we can't go, there was a fire there last night. Momma, it's a holiday today, no school, they told me.

But never a direct protest, never rebellion. I think of our others in their three-, four-year-oldness—the explosions, the tempers, the denunciations, the demands—and I feel suddenly ill. I put the iron down. What in me demanded that goodness in her? And what was the cost, the cost to her of such goodness?

The old man living in the back once said in his gentle way: "You should smile at Emily more when you look at her." What *was* in my face when I looked at her? I loved her. There were all the acts of love.

It was only with the others I remembered what he said, and it was the face of joy, and not of care or tightness or worry I turned to them—too late for Emily. She does not smile easily, let alone almost always as her brothers and sisters do. Her face is closed and sombre, but when she wants, how fluid. You must have seen it in her pantomimes, you spoke of her rare gift for comedy on the stage that rouses a laughter out of the audience so dear they applaud and applaud and do not want to let her go.

Where does it come from, that comedy? There was none of it in her when she came back to me that second time, after I had had to send her away again. She had a new daddy now to learn to love, and I think perhaps it was a better time.

Except when we left her alone nights, telling ourselves she was old enough.   *20*

"Can't you go some other time, Mommy, like tomorrow?" she would ask. "Will it be just a little while you'll be gone? Do you promise?"

The time we came back, the front door open, the clock on the floor in the hall. She rigid awake. "It wasn't just a little while. I didn't cry. Three times I called you, just three times, and then I ran downstairs to open the door so you could come faster. The clock talked loud. I threw it away, it scared me what it talked."

She said the clock talked loud again that night I went to the hospital to have Susan. She was delirious with the fever that comes before red measles, but she was fully conscious all the week I was gone and the week after we were home when she could not come near the new baby or me.

She did not get well. She stayed skeleton thin, not wanting to eat, and night after night she had nightmares. She would call for me, and I would rouse from exhaustion to sleepily call back: "You're all right, darling, go to sleep, it's just a dream," and if she still called, in a sterner voice, "now go to sleep, Emily, there's nothing to hurt you." Twice, only twice, when I had to get up for Susan anyhow, I went in to sit with her.

Now when it is too late (as if she would let me hold and comfort her   *25* like I do the others) I get up and go to her at once at her moan or restless stirring. "Are you awake, Emily? Can I get you something?" And the answer is always the same: "No, I'm all right, go back to sleep, Mother."

They persuaded me at the clinic to send her away to a convalescent home in the country where "she can have the kind of food and care you can't manage for her, and you'll be free to concentrate on the new baby." They still send children to that place. I see pictures on the society page of sleek young women planning affairs to raise money for it, or dancing at the affairs, or decorating Easter eggs or filling Christmas stockings for the children.

They never have a picture of the children so I do not know if the girls still wear those gigantic red bows and the ravaged looks on the every other Sunday when parents can come to visit "unless otherwise notified"—as we were notified the first six weeks.

Oh it is a handsome place, green lawns and tall trees and fluted flower beds. High up on the balconies of each cottage the children stand, the girls in their red bows and white dresses, the boys in white suits and giant red ties. The parents stand below shrieking up to be heard and the children shriek down to be heard, and between them the invisible wall "Not To Be Contaminated by Parental Germs or Physical Affection."

There was a tiny girl who always stood hand in hand with Emily. Her parents never came. One visit she was gone. "They moved her to Rose

Cottage," Emily shouted in explanation. "They don't like you to love anybody here."

She wrote once a week, the labored writing of a seven–year–old. "I   *30* am fine. How is the baby. If I write my leter nicly I will have a star. Love." There never was a star. We wrote every other day, letters she could never hold or keep but only hear read—once. "We simply do not have room for children to keep any personal possessions," they patiently explained when we pieced one Sunday's shrieking together to plead how much it would mean to Emily, who loved so to keep things, to be allowed to keep her letters and cards.

Each visit she looked frailer. "She isn't eating," they told us.

(They had runny eggs for breakfast or mush with lumps. Emily said later, I'd hold it in my mouth and not swallow. Nothing ever tasted good, just when they had chicken.)

It took us eight months to get her released home, and only the fact that she gained back so little of her seven lost pounds convinced the social worker.

I used to try to hold and love her after she came back, but her body would stay stiff, and after a while she'd push away. She ate little. Food sickened her, and I think much of life too. Oh she had physical lightness and brightness, twinkling by on skates, bouncing like a ball up and down up and down over the jump rope, skimming over the hill; but these were momentary.

She fretted about her appearance, thin and dark and foreign–looking   *35* at a time when every little girl was supposed to look or thought she should look a chubby blonde replica of Shirley Temple. The doorbell sometimes rang for her, but no one seemed to come and play in the house or be a best friend. Maybe because we moved so much.

There was a boy she loved painfully through two school semesters. Months later she told me how she had taken pennies from my purse to buy him candy. "Licorice was his favorite and I brought him some every day, but he still liked Jennifer better'n me. Why, Mommy?" The kind of question for which there is no answer.

School was a worry to her. She was not glib or quick in a world where glibness and quickness were easily confused with ability to learn. To her overworked and exasperated teachers she was an overconscientious "slow learner" who kept trying to catch up and was absent entirely too often.

I let her be absent, though sometimes the illness was imaginary. How different from my now-strictness about attendance with the others. I wasn't working. We had a new baby, I was home anyhow. Sometimes, after Susan grew old enough, I would keep her home from school, too, to have them all together.

Mostly Emily had asthma, and her breathing, harsh and labored, would fill the house with a curiously tranquil sound. I would bring the two old dresser mirrors and her boxes of collections to her bed. She would select beads and single earrings, bottle tops and shells, dried flowers and pebbles, old postcards and scraps, all sorts of oddments; then she and Susan would play Kingdom, setting up landscapes and furniture, peopling them with action.

Those were the only times of peaceful companionship between her   *40* and Susan. I have edged away from it, that poisonous feeling between them, that terrible balancing of hurts and needs I had to do between the two, and did so badly, those earlier years.

Oh there are conflicts between the others too, each one human, needing, demanding, hurting, taking—but only between Emily and Susan, no, Emily toward Susan that corroding resentment. It seems so obvious on the surface, yet it is not obvious. Susan, the second child, Susan, golden- and curly-haired and chubby, quick and articulate and assured, everything in appearance and manner Emily was not; Susan, not able to resist Emily's precious things, losing or sometimes clumsily breaking them; Susan telling jokes and riddles to company for applause while Emily sat silent (to say to me later: that was *my* riddle, Mother, I told it to Susan); Susan, who for all the five years' difference in age was just a year behind Emily in developing physically.

I am glad for that slow physical development that widened the difference between her and her contemporaries, though she suffered over it. She was too vulnerable for that terrible world of youthful competition, of preening and parading, of constant measuring of yourself against every other, of envy, "If I had that copper hair," "If I had that skin. . . ." She tormented herself enough about not looking like the others, there was enough of the unsureness, the having to be conscious of words before you speak, the constant caring—what are they thinking of me? without having it all magnified by the merciless physical drives.

Ronnie is calling. He is wet and I change him. It is rare there is such a cry now. That time of motherhood is almost behind me when the ear is not one's own but must always be racked and listening for the child cry, the child call. We sit for a while and I hold him, looking out over the city spread in charcoal with its soft aisles of light. "*Shoogily,*" he breathes and curls closer. I carry him back to bed, asleep. *Shoogily.* A funny word, a family word, inherited from Emily, invented by her to say: *comfort.*

In this and other ways she leaves her seal, I say aloud. And startle at my saying it. What do I mean? What did I start to gather together, to try and make coherent? I was at the terrible, growing years. War years. I do not remember them well. I was working, there were four smaller ones now, there was not time for her. She had to help be a mother, and housekeeper, and shopper. She had to set her seal. Mornings of crisis and near hysteria trying to get lunches packed, hair combed, coats and shoes found, everyone to school or Child Care on time, the baby ready for transportation. And always the paper scribbled on by a smaller one, the book looked at by Susan then mislaid, the homework not done. Running out to that huge school where she was one, she was lost, she was a drop; suffering over the unpreparedness, stammering and unsure in her classes.

There was so little time left at night after the kids were bedded down. She would struggle over books, always eating (it was in those years she developed her enormous appetite that is legendary in our family) and I would be ironing, or preparing food for the next day, or writing V-mail to Bill, or tending the baby. Sometimes, to make me laugh, or out of her despair, she would imitate happenings or types at school.

I think I said once: "Why don't you do something like this in the school amateur show?" One morning she phoned me at work, hardly understandable through the weeping: "Mother, I did it. I won, I won; they gave me first prize; they clapped and clapped and wouldn't let me go."

Now suddenly she was Somebody, and as imprisoned in her difference as she had been in anonymity.

She began to be asked to perform at other high schools, even in colleges, then at city and statewide affairs. The first one we went to, I only recognized her that first moment when thin, shy, she almost drowned herself into the curtains. Then: Was this Emily? The control, the command, the convulsing and deadly clowning, the spell, then the roaring, stamping audience, unwilling to let this rare and precious laughter out of their lives.

Afterwards: You ought to do something about her with a gift like that—but without money or knowing how, what does one do? We have left it all to her, and the gift has as often eddied inside, clogged and clotted, has been used and growing.

She is coming. She runs up the stairs two at a time with her light graceful step, and I know she is happy tonight. Whatever it was that occasioned your call did not happen today.

"Aren't you ever going to finish the ironing, Mother? Whistler painted his mother in a rocker. I'd have to paint mine standing over an ironing board." This is one of her communicative nights and she tells me everything and nothing as she fixes herself a plate of food out of the icebox.

She is so lovely. Why did you want me to come in at all? Why were you concerned? She will find her way.

She starts up the stairs to bed. "Don't get me up with the rest in the morning." "But I thought you were having midterms." "Oh, those," she comes back in, kisses me, and says quite lightly, "in a couple of years when we'll all be atom-dead they won't matter a bit."

She has said it before. She *believes* it. But because I have been dredging the past and all that compounds a human being is so heavy and meaningful in me, I cannot endure it tonight.

I will never total it all. I will never come in to say: She was a child seldom smiled at. Her father left me before she was a year old. I had to work her first six years when there was work, or I sent her home and to his relatives. There were years she had care she hated. She was dark and thin and foreign-looking in a world where the prestige went to blonde-ness and curly hair and dimples, she was slow where glibness was prized. She was a child of anxious, not proud, love. We were poor and could not afford for her the soil of easy growth. I was a young mother, I was a distracted mother. There were the other children pushing up, demand-ing. Her younger sister seemed all that she was not. There were years she did not want me to touch her. She kept too much in herself, her life was such she had to keep too much in herself. My wisdom came too late. She has much to her and probably nothing will come of it. She is a child of her age, of depression, of war, of fear.

Let her be. So all that is in her will not bloom—but in how many does it? There is still enough left to live by. Only help her to know—help make it so there is cause for her to know—that she is more than this dress on the ironing board, helpless before the iron.

---

1. Who do you think the speaker in this story is speaking to?
2. What do you think the situation is?
3. Do you think this story is about the mother or about Emily? What leads you to think so?
4. What does the mother tell you about herself as she speaks about Emily?
5. Except for one scene, this story is primarily narrative. Why do you think Olsen chose to concentrate on narration? Why does she change her approach in the one scene?
6. What dominant idea does this story lead you to?
7. Do you think the mother is a good mother or a bad mother? Does your judgment of her change as you read the story? If your judgment changes, what does Olsen do to make that happen?
8. Whether you think the mother is a good or a bad mother, do you sympathize with her? Why or why not?

～ꇾ *An Invitation to Write*

Write an essay, a short story, or a poem from the first-person point of view about someone you know well. As you write your piece, try to reflect the same sort of conflict that you see in the pieces you have just read.

The Objective Point of View

The *objective* point of view is like using a movie or video camera to present your dominant idea. You can take your audience anywhere, but like a camera, you can only provide your audience with the events that can be seen and heard at that moment and in that place. A camera cannot comment on the action, nor can it take the reader inside the characters' minds. Because emotions and thoughts are as closed to the readers as they would be to a camera, you are limited only to words and actions. Of course, because you are the writer, you choose the words and the actions to suggest thoughts, emotions, and your dominant idea. But you cannot step back from the plot and speak to your readers as you can if you use the omniscient and limited omniscient points of view. You cannot let your readers in on any of the characters' thoughts. Characterization and possibly description of the setting are the only tools you have to define your characters for your readers.

Working with a Reading

Read the following story and, alone or in your group, answer the questions that follow it.

HILLS LIKE WHITE ELEPHANTS

Ernest Hemingway

The hills across the valley of the Ebro° were long and white. On this side there was no shade and no trees and the station was between two lines of rails in the sun. Close against the side of the station there was the warm shadow of the building and a curtain, made of strings of bamboo beads, hung across the open door into the bar, to keep out flies. The American and the girl with him sat at a table in the shade, outside the building. It was very hot and the express from Barcelona would come in forty minutes. It stopped at this junction for two minutes and went on to Madrid.

"What should we drink?" the girl asked. She had taken off her hat and put it on the table.

"It's pretty hot," the man said.

"Let's drink beer."

"Dos cervezas," the man said into the curtain.

"Big ones?" a woman asked from the doorway.   5

"Yes. Two big ones."

The woman brought two glasses of beer and two felt pads. She put the felt pads and the beer glasses on the table and looked at the man and the girl. The girl was looking off at the line of hills. They were white in the sun and the country was brown and dry.

Ebro: river in the north of Spain

"They look like white elephants," she said.

"I've never seen one," the man drank his beer. *10*

"No, you wouldn't have."

"I might have," the man said. "Just because you say I wouldn't have doesn't prove anything."

The girl looked at the bead curtain. "They've painted something on it," she said. "What does it say?"

"Anis del Toro. It's a drink."

"Could we try it?" *15*

The man called "Listen" through the curtain. The woman came out from the bar.

"Four reales."

"We want two Anis del Toro."

"With water?"

"Do you want it with water?" *20*

"I don't know," the girl said. "Is it good with water?"

"It's all right."

"You want them with water?" asked the woman.

"Yes, with water."

"It tastes like licorice," the girl said and put the glass down. *25*

"That's the way with everything."

"Yes," said the girl. "Everything tastes of licorice. Especially all the things you've waited so long for, like absinthe."

"Oh, cut it out."

"You started it," the girl said. "I was being amused. I was having a fine time."

"Well, let's try and have a fine time." *30*

"All right. I was trying. I said the mountains looked like white elephants. Wasn't that bright?"

"That was bright."

"I wanted to try this new drink. That's all we do, isn't it—look at things and try new drinks?"

"I guess so."

The girl looked across at the hills. *35*

"They're lovely hills," she said. "They don't really look like white elephants. I just meant the coloring of their skin through the trees."

"Should we have another drink?"

"All right."

The warm wind blew the bead curtain against the table.

"The beer's nice and cool," the man said. *40*

"It's lovely," the girl said.

"It's really an awfully simple operation, Jig," the man said. "It's not really an operation at all."

The girl looked at the ground the table legs rested on.

"I know you wouldn't mind it, Jig. It's really not anything. It's just to let the air in."

The girl did not say anything.   *45*

"I'll go with you and I'll stay with you all the time. They just let the air in and then it's all perfectly natural."

"Then what will we do afterward?"

"We'll be fine afterward. Just like we were before."

"What makes you think so?"

"That's the only thing that bothers us. It's the only thing that's made   *50* us unhappy."

The girl looked at the bead curtain, put her hand out and took hold of two of the strings of beads.

"And you think then we'll be all right and be happy."

"I know we will. You don't have to be afraid. I've known lots of people that have done it."

"So have I," said the girl. "And afterward they were all so happy."

"Well, the man said, "if you don't want to you don't have to. I   *55* wouldn't have you do it if you didn't want to. But I know it's perfectly simple."

"And you really want to?"

"I think it's the best thing to do. But I don't want you to do it if you don't really want to."

"And if I do it you'll be happy and things will be like they were and you'll love me?"

"I love you now. You know I love you."

"I know. But if I do it, then it will be nice again if I say things are   *60* like white elephants, and you'll like it?"

"I'll love it. I love it now but I just can't think about it. You know how I get when I worry."

"If I do it you won't ever worry?"

"I won't worry about that because it's perfectly simple."

"Then I'll do it. Because I don't care about me."

"What do you mean?"   *65*

"I don't care about me."

"Well, I care about you."

"Oh, yes. But I don't care about me. And I'll do it and then every- thing will be fine."

"I don't want you to do it if you feel that way."

The girl stood up and walked to the end of the station. Across, on   *70* the other side, were fields of grain and trees along the banks of the Ebro. Far away, beyond the river, were mountains. The shadow of a cloud moved across the field of grain and she saw the river through the trees.

"And we could have all this," she said. "And we could have every- thing and every day we make it more impossible."

"What did you say?"

"I said we could have everything."

"We can have everything."

"No, we can't."   *75*

"We can have the whole world."

"No, we can't."

"We can go everywhere."

"No, we can't. It isn't ours any more."

"It's ours."   80

"No, it isn't. And once they take it away, you never get it back."

"But they haven't taken it away."

"We'll wait and see."

"Come on back in the shade," he said. "You mustn't feel that way."

"I don't feel any way," the girl said. "I just know things."   85

"I don't want you to do anything that you don't want to do—"

"Nor that isn't good for me," she said. "I know. Could we have another beer?"

"All right. But you've got to realize—"

"I realize," the girl said. "Can't we maybe stop talking?"

They sat down at the table and the girl looked across at the hills on   90
the dry side of the valley and the man looked at her and at the table.

"You've got to realize," he said, "that I don't want you to do it if you don't want to. I'm perfectly willing to go through with it if it means anything to you."

"Doesn't it mean anything to you? We could get along."

"Of course it does. But I don't want anybody but you. I don't want any one else. And I know it's perfectly simple."

"Yes, you know it's perfectly simple."

"It's all right for you to say that, but I do know it."   95

"Would you do something for me now?"

"I'd do anything for you."

"Would you please please please please please please please stop talking?"

He did not say anything but looked at the bags against the wall of the station. There were labels on them from all the hotels where they had spent nights.

"But I don't want you to," he said, "I don't care anything about it."   100

"I'll scream," the girl said.

The woman came out through the curtains with two glasses of beer and put them down on the damp felt pads. "The train comes in five minutes," she said.

"What did she say?" asked the girl.

"That the train is coming in five minutes."

The girl smiled brightly at the woman, to thank her.   105

"I'd better take the bags over to the other side of the station," the man said. She smiled at him.

"All right. Then come back and we'll finish the beer."

He picked up the two heavy bags and carried them around the station to the other tracks. He looked up the tracks but could not see the train. Coming back, he walked through the barroom, where people waiting for the train were drinking. He drank an Anis at the bar and looked at the people. They were all waiting reasonably for the train. He went out through the bead curtain. She was sitting at the table and smiled at him.

"Do you feel better?" he asked.

"I feel fine," she said. "There's nothing wrong with me. I feel fine."   *110*

---

1. The two characters in this story are having a conversation. What do you think the conversation is about? What does Hemingway provide you with to help you discover the subject of the conversation?

2. How would you define the two characters' relationship to each other? Who is the protagonist and who or what is the antagonist?

3. How would you define each of the characters?

4. At the beginning and at various times throughout the story, Hemingway describes the setting against which this conversation takes place. What does the setting have to do with the conversation?

5. Have you ever known anyone who acts like one of these characters? Has this story helped you to understand that person better?

❧ An Invitation to Write

Write an essay, a short story, a short play, or a poem from the objective point of view. In it, describe the behavior of one character or two characters interacting in such a way as to lead your readers toward a clear idea of what kind of person or people are involved and the nature of the conflict that surrounds them. Try to make your setting reflect the situation, as well.

Drama and Point of View

A dramatist is always restricted to the objective point of view. Drama is action driven by conflict that is played out in front of an audience that observes the action. Thus, the author can present only the actions and words of the characters in the drama. It is possible for the author to show what a character thinks by having him or her speak to the audience in what is called an *aside* or by having a character appear alone on stage to speak his or her thoughts aloud in a *soliloquy* (which roughly means "to speak alone"). However, even in these cases the author can present only the action and thoughts; he or she cannot directly interpret them for the audience.

❧ Working with a Reading

Read the following short play and, alone or with your group, answer the questions that follow it.

THE RED COAT

John Patrick Shanley

Night time on a side street. A street light shines down on some steps through a green tree. Moonlight mixes in the shadows. A seventeen year-old boy sits on the steps in a white shirt with a loosened skinny tie, black dress pants, and black shoes. He is staring off. His eyes are shining. A sixteen year-old girl enters, in neighborhood party clothes: short skirt, blouse, penny loafers.

JOHN Hi, Mary.

MARY Oh! I didn't see you there. You're hiding.

JOHN Not from you, Mary.

MARY Who from?

JOHN Oh, nobody. I was up at Susan's party.

MARY That's where I'm going.

JOHN Oh.

MARY Why did you leave?

JOHN No reason.

MARY You just gonna sit here?

JOHN For awhile.

MARY Well, I'm going in.

JOHN Oh. Okay . . . Oh! I'm not going in . . . I mean came out because
. . . Oh, go in!

MARY What's wrong with you, John?

JOHN I left the party because you weren't there. That's why I left the
party.

MARY Why'd ya leave the party 'cause I wasn't there?

JOHN I dunno.

MARY I'm going in.

JOHN I left the party 'cause I felt like everything I wanted was outside the
party . . . out here. There's a breeze out here, and the moon . . . look
at the way the moon is . . . and I knew you were outside somewhere,
too! So I came out and sat on the steps here and I thought that maybe
you'd come and I would be here . . . outside the party, on the steps, in
the moonlight . . . and those other people . . . the ones at the party . . .
wouldn't be here . . . but the night would be here . . . and you and me
would be talking on the steps in the night in the moonlight and I could
tell you . . .

MARY Tell me what?

JOHN How I feel!

MARY How you feel about what?

JOHN I don't know. I was looking out the window at the party . . . and I drank some wine . . . and I was looking out the window at the moon and I thought of you . . . and I could feel my heart . . . breaking.

MARY Joh . . .

JOHN I felt that wine and the moon and your face all pushing in my heart and I left the party and I came out here.

MARY Your eyes are all shiny.

JOHN I know. And I came out here looking for the moon and I saw that street light shining down through the leaves of that tree.

MARY Hey yeah! It does look pretty.

JOHN It's beautiful. I didn't know a street light could be beautiful. I've always thought of them as being cold and blue, you know? But this one's yellow . . . and it comes down through the leaves and the leaves are so green! Mary, I love you!

MARY Oh!

JOHN I shouldn't 've said it. I shouldn't 've said it.

MARY No, no. That's all right.

JOHN My heart's breaking. You must think I'm so stupid . . . but I can feel it breaking. I wish I could stop talking. I can't. I can't.

MARY I never heard you talking like this before.

JOHN That's 'cause this is outside the party and it's night and there's a moon up there . . . and a street light that's more beautiful than the sun! My God, the sidewalk's beautiful. Those bits of shiny stuff in the concrete . . . look how they're sparkling up the light!

MARY You're crying! You're crying over the sidewalk!

JOHN I love you, Mary!

MARY That's all right. But don't cry over the sidewalk. You're usually so quiet.

JOHN Okay. Okay.

(*A pause. Then John grabs Mary and kisses her.*)

MARY Oh . . . you used your tongue. (*He kisses her again.*) You . . . should we go into the party?

JOHN No.

MARY I got all dressed . . . I tasted the wine on your . . . mouth. You were waiting for me out here? I wasn't even going to come. I don't like Susan so much. I was going to stay home and watch a movie. What would you have done?

JOHN I don't know.

(*Kisses her again. She kisses him back.*)

MARY You go to St. Nicholas of Tolentine, don't you?

JOHN Yeah.

MARY I see you on the platform on a hundred and forty-ninth street sometimes.

JOHN I see you, too! Sometimes I just let the trains go by until the last
minute, hoping to see you.

MARY Really?

JOHN Yeah.

MARY I take a look around for you but I always get on my train. What
would you have done if I hadn't come?

JOHN I don't know. Walked around. I walk around a lot.

MARY Walk around where?

JOHN I walk around your block a lot. Sometimes I run into you.

MARY You mean that was *planned?* Wow! I always thought you were
coming from somewhere.

JOHN I love you, Mary. I can't believe I'm saying it . . . to you . . . out
loud. I love you.

MARY Kiss me again.

(They kiss.)

JOHN I've loved you for a long time.

MARY How long?

JOHN Months. Remember that big snowball fight?

MARY In the park?

JOHN Yeah. That's when it was. That's when I fell in love with you. You
were wearing a red coat.

MARY Oh, that coat! I've had that for ages and ages. I've had it since the
sixth grade.

JOHN Really?

MARY I have really special feelings for that coat. I feel like it's part of
me . . . like it stands for something . . . my childhood . . . something
like that.

JOHN You look nice in that coat. I think I sensed something about it . . .
the coat . . . it's special to me, too. It's so good to be able to talk to you
like this.

MARY Yeah, this is nice. That's funny how you felt that about my coat.
The red one. No one knows how I feel about that coat.

JOHN I think I do, Mary.

MARY Do you? If you understood about my red coat . . . that red coat is
like all the good things about when I was a kid . . . it's like I still have
all the good kid things when I'm in that red coat . . . it's like being
grown up and having your childhood, too. You know what it's like?
It's like being in one of those movies where you're safe, even when
you're in an adventure. Do you know what I mean? Sometimes, in a
movie the hero's doin' all this stuff that's dangerous, but you know,
becausa the kind of movie it is, that he's not gonna get hurt. Bein' in
that red coat is like that . . . like bein' safe in an adventure.

JOHN And that's the way you were in that snowball fight! It was like you
knew that nothing could go wrong!

MARY That's right! That's right! That's the way it feels! Oh, you do understand! It seems silly but I've always wanted someone to understand some things and that was one of them . . . the red coat.

JOHN I do understand! I do!

MARY I don't know. I don't know. I don't know about tomorrow, but . . . right this minute I . . . love you!

JOHN Oh, Mary!

MARY Oh, kiss me, John. Please!

JOHN You're crying!

MARY I didn't know. I didn't know two people could understand some things . . . share some things.

(They kiss.)

JOHN It must be terrible not to.

MARY What?

JOHN Be able to share things.

MARY It is! It is! But don't you remember? Only a few minutes ago we were alone. I feel like I could tell you anything. Isn't that crazy?

JOHN Do you want to go for a walk?

MARY No, no. Let's stay right here. Between the streetlight and the moon. Under the tree. Tell me that you love me.

JOHN I love you.

MARY I love you, too. You're good-looking, did you know that? Does your mother tell you that?

JOHN Yeah, she does.

MARY Your eyes are shining.

JOHN I know. I can feel them shining.

(The Lights Go Down Slowly.)

---

1. Describe the characters of John and Mary as you see them at the opening of the play.

2. What is the relationship of John and Mary like through the first third or so of the play? Is there a protagonist? An antagonist? Which is which?

3. Do that relationship and the roles John and Mary play change by the end of the play? If you see them changing, describe that change.

4. What role do you think the red coat plays in the relationship?

5. Does the red coat mean the same thing to John as it does to Mary?

6. Do John and Mary reveal to each other everything they are feeling and thinking? Does Shanley allow their actions and their speeches to reveal different feelings and motivations to you?

7. On the basis of what you have learned of these two people and your own experience, what do you think the chances are for the success of this relationship? What makes you think so?

 ## *An Invitation to Write*

Write a poem, an essay, a short story, or a short play that provides only the actions and words of one or more persons without narrating or interpreting for your audience. Make your description so clear that it will lead your audience to understand that character's feelings.

A Student Paper

The paper that follows uses narration to tell a story. When you have read it, answer the questions that follow it, alone or with your group.

AS GRANDPA LEAVES

Che J. Hsu

Grandpa called tonight—all the way from the other side of earth. I was studying when the unanticipated phone ring broke the silence. The years have streamed by since I last saw him, but the image of his back walking away from the train kept coming to my mind.

I went to visit my grandparents the summer before my family's immigration. Back then, they lived in an old house where I spent my happiest moments. This was the place where we used to have our family reunions, the place where my childhood memory was shaped. It was a year during which misfortunes came in pairs. Grandpa's lifelong friend died that summer, and the next morning was my departure to America.

I woke up in the dark on that morning and started packing my clothes. Grandpa had decided that he wasn't going to take me to the train station due to the death of his best friend. He asked my uncle to accompany me but then changed his mind. I was thirteen that year and had been on the train alone several times, so I told him that it was unnecessary, but he said, "Don't worry. I want to go and breathe some fresh air anyway."

We got to the station a few minutes early. The building was very old. I waited in line to buy the ticket while he was taking care of the luggage. Since we had more suitcases than normal, we had to pay the bell boy a little extra. Grandpa started to bargain with the bell boy. Being the overconfident boy I was, the words from Grandpa sounded dull and unskillful to me. I said to myself impatiently, "Grandpa! You are not going to get a good deal the way you talk. Just give him what he wants and let's go!"

When we got on the train, he picked a window seat for me. I covered   5
myself with a purple blanket he gave me because he insisted that I would get cold sitting right next to a window. He started to lecture me about how I should be careful in America. A couple of minutes later, a conductor came by. Grandpa asked him to take good care of me. I was laughing to myself while trying to hide the embarrassment by turning my head away. "Come on, Grandpa! All these people want is money. Why waste your energy? I'm a thirteen-year-old boy, don't you think I can take care of myself?" I thought.

"It's about time to leave, Grandpa," I said. He looked out the window saying, "Let me go buy some oranges. You stay here and don't move." I saw a couple of salespeople over on the first platform. To get there from my train he would have to cross some rail tracks and get over several platforms. Grandpa is fat, so I was a little worried. I asked him whether I should go, but he said no. I saw him, with a fishing cap, a wrinkled blue shirt, and a pair of old black pants, walking to the edge of the third platform, bending his old bones, and jumping off the platform without difficulty. He crossed the tracks and stopped in front of the five-foot concrete wall. He placed his hands on top of the platform and pushed his body half way up. His ball-shaped body tilted to the left as he struggled. He bent his knee over the platform and finally stood up. As I watched him, tears fell from my eyes. I wiped them off immediately, fearing that he might see the tears. When I looked out the window again, he was coming back with a bag full of oranges. He left the bag on the platform and jumped off. When he got to the edge of the nearest platform, I got up from the seat and rushed out of the train to help him. We walked back to the seat together. He dumped the bag on my coat and brushed the dirt off his clothes. A smile of satisfaction appeared on his face. He said, "Remember to give me a call when you get there."

I followed him out of the train as he was leaving. He turned around and said, "Go back in the train. It's going to leave pretty soon." I stood motionless, until the train started to move slowly. Metal wheels rolled over the cracks between the rails. I felt as if my legs were stuck in concrete. My eyes couldn't turn away from the tiny image of Grandpa's back as he merged into the crowd. As the train pulled me away faster and faster, tears started to pour again.

I was shocked when I saw my grandparents again a few years ago. They came to America to visit us. I got to the airport early on the day of their arrival. Time stopped when I found them. I almost ran into Grandpa's bosom, but I didn't because Grandpa's white hair surprised me. The warmth in his smile was still enchanting, and the clothes he wore were familiar, but his skin had wrinkled; his voice sounded weaker, and his eyes no longer glittered. Time! What have you done to him?

Two years have passed. Both my and Grandpa's lives have changed a lot. My family has moved several times, and now I am in college. Most of my time is spent away from home. My grandparents also moved out of the place where they lived most of their lives. The old house was replaced by a wide six-lane street. Under the pavement are ashes of the old house and my childhood memories. Grandpa called me from his new apartment.

Grandpa had written a letter after his visit. In the letter he said, "All   10 is good except my leg aches frequently. It becomes very inconvenient sometimes. Maybe my life is getting close to its end." After hanging up the phone, I took out Grandpa's letter from the drawer of my desk. As I was reading it, the image of his back kept coming to my mind again and again—with a black fishing cap, a wrinkled blue shirt, and a pair of old black pants, climbing and jumping from one platform to another. Oh God! When will I see him again?

---

1. Is the purpose of the narration in this piece just to tell you a story? Is another sort of dominant idea expressed through the narration? What do you think that dominant idea is?

2. This writer does not tell you everything. He links a number of incidents together and tells you three stories. What are the three stories, and how do they work together to lead you to the dominant idea?

3. The writer chooses to describe some of the surroundings, but he doesn't describe everything. What has he chosen to show you? What do his descriptions have to do with his dominant idea?

4. Suppose the writer had made all this material up? Would that make a difference to you? To the dominant idea?

FURTHER READINGS

On the following pages you will find readings that use narration as an organizational strategy. If your teacher assigns some or all of these readings or if you are inclined to read them on your own, pay attention to the ways the writers use narration to support their dominant ideas. Also, note how the writers use voice and style to engage your feelings, your interest, and your intellect.

Remember, these writers are writing to you—a fellow human being. They have chosen to tell you something about coping with the effort of being human in their worlds. See how their examples and ideas speak to your experience. See how the combination of your experiences and those the writers offer you might lead you to your own ideas about your world.

NO NAME WOMAN

Maxine Hong Kingston

"You must not tell anyone," my mother said, "what I am about to tell you. In China your father had a sister who killed herself. She jumped into the family well. We say that your father has all brothers because it is as if she had never been born.

"In 1924 just a few days after our village celebrated seventeen hurry-up weddings—to make sure that every young man who went 'out on the road' would responsibly come home—your father and his brothers and your grandfather and his brothers and your aunt's new husband sailed for America, the Gold Mountain. It was your grandfather's last trip. Those lucky enough to get contracts waved good-bye from the decks. They fed and guarded the stowaways and helped them off in Cuba, New York, Bali, Hawaii. 'We'll meet in California next year,' they said. All of them sent money home.

"I remember looking at your aunt one day when she and I were dressing; I had not noticed before that she had such a protruding melon of a stomach. But I did not think, 'She's pregnant,' until she began to look like other pregnant women, her shirt pulling and the white tops of her black pants showing. She could not have been pregnant, you see, because her husband had been gone for years. No one said anything. We did not discuss it. In early summer she was ready to have the child, long after the time when it could have been possible.

"The village had also been counting. On the night the baby was to be born the villagers raided our house. Some were crying. Like a great saw, teeth strung with lights, files of people walked zigzag across our land, tearing the rice. Their lanterns doubled in the disturbed black water, which drained away through the broken bunds. As the villagers closed in, we could see that some of them, probably men and women we knew well, wore white masks. The people with long hair hung it over their faces. Women with short hair made it stand up on end. Some had tied white bands around their foreheads, arms, and legs.

"At first they threw mud and rocks at the house. Then they threw eggs 5 and began slaughtering our stock. We could hear the animals scream their deaths—the roosters, the pigs, a last great roar from the ox. Familiar wild heads flared in our night windows; the villagers encircled us. Some of the faces stopped to peer at us, their eyes rushing like searchlights. The hands flattened against the panes, framed heads, and left red prints.

"The villagers broke in the front and the back doors at the same time, even though we had not locked the doors against them. Their knives dripped with the blood of our animals. They smeared blood on the doors and walls. One woman swung a chicken, whose throat she had slit, splattering blood in red arcs about her. We stood together in the middle of our house, in the family hall with the pictures and tables of the ancestors around us, and looked straight ahead.

"At that time the house had only two wings. When the men came back, we would build two more to enclose our courtyard and a third one to begin a second courtyard. The villagers pushed through both wings, even your grandparents' rooms, to find your aunt's, which was also mine until the men returned. From this room a new wing for one of the younger families would grow. They ripped up her clothes and shoes and broke her combs, grinding them underfoot. They tore her work from the loom. They scattered the cooking fire and rolled the new weaving in it. We could hear them in the kitchen breaking our bowls and banging the pots. They overturned the great waist-high earthenware jugs; duck eggs, pickled fruits, vegetables burst out and mixed in acrid torrents. The old woman from the next field swept a broom through the air and loosed the spirits-of-the-broom over our heads. 'Pig.' 'Ghost.' 'Pig,' they sobbed and scolded while they ruined our house.

"When they left, they took sugar and oranges to bless themselves. They cut pieces from the dead animals. Some of them took bowls that were not broken and clothes that were not torn. Afterward we swept up the rice and sewed it back up into sacks. But the smells from the spilled preserves lasted. Your aunt gave birth in the pigsty that night. The next morning when I went up for the water, I found her and the baby plugging up the family well.

"Don't let your father know that I told you. He denies her. Now that you have started to menstruate, what happened to her could happen to you. Don't humiliate us. You wouldn't like to be forgotten as if you had never been born. The villagers are watchful."

Whenever she had to warn us about life, my mother told stories that ran 10 like this one, a story to grow up on. She tested our strength to establish realities. Those in the emigrant generations who could not reassert brute survival died young and far from home. Those of us in the first American generations have had to figure out how the invisible world the emigrants built around our childhoods fit in solid America.

The emigrants confused the gods by diverting their curses, misleading them with crooked streets and false names. They must try to confuse their offspring as well, who, I suppose, threaten them in similar ways—always trying to get things straight, always trying to name the unspeakable. The Chinese I know hide their names; sojourners take new names when their lives change and guard their real names with silence.

Chinese-Americans, when you try to understand what things in you are Chinese, how do you separate what is peculiar to childhood, to poverty, insanities, one family, your mother who marked your growing with stories, from what is Chinese? What is Chinese tradition and what is the movies?

If I want to learn what clothes my aunt wore, whether flashy or ordinary, I would have to begin, "Remember Father's drowned-in-the-well sister?" I cannot ask that. My mother has told me once and for all the useful parts. She will add nothing unless powered by Necessity, a riverbank that guides her life. She plants vegetable gardens rather than lawns; she carries the odd-shaped tomatoes home from the fields and eats food left for the gods.

Whenever we did frivolous things, we used up energy; we flew high kites. We children came up off the ground over the melting cones our parents brought home from work and the American movie on New Year's Day—*Oh, You Beautiful Doll* with Betty Grable one year, and *She Wore a Yellow Ribbon* with John Wayne another year. After the one carnival ride each, we paid in guilt; our tired father counted his change on the dark walk home.

Adultery is extravagance. Could people who hatch their own chicks and eat the embryos and the heads for delicacies and boil the feet in vinegar for party food, leaving only the gravel, eating even the gizzard lining—could such people engender a prodigal aunt? To be a woman, to have a daughter in starvation time was a waste enough. My aunt could not have been the lone romantic who gave up everything for sex. Women in the old China did not choose. Some man had commanded her to lie with him and be his secret evil. I wonder whether he masked himself when he joined the raid on her family.   15

Perhaps she encountered him in the fields or on the mountain where the daughters-in-law collected fuel. Or perhaps he first noticed her in the marketplace. He was not a stranger because the village housed no strangers. She had to have dealings with him other than sex. Perhaps he worked an adjoining field, or he sold her the cloth for the dress she sewed and wore. His demand must have surprised, then terrified her. She obeyed him; she always did as she was told.

When the family found a young man in the next village to be her husband, she stood tractably beside the best rooster, his proxy, and promised before they met that she would be his forever. She was lucky that he was her age and she would be the first wife, an advantage secure now. The night she first saw him, he had sex with her. Then he left for America. She had almost forgotten what he looked like. When she tried to envision him, she only saw the black and white face in the group photograph the men had had taken before leaving.

The other man was not, after all, much different from her husband. They both gave orders: she followed. "If you tell your family, I'll beat you. I'll kill you. Be here again next week." No one talked sex, ever. And she might have separated the rapes from the rest of living if only she did not have to buy her oil from him or gather wood in the same forest. I want her fear to have lasted just as long as rape lasted so that the fear could have been contained. Not drawn-out fear. But women at sex hazarded birth and hence lifetimes. The fear did not stop but permeated everywhere. She told the man, "I think I'm pregnant." He organized the raid against her.

On night when my mother and father talked about their life back home, sometimes they mentioned an "outcast table" whose business they still seemed to be settling, their voices tight. In a commensal tradition, where food is precious, the powerful older people made wrongdoers eat alone. Instead of letting them start separate new lives like the Japanese, who could become samurais and geishas, the Chinese family, faces averted but eyes glowering sideways, hung on to the offenders and fed them leftovers. My aunt must have lived in the same house as my parents and eaten at an outcast table. My mother spoke about the raid as if she had seen it, when she and my aunt, a daughter-in-law to a different household, should not have been living together at all. Daughters-in-law lived with their husband's parents, not their own; a synonym for marriage in Chinese is "taking a daughter-in-law." Her husband's parents could have sold her, mortgaged her, stoned her. But they had sent her back to her own mother and father, a mysterious act hinting at disgraces not told me. Perhaps they had thrown her out to deflect the avengers.

She was the only daughter; her four brothers went with her father, husband, and uncles "out on the road" and for some years became western men. When the goods were divided among the family, three of the brothers took land, and the youngest, my father, chose an education. After my grandparents gave their daughter away to her husband's family, they had dispensed all the adventure and all the property. They expected her alone to keep the traditional ways, which her brothers, now among the barbarians, could fumble without detection. The heavy, deep-rooted women were to maintain the past against the flood, safe for returning. But the rare urge west had fixed upon our family, and so my aunt crossed boundaries not delineated in space.

The work of preservation demands that the feelings playing about in one's guts not be turned into action. Just watch their passing like cherry blossoms. But perhaps my aunt, my forerunner, caught in a slow life, let dreams grow and fade and after some months or years went toward what persisted. Fear at the enormities of the forbidden kept her desires delicate,

20

wire and bone. She looked at a man because she liked the way the hair was tucked behind his ears, or she liked the questionmark line of a long torso curving at the shoulder and straight at the hip. For warm eyes or a soft voice or a slow walk—that's all—a few hairs, a line, a brightness, a sound, a pace, she gave up family. She offered us up for a charm that vanished with tiredness, a pigtail that didn't toss when the wind died. Why, the wrong lighting could erase the dearest thing about him.

It could very well have been, however, that my aunt did not take subtle enjoyment of her friend, but, a wild woman, kept rollicking company. Imagining her free with sex doesn't fit, though. I don't know any women like that, or men either. Unless I see her life branching into mine, she gives me no ancestral help.

To sustain her being in love, she often worked at herself in the mirror, guessing at the colors and shapes that would interest him, changing them frequently in order to hit on the right combination. She wanted him to look back.

On a farm near the sea, a woman who tended her appearance reaped a reputation for eccentricity. All the married women blunt-cut their hair in flaps about their ears or pulled it back in tight buns. No nonsense. Neither style blew easily into heart-catching tangles. And at their weddings they displayed themselves in their long hair for the last time. "It brushed the backs of my knees," my mother tells me. "It was braided, and even so, it brushed the backs of my knees."

At the mirror my aunt combed individuality into her bob. A bun could   25
have been contrived to escape into black streamers blowing in the wind or in quiet wisps about her face, but only the older women in our picture album wear buns. She brushed her hair back from her forehead, tucking the flaps behind her ears. She looped a piece of thread, knotted into a circle between her index fingers and thumbs, and ran the double strand across her forehead. When she closed her fingers as if she were making a pair of shadow geese bite, the string twisted together catching the little hairs. Then she pulled the thread away from her skin, ripping the hairs out neatly, her eyes watering from the needles of pain. Opening her fingers, she cleaned the thread, then rolled it along her hairline and the tops of her eyebrows. My mother did the same to me and my sisters and herself. I used to believe that the expression "caught by the short hairs" meant a captive held with a depilatory string. It especially hurt at the temples, but my mother said we were lucky we didn't have to have our feet bound when we were seven. Sisters used to sit on their beds and cry together, she said, as their mothers or their slave removed the bandages for a few minutes each night and let the blood gush back into their veins. I hope that the man my aunt loved appreciated a smooth brow, that he wasn't just a tits-and-ass man.

Once my aunt found a freckle on her chin, at a spot that the almanac said predestined her for unhappiness. She dug it out with a hot needle and washed the wound with peroxide.

More attention to her looks than these pullings of hairs and pickings at spots would have caused gossip among the villagers. They owned work clothes and good clothes, and they wore good clothes for feasting the new seasons. But since a woman combing her hair hexes beginnings, my aunt rarely found an occasion to look her best. Women looked like great sea snails—the corded wood, babies, and laundry they carried were the whorls on their backs. The Chinese did not admire a bent back; goddesses and warriors stood straight. Still there must have been a marvelous freeing of beauty when a worker laid down her burden and stretched and arched.

Such commonplace loveliness, however, was not enough for my aunt. She dreamed of a lover for the fifteen days of New Year's, the time for families to exchange visits, money, and food. She plied her secret comb. And sure enough she cursed the year, the family, the village, and herself.

Even as her hair lured her imminent lover, many other men looked at her. Uncles, cousins, nephews, brothers would have looked, too, had they been home between journeys. Perhaps they had already been restraining their curiosity, and they left, fearful that their glances, like a field of nesting birds, might be startled and caught. Poverty hurt, and that was their first reason for leaving. But another, final reason for leaving the crowded house was the never-said.

She may have been unusually beloved, the precious only daughter, *30* spoiled and mirror-gazing because of the affection the family lavished on her. When her husband left, they welcomed the chance to take her back from the in-laws; she could live like the little daughter for just a while longer. There are stories that my grandfather was different from other people, "crazy ever since the little Jap bayoneted him in the head." He used to put his naked penis on the dinner table, laughing. And one day he brought home a baby girl, wrapped up inside his brown western-style great-coat. He had traded one of his sons, probably my father, the youngest, for her. My grandmother made him trade back. When he finally got a daughter of his own, he doted on her. They must have all loved her, except perhaps my father, the only brother who never went back to China, having once been traded for a girl.

Brothers and sisters, newly men and women, had to efface their sexual color and present plain miens. Disturbing hair and eyes, a smile like no other, threatened the ideal of five generations living under one roof. To focus blurs, people shouted face to face and yelled from room to room. The immigrants I know have loud voices, unmodulated to American tones even after years away from the village where they called their friendships out across the fields. I have not been able to stop my mother's screams in public libraries or over telephones. Walking erect (knees straight, toes pointed forward, not pigeon-toed, which is Chinese-feminine) and speaking in an inaudible voice, I have tried to turn myself American-feminine. Chinese communication was loud, public. Only sick people had to whisper. But at the dinner table, where the family members came nearest one another, no one could talk, not the outcasts nor any eaters. Every word that falls from the mouth is a coin lost. Silently they gave and accepted food with both hands. A preoccupied child who took his bowl with one hand got a sideways glare. A complete moment of total attention is due everyone alike. Children and lovers have no singularity here, but my aunt used a secret voice, a separate attentiveness.

She kept the man's name to herself throughout her labor and dying; she did not accuse him that he be punished with her. To save her inseminator's name she gave silent birth.

He may have been somebody in her own household, but intercourse with a man outside the family would have been no less abhorrent. All the village were kinsmen, and the titles shouted in loud country voices never let kinship be forgotten. Any man within visiting distance would have been neutralized as a lover—"brother," "younger brother," "older brother"— 115 relationship titles. Parents researched birth charts probably not so much to assure good fortune as to circumvent incest in a population that has but one hundred surnames. Everybody has eight million relatives. How useless then sexual mannerisms, how dangerous.

As if it came from an atavism deeper than fear, I used to add "brother" silently to boys' names. It hexed the boys, who would or would not ask me to dance, and made them less scary and as familiar and deserving of benevolence as girls.

But, of course, I hexed myself also—no dates. I should have stood up, both arms waving, and shouted out across libraries, "Hey, you! Love me back." I had no idea, though, how to make attraction selective, how to control its direction and magnitude. If I made myself American-pretty so that the five or six Chinese boys in the class fell in love with me, everyone else—the Caucasian, Negro, and Japanese boys—would too. Sisterliness, dignified and honorable, made much more sense.   *35*

Attraction eludes control so stubbornly that whole societies designed to organize relationships among people cannot keep order, not even when they bind people to one another from childhood and raise them together. Among the very poor and the wealthy, brothers married their adopted sisters, like doves. Our family allowed some romance, paying adult brides' prices and providing dowries so that their sons and daughters could marry strangers. Marriage promises to turn strangers into friendly relatives—a nation of siblings.

In the village structure, spirits shimmered among the live creatures, balanced and held in equilibrium by time and land. But one human being flaring up into violence could open up a black hole, a maelstrom that pulled in the sky. The frightened villagers, who depended on one another to maintain the real, went to my aunt to show her a personal, physical representation of the break she made in the "roundness." Misallying couples snapped off the future, which was to be embodied in true offspring. The villagers punished her for acting as if she could have a private life, secret and apart from them.

If my aunt had betrayed the family at a time of large grain yields and peace, when many boys were born, and wings were being built on many houses, perhaps she might have escaped such severe punishment. But the men—hungry, greedy, tired of planting in dry soil, cuckolded—had been forced to leave the village in order to send food-money home. There were ghost plagues, bandit plagues, wars with the Japanese, floods. My Chinese brother and sister had died of an unknown sickness. Adultery, perhaps only a mistake during good times, became a crime when the village needed food.

The round moon cakes and round doorways, the round tables of graduated size that fit one roundness inside another, round windows and rice bowls—these talismans had lost their power to warn this family of the law: a family must be whole, faithfully keeping the descent line by having sons to feed the old and the dead who in turn look after the family. The villagers came to show my aunt and lover-in-hiding a broken house. The villagers were speeding up the circling of events because she was too shortsighted to see that her infidelity had already harmed the village, that waves of consequences would return unpredictably, sometimes in disguise, as now, to hurt her. This roundness had to be made coin-sized so that she would see its circumference: punish her at the birth of her baby. Awaken her to the inexorable. People who refused fatalism because they could invent small resources insisted on culpability. Deny accidents and wrest fault from the stars.

After the villagers left, their lanterns now scattering in various directions toward home, the family broke their silence and cursed her. "Aiaa, we're going to die. Death is coming. Death is coming. Look what you've done. You've killed us. Ghost! Dead Ghost! Ghost! You've never been born." She ran out into the fields, far enough from the house so that she could no longer hear their voices, and pressed herself against the earth, her own land no more. When she felt the birth coming, she thought that she had been hurt. Her body seized together. "They've hurt me too much," she thought. "This is gall, and it will kill me." With forehead and knees against the earth, her body convulsed and then relaxed. She turned on her back, lay on the ground. The black well of sky and stars went out and out forever; her body and her complexity seemed to disappear. She was one of the stars, a bright dot in blackness, without home, without a companion, in eternal cold and silence. An agoraphobia rose in her, speeding higher and higher, bigger and bigger; she would not be able to contain it; there would be no end to fear.

Flayed, unprotected against space, she felt pain return, focusing her body. This pain chilled her—a cold, steady kind of surface pain. Inside, spasmodically, the other pain, the pain of the child, heated her. For hours she lay on the ground, alternately body and space. Sometimes a vision of normal comfort obliterated reality; she saw the family in the evening gambling at the dinner table, the young people massaging their elders' backs. She saw them congratulating one another, high joy on the mornings the rice shoots came up. When these pictures burst, the stars drew yet further apart. Black space opened.

40

She got to her feet to fight better and remembered that old-fashioned women gave birth in their pigsties to fool the jealous, paindealing gods, who do not snatch piglets. Before the next spasms could stop her, she ran to the pigsty, each step a rushing out into emptiness. She climbed over the fence and knelt in the dirt. It was good to have a fence enclosing her, a tribal person alone.

Laboring, this woman who had carried her child as a foreign growth that sickened her every day, expelled it at last. She reached down to touch the hot, wet, moving mass, surely smaller than anything human, and could feel that it was human after all—fingers, toes, nails, nose. She pulled it up on her belly, and it lay curled there, butt in the air, feet precisely tucked one under the other. She opened her loose shirt and buttoned the child inside. After resting, it squirmed and thrashed and she pushed it up to her breast. It turned its head this way and that until it found her nipple. There, it made little snuffling noises. She clenched her teeth at its preciousness, lovely as a young calf, a piglet, a little dog.

She may have gone to the pigsty as a last act of responsibility: she would protect this child as she had protected its father. It would look after her soul, leaving supplies on her grave. But how would this tiny child without family find her grave when there would be no marker for her anywhere, neither in the earth nor the family hall? No one would give her a family hall name. She had taken the child with her into the wastes. At its birth the two of them had felt the same raw pain of separation, a wound that only the family pressing tight could close. A child with no descent line would not soften her life but only trail after her, ghostlike, begging her to give it purpose. At dawn the villagers on their way to the fields would stand around the fence and look.

Full of milk, the little ghost slept. When it awoke, she hardened her breasts against the milk that crying loosens. Toward morning she picked up the baby and walked to the well.

Carrying the baby to the well shows loving. Otherwise abandon it. Turn its face into the mud. Mothers who love their children take them along. It was probably a girl; there is some hope of forgiveness for boys.

45

"Don't tell anyone you had an aunt. Your father does not want to hear her name. She has never been born." I have believed that sex was unspeakable and words so strong and fathers so frail that "aunt" would do my father mysterious harm. I have thought that my family, having settled among immigrants who had also been their neighbors in the ancestral land, needed to clean their name, and a wrong word would incite the kinspeople even here. But there is more to this silence: they want me to participate in her punishment. And I have.

In the twenty years since I heard this story I have not asked for details nor said my aunt's name; I do not know it. People who comfort the dead can also chase after them to hurt them further—a reverse ancestor worship. The real punishment was not the raid swiftly inflicted by the villagers, but the family's deliberately forgetting her. Her betrayal so maddened them, they saw to it that she would suffer forever, even after death. Always hungry, always needing, she would have to beg food from other ghosts, snatch and steal it from those whose living descendants give them gifts. She would have to fight the ghosts massed at crossroads for the buns a few thoughtful citizens leave to decoy her away from village and home so that the ancestral spirits could feast unharassed. At peace, they could act like gods, not ghosts, their descent lines providing them with paper suits and dresses, spirit money, paper houses, paper automobiles, chicken, meat, and rice into eternity—essences delivered up in smoke and flames, steam and incense rising from each rice bowl. In an attempt to make the Chinese care for people outside the family, Chairman Mao encourages us now to give our paper replicas to the spirits of outstanding soldiers and workers, no matter whose ancestors they may be. My aunt remains forever hungry. Goods are not distributed evenly among the dead.

My aunt haunts me—her ghost drawn to me because now, after fifty years of neglect, I alone devote pages of paper to her, though not origamied into houses and clothes. I do not think she always means me well. I am telling on her, and she was a spite suicide, drowning herself in the drinking water. The Chinese are always very frightened of the drowned one, whose weeping ghost, wet hair hanging and skin bloated, waits silently by the water to pull down a substitute.

THE YELLOW WALL-PAPER

Charlotte Perkins Gilman

It is very seldom that mere ordinary people like John and myself secure ancestral halls for the summer.

A colonial mansion, a hereditary estate, I would say a haunted house, and reach the height of romantic felicity—but that would be asking too much of fate!

Still I will proudly declare that there is something queer about it.

Else, why should it be let so cheaply? And why have stood so long untenanted?

John laughs at me, of course, but one expects that in marriage.   5

John is practical in the extreme. He has no patience with faith, an intense horror of superstition, and he scoffs openly at any talk of things not to be felt and seen and put down in figures.

John is a physician, and *perhaps*—(I would not say it to a living soul, of course, but this is dead paper and a great relief to my mind—) *perhaps* that is one reason I do not get well faster.

You see he does not believe I am sick!

And what can one do?

If a physician of high standing, and one's own husband, assures friends   *10*
and relatives that there is really nothing the matter with one but temporary
nervous depression—a slight hysterical tendency—what is one to do?

My brother is also a physician, and also of high standing, and he says the
same thing.

So I take phosphates or phosphites°—whichever it is, and tonics, and
journeys, and air, and exercise, and am absolutely forbidden to "work" until
I am well again.

Personally, I disagree with their ideas.

Personally, I believe that congenial work, with excitement and change,
would do me good.

But what is one to do?   *15*

I did write for a while in spite of them; but it *does* exhaust me a good
deal—having to be so sly about it, or else meet with heavy opposition.

I sometimes fancy that in my condition if I had less opposition and more
society and stimulus—but John says the very worst thing I can do is to think
about my condition, and I confess it always makes me feel bad.

So I will let it alone and talk about the house.

The most beautiful place! It is quite alone, standing well back from the
road, quite three miles from the village. It makes me think of English places
that you read about, for there are hedges and walls and gates that lock, and
lots of separate little houses for the gardeners and people.

There is a *delicious* garden! I never saw such a garden—large and shady,   *20*
full of box-bordered paths, and lined with long grape-covered arbors with
seats under them.

There were greenhouses, too, but they are all broken now.

There was some legal trouble, I believe, something about the heirs and
co-heirs; anyhow, the place has been empty for years.

That spoils my ghostliness, I am afraid, but I don't care—there is something strange about the house—I can feel it.

I even said so to John one moonlight evening, but he said what I felt
was a *draught,* and shut the window.

I get unreasonably angry with John sometimes. I'm sure I never used to   *25*
be so sensitive. I think it is due to this nervous condition.

But John says if I feel so, I shall neglect proper self-control; so I take
pains to control myself—before him, at least, and that makes me very tired.

I don't like our room a bit. I wanted one downstairs that opened on the
piazza and had roses all over the window, and such pretty old-fashioned
chintz hangings! But John would not hear of it.

He said there was only one window and not room for two beds, and no
near room for him if he took another.

---

phosphates or phosphites: "phosphate," a carbonated beverage of water, flavoring, and a small
amount of phosphoric acid

He is very careful and loving, and hardly lets me stir without special direction.

I have a schedule prescription for each hour in the day; he takes all care from me, and so I feel basely ungrateful not to value it more.

He said we came here solely on my account, that I was to have perfect rest and all the air I could get. "Your exercise depends on your strength, my dear," said he, "and your food somewhat on your appetite; but air you can absorb all the time." So we took the nursery at the top of the house.

It is a big, airy room, the whole floor nearly, with windows that look all ways, and air and sunshine galore. It was nursery first and then playroom and gymnasium, I should judge; for the windows are barred for little children, and there are rings and things in the walls.

The paint and paper look as if a boys' school had used it. It is stripped off—the paper—in great patches all around the head of my bed, about as far as I can reach, and in a great place on the other side of the room low down. I never saw a worse paper in my life.

One of those sprawling flamboyant patterns committing every artistic sin.

It is dull enough to confuse the eye in following, pronounced enough to constantly irritate and provoke study, and when you follow the lame uncertain curves for a little distance they suddenly commit suicide—plunge off at outrageous angles, destroy themselves in unheard of contradictions.

The color is repellent, almost revolting; a smouldering unclean yellow, strangely faded by the slow-turning sunlight.

It is a dull yet lurid orange in some places, a sickly sulphur tint in others.

No wonder the children hated it! I should hate it myself if I had to live in this room long.

There comes John, and I must put this away,—he hates to have me write a word.

We have been here two weeks, and I haven't felt like writing before, since that first day.

I am sitting by the window now, up in this atrocious nursery, and there is nothing to hinder my writing as much as I please, save lack of strength.

John is away all day, and even some nights when his cases are serious.

I am glad my case is not serious!

But these nervous troubles are dreadfully depressing.

John does not know how much I really suffer. He knows there is no *reason* to suffer, and that satisfies him.

Of course it is only nervousness. It does weigh on me so not to do my duty in any way!

I meant to be such a help to John, such a real rest and comfort, and here I am a comparative burden already!

Nobody would believe what an effort it is to do what little I am able,—to dress and entertain, and order things.

It is fortunate Mary is so good with the baby. Such a dear baby!

And yet I *cannot* be with him, it makes me so nervous.   *50*

I suppose John never was nervous in his life. He laughs at me so about this wall-paper!

At first he meant to repaper the room, but afterwards he said that I was letting it get the better of me, and that nothing was worse for a nervous patient than to give way to such fancies.

He said that after the wall-paper was changed it would be the heavy bedstead, and then the barred windows, and then that gate at the head of the stairs, and so on.

"You know the place is doing you good," he said, "and really, dear, I don't care to renovate the house just for a three months' rental."

"Then do let us go downstairs," I said, "there are such pretty rooms   *55*
there."

Then he took me in his arms and called me a blessed little goose, and said he would go down cellar, if I wished, and have it whitewashed into the bargain.

But he is right enough about the beds and windows and things.

It is an airy and comfortable room as any one need wish, and, of course, I would not be so silly as to make him uncomfortable just for a whim.

I'm really getting quite fond of the big room, all but that horrid paper.

Out of one window I can see the garden, those mysterious deep-shaded   *60*
arbors, the riotous old-fashioned flowers, and bushes and gnarly trees.

Out of another I get a lovely view of the bay and a little private wharf belonging to the estate. There is a beautiful shaded lane that runs down there from the house. I always fancy I see people walking in these numerous paths and arbors, but John has cautioned me not to give way to fancy in the least. He says that with my imaginative power and habit of story-making, a nervous weakness like mine is sure to lead to all manner of excited fancies, and that I ought to use my will and good sense to check the tendency. So I try.

I think sometimes that if I were only well enough to write a little it would relieve the press of ideas and rest me.

But I find I get pretty tired when I try.

It is so discouraging not to have any advice and companionship about my work. When I get really well, John says we will ask Cousin Henry and Julia down for a long visit; but he says he would as soon put fireworks in my pillow-case as to let me have those stimulating people about now.

I wish I could get well faster.   *65*

But I must not think about that. This paper looks to me as if it *knew* what a vicious influence it had!

There is a recurrent spot where the pattern lolls like a broken neck and two bulbous eyes stare at you upside down.

I get positively angry with the impertinence of it and the everlastingness. Up and down and sideways they crawl, and those absurd, unblinking eyes are everywhere. There is one place where two breadths didn't match, and the eyes go all up and down the line, one a little higher than the other.

I never saw so much expression in an inanimate thing before, and we all know how much expression they have! I used to lie awake as a child and get more entertainment and terror out of blank walls and plain furniture than most children could find in a toy-store.

I remember what a kindly wink the knobs of our big, old bureau used 70 to have, and there was one chair that always seemed like a strong friend.

I used to feel that if any of the other things looked too fierce I could always hop into that chair and be safe.

The furniture in this room is no worse than inharmonious, however, for we had to bring it all from downstairs. I suppose, when this was used as a playroom they had to take the nursery things out, and no wonder! I never saw such ravages as the children have made here.

The wall-paper, as I said before, is torn off in spots, and it sticketh closer than a brother—they must have had perseverance as well as hatred.

Then the floor is scratched and gouged and splintered, the plaster itself is dug out here and there, and this great heavy bed which is all we found in the room, looks as if it had been through the wars.

But I don't mind it a bit—only the paper. 75

There comes John's sister. Such a dear girl as she is, and so careful of me! I must not let her find me writing.

She is a perfect and enthusiastic housekeeper, and hopes for no better profession. I verily believe she thinks it is the writing which made me sick!

But I can write when she is out, and see her a long way off from these windows.

There is one that commands the road, a lovely shaded winding road, and one that just looks off over the country. A lovely country, too, full of great elms and velvet meadows.

This wall-paper has a kind of sub-pattern in a different shade, a particu- 80 larly irritating one, for you can only see it in certain lights, and not clearly then.

But in the places where it isn't faded and where the sun is just so—I can see a strange, provoking, formless sort of figure, that seems to skulk about behind that silly and conspicuous front design.

There's sister on the stairs!

Well, the Fourth of July is over! The people are all gone and I am tired out. John thought it might do me good to see a little company, so we just had mother and Nellie and the children down for a week.

Of course I didn't do a thing, Jennie sees to everything now.

But it tired me all the same. 85

John says if I don't pick up faster he shall send me to Weir Mitchell° in the fall.

Weir Mitchell: Silas Weir Mitchell (1829–1914), a Philadelphia neurologist-psychologist who introduced the "rest cure" for nervous diseases

But I don't want to go there at all. I had a friend who was in his hands once, and she says he is just like John and my brother, only more so!

Besides, it is such an undertaking to go so far.

I don't feel as if it was worth while to turn my hand over for anything, and I'm getting dreadfully fretful and querulous.

I cry at nothing, and cry most of the time.   *90*

Of course I don't when John is here, or anybody else, but when I am alone.

And I am alone a good deal just now. John is kept in town very often by serious cases, and Jennie is good and lets me alone when I want her to.

So I walk a little in the garden or down that lovely lane, sit on the porch under the roses, and lie down up here a good deal.

I'm getting really fond of the room in spite of the wall-paper. Perhaps *because* of the wall-paper.

It dwells in my mind so!   *95*

I lie here on this great immovable bed—it is nailed down, I believe—and follow that pattern about by the hour. It is as good as gymnastics, I assure you. I start, we'll say, at the bottom, down in the corner over there where it has not been touched, and I determine for the thousandth time that I *will* follow that pointless pattern to some sort of conclusion.

I know a little of the principle of design, and I know this thing was not arranged on any laws of radiation, or alternation, or repetition, or symmetry, or anything else that I ever heard of.

It is repeated, of course, by the breadths, but not otherwise.

Looked at in one way each breadth stands alone, the bloated curves and flourishes—a kind of "debased Romanesque" with *delirium tremens*° go waddling up and down in isolated columns of fatuity.

But, on the other hand, they connect diagonally, and the sprawling out-   *100* lines run off in great slanting waves of optic horror, like a lot of wallowing seaweeds in full chase.

The whole thing goes horizontally, too, at least it seems so, and I exhaust myself in trying to distinguish the order of its going in that direction.

They have used a horizontal breadth for a frieze, and that adds wonderfully to the confusion.

There is one end of the room where it is almost intact, and there, when the crosslights fade and the low sun shines directly upon it, I can almost fancy radiation after all,—the interminable grotesques seem to form around a common center and rush off in headlong plunges of equal distraction.

It makes me tired to follow it. I will take a nap I guess.

I don't know why I should write this.   *105*

I don't want to.

I don't feel able.

---

delirium tremens: mental confusion caused by alcohol poisoning and characterized by physical tremors and hallucinations

And I know John would think it absurd. But I *must* say what I feel and think in some way—it is such a relief!

But the effort is getting to be greater than the relief.

Half the time now I am awfully lazy, and lie down ever so much.   110

John says I mustn't lose my strength, and has me take cod liver oil and lots of tonics and things, to say nothing of ale and wine and rare meat.

Dear John! He loves me very dearly, and hates to have me sick. I tried to have a real earnest reasonable talk with him the other day, and tell him how I wish he would let me go and make a visit to Cousin Henry and Julia.

But he said I wasn't able to go, nor able to stand it after I got there; and I did not make out a very good case for myself, for I was crying before I had finished.

It is getting to be a great effort for me to think straight. Just this nervous weakness I suppose.

And dear John gathered me up in his arms, and just carried me upstairs   115
and laid me on the bed, and sat by me and read to me till it tired my head.

He said I was his darling and his comfort and all he had, and that I must take care of myself for his sake, and keep well.

He says no one but myself can help me out of it, that I must use my will and self-control and not let any silly fancies run away with me.

There's one comfort, the baby is well and happy, and does not have to occupy this nursery with the horrid wall-paper.

If we had not used it, that blessed child would have! What a fortunate escape! Why, I wouldn't have a child of mine, an impressionable little thing, live in such a room for worlds.

I never thought of it before, but it is lucky that John kept me here after   120
all, I can stand it so much easier than a baby, you see.

Of course I never mention it to them any more—I am too wise,—but I keep watch of it all the same.

There are things in that paper that nobody knows but me, or ever will.

Behind that outside pattern the dim shapes get clearer every day.

It is always the same shape, only very numerous.

And it is like a woman stooping down and creeping about behind that   125
pattern. I don't like it a bit. I wonder—I begin to think—I wish John would take me away from here!

It is so hard to talk with John about my case, because he is so wise, and because he loves me so.

But I tried it last night.

It was moonlight. The moon shines in all around just as the sun does.

I hate to see it sometimes, it creeps so slowly, and always comes in by one window or another.

John was asleep and I hated to waken him, so I kept still and watched   130
the moonlight on that undulating wall-paper till I felt creepy.

The faint figure behind seemed to shake the pattern, just as if she wanted to get out.

I got up softly and went to feel and see if the paper *did* move, and when I came back John was awake.

"What is it, little girl?" he said. "Don't go walking about like that— you'll get cold."

I thought it was a good time to talk, so I told him that I really was not gaining here, and that I wished he would take me away.

"Why, darling!" said he, "our lease will be up in three weeks, and I can't see how to leave before.   *135*

"The repairs are not done at home, and I cannot possibly leave town just now. Of course if you were in any danger, I could and would, but you really are better, dear, whether you can see it or not. I am a doctor, dear, and I know. You are gaining flesh and color, your appetite is better, I feel really much easier about you."

"I don't weigh a bit more," said I, "nor as much; and my appetite may be better in the evening when you are here, but it is worse in the morning when you are away!"

"Bless her little heart!" said he with a big hug, "she shall be as sick as she pleases! But now let's improve the shining hours by going to sleep, and talk about it in the morning!"

"And you won't go away?" I asked gloomily.

"Why, how can I, dear? It is only three weeks more and then we will   *140* take a nice little trip of a few days while Jennie is getting the house ready. Really dear you are better!"

"Better in body perhaps—" I began, and stopped short, for he sat up straight and looked at me with such a stern, reproachful look that I could not say another word.

"My darling," said he, "I beg of you, for my sake and for our child's sake, as well as for your own, that you will never for one instant let that idea enter your mind! There is nothing so dangerous, so fascinating, to a temperament like yours. It is a false and foolish fancy. Can you not trust me as a physician when I tell you so?"

So of course I said no more on that score, and we went to sleep before long. He thought I was asleep first, but I wasn't, and lay there for hours trying to decide whether that front pattern and the back pattern really did move together or separately.

On a pattern like this, by daylight, there is a lack of sequence, a defiance of law, that is a constant irritant to a normal mind.

The color is hideous enough, and unreliable enough, and infuriating   *145* enough, but the pattern is torturing.

You think you have mastered it, but just as you get well underway in following, it turns back-somersault and there you are. It slaps you in the face, knocks you down, and tramples upon you. It is like a bad dream.

The outside pattern is a florid arabesque, reminding one of a fungus. If you can imagine a toadstool in joints, an interminable string of toadstools, budding and sprouting in endless convolutions—why, that is something like it.

That is, sometimes!

There is one marked peculiarity about this paper, a thing nobody seems to notice but myself, and that is that it changes as the light changes.

When the sun shoots in through the east window—I always watch for that first long, straight ray—it changes so quickly that I never can quite believe it.

That is why I watch it always.

By moonlight—the moon shines in all night when there is a moon—I wouldn't know it was the same paper.

At night in any kind of light, in twilight, candlelight, lamplight, and worst of all by moonlight, it becomes bars! The outside pattern I mean, and the woman behind it is as plain as can be.

I didn't realize for a long time what the thing was that showed behind, that dim sub-pattern, but now I am quite sure it is a woman.

By daylight she is subdued, quiet. I fancy it is the pattern that keeps her so still. It is so puzzling. It keeps me quiet by the hour.

I lie down ever so much now. John says it is good for me, and to sleep all I can.

Indeed he started the habit by making me lie down for an hour after each meal.

It is a very bad habit I am convinced, for you see I don't sleep.

And that cultivates deceit, for I don't tell them I'm awake—O no!

The fact is I am getting a little afraid of John.

He seems very queer sometimes, and even Jennie has an inexplicable look.

It strikes me occasionally, just as a scientific hypothesis,—that perhaps it is the paper!

I have watched John when he did not know I was looking, and come into the room suddenly on the most innocent excuses, and I've caught him several times *looking at the paper!* And Jennie too. I caught Jennie with her hand on it once.

She didn't know I was in the room, and when I asked her in a quiet, a very quiet voice, with the most restrained manner possible, what she was doing with the paper—she turned around as if she had been caught stealing, and looked quite angry—asked me why I should frighten her so!

Then she said that the paper stained everything it touched, that she had found yellow smooches on all my clothes and John's, and she wished we would be more careful!

Did not that sound innocent? But I know she was studying that pattern, and I am determined that nobody shall find it out but myself!

Life is very much more exciting now than it used to be. You see I have something more to expect, to look forward to, to watch. I really do eat better, and am more quiet than I was.

John is so pleased to see me improve! He laughed a little the other day, and said I seemed to be flourishing in spite of my wall-paper.

I turned it off with a laugh. I had no intention of telling him it was *because* of the wall-paper—he would make fun of me. He might even want to take me away.

I don't want to leave now until I have found it out. There is a week   *170* more, and I think that will be enough.

I'm feeling ever so much better! I don't sleep much at night, for it is so interesting to watch developments; but I sleep a good deal in the daytime.

In the daytime it is tiresome and perplexing.

There are always new shoots on the fungus, and new shades of yellow all over it. I cannot keep count of them, though I have tried conscientiously.

It is the strangest yellow, that wall-paper! It makes me think of all the yellow things I ever saw—not beautiful ones like buttercups, but old foul, bad yellow things.

But there is something else about that paper—the smell! I noticed it the   *175* moment we came into the room, but with so much air and sun it was not bad. Now we have had a week of fog and rain, and whether the windows are open or not, the smell is here.

It creeps all over the house.

I find it hovering in the dining-room, skulking in the parlor, hiding in the hall, lying in wait for me on the stairs.

It gets into my hair.

Even when I go to ride, if I turn my head suddenly and surprise it—there is that smell!

Such a peculiar odor, too! I have spent hours in trying to analyze it, to   *180* find what it smelled like.

It is not bad—at first, and very gentle, but quite the subtlest, most enduring odor I ever met.

In this damp weather it is awful, I wake up in the night and find it hanging over me.

It used to disturb me at first. I thought seriously of burning the house—to reach the smell.

But now I am used to it. The only thing I can think of that it is like is the *color* of the paper! A yellow smell.

There is a very funny mark on this wall, low down, near the mopboard.   *185* A streak that runs round the room. It goes behind every piece of furniture, except the bed, a long, straight, even *smooch,* as if it had been rubbed over and over.

I wonder how it was done and who did it, and what they did it for, Round and round and round—round and round and round!—it makes me dizzy!

I really have discovered something at last.

Through watching so much at night, when it changes so, I have finally found out.

The front pattern *does* move—and no wonder! The woman behind shakes it!

Sometimes I think there are a great many women behind, and sometimes only one, and she crawls around fast, and her crawling shakes it all over.

Then in the very bright spots she keeps still, and in the very shady spots she just takes hold of the bars and shakes them hard.

And she is all the time trying to climb through. But nobody could climb through that pattern—it strangles so; I think that is why it has so many heads.

They get through, and then the pattern strangles them off and turns them upside down, and makes their eyes white!

If those heads were covered or taken off it would not be half so bad.

I think that woman gets out in the daytime!

And I'll tell you why—privately—I've seen her!

I can see her out of every one of my windows!

It is the same woman, I know, for she is always creeping, and most women do not creep by daylight.

I see her in that long shaded lane, creeping up and down. I see her in those dark grape arbors, creeping all around the garden.

I see her on that long road under the trees, creeping along, and when a carriage comes she hides under the blackberry vines.

I don't blame her a bit. It must be very humiliating to be caught creeping by daylight!

I always lock the door when I creep by daylight. I can't do it at night, for I know John would suspect something at once.

And John is so queer now, that I don't want to irritate him. I wish he would take another room! Besides, I don't want anybody to get that woman out at night but myself.

I often wonder if I could see her out of all the windows at once.

But, turn as fast as I can, I can only see out of one at one time.

And though I always see her, she *may* be able to creep faster than I can turn!

I have watched her sometimes away off in the open country, creeping as fast as a cloud shadow in a high wind.

If only that top pattern could be gotten off from the under one! I mean to try it, little by little.

I have found out another funny thing, but I shan't tell it this time! It does not do to trust people too much.

There are only two more days to get this paper off, and I believe John is beginning to notice. I don't like the look in his eyes.

And I heard him ask Jennie a lot of professional questions about me. She had a very good report to give.

She said I slept a good deal in the daytime.

John knows I don't sleep very well at night, for all I'm so quiet!

He asked me all sorts of questions, too, and pretended to be very loving and kind.

As if I couldn't see through him!   215

Still, I don't wonder he acts so, sleeping under this paper for three months.

It only interests me, but I feel sure John and Jennie are secretly affected by it.

Hurrah! This is the last day, but it is enough. John to stay in town over night, and won't be out until this evening.

Jennie wanted to sleep with me—the sly thing! But I told her I should undoubtedly rest better for a night all alone.

That was clever, for really I wasn't alone a bit! As soon as it was moon-   220
light and that poor thing began to crawl and shake the pattern, I got up and ran to help her.

I pulled and she shook, I shook and she pulled, and before morning we had peeled off yards of that paper.

A strip about as high as my head and half around the room.

And then when the sun came and that awful pattern began to laugh at me, I declared I would finish it to-day!

We go away to-morrow, and they are moving all my furniture down again to leave things as they were before.

Jennie looked at the wall in amazement, but I told her merrily that I did   225
it out of pure spite at the vicious thing.

She laughed and said she wouldn't mind doing it herself, but I must not get tired.

How she betrayed herself that time!

But I am here, and no person touches this paper but me,—not *alive!*

She tried to get me out of the room—it was too patent! But I said it was so quiet and empty and clean now that I believed I would lie down again and sleep all I could; and not to wake me even for dinner—I would call when I woke.

So now she is gone, and the servants are gone, and the things are gone,   230
and there is nothing left but that great bedstead nailed down, with the canvas mattress we found on it.

We shall sleep downstairs to-night, and take the boat home to-morrow.

I quite enjoy the room, now it is bare again.

How those children did tear about here!

This bedstead is fairly gnawed!

But I must get to work.   235

I have locked the door and thrown the key down into the front path.

I don't want to go out, and I don't want to have anybody come in, till John comes.

I want to astonish him.

I've got a rope up here that even Jennie did not find. If that woman does get out, and tries to get away, I can tie her!

But I forgot I could not reach far without anything to stand on! 240

This bed will *not* move!

I tried to lift and push it until I was lame, and then I got so angry I bit off a little piece at one corner—but it hurt my teeth.

Then I peeled off all the paper I could reach standing on the floor. It sticks horribly and the pattern just enjoys it! All those strangled heads and bulbous eyes and waddling fungus growths just shriek with derision!

I am getting angry enough to do something desperate. To jump out of the window would be admirable exercise, but the bars are too strong even to try.

Besides I wouldn't do it. Of course not. I know well enough that a step 245 like that is improper and might be misconstrued.

I don't like to *look* out of the windows even—there are so many of those creeping women, and they creep so fast.

I wonder if they all come out of that wall-paper as I did?

But I am securely fastened now by my well-hidden rope—you don't get *me* out in the road there!

I suppose I shall have to get back behind the pattern when it comes night, and that is hard!

It is so pleasant to be out in this great room and creep around as I please! 250

I don't want to go outside. I won't, even if Jennie asks me to.

For outside you have to creep on the ground, and everything is green instead of yellow.

But here I can creep smoothly on the floor, and my shoulder just fits in that long smooch around the wall, so I cannot lose my way.

Why there's John at the door!

It is no use, young man, you can't open it! 255

How he does call and pound!

Now he's crying for an axe.

It would be a shame to break down that beautiful door!

"John dear!" said I in the gentlest voice, "the key is down by the front steps, under a plaintain leaf!"

That silenced him for a few moments. 260

Then he said—very quietly indeed. "Open the door, my darling!"

"I can't," said I. "The key is down by the front door under a plaintain leaf!"

And then I said it again, several times, very gently and slowly, and said it so often that he had to go and see, and he got it of course, and came in. He stopped short by the door.

"What is the matter?" he cried. "For God's sake, what are you doing!"

I kept on creeping just the same, but I looked at him over my shoulder. 265

"I've got out at last," said I, "in spite of you and Jane. And I've pulled off most of the paper, so you can't put me back!"

Now why should that man have fainted? But he did, and right across my path by the wall, so that I had to creep over him every time!

THE LOVE SONG OF
J. ALFRED PRUFROCK

T. S. Eliot

S'io credessi che mia risposta fosse
A persona che mai tornasse al mondo,
Questa fiamma staria senza più scosse.
Ma perciocchè giammai di questo fondo
Non tornò vivo alcun, s'i'odo il vero,
Senza tema d'infamia ti rispondo.°

    Let us go then, you and I,
When the evening is spread out against the sky
Like a patient etherized upon a table;
Let us go, through certain half-deserted streets,
The muttering retreats   5
Of restless nights in one-night cheap hotels
And sawdust restaurants with oyster-shells:
Streets that follow like a tedious argument
Of insidious intent
To lead you to an overwhelming question . . .   10

Oh, do not ask, "What is it?"
Let us go and make our visit.

In the room the women come and go
Talking of Michelangelo.

    The yellow fog that rubs its back upon the window panes,   15
The yellow smoke that rubs its muzzle on the window panes
Licked its tongue into the corners of the evening,
Lingered upon the pools that stand in drains,
Let fall upon its back the soot that falls from chimneys,
Slipped by the terrace, made a sudden leap,   20
And seeing that it was a soft October night,
Curled once about the house, and fell asleep.

S'io credessi . . . rispondo: Dante's *Inferno,* XXVII, 58–63. In the Eighth Chasm of the Inferno,
Dante and Virgil meet Guido da Montefeltro, one of the False Counselors, who is punished
by being enveloped in an eternal flame. When Dante asks Guido to tell his life story, the spirit
replies: "If I thought that my answer were to one who might ever return to the world, this
flame would shake no more; but since from this depth none ever returned alive, if what I hear
is true, I answer you without fear of infamy."

And indeed there will be time°
For the yellow smoke that slides along the street,
Rubbing its back upon the window panes;   25
There will be time, there will be time
To prepare a face to meet the faces that you meet;
There will be time to murder and create,
And time for all the works and days° of hands
That lift and drop a question on your plate: 30
Time for you and time for me,
And time yet for a hundred indecisions,
And for a hundred visions and revisions,
Before the taking of a toast and tea.

In the room the women come and go   35
Talking of Michelangelo.

And indeed there will be time
To wonder, "Do I dare?" and, "Do I dare?"—
Time to turn back and descend the stair,
With a bald spot in the middle of my hair—   40
(They will say: "How his hair is growing thin!")
My morning coat, my collar mounting firmly to the chin,
My necktie rich and modest, but asserted by a simple pin—
(They will say: "But how his arms and legs are thin!")
Do I dare   45
Disturb the universe?
In a minute there is time
For decisions and revisions which a minute will reverse.

For I have known them already, known them all:
Have known the evenings, mornings, afternoons,   50
I have measured out my life with coffee spoons;
I know the voices dying with a dying fall
Beneath the music from a farther room.
So how should I presume?

And I have known the eyes already, known them all—   55
The eyes that fix you in a formulated phrase.
And when I am formulated, sprawling on a pin,
When I am pinned and wriggling on the wall,
Then how should I begin
To spit out all the butt-ends of my days and ways?   60
And how should I presume?

---

23. *there will be time:* an allusion to Ecclesiastes 3:1–8: "To everything there is a season, and
a time to every purpose under heaven . . ."
29. *works and days:* Hesiod's eighth century B.C. poem *Works and Days* gave practical advice
on how to conduct one's life in accordance with the seasons.

And I have known the arms already, known them all—
Arms that are braceleted and white and bare
(But in the lamplight, downed with light brown hair!)
   Is it perfume from a dress   65
   That makes me so digress?
Arms that lie along a table, or wrap about a shawl.
   And should I then presume?
     And how should I begin?

          · · · · ·

   Shall I say, I have gone at dusk through narrow streets,   70
And watched the smoke that rises from the pipes
Of lonely men in shirtsleeves, leaning out of windows? . . .

I should have been a pair of ragged claws,
Scuttling across the floor of silent seas.

          · · · · ·

   And the afternoon, the evening, sleeps so peacefully!   75
Smoothed by long fingers,
Asleep . . . tired . . . or it malingers,
Stretched on the floor, here beside you and me.
Should I, after tea and cakes and ices,
Have the strength to force the moment to its crisis?   80
But though I have wept and fasted, wept and prayed,
Though I have seen my head (grown slightly bald) brought in upon
   a platter,°
I am no prophet—and here's no great matter;
I have seen the moment of my greatness flicker,
And I have seen the eternal Footman hold my coat, and snicker,   85
   And in short, I was afraid.

   And would it have been worth it, after all,
After the cups, the marmalade, the tea,
Among the porcelain, among some talk of you and me,
Would it have been worth while   90
To have bitten off the matter with a smile,
To have squeezed the universe into a ball°
To roll it toward some overwhelming question,
To say: "I am Lazarus,° come from the dead,

---

82. *head . . . upon a platter:* At Salome's request, Herod had John the Baptist decapitated and
had the severed head delivered to her on a platter (see Matt. 14:1–12 and Mark 6:17–29).
92. *squeezed the universe into a ball:* See Marvell's "To His Coy Mistress," lines 41–42: "Let
us roll all our strength and all / Our sweetness up into one ball."
94. *Lazarus:* The brother of Mary and Martha who was raised from the dead by Jesus (John
11:1–44). In Luke 16:19–31, a rich man asks that another Lazarus return from the dead to
warn the living about their treatment of the poor.

Come back to tell you all, I shall tell you all"—   95
If one, settling a pillow by her head,
    Should say: "That is not what I meant at all;
        That is not it, at all."

  And would it have been worth it, after all,
Would it have been worth while,   100
After the sunsets and the dooryards and the sprinkled streets,
After the novels, after the teacups, after the skirts that trail along the
        floor—
And this, and so much more?—
It is impossible to say just what I mean!
But as if a magic lantern threw the nerves in patterns on a screen: 105
Would it have been worth while
If one, settling a pillow or throwing off a shawl,
And turning toward the window, should say: "That is not it at all,
        That is not what I meant, at all."   110
                        . . . . .

    No! I am not Prince Hamlet, nor was meant to be;
Am an attendant lord,° one that will do
To swell a progress,° start a scene or two
Advise the prince: withal, an easy tool,
Deferential, glad to be of use,   115
Politic, cautious, and meticulous;
Full of high sentence, but a bit obtuse;
At times, indeed, almost ridiculous—
Almost, at times, the Fool.

I grow old . . . I grow old . . .   120
I shall wear the bottoms of my trowsers rolled.

    Shall I part my hair behind? Do I dare to eat a peach?
I shall wear white flannel trowsers, and walk upon the beach.
I have heard the mermaids singing, each to each.
I do not think that they will sing to me.   125

I have seen them riding seaward on the waves,
Combing the white hair of the waves blown back
When the wind blows the water white and black.

We have lingered in the chambers of the sea
By seagirls wreathed with seaweed red and brown,   130
Till human voices wake us, and we drown.

---

112. *attendant lord:* like Polonius in Shakespeare's *Hamlet*
113. *progress:* state procession

THE FLEA

John Donne

Mark but this flea, and mark in this°
How little that which thou deny'st me is;
It sucked me first, and now sucks thee,
And in this flea our two bloods mingled be;
Thou know'st that this cannot be said   5
A sin, nor shame, nor loss of maidenhead,°
    Yet this enjoys before it woo,
    And pampered swells with one blood made of two,
    And this, alas, is more than we would do.°

Oh stay, three lives in one flea spare,   10
Where we almost, yea more than, married are.
This flea is you and I, and this
Our marriage bed, and marriage temple is;
Though parents grudge, and you, we're met
And cloistered in these living walls of jet.   15
    Though use° make you apt to kill me,
    Let not to that, self-murder added be,
    And sacrilege, three sins in killing three.

Cruel and sudden, hast thou since
Purpled thy nail in blood of innocence?   20
Wherein could this flea guilty be,
Except in that drop which is sucked from thee?
Yet thou triumph'st, and say'st that thou
Find'st not thyself, nor me, the weaker now;
    'Tis true; then learn how false, fears be;   25
    Just so much honor, when thou yield'st to me,
    Will waste, as this flea's death took life from thee.

---

1. *mark in this:* take note of the moral lesson in this object
6. *maidenhead:* hymen
9. *more than we would do:* i.e., if we do not join our blood in conceiving a child
16. *use:* habit

THE ROAD NOT TAKEN

Robert Frost

Two roads diverged in a yellow wood,
And sorry I could not travel both
And be one traveler, long I stood
And looked down one as far as I could
To where it bent in the undergrowth;   5

Then took the other, as just as fair,
And having perhaps the better claim,
Because it was grassy and wanted wear;
Though as for that the passing there
Had worn them really about the same,   10

And both that morning equally lay
In leaves no step had trodden black.
Oh, I kept the first for another day!
Yet knowing how way leads on to way,
I doubted if I should ever come back.   15

I shall be telling this with a sigh
Somewhere ages and ages hence:
Two roads diverged in a wood, and I—
I took the one less traveled by,
And that has made all the difference.   20

THE FISH

Elizabeth Bishop

I caught a tremendous fish
and held him beside the boat
half out of water, with my hook
fast in a corner of his mouth.
He didn't fight.   5
He hadn't fought at all.
He hung a grunting weight,
battered and venerable
and homely. Here and there

his brown skin hung in strips   10
like ancient wallpaper,
and its pattern of darker brown
was like wallpaper:
shapes like full-blown roses
stained and lost through age.   15
He was speckled with barnacles,
fine rosettes of lime,
and infested
with tiny white sea-lice,
and underneath two or three   20
rags of green weed hung down.
While his gills were breathing in
the terrible oxygen
—the frightening gills,
fresh and crisp with blood,   25
that can cut so badly—
I thought of the coarse white flesh
packed in like feathers,
the big bones and the little bones,
the dramatic reds and blacks   30
of his shiny entrails,
and the pink swim-bladder
like a big peony.
I looked into his eyes
which were far larger than mine   35
but shallower, and yellowed,
the irises backed and packed
with tarnished tinfoil
seen through the lenses
of old scratched isinglass.°   40
They shifted a little, but not
to return my stare.
—It was more like the tipping
of an object toward the light.
I admired his sullen face,   45
the mechanism of his jaw,
and then I saw
that from his lower lip
—if you could call it a lip—
grim, wet, and weaponlike,   50
hung five old pieces of fish-line,
or four and a wire leader

---

40. *isinglass:* mica

with the swivel still attached,
with all their five big hooks
grown firmly in his mouth.   55
A green line, frayed at the end
where he broke it, two heavier lines,
and a fine black thread
still crimped from the strain and snap
when it broke and he got away.   60
Like medals with their ribbons
frayed and wavering,
a five-haired beard of wisdom
trailing from his aching jaw.
I stared and stared   65
and victory filled up
the little rented boat,
from the pool of bilge
where oil had spread a rainbow
around the rusted engine   70
to the bailer rusted orange,
the sun-cracked thwarts,
the oarlocks on their strings,
the gunnels—until everything
was rainbow, rainbow, rainbow!   75
And I let the fish go.

DULCE ET DECORUM EST°

Wilfred Owen

Bent double, like old beggars under sacks,
Knock-kneed, coughing like hags, we cursed through sludge,
Till on the haunting flares we turned our backs
And towards our distant rest began to trudge.
Men marched asleep. Many had lost their boots   5
But limped on, blood-shod. All went lame; all blind;
Drunk with fatigue; deaf even to the hoots
Of tired, outstripped Five-Nines that dropped behind.

Gas! GAS! Quick, boys!—An ecstasy of fumbling,
Fitting the clumsy helmets just in time;   10
But someone still was yelling out and stumbling,

Title. *Dulce et decorum est pro patria mori:* Latin, "It is sweet and fitting to die for one's country."

And flound'ring like a man in fire or lime . . .
Dim, through the misty panes and thick green light,
As under a green sea, I saw him drowning.

In all my dreams, before my helpless sight,   15
He plunges at me, guttering, choking, drowning.

If in some smothering dreams you too could pace
Behind the wagon that we flung him in,
And watch the white eyes writhing in his face,
His hanging face, like a devil's sick of sin;   20
If you could hear, at every jolt, the blood
Come gargling from the froth-corrupted lungs,
Obscene as cancer, bitter as the cud
Of vile, incurable sores on innocent tongues,—
My friend, you would not tell with such high zest   25
To children ardent for some desperate glory,
The old Lie: Dulce et decorum est
Pro patria mori.

12

Describing a Process: Showing Your Reader How Something Is Done

Duckling Rouennaise

Unless you choke your duck, pluck the down on its breast immediately afterward and cook it within 24 hours, you cannot lay claim to having produced an authentic Rouen duck. The first two steps assure the dark red flesh and the special flavor of this dish. If, as is likely, duck-strangling will bring you into local disrepute, you may waive the sturdy peasant preliminaries and serve a modified version. . . .

Clean:
> A duckling

reserving the liver. Free it from the gall. Tuck the liver into the body cavity. Use a spit or rotisserie to roast the duck only 20 to 22 minutes in all. Only the breast and the legs, if tender, are reserved and kept warm. The rest of the carcass is pressed. . . .

Meanwhile melt:
> 2 tablespoons butter

When the fat reaches the point of fragrance, add and simmer:
> 1 finely minced onion
> 3/4 cup Burgundy

When the duckling is done, remove and crush the liver and add to the reduced wine mixture. Poach it gently in the wine with the drippings from the pressed carcass. Add several tablespoons of:
> Paté de Foie de Volaille
> Season to taste

Slice the breast lengthwise into about 20 thin strips and put them in a chafing dish. Should you want to serve the legs, they must at this point be removed and grilled, as they are too raw without further cooking.

We prefer to utilize them later in some other dish, so the breast can be served "*à point.*"°

Cover the sliced meat quickly with the hot liver sauce and serve immediately from the chafing dish at table.

When you describe a process, you take an activity that you want your audience to know about and break it down into its component parts, showing how the parts connect with each other in a logical sequence. A recipe—such as this one from Rombauer and Becker's *The Joy of Cooking*—is one of the simplest and most familiar forms of describing a process.

When you look at your first draft, you might find that it suggests that your dominant idea will be best served if your audience learns how to undertake a process or how a process occurs. In the first case, you write a set of directions, speaking directly or indirectly to the audience in the second person ("you"). You can find examples of this sort of writing posted in restaurants or by swimming pools, where people need to know how to do the Heimlich maneuver or how to give cardiopulmonary resuscitation. You'll find this sort of process description written in the plainest possible way, in the simplest possible language. When you choose to write the description of a process with the aim of showing your readers how to do something important, it is likely that you don't want to direct their attention to your language or your imagery.

You might discover that your draft suggests that you write a process description that explains a process to your audience as a way of supporting or clarifying your dominant idea. This use of process description generally speaks to the audience in the third person ("he," "she," or "they"). Such an approach does not propose to tell your reader how to do something but tells him or her how something will be, is being, or has been done by other people. Because such a description is linked to a dominant idea that is probably meant to engage the readers' interest and create or speak to their emotions and thoughts, imagery and the sort of language a writer chooses to create a response in his or her readers become an important issue.

For example, you might decide to write about how a local landfill is being turned into an ecological hazard, and so you decide to describe how the company that owns the landfill disposes of hazardous materials. But because you probably intend to move your audience to take action against the process, you might consider using imagery and examples that will move your audience in the direction you intend.

When you ask your reader to examine a process, you may find yourself first either identifying that process as part of a larger class of processes or contrasting it with similar processes. In the first case, showing how the process you've chosen to describe "fits in" with a larger process might

---

à point: French for "rare"

strengthen your dominant idea. For example, in writing about "hell week" in a fraternity or sorority initiation, you might find yourself placing that period in the larger process of being a pledge. This organizational approach is called *classification,* and it is discussed in Chapter 14. In another writing situation, you might find that your dominant idea becomes clearer when you distinguish your process from similar procedures. For example, studying for a literature exam and studying for a statistics exam might appear similar on the surface, but it might be important for you to make the differences apparent to your reader so that you can make your dominant idea as clear as possible. If you should choose to write a paper on the disposal of hazardous materials, you might find that you need to show your reader that this sort of disposal is in a different class than the disposal of household garbage. This organizational strategy is called *comparison and contrast;* it is the subject of Chapter 13.

In addition, because describing a process commits you to presenting the parts of that process to your audience, you almost always have to make sense of those parts by showing their relation to each other and to the sequence in which they occur. That means that the analysis of a process is also narration. Of course, since a process happens someplace and depends upon certain objects to complete itself, you usually have to describe the necessary materials as well as the relevant surroundings. Often you will find that description is a part of analyzing a process.

Working with the Readings

Read the following selections and, alone or with your group, answer the questions that follow each one.

NAMING OF PARTS

Henry Reed

To-day we have naming of parts. Yesterday,
We had daily cleaning. And to-morrow morning,
We shall have what to do after firing. But to-day,
To-day we have naming of parts. Japonica°
Glistens like coral in all of the neighboring gardens,   5
And to-day we have naming of parts.

Japonica: a tropical flower

This is the lower sling swivel. And this
Is the upper sling swivel, whose use you will see,
When you are given your slings. And this is the piling swivel,
Which in your case you have not got. The branches   10
Hold in the gardens their silent, eloquent gesture,
   Which in our case we have not got.

This is the safety catch, which is always released
With an easy flick of the thumb. And please do not let me
See anyone using his finger. You can do it quite easy   15
If you have any strength in your thumb. The blossoms
Are fragile and motionless, never letting anyone see
   Any of them using his finger.

And this you can see is the bolt. The purpose of this
Is to open the breech, as you see. We can slide it   20
Rapidly backwards and forwards: we call this
Easing the spring. And rapidly backwards and forwards
The early bees are assaulting and fumbling the flowers:
   They call it easing the Spring.

They call it easing the Spring: it is perfectly easy   25
If you have any strength in your thumb: like the bolt,
And the breech, and the cocking piece, and the point of balance,
Which in our case we have not got; and the almond-blossom
Silent in all of the gardens and the bees going backwards and forwards,
   For today we have naming of parts.   30

---

1. What is the situation in this poem? What exposition along the way does Reed give you to help you grasp the situation?

2. The events in this poem take place in a setting. What descriptive material does the author give you to help you visualize the setting? What relevance does the descriptive material have to the author's dominant idea?

3. How many points of view are there in this poem? How many speakers? Can you define each point of view?

4. What process or processes are analyzed, and who is doing the analysis?

5. What does the author do to help you distinguish one process from another?

6. What are the differences between the processes? How does the author use single words to carry two meanings to show you these differences?

7. How does the difference between the processes and the way they are presented, as well as the background against which these processes are set, lead you to a dominant idea?

A FEW WORDS ABOUT BREASTS: SHAPING UP ABSURD

Nora Ephron

[handwritten: → neither male or female]

   I have to begin with a few words about androgyny. In grammar school, in the fifth and sixth grades, we were all tyrannized by a rigid set of rules that supposedly determined whether we were boys or girls. The episode in *Huckleberry Finn* where Huck is disguised as a girl and gives himself away by the way he threads a needle and catches a ball—that kind of thing. We learned that the way you sat, crossed your legs, held a cigarette and looked at your nails, your wristwatch, the way you did these things instinctively was absolute proof of your sex. Now obviously most children did not take this literally, but I did. I thought that just one slip, just one incorrect cross of my legs or flick of an imaginary cigarette ash would turn me from whatever I was into the other thing; that would be all it took, really. Even though I was outwardly a girl and had many of the trappings generally associated with the field of girldom—a girl's name, for example, and dresses, my own telephone, an autograph book—I spent the early years of my adolescence absolutely certain that I might at any point gum it up. I did not feel at all like a girl. I was boyish. I was athletic, ambitious, outspoken, competitive, noisy, rambunctious. I had scabs on my knees and my socks slid into my loafers and I could throw a football. I wanted desperately not to be that way, not to be a mixture of both things but instead just one, a girl, a definite indisputable girl. As soft and pink as a nursery. And nothing would do that for me, I felt, but breasts.

   I was about six months younger than everyone in my class, and so for about six months after it began, for six months after my friends had begun to develop—that was the word we used, develop—I was not particularly worried. I would sit in the bathtub and look down at my breasts and know that any day now, any second now, they would start growing like everyone else's. They didn't. "I want to buy a bra," I said to my mother one night. "What for?" she said. My mother was really hateful about bras, and by the time my third sister had gotten to the point where she was ready to want one, my mother had worked the whole business into a comedy routine. "Why not use a Band-Aid instead?" she would say. It was a source of great pride to my mother that she had never even had to wear a brassiere until she had her fourth child, and then only because her gynecologist made her. It was incomprehensible to me that anyone would ever be proud of something like that. It was the 1950s, for God's sake. Jane Russell. Cashmere sweaters. Couldn't my mother see that? *"I am too old to wear an undershirt."* Screaming. Weeping. Shouting. "Then don't wear an undershirt," said my mother. "But I want to buy a bra." "What for?"

I suppose that for most girls, breasts, brassieres, that entire thing, has more trauma, more to do with the coming of adolescence, of becoming a woman, than anything else. Certainly more than getting your period, although that too was traumatic, symbolic. But you could *see* breasts; they were there; they were visible. Whereas a girl could claim to have her period for months before she actually got it and nobody would ever know the difference. Which is exactly what I did. All you had to do was make a great fuss over having enough nickels for the Kotex machine and walk around clutching your stomach and moaning for three to five days a month about The Curse and you could convince anybody. There is a school of thought somewhere in the women's lib/women's mag/gynecology establishment that claims that menstrual cramps are purely psychological, and I lean toward it. Not that I didn't have them finally. Agonizing cramps, heating-pad cramps, go–down–to–the–school–nurse–and–lie–on–the–cot cramps. But unlike any pain I have ever suffered, I adored the pain of cramps, welcomed it, wallowed in it, bragged about it. "I can't go. I have cramps." "I can't do that. I have cramps." And most of all, gigglingly, blushingly: "I can't swim. I have cramps." Nobody ever used the hard-core word. Menstruation. God, what an awful word. Never that. "I have cramps."

The morning I first got my period, I went into my mother's bedroom to tell her. And my mother, my utterly-hateful-about-bras mother, burst into tears. It was really a lovely moment, and I remember it so clearly not just because it was one of the two times I ever saw my mother cry on my account (the other was when I was caught being a six-year-old kleptomaniac), but also because the incident did not mean to me what it meant to her. Her little girl, her firstborn, had finally become a woman. That was what she was crying about. My reaction to the event, however, was that I might well be a woman in some scientific, textbook sense (and could at least stop faking every month and stop wasting all those nickels). But in another sense—in a visible sense—I was as androgynous and as liable to tip over into boyhood as ever.

I started with a 28AA bra. I don't think they made them any smaller in those days, although I gather that now you can buy bras for five year olds that don't have any cups whatsoever in them; trainer bras they are called. My first brassiere came from Robinson's Department Store in Beverly Hills. I went there alone, shaking, positive they would look me over and smile and tell me to come back next year. An actual fitter took me into the dressing room and stood over me while I took off my blouse and tried the first one on. The little puffs stood out on my chest. "Lean over," said the fitter (to this day I am not sure what fitters in bra departments do except to tell you to lean over). I leaned over, with the fleeting hope that my breasts would miraculously fall out of my body and into the puffs. Nothing.

"Don't worry about it," said my friend Libby some months later, when things had not improved. "You'll get them after you're married."

"What are you talking about?" I said.

"When you get married," Libby explained, "your husband will touch your breasts and rub them and kiss them and they'll grow."

That was the killer. Necking I could deal with. Intercourse I could deal with. But it had never crossed my mind that a man was going to touch my breasts, that breasts had something to do with all that, petting, my God they never mentioned petting in my little sex manual about fertilization of the ovum. I became dizzy. For I knew instantly—as naïve as I had been only a moment before—that only part of what she was saying was true: the touching, rubbing, kissing part, not the growing part. And I knew that no one would ever want to marry me. I had no breasts. I would never have breasts.

My best friend in school was Diana Raskob. She lived a block from   *10* me in a house full of wonders. English muffins, for instance. The Raskobs were the first people in Beverly Hills to have English muffins for breakfast. They also had an apricot tree in the back, and a badminton court, and a subscription to *Seventeen* magazine, and hundreds of games like Sorry and Parcheesi and Treasure Hunt and Anagrams. Diana and I spent three or four afternoons a week in their den reading and playing and eating. Diana's mother's kitchen was full of the most colossal assortment of junk food I have ever been exposed to. My house was full of apples and peaches and milk and homemade chocolate-chip cookies—which were nice, and good for you, but-not-right-before-dinner-or-you'll-spoil-your-appetite. Diana's house had nothing in it that was good for you, and what's more, you could stuff it in right up until dinner and nobody cared. Bar-B-Q potato chips (they were the first in them, too), giant bottles of ginger ale, fresh popcorn with melted butter, hot fudge sauce on Baskin-Robbins jamoca ice cream, powdered-sugar doughnuts from Van de Kamps. Diana and I had been best friends since we were seven; we were about equally popular in school (which is to say, not particularly), we had about the same success with boys (extremely intermittent) and we looked much the same. Dark. Tall. Gangly.

It is September, just before school begins. I am eleven years old, about to enter the seventh grade, and Diana and I have not seen each other all summer. I have been to camp and she has been somewhere like Banff with her parents. We are meeting, as we often do, on the street midway between our two houses and we will walk back to Diana's and eat junk and talk about what has happened to each of us that summer. I am walking down Walden Drive in my jeans and my father's shirt hanging out and my old red loafers with the socks falling into them and coming toward me is . . . I take a deep breath . . . a young woman. Diana. Her hair is curled and she has a waist and hips and a bust and she is wearing a straight skirt, an article of clothing I have been repeatedly told that I will be unable to wear until I have the hips to hold it up. My jaw drops, and suddenly I am crying, crying hysterically, can't catch my breath sobbing. My best friend has betrayed me. She has gone ahead without me and done it. She has shaped up.

Here are some things I did to help:

Bought a Mark Eden Bust Developer.

Slept on my back for four years.

Splashed cold water on them every night because some French actress   15
said in *Life* magazine that that was what *she* did for her perfect bustline.

Ultimately, I resigned myself to a bad toss and began to wear padded bras. I think about them now, think about all those years in high school I went around in them, my three padded bras, every single one of them with different sized breasts. Each time I changed bras I changed sizes: one week nice perky but not too obtrusive breasts, the next medium-sized slightly pointed ones, the next week knockers, true knockers; all the time, whatever size I was, carrying around this rubberized appendage on my chest that occasionally crashed into a wall and was poked inward and had to be poked outward—I think about all that and wonder how anyone kept a straight face through it. My parents, who normally had no re-straints about needling me—why did they say nothing as they watched my chest go up and down? My friends, who would periodically inspect my breasts for signs of growth and reassure me—why didn't they at least counsel consistency?

And the bathing suits. I die when I think about the bathing suits. That was the era when you could lay an uninhabited bathing suit on the beach and someone would make a pass at it. I would put one on, an absurd swimsuit with its enormous bust built into it, the bones from the suit stabbing me in the rib cage and leaving little red welts on my body, and there I would be, my chest plunging straight downward absolutely vertically from my collarbone to the top of my suit and then suddenly, wham, out came all that padding and material and wiring absolutely horizontally.

Buster Klepper was the first boy who ever touched them. He was my boyfriend my senior year of high school. There is a picture of him in my high-school yearbook that makes him look quite attractive in a Jewish, horn-rimmed glasses sort of way, but the picture does not show the pimples, which were air-brushed out, or the dumbness. Well, that isn't really fair. He wasn't dumb. He just wasn't terribly bright. His mother refused to accept it, refused to accept the relentlessly average report cards, refused to deal with her son's inevitable destiny in some junior college or other. "He was tested," she would say to me, apropos of nothing, "and it came out 145. That's near-genius." Had the word underachiever been coined, she probably would have lobbed that one at me, too. Anyway, Buster was really very sweet—which is, I know, damning with faint praise, but there it is. I was the editor of the front page of the high-school newspaper and he was editor of the back page; we had to work together, side by side, in the print shop, and that was how it started. On our first date, we went to see *April Love* starring Pat Boone. Then we started going together. Buster had a green coupe, a 1950 Ford with an engine he had handchromed until it shone, dazzled, reflected the image of anyone who looked into it, anyone usually being Buster polishing it or the gas-station attendants he constantly asked to check the oil in order for them to be overwhelmed by the sparkle on the valves. The car also had a boot stretched over the back seat for reasons I never understood; hanging from the rearview mirror, as was the custom, was a pair of angora dice. A previous girl friend named Solange who was famous throughout Beverly Hills High School for having no pigment in her right eyebrow had knitted them for him. Buster and I would ride around town, the two of us seated to the left of the steering wheel. I would shift gears. It was nice.

There was necking. Terrific necking. First in the car, overlooking Los Angeles from what is now the Trousdale Estates. Then on the bed of his parents' cabana at Ocean House. Incredibly wonderful, frustrating necking, I loved it, really, but no further than necking, please don't, please, because there I was absolutely terrified of the general implications of going-a-step-further with a near-dummy and also terrified of his finding out there was next to nothing there (which he knew, of course; he wasn't that dumb).

I broke up with him at one point. I think we were apart for about   *20* two weeks. At the end of that time I drove down to see a friend at a boarding school in Palos Verdes Estates and a disc jockey played *April Love* on the radio four times during the trip. I took it as a sign. I drove straight back to Griffith Park to a golf tournament Buster was playing in (he was the sixth-seeded teen-age golf player in Southern California) and presented myself back to him on the green of the 18th hole. It was all very dramatic. That night we went to a drive-in and I let him get his hand under my protuberances and onto my breasts. He really didn't seem to mind at all.

"Do you want to marry my son?" the woman asked me.
"Yes," I said.
I was nineteen years old, a virgin, going with this woman's son, this big strange woman who was married to a Lutheran minister in New Hampshire and pretended she was Gentile and had this son, by her first husband, this total fool of a son who ran the hero-sandwich concession at Harvard Business School and whom

*for one moment one December in New Hampshire I said—as much out of polite-
ness as anything else—that I wanted to marry.*

*"Fine," she said. "Now, here's what you do. Always make sure you're
on top of him so you won't seem so small. My bust is very large, you see, so I
always lie on my back to make it look smaller, but you'll have to be on top most
of the time."*

I nodded. "Thank you," I said.

*"I have a book for you to read," she went on. "Take it with you when you
leave. Keep it." She went to the bookshelf, found it, and gave it to me. It was a
book on frigidity.*

"Thank you," I said.

25

That is a true story. Everything in this article is a true story, but I feel
I have to point out that that story in particular is true. It happened on
December 30, 1960. I think about it often. When it first happened, I
naturally assumed that the woman's son, my boyfriend, was responsible. I
invented a scenario where he had had a little heart-to-heart with his
mother and had confessed that his only objection to me was that my
breasts were small; his mother then took it upon herself to help out. Now
I think I was wrong about the incident. The mother was acting on her
own, I think: that was her way of being cruel and competitive under the
guise of being helpful and maternal. You have small breasts, she was saying; therefore you will never make him as happy as I have. Or you have
small breasts; therefore you will doubtless have sexual problems. Or you
have small breasts; therefore you are less woman than I am. She was, as it
happens, only the first of what seems to me to be a never-ending string
of women who have made competitive remarks to me about breast size.
"I would love to wear a dress like that," my friend Emily says to me, "but
my bust is too big." Like that. Why do women say these things to me?
Do I attract these remarks the way other women attract married men or
alcoholics or homosexuals? This summer, for example. I am at a party in
East Hampton and I am introduced to a woman from Washington. She is
a minor celebrity, very pretty and Southern and blonde and outspoken
and I am flattered because she has read something I have written. We are
talking animatedly, we have been talking no more than five minutes,
when a man comes up to join us. "Look at the two of us," the woman
says to the man, indicating me and her. "The two of us together couldn't
fill an A cup." Why does she say that? It isn't even true, dammit, so why?
Is she even more addled than I am on this subject? Does she honestly
believe there is something wrong with her size breasts, which, it seems to
me, now that I look hard at them, are just right. Do I unconsciously bring
out competitiveness in women? In that form? What did I do to deserve it?

As for men.

There were men who minded and let me know they minded. There   30
were men who did not mind. In any case, I always minded.

And even now, now that I have been countlessly reassured that my
figure is a good one, now that I am grown up enough to understand that

most of my feelings have very little to do with the reality of my shape, I am nonetheless obsessed by breasts. I cannot help it. I grew up in the terrible Fifties—with rigid stereotypical sex roles, the insistence that men be men and dress like men and women be women and dress like women, the intolerance of androgyny—and I cannot shake it, cannot shake my feelings of inadequacy. Well, that time is gone, right? All those exaggerated examples of breast worship are gone, right? Those women were freaks, right? I know all that. And yet, here I am, stuck with the psychological remains of it all, stuck with my own peculiar version of breast worship. You probably think I am crazy to go on like this: here I have set out to write a confession that is meant to hit you with the shock of recognition and instead you are sitting there thinking I am thoroughly warped. Well, what can I tell you? If I had had them, I would have been a completely different person. I honestly believe that.

After I went into therapy, a process that made it possible for me to tell total strangers at cocktail parties that breasts were the hang-up of my life, I was often told that I was insane to have been bothered by my condition. I was also frequently told, by close friends, that I was extremely boring on the subject. And my girl friends, the ones with nice big breasts, would go on endlessly about how their lives had been far more miserable than mine. Their bra straps were snapped in class. They couldn't sleep on their stomachs. They were stared at whenever the word "mountain" cropped up in geography. And *Evangeline,* good God what they went through every time someone had to stand up and recite the Prologue to Longfellow's *Evangeline:* "*. . . stand like druids of eld . . . /with beards that rest on their bosoms.* " It was much worse for them, they tell me. They had a terrible time of it, they assure me. I don't know how lucky I was, they say.

I have thought about their remarks, tried to put myself in their place, considered their point of view. I think they are full of shit.

---

1. What process does Ephron describe and analyze in her essay?

2. Throughout her analysis, Ephron presents you with a number of characters: her mother, Diana Raskob, and Buster Klepper, among others. How do her descriptions of these characters function in her essay?

3. Ephron describes a process that created a good deal of pain and anxiety for her, but her presentation is humorous for the most part. Do you think humor is an appropriate tone here? What effect does it have for you as her audience?

4. Ephron's essay is informal in its approach to its subject. What do you find that makes it so? Is informality effective for what you see to be her purposes?

5. What dominant idea do you see emerging from Ephron's essay?

An Invitation to Write

Both Reed's poem and Ephron's essay show a process (or contrasting processes) as a way of defining a difference in values held by different people. Think of a situation you've witnessed or experienced that grew out of such a conflict. Write an essay, a short story, a poem, or a short drama in which you show a process occurring from the point of view of a person in the middle of it. Use your description of that process to reflect a dominant idea about the conflict.

A Student Paper

When you have read this paper, answer the questions that follow it, alone or with your group.

THREE-HUNDRED-AND-SIXTY SECONDS
Erik Ehn

The beads of sweat glided down my forehead and onto my nose, where they hung for a moment and then dropped to puddle on the floor. I was up in three rounds but was I ready for the most important three-hundred-and-sixty seconds of my nine-year career? I had prepared for this moment since the fourth grade. I had endured hundreds of matches, dieting, and nine years of brutal practice to reach the point where I stood at the end of my final season at 125 pounds.

Good and bad memories ran through my head. My first victory as the lightest member of the elementary school wrestling team was as vivid and important as the match that now awaited me. That feeling of victory and accomplishment I experienced as a 57-pound champion had never been equaled. I could close my eyes and still see my raised hand in front of classmates and parents, and, most important, my coach whose smile lifted the ends of his mustache as in one great swoop this huge, round coach rocketed my 57 pounds up into the air and squeezed me until I was blue. "That a way, E!" still echoes in my mind.

All of the same people were in attendance this night. The gymnasium was packed from wall to wall with a sea of heads and shoulders and late-comers struggling through the rows to find a seat. Across the mat was the home team crowd—strong, fiery, and numerous. Friends who had all driven to the other side of town just to see me wrestle tried to catch my attention in the middle of the chaos of the stomping, the muffled clapping of the cheerleaders' white gloves, and chants of "Pin for the WIN." Administrators and teachers circled the gym like hawks. These same adults and peers had watched me grow up, led me in Boy Scouts, driven me to soccer and baseball games. My first wrestling coach and all my teammates were sitting in a hot and stuffy gym just to see me wrestle for three two-minute rounds.

The tremor of the fear of losing played through me as I stood in front of all these friends and my family. Losing did not mean that I would be anything less, but winning entitled me to prove myself in front of the people I respected the most. What kind of excuses would I use to teachers and friends who would inquire tomorrow about tonight's match? Losing could cost my team the entire match.

The team needed my three team points for a win, a strong chance to maintain our first place league finish, and to hold our title as California State Champions for the fourth season in a row. What was I saying? "How can I lose?"

At times the pressure I forced on myself reached such intensity that I would catch myself losing track of the long orange hand as it ticked away on the scoreboard. I went through my stretching as I always did when I was nervous before a match—hamstring left—hamstring right—left leg back—lean back—right leg back—lean back. . . . It was a routine that had become natural and thoughtless, like breathing. It was more of a mental preparation for the match. I had gone through the same stretches in the same order countless times before every match.

Although my eyes were focused on the mat at all times, my awareness of the crowd never left me as I braced for my match. It felt awkward to think that all these people were here for me. Why couldn't they just have stayed home or asked me how things went the next day? This was just another match. In three two-minute periods—three-hundred-and-sixty seconds—everything would be over, my match, season, and wrestling years. Would I end my nine years of dedication and hard work with a loss in front of everyone I respected? I couldn't think of a more humiliating outcome.

I stretched again and thought about the dedication and hours of grueling dieting over nine years. My mom's grilled chicken breasts, the whole-grain rice from the specialty health store, the Healthy Choice dinners that I despised for the 3 grams of fat they contained, and the rice cakes that crunched and tasted like Styrofoam packing had almost driven me to insanity by the end of each wrestling season.

Would my dedication pay off in a victory or would I go home disappointed, with one bad memory of wrestling for the rest of my life? Had I put in enough time between my collegiate wrestling in high school and freestyle wrestling on weekends during the summer? I had stayed after practice every day to work on refining my moves, climbing the ropes without using my legs, and running sprints to the point that I couldn't stand or spilled my guts into the trash can. Had I made the extra effort to

5

be the better wrestler, or had I missed an extra push-up or sit-up some-where? In 30 seconds I would know.

The thirty-second mark was my signal to remove my warm-up bot-toms. First came the right leg, then came the left, and I neatly folded my pants. I pulled up my right knee pad. I pulled my right arm through my sleeve, and I pulled my singlet strap over my shoulder followed by the same sequence with my left arm. I removed everything and placed it with respect to specific order and with attention to the time remaining on the scoreboard. I made sure I was never caught off guard by the sharp vibrat-ing discord of the buzzer reminding me it was my match.

With ten seconds left, I took off the final article and made a final stretch, nothing out of order. My teammate walked off the mat and slapped my back as he fell into his chair. The blue warm-up tops of my teammates hovering around me and my coach had hidden my presence from the crowd and opponents.

"We need your win" were my coach's final words. We both knew what I had to do, so little needed to be said. I was the only one who could win this match no matter what my coach instructed from his mat-side seat. A quick glance caught the pleading eyes of my parents amidst the concentrated stare of the crowd. The sweaty palms of wrestlers on my back added to my emotions as my teammates yelled my last name, send-ing me out under the only light in the entire gym.

A surge of cheers and applause was interrupted by the referee's in-structions. "Shake hands, gentlemen," announced the referee as the heat from the light overhead penetrated my skin and my energy swelled. It was all standard procedure to me as I squeezed my opponent's hand with both of mine. I remember the whistle blowing, and the knots that had twisted and turned my stomach, making it difficult to swallow, disap-peared. From that point on, the smashing of heads, the pulling on arms and legs as if I was trying to get to the surface for air, and the handfuls of muscle and bone all blend together. The sounds of the coach's directions covered over by the crowd's screams completely disappeared, and it was just my opponent, the referee, and me.

Walking off the mat after the final whistle had blown was the longest fifteen feet I have ever walked. I was dizzy and I had completely depleted my strength and energy to the point that I relied on two teammates at my sides to lean on so that I didn't fall out of my chair. My head was tilted, resting on my shoulder, attached to a limp neck and blurry vision. At the end of the last match the final team score was 33 to 32. Our crosstown rivals went home defeated once again. My win had made the difference. If I had lost or even tied, the songs of "We will rock you" and "We are the Champions" and the excitement of the bus ride home would have been absent.

To this day I wonder what would have happened if I had lost and let myself and the team down. Would I still be proud that I had devoted myself and a significant portion of my life to wrestling? Would I feel the same about my devotion to the sport, win or lose? Did I really feel different around my friends and family in victory or defeat?

The answer that was clear despite all my concerns and questions was that I had given all that I could. I didn't see a moment when I might have said to myself, "I could have done that little extra," or "Why didn't I finish it?" For nine years I had practiced, struggled, and devoted my time to a goal that was more important than just one three-hundred-and-sixty-second match. I was proud of what I had accomplished in wrestling win or lose because of the tenacious dedication and toil I had given to the sport. I had given quality time and relentless effort to a sport that had cultivated the type of growth that taught me more than just to win.

I walked away from the match with sore muscles but a proud spirit. Not until a full year later did I realize that my devotion up to that match taught me more than the match itself. Every job, task, and goal I had taken on had to be accomplished with the type of dedication and sincerity that I had experienced through wrestling. My defeats have been more important than my victories because there is more to learn and respect. Oftentimes a defeat has made me a stronger person. Recently I was defeated running for Associated Student Body Board of Directors. I was extremely disappointed and discouraged after losing the election. One week later, I am able to look back on the election and see the speaking skills, understanding of school politics, and friends I have made.

To be able and willing to give full effort to the last ounce of energy is demanding and time-consuming. My dedication to nine years of wrestling has been the kind of effort and price I have always enjoyed and which has taught me my most important lessons. When I look back on my actions through moments like my first and final match, and more importantly my losses and victories today, it's clear why we should look beyond our triumphs and defeats and concentrate on what is gained from the experience.

---

1. What do you think is the writer's dominant idea in this paper?

2. How does the writer use his primary organizational approach to support his dominant idea?

3. What other organizational approaches do you find the writer using to support his dominant idea? How does he integrate them with the primary approach?

4. If this writer were in your group or if you were editing his paper, what suggestions would you have for him that would make his writing better? Why do you think your suggestions would be effective?

On the following pages you will find readings that use description of a process as an organizational strategy. If your teacher assigns some or all of these readings or if you are inclined to read them on your own, pay attention to the ways the writers use the description of a process to support their dominant ideas. Also, note how the writers use voice and style to engage your feelings, your interest, and your intellect.

Remember, these writers are writing to you—a fellow human being. They have chosen to tell you something about coping with the effort of being human in their worlds. See how their examples and ideas speak to your experience. See how the combination of your experiences and those the writers offer you might lead you to your own ideas about your world.

MY FIRST CONK

Malcolm X

Shorty soon decided that my hair was finally long enough to be conked. He had promised to school me in how to beat the barbershops' three- and four-dollar price by making up congolene, and then conking ourselves.

I took the little list of ingredients he had printed out for me, and went to a grocery store, where I got a can of Red Devil lye, two eggs, and two medium-sized white potatoes. Then at a drugstore near the poolroom, I asked for a large jar of Vaseline, a large bar of soap, a large-toothed comb and a fine-toothed comb, one of those rubber hoses with a metal spray-head, a rubber apron and a pair of gloves.

"Going to lay on that first conk?" the drugstore man asked me. I proudly told him, grinning, "Right!"

Shorty paid six dollars a week for a room in his cousin's shabby apartment. His cousin wasn't at home. "It's like the pad's mine, he spends so much time with his woman," Shorty said. "Now, you watch me—"

He peeled the potatoes and thin-sliced them into a quart-sized Mason fruit jar, then started stirring them with a wooden spoon as he gradually poured in a little over half the can of lye. "Never use a metal spoon; the lye will turn it black," he told me.

A jelly-like, starchy-looking glop resulted from the lye and potatoes, and Shorty broke in the two eggs, stirring real fast—his own conk and dark face bent down close. The congolene turned pale-yellowish. "Feel the jar," Shorty said. I cupped my hand against the outside, and snatched it away.

"Damn right, it's hot, that's the lye," he said. "So you know it's going to burn when I comb it in—it burns bad. But the longer you can stand it, the straighter the hair."

He made me sit down, and he tied the string of the new rubber apron tightly around my neck, and combed up my bush of hair. Then, from the big Vaseline jar, he took a handful and massaged it hard all through my hair and into the scalp. He also thickly Vaselined my neck, ears and forehead. "When I get to washing out your head, be sure to tell me anywhere you feel any little stinging," Shorty warned me, washing his hands, then pulling on the rubber gloves, and tying on his own rubber apron. "You always got to remember that any congolene left in burns a sore into your head."

The congolene just felt warm when Shorty started combing it in. But then my head caught fire.

I gritted my teeth and tried to pull the sides of the kitchen table together. The comb felt as if it was raking my skin off.

My eyes watered, my nose was running. I couldn't stand it any longer; I bolted to the washbasin. I was cursing Shorty with every name I could think of when he got the spray going and started soap-lathering my head.   10

He lathered and spray-rinsed, lathered and spray-rinsed, maybe ten or twelve times, each time gradually closing the hot-water faucet, until the rinse was cold, and that helped some.

"You feel any stinging spots?"

"No," I managed to say. My knees were trembling.

"Sit back down, then. I think we got it all out okay."

The flame came back as Shorty, with a thick towel, started drying my   15
head, rubbing hard. "*Easy, man, easy!*" I kept shouting.

"The first time's always worst. You get used to it better before long. You took it real good, homeboy. You got a good conk."

When Shorty let me stand up and see in the mirror, my hair hung down in limp, damp strings. My scalp still flamed, but not as badly; I could bear it. He draped the towel around my shoulders, over my rubber apron, and began again Vaselining my hair.

I could feel him combing, straight back, first the big comb, then the fine-tooth one.

Then, he was using a razor, very delicately, on the back of my neck. Then finally, shaping the sideburns.

My first view in the mirror blotted out the hurting. I'd seen some pretty   20
conks, but when it's the first time, on your *own* head, the transformation, after the lifetime of kinks, is staggering.

The mirror reflected Shorty behind me. We both were grinning and sweating. And on top of my head was this thick, smooth sheen of shining red hair—real red—as straight as any white man's.

How ridiculous I was! Stupid enough to stand there simply lost in admiration of my hair now looking "white," reflected in the mirror in Shorty's room. I vowed that I'd never again be without a conk, and I never was for many years.

This was my first really big step toward self-degradation: when I endured all of that pain, literally burning my flesh to have it look like a white man's hair. I had joined that multitude of Negro men and women in America who are brainwashed into believing that the black people are "inferior"—and white people "superior"—that they will even violate and mutilate their God-created bodies to try to look "pretty" by white standards.

Look around today, in every small town and big city, from two-bit catfish and soda-pop joints into the "integrated" lobby of the Waldorf-Astoria, and you'll see conks on black men. And you'll see black women wearing these green and pink and purple and red and platinum-blonde wigs. They're all more ridiculous than a slapstick comedy. It makes you wonder if the Negro has completely lost his sense of identity, lost touch with himself.

You'll see the conk worn by many, many so-called "upper class" Negroes, and, as much as I hate to say it about them, on all too many Negro entertainers. One of the reasons that I've especially admired some of them, like Lionel Hampton and Sidney Poitier, among others, is that they have kept their natural hair and fought to the top. I admire any Negro man who has never had himself conked, or who has had the sense to get rid of it as I finally did. *25*

I don't know which kind of self-defacing conk is the greater shame— the one you'll see on the heads of the black so-called "middle class" and "upper class," who ought to know better, or the one you'll see on the heads of the poorest, most downtrodden, ignorant black men. I mean the legal-minimum-wage ghetto-dwelling kind of Negro, as I was when I got my first one. It's generally among these poor fools that you'll see a black kerchief over the man's head, like Aunt Jemima; he's trying to make his conk last longer, between trips to the barbershop. Only for special occasions is this kerchief-protected conk exposed—to show off how "sharp" and "hip" its owner is. The ironic thing is that I have never heard any woman, white or black, express any admiration for a conk. Of course, any white woman with a black man isn't thinking about his hair. But I don't see how on earth a black woman with any race pride could walk down the street with any black man wearing a conk—the emblem of his shame that he is black.

To my own shame, when I say all of this I'm talking first of all about myself—because you can't show me any Negro who ever conked more faithfully than I did. I'm speaking from personal experience when I say of any black man who conks today, or any white-wigged black woman, that if they gave the brains in their heads just half as much attention as they do their hair, they would be a thousand times better off.

PATRIOTISM

Yukio Mishima

In the twenty-eighth of February, 1936 (on the third day, that is, of the February Incident°), Lieutenant Shinji Takeyama of the Konoe Transport Battalion—profoundly disturbed by the knowledge that his closest colleagues had been with the mutineers from the beginning, and indignant at the imminent prospect of Imperial troops attacking Imperial troops—took his officer's sword and ceremonially disemboweled himself in the eight-mat room of his private residence in the sixth block of Aoba-chō, in Yotsuya Ward. His wife, Reiko, followed him, stabbing herself to death. The lieutenant's farewell note consisted of one sentence: "Long live the Imperial Forces." His wife's, after apologies for her unfilial conduct in thus preceding her parents to the grave, concluded: "The day which, for a soldier's wife, had to come, has come. . . ." The last moments of this heroic and dedicated couple were such as to make the gods themselves weep. The lieutenant's age, it should be noted, was thirty-one, his wife's twenty-three; and it was not half a year since the celebration of their marriage.

2

Those who saw the bride and bridegroom in the commemorative photograph—perhaps no less than those actually present at the lieutenant's wedding—had exclaimed in wonder at the bearing of this handsome couple. The lieutenant, majestic in military uniform, stood protectively beside his bride, his right hand resting upon his sword, his officer's cap held at his left side. His expression was severe, and his dark brows and wide-gazing eyes well conveyed the clear integrity of youth. For the beauty of the bride in her white over-robe no comparisons were adequate. In the eyes, round beneath soft brows, in the slender, finely shaped nose, and in the full lips, there was both sensuousness and refinement. One hand, emerging shyly from a sleeve of the over-robe, held a fan, and the tips of the fingers, clustering delicately, were like the bud of a moonflower.

After the suicide, people would take out this photograph and examine it, and sadly reflect that too often there was a curse on these seemingly flawless unions. Perhaps it was no more than imagination, but looking at the

---

February Incident: On February 26, 1936, a long period of political turmoil culminated in an attempted coup led by young officers. Units commanded by the rebels seized and held central Tokyo for a number of days, and numerous high-ranking government officials, including Lord Privy Seal Saitō, were assassinated. The mutiny was crushed by loyal troops, and the leaders were executed.

picture after the tragedy it almost seemed as if the two young people before the gold–lacquered screen were gazing, each with equal clarity, at the deaths which lay before them.

Thanks to the good offices of their go–between, Lieutenant General Ozeki, they had been able to set themselves up in a new home at Aoba–chō in Yotsuya. "New home" is perhaps misleading. It was an old three–room rented house backing onto a small garden. As neither the six– nor the four–and–a–half–mat room downstairs was favored by the sun, they used the up-stairs eight–mat room as both bedroom and guest room. There was no maid, so Reiko was left alone to guard the house in her husband's absence.

The honeymoon trip was dispensed with on the grounds that these were   5
times of national emergency. The two of them had spent the first night of their marriage at this house. Before going to bed, Shinji, sitting erect on the floor with his sword laid before him, had bestowed upon his wife a soldierly lecture. A woman who had become the wife of a soldier should know and resolutely accept that her husband's death might come at any moment. It could be tomorrow. It could be the day after. But, no matter when it came—he asked—was she steadfast in her resolve to accept it? Reiko rose to her feet, pulled open a drawer of the cabinet, and took out what was the most prized of her new possessions, the dagger her mother had given her. Returning to her place, she laid the dagger without a word on the mat be-fore her, just as her husband had laid his sword. A silent understanding was achieved at once and the lieutenant never again sought to test his wife's resolve.

In the first few months of her marriage Reiko's beauty grew daily more radiant, shining serene like the moon after rain.

As both were possessed of young, vigorous bodies, their relationship was passionate. Nor was this merely a matter of the night. On more than one occasion, returning home straight from maneuvers, and begrudging even the time it took to remove his mud–splashed uniform, the lieutenant had pushed his wife to the floor almost as soon as he had entered the house. Reiko was equally ardent in her response. For a little more or a little less than a month, from the first night of their marriage Reiko knew happiness, and the lieutenant, seeing this, was happy too.

Reiko's body was white and pure, and her swelling breasts conveyed a firm and chaste refusal; but, upon consent, those breasts were lavish with their intimate, welcoming warmth. Even in bed these two were frighten-ingly and awesomely serious. In the very midst of wild, intoxicating pas-sions, their hearts were sober and serious.

By day the lieutenant would think of his wife in the brief rest periods between training; and all day long, at home, Reiko would recall the image of her husband. Even when apart, however, they had only to look at the wedding photograph for their happiness to be once more confirmed. Reiko felt not the slightest surprise that a man who had been a complete stranger until a few months ago should now have become the sun about which her whole world revolved.

All these things had a moral basis, and were in accordance with the   *10*
Education Rescript's° injunction that "husband and wife should be harmonious." Not once did Reiko contradict her husband, nor did the lieutenant
ever find reason to scold his wife. On the god shelf below the stairway,
alongside the tablet from the Great Ise Shrine,° were set photographs of their
Imperial Majesties, and regularly every morning, before leaving for duty, the
lieutenant would stand with his wife at this hallowed place and together they
would bow their heads low. The offering water was renewed each morning,
and the sacred sprig of *sasaki* was always green and fresh. Their lives were
lived beneath the solemn protection of the gods and were filled with an
intense happiness which set every fiber in their bodies trembling.

3

Although Lord Privy Seal Saitō's house was in their neighborhood, neither of them heard any noise of gunfire on the morning of February 26. It
was a bugle, sounding muster in the dim, snowy dawn, when the ten-
minute tragedy had already ended, which first disrupted the lieutenant's
slumbers. Leaping at once from his bed, and without speaking a word, the
lieutenant donned his uniform, buckled on the sword held ready for him by
his wife, and hurried swiftly out into the snow-covered streets of the still
darkened morning. He did not return until the evening of the twenty-
eighth.

Later, from the radio news, Reiko learned the full extent of this sudden
eruption of violence. Her life throughout the subsequent two days was lived
alone, in complete tranquility, and behind locked doors.

In the lieutenant's face, as he hurried silently out into the snowy morning, Reiko had read the determination to die. If her husband did not return,
her own decision was made: she too would die. Quietly she attended to the
disposition of her personal possessions. She chose her sets of visiting kimo-
nos as keepsakes for friends of her schooldays, and she wrote a name and
address on the stiff paper wrapping in which each was folded. Constantly
admonished by her husband never to think of the morrow, Reiko had not
even kept a diary and was now denied the pleasure of assiduously rereading
her record of the happiness of the past few months and consigning each page
to the fire as she did so. Ranged across the top of the radio were a small
china dog, a rabbit, a squirrel, a bear, and a fox. There were also a small vase
and a water pitcher. These comprised Reiko's one and only collection. But
it would hardly do, she imagined, to give such things as keepsakes. Nor again

---

Education Rescript: a code promulgated during the Meiji, the reign of Emperor Mutsuhito
which lasted from 1867 to 1912. The period is regarded as a historic era in the development
of modern Japan.
Great Ise Shrine: The highest ranking shrine in Japan. The emperor's ancestors were buried
there.

would it be quite proper to ask specifically for them to be included in the coffin. It seemed to Reiko, as these thoughts passed through her mind, that the expressions on the small animals' faces grew even more lost and forlorn.

Reiko took the squirrel in her hand and looked at it. And then, her thoughts turning to a realm far beyond these childlike affections, she gazed up into the distance at the great sunlike principle which her husband embodied. She was ready, and happy, to be hurtled along to her destruction in that gleaming sun chariot—but now, for these few moments of solitude, she allowed herself to luxuriate in this innocent attachment to trifles. The time when she had genuinely loved these things, however, was long past. Now she merely loved the memory of having once loved them, and their place in her heart had been filled by more intense passions, by a more frenzied happiness. . . . For Reiko had never, even to herself, thought of those soaring joys of the flesh as a mere pleasure. The February cold, and the icy touch of the china squirrel, had numbed Reiko's slender fingers; yet, even so, in her lower limbs, beneath the ordered repetition of the pattern which crossed the skirt of her trim *meisen* kimono, she could feel now, as she thought of the lieutenant's powerful arms reaching out toward her, a hot moistness of the flesh which defied the snows.

She was not in the least afraid of the death hovering in her mind. Waiting alone at home, Reiko firmly believed that everything her husband was feeling or thinking now, his anguish and distress, was leading her—just as surely as the power in his flesh—to a welcome death. She felt as if her body could melt away with ease and be transformed to the merest fraction of her husband's thought. 15

Listening to the frequent announcements on the radio, she heard the names of several of her husband's colleagues mentioned among those of the insurgents. This was news of death. She followed the developments closely, wondering anxiously, as the situation became daily more irrevocable, why no Imperial ordinance was sent down, and watching what had at first been taken as a movement to restore the nation's honor come gradually to be branded with the infamous name of mutiny. There was no communication from the regiment. At any moment, it seemed, fighting might commence in the city streets where the remains of the snow still lay.

Toward sundown on the twenty-eighth Reiko was startled by a furious pounding on the front door. She hurried downstairs. As she pulled with fumbling fingers at the bolt, the shape dimly outlined beyond the frosted-glass panel made no sound, but she knew it was her husband. Reiko had never known the bolt on the sliding door to be so stiff. Still it resisted. The door just would not open.

In a moment, almost before she knew she had succeeded, the lieutenant was standing before her on the cement floor inside the porch, muffled in a khaki greatcoat, his top boots heavy with slush from the street. Closing the door behind him, he returned the bolt once more to its socket. With what significance, Reiko did not understand.

"Welcome home."

Reiko bowed deeply, but her husband made no response. As he had   20
already unfastened his sword and was about to remove his greatcoat, Reiko
moved around behind to assist. The coat, which was cold and damp and had
lost the odor of horse dung it normally exuded when exposed to the sun,
weighed heavily upon her arm. Draping it across a hanger, and cradling the
sword and leather belt in her sleeves, she waited while her husband removed
his top boots and then followed behind him into the "living room." This
was the six-mat room downstairs.

Seen in the clear light from the lamp, her husband's face, covered with
a heavy growth of bristle, was almost unrecognizably wasted and thin. The
cheeks were hollow, their luster and resilience gone. In his normal good
spirits he would have changed into old clothes as soon as he was home and
have pressed her to get supper at once, but now he sat before the table still
in his uniform, his head dropping dejectedly. Reiko refrained from asking
whether she should prepare the supper.

After an interval the lieutenant spoke.

"I knew nothing. They hadn't asked me to join. Perhaps out of consideration, because I was newly married. Kano, and Homma too, and
Yamaguchi."

Reiko recalled momentarily the faces of high-spirited young officers,
friends of her husband, who had come to the house occasionally as guests.

"There may be an Imperial ordinance sent down tomorrow. They'll be   25
posted as rebels, I imagine. I shall be in command of a unit with orders to
attack them. . . . I can't do it. It's impossible to do a thing like that."

He spoke again.

"They've taken me off guard duty, and I have permission to return
home for one night. Tomorrow morning, without question, I must leave to
join the attack. I can't do it, Reiko."

Reiko sat erect with lowered eyes. She understood clearly that her husband had spoken of his death. The lieutenant was resolved. Each word, being rooted in death, emerged sharply and with powerful significance against
this dark, unmovable background. Although the lieutenant was speaking of
his dilemma, already there was no room in his mind for vacillation.

However, there was a clarity, like the clarity of a stream fed from melting
snows, in the silence which rested between them. Sitting in his own home
after the long two-day ordeal, and looking across at the face of his beautiful
wife, the lieutenant was for the first time experiencing true peace of mind.
For he had at once known, though she said nothing, that his wife divined
the resolve which lay beneath his words.

"Well, then . . ." The lieutenant's eyes opened wide. Despite his ex-   30
haustion they were strong and clear, and now for the first time they looked
straight into the eyes of his wife. "Tonight I shall cut my stomach."

Reiko did not flinch.

Her round eyes showed tension, as taut as the clang of a bell.

"I am ready," she said. "I ask permission to accompany you."

The lieutenant felt almost mesmerized by the strength in those eyes. His words flowed swiftly and easily, like the utterances of a man in delirium, and it was beyond his understanding how permission in a matter of such weight could be expressed so casually.

"Good. We'll go together. But I want you as a witness, first, for my own suicide. Agreed?"

35

When this was said a sudden release of abundant happiness welled up in both their hearts. Reiko was deeply affected by the greatness of her husband's trust in her. It was vital for the lieutenant, whatever else might happen, that there should be no irregularity in his death. For that reason there had to be a witness. The fact that he had chosen his wife for this was the first mark of his trust. The second, and even greater mark, was that though he had pledged that they should die together he did not intend to kill his wife first—he had deferred her death to a time when he would no longer be there to verify it. If the lieutenant had been a suspicious husband, he would doubtless, as in the usual suicide pact, have chosen to kill his wife first.

When Reiko said, "I ask permission to accompany you," the lieutenant felt these words to be the final fruit of the education which he had himself given his wife, starting on the first night of their marriage, and which had schooled her, when the moment came, to say what had to be said without a shadow of hesitation. This flattered the lieutenant's opinion of himself as a self-reliant man. He was not so romantic or conceited as to imagine that the words were spoken spontaneously, out of love for her husband.

With happiness welling almost too abundantly in their hearts, they could not help smiling at each other. Reiko felt as if she had returned to her wedding night.

Before her eyes was neither pain nor death. She seemed to see only a free and limitless expanse opening out into vast distances.

"The water is hot. Will you take your bath now?"

40

"Ah yes, of course."

"And supper . . . ?"

The words were delivered in such level, domestic tones that the lieutenant came near to thinking, for the fraction of a second, that everything had been a hallucination.

"I don't think we'll need supper. But perhaps you could warm some sake?"

"As you wish."

45

As Reiko rose and took a *tanzen* gown from the cabinet for after the bath, she purposely directed her husband's attention to the opened drawer. The lieutenant rose, crossed to the cabinet, and looked inside. From the ordered array of paper wrappings he read, one by one, the addresses of the keepsakes. There was no grief in the lieutenant's response to this demonstration of heroic resolve. His heart was filled with tenderness. Like a husband who is proudly shown the childish purchases of a young wife, the lieutenant, overwhelmed by affection, lovingly embraced his wife from behind and implanted a kiss upon her neck.

Reiko felt the roughness of the lieutenant's unshaven skin against her neck. This sensation, more than being just a thing of this world, was for Reiko almost the world itself, but now—with the feeling that it was soon to be lost forever—it had freshness beyond all her experience. Each moment had its own vital strength, and the senses in every corner of her body were reawakened. Accepting her husband's caresses from behind, Reiko raised herself on the tips of her toes, letting the vitality seep through her entire body.

"First the bath, and then, after some sake . . . lay out the bedding upstairs, will you?"

The lieutenant whispered the words into his wife's ear. Reiko silently nodded.

Flinging off his uniform, the lieutenant went to the bath. To faint back- 50
ground noises of slopping water Reiko tended the charcoal brazier in the living room and began the preparations for warming the sake.

Taking the *tanzen,* a sash, and some underclothes, she went to the bathroom to ask how the water was. In the midst of a coiling cloud of steam the lieutenant was sitting cross-legged on the floor, shaving, and she could dimly discern the rippling movements of the muscles on his damp, powerful back as they responded to the movement of his arms.

There was nothing to suggest a time of any special significance. Reiko, going busily about her tasks, was preparing side dishes from odds and ends in stock. Her hands did not tremble. If anything, she managed even more efficiently and smoothly than usual. From time to time, it is true, there was strange throbbing deep within her breast. Like distant lightning, it had a moment of sharp intensity and then vanished without trace. Apart from that, nothing was in any way out of the ordinary.

The lieutenant, shaving in the bathroom, felt his warmed body miraculously healed at last of the desperate tiredness of the days of indecision and filled—in spite of the death which lay ahead—with pleasurable anticipation. The sound of his wife going about her work came to him faintly. A healthy physical craving, submerged for two days, reasserted itself.

The lieutenant was confident there had been no impurity in that joy they had experienced when resolving upon death. They had both sensed at that moment—though not, of course, in any clear and conscious way—that those permissible pleasures which they shared in private were once more beneath the protection of Righteousness and Divine Power, and of a complete and unassailable morality. On looking into each other's eyes and discovering there an honorable death, they had felt themselves safe once more behind steel walls which none could destroy, encased in an impenetrable armor of Beauty and Truth. Thus, so far from seeing any inconsistency or conflict between the urges of his flesh and the sincerity of his patriotism, the lieutenant was even able to regard the two as parts of the same thing.

Thrusting his face close to the dark, cracked, misted wall mirror, the   55
lieutenant shaved himself with great care. This would be his death face.
There must be no unsightly blemishes. The clean-shaven face gleamed once
more with a youthful luster, seeming to brighten the darkness of the mirror.
There was a certain elegance, he even felt, in the association of death with
this radiantly healthy face.

Just as it looked now, this would become his death face! Already, in fact,
it had half departed from the lieutenant's personal possession and had become the bust above a dead soldier's memorial. As an experiment he closed
his eyes tight. Everything was wrapped in blackness, and he was no longer a
living, seeing creature.

Returning from the bath, the traces of the shave glowing faintly blue
beneath his smooth cheeks, he seated himself beside the now well-kindled
charcoal brazier. Busy though Reiko was, he noticed, she had found time
lightly to touch up her face. Her cheeks were gay and her lips moist. There
was no shadow of sadness to be seen. Truly, the lieutenant felt, as he saw this
mark of his young wife's passionate nature, he had chosen the wife he ought
to have chosen.

As soon as the lieutenant had drained his sake cup he offered it to Reiko.
Reiko had never before tasted sake, but she accepted without hesitation and
sipped timidly.

"Come here," the lieutenant said.

Reiko moved to her husband's side and was embraced as she leaned   60
backward across his lap. Her breast was in violent commotion, as if sadness,
joy, and the potent sake were mingling and reacting within her. The lieutenant looked down into his wife's face. It was the last face he would see in
this world, the last face he would see of his wife. The lieutenant scrutinized
the face minutely, with the eyes of a traveler bidding farewell to splendid
vistas which he will never revisit. It was a face he could not tire of looking at—the features regular yet not cold, the lips lightly closed with a soft
strength. The lieutenant kissed those lips, unthinkingly. And suddenly,
though there was not the slightest distortion of the face into the unsightliness
of sobbing, he noticed that tears were welling slowly from beneath the long
lashes of the closed eyes and brimming over into a glistening stream.

When, a little later, the lieutenant urged that they should move to the
upstairs bedroom, his wife replied that she would follow after taking a bath.
Climbing the stairs alone to the bedroom, where the air was already warmed
by the gas heater, the lieutenant lay down on the bedding with arms outstretched and legs apart. Even the time at which he lay waiting for his wife
to join him was no later and no earlier than usual.

He folded his hands beneath his head and gazed at the dark boards of
the ceiling in the dimness beyond the range of the standard lamp. Was it
death he was now waiting for? Or a wild ecstasy of the senses? The two
seemed to overlap, almost as if the object of this bodily desire was death
itself. But, however that might be, it was certain that never before had the
lieutenant tasted such total freedom.

There was the sound of a car outside the window. He could hear the screech of its tires skidding in the snow piled at the side of the street. The sound of its horn re-echoed from near-by walls. . . . Listening to these noises he had the feeling that this house rose like a solitary island in the ocean of a society going as restlessly about its business as ever. All around, vastly and untidily, stretched the country for which he grieved. He was to give his life for it. But would that great country, with which he was prepared to remonstrate to the extent of destroying himself, take the slightest heed of his death? He did not know; and it did not matter. His was a battlefield without glory, a battlefield where none could display deeds of valor: it was the front line of the spirit.

Reiko's footsteps sounded on the stairway. The steep stairs in this old house creaked badly. There were fond memories in that creaking, and many a time, while waiting in bed, the lieutenant had listened to its welcome sound. At the thought that he would hear it no more he listened with intense concentration, striving for every corner of every moment of this precious time to be filled with the sound of those soft footfalls on the creaking stairway. The moments seemed transformed to jewels, sparkling with inner light.

Reiko wore a Nagoya sash about the waist of her *yukata,* but as the lieutenant reached toward it, its redness sobered by the dimness of the light, Reiko's hand moved to his assistance and the sash fell away, slithering swiftly to the floor. As she stood before him, still in her *yukata,* the lieutenant inserted his hands through the side slits beneath each sleeve, intending to embrace her as she was; but at the touch of his finger tips upon the warm naked flesh, and as the armpits closed gently about his hands, his whole body was suddenly aflame.

Neither spoke the thought, but their hearts, their bodies, and their pounding breasts blazed with the knowledge that this was the very last time. It was as if the words "The Last Time" were spelled out, in invisible brushstrokes, across every inch of their bodies.

The lieutenant drew his wife close and kissed her vehemently. As their tongues explored each other's mouths, reaching out into the smooth, moist interior, they felt as if the still unknown agonies of death had tempered their senses to the keenness of red-hot steel. The agonies they could not yet feel, the distant pains of death, had refined their awareness of pleasure.

"This is the last time I shall see your body," said the lieutenant. "Let me look at it closely." And, tilting the shade on the lampstand to one side, he directed the rays along the full length of Reiko's outstretched form.

Reiko lay still with her eyes closed. The light from the low lamp clearly revealed the majestic sweep of her white flesh. The lieutenant, not without a touch of egocentricity, rejoiced that he would never see this beauty crumble in death.

At his leisure, the lieutenant allowed the unforgettable spectacle to engrave itself upon his mind. With one hand he fondled the hair, with the other he softly stroked the magnificent face, implanting kisses here and there where his eyes lingered. The quiet coldness of the high, tapering forehead,

65

70

the closed eyes with their long lashes beneath faintly etched brows, the set of the finely shaped nose, the gleam of teeth glimpsed between full, regular lips, the soft cheeks and the small, wise chin . . . these things conjured up in the lieutenant's mind the vision of a truly radiant death face, and again and again he pressed his lips tight against the white throat—where Reiko's own hand was soon to strike—and the throat reddened faintly beneath his kisses. Returning to the mouth he laid his lips against it with the gentlest of pressures, and moved them rhythmically over Reiko's with the light rolling motion of a small boat. If he closed his eyes, the world became a rocking cradle.

Wherever the lieutenant's eyes moved his lips faithfully followed. The high, swelling breasts, surmounted by nipples like the buds of a wild cherry, hardened as the lieutenant's lips closed about them. The arms flowed smoothly downward from each side of the breast, tapering toward the wrists, yet losing nothing of their roundness or symmetry, and at their tips were those delicate fingers which had held the fan at the wedding ceremony. One by one, as the lieutenant kissed them, the fingers withdrew behind their neighbor as if in shame. . . . The natural hollow curving between the bosom and the stomach carried in its lines a suggestion not only of softness but of resilient strength, and while it gave forewarning of the rich curves spreading outward from here to the hips it had, in itself, an appearance only of restraint and proper discipline. The whiteness and richness of the stomach and hips was like milk brimming in a great bowl, and the sharply shadowed dip of the navel could have been the fresh impress of a raindrop, fallen there that very moment. Where the shadows gathered more thickly, hair clustered, gentle and sensitive, and as the agitation mounted in the now no longer passive body there hung over this region a scent like the smoldering of fragrant blossoms, growing steadily more pervasive.

At length, in a tremulous voice, Reiko spoke.

"Show me. . . . Let me look too, for the last time."

Never before had he heard from his wife's lips so strong and unequivocal a request. It was as if something which her modesty had wished to keep hidden to the end had suddenly burst its bonds of constraint. The lieutenant obediently lay back and surrendered himself to his wife. Lithely she raised her white, trembling body, and—burning with an innocent desire to return to her husband what he had done for her—placed two white fingers on the lieutenant's eyes, which gazed fixedly up at her, and gently stroked them shut.

Suddenly overwhelmed by tenderness, her cheeks flushed by a dizzying uprush of emotion, Reiko threw her arms about the lieutenant's close-cropped head. The bristly hairs rubbed painfully against her breast, the prominent nose was cold as it dug into her flesh, and his breath was hot. Relaxing her embrace, she gazed down at her husband's masculine face. The severe brows, the closed eyes, the splendid bridge of the nose, the shapely lips drawn firmly together . . . the blue, cleanshaven cheeks reflecting the light and gleaming smoothly. Reiko kissed each of these. She kissed the broad nape of the neck, the strong, erect shoulders, the powerful chest with

75

its twin circles like shields and its russet nipples. In the armpits, deeply shad-owed by the ample flesh of the shoulders and chest, a sweet and melancholy odor emanated from the growth of hair, and in the sweetness of this odor was contained, somehow, the essence of young death. The lieutenant's na-ked skin glowed like a field of barley, and everywhere the muscles showed in sharp relief, converging on the lower abdomen about the small, unassum-ing navel. Gazing at the youthful, firm stomach, modestly covered by a vig-orous growth of hair, Reiko thought of it as it was soon to be, cruelly cut by the sword, and she laid her head upon it, sobbing in pity, and bathed it with kisses.

At the touch of his wife's tears upon his stomach the lieutenant felt ready to endure with courage the cruelest agonies of his suicide.

What ecstasies they experienced after these tender exchanges may well be imagined. The lieutenant raised himself and enfolded his wife in a pow-erful embrace, her body now limp with exhaustion after her grief and tears. Passionately they held their faces close, rubbing cheek against cheek. Reiko's body was trembling. Their breasts, moist with sweat, were tightly joined, and every inch of the young and beautiful bodies had become so much one with the other that it seemed impossible there should ever again be a sepa-ration. Reiko cried out. From the heights they plunged into the abyss, and from the abyss they took wing and soared once more to dizzying heights. The lieutenant panted like the regimental standard-bearer on a route march. . . . As one cycle ended, almost immediately a new wave of passion would be generated, and together—with no trace of fatigue—they would climb again in a single breathless movement to the very summit.

4

When the lieutenant at last turned away, it was not from weariness. For one thing, he was anxious not to undermine the considerable strength he would need in carrying out his suicide. For another, he would have been sorry to mar the sweetness of these last memories by overindulgence.

Since the lieutenant had clearly desisted, Reiko too, with her usual compliance, followed his example. The two lay naked on their backs, with fingers interlaced, staring fixedly at the dark ceiling. The room was warm from the heater, and even when the sweat had ceased to pour from their bodies they felt no cold. Outside, in the hushed night, the sounds of passing traffic had ceased. Even the noises of the trains and streetcars around Yotsuya station did not penetrate this far. After echoing through the region bounded by the moat, they were lost in the heavily wooded park fronting the broad driveway before Akasaka Palace. It was hard to believe in the tension grip-ping this whole quarter, where the two factions of the bitterly divided Im-perial Army now confronted each other, poised for battle.

Savoring the warmth glowing within themselves, they lay still and re-called the ecstasies they had just known. Each moment of the experience

80

was relived. They remembered the taste of kisses which had never wearied, the touch of naked flesh, episode after episode of dizzying bliss. But already, from the dark boards of the ceiling, the face of death was peering down. These joys had been final, and their bodies would never know them again. Not that joy of this intensity—and the same thought had occurred to them both—was ever likely to be reexperienced, even if they should live on to old age.

The feel of their fingers intertwined—this too would soon be lost. Even the wood-grain patterns they now gazed at on the dark ceiling boards would be taken from them. They could feel death edging in, nearer and nearer. There could be no hesitation now. They must have the courage to reach out to death themselves, and to seize it.

"Well, let's make our preparations," said the lieutenant. The note of determination in the words was unmistakable, but at the same time Reiko had never heard her husband's voice so warm and tender.

After they had risen, a variety of tasks awaited them.

The lieutenant, who had never once before helped with the bedding,   85
now cheerfully slid back the door of the closet, lifted the mattress across the room by himself, and stowed it away inside.

Reiko turned off the gas heater and put away the lamp standard. During the lieutenant's absence she had arranged this room carefully, sweeping and dusting it to a fresh cleanness, and now—if one overlooked the rosewood table drawn into one corner—the eight-mat room gave all the appearance of a reception room ready to welcome an important guest.

"We've seen some drinking here, haven't we? With Kanō and Homma and Noguchi. . . ."

"Yes, they were great drinkers, all of them."

"We'll be meeting them before long, in the other world. They'll tease us, I imagine, when they find I've brought you with me."

Descending the stairs, the lieutenant turned to look back into this calm   90
clean room, now brightly illuminated by the ceiling lamp. There floated across his mind the faces of the young officers who had drunk there, and laughed, and innocently bragged. He had never dreamed then that he would one day cut open his stomach in this room.

In the two rooms downstairs husband and wife busied themselves smoothly and serenely with their respective preparations. The lieutenant went to the toilet, and then to the bathroom to wash. Meanwhile Reiko folded away her husband's padded robe, placed his uniform tunic, his trousers, and a newly cut bleached loincloth in the bathroom, and set out sheets of paper on the living-room table for the farewell notes. Then she removed the lid from the writing box and began rubbing ink from the ink tablet. She had already decided upon the wording of her own note.

Reiko's fingers pressed hard upon the cold gilt letters of the ink tablet, and the water in the shallow well at once darkened, as if a black cloud had spread across it. She stopped thinking that this repeated action, this pressure from her fingers, this rise and fall of faint sound, was all and solely for death. It was a routine domestic task, a simple paring away of time until death should finally stand before her. But somehow, in the increasingly smooth motion of the tablet rubbing on the stone, and in the scent from the thickening ink, there was unspeakable darkness.

Neat in his uniform, which he now wore next to his skin, the lieutenant emerged from the bathroom. Without a word he seated himself at the table, bolt upright, took a brush in his hand, and stared undecidedly at the paper before him.

Reiko took a white silk kimono with her and entered the bathroom. When she reappeared in the living room, clad in the white kimono and with her face lightly made up, the farewell note lay completed on the table beneath the lamp. The thick black brushstrokes said simply:

"Long Live the Imperial Forces—Army Lieutenant Takeyama Shinji." *95*

While Reiko sat opposite him writing her own note, the lieutenant gazed in silence, intensely serious, at the controlled movement of his wife's pale fingers as they manipulated the brush.

With their respective notes in their hands—the lieutenant's sword strapped to his side, Reiko's small dagger thrust into the sash of her white kimono—the two of them stood before the god shelf and silently prayed. Then they put out all the downstairs lights. As he mounted the stairs the lieutenant turned his head and gazed back at the striking, white-clad figure of his wife, climbing behind him, with lowered eyes, from the darkness beneath.

The farewell notes were laid side by side in the alcove of the upstairs room. They wondered whether they ought not to remove the hanging scroll, but since it had been written by their go-between, Lieutenant General Ozeki, and consisted, moreover, of two Chinese characters signifying "Sincerity," they left it where it was. Even if it were to become stained with splashes of blood, they felt that the lieutenant general would understand.

The lieutenant sitting erect with his back to the alcove, laid his sword on the floor before him.

Reiko sat before him, a mat's width away. With the rest of her so severely white the touch of rouge on her lips seemed remarkably seductive. *100*

Across the dividing mat they gazed intently into each other's eyes. The lieutenant's sword lay before his knees. Seeing it, Reiko recalled their first night and was overwhelmed with sadness. The lieutenant spoke, in a hoarse voice:

"As I have no second to help me I shall cut deep. It may look unpleasant, but please do not panic. Death of any sort is a fearful thing to watch. You must not be discouraged by what you see. Is that all right?"

"Yes."

Reiko nodded deeply.

Looking at the slender white figure of his wife the lieutenant experi- *105*
enced a bizarre excitement. What he was about to perform was an act in his

public capacity as a soldier, something he had never previously shown his wife. It called for a resolution equal to the courage to enter battle; it was a death of no less degree and quality than death in the front line. It was his conduct on the battlefield that he was now to display.

Momentarily the thought led the lieutenant to a strange fantasy. A lonely death on the battlefield, a death beneath the eyes of his beautiful wife . . . in the sensation that he was now to die in these two dimensions, realizing an impossible union of them both, there was sweetness beyond words. This must be the very pinnacle of good fortune, he thought. To have every moment of his death observed by those beautiful eyes—it was like being borne to death on a gentle, fragrant breeze. There was some special favor here. He did not understand precisely what it was, but it was a domain unknown to others: a dispensation granted to no one else had been permitted to himself. In the radiant, bridelike figure of his white-robed wife the lieutenant seemed to see a vision of all those things he had loved and for which he was to lay down his life—the Imperial Household, the Nation, the Army Flag. All these, no less than the wife who sat before him, were presences observing him closely with clear and never-faltering eyes.

Reiko too was gazing intently at her husband, so soon to die, and she thought that never in this world had she seen anything so beautiful. The lieutenant always looked well in uniform, but now, as he contemplated death with severe brows and firmly closed lips, he revealed what was perhaps masculine beauty at its most superb.

"It's time to go," the lieutenant said at last.

Reiko bent her body low to the mat in a deep bow. She could not raise her face. She did not wish to spoil her make-up with tears, but the tears could not be held back.

When at length she looked up she saw hazily through the tears that her   *110* husband had wound a white bandage around the blade of his now unsheathed sword, leaving five or six inches of naked steel showing at the point.

Resting the sword in its cloth wrapping on the mat before him, the lieutenant rose from his knees, resettled himself cross-legged, and unfastened the hooks of his uniform collar. His eyes no longer saw his wife. Slowly, one by one, he undid the flat brass buttons. The dusky brown chest was revealed, and then the stomach. He unclasped his belt and undid the buttons of his trousers. The pure whiteness of the thickly coiled loincloth showed itself. The lieutenant pushed the cloth down with both hands, further to ease his stomach, and then reached for the white-bandaged blade of his sword. With his left hand he massaged his abdomen, glancing downward as he did so.

To reassure himself on the sharpness of his sword's cutting edge the lieutenant folded back the left trouser flap, exposing a little of his thigh, and lightly drew the blade across the skin. Blood welled up in the wound at once, and several streaks of red trickled downward, glistening in the strong light.

It was the first time Reiko had ever seen her husband's blood, and she felt a violent throbbing in her chest. She looked at her husband's face. The lieutenant was looking at the blood with calm appraisal. For a moment—though thinking at the same time that it was hollow comfort—Reiko experienced a sense of relief.

The lieutenant's eyes fixed his wife with an intense, hawk-like stare. Moving the sword around to his front, he raised himself slightly on his hips and let the upper half of his body lean over the sword point. That he was mustering his whole strength was apparent from the angry tension of the uniform at his shoulders. The lieutenant aimed to strike deep into the left of his stomach. His sharp cry pierced the silence of the room.

Despite the effort he had himself put into the blow, the lieutenant had the impression that someone else had struck the side of his stomach agonizingly with a thick rod of iron. For a second or so his head reeled and he had no idea what had happened. The five or six inches of naked point had vanished completely into his flesh, and the white bandage, gripped in his clenched fist, pressed directly against his stomach.

He returned to consciousness. The blade had certainly pierced the wall of the stomach, he thought. His breathing was difficult, his chest thumped violently, and in some far deep region, which he could hardly believe was a part of himself, a fearful and excruciating pain came welling up as if the ground had split open to disgorge a boiling stream of molten rock. The pain came suddenly nearer, with terrifying speed. The lieutenant bit his lower lip and stifled an instinctive moan.

Was this *seppuku?*—he was thinking. It was a sensation of utter chaos, as if the sky had fallen on his head and the world was reeling drunkenly. His will power and courage, which had seemed so robust before he made the incision, had now dwindled to something like a single hairlike thread of steel, and he was assailed by the uneasy feeling that he must advance along this thread, clinging to it with desperation. His clenched fist had grown moist. Looking down, he saw that both his hand and the cloth were drenched in blood. His loincloth too was dyed a deep red. It struck him as incredible that, amidst this terrible agony, things which could be seen could still be seen, and existing things existed still.

The moment the lieutenant thrust the sword into his left side and she saw the deathly pallor fall across his face, like an abruptly lowered curtain, Reiko had to struggle to prevent herself from rushing to his side. Whatever happened, she must watch. She must be a witness. That was the duty her husband had lain upon her. Opposite her, a mat's space away, she could clearly see her husband biting his lip to stifle the pain. The pain was there, with absolute certainty, before her eyes. And Reiko had no means of rescuing him from it.

The sweat glistened on her husband's forehead. The lieutenant closed his eyes, and then opened them again, as if experimenting. The eyes had lost their luster, and seemed innocent and empty like the eyes of a small animal.

115

The agony before Reiko's eyes burned as strong as the summer sun,   *120*
utterly remote from the grief which seemed to be tearing herself apart
within. The pain grew steadily in stature, stretching upward. Reiko felt that
her husband had already become a man in a separate world, a man whose
whole being had been resolved into pain, a prisoner in a cage of pain where
no hand could reach out to him. But Reiko felt no pain at all. Her grief was
not pain. As she thought about this, Reiko began to feel as if someone had
raised a cruel wall of glass high between herself and her husband.

Ever since her marriage her husband's existence had been her own existence, and every breath of his had been a breath drawn by herself. But
now, while her husband's existence in pain was a vivid reality, Reiko could
find in this grief of hers no certain proof at all of her own existence.

With only his right hand on the sword the lieutenant began to cut sideways across his stomach. But as the blade became entangled with the entrails
it was pushed constantly outward by their soft resilience; and the lieutenant
realized that it would be necessary, as he cut, to use both hands to keep the
point pressed deep into his stomach. He pulled the blade across. It did not
cut as easily as he had expected. He directed the strength of his whole body
into his right hand and pulled again. There was a cut of three or four inches.

The pain spread slowly outward from the inner depths until the whole
stomach reverberated. It was like the wild clanging of a bell. Or like a thousand bells which jangled simultaneously at every breath he breathed and
every throb of his pulse, rocking his whole being. The lieutenant could no
longer stop himself from moaning. But by now the blade had cut its way
through to below the navel, and when he noticed this he felt a sense of
satisfaction, and a renewal of courage.

The volume of blood had steadily increased, and now it spurted from
the wound as if propelled by the beat of the pulse. The mat before the
lieutenant was drenched red with splattered blood, and more blood over-
flowed onto it from pools which gathered in folds of the lieutenant's khaki
trousers. A spot, like a bird, came flying across to Reiko and settled on the
lap of her white silk kimono.

By the time the lieutenant had at last drawn the sword across to the right   *125*
side of his stomach, the blade was already cutting shallow and had revealed
its naked tip, slippery with blood and grease. But, suddenly stricken by a fit
of vomiting, the lieutenant cried out hoarsely. The vomiting made the fierce
pain fiercer still, and the stomach, which had thus far remained firm and
compact, now abruptly heaved, opening wide its wound, and the entrails
burst through, as if the wound too were vomiting. Seemingly ignorant of
their master's suffering, the entrails gave an impression of robust health and
almost disagreeable vitality as they slipped smoothly out and spilled over into
the crotch. The lieutenant's head dropped, his shoulders heaved, his eyes
opened to narrow slits, and a thin trickle of saliva dribbled from his mouth.
The gold markings on his epaulettes caught the light and glinted.

Blood was scattered everywhere. The lieutenant was soaked in it to his
knees, and he sat now in a crumpled and listless posture, one hand on the

floor. A raw smell filled the room. The lieutenant, his head drooping, retched repeatedly, and the movement showed vividly in his shoulders. The blade of the sword, now pushed back by the entrails and exposed to its tip, was still in the lieutenant's right hand.

It would be difficult to imagine a more heroic sight than that of the lieutenant at this moment, as he mustered his strength and flung back his head. The movement was performed with sudden violence, and the back of his head struck with a sharp crack against the alcove pillar. Reiko had been sitting until now with her face lowered, gazing in fascination at the tide of blood advancing toward her knees, but the sound took her by surprise and she looked up.

The lieutenant's face was not the face of a living man. The eyes were hollow, the skin parched, the once so lustrous cheeks and lips the color of dried mud. The right hand alone was moving. Laboriously gripping the sword, it hovered shakily in the air like the hand of a marionette and strove to direct the point at the base of the lieutenant's throat. Reiko watched her husband make this last, most heart-rending, futile exertion. Glistening with blood and grease, the point was thrust at the throat again and again. And each time it missed its aim. The strength to guide it was no longer there. The straying point struck the collar and the collar badges. Although its hooks had been unfastened, the stiff military collar had closed together again and was protecting the throat.

Reiko could bear the sight no longer. She tried to go to her husband's help, but she could not stand. She moved through the blood on her knees, and her white skirts grew deep red. Moving to the rear of her husband, she helped no more than by loosening the collar. The quivering blade at last contacted the naked flesh of the throat. At that moment Reiko's impression was that she herself had propelled her husband forward; but that was not the case. It was movement planned by the lieutenant himself, his last exertion of strength. Abruptly he threw his body at the blade, and the blade pierced his neck, emerging at the nape. There was a tremendous spurt of blood and the lieutenant lay still, cold blue-tinged steel protruding from his neck at the back.

5

Slowly, her socks slippery with blood, Reiko descended the stairway. The upstairs room was now completely still.

Switching on the ground-floor lights, she checked the gas jet and the main gas plug and poured water over the smoldering, half-buried charcoal in the brazier. She stood before the upright mirror in the four-and-a-half-mat room and held up her skirts. The bloodstains made it seem as if a bold, vivid pattern was printed across the lower half of her white kimono. When she sat down before the mirror, she was conscious of the dampness and coldness of her husband's blood in the region of her thighs, and she shivered. Then, for a long while, she lingered over her toilet preparations. She applied

130

the rouge generously to her cheeks, and her lips too she painted heavily. This was no longer make-up to please her husband. It was make-up for the world which she would leave behind, and there was a touch of the magnificent and the spectacular in her brushwork. When she rose, the mat before the mirror was wet with blood. Reiko was not concerned about this.

Returning from the toilet, Reiko stood finally on the cement floor of the porchway. When her husband had bolted the door here last night it had been in preparation for death. For a while she stood immersed in the consideration of a simple problem. Should she now leave the bolt drawn? If she were to lock the door, it could be that the neighbors might not notice their suicide for several days. Reiko did not relish the thought of their two corpses putrifying before discovery. After all, it seemed it would be best to leave it open. . . . She released the bolt, and also drew open the frosted-glass door a fraction. . . . At once a chill wind blew in. There was no sign of anyone in the midnight streets and stars glittered ice-cold through the trees in the large house opposite.

Leaving the door as it was, Reiko mounted the stairs. She had walked here and there for some time and her socks were no longer slippery. About halfway up, her nostrils were already assailed by a peculiar smell.

The lieutenant was lying on his face in a sea of blood. The point protruding from his neck seemed to have grown even more prominent than before. Reiko walked heedlessly across the blood. Sitting beside the lieutenant's corpse, she stared intently at the face, which lay on one cheek on the mat. The eyes were opened wide, as if the lieutenant's attention had been attracted by something. She raised the head, folding it in her sleeve, wiped the blood from the lips, and bestowed a last kiss.

Then she rose and took from the closet a new white blanket and a waist   *135* cord. To prevent any derangement of her skirts, she wrapped the blanket about her waist and bound it firmly with the cord.

Reiko sat herself on a spot about one foot distant from the lieutenant's body. Drawing the dagger from her sash, she examined its dully gleaming blade intently, and held it to her tongue. The taste of the polished steel was slightly sweet.

Reiko did not linger. When she thought how the pain which had previously opened such a gulf between herself and her dying husband was now to become a part of her own experience, she saw before her only the joy of herself entering a realm her husband had already made his own. In her husband's agonized face there had been something inexplicable which she was seeing for the first time. Now she would solve that riddle. Reiko sensed that at last she too would be able to taste the true bitterness and sweetness of that great moral principle in which her husband believed. What had until now been tasted only faintly through her husband's example she was about to savor directly with her own tongue.

Reiko rested the point of the blade against the base of her throat. She thrust hard. The wound was only shallow. Her head blazed, and her hands shook uncontrollably. She gave the blade a strong pull sideways. A warm substance flooded into her mouth, and everything before her eyes reddened, in a vision of spouting blood. She gathered her strength and plunged the point of the blade deep into her throat.

AFTER WEEKS OF WATCHING THE ROOF LEAK

Gary Snyder

After weeks of watching the roof leak
        I fixed it tonight
by moving a single board

THE EMPEROR OF ICE-CREAM

Wallace Stevens

Call the roller of big cigars,
The muscular one, and bid him whip
In kitchen cups concupiscent° curds.
Let the wenches dawdle in such dress
As they are used to wear, and let the boys   5
Bring flowers in last month's newspapers.
Let be be finale of seem.
The only emperor is the emperor of ice-cream.

Take from the dresser of deal,
Lacking the three glass knobs, that sheet   10
On which she embroidered fantails once
And spread it so as to cover her face.
If her horny feet protrude, they come
To show how cold she is, and dumb.
Let the lamp affix its beam.   15
The only emperor is the emperor of ice-cream.

---

3. *concupiscent:* sensual

TRACT

William Carlos Williams

I will teach you my townspeople
how to perform a funeral—
for you have it over a troop
of artists—
unless one should scour the world— 5
you have the ground sense necessary.

See! the hearse leads.
I begin with a design for a hearse.
For Christ's sake not black—
nor white either—and not polished! 10
Let it be weathered—like a farm wagon—
with gilt wheels (this could be
applied fresh at small expense)
or no wheels at all:
a rough dray° to drag over the ground. 15

Knock the glass out!
My God—glass, my townspeople!
For what purpose? Is it for the dead
to look out or for us to see
how well he is housed or to see 20
the flowers or the lack of them—
or what?
To keep the rain and snow from him?
He will have a heavier rain soon:
pebbles and dirt and what not. 25
Let there be no glass—
and no upholstery, phew!
and no little brass rollers
and small easy wheels on the bottom—
my townspeople what are you thinking of? 30

A rough plain hearse then
with gilt wheels and no top at all.
On this the coffin lies
by its own weight.

---

15. *dray:* a low cart, without sides or wheels; a sledge

No wreaths please— 35
especially no hot house flowers.
Some common memento is better,
something he prized and is known by:
his old clothes—a few books perhaps—
God knows what! You realize 40
how we are about these things
my townspeople—
something will be found—anything
even flowers if he had come to that.
So much for the hearse. 45

For heaven's sake though see to the driver!
Take off the silk hat; In fact
that's no place at all for him—
up there unceremoniously
dragging our friend out to his own dignity! 50
Bring him down—bring him down!
Low and inconspicuous! I'd not have him ride
on the wagon at all—damn him—
the undertaker's understrapper!
Let him hold the reins 55
and walk at the side
and inconspicuously too!

Then briefly as to yourselves:
Walk behind—as they do in France,
seventh class, or if you ride 60
Hell take curtains! Go with some show
of inconvenience; sit openly—
to the weather as to grief.
Or do you think you can shut grief in?
What—from us? We who have perhaps 65
nothing to lose? Share with us
share with us—it will be money
in your pockets.
                    Go now
I think you are ready. 70

I HEARD A FLY BUZZ

Emily Dickinson

I heard a Fly buzz—when I died—
The Stillness in the Room
Was like the Stillness in the Air—
Between the Heaves of Storm—

The Eyes around—had wrung them dry—   5
And Breaths were gathering firm
For that last Onset—when the King
Be witnessed—in the Room—

I willed my Keepsakes—Signed away
What portion of me be   10
Assignable—and then it was
There interposed a Fly—

With Blue—uncertain stumbling Buzz—
Between the light—and me—
And then the Windows failed—and then   15
I could not see to see—

13

Comparing and Contrasting: Showing Your Reader Likenesses and Differences

Imagine that one day a friend approaches you and asks you whether she should take Professor Easygrade's class or Professor Hardnose's class in Custodial Engineering. After some consideration, you tell your friend to take Professor Hardnose's class because Professor Hardnose has a more comprehensive knowledge of solvents and soaps than Professor Easygrade has. You add that although Professor Easygrade is much friendlier and more approachable and his exams are easier, if your friend wants to be successful in her chosen field, it would be a better idea to choose the more demanding professor because he or she knows the field better and expects more serious work from the students.

To help your friend, you had to arrive at a conclusion, or a dominant idea, by examining two alternatives, comparing or contrasting them in terms of the most important issues relative to the question, and arriving at a conclusion. When you do this in a piece of writing, you compare and contrast to support your dominant idea.

When you read your first draft or watch your second draft develop, you might find that your draft suggests a dominant idea that leads you to consider focusing on the likenesses or differences between two objects, locations, processes, persons, or ideas. Or you might discover that a comparison or a contrast or both might help you clarify a subordinate idea that will lead your reader to see your dominant idea in more detail.

Working with the Readings

Read the following poems and, alone or with your group, answer the questions that follow.

RICHARD CORY

Edwin Arlington Robinson

> Whenever Richard Cory went down town,
> We people on the pavement looked at him:
> He was a gentleman from sole to crown,
> Clean favored° and imperially slim.
>
> And he was always quietly arrayed,   5
> And he was always human when he talked;
> But still he fluttered pulses when he said,
> "Good-morning," and he glittered when he walked.
>
> And he was rich—yes, richer than a king—
> And admirably schooled in every grace: 10
> In fine,° we thought that he was everything
> To make us wish that we were in his place.
>
> So on we worked, and waited for the light,
> And went without the meat, and cursed the bread;
> And Richard Cory, one calm summer night,   15
> Went home and put a bullet through his head.

---

1. Does this poem show likenesses (comparisons) or differences (contrasts)?
2. Who or what is being compared or contrasted?
3. What characteristics does Robinson have his speaker focus on?
4. What other organizational approaches does Robinson use in "Richard Cory" to arrive at his dominant idea? How are those approaches connected to the central comparison or contrast?
5. How does the speaker feel about these likenesses or differences?
6. Although there is no *direct* statement of a dominant idea in the poem, can you see an idea growing from the relationship between the speaker and what he or she observes?

Now read the following poem. On your own or in your group, decide, by comparing and contrasting the two versions of the tale of Richard Cory, which one you think is more effective and more pleasing. Give reasons for your answer.

---

4. *clean favored:* handsome
11. *in fine:* in short

RICHARD CORY

Paul Simon

They say that Richard Cory owns one half of this whole town,
With political connections to spread his wealth around.
Born into society, a banker's only child,
He had everything a man could want: power, grace and style

But I work in his factory   5
And I curse the life I'm living
And I curse my poverty
And I wish that I could be
Oh, I wish that I could be,
Oh, I wish that I could be   10
Richard Cory

The papers print his picture almost everywhere he goes:
Richard Cory at the opera, Richard Cory at a show.
And the rumor of his parties and the orgies on his yacht!
Oh, he surely must be happy with everything he's got.   15

But I work in his factory
And I curse the life I'm living
And I curse my poverty
And I wish that I could be
Oh, I wish that I could be,   20
Oh, I wish that I could be
Richard Cory

He freely gave to charity, he had the common touch,
And they were grateful for his patronage and thanked him
     very much,
So my mind was filled with wonder when the evening   25
     headlines read:
"Richard Cory went home last night and put a bullet through
     his head."

But I work in his factory
And I curse the life I'm living
And I curse my poverty
And I wish that I could be,   30
Oh, I wish that I could be,
Oh, I wish that I could be
Richard Cory

As with the other ways of organizing your ideas that you have learned so far, you have choices in the way you can arrange your comparisons and your contrasts. These choices depend on your dominant idea and on your audience. First of all, you need to decide whether to emphasize likenesses or differences, although in some cases, a balance of the two might be most effective. In addition, you have significant organizational choices to make.

Working with the Readings

Read the following poem, which exemplifies how a writer can use contrast. Alone or in your group, answer the questions that follow it.

SATURDAY'S CHILD

Countee Cullen

Some are teethed on a silver spoon,
With the stars hung for a rattle;
I cut my teeth as the black raccoon—
For implements of battle.

Some are swaddled in silk and down,   5
And heralded by a star;
They swathed my limbs in a sackcloth gown
On a night that was black as tar.

For some, godfather and goddame
The opulent fairies be;   10
Dame Poverty gave me my name,
And Pain godfathered me.

For I was born on a Saturday—
"Bad time for planting a seed,"
Was all my father had to say,   15
And "One more mouth to feed."

Death cut the strings that gave me life,
And handed me to Sorrow,
The only kind of middle wife
My folks could beg or borrow.   20

1. What is Cullen comparing or contrasting? (A reminder: Cullen was an African American poet.)
2. What is the dominant idea that grows from Cullen's poem?

3. In presenting his dominant idea, Cullen chooses certain facts to contrast with other facts to lead you toward a dominant idea. How do the facts support that idea?

4. In presenting his idea, does Cullen arrange his contrast by presenting one side completely and then the other, or does he describe the two sides by giving you part of one and then the corresponding part of the other? After you've decided which approach Cullen uses, try to imagine the same poem using the other approach. Which one seems to be the most effective? Why?

5. Do you think the fact that Cullen was African-American affects his tone and choice of words? Where do you see this?

6. Think of a situation you have faced in which a contrast like Cullen's might make your response to that situation clear. Note the contrasts and see what dominant idea they lead you toward.

Here is another example of comparing and contrasting. When you have read the poem, answer the questions that follow it.

WHEN I HEARD THE LEARN'D ASTRONOMER

Walt Whitman

When I heard the learn'd astronomer,
When the proofs, the figures were ranged in columns before me,
When I was shown the charts and diagrams, to add, divide, and measure them,
When I sitting heard the astronomer where he lectured with much applause in the lecture-room,
How soon unaccountable I became tired and sick,   5
Till rising and gliding out I wander'd off by myself,
In the mystical moist night air, and from time to time,
Look'd up in perfect wonder at the stars.

1. What is Whitman comparing or contrasting, and how does his comparison or contrast lead you to a dominant idea?

2. Does this poem have a plot? Is the plot created by characters?

3. Does Whitman arrange his elements in the same way Cullen did, or does he choose a different way of arranging them? Try imagining

Whitman's poem using another form of arrangement. Would the poem then be more or less effective than Whitman's version?

4. Does Whitman use other techniques to support his comparison or contrast? To begin, you might look at issues such as the words, sounds, and grammar of the poem.

As you've seen, Whitman and Cullen organize their points in two different ways. Whitman approaches his idea and organizes his points by completely presenting one of the objects he is contrasting and then moving on to the other:

Astronomer
Lecture room
Proofs, figures, etc.

Speaker
Outside
Night air, stars, etc.

Cullen organizes his ideas by breaking each one down into its significant component parts and presenting the contrasts between each part separately:

Teething
Silver spoon, etc.
Black raccoon

Swaddling
Silk and down
Sackcloth gown

Godparents
Opulent fairies
Dame Poverty

For showing your reader likenesses and differences, these are the primary approaches. Which one you choose is often a matter of which one your dominant idea suggests to you. As a general rule, the more complex the material you have chosen, the wiser it is to focus on each significant characteristic of each object separately rather than to discuss each object as a whole. You risk losing your reader if you ask him or her to keep too many ideas in mind at once.

However, you do not always have to present every element in equal detail to make your dominant idea clear. If you deal with one element of a comparison in enough concrete, specific detail, you may find it unnecessary to write very much about the other element to make your point. In Robinson's "Richard Cory," for example, the poet chooses details to tell you what you need to know about the speaker *and* about Richard Cory through the way the people of the town see Cory.

To take another example, in "A Nice Place to Visit," Russell Baker contrasts New York and Toronto, choosing three aspects of the two cities. Notice how little he writes about New York. Nevertheless, his point is absolutely clear because his description of Toronto is so concrete:

> Consider the garbage picture. It seems never to have occurred to anybody in Toronto that garbage exists to be heaved into the streets. One can drive for miles without seeing so much as a banana peel in the gutter or a discarded newspaper whirling in the wind.
>
> Nor has Toronto learned about dogs. A check with the authorities confirmed that, yes, there are indeed dogs resident in Toronto, but one would never realize it by walking the sidewalks. Our delegation was shocked by the presumption of a town's calling itself a city, much less a great city, when it obviously knows nothing of either garbage or dogs.
>
> The subway, on which Toronto prides itself, was a laughable imitation of the real thing. The subway cars were not only spotlessly clean, but also fully illuminated. So were the stations. To New Yorkers, it was embarrassing, and we hadn't the heart to tell the subway authorities that they were light-years away from greatness.
>
> We did, however, tell them about spray paints and how effectively a few hundred children equipped with spray-paint cans could at least give their subway the big-city look.

ANALOGY: A SPECIAL USE OF LIKENESS

There will be times in your writing when you discover that to create the background for your idea or to develop your idea you must describe a concept, an object, or a process that few of your readers are familiar with. One way of solving this problem is to create an *analogy:* to compare the unfamiliar to something that your readers already understand. For example, some people who face a computer for the first time are reassured by being told that in some ways it is like a screwdriver or a hammer: It is a tool that will do only what the operator tells it to do.

One note of caution. Although an analogy is very effective for making the unfamiliar familiar, its usefulness is limited. You cannot prove a point with an analogy because its two elements are, after all, different. If you push your analogy too far, your result could be ridiculous. You can't, for example, saw a piece of wood or drive a screw with a computer. Possibly in a beginning biology class your teacher used the image of a water pump to show you how the heart works. This analogy does not mean, however, that when a person has a heart attack, his pump needs to be oiled.

◥ *Working with a Reading*

Read the following selection and, alone or with your group, answer the questions that follow it.

SOJOURNER

Annie Dillard

If survival is an art, then mangroves are artists of the beautiful: not only that they exist at all—smooth-barked, glossy-leaved, thickets of lapped mystery—but that they can and do exist as floating islands, as trees upright and loose, alive and homeless on the water.

I have seen mangroves, always on tropical ocean shores, in Florida and in the Galápagos. There is the red mangrove, the yellow, the button, and the black. They are all short, messy trees, waxy-leaved, laced all over with aerial roots, woody arching buttresses, and weird leathery berry pods. All this tangles from a black muck soil, a black muck matted like a mud-sopped rag, a muck without any other plants, shaded, cold to the touch, tracked at the water's edge by herons and nosed by sharks.

It is these shoreline trees which, by a fairly common accident, can become floating islands. A hurricane flood or a riptide can wrest a tree from the shore, or from the mouth of a tidal river, and hurl it into the ocean. It floats. It is a mangrove island, blown.

There are floating islands on the planet; it amazes me. Credulous Pliny described some islands thought to be mangrove islands floating on a river. The people called these river islands *the dancers,* "because in any consort of musicians singing, they stir and move at the stroke of the feet, keeping time and measure."

Trees floating on rivers are less amazing than trees floating on the poisonous sea. A tree cannot live in salt. Mangrove trees exude salt from their leaves; you can see it, even on shoreline black mangroves, as a thin white crust. Lick a leaf and your tongue curls and coils; your mouth's a heap of salt.   5

Nor can a tree live without soil. A hurricane-born mangrove island may bring its own soil to the sea. But other mangrove trees make their own soil—and their own islands—from scratch. These are the ones which interest me. The seeds germinate in the fruit on the tree. The germinated embryo can drop anywhere—say, onto a dab of floating muck. The heavy root end sinks; a leafy plumule unfurls. The tiny seedling, afloat, is on its way. Soon aerial roots shooting out in all directions trap debris. The sapling's networks twine, the interstices narrow, and water calms in the lee. Bacteria thrive on organic broth; amphipods swarm. These creatures grow and die at the trees' wet feet. The soil thickens, accumulating rainwater, leaf rot, seashells, and guano; the island spreads.

More seeds and more muck yield more trees on the new island. A society grows, interlocked in a tangle of dependencies. The island rocks less in the swells. Fish throng to the backwaters stilled in snarled roots.

Soon, Asian mudskippers—little four-inch fish—clamber up the mangrove roots into the air and peer about from periscope eyes on stalks, like snails. Oysters clamp to submersed roots, as do starfish, dog whelk, and the creatures that live among tangled kelp. Shrimp seek shelter there, limpets a holdfast, pelagic birds a rest.

And the mangrove island wanders on, afloat and adrift. It walks teetering and wanton before the wind. Its fate and direction are random. It may bob across an ocean and catch on another mainland's shores. It may starve or dry while it is still a sapling. It may topple in a storm, or pitchpole. By the rarest of chances, it may stave into another mangrove island in a crash of clacking roots, and mesh. What it is most likely to do is drift anywhere in the alien ocean, feeding on death and growing, netting a makeshift soil as it goes, shrimp in its toes and terns in its hair.

We could do worse.

I alternate between thinking of a planet as home—dear and familiar   *10*
stone hearth and garden—and as a hard land of exile in which we are all sojourners. Today I favor the latter view. The word "sojourner" occurs often in the English Old Testament. It invokes a nomadic people's sense of vagrancy, a praying people's knowledge of estrangement, a thinking people's intuition of sharp loss: "For we are strangers before thee, and sojourners, as were all our fathers: our days on the earth are as a shadow, and there is none abiding."

We don't know where we belong, but in times of sorrow it doesn't seem to be here, here with these silly pansies and witless mountains, here with sponges and hard-eyed birds. In times of sorrow the innocence of the other creatures—from whom and with whom we evolved—seems a mockery. Their ways are not our ways. We seem set among them as among lifelike props for a tragedy—or a broad lampoon—on a thrust rock stage.

It doesn't seem to be here that we belong, here where space is curved, the earth is round, we're all going to die, and it seems as wise to stay in bed as budge. It is strange here, not quite warm enough, or too warm, too leafy, or inedible, or windy, or dead. It is not, frankly, the sort of home for people one would have thought of—although I lack the fancy to imagine another.

The planet itself is a sojourner in airless space, a wet ball flung across nowhere. The few objects in the universe scatter. The coherence of matter dwindles and crumbles toward stillness. I have read, and repeated, that our solar system as a whole is careering through space toward a point east of Hercules. Now I wonder: what could that possibly mean, east of Hercules? Isn't space curved? When we get "there," how will our course change, and why? Will we slide down the universe's inside arc like mud slung at a wall? Or what sort of welcoming shore is this east of Hercules? Surely we don't anchor there, and disembark, and sweep into dinner with our host. Does someone cry, "Last stop, last stop"? At any rate, east of

Hercules, like east of Eden, isn't a place to call home. It is a course without direction; it is "out." And we are cast.

These are enervating thoughts, the thoughts of despair. They crowd back, unbidden, when human life as it unrolls goes ill, when we lose control of our lives or the illusion of control, and it seems that we are not moving toward any end but merely blown. Our life seems cursed to be a wiggle merely, and a wandering without end. Even nature is hostile and poisonous, as though it were impossible for our vulnerability to survive on these acrid stones.

Whether these thoughts are true or not I find less interesting than the   15
possibilities for beauty they may hold. We are down here in time, where beauty grows. Even if things are as bad as they could possibly be, and as meaningless, then matters of truth are themselves indifferent; we may as well please our sensibilities and, with as much spirit as we can muster, go out with a buck and wing.

The planet is less like an enclosed spaceship—spaceship earth—than it is like an exposed mangrove island beautiful and loose. We the people started small and have since accumulated a great and solacing muck of soil, of human culture. We are rooted in it; we are bearing it with us across nowhere. The word "nowhere" is our cue: the consort of musicians strikes up, and we in the chorus stir and move and start twirling our hats. A mangrove island turns drift to dance. It creates its own soil as it goes, rocking over the salt sea at random, rocking day and night and round the sun, rocking round the sun and out toward east of Hercules.

---

1. What do you think is Dillard's dominant idea?
2. Do you think the dominant idea itself is concrete (tied to specific realities or actual events) or abstract (apart from specific realities or actual events)?
3. What is the analogy that Dillard creates for her essay?
4. How does that analogy work in her essay?
5. Dillard's analogy takes half the essay, and in it she writes a lot of concrete description. Do you think all of that description is necessary?
6. How does the last paragraph of Dillard's essay function in terms of what she has done up to that point?

METAPHOR AND SIMILE: IMAGINATIVE ANALOGIES AND FIGURATIVE LANGUAGE

Metaphors and similes are called "figurative language." Figurative language is language that is not meant to be taken literally. Specifically, metaphors and similes are comparisons of two objects that are usually not at all like each other. A *simile* makes a comparison *explicit* by using the word *like* or *as*. A *metaphor suggests* its comparison by referring to one of its elements as if it *were* the other.

Writers use metaphors and similes to appeal to your imagination, to invite you to see familiar objects or people in a way you had not thought of before. A new combination of images invites you to go past the literal facts and to look at the writer's subject from a different point of view that takes you beneath the surface of his or her material. By appealing to your imagination, writers use metaphors to suggest far more than the literal words themselves can.

It is easy to assume that metaphors and similes are the exotic inventions and exclusive property of professional writers, especially poets, and that a person must have some sort of special training to understand them. However, you already know and use figurative language. If you listen to the words flying around you, you will hear metaphors and similes packed into every speech. When a person wants to describe another, attractive person of the opposite sex, that person may be "a fox," "a hunk," "a babe," or "a stud." Few people hearing such a statement take it literally. A car which breaks down a lot is "a lemon" or "a dog," yet no one expects to see either a piece of fruit or an animal being driven around town. Advertisements are packed with metaphors and similes that are meant to suggest ideas and attitudes to their audience. A deodorant can leave you smelling fresh as a summer's day. Even the names of products are figures of speech. Drivers can climb into a Mustang, an Eagle, an Eclipse, or a Saturn. People can suds up with Irish Spring, Ivory, or Zest. They can wash their laundry in Tide, then soften it with Downy while they munch on Screaming Yellow Zonkers, Ding-Dongs, or Ho-Ho's.

✒ *Working with a Reading*

Alone or with your group, read the following advertisement and point out the metaphors or similes in it. Since you cannot take the figurative language literally, define what that language suggests to you about the product and what it might do for the person who buys it.

> As sparkling and seductive
> as a sunlit garden
> in the south of France.
> Le parfum lalique is now
> brought to light in a
> limited edition parfum
> flacon or precious crystal.

For the next day or so be on the lookout for metaphors and similes. Listen to people speaking to you or listen to other people's conversations.

Listen to the radio or listen carefully as you watch television. As you read, look for figurative language.

Collect three examples that strike you as being especially effective. Analyze them in terms of what they suggest about their subject without making their statement literally.

If you're working in a group, choose the most interesting of your three examples and explain it to your group. The group should then pick the most interesting of the members' examples, analyze it again, and report the results to the class.

If you're working alone, choose the most interesting example and be prepared to analyze it for your class.

 An Invitation to Write

Write an advertisement for an object that is familiar and insignificant to you. Using figurative language, make the object both interesting and desirable to your audience.

Sometimes, as in the following readings, the writer uses a metaphor or a series of metaphors to suggest an idea, intensity of feeling, or associated emotions in a line or two as part of the thematic development of his or her idea.

Working with the Readings

Read the following four selections and, alone or with your group, answer the questions that follow each one.

QUESTION

May Swenson

Body my house
my horse my hound
what will I do
when you are fallen

Where will I sleep
How will I ride
What will I hunt

Where can I go
without my mount
all eager and quick   *10*
How will I know
in thicket ahead
is danger or treasure
when Body my good
bright dog is dead   *15*

How will it be
to lie in the sky
without roof or door
and wind for an eye

With cloud for shift   *20*
how will I hide?

---

1. Describe the metaphors Swenson presents in the first stanza of her poem. What is she speaking about? What does she compare it to?

2. How are these metaphors like each other?

3. In the second stanza Swenson allows a new metaphor to grow from the metaphor that she presented in the first stanza. What is it?

4. What kind of behavior does Swenson use these metaphors to speak about? What does she suggest about that behavior through her metaphors?

5. What metaphor does Swenson return to in the last stanza? What does she use that metaphor to suggest to you in that stanza?

6. What is Swenson's dominant idea in "Question"? How do the metaphors help her present her ideas to you?

7. Can you apply Swenson's subject and the metaphors she uses to experiences and attitudes in your life?

Other writers may make a whole poem of a single metaphor.

TAKING THE HANDS
OF SOMEONE YOU LOVE

Robert Bly

> Taking the hands of someone you love,
> You see they are delicate cages . . .
> Tiny birds are singing
> In the secluded prairies
> And in the deep valleys of the hand.   5

---

1. What does this metaphor tell you about how the speaker feels about the person he loves?
2. Why do you think the speaker focuses on the other person's hands and the act of taking them?
3. What does the metaphor lead you to feel about taking the hands of someone you love?

Sometimes a writer may use metaphor at many levels, as Sylvia Plath does in this poem.

METAPHORS

Sylvia Plath

> I'm a riddle in nine syllables.
> An elephant, a ponderous house,
> A melon strolling on two tendrils.
> O red fruit, ivory, fine timbers!
> This loaf's big with its yeasty rising.   5
> Money's new-minted in this fat purse.
> I'm a means, a stage, a cow in calf.
> I've eaten a bag of green apples,
> Boarded the train there's no getting off.

---

1. Look at the form of this poem. How many lines does the poem have? How many syllables can you find in each line?

2. Each line contains a different metaphor. What ideas and images tie them together? How does each express what Plath feels about herself at the time of the poem?

3. If you have not thought about it yet, what is the answer to the riddle? How do all the metaphors in the poem, including the form of the poem itself, lead you to this answer?

Writers of prose, both fiction and nonfiction, also use metaphor to clarify their ideas, to make them more interesting for their audience, and to suggest further ideas.

I HAVE A DREAM

Martin Luther King, Jr.

I am happy to join with you today in what will go down in history as the greatest demonstration for freedom in the history of our nation.

Five score years ago, a great American, in whose symbolic shadow we stand today, signed the Emancipation Proclamation. This momentous decree came as a great beacon light of hope to millions of Negro slaves who had been seared in the flames of withering injustice. It came as a joyous daybreak to end the long night of their captivity. But one hundred years later, the Negro still is not free. One hundred years later, the life of the Negro is still sadly crippled by the manacles of segregation and the chains of discrimination. One hundred years later, the Negro lives on a lonely island of poverty in the midst of a vast ocean of material prosperity. One hundred years later, the Negro is still anguished in the corners of American society and finds himself in exile in his own land. And so we have come here today to dramatize a shameful condition.

In a sense we have come to our nation's capital to cash a check. When the architects of our republic wrote the magnificent words of the Constitution and the Declaration of Independence, they were signing a promissory note to which every American was to fall heir. This note was the promise that all men—yes, Black men as well as white men—would be guaranteed the inalienable rights of life, liberty, and the pursuit of happiness.

It is obvious today that America has defaulted on this promissory note insofar as her citizens of color are concerned. Instead of honoring this sacred obligation, America has given the Negro people a bad check, a check which has come back marked "insufficient funds." But we refuse to believe that the bank of justice is bankrupt. We refuse to believe that there are insufficient funds in the great vaults of opportunity of this nation; and so we have come to cash this check, a check that will give us upon demand the riches of freedom and the security of justice.

We have also come to this hallowed spot to remind America of the   5
fierce urgency of *now*. This is no time to engage in the luxury of cooling off or to take the tranquilizing drug of gradualism. *Now* is the time to make real promises of democracy. *Now* is the time to rise from the dark and desolate valley of segregation to the sunlit path of racial justice. *Now* is the time to lift our nation from the quicksands of racial injustice to the solid rock of brotherhood. *Now* is the time to make justice a reality for all of God's children.

It would be fatal for the nation to overlook the urgency of the moment. This sweltering summer of the Negro's legitimate discontent will not pass until there is an invigorating autumn of freedom and equality. Nineteen sixty-three is not an end, but a beginning. And those who hope that the Negro needed to blow off steam and will now be content will have a rude awakening if the nation returns to business as usual. There will be neither rest nor tranquility in America until the Negro is granted his citizenship rights. The whirlwinds of revolt will continue to shake the foundations of our nation until the bright day of justice emerges.

But there is something that I must say to my people who stand on the warm threshold which leads into the palace of justice. In the process of gaining our rightful place, we must not be guilty of wrongful deeds. Let us not seek to satisfy our thirst for freedom by drinking from the cup of bitterness and hatred. We must forever conduct our struggle on the high plane of dignity and discipline. We must not allow our creative protest to degenerate into physical violence. Again and again we must rise to the majestic heights of meeting physical force with soul force. And the marvelous new militancy which has engulfed the Negro community must not lead us to a distrust of all white people; for many of our white brothers, as evidenced by their presence here today, have come to realize that their destiny is tied up with our destiny, and they have come to realize that their freedom is inextricably bound to our freedom.

We cannot walk alone. And as we walk we must make the pledge that we shall always march ahead. We cannot turn back. There are those who are asking the devotees of civil rights, "When will you be satisfied?" We can never be satisfied as long as the Negro is the victim of the unspeakable horrors of police brutality. We can never be satisfied as long as our bodies, heavy with the fatigue of travel, cannot gain lodging in the motels of the highways and the hotels of the cities. We cannot be satisfied as long as the Negro's basic mobility is from a smaller ghetto to a larger one. We can never be satisfied as long as our children are stripped of their selfhood and robbed of their dignity by signs stating "For Whites Only."

We cannot be satisfied as long as the Negro in Mississippi cannot vote and a Negro in New York believes he has nothing for which to vote. No, no, we are not satisfied, and we will not be satisfied until justice rolls down like waters and righteousness like a mighty stream.

I am not unmindful that some of you have come here out of great trials and tribulations. Some of you have come fresh from narrow jail cells. Some of you have come from areas where your quest for freedom left you battered by the storms of persecution and staggered by the winds of police brutality. You have been the veterans of creative suffering. Continue to work with the faith that unearned suffering is redemptive.

Go back to Mississippi, and go back to Alabama. Go back to South   10 Carolina. Go back to Georgia. Go back to Louisiana. Go back to the slums and ghettos of our Northern cities, knowing that somehow this situation can and will be changed. Let us not wallow in the valley of despair.

I say to you today, my friends, even though we face the difficulties of today and tomorrow, I still have a dream. It is a dream deeply rooted in the American dream. I have a dream that one day this nation will rise up and live out the true meaning of its creed: "We hold these truths to be self-evident, that all men are created equal." I have a dream that one day, on the red hills of Georgia, sons of former slaves and the sons of former slave owners will be able to sit down together at the table of brotherhood. I have a dream that one day even the state of Mississippi, a state sweltering with the heat of injustice, sweltering with the heat of oppression, will be transformed into an oasis of freedom and justice. I have a dream that my four little children will one day live in a nation where they will not be judged by the color of their skin, but by the content of their character.

I have a dream today. I have a dream that one day down in Alabama—with its vicious racists, with its governor's lips dripping with the words of interposition and nullification—one day right there in Alabama, little Black boys and Black girls will be able to join hands with little white boys and white girls as sisters and brothers.

I have a dream today. I have a dream that one day every valley shall be exalted and every hill and mountain shall be made low, the rough places will be made plain and the crooked places will be made straight, and the glory of the Lord shall be revealed, and all flesh shall see it together.

This is our hope. This is the faith that I go back to the South with. And with this faith we will be able to hew out of the mountain of despair a stone of hope. With this faith we will be able to transform the jangling discords of our nation into a beautiful symphony of brotherhood. With this faith we will be able to work together, to play together, to struggle together, to go to jail together, to stand up for freedom together, knowing that we will be free one day.

And this will be the day—this will be the day when all of God's   *15*
children will be able to sing with new meaning:

> My country, 'tis of thee,
> Sweet land of liberty,
>   Of thee I sing;
> Land where my fathers died,
> Land of the Pilgrim's pride,
> From every mountainside
>   Let freedom ring.

And if America is to be a great nation, this must become true.

And so let freedom ring from the prodigious hilltops of New Hampshire. Let freedom ring from the mighty mountains of New York. Let freedom ring from the heightening Alleghenies of Pennsylvania. Let freedom ring from the snow-capped Rockies of Colorado. Let freedom ring from the curvaceous slopes of California.

But not only that. Let freedom ring from Stone Mountain of Georgia. Let freedom ring from Lookout Mountain of Tennessee. Let freedom ring from every hill and molehill of Mississippi. "From every mountainside let freedom ring."

And when this happens—when we allow freedom to ring, when we let it ring from every village and every hamlet, from every state and every city—we will be able to speed up that day when all of God's children, Black men and white men, Jews and Gentiles, Protestants and Catholics, will be able to join hands and sing in the words of the old Negro spiritual: "Free at last! Free at last! Thank God Almighty. We are free at last!"

---

1. What is King's dominant idea as you understand it?

2. Look carefully at King's speech/essay. Does his figurative language imply a consistent theme? If you see a theme in his use of figurative language, how does it support his dominant idea?

3. Take any paragraph in the speech/essay that you find particularly effective and substitute literal statements for the figurative language. How has the paragraph been changed? Do you find the literal version better or worse than the original? Why?

❧ *An Invitation to Write*

Choose a subject that is as important to you as the subjects in the preceding poems and essay were to their writers. Using a metaphor or a series of metaphors, write a poem or a short piece of prose that communicates your feeling to your reader.

PERSONIFICATION

Personification is a special sort of metaphor. The writer using personification gives human attributes to nonhuman objects. Our everyday language is full of personification. For example, the sun might shine down *cheerfully* on a day that *promises* to be pleasant. Or on a cloudy day that *frowns* down upon you, you realize that the test you have to take later will *challenge* you more than you thought it would. In these ways, personification takes abstract notions and gives them a human face that speaks to the reader's experience in terms that he or she knows and can respond to.

 Working with a Reading

Read the following poem and, alone or with your group, answer the questions that follow it.

A BLESSING

James Wright

> Just off the highway to Rochester, Minnesota,
> Twilight bounds softly forth on the grass.
> And the eyes of those two Indian ponies
> Darken with kindness.
> They have come gladly out of the willows   5
> To welcome my friend and me.
> We step over the barbed wire into the pasture
> Where they have been grazing all day, alone.
> They ripple tensely, they can hardly contain their happiness
> That we have come.   10
> They bow shyly as wet swans. They love each other.
> There is no loneliness like theirs.
> At home once more,
> They begin munching the young tufts of spring in the darkness.
> I would like to hold the slenderer one in my arms,   15
> For she has walked over to me
> And nuzzled my left hand.
> She is black and white,
> Her mane falls wild on her forehead,
> And the light breeze moves me to caress her long ear   20
> That is delicate as the skin over a girl's wrist.
> Suddenly I realize
> That if I stepped out of my body I would break
> Into blossom.

1. Find examples of personification, metaphor, and simile in this poem. How do these examples of figurative language work together to show you how the narrator feels in this situation?

2. What do the instances of personification and uses of metaphor and simile tell you about the relationship between the speaker and the horses?

3. What idea or attitude do the details and images—along with the metaphors, similes, and personification—lead you to?

An Invitation to Write

Think of a situation in which you found yourself dealing with a non-human object. Would personification help you to make your feelings about that situation clearer to others? Try writing a paragraph or two in poetry or prose that uses personification to make those feelings clear to your reader.

A Student Paper

When you have read this paper, answer the questions that follow it, alone or with your group.

REVERSE DISCRIMINATION

Donald L. Rose

The air around the elementary school is filled with the smell of hot macadam. A bell rings like a warning of a jailbreak to prison guards. Soon the line-painted surface of the play yard is filled with screaming kids. As I run to my favorite spot to play kickball, my best friend is selecting team partners. I advise him to avoid the Mexican kid so that the other team will get him and lose the game.

Now I've grown to my early teens. As I walk with my friends down the corridors of the junior high, I feel invincible. We walk through the building whispering, laughing, telling ethnic jokes and making racial slurs about the brown kids. We believe only white kids should be allowed in my school. Any other color of people makes it dirty. I wouldn't associate with them nor would I talk to them voluntarily. To me they were of lower status in society and didn't deserve to be in my company. They were the obvious root of all the problems that the community and the school were having with violence and graffiti.

The second week of high school has started, and I'm sitting talking to a friend. She is a cheerleader with blonde hair and tanned skin. We are talking about an injury that I incurred during football practice a few days earlier. She tells me that I have a female admirer who would like very much to meet me. She's the girl of my dreams. Her name is Helen, a petite brunette with blue eyes that make my heart pound and a body that would bring most guys to their knees. We talk for the rest of the lunch period, and I walk her to class. As she walks away, I think to myself that I can't wait to see her again. The only time I do see her is at school, where we spend all of our free time together.

A few weeks go by, and Helen wants me to meet her mom. As we arrive at her house I feel so nervous that my stomach is tied up in knots, my heart is pounding, and I can feel my body shaking to my heartbeat. Helen's mom resembles Helen in stature and has the same brown hair. She smiles and speaks to me, but I don't understand. I beg her pardon and ask her to repeat herself. Then it hits me. She is speaking Spanish. Helen looks at me as I stand there speechless and says to me, "My mom says, 'Hi. Come in and have a seat.' I think she likes you."

I feel sick to my stomach and a lump has grown in my throat, not   5
because Helen's mom speaks Spanish, or that my girlfriend is Mexican, but because of the things I've said and thought about Mexicans all my life. I've treated them badly all of these years, and suddenly I don't have any reasons to justify what I've done. The guilt overwhelms me, and I make an excuse to leave.

As I leave the house and drive home, a sinking feeling overwhelms me. Guilt for all those years sets in. The next day I don't see other races of people. I see people. I feel like a new person, without prejudice. Now I look past the color of people's skin and see them for what they really are. When I see Helen, I apologize for leaving so abruptly and explain to her what I felt then and how I feel now. She assures me in a very sweet way that I am not the first to be shocked that she is Mexican. Her blue eyes and fair skin threw off my estimate of her ethnic background.

Helen asks me if I would like to meet her father. Feeling cured of my racial prejudices, I agree that it would be a good idea. Once inside the house I meet a thin, tall dark man of about six feet. He is dressed in a suit and tie, and as I approach him he stands and waits for Helen to introduce us. She introduces him as Bill, her father. He greets me with a handshake and speaks to me in English. I am pleasantly surprised and begin to feel relaxed and confident. He offers me a seat and to get me a soda. When he gets to the kitchen, I hear a discussion break out in Spanish between Helen, her mom, and Bill. I don't think anything of it until it seems they are arguing. After a few minutes Helen walks out of the kitchen with tears in her eyes. She tells me that her father is very disappointed in her because he doesn't want her dating white boys. I leave the house without saying good-bye. I fly out to my car in a rage. Helen apologizes to me the following day for what happened, and I apologize to her for leaving the way I did. We agree that we will continue to see each other only at school.

Being called a "white boy" by a man who looks as if he has a good education and is older than I brought out feelings of anger in me that I've never felt before. This experience made me realize what it's like to be discriminated against. Discrimination goes both ways, and in either case it doesn't contribute to the growth and understanding between different people.

---

1. What is this writer's dominant idea?
2. If the writer uses comparison and contrast as a dominant organizational strategy, what other organizational strategies does he use to develop and support his dominant idea?
3. How does this writer introduce his piece of writing? Do you think the introduction is effective?
4. When and how does this writer present his dominant idea? Do you think this is an effective way to present it?
5. Do the writer's examples support his dominant idea adequately?
6. If this writer were a member of your group or if you had the chance to speak with him about his paper, what suggestions would you have for him to help him make his paper more effective?

FURTHER READINGS

On the following pages you will find readings that use comparison and contrast as an organizational strategy. If your teacher assigns some or all of these readings or if you are inclined to read them on your own, pay attention to the ways the writers use comparison and contrast to support their dominant ideas. Also, note how the writers use voice and style to engage your feelings, your interest, and your intellect.

Remember, these writers are writing to you—a fellow human being. They have chosen to tell you something about coping with the effort of being human in their worlds. See how their examples and ideas speak to your experience. See how the combination of your experiences and those the writers offer you might lead you to your own ideas about your world.

MY HORSE

Barry Lopez

It is curious that Indian warriors on the northern plains in the nineteenth century, who were almost entirely dependent on the horse for mobility and status, never gave their horses names. If you borrowed a man's horse and went off raiding for other horses, however, or if you lost your mount in battle and then jumped on mine and counted coup° on an enemy—well, those horses would have to be shared with the man whose horse you borrowed, and that coup would be mine, not yours. Because even if I gave him no name, he was my horse.

If you were a Crow warrior and I a young Teton Sioux out after a warrior's identity and we came over a small hill somewhere in the Montana prairie and surprised each other, I could tell a lot about you by looking at your horse.

Your horse might have feathers tied in his mane, or in his tail, or a medicine bag tied around his neck. If I knew enough about the Crow, and had looked at you closely, I might make some sense of the decoration, even guess who you were if you were well-known. If you had painted your horse I could tell even more, because we both decorated our horses with signs that meant the same things. Your white handprints high on his flanks would tell me you had killed an enemy in a hand-to-hand fight. Small horizontal lines stacked on your horse's foreleg, or across his nose, would tell me how many

---

counting coup: the custom among the Plains Indians of striking or touching an enemy as a sign of courage

times you had counted coup. Horse hoof marks on your horse's rump, or three-sided boxes, would tell me how many times you had stolen horses. If there was a bright red square on your horse's neck I would know you were leading a war party and that there were probably others out there in the coulees behind you.

You might be painted all over as blue as the sky and covered with white dots, with your horse painted the same way. Maybe hailstorms were your power—or if I chased you a hailstorm might come down and hide you. There might be lightning bolts on the horse's legs and flanks, and I would wonder if you had lightning power, or a slow horse. There might be white circles around your horse's eyes to help him see better.

Or you might be like Crazy Horse,° with no decoration, no marks on   5
your horse to tell me anything, only a small lightning bolt on your cheek, a piece of turquoise tied behind your ear.

You might have scalps dangling from your rein.

I could tell something about you by your horse. All this would come to me in a few seconds. I might decide this was my moment and shout my war cry—*Hoka hey!* Or I might decide you were like the grizzly bear: I would raise my weapon to you in salute and go my way, to see you again when I was older.

I do not own a horse. I am attached to a truck, however, and I have come to think of it in a similar way. It has no name; it never occurred to me to give it a name. It has little decoration; neither of us is partial to decoration. I have a piece of turquoise in the truck because I had heard once that some of the southwestern tribes tied a small piece of turquoise in a horse's hock to keep him from stumbling. I like the idea. I also hang sage in the truck when I go on a long trip. But inside, the truck doesn't look much different from others that look just like it on the outside. I like it that way. Because I like my privacy.

For two years in Wyoming I worked on a ranch wrangling horses. The horse I rode when I had to have a good horse was a quarter horse and his name was Coke High. This name came with him. At first I thought he'd been named for the soft drink. I'd known stranger names given to horses by whites. Years later I wondered if some deviant Wyoming cowboy wise to cocaine had not named him. Now I think he was probably named after a rancher, an historical figure of the region. I never asked the people who owned him for fear of spoiling the spirit of my inquiry.

We were running over a hundred horses on this ranch. They all had   10
names. After a few weeks I knew all the horses and the names too. You had to. No one knew how to talk about the animals or put them in order or tell

---

Crazy Horse: A Sioux chief (1849?–1877) born in Nebraska; he fought General Custer at the Little Big Horn.

the wranglers what to do unless they were using the names—Princess, Big Red, Shoshone, Clay.

My truck is named Dodge. The name came with it. I don't know if it was named after the town or the verb or the man who invented it. I like it for a name. Perfectly anonymous, like Rex for a dog, or Old Paint. You can't tell anything with a name like that.

The truck is a van. I call it a truck because it's not a car and because "van" is a suburban sort of consumer word, like "oxford loafer," and I don't like the sound of it. On the outside it looks like any other Dodge Sportsman 300. It's a dirty tan color. There are a few body dents, but it's never been in a wreck. I tore the antenna off against a tree on a pinched mountain road. A boy in Midland, Texas, rocked one of my rear view mirrors off. A logging truck in Oregon squeeze-fired a piece of debris off the road and shattered my windshield. The oil pan and gas tank are pug-faced from high-centering on bad roads. (I remember a horse I rode for a while named Targhee whose hocks were scarred from tangles in barbed wire when he was a colt and who spooked a lot in high grass, but these were not like "dents." They were more like bad tires.)

I like to travel. I go mostly in the winter and mostly on two-lane roads. I've driven the truck from Key West to Vancouver, British Columbia, and from Yuma to Long Island over the past four years. I used to ride Coke High only about five miles every morning when we were rounding up horses. Hard miles of twisting and turning. About six hundred miles a year. Then I'd turn him out and ride another horse for the rest of the day. That's what was nice about having a remuda.° You could do all you had to do and not take it all out on your best horse. Three car family.

My truck came with a lot of seats in it and I've never really known what to do with them. Sometimes I put the seats in and go somewhere with a lot of people, but most of the time I leave them out. I like riding around with the empty cavern of space behind my head. I know it's something with a history to it, that there's truth in it, because I always rode a horse the same way—with empty saddle bags. In case I found something. The possibility of finding something is half the reason for being on the road.

The value of anything comes to me in its use. If I am not using some- 15 thing it is of no value to me and I give it away. I wasn't always that way. I used to keep everything I owned—just in case. I feel good about the truck because it gets used. A lot. To haul hay and firewood and lumber and rocks and garbage and animals. Other people have used it to haul furniture and freezers and dirt and recycled newspapers. And to move from one house to another. When I lend it for things like that I don't look to get anything back but some gas (if we're going to be friends). But if you go way out in the

---

remuda: in the Southwest, a herd of horses from which ranch hands choose their mounts

country to a dump and pick up the things you can still find out there (once a load of cedar shingles we sold for $175 to an architect) I expect you to leave some of those things around my place when you come back—if I need them.

When I think back, maybe the nicest thing I ever put in that truck was timber wolves. It was a long night's drive from Oregon up into British Columbia. We were all very quiet about it; it was like moving clouds across the desert.

Sometimes something won't fit in the truck and I think about improving it—building a different door system, for example. I am forever going to add better gauges on the dash and a pair of driving lamps and a sunroof, but I never get around to doing any of it. I remember I wanted to improve Coke High once too, especially the way he bolted like a greyhound through patches of cottonwood on a river flat. But all I could do with him was to try to rein him out of it. Or hug his back.

Sometimes, road-stoned in a blur of country like southwestern Wyoming or North Dakota, I talk to the truck. It's like wandering on the high plains under a summer sun, on plains where, George Catlin° wrote, you were "out of sight of land." I say what I am thinking out loud, or point at things along the road. It's a crazy, sun-stroked sort of activity, a sure sign it's time to pull over, to go for a walk, to make a fire and have some tea, to lie in the shade of the truck.

I've always wanted to pat the truck. It's basic to the relationship. But it never works.

I remember when I was on the ranch, just at sunrise, after I'd saddled   *20* Coke High, I'd be huddled down in my jacket smoking a cigarette and looking down into the valley, along the river where the other horses had spent the night. I'd turn to Coke and run my hand down his neck and slap-pat him on the shoulder to say I was coming up. It made a bond, an agreement we started the day with.

I've thought about that a lot with the truck, because we've gone out together at sunrise on so many mornings. I've even fumbled around trying to do it. But metal won't give.

The truck's personality is mostly an expression of two ideas: "with-you" and "alone." When Coke High was "with-you" he and I were the same animal. We could have cut a rooster out of a flock of chickens, we were so in tune. It's the same with the truck: rolling through Kentucky on a hilly two-lane road, three in the morning under a full moon and no traffic. Picture it. You roll like water.

There are other times when you are with each other but there's no connection at all. Coke got that way when he was bored and we'd fight each other about which way to go around a tree. When the truck gets like

---

George Catlin: American artist and writer (1796–1872) who lived among the Indians

that—"alone"—it's because it feels its Detroit fat-ass design dragging at its heart and making a fool out of it.

I can think back over more than a hundred nights I've slept in the truck, sat in it with a lamp burning, bundled up in a parka, reading a book. It was always comfortable. A good place to wait out a storm. Like sleeping inside a buffalo.

The truck will go past 100,000 miles soon. I'll rebuild the engine and put a different transmission in it. I can tell from magazine advertisements that I'll never get another one like it. Because every year they take more of the heart out of them. One thing that makes a farmer or a rancher go sour is a truck that isn't worth a shit. The reason you see so many old pickups in ranch country is because these are the only ones with any heart. You can count on them. The weekend rancher runs around in a new pickup with too much engine and not enough transmission and with the wrong sort of tires because he can afford anything, even the worst. A lot of them have names for their pickups too.

My truck has broken down, in out of the way places at the worst of times. I've walked away and screamed the foulness out of my system and gotten the tools out. I had to fix a water pump in a blizzard in the Panamint Mountains in California once. It took all day with the Coleman stove burning under the engine block to keep my hands from freezing. We drifted into Beatty, Nevada, that night with it jury-rigged together with—I swear— baling wire, and we were melting snow as we went and pouring it in to compensate for the leaks.

There is a dent next to the door on the driver's side I put there one sweltering night in Miami. I had gone to the airport to meet my wife, whom I hadn't seen in a month. My hands were so swollen with poison ivy blisters I had to drive with my wrists. I had shut the door and was locking it when the window fell off its runner and slid down inside the door. I couldn't leave the truck unlocked because I had too much inside I didn't want to lose. So I just kicked the truck a blow in the side and went to work on the window. I hate to admit kicking the truck. It's like kicking a dog, which I've never done.

Coke High and I had an accident once. We hit a badger hole at a full gallop. I landed on my back and blacked out. When I came to, Coke High was about a hundred yards away. He stayed a hundred yards away for six miles, all the way back to the ranch.

I want to tell you about carrying those wolves, because it was a fine thing. There were ten of them. We had four in the truck with us in crates and six in a trailer. It was a five hundred mile trip. We went at night for the cool air and because there wouldn't be as much traffic. I could feel from the way the truck rolled along that its heart was in the trip. It liked the wolves inside it, the sweet odor that came from the crates. I could feel that same

tireless wolf–lope developing in its wheels; it was like you might never have
to stop for gas, ever again.

The truck gets very self–focused when it works like this; its heart is   *30*
strong and it's good to be around it. It's good to be *with* it. You get the same
feeling when you pull someone out of a ditch. Coke High and I pulled a
Volkswagen out of the mud once, but Coke didn't like doing it very much.
Speed, not strength, was his center. When the guy who owned the car
thanked us and tried to pat Coke, the horse snorted and swung away, trying
to preserve his distance, which is something a horse spends a lot of time on.

So does the truck.

Being distant lets the truck get its heart up. The truck has been cold and
alone in Montana at 38 below zero. It's climbed horrible, eroded roads in
Idaho. It's been burdened beyond overloading, and made it anyway. I've asked
it to do these things because they build heart, and without heart all you have
is a machine. You have nothing. I don't think people in Detroit know anything at all about heart. That's why everything they build dies so young.

One time in Arizona the truck and I came through one of the worst
storms I've ever been in, an outrageous, angry blizzard. But we went down
the road, right through it. You couldn't explain our getting through by the
sort of tires I had on the truck, or the fact that I had chains on, or was a good
driver, or had a lot of weight over my drive wheels or a good engine, because it was more than this. It was a contest between the truck and the
blizzard—and the truck wouldn't quit. I could have gone to sleep and the
truck would have just torn a road down Interstate 40 on its own. It scared
the hell out of me; but it gave me heart, too.

We came off the Mogollon Rim that night and out of the storm and
headed south for Phoenix. I pulled off the road to sleep for a few hours, but
before I did I got out of the truck. It was raining. Warm rain. I tied a short
piece of red avalanche cord into the grill. I left it there for a long time, like
an eagle feather on a horse's tail. It flapped and spun in the wind. I could
hear it ticking against the grill when I drove.

When I have to leave that truck I will just raise up my left arm—*Hoka*   *35*
hey!—and walk away.

THE DIFFERENCES BETWEEN MEN AND WOMEN

Phyllis Schlafly

The first requirement for the acquisition of power by the Positive
Woman is to understand the differences between men and women. Your
outlook on life, your faith, your behavior, your potential for fulfillment, all
are determined by the parameters of your original premise. The Positive

Woman starts with the assumption that the world is her oyster. She rejoices in the creative capability within her body and the power potential of her mind and spirit. She understands that men and women are different, and that those very differences provide the key to her success as a person and fulfillment as a woman.

The women's liberationist, on the other hand, is imprisoned by her own negative view of herself and of her place in the world around her. This view of women was most succinctly expressed in an advertisement designed by the principal women's liberationist organization, the National Organization for Women (NOW), and run in many magazines and newspapers and as spot announcements on many television stations. The advertisement showed a darling curlyheaded girl with the caption: "This healthy, normal baby has a handicap. She was born female."

This is the self-articulated, dog-in-the-manger, chip-on-the-shoulder, fundamental dogma of the women's liberation movement. Someone—it is not clear who, perhaps God, perhaps the "Establishment," perhaps a conspiracy of male chauvinist pigs—dealt women a foul blow by making them female. It becomes necessary, therefore, for women to agitate and demonstrate and hurl demands on society in order to wrest from an oppressive male-dominated social structure the status that has been wrongfully denied to women through the centuries.

By its very nature, therefore, the women's liberation movement precipitates a series of conflict situations—in the legislatures, in the courts, in the schools, in industry—with man targeted as the enemy. Confrontation replaces cooperation as the watchword of all relationships. Women and men become adversaries instead of partners.

The second dogma of the women's liberationists is that, of all the injus- 5 tices perpetrated upon women through the centuries, the most oppressive is the cruel fact that women have babies and men do not. Within the confines of the women's liberationist ideology, therefore, the abolition of this overriding inequality of women becomes the primary goal. This goal must be achieved at any and all costs—to the woman herself, to the baby, to the family, and to society. Women must be made equal to men in their ability *not* to become pregnant and *not* to be expected to care for babies they may bring into the world.

This is why women's liberationists are compulsively involved in the drive to make abortion and child-care centers for all women, regardless of religion or income, both socially acceptable and government-financed. Former congresswoman Bella Abzug has defined the goal: "to enforce the constitutional right of females to terminate pregnancies that they do not wish to continue."

If man is targeted as the enemy, and the ultimate goal of women's liberation is independence from men and the avoidance of pregnancy and its consequences, then lesbianism is logically the highest form in the ritual of women's liberation. Many, such as Kate Millett, come to this conclusion, although many others do not.

The Positive Woman will never travel that dead-end road. It is self-evident to the Positive Woman that the female body with its baby-producing organs was not designed by a conspiracy of men but by the Divine Architect of the human race. Those who think it is unfair that women have babies, whereas men cannot, will have to take up their complaint with God because no other power is capable of changing that fundamental fact. On some college campuses, I have been assured that other methods of reproduction will be developed. But most of us must deal with the real world rather than with the imagination of dreamers.

Another feature of the woman's natural role is the obvious fact that women can breast-feed babies and men cannot. This functional role was not imposed by conspiratorial males seeking to burden women with confining chores but must be recognized as part of the plan of the Divine Architect for the survival of the human race through the centuries and in the countries that know no pasteurization of milk or sterilization of bottles.

The Positive Woman looks upon her femaleness and her fertility as part   10
of her purpose, her potential, and her power. She rejoices that she has a capability for creativity that men can never have.

The third basic dogma of the women's liberation movement is that there is no difference between male and female except the sex organs, and that all those physical, cognitive, and emotional differences you *think* are there, are merely the result of centuries of restraints imposed by a male-dominated society and sex-stereotyped schooling. The role imposed on women is, by definition, inferior, according to the women's liberationists.

The Positive Woman knows that, while there are some physical competitions in which women are better (and can command more money) than men, including those that put a premium on grace and beauty, such as figure skating, the superior physical strength of males over females in competitions of strength, speed, and short-term endurance is beyond rational dispute.

In the Olympic Games, women not only cannot win any medals in competition with men, the gulf between them is so great that they cannot even qualify for the contests with men. No amount of training from infancy can enable women to throw the discus as far as men, or to match men in push-ups or in lifting weights. In track and field events, individual male records surpass those of women by 10 to 20 percent.

Female swimmers today are beating Johnny Weissmuller's records, but today's male swimmers are better still. Chris Evert can never win a tennis match against Jimmy Connors. If we removed lady's tees from golf courses, women would be out of the game. Putting women in football or wrestling matches can only be an exercise in laughs.

The Olympic Games, whose rules require strict verification to ascertain   15
that no male enters a female contest and, with his masculine advantage, unfairly captures a woman's medal, formerly insisted on a visual inspection of the contestants' bodies. Science, however, has discovered that men and women are so innately different physically that their maleness/femaleness

can be conclusively established by means of a simple skin test of fully clothed persons.

The Positive Woman remembers the essential validity of the old prayer: "Lord, give me the strength to change what I can change, the serenity to accept what I cannot change, and the wisdom to discern the difference." The women's liberationists are expending their time and energies erecting a make-believe world in which they hypothesize that *if* schooling were gender-free, and *if* the same money were spent on male and female sports programs, and *if* women were permitted to compete on equal terms, *then* they would prove themselves to be physically equal. Meanwhile, the Positive Woman has put the ineradicable physical differences into her mental computer, programmed her plan of action, and is already on the way to personal achievement.

Thus, while some militant women spend their time demanding more money for professional sports, ice skater Janet Lynn, a truly Positive Woman, quietly signed the most profitable financial contract in the history of women's athletics. It was not the strident demands of the women's liberationists that brought high prizes to women's tennis, but the discovery by sports promoters that beautiful female legs gracefully moving around the court made women's tennis a highly marketable television production to delight male audiences. . . .

Despite the claims of the women's liberation movement, there are countless physical differences between men and women. The female body is 50 to 60 percent water, the male 60 to 70 percent water, which explains why males can dilute alcohol better than women and delay its effect. The average woman is about 25 percent fatty tissue, while the male is 15 percent, making women more buoyant in water and able to swim with less effort. Males have a tendency to color blindness. Only 5 percent of persons who get gout are female. Boys are born bigger. Women live longer in most countries of the world, not only in the United States where we have a hard-driving competitive pace. Women excel in manual dexterity, verbal skills, and memory recall.

Does the physical advantage of men doom women to a life of servility and subservience? The Positive Woman knows that she has a complementary advantage which is at least as great—and, in the hands of a skillful woman, far greater. The Divine Architect who gave men a superior strength to lift weights also gave women a different kind of superior strength.

The women's liberationists and their dupes who try to tell each other   *20* that the sexual drive of men and women is really the same, and that it is only societal restraints that inhibit women from an equal desire, an equal enjoyment, and an equal freedom from the consequences, are doomed to frustration forever. It just isn't so, and pretending cannot make it so. The differences are not a woman's weakness but her strength. . . .

The differences between men and women are also emotional and psychological. Without woman's innate maternal instinct, the human race would have died out centuries ago. There is nothing so helpless in all earthly life as the newborn infant. It will die within hours if not cared for. Even in the most primitive, uneducated societies, women have always cared for their newborn babies. They didn't need any schooling to teach them how. They didn't need any welfare workers to tell them it is their social obligation. Even in societies to whom such concepts as "ought," "social responsibility," and "compassion for the helpless" were unknown, mothers cared for their new babies.

Why? Because caring for a baby serves the natural maternal need of a woman. Although not nearly so total as the baby's need, the woman's need is nonetheless real.

The overriding psychological need of a woman is to love something alive. A baby fulfills this need in the lives of most women. If a baby is not available to fill that need, women search for a baby-substitute. This is the reason why woman have traditionally gone into teaching and nursing careers. They are doing what comes naturally to the female psyche. The schoolchild or the patient of any age provides an outlet for a woman to express her natural maternal need.

This is not to say that every woman must have a baby in order to be fulfilled. But it is to say that fulfillment for most women involves expressing their natural maternal urge by loving and caring for someone.

The women's liberation movement complains that traditional stereo-   25
typed roles assume that women are "passive" and that men are "aggressive." The anomaly is that a woman's most fundamental emotional need is not passive at all, but active. A woman naturally seeks to love affirmatively and to show that love in an active way by caring for the object of her affections.

One of the strangest quirks of women's liberationists is their complaint that societal restraints prevent men from crying in public or showing their emotions, but permit women to do so, and that therefore we should "liberate" men to enable them, too, to cry in public. The public display of fear, sorrow, anger, and irritation reveals a lack of self-discipline that should be avoided by the Positive Woman just as much as by the Positive Man. Maternal love, however, is not a weakness but a manifestation of strength and service, and it should be nurtured by the Positive Woman.

Finally, women are different from men in dealing with the fundamentals of life itself. Men are philosophers, women are practical, and 'twas ever thus. Men may philosophize about how life began and where we are heading; women are concerned about feeding the kids today. No woman would ever, as Karl Marx did, spend years reading political philosophy in the British Museum while her child starved to death. Women don't take naturally to a search for the intangible and the abstract. The Positive Woman knows who she is and where she is going, and she will reach her goal because the longest journey starts with a very practical first step.

Amaury de Riencourt, in his book *Sex and Power in History*, shows that a successful society depends on a delicate balancing of different male and female factors, and that the women's liberation movement, which promotes unisexual values and androgyny, contains within it "a social and cultural death wish and the end of the civilization that endorses it."

One of the few scholarly works dealing with woman's role, *Sex and*

Power in History synthesizes research from a variety of disciplines—sociology, biology, history, anthropology, religion, philosophy, and psychology. De Riencourt traces distinguishable types of women in different periods in history, from prehistoric to modern times. The "liberated" Roman matron, who is most similar to the present-day feminist, helped bring about the fall of Rome through her unnatural emulation of masculine qualities, which resulted in a large-scale breakdown of the family and ultimately of the empire.

De Riencourt examines the fundamental, inherent differences between men and women. He argues that man is the more aggressive, rational, mentally creative, analytical-minded sex because of his early biological role as hunter and provider. Woman, on the other hand, represents stability, flexibility, reliance on intuition, and harmony with nature, stemming from her procreative function.

Where man is discursive, logical, abstract, or philosophical, woman tends to be emotional, personal, practical, or mystical. Each set of qualities is vital and complements the other. Among the many differences explained in de Riencourt's book are the following:

> Women tend more toward conformity than men—which is why they often excel in such disciplines as spelling and punctuation where there is only one correct answer, determined by social authority. Higher intellectual activities, however, require a mental independence and power of abstraction that they usually lack, not to mention a certain form of aggressive boldness of the imagination which can only exist in a sex that is basically aggressive for biological reasons. . . .

An effort to eliminate the differences by social engineering or legislative or constitutional tinkering cannot succeed, which is fortunate, but social relationships and spiritual values can be ruptured in the attempt. Thus the role reversals being forced upon high school students, under which guidance counselors urge reluctant girls to take "shop" and boys to take "home economics," further confuse a generation already unsure about its identity. They are as wrong as efforts to make a left-handed child right-handed.

BLOOD-BURNING MOON

Jean Toomer

1

Up from the skeleton stone walls, up from the rotting floor boards and the solid hand-hewn beams of oak of the pre-war cotton factory, dusk came. Up from the dusk the full moon came. Glowing like a fired pine-knot, it illumined the great door and soft showered the Negro shanties aligned along the single street of factory town. The full moon in the great door was an omen. Negro women improvised songs against its spell.

Louisa sang as she came over the crest of the hill from the white folks' kitchen. Her skin was the color of oak leaves on young trees in fall. Her breasts, firm and up-pointed like ripe acorns. And her singing had the low murmur of winds in fig trees. Bob Stone, younger son of the people she worked for, loved her. By the way the world reckons things, he had won her. By measure of that warm glow which came into her mind at thought of him, he had won her. Tom Burwell, whom the whole town called Big Boy, also loved her. But working in the fields all day, and far away from her, gave him no chance to show it. Though often enough of evenings he had tried to. Somehow, he never got along. Strong as he was with hands upon the ax or plow, he found it difficult to hold her. Or so he thought. But the fact was that he held her to factory town more firmly than he thought for. His black balanced, and pulled against, the white of Stone, when she thought of them. And her mind was vaguely upon them as she came over the crest of the hill, coming from the white folks' kitchen. As she sang softly at the evil face of the full moon.

A strange stir was in her. Indolently, she tried to fix upon Bob or Tom as the cause of it. To meet Bob in the canebrake, as she was going to do an hour or so later, was nothing new. And Tom's proposal which she felt on its way to her could be indefinitely put off. Separately, there was no unusual significance to either one. But for some reason, they jumbled when her eyes gazed vacantly at the rising moon. And from the jumble came the stir that was strangely within her. Her lips trembled. The slow rhythm of her song grew agitant and restless. Rusty black and tan spotted hounds, lying in the dark corners of porches or prowling around back yards, put their noses in the air and caught its tremor. They began plaintively to yelp and howl. Chickens woke up and cackled. Intermittently, all over the countryside dogs barked and roosters crowed as if heralding a weird dawn or some ungodly awakening. The women sang lustily. Their songs were cotton-wads to stop their ears. Louisa came down into factory town and sank wearily upon the step before her home. The moon was rising towards a thick cloud-bank which soon would hide it.

Red nigger moon. Sinner!
Blood-burning moon. Sinner!
Come out that fact'ry door.

2

Up from the deep dusk of a cleared spot on the edge of the forest a mellow glow arose and spread fan-wise into the low-hanging heavens. And all around the air was heavy with the scent of boiling cane. A large pile of cane-stalks lay like ribboned shadows upon the ground. A mule, harnessed to a pole, trudged lazily round and round the pivot of the grinder. Beneath a swaying oil lamp, a Negro alternately whipped out at the mule, and fed cane-stalks to the grinder. A fat boy waddled pails of fresh ground juice between the grinder and the boiling stove. Steam came from the copper boiling pan. The scent of cane came from the copper pan and drenched the forest and the hill that sloped to factory town, beneath its fragrance. It drenched the men in circle seated around the stove. Some of them chewed at the white pulp of stalks, but there was no need for them to, if all they wanted was to taste the cane. One tasted it in factory town. And from factory town one could see the soft haze thrown by the glowing stove upon the low-hanging heavens.

Old David Georgia stirred the thickening syrup with a long ladle, and   5 ever so often drew it off. Old David Georgia tended his stove and told tales about the white folks, about moonshining and cotton picking, and about sweet nigger gals, to the men who sat there about his stove to listen to him. Tom Burwell chewed cane-stalk and laughed with the others till some one mentioned Louisa. Till some one said something about Louisa and Bob Stone, about the silk stockings she must have gotten from him. Blood ran up Tom's neck hotter than the glow that flooded from the stove. He sprang up. Glared at the men and said, "She's my gal." Will Manning laughed. Tom strode over to him. Yanked him up and knocked him to the ground. Several of Manning's friends got up to fight for him. Tom whipped out a long knife and would have cut them to shreds if they hadnt ducked into the woods. Tom had had enough. He nodded to Old David Georgia and swung down the path to factory town. Just then, the dogs started barking and the roosters began to crow. Tom felt funny. Away from the fight, away from the stove, chill got to him. He shivered. He shuddered when he saw the full moon rising towards the cloud-bank. He who didnt give a godam for the fears of old women. He forced his mind to fasten on Louisa. Bob Stone. Better not be. He turned into the street and saw Louisa sitting before her home. He went towards her, ambling, touched the brim of a marvelously shaped, spotted, felt hat, said he wanted to say something to her, and then found that he didnt know what he had to say, or if he did, that he couldnt say it. He shoved his big fists in his overalls, grinned, and started to move off.

"Youall want me, Tom?"

"Thats what us wants, sho, Louisa."

"Well, here I am—"

"An here I is, but that aint ahelpin none, all th same."

"You wanted to say something? . ."   10

"I did that, sho. But words is like th spots on dice: no matter how y fumbles em, there's times when they jes wont come. I dunno why. Seems like th love I feels fo yo done stole m tongue. I got it now. Whee! Louisa, honey, I oughtnt tell y, I feel I oughtnt cause yo is young an goes t church an I has had other gals, but Louisa I sho do love y. Lil gal, Ise watched y from them first days when youall sat right here befo yo door befo th well an sang sometimes in a way that like t broke m heart. Ise carried y with me into th fields, day after day, an after that, an I sho can plow when yo is there, an I can pick cotton. Yassur! Come near beatin Barlo yesterday. I sho did. Yassur! An next year if ole Stone'll trust me, I'll have a farm. My own. My bales will buy yo what y gets from white folks now. Silk stockings an purple dresses—course I dont believe what some folks been whisperin as t how y gets them things now. White folks always did do for niggers what they likes. An they jes cant help alikin yo, Louisa. Bob Stone likes y. Course he does. But not th way folks is awhisperin. Does he, hon?"

"I dont know what you mean, Tom."

"Course y dont. Ise already cut two niggers. Had t hon, t tell em so. Niggers always tryin t make somethin out a nothin. An then besides, white folks aint up t them tricks so much nowadays. Godam better not be. Leastawise not with yo. Cause I wouldnt stand f it. Nassur."

"What would you do, Tom?"

"Cut him jes like I cut a nigger."   15

"No, Tom—"

"I said I would an there aint no mo to it. But that aint th talk f now. Sing, honey Louisa, an while I'm listenin t y I'll be makin love."

Tom took her hand in his. Against the tough thickness of his own, hers felt soft and small. His huge body slipped down to the step beside her. The full moon sank upward into the deep purple of the cloud-bank. An old woman brought a lighted lamp and hung it on the common well whose bulky shadow squatted in the middle of the road, opposite Tom and Louisa. The old woman lifted the well-lid, took hold the chain, and began drawing up the heavy bucket. As she did so, she sang. Figures shifted, restlesslike, between lamp and window in the front rooms of the shanties. Shadows of the figures fought each other on the gray dust of the road. Figures raised the windows and joined the old woman in song. Louisa and Tom, the whole street, singing:

> Red nigger moon. Sinner!
> Blood-burning moon. Sinner!
> Come out that fact'ry door.

3

Bob Stone sauntered from his veranda out into the gloom of fir trees and magnolias. The clear white of his skin paled, and the flush of his cheeks turned purple. As if to balance this outer change, his mind became consciously a white man's. He passed the house with its huge open hearth which, in the days of slavery, was the plantation cookery. He saw Louisa bent over that hearth. He went in as a master should and took her. Direct, honest, bold. None of this sneaking that he had to go through now. The contrast was repulsive to him. His family had lost ground. Hell no, his family still owned the niggers, practically. Damned if they did, or he wouldnt have to duck around so. What would they think if they knew? His mother? His sister? He shouldnt mention them, shouldnt think of them in this connection. There in the dusk he blushed at doing so. Fellows about town were all right, but how about his friends up North? He could see them incredible, repulsed. They didnt know. The thought first made him laugh. Then, with their eyes still upon him, he began to feel embarrassed. He felt the need of explaining things to them. Explain hell. They wouldnt understand, and moreover, who ever heard of a Southerner getting on his knees to any Yankee, or anyone. No sir. He was going to see Louisa to-night, and love her. She was lovely—in her way. Nigger way. What way was that? Damned if he knew. Must know. He'd known her long enough to know. Was there something about niggers that you couldnt know? Listening to them at church didnt tell you anything. Looking at them didnt tell you anything. Talking to them didnt tell you anything—unless it was gossip, unless they wanted to talk. Of course, about farming, and licker, and craps—but those werent nigger. Nigger was something more. How much more? Something to be afraid of, more? Hell no. Who ever heard of being afraid of a nigger? Tom Burwell. Cartwell had told him that Tom went with Louisa after she reached home. No sir. No nigger had ever been with his girl. He'd like to see one try. Some position for him to be in. Him, Bob Stone, of the old Stone family, in a scrap with a nigger over a nigger girl. In the good old days. . . Ha! Those were the days. His family had lost ground. Not so much, though. Enough for him to have to cut through old Lemon's canefield by way of the woods, that he might meet her. She was worth it. Beautiful nigger gal. Why nigger? Why not, just gal? No, it was because she was nigger that he went to her. Sweet. . . The scent of boiling cane came to him. Then he saw the rich glow of the stove. He heard the voices of the men circled around it. He was about to skirt the clearing when he heard his own name mentioned. He stopped. Quivering. Leaning against a tree, he listened.

"Bad nigger. Yassur, he sho is one bad nigger when he gets started."   20

"Tom Burwell's been on th gang three times fo cuttin men."

"What y think he's agwine t do t Bob Stone?"

"Dunno yet. He aint found out. When he does—Baby!"

"Aint no tellin."

"Young Stone aint no quitter an I ken tell y that. Blood of th old uns in   25
his veins."

"Thats right. He'll scrap, sho."

"Be gettin too hot f niggers round this away."

"Shut up, nigger. Y dont know what y talkin bout."

Bob Stone's ears burned as though he had been holding them over the stove. Sizzling heat welled up within him. His feet felt as if they rested on red-hot coals. They stung him to quick movement. He circled the fringe of the glowing. Not a twig cracked beneath his feet. He reached the path that led to factory town. Plunged furiously down it. Halfway along, a blindness within him veered him aside. He crashed into the bordering canebrake. Cane leaves cut his face and lips. He tasted blood. He threw himself down and dug his fingers in the ground. The earth was cool. Cane-roots took the fever from his hands. After a long while, or so it seemed to him, the thought came to him that it must be time to see Louisa. He gŏt to his feet and walked calmly to their meeting place. No Louisa. Tom Burwell had her. Veins in his forehead bulged and distended. Saliva moistened the dried blood on his lips. He bit down on his lips. He tasted blood. Not his own blood; Tom Burwell's blood. Bob drove through the cane and out again upon the road. A hound swung down the path before him towards factory town. Bob couldnt see it. The dog loped aside to let him pass. Bob's blind rushing made him stumble over it. He fell with a thud that dazed him. The hound yelped. Answering yelps came from all over the countryside. Chickens cackled. Roosters crowed, heralding the bloodshot eyes of southern awakening. Singers in the town were silenced. They shut their windows down. Palpitant between the rooster crows, a chill hush settled upon the huddled forms of Tom and Louisa. A figure rushed from the shadow and stood before them. Tom popped to his feet.

"Whats y want?"   30

"I'm Bob Stone."

"Yassur—an I'm Tom Burwell. Whats y want?"

Bob lunged at him. Tom side-stepped, caught him by the shoulder, and flung him to the ground. Straddled him.

"Let me up."

"Yassur—but watch yo doins,° Bob Stone."   35

A few dark figures, drawn by the sound of scuffle, stood about them. Bob sprang to his feet.

"Fight like a man, Tom Burwell, an I'll lick y."

Again he lunged. Tom side-stepped and flung him to the ground. Strad-dled him.

"Get off me, you godam nigger you."

"Yo sho has started somethin now. Get up."   40

Tom yanked him up and began hammering at him. Each blow sounded as if it smashed into a precious, irreplaceable soft something. Beneath them, Bob staggered back. He reached in his pocket and whipped out a knife.

"Thats my game, sho."

Blue flash, a steel blade slashed across Bob Stone's throat. He had a sweetish sick feeling. Blood began to flow. Then he felt a sharp twitch of pain. He let his knife drop. He slapped one hand against his neck. He pressed the other on top of his head as if to hold it down. He groaned. He turned, and staggered towards the crest of the hill in the direction of white town. Negroes who had seen the fight slunk into their homes and blew the lamps out. Louisa, dazed, hysterical, refused to go indoors. She slipped, crumbled, her body loosely propped against the woodwork of the well. Tom Burwell leaned against it. He seemed rooted there.

Bob reached Broad Street. White men rushed up to him. He collapsed in their arms.

"Tom Burwell. . . ."   45

---

doins: actions

White men like ants upon a forage rushed about. Except for the taut hum of their moving, all was silent. Shotguns, revolvers, rope, kerosene, torches. Two high-powered cars with glaring search-lights. They came together. The taut hum rose to a low roar. Then nothing could be heard but the flop of their feet in the thick dust of the road. The moving body of their silence preceded them over the crest of the hill into factory town. It flattened the Negroes beneath it. It rolled to the wall of the factory, where it stopped. Tom knew that they were coming. He couldnt move. And then he saw the search-lights of the two cars glaring down on him. A quick shock went through him. He stiffened. He started to run. A yell went up from the mob. Tom wheeled about and faced them. They poured down on him. They swarmed. A large man with dead-white face and flabby cheeks came to him and almost jabbed a gun-barrel through his guts.

"Hands behind y, nigger."

Tom's wrists were bound. The big man shoved him to the well. Burn him over it, and when the woodwork caved in, his body would drop to the bottom. Two deaths for a godam nigger. Louisa was driven back. The mob pushed in. Its pressure, its momentum was too great. Drag him to the factory. Wood and stakes already there. Tom moved in the direction indicated. But they had to drag him. They reached the great door. Too many to get in there. The mob divided and flowed around the walls to either side. The big man shoved him through the door. The mob pressed in from the sides. Taut humming. No words. A stake was sunk into the ground. Rotting floor boards piled around it. Kerosene poured on the rotting floor boards. Tom bound to the stake. His breast was bare. Nails' scratches let little lines of blood trickle down and mat into the hair. His face, his eyes were set and stony. Except for irregular breathing, one would have thought him already dead. Torches were flung onto the pile. A great flare muffled in black smoke shot upward. The mob yelled. The mob was silent. Now Tom could be seen within the flames. Only his head, erect, lean, like a blackened stone. Stench of burning flesh soaked the air. Tom's eyes popped. His head settled downward. The mob yelled. Its yell echoed against the skeleton stone walls and sounded like a hundred yells. Like a hundred mobs yelling. Its yell thudded against the thick front wall and fell back. Ghost of a yell slipped through the flames and out the great door of the factory. It fluttered like a dying thing down the single street of factory town. Louisa, upon the step before her home, did not hear it, but her eyes opened slowly. They saw the full moon glowing in the great door. The full moon, an evil thing, an omen, soft showering the homes of folks she knew. Where were they, these people? She'd sing, and perhaps they'd come out and join her. Perhaps Tom Burwell would come. At any rate, the full moon in the great door was an omen which she must sing to:

Red nigger moon. Sinner!
Blood-burning moon. Sinner!
Come out that fact'ry door.

THAT EVENING SUN

William Faulkner

I

Monday is no different from any other weekday in Jefferson now. The streets are paved now, and the telephone and electric companies are cutting down more and more of the shade trees—the water oaks, the maples and locusts and elms—to make room for iron poles bearing clusters of bloated and ghostly and bloodless grapes, and we have a city laundry which makes the rounds on Monday morning, gathering the bundles of clothes into bright-colored, specially-made motor cars: the soiled wearing of a whole week now flees apparitionlike behind alert and irritable electric horns, with a long diminishing noise of rubber and asphalt like tearing silk, and even the Negro women who still take in white people's washing after the old custom, fetch and deliver it in automobiles.

But fifteen years ago, on Monday morning the quiet, dusty, shady streets would be full of Negro women with, balanced on their steady, turbaned heads, bundles of clothes tied up in sheets, almost as large as cotton bales, carried so without touch of hand between the kitchen door of the white house and the blackened washpot beside a cabin door in Negro Hollow.

Nancy would set her bundle on the top of her head, then upon the bundle in turn she would set the black straw sailor hat which she wore winter and summer. She was tall, with a high, sad face sunken a little where her teeth were missing. Sometimes we would go a part of the way down the lane and across the pasture with her, to watch the balanced bundle and the hat that never bobbed nor wavered, even when she walked down into the ditch and up the other side and stooped through the fence. She would go down on her hands and knees and crawl through the gap, her head rigid, uptilted, the bundle steady as a rock or a balloon, and rise to her feet again and go on.

Sometimes the husbands of the washing women would fetch and deliver the clothes, but Jesus never did that for Nancy, even before father told him to stay away from our house, even when Dilsey was sick and Nancy would come to cook for us.

And then about half the time we'd have to go down the lane to Nancy's   5
cabin and tell her to come on and cook breakfast. We would stop at the ditch, because father told us to not have anything to do with Jesus—he was a short black man, with a razor scar down his face—and we would throw rocks at Nancy's house until she came to the door, leaning her head around it without any clothes on.

"What yawl mean, chunking my house?" Nancy said. "What you little devils mean?"

"Father says for you to come on and get breakfast," Caddy said. "Father says it's over a half an hour now, and you've got to come this minute."

"I aint studying no breakfast," Nancy said. "I going to get my sleep out."

"I bet you're drunk," Jason said. "Father says you're drunk. Are you drunk, Nancy?"

"Who says I is?" Nancy said. "I got to get my sleep out. I aint studying   10
no breakfast."

So after a while we quit chunking the cabin and went back home. When she finally came, it was too late for me to go to school. So we thought it was whisky until that day they arrested her again and they were taking her to jail and they passed Mr. Stovall. He was the cashier in the bank and a deacon in the Baptist church, and Nancy began to say:

"When you going to pay me, white man? When you going to pay me, white man? It's been three times now since you paid me a cent—" Mr. Stovall knocked her down, but she kept on saying, "When you going to pay me, white man? It's been three times now since—" until Mr. Stovall kicked her in the mouth with his heel and the marshal caught Mr. Stovall back, and Nancy lying in the street, laughing. She turned her head and spat out some blood and teeth and said, "It's been three times now since he paid me a cent."

That was how she lost her teeth, and all that day they told about Nancy and Mr. Stovall, and all that night the ones that passed the jail could hear Nancy singing and yelling. They could see her hands holding to the window bars, and a lot of them stopped along the fence, listening to her and to the jailer trying to make her stop. She didn't shut up until almost daylight, when the jailer began to hear a bumping and scraping upstairs and he went up there and found Nancy hanging from the window bar. He said that it was cocaine and not whisky, because no nigger would try to commit suicide unless he was full of cocaine, because a nigger full of cocaine wasn't a nigger any longer.

The jailer cut her down and revived her; then he beat her, whipped her. She had hung herself with her dress. She had fixed it all right, but when they arrested her she didn't have on anything except a dress and so she didn't have anything to tie her hands with and she couldn't make her hands let go of the window ledge. So the jailer heard the noise and ran up there and found Nancy hanging from the window, stark naked, her belly already swelling out a little, like a little balloon.

When Dilsey was sick in her cabin and Nancy was cooking for us, we   15
could see her apron swelling out: that was before father told Jesus to stay away from the house. Jesus was in the kitchen, sitting behind the stove, with his razor scar on his black face like a piece of dirty string. He said it was a watermelon that Nancy had under her dress.

"It never come off of your vine, though," Nancy said.

"Off of what vine?" Caddy said.

"I can cut down the vine it did come off of," Jesus said.

"What makes you want to talk like that before these chillen?" Nancy said. "Whyn't you go to work? You done et. You want Mr Jason to catch you hanging around his kitchen, talking that way before these chillen?"

"Talking what way?" Caddy said. "What vine?"   20

"I cant hang around white man's kitchen," Jesus said. "But white man can hang around mine. White man can come in my house, but I cant stop him. When white man want to come in my house, I aint got no house. I cant stop him, but he cant kick me outen it. He cant do that."

Dilsey was still sick in her cabin. Father told Jesus to stay off our place. Dilsey was still sick. It was a long time. We were in the library after supper.

"Isn't Nancy through in the kitchen yet?" mother said. "It seems to me that she has had plenty of time to have finished the dishes."

"Let Quentin go and see," father said. "Go and see if Nancy is through, Quentin. Tell her she can go on home."

I went to the kitchen. Nancy was through. The dishes were put away   25
and the fire was out. Nancy was sitting in a chair, close to the cold stove. She looked at me.

"Mother wants to know if you are through," I said.

"Yes," Nancy said. She looked at me. "I done finished." She looked at me.

"What is it?" I said. "What is it?"

"I aint nothing but a nigger," Nancy said. "It aint none of my fault."

She looked at me, sitting in the chair before the cold stove, the sailor   30
hat on her head. I went back to the library. It was the cold stove and all, when you think of a kitchen being warm and busy and cheerful. And with a cold stove and the dishes all put away, and nobody wanting to eat at that hour.

"Is she through?" mother said.

"Yessum," I said.

"What is she doing?" mother said.

"She's not doing anything. She's through."

"I'll go and see," father said.   35

"Maybe she's waiting for Jesus to come and take her home," Caddy said.

"Jesus is gone," I said. Nancy told us how one morning she woke up and Jesus was gone.

"He quit me," Nancy said. "Done gone to Memphis, I reckon. Dodging them city po-lice for a while, I reckon."

"And a good riddance," father said. "I hope he stays there."

"Nancy's scaired of the dark," Jason said.   40

"So are you," Caddy said.

"I'm not," Jason said.

"Scairy cat," Caddy said.

"I'm not," Jason said.

"You, Candace!" mother said. Father came back.   45

"I am going to walk down the lane with Nancy," he said. "She says that Jesus is back."

"Has she seen him?" mother said.

"No. Some Negro sent her word that he was back in town. I wont be long."

"You'll leave me alone, to take Nancy home?" mother said. "Is her safety more precious to you than mine?"

"I wont be long," father said.   *50*

"You'll leave these children unprotected, with that Negro about?"

"I'm going too," Caddy said. "Let me go, Father."

"What would he do with them, if he were unfortunate enough to have them?" father said.

"I want to go, too," Jason said.

"Jason!" mother said. She was speaking to father. You could tell that by   *55* the way she said the name. Like she believed that all day father had been trying to think of doing the thing she wouldn't like the most, and that she knew all the time that after a while he would think of it. I stayed quiet, because father and I both knew that mother would want him to make me stay with her if she just thought of it in time. So father didn't look at me. I was the oldest. I was nine and Caddy was seven and Jason was five.

"Nonsense," father said. "We wont be long."

Nancy had her hat on. We came to the lane. "Jesus always been good to me," Nancy said. "Whenever he had two dollars, one of them was mine." We walked in the lane. "If I can just get through the lane," Nancy said, "I be all right then."

The lane was always dark. "This is where Jason got scared on Hallowe'en," Caddy said.

"I didn't," Jason said.

"Cant Aunt Rachel do anything with him?" father said. Aunt Rachel   *60* was old. She lived in a cabin beyond Nancy's, by herself. She had white hair and she smoked a pipe in the door, all day long; she didn't work any more. They said she was Jesus' mother. Sometimes she said she was and sometimes she said she wasn't any kin to Jesus.

"Yes, you did," Caddy said. "You were scairder than Frony. You were scairder than T.P. even. Scairder than niggers."

"Cant nobody do nothing with him," Nancy said. "He say I done woke up the devil in him and aint but one thing going to lay it down again."

"Well, he's gone now," father said. "There's nothing for you to be afraid of now. And if you'd just let white men alone."

"Let what white men alone?" Caddy said. "How let them alone?"

"He aint gone nowhere," Nancy said. "I can feel him. I can feel him   *65* now, in this lane. He hearing us talk, every word, hid somewhere, waiting. I aint seen him, and I aint going to see him again but once more, with that razor in his mouth. That razor on that string down his back, inside his shirt. And then I aint going to be even surprised."

"I wasn't scaired," Jason said.

"If you'd behave yourself, you'd have kept out of this," father said. "But it's all right now. He's probably in St. Louis now. Probably got another wife by now and forgot all about you."

"If he has, I better not find out about it," Nancy said. "I'd stand there right over them, and every time he wropped her, I'd cut that arm off. I'd cut his head off and I'd slit her belly and I'd shove—"

"Hush," father said.

"Slit whose belly, Nancy?" Caddy said.   70

"I wasn't scaired," Jason said. "I'd walk right down this lane by myself."

"Yah," Caddy said. "You wouldn't dare to put your foot down in it if we were not here too."

II

Dilsey was still sick, so we took Nancy home every night until mother said, "How much longer is this going on? I to be left alone in this big house while you take home a frightened Negro?"

We fixed a pallet in the kitchen for Nancy. One night we waked up, hearing the sound. It was not singing and it was not crying, coming up the dark stairs. There was a light in mother's room and we heard father going down the hall, down the back stairs, and Caddy and I went into the hall. The floor was cold. Our toes curled away from it while we listened to the sound. It was like singing and it wasn't like singing, like the sounds that Negroes make.

Then it stopped and we heard father going down the back stairs, and we   75
went to the head of the stairs. Then the sound began again, in the stairway, not loud, and we could see Nancy's eyes halfway up the stairs, against the wall. They looked like cat's eyes do, like a big cat against the wall, watching us. When we came down the steps to where she was, she quit making the sound again, and we stood there until father came back up from the kitchen, with his pistol in his hand. He went back down with Nancy and they came back with Nancy's pallet.

We spread the pallet in our room. After the light in mother's room went off, we could see Nancy's eyes again. "Nancy," Caddy whispered, "are you asleep, Nancy?"

Nancy whispered something. It was oh or no, I dont know which. Like nobody had made it, like it came from nowhere and went nowhere, until it was like Nancy was not there at all; that I had looked so hard at her eyes on the stairs that they had got printed on my eyeballs, like the sun does when you have closed your eyes and there is no sun. "Jesus," Nancy whispered. "Jesus."

"Was it Jesus?" Caddy said. "Did he try to come into the kitchen?"

"Jesus," Nancy said. Like this: Jeeeeeeeeeeeeeeeesus, until the sound went out, like a match or a candle does.

"It's the other Jesus she means," I said.   80

"Can you see us, Nancy?" Caddy whispered. "Can you see our eyes too?"

"I aint nothing but a nigger," Nancy said. "God knows. God knows."

"What did you see down there in the kitchen?" Caddy whispered. "What tried to get in?"

"God knows," Nancy said. We could see her eyes. "God knows."

Dilsey got well. She cooked dinner. "You'd better stay in bed a day or   85
two longer," father said.

"What for?" Dilsey said. "If I had been a day later, this place would be to rack and ruin. Get on out of here now, and let me get my kitchen straight again."

Dilsey cooked supper too. And that night, just before dark, Nancy came into the kitchen.

"How do you know he's back?" Dilsey said. "You aint seen him."

"Jesus is a nigger," Jason said.

"I can feel him," Nancy said. "I can feel him laying yonder in the   90
ditch."

"Tonight?" Dilsey said. "Is he there tonight?"

"Dilsey's a nigger too," Jason said.

"You try to eat something," Dilsey said.

"I dont want nothing," Nancy said.

"I aint a nigger," Jason said.   95

"Drink some coffee," Dilsey said. She poured a cup of coffee for Nancy. "Do you know he's out there tonight? How come you know it's tonight?"

"I know," Nancy said. "He's there, waiting. I know. I done lived with him too long. I know what he's fixing to do fore he know it himself."

"Drink some coffee," Dilsey said. Nancy held the cup to her mouth and blew into the cup. Her mouth pursed out like a spreading adder's, like a rubber mouth, like she had blown all the color out of her lips with blowing the coffee.

"I aint a nigger," Jason said. "Are you a nigger, Nancy?"

"I hellborn, child," Nancy said. "I wont be nothing soon. I going back   100
where I come from soon."

III

She began to drink the coffee. While she was drinking, holding the cup in both hands, she began to make the sound again. She made the sound into the cup and the coffee sploshed out onto her hands and her dress. Her eyes looked at us and she sat there, her elbows on her knees, holding the cup in both hands, looking at us across the wet cup, making the sound. "Look at Nancy," Jason said. "Nancy cant cook for us now. Dilsey's got well now."

"You hush up," Dilsey said. Nancy held the cup in both hands, looking at us, making the sound, like there were two of them: one looking at us and the other making the sound. "Whyn't you let Mr Jason telefoam the marshal?" Dilsey said. Nancy stopped then, holding the cup in her long brown hands. She tried to drink some coffee again, but it sploshed out of the cup, onto her hands and her dress, and she put the cup down. Jason watched her.

"I cant swallow it," Nancy said. "I swallows but it wont go down me."

"You go down to the cabin," Dilsey said. "Frony will fix you a pallet and I'll be there soon."

"Wont no nigger stop him," Nancy said.   *105*

"I aint a nigger," Jason said. "Am I, Dilsey?"

"I reckon not," Dilsey said. She looked at Nancy. "I dont reckon so. What you going to do, then?"

Nancy looked at us. Her eyes went fast, like she was afraid there wasn't time to look, without hardly moving at all. She looked at us, at all three of us at one time. "You member that night I stayed in yawls' room?" she said. She told about how we waked up early the next morning, and played. We had to play quiet, on her pallet, until father woke up and it was time to get breakfast. "Go and ask your maw to let me stay here tonight," Nancy said. "I wont need no pallet. We can play some more."

Caddy asked mother. Jason went too. "I cant have Negroes sleeping in the bedrooms," mother said. Jason cried. He cried until mother said he couldn't have any dessert for three days if he didn't stop. Then Jason said he would stop if Dilsey would make a chocolate cake. Father was there.

"Why dont you do something about it?" mother said. "What do we   *110* have officers for?"

"Why is Nancy afraid of Jesus?" Caddy said. "Are you afraid of father, mother?"

"What could the officers do?" father said. "If Nancy hasn't seen him, how could the officers find him?"

"Then why is she afraid?" mother said.

"She says he is there. She says she knows he is there tonight."

"Yet we pay taxes," mother said. "I must wait here alone in this big   *115* house while you take a Negro woman home."

"You know that I am not lying outside with a razor," father said.

"I'll stop if Dilsey will make a chocolate cake," Jason said. Mother told us to go out and father said he didn't know if Jason would get a chocolate cake or not, but he knew what Jason was going to get in about a minute. We went back to the kitchen and told Nancy.

"Father said for you to go home and lock the door, and you'll be all right," Caddy said. "All right from what, Nancy? Is Jesus mad at you?" Nancy was holding the coffee cup in her hands again, her elbows on her knees and her hands holding the cup between her knees. She was looking into the cup. "What have you done that made Jesus mad?" Caddy said. Nancy let the cup go. It didn't break on the floor, but the coffee spilled out, and Nancy sat there with her hands still holding the shape of the cup. She began to make the sound again, not loud. Not singing and not unsinging. We watched her.

"Here," Dilsey said. "You quit that, now. You get aholt of yourself. You wait here. I going to get Versh to walk home with you." Dilsey went out.

We looked at Nancy. Her shoulders kept shaking, but she quit making the sound. We watched her. "What's Jesus going to do to you?" Caddy said. "He went away."

Nancy looked at us. "We had fun that night I stayed in yawls' room, didn't we?"

"I didn't," Jason said. "I didn't have any fun."

"You were alseep in mother's room," Caddy said. "You were not there."

"Let's go down to my house and have some more fun," Nancy said.

"Mother wont let us," I said. "It's too late now."

"Dont bother her," Nancy said. "We can tell her in the morning. She wont mind."

"She wouldn't let us," I said.

"Dont ask her now," Nancy said. "Dont bother her now."

"She didn't say we couldn't go," Caddy said.

"We didn't ask," I said.

"If you go, I'll tell," Jason said.

"We'll have fun," Nancy said. "They won't mind, just to my house. I been working for yawl a long time. They won't mind."

"I'm not afraid to go," Caddy said. "Jason is the one that's afraid. He'll tell."

"I'm not," Jason said.

"Yes, you are," Caddy said. "You'll tell."

"I won't tell," Jason said. "I'm not afraid."

"Jason ain't afraid to go with me," Nancy said. "Is you, Jason?"

"Jason is going to tell," Caddy said. The lane was dark. We passed the pasture gate. "I bet if something was to jump out from behind that gate, Jason would holler."

"I wouldn't," Jason said. We walked down the lane. Nancy was talking loud.

"What are you talking so loud for, Nancy?" Caddy said.

"Who, me?" Nancy said. "Listen at Quentin and Caddy and Jason saying I'm talking loud."

"You talk like there was five of us here," Caddy said. "You talk like father was here too."

"Who; me talking loud, Mr Jason?" Nancy said.

"Nancy called Jason 'Mister,'" Caddy said.

"Listen how Caddy and Quentin and Jason talk," Nancy said.

"We're not talking loud," Caddy said. "You're the one that's talking like father—"

"Hush," Nancy said; "hush, Mr Jason."

"Nancy called Jason 'Mister' aguh—"

"Hush," Nancy said. She was talking loud when we crossed the ditch and stooped through the fence where she used to stoop through with the clothes on her head. Then we came to her house. We were going fast then. She opened the door. The smell of the house was like the lamp and the smell of Nancy was like the wick, like they were waiting for one another to begin to smell. She lit the lamp and closed the door and put the bar up. Then she quit talking loud, looking at us.

"What're we going to do?" Caddy said. 150

"What do yawl want to do?" Nancy said.

"You said we would have some fun," Caddy said.

There was something about Nancy's house; something you could smell besides Nancy and the house. Jason smelled it, even. "I don't want to stay here," he said. "I want to go home."

"Go home, then," Caddy said.

"I don't want to go by myself," Jason said. 155

"We're going to have some fun," Nancy said.

"How?" Caddy said.

Nancy stood by the door. She was looking at us, only it was like she had emptied her eyes, like she had quit using them. "What do you want to do?" she said.

"Tell us a story," Caddy said. "Can you tell a story?"

"Yes," Nancy said. 160

"Tell it," Caddy said. We looked at Nancy. "You don't know any stories."

"Yes," Nancy said. "Yes, I do."

She came and sat in a chair before the hearth. There was a little fire there. Nancy built it up, when it was already hot inside. She built a good blaze. She told a story. She talked like her eyes looked, like her eyes watching us and her voice talking to us did not belong to her. Like she was living somewhere else, waiting somewhere else. She was outside the cabin. Her voice was inside and the shape of her, the Nancy that could stoop under a barbed wire fence with a bundle of clothes balanced on her head as though without weight, like a balloon, was there. But that was all. "And so this here queen come walking up to the ditch, where that bad man was hiding. She was walking up to the ditch, and she say, 'If I can just get past this here ditch,' was what she say . . ."

"What ditch?" Caddy said. "A ditch like that one out there? Why did a queen want to go into a ditch?"

"To get to her house," Nancy said. She looked at us. "She had to cross 165 the ditch to get into her house quick and bar the door."

"Why did she want to go home and bar the door?" Caddy said.

IV

Nancy looked at us. She quit talking. She looked at us. Jason's legs stuck straight out of his pants where he sat on Nancy's lap. "I don't think that's a good story," he said. "I want to go home."

"Maybe we had better," Caddy said. She got up from the floor. "I bet they are looking for us right now." She went toward the door.

"No," Nancy said. "Don't open it." She got up quick and passed Caddy. She didn't touch the door, the wooden bar.

"Why not?" Caddy said.   170

"Come back to the lamp," Nancy said. "We'll have fun. You don't have to go."

"We ought to go," Caddy said. "Unless we have a lot of fun." She and Nancy came back to the fire, the lamp.

"I want to go home," Jason said. "I'm going to tell."

"I know another story," Nancy said. She stood close to the lamp. She looked at Caddy, like when your eyes look up at a stick balanced on your nose. She had to look down to see Caddy, but her eyes looked like that, like when you are balancing a stick.

"I won't listen to it," Jason said. "I'll bang on the floor."   175

"It's a good one," Nancy said. "It's better than the other one."

"What's it about?" Caddy said. Nancy was standing by the lamp. Her hand was on the lamp, against the light, long and brown.

"Your hand is on that hot globe," Caddy said. "Don't it feel hot to your hand?"

Nancy looked at her hand on the lamp chimney. She took her hand away, slow. She stood there, looking at Caddy, wringing her long hand as though it were tied to her wrist with a string.

"Let's do something else," Caddy said.   180

"I want to go home," Jason said.

"I got some popcorn," Nancy said. She looked at Caddy and then at Jason and then at me and then at Caddy again. "I got some popcorn."

"I don't like popcorn," Jason said. "I'd rather have candy."

Nancy looked at Jason. "You can hold the popper." She was still wringing her hand; it was long and limp and brown.

"All right," Jason said. "I'll stay a while if I can do that. Caddy can't   185
hold it. I'll want to go home again if Caddy holds the popper."

Nancy built up the fire. "Look at Nancy putting her hands in the fire," Caddy said. "What's the matter with you, Nancy?"

"I got popcorn," Nancy said. "I got some." She took the popper from under the bed. It was broken. Jason began to cry.

"Now we can't have any popcorn," he said.

"We ought to go home, anyway," Caddy said. "Come on, Quentin."

"Wait," Nancy said; "wait. I can fix it. Don't you want to help me   190
fix it?"

"I don't think I want any," Caddy said. "It's too late now."

"You help me, Jason," Nancy said. "Don't you want to help me?"

"No," Jason said. "I want to go home."

"Hush," Nancy said; "hush. Watch. Watch me. I can fix it so Jason can hold it and pop the corn." She got a piece of wire and fixed the popper.

"It won't hold good," Caddy said.   195

"Yes, it will," Nancy said. "Yawl watch. Yawl help me shell some corn."

The popcorn was under the bed too. We shelled it into the popper and Nancy helped Jason hold the popper over the fire.

"It's not popping," Jason said. "I want to go home."

"You wait," Nancy said. "It'll begin to pop. We'll have fun then." She was sitting close to the fire. The lamp was turned up so high it was beginning to smoke.

"Why don't you turn it down some?" I said.   *200*

"It's all right," Nancy said. "I'll clean it. Yawl wait. The popcorn will start in a minute."

"I don't believe it's going to start," Caddy said. "We ought to start home, anyway. They'll be worried."

"No," Nancy said. "It's going to pop. Dilsey will tell um yawl with me. I been working for yawl long time. They won't mind if yawl at my house. You wait, now. It'll start popping any minute now."

Then Jason got some smoke in his eyes and he began to cry. He dropped the popper into the fire. Nancy got a wet rag and wiped Jason's face, but he didn't stop crying.

"Hush," she said. "Hush." But he didn't hush. Caddy took the popper   *205* out of the fire.

"It's burned up," she said. "You'll have to get some more popcorn, Nancy."

"Did you put all of it in?" Nancy said.

"Yes," Caddy said. Nancy looked at Caddy. Then she took the popper and opened it and poured the cinders into her apron and began to sort the grains, her hands long and brown, and we watching her.

"Haven't you got any more?" Caddy said.

"Yes," Nancy said; "yes. Look. This here ain't burnt. All we need to do   *210* is—"

"I want to go home," Jason said. "I'm going to tell."

"Hush," Caddy said. We all listened. Nancy's head was already turned toward the barred door, her eyes filled with red lamplight. "Somebody is coming," Caddy said.

Then Nancy began to make that sound again, not loud, sitting there above the fire, her long hands dangling between her knees; all of a sudden water began to come out on her face in big drops, running down her face, carrying in each one a little turning ball of firelight like a spark until it dropped off her chin. "She's not crying," I said.

"I ain't crying," Nancy said. Her eyes were closed. "I ain't crying. Who is it?"

"I don't know," Caddy said. She went to the door and looked out.   *215* "We've got to go now," she said. "Here comes father."

"I'm going to tell," Jason said. "Yawl made me come."

The water still ran down Nancy's face. She turned in her chair. "Listen. Tell him. Tell him we going to have fun. Tell him I take good care of yawl until in the morning. Tell him to let me come home with yawl and sleep on the floor. Tell him I won't need no pallet. We'll have fun. You member last time how we had so much fun?"

"I didn't have fun," Jason said. "You hurt me. You put smoke in my eyes. I'm going to tell."

V

Father came in. He looked at us. Nancy did not get up.

"Tell him," she said.   220

"Caddy made us come down here," Jason said. "I didn't want to."

Father came to the fire. Nancy looked up at him. "Can't you go to Aunt Rachel's and stay?" he said. Nancy looked up at father, her hands between her knees. "He's not here," father said. "I would have seen him. There's not a soul in sight."

"He in the ditch," Nancy said. "He waiting in the ditch yonder."

"Nonsense," father said. He looked at Nancy. "Do you know he's there?"

"I got the sign," Nancy said.   225

"What sign?"

"I got it. It was on the table when I come in. It was a hogbone, with blood meat still on it, laying by the lamp. He's out there. When yawl walk out that door, I gone."

"Gone where, Nancy?" Caddy said.

"I'm not a tattletale," Jason said.

"Nonsense," father said.   230

"He out there," Nancy said. "He looking through that window this minute, waiting for yawl to go. Then I gone."

"Nonsense," father said. "Lock up your house and we'll take you on to Aunt Rachel's."

"'Twont do no good," Nancy said. She didn't look at father now, but he looked down at her, at her long, limp, moving hands. "Putting it off wont do no good."

"Then what do you want to do?" father said.

"I don't know," Nancy said. "I can't do nothing. Just put it off. And that   235 don't do no good. I reckon it belong to me. I reckon what I going to get ain't no more than mine."

"Get what?" Caddy said. "What's yours?"

"Nothing," father said. "You all must get to bed."

"Caddy made me come," Jason said.

"Go on to Aunt Rachel's," father said.

"It won't do no good," Nancy said. She sat before the fire, her elbows   240 on her knees, her long hands between her knees. "When even your own kitchen wouldn't do no good. When even if I was sleeping on the floor in the room with your chillen, and the next morning there I am, and blood—"

"Hush," father said. "Lock the door and put out the lamp and go to bed."

"I scared of the dark," Nancy said. "I scared for it to happen in the dark."

"You mean you're going to sit right here with the lamp lighted?" father said. Then Nancy began to make the sound again, sitting before the fire, her long hands between her knees. "Ah, damnation," father said. "Come along, chillen. It's past bedtime."

"When yawl go home, I gone," Nancy said. She talked quieter now, and her face looked quiet, like her hands. "Anyway, I got my coffin money saved up with Mr. Lovelady." Mr. Lovelady was a short, dirty man who collected the Negro insurance, coming around to the cabins or the kitchens every Sunday morning, to collect fifteen cents. He and his wife lived at the hotel. One morning his wife committed suicide. They had a child, a little girl. He and the child went away. After a week or two he came back alone. We would see him going along the lanes and the back streets on Saturday mornings.

"Nonsense," father said. "You'll be the first thing I'll see in the kitchen tomorrow morning."   *245*

"You'll see what you'll see, I reckon," Nancy said. "But it will take the Lord to say what that will be."

VI

We left her sitting before the fire.

"Come and put the bar up," father said. But she didn't move. She didn't look at us again, sitting quietly there between the lamp and the fire. From some distance down the lane we could look back and see her through the open door.

"What, Father?" Caddy said. "What's going to happen?"

"Nothing," father said. Jason was on father's back, so Jason was the tallest   *250*
of all of us. We went down into the ditch. I looked at it, quiet. I couldn't see much where the moonlight and the shadows tangled.

"If Jesus is hid here, he can see us, cant he?" Caddy said.

"He's not there," father said. "He went away a long time ago."

"You made me come," Jason said, high; against the sky it looked like father had two heads, a little one and a big one. "I didn't want to."

We went up out of the ditch. We could still see Nancy's house and the open door, but we couldn't see Nancy now, sitting before the fire with the door open, because she was tired. "I just done got tired," she said. "I just a nigger. It ain't no fault of mine."

But we could hear her, because she began just after we came up out of   *255*
the ditch, the sound that was not singing and not unsinging. "Who will do our washing now, Father?" I said.

"I'm not a nigger," Jason said, high and close above father's head.

"You're worse," Caddy said, "you are a tattletale. If something was to jump out, you'd be scairder than a nigger."

"I wouldn't," Jason said.

"You'd cry," Caddy said.

"Caddy," father said.

"I wouldn't," Jason said.

"Scairy cat," Caddy said.

"Candace!" father said.

260

YOU FIT INTO ME

Margaret Atwood

you fit into me
like a hook into an eye

a fish hook
an open eye

THE NAKED AND THE NUDE

Robert Graves

For me, the naked and the nude
(By lexicographers construed
As synonyms that should express
The same deficiency of dress
Or shelter) stand as wide apart   5
As love from lies, or truth from art.

Lovers without reproach will gaze
On bodies naked and ablaze;
The hippocratic eye° will see
In nakedness, anatomy;   10
And naked shines the Goddess when
She mounts her lion among men.

---

9. *hippocratic eye:* doctor's eye

The nude are bold, the nude are sly
To hold each treasonable eye.
While draping by a showman's trick   15
Their dishabille° in rhetoric,
They grin a mock–religious grin
Of scorn at those of naked skin.

The naked, therefore, who compete
Against the nude may know defeat;   20
Yet when they both together tread
The briary pastures of the dead,
By Gorgons with long whips pursued,
How naked go the sometime nude!

MY MISTRESS' EYES ARE NOTHING LIKE THE SUN

William Shakespeare

My mistress' eyes are nothing like the sun;
Coral is far more red than her lips' red;
If snow be white, why then her breasts are dun;
If hairs be wires, black wires grow on her head.
I have seen roses damasked,° red and white,   5
But no such roses see I in her cheeks;
And in some perfumes is there more delight
Than in the breath that from my mistress reeks.
I love to hear her speak, yet well I know
That music hath a far more pleasing sound;   10
I grant I never saw a goddess go;
My mistress, when she walks, treads on the ground.
And yet, by heaven, I think my love as rare
As any she belied with false compare.

---

16. *dishabille:* state of undress
5. *damasked:* reference to the damask rose, which is pink

THE MAN IN A CASE

Wendy Wasserstein

List of Characters
Byelinkov
Varinka

Scene

A small garden in the village of Mironitski. 1898.

> (*Byelinkov is pacing. Enter Varinka out of breath.*)

BYELINKOV You are ten minutes late.

VARINKA The most amazing thing happened on my way over here. You know the woman who runs the grocery store down the road. She wears a black wig during the week, and a blond wig on Saturday nights. And she has the daughter who married an engineer in Moscow who is doing very well thank you and is living, God bless them, in a three-room apartment. But he really is the most boring man in the world. All he talks about is his future and his station in life. Well, she heard we were to be married and she gave me this basket of apricots to give to you.

BYELINKOV That is a most amazing thing!

VARINKA She said to me, Varinka, you are marrying the most honorable man in the entire village. In this village he is the only man fit to speak with my son-in-law.

BYELINKOV I don't care for apricots. They give me hives.

VARINKA I can return them. I'm sure if I told her they give you hives she would give me a basket of raisins or a cake.

BYELINKOV I don't know this woman or her pompous son-in-law. Why would she give me her cakes?

VARINKA She adores you!

BYELINKOV She is emotionally loose.

VARINKA She adores you by reputation. Everyone adores you by reputation. I tell everyone I am to marry Byelinkov, the finest teacher in the country.

BYELINKOV You tell them this?

VARINKA If they don't tell me first.

BYELINKOV Pride can be an imperfect value.

VARINKA It isn't pride. It is the truth. You are a great man!

BYELINKOV I am the master of Greek and Latin at a local school at the end of the village of Mironitski.

> (*Varinka kisses him*)

VARINKA And I am to be the master of Greek and Latin's wife!

BYELINKOV Being married requires a great deal of responsibility. I hope I am able to provide you with all that a married man must properly provide a wife.

VARINKA We will be very happy.

BYELINKOV Happiness is for children. We are entering into a social contract, an amicable agreement to provide us with a secure and satisfying future.

VARINKA You are so sweet! You are the sweetest man in the world!

BYELINKOV I'm a man set in his ways who saw a chance to provide himself with a small challenge.

VARINKA Look at you! Look at you! Your sweet round spectacles, your dear collar always starched, always raised, your perfectly pressed pants always creasing at right angles perpendicular to the floor, and my most favorite part, the sweet little galoshes, rain or shine, just in case. My Byelinkov, never taken by surprise. Except by me.

BYELINKOV You speak about me as if I were your pet.

VARINKA You are my pet! My little school mouse.

BYELINKOV A mouse?

VARINKA My sweetest dancing bear with galoshes, my little stale babka.°

BYELINKOV A stale babka?

VARINKA I am not Pushkin.°

BYELINKOV (*Laughs*) That depends what you think of Pushkin.

VARINKA You're smiling. I knew I could make you smile today.

BYELINKOV I am a responsible man. Every day I have for breakfast black bread, fruit, hot tea, and every day I smile three times. I am halfway into my translation of the *Aeneid*° from classical Greek hexameter into Russian alexandrines. In twenty years I have never been late to school. I am a responsible man, but no dancing bear.

VARINKA Dance with me.

BYELINKOV Now? It is nearly four weeks before the wedding!

VARINKA It's a beautiful afternoon. We are in your garden. The roses are in full bloom.

BYELINKOV The roses have beetles.

VARINKA Dance with me!

BYELINKOV You are a demanding woman.

VARINKA You chose me. And right. And left. And turn. And right. And left.

BYELINKOV And turn. Give me your hand. You dance like a school mouse. It's a beautiful afternoon! We are in my garden. The roses are in full bloom! And turn. And turn. (*Twirls Varinka around*)

VARINKA I am the luckiest woman!

(*Byelinkov stops dancing*)

---

babka: cake with almonds and raisins
Pushkin: Alexander Pushkin (1799–1837), Russian poet
Aeneid: Latin epic poem by the Roman poet Virgil (70–19 B.C.)

Why are you stopping?

BYELINKOV To place a lilac in your hair. Every year on this day I will place a lilac in your hair.

VARINKA Will you remember?

BYELINKOV I will write it down. (*Takes a notebook from his pocket*) Dear Bye-linkov, don't forget the day a young lady, your bride, entered your garden, your peace, and danced on the roses. On that day every year you are to place a lilac in her hair.

VARINKA I love you.

BYELINKOV It is convenient we met.

VARINKA I love you.

BYELINKOV You are a girl.

VARINKA I am thirty.

BYELINKOV But you think like a girl. That is an attractive attribute.

VARINKA Do you love me?

BYELINKOV We've never spoken about housekeeping.

VARINKA I am an excellent housekeeper. I kept house for my family on the farm in Gadyatchsky. I can make a beetroot soup with tomatoes and au-bergines which is so nice. Awfully awfully nice.

BYELINKOV You are fond of expletives.

VARINKA My beet soup, sir, is excellent!

BYELINKOV Please don't be cross. I too am an excellent housekeeper. I have a place for everything in the house. A shelf for each pot, a cubby for every spoon, a folder for favorite recipes. I have cooked for myself for twenty years. Though my beet soup is not outstanding, it is sufficient.

VARINKA I'm sure it's very good.

BYELINKOV No. It is awfully, awfully not. What I am outstanding in, how-ever, what gives me greatest pleasure, is preserving those things which are left over. I wrap each tomato slice I haven't used in a wet cloth and place it in the coolest corner of the house. I have had my shoes for seven years because I wrap them in the galoshes you are so fond of. And every night before I go to sleep I wrap my bed in quilts and curtains so I never catch a draft.

VARINKA You sleep with curtains on your bed?

BYELINKOV I like to keep warm.

VARINKA I will make you a new quilt.

BYELINKOV No. No new quilt. That would be hazardous.

VARINKA It is hazardous to sleep under curtains.

BYELINKOV Varinka, I don't like change very much. If one works out the arithmetic the final fraction of improvement is at best less than an eighth of value over the total damage caused by disruption. I never thought of marrying till I saw your eyes dancing among the familiar faces at the head-master's tea. I assumed I would grow old preserved like those which are left over, wrapped suitably in my case of curtains and quilts.

VARINKA Byelinkov, I want us to have dinners with friends and summer country visits. I want people to say, "Have you spent time with Varinka

and Byelinkov? He is so happy now that they are married. She is just what
he needed."

BYELINKOV You have already brought me some happiness. But I never was
a sad man. Don't ever think I thought I was a sad man.

VARINKA My sweetest darling, you can be whatever you want! If you are
sad, they'll say she talks all the time, and he is softspoken and kind.

BYELINKOV And if I am difficult?

VARINKA Oh, they'll say he is difficult because he is highly intelligent. All
great men are difficult. Look at Lermontov, Tchaikovsky, Peter the Great.

BYELINKOV Ivan the Terrible.°

VARINKA Yes, him too.

BYELINKOV Why are you marrying me? I am none of these things.

VARINKA To me you are.

BYELINKOV You have imagined this. You have constructed an elaborate romance for yourself. Perhaps you are the great one. You are the one with
the great imagination.

VARINKA Byelinkov, I am a pretty girl of thirty. You're right, I am not a
woman. I have not made myself into a woman because I do not deserve
that honor. Until I came to this town to visit my brother I lived on my
family's farm. As the years passed I became younger and younger in fear
that I would never marry. And it wasn't that I wasn't pretty enough or
sweet enough, it was just that no man ever looked at me and saw a wife.
I was not the woman who would be there when he came home. Until I
met you I thought I would lie all my life and say I never married because
I never met a man I loved. I will love you, Byelinkov. And I will help you
to love me. We deserve the life everyone else has. We deserve not to be
different.

BYELINKOV Yes. We are the same as everyone else.

VARINKA Tell me you love me.

BYELINKOV I love you.

VARINKA (*Takes his hands*) We will be very happy. I am very strong. (*Pauses*)
It is time for tea.

BYELINKOV It is too early for tea. Tea is at half past the hour.

VARINKA Do you have heavy cream? It will be awfully nice with apricots.

BYELINKOV Heavy cream is too rich for teatime.

VARINKA But today is special. Today you placed a lilac in my hair. Write in
your note pad. Every year we will celebrate with apricots and heavy
cream. I will go to my brother's house and get some.

BYELINKOV But your brother's house is a mile from here.

VARINKA Today it is much shorter. Today my brother gave me his bicycle
to ride. I will be back very soon.

Lermontov . . . Ivan the Terrible: Mikhail Lermontov (1814–41), poet and novelist; Peter Ilich
Tchaikovsky (1840–93), composer; Peter the Great (1672–1725) and Ivan the Terrible
(1530–84), czars credited with making Russia a great European power

BYELINKOV You rode to my house by bicycle! Did anyone see you!

VARINKA Of course. I had such fun. I told you I saw the grocery store lady with the son-in-law who is doing very well thank you in Moscow, and the headmaster's wife.

BYELINKOV You saw the headmaster's wife!

VARINKA She smiled at me.

BYELINKOV Did she laugh or smile?

VARINKA She laughed a little. She said, "My dear, you are very progressive to ride a bicycle." She said you and your fiancé Byelinkov must ride together sometime. I wonder if he'll take off his galoshes when he rides a bicycle.

BYELINKOV She said that?

VARINKA She adores you. We had a good giggle.

BYELINKOV A woman can be arrested for riding a bicycle. That is not progressive, it is a premeditated revolutionary act. Your brother must be awfully, awfully careful on behalf of your behavior. He has been careless—oh so careless—in giving you the bicycle.

VARINKA Dearest Byelinkov, you are wrapping yourself under curtains and quilts! I made friends on the bicycle.

BYELINKOV You saw more than the headmaster's wife and the idiot grocery woman.

VARINKA She is not an idiot.

BYELINKOV She is a potato-vending, sausage-armed fool!

VARINKA Shhhh! My school mouse. Shhh!

BYELINKOV What other friends did you make on this bicycle?

VARINKA I saw students from my brother's classes. They waved and shouted, "Anthropos in love! Anthropos in love!!"

BYELINKOV Where is that bicycle?

VARINKA I left it outside the gate. Where are you going?

BYELINKOV (*Muttering as he exits*) Anthropos in love, anthropos in love.

VARINKA They were cheering me on. Careful, you'll trample the roses.

BYELINKOV (*Returning with the bicycle*) Anthropos is the Greek singular for man. Anthropos in love translates as the Greek and Latin master in love. Of course they cheered you. Their instructor, who teaches them the discipline and contained beauty of the classics, is in love with a sprite on a bicycle. It is a good giggle, isn't it? A very good giggle! I am returning this bicycle to your brother.

VARINKA But it is teatime.

BYELINKOV Today we will not have tea.

VARINKA. But you will have to walk back a mile.

BYELINKOV I have my galoshes on. (*Gets on the bicycle*) Varinka, we deserve not to be different. (*Begins to pedal. The bicycle doesn't move*)

VARINKA Put the kickstand up.

BYELINKOV I BEG YOUR PARDON.

VARINKA (*Giggling*) Byelinkov, to make the bicycle move, you must put the kickstand up.

(*Byelinkov puts it up and awkwardly falls off the bicycle as it moves*)

(*Laughing*) Ha ha ha. My little school mouse. You look so funny! You are the sweetest dearest man in the world. Ha ha ha!

(*Pause*)

BYELINKOV Please help me up. I'm afraid my galosh is caught.

VARINKA (*Trying not to laugh*). Your galosh is caught! (*Explodes in laughter again*) Oh, you are so funny! I do love you so. (*Helps Byelinkov up*) You were right, my pet, as always. We don't need heavy cream for tea. The fraction of improvement isn't worth the damage caused by the disruption.

BYELINKOV Varinka, it is still too early for tea. I must complete two stanzas of my translation before late afternoon. That is my regular schedule.

VARINKA Then I will watch while you work.

BYELINKOV No. You had a good giggle. That is enough.

VARINKA Then while you work I will work too. I will make lists of guests for our wedding.

BYELINKOV I can concentrate only when I am alone in my house. Please take your bicycle home to your brother.

VARINKA But I don't want to leave you. You look so sad.

BYELINKOV I never was a sad man. Don't ever think I was a sad man.

VARINKA Byelinkov, it's a beautiful day, we are in your garden. The roses are in bloom.

BYELINKOV Allow me to help you on to your bicycle. (*Takes Varinka's hand as she gets on the bike*)

VARINKA You are such a gentleman. We will be very happy.

BYELINKOV You are very strong. Good day, Varinka.

(*Varinka pedals off. Byelinkov, alone in the garden, takes out his pad and rips up the note about the lilac, strews it over the garden, then carefully picks up each piece of paper and places them all in a small envelope as lights fade to black*)

14

Classification and Analysis: Grouping and Dismantling

CLASSIFICATION

You classify and analyze constantly. Everybody does. *Classification* takes an undifferentiated collection of objects, ideas, or actions and by applying a single principle—a single way of categorizing them—sorts them into manageable groups.

For example, if you shop for a new car, you most likely arrive at your decision by working through a number of levels of choice and a number of ways of looking at the problem that are based on classification. You might begin by deciding what size of car you want and then group the available cars into classes, such as subcompact, compact, mid-size, and full-size. Then you might consider types such as sports cars, coupes, sedans, and wagons.

Once you have decided what size and type suits you best, you might consider the amount of money you have available to spend on the car and then separate the cars of the type you have decided you want into two groups: those you can afford and those you cannot afford. Having settled on the group composed of the types of cars that you can afford, you might read a magazine which evaluates the cars according to how dependable they are and the cost and frequency of repairs of a particular model. On the basis of your reading, you settle on a car, or a few cars, that you want. Thus you break a large assortment of objects into smaller and smaller groups until you arrive at a limited group from which you make your choice. In general, when you classify, you aim to group a collection of objects or people according to type or kind.

As the car-selection example shows, a person can use more than one principle of classification to help him or her make a decision or support a position. But it is also true that if you move from one basis of classification to another before you are finished with the first, it's easy to become confused—and to confuse your reader. It is especially important to remember that when you choose classification for a portion of your support for your dominant idea, you must use a single principle consistently, sticking with it until you have completed it. For example, say you are recommending a restaurant to a friend and you begin by telling your friend about the types of restaurants in town. You mention delis, Italian restaurants, Chinese restaurants, Greek restaurants, and steakhouses. Suddenly, you begin telling your friend what meals in some of these restaurants cost, but before you finish talking about price, you start to mention the locations of the various restaurants. In the middle of talking about location, you mention that there are also Thai restaurants and vegetarian restaurants. Your "recommendation" has probably not helped your friend a great deal.

Exercise

Alone or with your group, discover at least five different principles by which you could classify the following groups:

1. The members of your class
2. Teachers
3. Your friends
4. Colleges and universities
5. Movies

Now, choose one of the groups and see if each of the different ways you classified the members of that group suggests topics and a possible dominant idea. How do the topics and dominant ideas differ among the various principles of classification?

Working with the Readings

Read the following selections and, alone or with your group, answer the questions that follow each one.

SONG IN TIME OF PLAGUE

Thomas Nashe

> Adieu, farewell, earth's bliss;
> This world uncertain is;
> Fond are life's lustful joys;
> Death proves them all but toys;
> None from his darts can fly;
> I am sick, I must die.
>   Lord have mercy on us!

5

Rich men, trust not in wealth,
Gold cannot buy you health;
Physic° himself must fade.   *10*
All things to end are made,
The plague full swift goes by;
I am sick, I must die.
    Lord have mercy on us!

Beauty is but a flower   *15*
Which wrinkles will devour;
Brightness falls from the air;
Queens have died young and fair;
Dust hath closed Helen's° eye.   *20*
I am sick, I must die.
    Lord have mercy on us!

Strength stoops unto the grave,
Worms feed on Hector° brave;
Swords may not fight with fate,
Earth still holds ope her gate.   *25*
"Come, come!" the bells° do cry.
I am sick, I must die.
    Lord have mercy on us.

Wit with his wantonness°
Tasteth death's bitterness;   *30*
Hell's executioner
Hath no ears for to hear
What vain art can reply.
I am sick, I must die.
    Lord have mercy on us.   *35*

Haste, therefore, each degree,
To welcome destiny;
Heaven is our heritage,
Earth but a player's stage;
Mount we unto the sky.   *40*
I am sick, I must die.
    Lord have mercy on us.

---

10. *physic:* medicine
19. *Helen:* Helen of Troy, whose beauty caused the Trojan War
23. *Hector:* the Trojan hero of the Trojan War
26. *bells:* the passing bells, rung when someone dies
29. *Wit with his wantonness:* intelligence, with its contempt for convention

1. What principle of classification does Nashe use to group the members of a class as large as all of humanity? Name each of the classes.

2. Note where Nashe chooses description to characterize each class. Do you find a consistent theme connecting the descriptions in stanzas 2–5 that suggests a dominant idea?

3. What information does Nashe give you in the first stanza? What do you think is the purpose of this information?

4. What does Nashe use the last stanza for?

5. *An experiment:* Alone or in your group, take stanzas 2–6 of Nashe's poem and change the qualities defined in each stanza, substituting their opposites for each of them. (You don't have to write poetry to do this. You can simply make lists.) How do the changes in the qualities affect the dominant idea?

CINEMATYPES

Susan Allen Toth

Aaron takes me only to art films. That's what I call them, anyway: strange movies with vague poetic images I don't always understand, long dreamy movies about a distant Technicolor past, even longer black-and-white movies about the general meaninglessness of life. We do not go unless at least one reputable critic has found the cinematography superb. We went to *The Devil's Eye,*° and Aaron turned to me in the middle and said, "My God, this is *funny.*" I do not think he was pleased.

When Aaron and I go to the movies, we drive our cars separately and meet by the box office. Inside the theater he sits tentatively in his seat, ready to move if he can't see well, poised to leave if the film is disappointing. He leans away from me, careful not to touch the bare flesh of his arm against the bare flesh of mine. Sometimes he leans so far I am afraid he may be touching the woman on his other side. If the movie is very good, he leans forward, too, peering between the heads of the couple in front of us. The light from the screen bounces off his glasses; he gleams with intensity, sitting there on the edge of his seat, watching the screen. Once I tapped him on the arm so I could whisper a comment in his ear. He jumped.

The Devil's Eye: 1960 satiric comedy by Swedish director Ingmar Bergman, generally known for the starkness and seriousness of his films

After *Belle de Jour*° Aaron said he wanted to ask me if he could stay overnight. "But I can't," he shook his head mournfully before I had a chance to answer, "because I know I never sleep well in strange beds." Then he apologized for asking. "It's just that after a film like that," he said, "I feel the need to assert myself."

Pete takes me only to movies that he thinks have redeeming social value. He doesn't call them "films." They tend to be about poverty, war, injustice, political corruption, struggling unions in the 1930s, and the military-industrial complex. Pete doesn't like propaganda movies, though, and he doesn't like to be too depressed, either. We stayed away from *The Sorrow and the Pity;*° it would be, he said, just too much. Besides, he assured me, things are never that hopeless. So most of the movies we see are made in Hollywood. Because they are always topical, these movies offer what Peter calls "food for thought." When we saw *Coming Home,*° Pete's jaw set so firmly with the first half-hour that I knew we would end up at Poppin' Fresh Pies afterward.

When Pete and I go to the movies, we take turns driving so no one   5
owes anyone else anything. We leave the car far from the theater so we don't have to pay for a parking space. If it's raining or snowing, Pete offers to let me off at the door, but I can tell he'll feel better if I go with him while he finds a spot, so we share the walk too. Inside the theater Pete will hold my hand when I get scared if I ask him. He puts my hand firmly on his knee and covers it completely with his own hand. His knee never twitches. After a while, when the scary part is past, he loosens his hand slightly and I know that is a signal to take mine away. He sits companionably close, letting his jacket just touch my sweater, but he does not infringe. He thinks I ought to know he is there if I need him.

One night, after *The China Syndrome,*° I asked Pete if he wouldn't like to stay for a second drink, even though it was past midnight. He thought a while about that, considering my offer from all possible angles, but finally he said no. Relationships today, he said, have a tendency to move too quickly.

Sam likes movies that are entertaining. By that he means movies that Will Jones in the *Minneapolis Tribune* loved and either *Time* or *Newsweek* rather liked; also movies that do not have sappy love stories, are not musicals, do not have subtitles, and will not force him to think. He does not go to movies to think. He liked *California Suite* and *The Seduction of Joe*

Belle de Jour: sensual 1967 movie by Spanish director Luis Buñuel, in which the glamorous actress Catherine Deneuve plays the role of a prostitute
The Sorrow and the Pity: 1972 documentary by Marcel Ophuls about France during the Nazi occupation
Coming Home: 1978 film of a wounded Vietnam veteran returning home
The China Syndrome: 1979 movie warning against the dangers of nuclear power plants

Tynan,° though the plots, he said, could have been zippier. He saw it all coming too far in advance, and that took the fun out. He doesn't like to know what is going to happen. "I just want my brain to be tickled," he says. It is very hard for me to pick out movies for Sam.

When Sam takes me to the movies, he pays for everything. He thinks that's what a man ought to do. But I buy my own popcorn, because he doesn't approve of it; the grease might smear his flannel slacks. Inside the theater, Sam makes himself comfortable. He takes off his jacket, puts one arm around me, and all during the movie he plays with my hand, stroking my palm, beating a small tattoo on my wrist. Although he watches the movie intently, his body operates on instinct. Once I inclined my head and kissed him lightly just behind his ear. He beat a faster tattoo on my wrist, quick and musical, but he didn't look away from the screen.

When Sam takes me home from the movies, he stands outside my door and kisses me long and hard. He would like to come in, he says regretfully, but his steady girlfriend in Duluth wouldn't like it. When the *Tribune* gives a movie four stars, he has to save it to see with her. Otherwise her feelings might be hurt.

I go to some movies by myself. On rainy Sunday afternoons I often sneak into a revival house or a college auditorium for old Technicolor musicals, *Kiss Me Kate, Seven Brides for Seven Brothers, Calamity Jane,* even, once, *The Sound of Music.* Wearing saggy jeans so I can prop my feet on the seat in front, I sit toward the rear where no one can see me. I eat large handfuls of popcorn with double butter. Once the movie starts, I feel completely at home. Howard Keel and I are old friends; I grin back at him on the screen. I know the sound tracks by heart. Sometimes when I get really carried away I hum along with Kathryn Grayson, remembering how I once thought I would fill out a formal like that. I am rather glad now I never did. Skirts whirl, feet tap, acrobatic young men perform impossible feats, and then the camera dissolves into a dream sequence I know I can comfortably follow. It is not, thank God, Bergman.

If I can't find an old musical, I settle for Hepburn and Tracy, vintage Grant or Gable, on adventurous days Claudette Colbert or James Stewart. Before I buy my ticket I make sure it will all end happily. If necessary, I ask the girl at the box office. I have never seen *Stella Dallas* or *Intermezzo.*° Over the years I have developed other peccadilloes: I will, for example, see anything that is redeemed by Thelma Ritter. At the end of *Daddy Long Legs* I wait happily for the scene when Fred Clark, no longer angry, at last pours Thelma a convivial drink. They smile at each other, I smile

10

California Suite and *The Seduction of Joe Tynan:* popular 1979 movies, both starring Alan Alda, among others

Stella Dallas or *Intermezzo:* two very sentimental movies of the 1930s

at them, I feel they are smiling at me. In the movies I go to by myself, the men and women always like each other.

---

1. What do you think Toth's dominant idea is?
2. What, exactly, does Toth classify in her essay?
3. How does her classification(s) support her dominant idea?
4. Does Toth use her classes to establish likenesses and differences? What purposes do the likenesses and differences serve for her?

～ゞ *An Invitation to Write*

You've seen how Nashe and Toth take a large, undifferentiated group and lead you to a conclusion about that group by arranging the members of that group according to a principle or a combination of principles that reflects their dominant ideas and by describing each group in terms of their dominant ideas. Using your own observation of an equally large group, write a draft of an essay, a poem, or a story that classifies the members of that group and describes each class so as to reflect your dominant idea about the group.

ANALYSIS

Analysis divides a subject into its component parts. This organizational strategy starts with a single object, idea, or action and applies a single principle—a way of looking at it—to break the object, idea, or action down into smaller, related parts.

If you have studied biology, you have probably dissected an animal. The purpose of dissection is to learn how an organism is put together by taking it apart and identifying the relationship between the parts. Analysis can also be used to dissect an event, a situation, or an idea with the purpose of showing the relationships between the parts in order to make a dominant idea clear. At other times, you might use analysis as a subordinate part of your paper—as support for a dominant idea.

Like classification, analysis must use one principle at a time. Changing the principle on which you have based your analysis before you have completed using it and then returning to it later will most likely confuse your reader and give him or her the impression that you cannot present your ideas clearly. However, it is possible to use more than one analytic approach to make your dominant idea clear. To return to the example of buying a car, you might define the reason you want a particular car in terms of both comfort and dependability. Looking at a specific car, you find that the seats are comfortable, the instruments are legible, and there is enough head and leg room for you. You have then analyzed the car in terms of comfort. When you apply the principle of dependability, you discover that there is no history of extensive repairs or of recalls due to the engine or the transmission.

It's equally important to complete your analysis at one level of generality before you move to a more specific level. For example, when you dissected an animal in biology, most likely you began by examining the various general systems that made up that animal. You looked at the circulatory system, the nervous system, the digestive system, etc. After that, you inspected each system more closely, identifying each part of that system—veins, arteries, capillaries, among others, in the circulatory system. You might have taken one more step, examining a single part of the system and exploring how its parts worked together.

᷊᷅ *Exercise*

Alone or with your group, discover at least five different principles by which you could analyze each of the following objects:

1. Your class

2. A teacher

3. A friend

4. A college or university

5. A movie

Now choose one of the subjects and two of the principles you used to analyze it. Derive a topic and a possible dominant idea from each of the two analytic principles. How does each different principle of analysis lead to a different dominant idea?

As soon as you begin to work with classification and analysis, it will probably occur to you that, a great deal of the time, the two processes look so much like each other that it's difficult to tell them apart. Often, as you draft a piece of writing, your dominant idea might suggest classifying or analyzing your material as a useful means of support. Or the dominant idea might suggest one or the other or a combination of the two as a central organizational strategy. Once you have decided on the relevant classes, you must make those classes clear to your audience by describing and defining their parts. When you come to the point at which you place objects in certain classes, you have to show your audience why those objects fit the classes you have chosen. To make your choices clear, you might need to show how certain elements of the objects you have grouped into various classes fit into those classes. When you have reached this stage, you have begun to analyze.

Look at Nashe's poem (page 544) again. See how he first establishes his classes, then analyzes each member he places in a class in terms of its characteristics.

 Working with the Readings

Read the following selections, paying particular attention to the way the writers define the classes they have chosen and how they show how their examples fit the classes—how these writers effectively combine classification and analysis. Then, alone or with your group, answer the questions that follow each selection.

THE EMBARRASSMENT-DREAM OF NAKEDNESS

Sigmund Freud

In a dream in which one is naked or scantily clad in the presence of strangers, it sometimes happens that one is not in the least ashamed of one's condition. But the dream of nakedness demands our attention only when shame and embarrassment are felt in it, when one wishes to escape or to hide, and when one feels the strange inhibition of being unable to stir from the spot, and of being utterly powerless to alter the painful situation. . . . I believe that the great majority of my readers will at some time have found themselves in this situation in a dream.

The nature and manner of the exposure is usually rather vague. The dreamer will say, perhaps, "I was in my chemise," but this is rarely a clear image; in most cases the lack of clothing is so indeterminate that it is described in narrating the dream by an alternative: "I was in my chemise or my petticoat." As a rule the deficiency in clothing is not serious enough to justify the feeling of shame attached to it. For a man who has served in the army, nakedness is often replaced by a manner of dressing that is contrary to regulations. "I was in the street without my sabre, and I saw some officers approaching," or "I had no collar," or "I was wearing checked civilian trousers," etc.

The persons before whom one is ashamed are almost always strangers, whose faces remain indeterminate. It never happens, in the typical dream, that one is reproved or even noticed on account of the lack of clothing which causes one such embarrassment. On the contrary, the people in the dream appear to be quite indifferent; or, as I was able to note in one particularly vivid dream, they have stiff and solemn expressions. This gives us food for thought.

The dreamer's embarrassment and the spectator's indifference constitute a contradiction such as often occurs in dreams. It would be more in keeping with the dreamer's feelings if the strangers were to look at him in astonishment, or were to laugh at him, or be outraged. I think, however, that this obnoxious feature has been displaced by wish–fulfillment, while the embarrassment is for some reason retained, so that the two components are not in agreement. We have an interesting proof that the dream which is partially distorted by wish–fulfillment has not been properly understood; for it has been made the basis of a fairy-tale familiar to us all in Andersen's version of *The Emperor's New Clothes*. . . . In Andersen's fairy-tale we are told of two imposters who weave a costly garment for the Emperor, which shall, however, be visible only to the good and true. The Emperor goes forth clad in this invisible garment, and since the imaginary fabric serves as a sort of touchstone, the people are frightened into behaving as though they did not notice the Emperor's nakedness.

But this is really the situation in our dream. . . . The imposter is the dream, the Emperor is the dreamer himself, and the moralizing tendency betrays a hazy knowledge of the fact that there is a question, in the latent dream-content, of forbidden wishes, victims of repressions. The connection in which such dreams appear during my analyses of neurotics proves beyond a doubt that a memory of the dreamer's earliest childhood lies at the foundation of the dream. Only in our childhood was there a time when we were seen by our relatives, as well as by strange nurses, servants and visitors, in a state of insufficient clothing, and at that time we were not ashamed of our nakedness. In the case of many rather older children it may be observed that being undressed has an exciting effect upon them, instead of making them feel ashamed. They laugh, leap about, slap or thump their own bodies; the mother, or whoever is present, scolds them, saying: "Fie, that is shameful—you mustn't do that!" Children often show a desire to display themselves; it is hardly possible to pass through a village in country districts without meeting a two- or three-year-old child who lifts up his or her blouse or frock before the traveller, possibly in his honour. One of my patients has retained in his conscious memory a scene from his eighth year, in which, after undressing for bed, he wanted to dance into his little sister's room in his shirt, but was prevented by the servant. In the history of the childhood of neurotics exposure before children of the opposite sex plays a prominent part; in paranoia the delusion of being observed while dressing and undressing may be directly traced to these experiences; and among those who have remained perverse there is a class in whom the childish impulse is accentuated into a symptom: the class of *exhibitionists*.

This age of childhood, in which the sense of shame is unknown, seems a paradise when we look back upon it later, and paradise itself is nothing but the mass-phantasy of the childhood of the individual. This is why in paradise men are naked and unashamed, until the moment arrives when shame and fear awaken; expulsion follows, and sexual life and cultural development begin. Into this paradise dreams can take us back every night; we have already ventured the conjecture that the impressions of our earliest childhood (from the prehistoric period° until about the end of the third year) crave reproduction for their own sake, perhaps without further reference to their content, so that their repetition is a wish-fulfillment. Dreams of nakedness, then, are *exhibition-dreams.*

The nucleus of an exhibition-dream is furnished by one's own person, which is seen not as that of a child, but as it exists in the present, and by the idea of scanty clothing which emerges indistinctly, owing to the superimposition of so many later situations of being partially clothed, or out of consideration for the censorship;° to these elements are added the persons in whose presence one is ashamed. I know of no example in which the actual spectators of these infantile exhibitions reappear in a dream; for a dream is hardly ever a simple recollection. Strangely enough, those persons who are the objects of our sexual interest in childhood are omitted from all reproductions, in dreams, in hysteria or in obsessional neurosis; paranoia alone restores the spectators, and is fanatically convinced of their presence, although they remain unseen. The substitute for these persons offered by the dream, the "number of strangers" who take no notice of the spectacle offered them, is precisely the *counter-wish* to that single intimately-known person for whom the exposure was intended. "A number of strangers," moreover, often occur in dreams in all sorts of other connections; as a *counter-wish* they always signify "a secret." It will be seen that even that restriction of the old state of affairs that occurs in paranoia complies with this counter-tendency. One is no longer alone; one is quite positively being watched; but the spectators are a "number of strange, curiously indeterminate people."

Furthermore, repression finds a place in the exhibition-dream. For the disagreeable sensation of the dream is, of course, the reaction . . . to the fact that the exhibitionistic scene which has been condemned by the censorship has nevertheless succeeded in presenting itself. The only way to avoid this sensation would be to refrain from reviving the scene.

In a later chapter we shall deal once again with the feeling of inhibition. In our dreams it represents to perfection *a conflict of the will, a denial.* According to our unconscious purpose, the exhibition is to proceed; according to the demands of the censorship, it is come to an end.

The relation of our typical dreams to fairy-tales and other fiction and poetry is neither sporadic nor accidental. Sometimes the penetrating insight of the poet has analytically recognized the process of transformation of which the poet is otherwise the instrument, and has followed it up in

10

---

prehistoric period: the period of infancy before the child begins to have a conscious memory
censorship: the inhibiting function or agency of the mind, which acts like a censor in preventing the open emergence of unconscious materials into consciousness, or admits them only under disguises so that they are unrecognizable

the reverse direction; that is to say, has traced a poem to a dream. A friend has called my attention to the following passage in G. Keller's *Der Grüne Heinrich:* "I do not wish, dear Lee, that you should ever come to realize from experience the exquisite and piquant truth in the situation of Odysseus, when he appears, naked and covered with mud, before Nausicaä and her playmates!° Would you like to know what it means? Let us for a moment consider the incident closely. If you are ever parted from your home, and from all that is dear to you, and wander about in a strange country; if you have seen much and experienced much; if you have cares and sorrows, and are, perhaps, utterly wretched and forlorn, you will some night inevitably dream that you are approaching your home; you will see it shining and glittering in the loveliest colours; lovely and gracious figures will come to meet you; and then you will suddenly discover that you are ragged, naked, and covered with dust. An indescribable feeling of shame and fear overcomes you; you try to cover yourself, to hide, and you wake up bathed in sweat. As long as humanity exists, this will be the dream of the care-laden, tempest-tossed man, and thus Homer has drawn this situation from the profoundest depth of the eternal nature of humanity."

What are the profoundest depths of the eternal nature of humanity, which the poet commonly hopes to awaken in his listeners, but these stirrings of the psychic life which are rooted in that age of childhood, which subsequently becomes prehistoric? Childish wishes, now suppressed and forbidden, break into the dream behind the unobjectionable and permissibly conscious wishes of the homeless man, and it is for this reason that the dream which is objectified in the legend of Nausicaä regularly develops into an anxiety-dream.

---

1. What do you think Freud's dominant idea is?

2. Identify the points at which Freud uses classification to organize his material and the points at which he uses analysis. How do these approaches work together to support his dominant idea?

3. This selection is excerpted from Freud's book *The Interpretation of Dreams,* which was published in 1899. How do you think Freud's audience might have responded to some of the material in this essay? How does he anticipate his audience's responses and account for them?

Nausicaä: In the sixth book of the *Odyssey,* Odysseus, who has been thrown by shipwreck on the shore of the land of the Phaeacians, is discovered in his nakedness and wretchedness by Nausicaä, the young princess of the Phaeacians, who devises means to escort him to her father, the king.

THE SECRETARY CHANT

Marge Piercy

My hips are a desk.
From my ears hang
chains of paper clips.
Rubber bands form my hair.
My breasts are wells of mimeograph ink.   5
My feet bear casters.
Buzz. Click.
My head is a badly organized file.
My head is a switchboard
where crossed lines crackle.   10
Press my fingers
and in my eyes appear
credit and debit.
Zing. Tinkle.
My navel is a reject button.   15
From my mouth issue canceled reams.
Swollen, heavy, rectangular
I am about to be delivered
of a baby
Xerox machine.   20
File me under W
because I wonce
was
a woman.

---

1. Anatomy is a form of analysis that breaks an object down into its component parts. How does the secretary anatomize herself?

2. The speaker chooses certain parts of her anatomy. Why these and not others? Does this selection suggest an analytic principle to you?

3. What do those parts of her anatomy become? Since you cannot take these statements literally, what technique does Piercy use here? How does that technique affect the way you see this person?

4 What is the effect of the misspelled word in line 22?

5. Do all of the elements of the analysis lead you to see the speaker as part of a particular class? How does the relationship between how she classifies herself and what she really is lead you to a dominant idea? What do you think that idea is?

❧ *An Invitation to Write*

In the readings in this chapter, you have seen writers examine human behavior and classify it in significant ways to narrow their field of investigation. Then they have analyzed the classes as a way of supporting a dominant idea.

Looking around you, find a subject that you feel a need to write about. Place that subject in its surroundings by classifying it. Then show how its parts work together. Use these two organizational schemes to develop a dominant idea.

Alternatively, you might find that a situation you are in the middle of or that you see another person caught in is important enough to create a need to write for you. Look at the parts of that situation and their relationship to each other as a way of making your dominant idea regarding that situation clear to your reader.

❧ *A Student Paper*

When you have read this paper, answer the questions that follow it, alone or with your group.

THE EFFECTS OF TELEVISION

Kimberly Coca

I went home last weekend because I thought that I would have the time and the peace and quiet to get some homework done. But wait. On Saturday morning, just as I had settled down at my old, familiar desk: "Vrooom. Crash. I'll get Ted! You wait over there!" It was that blasted television in my little brother's room. It seemed that every time I tried to study, there was background noise from that television.

Before the late 1940s, people did not have to deal with noise from a television. When the very first home television set was turned on, lives changed. Television has added to our world in a positive way, offering educational programs like *Nova* and *Contact*. These programs promote the advancement of technology and encourage the spread of knowledge. *Contact* teaches people about new inventions, and *Nova* introduces them to the latest scientific advances. On the other hand, there have been some negative consequences that accompanied the positive ones. For example, television has created the "couch potato." It has also provided poor role models to our youth and has desensitized people to violence. Television has affected each person who owns or has ever watched one by molding their attitudes and lifestyles.

While I tried to do my homework, it became clear to me that programs on television have influenced the lives of my family members. Fed up with the TV blasting in the next room, I struggled to find a place in my house free of the impact of television. I found it impossible to get away from the annoying sound of the television that seemed to permeate the air in every room. In each room I entered, I caught a glimpse of the different ways television shapes our lives.

As I entered the living room, I looked over at my mom and saw how engrossed she was in *The Oprah Winfrey Show*. I remembered that my mom used to go outside and garden, or we would take nice long walks together. Now, however, immediately after she gets home from work, on goes the television. It seems my mom, like so many people, is often willing to give up interacting with her family in order to watch her favorite program and listen to people she does not know talk about their problems.

Before television became such a hot item, families used to spend 5 more time doing things together. It used to be common to see a family together at the park: talking, playing, and sharing their thoughts. Or they would take a drive together on a weekend afternoon. With the invasion of television in the home, the scene has changed. Most families have been mesmerized by television; they become so absorbed in a program that it is now common for family members to sit together for hours without even speaking a word to each other.

Of all those affected by television, I would have to say that children are shaped the most by what they see. I tromped into the playroom, trying to get away from the noise of Oprah telling me what I should and shouldn't do. I was almost trampled by my younger brother, who was chasing our family dog. I stopped my brother and asked him what it was that he was doing. He explained that he was "gonna karate-chop Spot just like the Ninja Turtles." He then quoted Bart Simpson, saying, "Outta my way, man!"

Characters like the Ninja Turtles and Bart Simpson are poor role models for our youth. Although they are supposed to stand for good and justice, the Ninja Turtles are bad examples for our children because they automatically use violence instead of working their problems out in a more reasonable way. This show gives children the idea that if someone is bothering them, then using force will solve the problem. Bart Simpson is rude, irresponsible, and insensitive. Bart always cuts people down and shows no respect for adults. On one episode of *The Simpsons* he even told a teacher to "Can it!" These are not the type of attitudes I want my children to adopt. I left the playroom. I could tell I was not going to get any studying done in that part of the house. How about the den?

As I made my way down the hall to the den, I could hear my dad yelling, "Get 'em, punch 'em, knock 'em out!" It was apparent to me that he was watching a wrestling match. I stepped inside the den and saw my dad smiling as Mean Man Maloney's opponent was knocked across the ring, landing flat on his back. I couldn't help but feel a little disappointed by my father's reaction to such violence. People nowadays seem to think it is exciting when a "bad guy," or any guy for that matter, gets pounded.

The pleasure that arises in some viewers as a result of death or pain inflicted on a character bothers me. I don't like the fact that so many people get a thrill out of watching killing or violence on television. For example, the other day as I was passing through the upstairs lounge of my residence hall at school, I was amazed by the enthusiasm shown by most of the audience as Don Johnson shot and killed an intruder on *Miami Vice*. It is this type of behavior that causes me to question the control television has over peoples' attitudes.

I left the den, still trying to find a quiet place to study. Now, where 10 should I study? Definitely outside. If I could escape the noise caused by television and the effects it had on my family, I could get busy on my work. Just as I was about to sit down on the front porch and begin reading, my dog tore out of the front door followed by my brother, who was carrying a large "He Man" stick. He was shouting, "By the powers of Greystone!"

I never did get to start my work, but I learned that the influence of television on my family is varied and far-reaching. Because television plays such a large role in the development of our attitudes, many of them destructive or negative, I believe it is important that we are careful when we choose the programs we watch and that we carefully budget the amount of time we spend watching them.

---

1. What is this writer's dominant idea?
2. If the writer uses classification and analysis as an overall organizational strategy, what other organizational strategies does she use to arrange her ideas and examples?
3. How does this writer introduce her piece of writing? Do you think that her technique is effective?
4. Is the writer's conclusion effective?
5. Do the writer's examples support her dominant idea adequately?
6. If this writer were a member of your group or if you had the chance to speak with her about her paper, what suggestions would you have for her to help her make her paper more effective?

On the following pages you will find readings that use classification and analysis as an organizational strategy. If your teacher assigns some or all of these readings or if you are inclined to read them on your own, pay attention to the ways the writers use classification and analysis to support their dominant ideas. Also, note how the writers use voice and style to engage your feelings, your interest, and your intellect.

Remember, these writers are writing to you—a fellow human being. They have chosen to tell you something about coping with the effort of being human in their worlds. See how their examples and ideas speak to your experience. See how the combination of your experiences and those the writers offer you might lead you to your own ideas about your world.

SCHOOL

Garrison Keillor

School gave us marks every nine weeks, three marks for each subject: work, effort, and conduct. Effort was the important one, according to my mother, because that mark showed if you had gumption and stick-to-itiveness, and effort was my poorest showing. I was high in conduct except when dared to do wrong by other boys, and then I was glad to show what I could do. Pee on the school during recess? You don't think I would? Open the library door, yell "Boogers!" and run? Well, I showed them. I was not the one who put a big gob on the classroom doorknob during lunch though, the one that Darla Ingqvist discovered by putting her hand on it. Of all the people you'd want to see touch a giant gob, Darla was No. 1. She yanked her hand back just as Brian said, "Snot on you!" but she already knew. She couldn't wipe it off on her dress because she wore such nice dresses so she burst into tears and tore off to the girls' lavatory. Mrs. Meiers blamed me because I laughed. Brian, who did it, said, "That was a mean thing to do, shame on you" and I sat down on the hall floor and laughed myself silly. It was so *right* for Darla to be the one who got a gob in her hand. She was a jumpy, chatty little girl who liked to bring money to school and show it to everyone. Once a five-dollar bill—we never had a five-dollar bill, so all the kids crowded around to see it. That was what she wanted. She made us stand in line. It was dumb. All those dumb girls took turns holding it and saying what they would do if they had one, and then Darla said she had $400 in her savings account. "Liar, liar, pants on fire," Brian said, but we all knew she probably did have $400. Later Brian said, "I wish I had her five dollars and she had a feather in her butt, and we'd both be tickled," which made me feel a little better, but putting the gob on the knob, knowing that Darla was monitor and had the privilege of opening the door, *that* was a stroke of genius. I almost didn't mind Mrs. Meiers making me sit in the cloakroom for an hour. I put white paste on slips of paper and put them in the pockets of Darla's coat, hoping she'd think it was more of the same. . . .

I liked Mrs. Meiers a lot, though. She was a plump lady with bags of fat on her arms that danced when she wrote on the board: we named them Hoppy and Bob. That gave her a good mark for friendliness in my book, whereas Miss Conway of fourth grade struck me as suspiciously thin. What was her problem? Nerves, I suppose. She bit her lips and squinted and snaked her skinny hand into her dress to shore up a strap, and she was easily startled by loud noises. Two or three times a day, Paul or Jim or Lance would let go with a book, dropping it flat for maximum whack, and yell, "Sorry, Miss Conway!" as the poor woman jerked like a fish on the line. It could be done by slamming a door or dropping the window, too, or even scraping a chair, and once a loud slam made *her* drop a stack of books, which gave us a double jerk. It worked better if we were very quiet before the noise. Often, the class would be so quiet, our little heads bent over our work, that she would look up and congratulate us on our excellent behavior, and when she looked back down at her book, *wham!* and she did the best jerk we had ever seen. There were five classes of spasms: The Jerk, The Jump, The High Jump, the Pants Jump, and The Loopdeloop, and we knew when she was prime for the big one. It was after we had put her through a hard morning workout, including several good jumps, and a noisy lunch period, and she had lectured us in her thin weepy voice, then we knew she was all wound up for the Loopdeloop. All it required was an extra effort: *throwing* a dictionary flat at the floor or dropping the globe, which sounded like a car crash.

We thought about possibly driving Miss Conway to a nervous breakdown, an event we were curious about because our mothers spoke of it often. "You're driving me to a nervous breakdown!" they'd yell, but then, to prevent one, they'd grab us and shake us silly. Miss Conway seemed a better candidate. We speculated about what a breakdown might include— some good jumps for sure, maybe a couple hundred, and talking gibberish with spit running down her chin.

Miss Conway's nervous breakdown was prevented by Mrs. Meiers, who got wind of it from one of the girls—Darla, I think. Mrs. Meiers sat us boys down after lunch period and said that if she heard any more loud noises from Room 4, she would keep us after school for a half hour. "Why not the girls?" Lance asked. "Because I know that you boys can accept responsibility," Mrs. Meiers said. And that was the end of the jumps, except for one accidental jump when a leg gave way under the table that held Mr. Bugs the rabbit in his big cage. Miss Conway screamed and left the room, Mrs. Meiers stalked in, and we boys sat in Room 3 from 3:00 to 3:45 with our hands folded on our desks, and remembered that last Loopdeloop, how satisfying it was, and also how sad it was, being the last. Miss Conway had made some great jumps.

THE THREE NEW YORKS

E. B. White

There are roughly three New Yorks. There is, first, the New York of the man or woman who was born here, who takes the city for granted and accepts it size and its turbulence as natural and inevitable. Second, there is the New York of the commuter—the city that is devoured by locusts each day and spat out each night. Third, there is the New York of the person who was born somewhere else and came to New York in quest of something. Of these three trembling cities the greatest is the last—the city of final destination, the city that is a goal. It is this third city that accounts for New York's high-strung disposition, its poetical deportment, its dedication to the arts, and its incomparable achievements. Commuters give the city its tidal restlessness; natives give it solidity and continuity; but the settlers give it passion. And whether it is a farmer arriving from Italy to set up a small grocery store in a slum, or a young girl arriving from a small town in Mississippi to escape the indignity of being observed by her neighbors, or a boy arriving from the Corn Belt with a manuscript in his suitcase and a pain in his heart, it makes no difference; each embraces New York with the intense excitement of first love, each absorbs New York with the fresh eyes of an adventurer, each generates heat and light to dwarf the Consolidated Edison Company.

The commuter is the queerest bird of all. The suburb he inhabits has no essential vitality of its own and is a mere roost where he comes at day's end to go to sleep. Except in rare cases, the man who lives in Mamaroneck or Little Neck or Teaneck, and works in New York, discovers nothing much about the city except the time of arrival and departure of trains and buses, and the path to a quick lunch. He is deskbound, and has never, idly roaming in the gloaming, stumbled suddenly on Belvedere Tower in the Park, seen the ramparts rise sheer from the water of the pond, and the boys along the shore fishing for minnows, girls stretched out negligently on the shelves of the rocks; he has never come suddenly on anything at all in New York as a loiterer, because he has had no time between trains. He has fished in Manhattan's wallet and dug out coins, but has never listened to Manhattan's breathing, never awakened to its morning, never dropped off to sleep in its night. About 400,000 men and women come charging onto the Island each weekday morning, out of the mouths of tubes and tunnels. Not many among them have ever spent a drowsy afternoon in the great rustling oaken silence of the reading room of the Public Library, with the book elevator (like an old water wheel) spewing out books onto the trays. They tend their furnaces in Westchester and in Jersey, but have never seen the furnaces of the Bowery, the fires that burn in oil drums on zero winter nights. They may work in the financial district downtown and never see the extravagant plantings of Rockefeller Center—the daffodils and grape hyacinths and birches of the flags trimmed to the wind on a fine morning in spring. Or they may work in a midtown office and may let a whole year swing round without sighting Governor's Island from the sea wall. The commuter dies with tremendous mileage to his credit, but he is no rover. His entrances and exits are more devious than those in a prairie-dog village; and he calmly plays bridge while his train is buried in the mud at the bottom of the East River. The Long Island Rail Road alone carried forty million commuters last year; but many of them were the same fellow retracing his steps.

The terrain of New York is such that a resident sometimes travels farther, in the end, than a commuter. The journey of the composer Irving Berlin from Cherry Street in the lower East Side to an apartment uptown was through an alley and was only three or four miles in length; but it was like going three times around the world.

THE GIRLS IN THEIR SUMMER DRESSES

Irwin Shaw

Fifth Avenue was shining in the sun when they left the Brevoort.° The sun was warm, even though it was February, and everything looked like Sunday morning—the buses and the well-dressed people walking slowly in couples and the quiet buildings with the windows closed.

Michael held Frances' arm tightly as they walked toward Washington Square° in the sunlight. They walked lightly, almost smiling, because they had slept late and had a good breakfast and it was Sunday. Michael unbuttoned his coat and let it flap around him in the mild wind.

"Look out," Frances said as they crossed Eighth Street. "You'll break your neck." Michael laughed and Frances laughed with him.

"She's not so pretty," Frances said. "Anyway, not pretty enough to take a chance of breaking your neck."

Brevoort: a hotel on lower Fifth Avenue in New York
Washington Square: a park at the south end of Fifth Avenue

Michael laughed again. "How did you know I was looking at her?" 5

Frances cocked her head to one side and smiled at her husband under the brim of her hat. "Mike, darling," she said.

"O.K.," he said. "Excuse me."

Frances patted his arm lightly and pulled him along a little faster toward Washington Square. "Let's not see anybody all day," she said. "Let's just hang around with each other. You and me. We're always up to our neck in people, drinking their Scotch or drinking our Scotch; we only see each other in bed. I want to go out with my husband all day long. I want him to talk only to me and listen only to me."

"What's to stop us?" Michael asked.

"The Stevensons. They want us to drop by around one o'clock and 10
they'll drive us into the country."

"The cunning Stevensons," Mike said. "Transparent. They can whistle. They can go driving in the country by themselves."

"Is it a date?"

"It's a date."

Frances leaned over and kissed him on the tip of the ear.

"Darling," Michael said, "this is Fifth Avenue." 15

"Let me arrange a program," Frances said. "A planned Sunday in New York for a young couple with money to throw away."

"Go easy."

"First let's go to the Metropolitan Museum of Art," Frances suggested, because Michael had said during the week he wanted to go. "I haven't been there in three years and there're at least ten pictures I want to see again. Then we can take the bus down to Radio City and watch them skate. And later we'll go down to Cavanagh's and get a steak as big as a blacksmith's apron, with a bottle of wine, and after that there's a French picture at the Filmarte that everybody says—say, are you listening to me?"

"Sure," he said. He took his eyes off the hatless girl with the dark hair, cut dancer-style like a helmet, who was walking past him.

"That's the program for the day," Frances said flatly. "Or maybe you'd 20
just rather walk up and down Fifth Avenue."

"No," Michael said. "Not at all."

"You always look at other women," Frances said. "Everywhere. Every damned place we go."

"No, darling," Michael said, "I look at everything. God gave me eyes and I look at women and men in subway excavations and moving pictures and the little flowers of the field. I casually inspect the universe."

"You ought to see the look in your eye," Frances said, "as you casually inspect the universe on Fifth Avenue."

"I'm a happily married man." Michael pressed her elbow tenderly. "Ex- 25
ample for the whole twentieth century—Mr. and Mrs. Mike Loomis. Hey, let's have a drink," he said, stopping.

"We just had breakfast."

"Now listen, darling," Mike said, choosing his words with care, "it's a nice day and we both felt good and there's no reason why we have to break it up. Let's have a nice Sunday."

"All right. I don't know why I started this. Let's drop it. Let's have a good time."

They joined hands consciously and walked without talking among the baby carriages and the old Italian men in their Sunday clothes and the young women with Scotties in Washington Square Park.

"At least once a year everyone should go to the Metropolitan Museum of Art," Frances said after a while, her tone a good imitation of the tone she had used at breakfast and at the beginning of their walk. "And it's nice on Sunday. There're a lot of people looking at the pictures and you get the feeling maybe Art isn't on the decline in New York City, after all—" 30

"I want to tell you something," Michael said very seriously. "I have not touched another woman. Not once. In all the five years."

"All right," Frances said.

"You believe that, don't you?"

"All right."

They walked between the crowded benches, under the scrubby city-park trees. 35

"I try not to notice it," Frances said, "but I feel rotten inside, in my stomach, when we pass a woman and you look at her and I see that look in your eye and that's the way you looked at me the first time. In Alice Maxwell's house. Standing there in the living room, next to the radio, with a green hat on and all those people."

"I remember the hat," Michael said.

"The same look," Frances said. "And it makes me feel bad. It makes me feel terrible."

"Sh-h-h, please, darling, sh-h-h."

"I think I would like a drink now," Frances said. 40

They walked over to a bar on Eighth Street, not saying anything, Michael automatically helping her over curbstones and guiding her past automobiles. They sat near a window in the bar and the sun streamed in and there was a small, cheerful fire in the fireplace. A little Japanese waiter came over and put down some pretzels and smiled happily at them.

"What do you order after breakfast?" Michael asked.

"Brandy, I suppose," Frances said.

"Courvoisier," Michael told the waiter. "Two Courvoisiers."

The waiter came with the glasses and they sat drinking the brandy in the sunlight. Michael finished half his and drank a little water. 45

"I look at women," he said. "Correct. I don't say it's wrong or right. I look at them. If I pass them on the street and I don't look at them, I'm fooling you, I'm fooling myself."

"You look at them as though you want them," Frances said, playing with her brandy glass. "Every one of them."

"In a way," Michael said, speaking softly and not to his wife, "in a way that's true. I don't do anything about it, but it's true."

"I know it. That's why I feel bad."

"Another brandy," Michael called. "Waiter, two more brandies."   *50*

He sighed and closed his eyes and rubbed them gently with his fingers. "I love the way women look. One of the things I like best about New York is the battalions of women. When I first came to New York from Ohio that was the first thing I noticed, the million wonderful women, all over the city. I walked around with my heart in my throat."

"A kid," Frances said. "That's a kid's feeling."

"Guess again," Michael said. "Guess again. I'm older now. I'm a man getting near middle age, putting on a little fat, and I still love to walk along Fifth Avenue at three o'clock on the east side of the street between Fiftieth and Fifty-seventh Streets. They're all out then, shopping, in their furs and their crazy hats, everything all concentrated from all over the world into seven blocks—the best furs, the best clothes, the handsomest women, out to spend money and feeling good about it."

The Japanese waiter put the two drinks down, smiling with great happiness.

"Everything is all right?" he asked.   *55*

"Everything is wonderful," Michael said.

"If it's just a couple of fur coats," Frances said, "and forty-five dollar hats—"

"It's not the fur coats. Or the hats. That's just the scenery for that particular kind of woman. Understand," he said, "you don't have to listen to this."

"I want to listen."

"I like the girls in the offices. Neat with their eyeglasses, smart, chipper,   *60* knowing what everything is about. I like the girls on Forty-fourth Street at lunchtime, the actresses, all dressed up on nothing a week. I like the salesgirls in the stores, paying attention to you first because you're a man, leaving the lady customers waiting. I got all this stuff accumulated in me because I've been thinking about it for ten years and now you've asked for it and here it is."

"Go ahead," Frances said.

"When I think of New York City, I think of all the girls on parade in the city. I don't know whether it's something special with me or whether every man in the city walks around with the same feeling inside him, but I feel as though I'm at a picnic in this city. I like to sit near the women in the theatres, the famous beauties who've taken six hours to get ready and look it. And the young girls at the football games, with the red cheeks, and when the warm weather comes, the girls in their summer dresses." He finished his drink. "That's the story."

Frances finished her drink and swallowed two or three times extra. "You say you love me?"

"I love you."

"I'm pretty, too," Frances said. "As pretty as any of them." 65
"You're beautiful," Michael said.

"I'm good for you," Frances said pleading. "I've made a good wife, a good housekeeper, a good friend. I'd do any damn thing for you."

"I know," Michael said. He put his hand out and grasped hers.

"You'd like to be free to—" Frances said.

"Sh-h-h." 70

"Tell the truth." She took her hand away from under his.

Michael flicked the edge of his glass with his finger. "O.K.," he said gently. "Sometimes I feel I would like to be free."

"Well," Frances said, "any time you say."

"Don't be foolish." Michael swung his chair around to her side of the table and patted her thigh.

She began to cry silently into her handkerchief, bent over just enough 75
so that nobody else in the bar would notice. "Someday," she said, crying, "you're going to make a move."

Michael didn't say anything. He sat watching the bartender slowly peel a lemon.

"Aren't you?" Frances asked harshly. "Come on, tell me. Talk. Aren't you?"

"Maybe," Michael said. He moved his chair back again. "How the hell do I know?"

"You know," Frances persisted. "Don't you know?"

"Yes," Michael said after a while, "I know." 80

Frances stopped crying then. Two or three snuffles into the handkerchief and she put it away and her face didn't tell anything to anybody. "At least do me one favor," she said.

"Sure."

"Stop talking about how pretty this woman is or that one. Nice eyes, nice breasts, a pretty figure, good voice." She mimicked his voice. "Keep it to yourself. I'm not interested."

Michael waved to the waiter. "I'll keep it to myself," he said.

Frances flicked the corners of her eyes. "Another brandy," she told the 85
waiter.

"Two," Michael said.

"Yes, ma'am, yes, sir," said the waiter, backing away.

Frances regarded Michael coolly across the table. "Do you want me to call the Stevensons?" she asked. "It'll be nice in the country."

"Sure," Michael said. "Call them."

She got up from the table and walked across the room toward the 90
telephone. Michael watched her walk, thinking what a pretty girl, what nice legs.

HOW DO I LOVE THEE?

Elizabeth Barrett Browning

How do I love thee? Let me count the ways.
I love thee to the depth and breadth and height
My soul can reach, when feeling out of sight
For the ends of Being and ideal Grace.
I love thee to the level of everyday's   5
Most quiet need, by sun and candle-light.
I love thee freely, as men strive for Right;
I love thee purely, as they turn from Praise.
I love thee with the passion put to use
In my old griefs, and with my childhood's faith.   10
I love thee with a love I seemed to lose
With my lost saints—I love thee with the breath,
Smiles, tears, of all my life!—and, if God choose,
I shall but love thee better after death.

DO NOT GO GENTLE INTO THAT GOOD NIGHT

Dylan Thomas

Do not go gentle into that good night,
Old age should burn and rave at close of day;
Rage, rage against the dying of the light.

Though wise men at their end know dark is right,
Because their words had forked no lightning they   5
Do not go gentle into that good night.

Good men, the last wave by, crying how bright
Their frail deeds might have danced in a green bay,
Rage, rage against the dying of the light.

Wild men who caught and sang the sun in flight,   10
And learn, too late, they grieved it on its way,
Do not go gentle into that good night.

Grave men, near death, who see with blinding sight
Blind eyes could blaze like meteors and be gay,
Rage, rage against the dying of the light.   15

And you, my father, there on the sad height,
Curse, bless, me now with your fierce tears, I pray.
Do not go gentle into that good night.
Rage, rage against the dying of the light.

BUT HE WAS COOL
or: he even stopped for green lights
Haki R. Mudhubuti

super–cool
ultrablack
a tan / purple
had a beautiful shade
he had a double-natural   5
that wd put the sisters to shame.
his dashikis were tailor made
& his beads were imported sea shells
   (from some blk / country i never heard of)
he was triple-hip.   10
his tikis were hand carved
out of ivory
& came express from the motherland.
he would greet u in swahili
& say good-bye in yoruba.   15

woooooooooooo-jim he bes so cool & ill tel li gent
   cool-cool is so cool he was un-cooled by other niggers' cool
   cool-cool ultracool was bop-cool / ice box cool so cool cold cool
   his wine didn't have to be cooled, him was air conditioned cool
   cool-cool / real cool made me cool—ain't that cool   20
   cool-cool so cool him nick-named refrigerator.

cool-cool so cool
he didn't know,
after detroit, newark, chicago &c.,
we had to hip   25
   cool-cool / super-cool / real cool
   that
to be black
is
to be   30
very-hot.

POT ROAST

Mark Strand

I gaze upon the roast,
that is sliced and laid out
on my plate
and over it
I spoon the juices   5
of carrot and onion.
And for once I do not regret
the passage of time.

I sit by a window
that looks   10
on the soot-stained brick of buildings
and do not care that I see
no living thing—not a bird,
not a branch in bloom,
not a soul moving   15
in the rooms
behind the dark panes.
These days when there is little
to love or to praise
one could do worse   20
than yield
to the power of food.
So I bend
to inhale
the steam that rises   25
from my plate, and I think
of the first time
I tasted a roast
like this.
It was years ago   30
in Seabright,
Nova Scotia;
my mother leaned
over my dish and filled it
and when I finished   35
filled it again.
I remember the gravy,
its odor of garlic and celery,

and sopping it up
with pieces of bread.   40

And now
I taste it again.
The meat of memory.
The meat of no change.
I raise my fork in praise,   45
and I eat.

15

Cause and Effect: Showing Your Reader the Connections between Events

As you write a draft and work toward discovering your dominant idea, you may find that your writing suggests showing your audience how an event or condition has led or might lead to another or how an event or condition is the result of a previous state of affairs. For example, your dominant idea might grow from your finding that there are too few classes at your school to meet student demand. Your dominant idea suggests that as a result of that shortage students are delayed in their progress toward graduation, spending more of their time and their and their parents' money in college than you believe they should. In that case, your dominant idea suggests a cause-and-effect relationship between a set of events, a relationship in which one event leads to another—in which the second event is the result of the first, the third event is the result of the first two, and so on.

Looking critically at your dominant idea—and remembering that your audience might not see the events in the same way as you do—might lead you to decide that simply stating the relationship between these events is not enough. You might discover that you need to give your reader a reason for being concerned about that connection, as well as giving him or her the idea that something might be done about its consequences.

In the example of the class shortage, you might add the following ideas to the core relationship: Because students are being delayed in their progress toward graduation, they and their families incur extra expenses that they might not be able to afford. Digging deeper into the causes of this problem, you conclude that this predicament results from an inadequate university budget, from inefficient allocation of the resources in the budget, or perhaps from both.

THE CAUSE-AND-EFFECT CHAIN: AN EXAMPLE

Summing up your exploration of your original dominant idea, you find that you've discovered the following chain of cause-and-effect relationships:

Because	there is not enough money in the budget, or the money is not allocated properly, or both,
the *effect* is that	there are not enough classes to meet student demand.
Because	there are not enough classes to meet student demand,
the *effect* is that	students must remain in school longer than necessary.
Because	students must remain in school longer than necessary,
the *effect* is that	students and their families have to carry an unnecessary and possibly damaging financial burden.
Therefore	it would benefit the students as well as their families to allocate more money or reallocate money in the present budget to build new classrooms.

Most writers discover that showing an audience a sequence of events in terms of the connections between those events allows them to focus their readers' attention upon an issue that defines the relationship between those events and that reflects the dominant idea. The previous example suggests that the drain upon a student's time and his or her family's financial resources results from a connected series of events or conditions, all of which result from a combination of inadequate budget and inept money management. When a writer has discovered and shown his or her audience the chain of causes and effects, the dominant idea suggests itself as a way of responding to the causal relationship. In this case, the response suggests finding additional sources of revenue, making certain the individuals in charge of the budget are doing their jobs correctly, or both.

Sequence of Events Versus Causality

A warning: Simply describing a chain of causes and effects does not necessarily lead to your readers' understanding or accepting your dominant idea. You need to convince your readers that both the events you describe and the relationships between them that you suggest have a basis in fact. Your readers need to be certain that the conditions or events on which you base your dominant idea *really* exist and that there *really* is a causal relationship that ties the events or conditions together.

Although this warning probably seems obvious, in your day-to-day life you run into many statements about connections between events and the reasons for those connections. When you examine those statements critically, you may find that many of them seem to ignore this caution either accidentally or deliberately. Such assertions confuse a sequence of events with a causal relationship. Often, such a false chain of reasoning is a device unscrupulous writers use to manipulate an audience into believing an idea that is not necessarily truthful. A TV advertisement for a brand of coffee begins with a woman's feeling inadequate because her husband takes a second cup of coffee at her friend's house although he never takes a second cup of the coffee she has made. As a result, she doubts her adequacy as a wife and as a woman and feels jealousy toward her friend. In the next scene, she has switched to her friend's brand of coffee. Her husband happily takes a second cup and compliments her on the excellence of her coffee. As a result, she feels adequate as a woman and as a wife. The advertisement tries to lead the viewer to believe that switching brands of coffee will cure the ills of an unhappy marriage—a case of sequence being intentionally confused with causation. Superstitions are cases of unintentionally confused thinking about causes and effects. There is no reason to think that breaking a mirror will cause seven years of bad luck or that finding a penny will cause you to have good luck.

If you choose to write a paper that has a cause-and-effect relationship as its dominant idea, consider how many other organizational schemes might contribute to your point. For example, if the chain of events you've chosen to present depends on a setting, you might have to describe the surroundings and how the surroundings contributed to the actions. If people and their actions are involved, you might find yourself narrating a series of actions. In order to distinguish one element of your idea from another, similar one, you might have to establish a contrast, or you might have to show some resemblances. And another way of looking at cause and effect is to see it as the analysis of a situation in terms of the elements that created it.

Working with the Readings

Read the following pieces of writing and, alone or with your group, answer the questions that follow each one.

HARLEM

Langston Hughes

> *What happens to a dream deferred?*
>
> Does it dry up
> like a raisin in the sun?
> Or fester like a sore—
> And then run?   5

Does it stink like rotten meat?
Or crust and sugar over—
like a syrupy sweet?

Maybe it just sags
like a heavy load.   10

Or does it explode?

---

1. This poem uses metaphor to establish the causes leading to a possible effect. What consistent image or idea can you find in the metaphors?

2. Do the metaphors suggest to you a state of mind or a set of feelings that explains the possibility of an explosion in the last line, that helps you to understand the possibility of a cause-and-effect relationship?

3. Why do you think Hughes, an African American who lived through the first half of the twentieth century, presents this cause-and-effect argument to you? Why does he use metaphors instead of directly saying what he means?

4. Can you think of a time when you or someone you know well had a dream that you, he, or she had to defer? Did it dry up? Was there the possibility of an explosion? If the dream dried up, what caused it to do so? Could the reasons the dream withered have led to an explosion? Why?

CHILDREN OF A MARRIAGE

Richard Rodriguez

What is culture?

The immigrant shrugs. Latin American immigrants come to the United States with only the things they need in mind—not abstractions like culture. Money. They need dollars. They need food. Maybe they need to get out of the way of bullets.

Most of us who concern ourselves with Hispanic-American culture, as painters, musicians, writers—or as sons and daughters—are the children of immigrants. We have grown up on this side of the border, in the land of Elvis Presley and Thomas Edison; our lives are prescribed by the mall, by the DMV and the Chinese restaurant. Our imaginations yet vascillate between an Edenic Latin America (the blue door)—which nevertheless betrayed our parents—and the repellent plate glass of a real American city—which has been good to us.

Hispanic-American culture is where the past meets the future. Hispanic-American culture is not an Hispanic milestone only, not simply a celebration at the crossroads. America transforms into pleasure what America cannot avoid. Is it any coincidence that at a time when Americans are troubled by the encroachment of the Mexican desert, Americans discover a chic in cactus, in the decorator colors of the Southwest? In sand?

Hispanic-American culture of the sort that is now showing (the teen movie, the rock song) may exist in an hourglass; may in fact be irrelevant to the epic. The U.S. Border Patrol works through the night to arrest the flow of illegal immigrants over the border, even as Americans wait in line to get into *La Bamba*. Even as Americans vote to declare, once and for all, that English shall be the official language of the United States, Madonna starts recording in Spanish.

But then so is Bill Cosby's show irrelevant to the 10 o'clock news, where families huddle together in fear on porches, pointing at the body of the slain boy bagged in tarpoline. Which is not to say that Bill Cosby or Michael Jackson is irrelevant to the future or without neo-Platonic influence. Like players within the play, they prefigure, they resolve. They make black and white audiences aware of a bond that may not yet exist.

Before a national TV audience, Rita Moreno tells Geraldo Rivera that her dream as an actress is to play a character rather like herself: "I speak English perfectly well . . . I'm not dying from poverty . . . I want to play *that* kind of Hispanic woman, which is to say, an American citizen." This is an actress talking, these are sho-biz pieties. But Moreno expresses as well the general Hispanic-American predicament. Hispanics want to belong to America without betraying the past.

Hispanics fear losing ground in any negotiation with the American city. We come from an expansive, an intimate culture that has been judged second-rate by the United States of America. For reasons of pride, therefore, as much as of affection, we are reluctant to give up our past. Hispanics often express a fear of "losing" culture. Our fame in the United States has been our resistance to assimilation.

The symbol of Hispanic culture has been the tongue of flame— Spanish. But the remarkable legacy Hispanics carry from Latin America is not language—an inflatable skin—but breath itself, capacity of soul, an inclination to live. The genius of Latin America is the habit of synthesis.

We assimilate. Just over the border there is the example of Mexico, the country from which the majority of U.S. Hispanics come. Mexico is mestizo—Indian and Spanish. Within a single family, Mexicans are light-skinned and dark. It is impossible for the Mexican to say, in the scheme of things, where the Indian begins and the Spaniard surrenders.

In culture as in blood, Latin America was formed by a rape that became a marriage. Due to the absorbing generosity of the Indian, European culture took on new soil. What Latin America knows is that people create one another as they marry. In the music of Latin America you will hear the litany of bloodlines—the African drum, the German accordion, the cry from the minaret.

The United States stands as the opposing New World experiment. In North America the Indian and the European stood apace. Whereas Latin America was formed by a medieval Catholic dream of one world—of meltdown conversion—the United States was built up from Protestant individualism. The American melting pot washes away only embarrassment; it is the necessary initiation into public life. The American faith is that our national strength derives from separateness, from "diversity." The glamour of the United States is a carnival promise: You can lose weight, get rich as Rockefeller, tough up your roots, get a divorce.

Immigrants still come for the promise. But the United States wavers in its faith. As long as there was space enough, sky enough, as long as economic success validated individualism, loneliness was not too high a price to pay. (The cabin on the prairie or the Sony Walkman.)

As we near the end of the American century, two alternative cultures beckon the American imagination—both highly communal cultures— the Asian and the Latin American. The United States is a literal culture. Americans devour what we might otherwise fear to become. Sushi will make us corporate warriors. Combination Plate No. 3, smothered in mestizo gravy, will burn a hole in our hearts.

Latin America offers passion. Latin America has a life—I mean *life*—big clouds, unambiguous themes, death, birth, faith, that the United States, for all its quality of life, seems without now. Latin America offers communal riches: an undistressed leisure, a kitchen table, even a full sorrow. Such is the solitude of America, such is the urgency of American need, Americans reach right past a fledgling, homegrown Hispanic-American culture for the real thing—the darker bottle of Mexican beer; the denser novel of a Latin American master.   15

For a long time, Hispanics in the United States withheld from the United States our Latin American gift. We denied the value of assimilation. But as our presence is judged less foreign in America, we will produce a more generous art, less timid, less parochial. Carlos Santana, Luis Valdez, Linda Ronstadt—Hispanic-Americans do not have a "pure" Latin American art to offer. Expect bastard themes, expect ironies, comic conclusions. For we live on this side of the border, where Kraft manufactures bricks of "Mexican style" Velveeta, and where Jack in the Box serves "Fajita Pita."

The flame-red Chevy floats a song down the Pan American Highway: From a rolled-down window, the grizzled voice of Willie Nelson rises in disembodied harmony with the voice of Julio Iglesias. Gabby Hayes and Cisco are thus resolved.

Expect marriage. We will change America even as we will be changed. We will disappear with you into a new miscegenation.

Along the border, real conflicts remain. But the ancient tear separating Europe from itself—the Catholic Mediterranean from the Protestant north—may yet heal itself in the New World. For generations, Latin America has been the place—the bed—of a confluence of so many races and cultures that Protestant North America shuddered to imagine it.

Imagine it.

20

------

1. What do you think is Rodriguez's dominant idea?

2. What organizational strategies does Rodriguez use to support his dominant idea? What is his overall strategy? What strategies does he use to support his overall strategy?

3. What audience does Rodriguez imagine for his piece of writing? What choices does he make to adapt his dominant idea and its support to his audience?

4. How do you think Rodriguez feels about what he writes about? What do you find him doing in his writing to reflect those feelings?

5. Rodriguez concludes his essay with a single sentence. What effect do you think he intends that abrupt conclusion to have on his audience?

THE WAR AT HOME

Lewis Shiner

Ten of us in the back of a Huey, assholes clenched like fists, C-rations turned to sno-cones in our bellies. Tracers float up at us, swollen, sizzling with orange light, like one dud firecracker after another. Ahead of us the gunships pound Landing Zone Dog with everything they have, flex guns, rockets, and 50-calibers, while the artillery screams overhead and the Air Force A1-Es strafe the clearing into kindling.

We hover over the LZ in the sudden phosphorus dawn of a flare, screaming, "Land, you fucker, land!" while the tracers close in, the shell of the copter ticking like a clock as the thumb-sized rounds go through her, ripping the steel like paper, spattering somebody's brains across the aft bulkhead.

Then falling into the knee-high grass, the air humming with bullets and stinking of swamp ooze and gasoline and human shit and blood. Spinning wildly, my finger jamming down the trigger of the M-16, not caring anymore where the bullets go.

And waking up in my own bed, Clare beside me, shaking me, hissing, "Wake up, wake up for Christ's sake."

I sat up, the taste of it still in my lungs, hands twitching with ber-   5
serker frenzy. "'M okay," I mumbled, "Nightmare. I was back in Nam."
    "What?"
    "Flashback," I said. "The war."
    "What are you talking about? You weren't in the war."
    I looked at my hands and remembered. It was true. I'd never even
been in the Army, never set foot in Vietnam.

    Three months earlier we'd been shooting an Eyewitness News series   10
on Vietnamese refugees. His name was Nguyen Ky Duk, former ARVN
colonel, now a fry cook at Jack in the Box. "You killed my country," he
said. "All of you. Americans, French, Japanese. Like you would kill a dog
because you thought it might have, you know, rabies. Just kill it and
throw it in a ditch. It was a living thing, and now it is dead."
    The afternoon of the massacre we got raw footage over the wire.
About a dozen of us crowded the monitor and stared at the shattered
windows of the Safeway, the mounds of cartridges, the bloodstains and
the puddles of congealing food.
    "What was it he said?"
    "Something about 'gooks.' 'You're all fucking gooks, just like the
others, and now I'll kill you too,' something like that."
    "But he wasn't in Nam. They talked to his wife."
    "So why'd he do it?"   15
    "He was a gun nut. Black market shit, like that M–16 he had. Camo
clothes, the whole nine yards. A nut."
    I walked down the hall, past the lines of potted ferns and bamboo,
and bought a Coke from the machine. I could still remember the dream,
the feel of the M–16 in my hands, the rage, the fear.

    "Like it?" Clare asked. She turned slowly, the loose folds of her black
cotton pajamas fluttering, her face hidden by the conical straw hat.
    "No," I said. "I don't know. It makes me feel weird."
    "It's fashion," she said. "Fashion's supposed to make you feel weird."   20
    I walked away from her, through the sliding glass door and into the
back yard. The grass had grown a foot or more without my noticing, and
strange plants had come up between the flowers, suffocating them in
sharp fronds and broad green leaves.

    "Did you go?"
    "No," I said. "I was I–Y. Underweight, if you can believe that." But
in fact I was losing weight again, the muscles turning stringy under sallow skin.
    "Me either. My dad got a shrink to write me a letter. I did the
marches, Washington and all that. But you know something? I feel weird
about not going. Kind of guilty, somehow. Even though we shouldn't

ever have been there, even though we were burning villages and fragging our own guys. I feel like . . . I don't know. Like I missed something. Something important."

"Maybe not," I said. Through cracked glass I could see the sunset   25
thickening the trees.

"What do you mean?"

I shrugged. I wasn't sure myself. "Maybe it's not too late," I said.

I walk through the haunted streets of my town, sweltering in the January heat. The jungle arches over me; children's voices in the distance chatter in their weird pidgin Vietnamese. The TV station is a crumbling ruin and none of us feel comfortable there any longer. We work now in a thatched hut with a mimeo machine.

The air is humid, fragrant with anticipation. Soon the planes will come and it will begin in earnest.

------

1. What kind of a world does Shiner describe in the last short section of his story?
2. This story breaks into five short sections, with the first four leading you to the last section. How do they do that? Can you find a theme, a redundant subject, that connects all the sections?
3. Through whose eyes do you see the events of this story? Are you outside the narrator's experience, watching him act and think, or are you someplace else? What does the writer's placement of you suggest about the events of the story?
4. What do you think the dominant idea of Shiner's story is? What events and thoughts lead you to that idea?

An Invitation to Write

As you go through your day, look around you (or within yourself) for situations that seem to create problems for you or for others and examine them for the reasons they happen and the results they might lead to. Wait for the idea that is important enough to you to give you the "felt sense" that you need to write something about it. Write a draft of a paper and watch for a dominant idea that explains the situation you've chosen in terms of causes and effects.

A Student Paper

When you have read this paper, answer the questions that follow it, alone or with your group.

TRANSCENDING RACE

Jeremiah Miller

"DOWN!" I yell as I throw my already exhausted body to the wrestling mat. As I jump back to my feet, I hear the wrestling team shout "TWELVE!" Still sprinting in place, I look around our wrestling room with pride. I see the windows of the room have already fogged up, as I expected they would have after two-and-a-half hours of grueling practice. "DOWN! THIRTEEN!" Our room would be dark without the two spotlights focused on me from thirty feet above. Still running in place, maybe a little more slowly now, I try to calculate how much weight I have lost so far in practice. I estimate seven pounds. "DOWN! FOURTEEN!" I am most likely within four pounds of my wrestling weight, 171 pounds, and all I can think about is how badly I wish practice were over and how thirsty I am. "DOWN! FIFTEEN!"

Coach tells me to switch places with Hobbes. His real name is Ben Spencer, I gave him the name "Hobbes" after Calvin's tiger in everyone's favorite comic strip. Besides being one of the valley's best 152-pounders, he is my best friend. As he takes his place under the spotlights, I fill his space in the front line of weary wrestlers who are still running in place. "O.K., guys, let's do thirty push-ups first, then finish up with ten handstand push-ups," yells Hobbes. I groan, "Handstand push-ups at the very end of practice? I'm going to kill you for this later." He points to the spot on the wall where the names of past state champions hang, along with a sign that reads CHAMPIONS ARE MADE NOT BORN. This shuts me up.

Thirty minutes later practice ends and I strip down so I can weigh myself. The scale reads 172. Coach asks me how much I weigh. I'm beaming as I say, "One-seventy-two, Coach. I had a ten-pound practice."

Just then at the other end of the room two wrestlers start yelling at each other. One of them, Hobbes, pushes Steve, our 140-pound man. I run over to the squabble and pull Hobbes away from Steve. Being in a sour mood myself, not having eaten anything solid for two days, I say, "What the hell's wrong with you? He's on your team. Leave him alone." Steve had been bragging about being three pounds underweight to Hobbes. This means that Steve can eat tonight, while Hobbes, who is four pounds over, will most likely be starving for three days. With Thanksgiving two days away he is not happy.

As you can tell, wrestling is a very demanding sport both mentally—try starving yourself through the holiday season—and physically—try waking up at 5:30 a.m. and running two pounds off after not having eaten much of anything for at least two days.

5

In the five years that I have been involved with the sport I have never heard a wrestler pass a judgment based on ethnicity on another wrestler. It isn't that all wrestlers are unbiased and open-minded. Some of the most bullish people that I have known are wrestlers. The reason is respect. Every good wrestler knows not to underestimate his opponent in any way. This mistake, if made once, is not repeated. The other reason for the mutual respect shared by all wrestlers is the knowledge of what each man must go through in practice just to be able to compete.

The practices held at my alma mater, South Hills High School, are probably among the toughest in the state. But I know that in schools throughout California practices similar to ours take place and that other wrestlers, whether they are black like Hobbes or white like me or Hispanic like half of my team, sweat the same sweat as I, bleed the same blood as I, and cry the same tears that I have cried in my quest to be the best.

As I write these words, I am writing what I have always known, what Hobbes has always known, and what anyone involved in the sport of wrestling has always known. I feel as if I am putting down on paper the legacy that wrestling has left me and many others. As my ten-year-old brother looks at his new pair of wrestling shoes and gives me a big hug, I think ahead to the day that he will experience what I have felt. I wonder if this open-mindedness will have spread to other areas of his life as it has for me. Only time will tell.

---

1. What is this writer's dominant idea?

2. Do you think the writer was wise to wait so long to state that idea?

3. If this writer uses cause and effect as his overall organizing strategy, what other organizational approaches does he use to support his dominant idea?

4. Is the writer's conclusion effective?

5. If this writer were a member of your group or if you had the chance to speak with him about his paper, what suggestions would you have for him to help him make his paper more effective?

FURTHER READINGS

On the following pages you will find readings that use cause and effect as an organizational strategy. If your teacher assigns some or all of these readings or if you are inclined to read them on your own, pay attention to the ways the writers use cause and effect to support their dominant ideas. Also, note how the writers use voice and style to engage your feelings, your interest, and your intellect.

Remember, these writers are writing to you—a fellow human being. They have chosen to tell you something about coping with the effort of being human in their worlds. See how their examples and ideas speak to your experience. See how the combination of your experiences and those the writers offer you might lead you to your own ideas about your world.

WHERE AIDS BEGAN

Randy Shilts

By October 2, 1985, the morning Rock Hudson died, the word was familiar to almost every household in the Western world.

AIDS.

Acquired Immune Deficiency Syndrome had seemed a comfortably distant threat to most of those who had heard of it before, the misfortune of people who fit into rather distinct classes of outcasts and social pariahs. But suddenly, in the summer of 1985, when a movie star was diagnosed with the disease and the newspapers couldn't stop talking about it, the AIDS epidemic became palpable and the threat loomed everywhere.

Suddenly there were children with AIDS who wanted to go to school, laborers with AIDS who wanted to work, and researchers who wanted funding, and there was a threat to the nation's public health that could no longer be ignored. Most significantly, there were the first glimmers of awareness that the future would always contain this strange new word. AIDS would become a part of American culture and indelibly change the course of our lives.

The implications would not be fleshed out for another few years, but   5
on that October day in 1985 the first awareness existed just the same. Rock Hudson riveted America's attention upon this deadly new threat for the first time, and his diagnosis became a demarcation that would separate the history of America before AIDS from the history that came after.

The timing of this awareness, however, reflected the unalterable tragedy at the heart of the AIDS epidemic: By the time America paid attention to the disease, it was too late to do anything about it. The virus was already pandemic in the nation, having spread to every corner of the North American continent. The tide of death that would later sweep America could, perhaps, be slowed, but it could not be stopped.

The AIDS epidemic, of course, did not arise full grown from the biological landscape; the problem had been festering throughout the decade. The death tolls of the late 1980s are not startling new developments but an unfolding of events predicted for many years. There had been a time when much of this suffering could have been prevented, but by 1985 that time had passed. Indeed, on the day the world learned that Rock Hudson was stricken, some 12,000 Americans were already dead or dying of AIDS and hundreds of thousands more were infected with the virus that caused the disease. But few had paid any attention to this; nobody, it seemed, had cared about them.

The bitter truth was that AIDS did not just happen to America—it was allowed to happen by an array of institutions, all of which failed to perform their appropriate tasks to safeguard the public health. This failure of the system leaves a legacy of unnecessary suffering that will haunt the Western world for decades to come.

There was no excuse, in this country and in this time, for the spread of a deadly new epidemic. For this was a time in which the United States boasted the world's most sophisticated medicine and the world's most extensive public health system, geared to eliminate such pestilence from our national life. When the virus appeared, the world's richest nation housed the most lavishly financed scientific research establishments—both inside the vast governmental health bureaucracy and in other institutions—to investigate new diseases and quickly bring them under control. And making sure that government researchers and public health agencies did their jobs were the world's most unfettered and aggressive media, the public's watchdogs. Beyond that, the group most affected by the epidemic, the gay community, had by then built a substantial political infrastructure, particularly in cities where the disease struck first and most virulently. Leaders were in place to monitor the gay community's health and survival interests.

But from 1980, when the first isolated gay men began falling ill from 10 strange and exotic ailments, nearly five years passed before all these institutions—medicine, public health, the federal and private scientific research establishments, the mass media, and the gay community's leadership—mobilized the way they should in a time of threat. The story of these first five years of AIDS in America is a drama of national failure, played out against a backdrop of needless death.

People died while Reagan administration officials ignored pleas from government scientists and did not allocate adequate funding for AIDS research until the epidemic had already spread throughout the country.

People died while scientists did not at first devote appropriate attention to the epidemic because they perceived little prestige to be gained in studying a homosexual affliction. Even after this denial fades, people died while some scientists, most notably those in the employ of the United States government, competed rather than collaborated in international research efforts, and so diverted attention and energy away from the central struggle against the disease itself.

People died while public health authorities and the political leaders who guided them refused to take the tough measures necessary to curb the epidemic's spread, opting for political expediency over the public health.

And people died while gay community leaders played politics with the disease, putting political dogma ahead of the preservation of human life.

People died and nobody paid attention because the mass media did not   15
like covering stories about homosexuals and was especially skittish about stories that involved gay sexuality. Newspapers and television largely avoided discussion of the disease until the death toll was too high to ignore and the casualties were no longer just the outcasts. Without the media to fulfill its role as public guardian, everyone else was left to deal—and not deal—with AIDS as they saw fit.

In those early years, the federal government viewed AIDS as a budget problem, local public health officials saw it as a political problem, gay leaders considered AIDS a public relations problem, and the news media regarded it as a homosexual problem that wouldn't interest anybody else. Consequently, few confronted AIDS for what it was, a profoundly threatening medical crisis.

Fighting against this institutional indifference were a handful of heroes from disparate callings. Isolated teams of scientists in research centers in America and Europe risked their reputation and often their jobs to pioneer early research on AIDS. There were doctors and nurses who went far beyond the call of duty to care for its victims. Some public health officials struggled valiantly to have the epidemic addressed in earnest. A handful of gay leaders withstood vilification to argue forcefully for a sane community response to the epidemic and to lobby for the funds that provided the first breakthroughs in research. And there were many victims of the epidemic who fought rejection, fear, isolation, and their own deadly prognoses to make people understand and to make people care.

Because of their efforts, the story of politics, people, and the AIDS epidemic is, ultimately, a tale of courage as well as cowardice, compassion as well as bigotry, inspiration as well as venality, and redemption as well as despair.

It is a tale that bears telling, so that it will never happen again, to any people, anywhere.

Christmas Eve, 1976

Kinshasa, Zaire

The hot African sky turned black and sultry; it wasn't like Christmas   20
at all.

The unrelenting mugginess of the equatorial capital made Dr. Ib Bygbjerg even lonelier for Denmark. In the kitchen, Dr. Grethe Rask, determined to assuage her young colleague's homesickness, began preparing an approximation of the dinner with which Danes traditionally begin their Christmas observance, the celebration known through centuries of custom as the Feast of the Hearts.

The preparations brought back memories of the woman's childhood in Thisted, the ancient Jutland port nestled on the Lim Fjord not far from the North Sea. As the main course, Grethe Rusk knew, there needed to be something that flies. In Jutland that would mean goose or duck; in Zaire, chicken would have to suffice. As she began preparing the fowl, Grethe again felt the familiar fatigue wash over her. She had spent the last two years haunted by weariness, and by now, she knew she couldn't fight it.

Grethe collapsed on her bed. She had been among the Danish doctors who came to replace the Belgian physicians who were no longer welcome in this new nation eager to forget its recent colonial incarnation as the Belgian Congo. Grethe had first gone there in 1964, returning to Europe for training in stomach surgery and tropical diseases. She had spent the last four years in Zaire but, despite all this time in Africa, she remained unmistakably from the Danish stock who proudly announce themselves as north of the fjord. To be north of the Lim Fjord was to be direct and decisive, independent and plainspoken. The Jutlanders born south of the stretch of water that divides the Danish peninsula tend toward weakness, as anyone north of the fjord might explain. Far from the kings in Copenhagen, these hardy northern people had nurtured their collective heritage for centuries. Grethe Rask from Thisted mirrored this.

It explained why she was here in Zaire, 5,000 miles from where she might forge a lucrative career as a surgeon in the sprawling modern hospitals of Copenhagen. Such a cosmopolitan career meant people looking over her shoulder, giving orders. Grethe preferred the work she had done at a primitive hospital in the remote village of Abumombazi in the north of Zaire. She alone was in charge there.

The hospital conditions in Abumombazi were not as deplorable as in other parts of the country. A prominent Zairian general came from the region. He had had the clout to attract a white doctor to the village, and there, with Belgian nuns, Grethe worked with what she could beg and borrow. This was Central Africa, after all, and even a favored clinic would never have such basics as sterile rubber gloves or disposable needles. You just used needles again and again until they wore out; once gloves had worn through, you risked dipping your hands in your patient's blood because that was what needed to be done. The lack of rudimentary supplies meant that a surgeon's work had risks that doctors in the developed world could not imagine, particularly because the undeveloped part, specifically Central Africa, seemed to sire new diseases with nightmarish regularity. Earlier that year, not far from Abumombazi, in a village along the Ebola River on the Zaire-Sudan border, a virulent outbreak of a horrifying new disease had demonstrated the dangers of primitive medicine and new viruses. A trader from the village of Enzara, suffering from fevers and profuse, uncontrollable bleeding, had come to the teaching hospital for nurses in Maridi. The man apparently had picked up the disease sexually. Within days, however, 40 percent of the student nurses in Maridi were stricken with the fever, transmitted by contact with the patient's infected blood either through standard care procedures or through accidental needle-sticks.

Frightened African health officials swallowed their pride and called the World Health Organization, who came with a staff from the American Centers for Disease Control. By the time the young American doctors arrived, thirty-nine nurses and two doctors were dead. The CDC doctors worked quickly, isolating all patients with fevers. Natives were infuriated when the Americans banned the traditional burials of the victims since the ritual bathing of the bodies was clearly spreading the disease further. Within weeks, however, the epidemic was under control. In the end, the Ebola Fever virus, as it came to be known, killed 53 percent of the people it infected, seizing 153 lives before it disappeared as suddenly and mysteriously as it had arisen. Sex and blood were two horribly efficient ways to spread a new virus, and years later, a tenuous relief would fill the voices of doctors who talked of how fortunate it was for humankind that this new killer had awakened in this most remote corner of the world and had been stamped out so quickly. A site just a bit closer to regional crossroads could have unleashed a horrible plague. With modern roads and jet travel, no corner of the earth was very remote anymore; never again could diseases linger undetected for centuries among a distant people without finding some route to fan out across the planet.

The battle between humans and disease was nowhere more bitterly fought than here in the fetid equatorial climate, where heat and humidity fuel the generation of new life forms. One historian has suggested that humans, who first evolved in Africa eons ago, migrated north to Asia and Europe simply to get to climates that were less hospitable to the deadly microbes the tropics so efficiently bred.

Here, on the frontiers of the world's harshest medical realities, Grethe Rask tended the sick. In her three years in Abumombazi, she had bullied and cajoled people for the resources to build her jungle hospital, and she was loved to the point of idolization by the local people. Then, she returned to the Danish Red Cross Hospital, the largest medical institution in the bustling city of Kinshasa, where she assumed the duties of chief surgeon. Here she met Ib Bygbjerg, who had returned from another rural outpost in the south. Bygbjerg's thick dark hair and small compact frame belied his Danish ancestry, the legacy, he figured, of some Spanish sailor who made his way to Denmark centuries ago. Grethe Rask had the features one would expect of a woman from Thisted, high cheekbones and blond hair worn short in a cut that some delicately called mannish.

To Bygbjerg's eye, on that Christmas Eve, there were troubling things to note about Grethe's appearance. She was thin, losing weight from a mysterious diarrhea. She had been suffering from the vague yet persistent malaise for two years now, since her time in the impoverished northern villages. In

1975, the problem had receded briefly after drug treatments, but for the past year, nothing had seemed to help. The surgeon's weight dropped further, draining and weakening her with each passing day.

Even more alarming was the disarray in the forty-six-year-old woman's lymphatic system, the glands that play the central role in the body's never-ending fight to make itself immune from disease. All of Grethe's lymph glands were swollen and had been for nearly two years. Normally, a lymph node might swell here or there to fight this or that infection, revealing a small lump on the neck, under an arm, or perhaps, in the groin. There didn't seem to be any reason for her glands to swell; there was no precise infection anywhere, much less anything that would cause such a universal enlargement of the lymph nodes all over her body.

And the fatigue. It was the most disconcerting aspect of the surgeon's malaise. Of course, in the best of times, this no-nonsense woman from north of the fjord did not grasp the concept of relaxation. Just that day, for example, she had not been scheduled to work, but she put in a full shift, anyway; she was always working, and in this part of the world nobody could argue because there was always so much to be done. But the weariness, Bygbjerg could tell, was not bred by overwork. Grethe had always been remarkably healthy, throughout her arduous career. No, the fatigue was something darker; it had become a constant companion that weighted her every move, mocking the doctor's industry like the ubiquitous cackling of the hyena on the savannah.

Though she was neither sentimental nor particularly Christian, Grethe Rask had wanted to cheer her young colleague; instead, she lay motionless, paralyzed again. Two hours later, Grethe stirred and began, halfheartedly, to finish dinner. Bygbjerg was surprised that she was so sick then that she could not muster the strength to stay awake for something as special as the Feast of the Hearts.

A QUESTION OF MANHOOD

Robert Ragaini

I was jolted out of my sleep one morning last summer by the sounds of shouting male voices and loud rock music. At first I assumed that the noise was coming from the tiny, one-man police station next door where kids with nothing to do sometimes gather, but this music was more raucous, the voices more pugnacious than those usually heard in the quiet family summer community where I have rented for the last four seasons.

Most often the earliest sounds are of children calling to each other or their parents, shrill and happy, impatient to get at the day, not a bad thing to hear at 8 or 8:30. This was different. It was 6:30. With a flick of a switch the silence had been broken by a radio at high volume and unrestrained yelling and laughter. As I became more awake, I realized that the din was coming from the house to the right of mine. I was surprised because, although this was a new rental and I didn't know my neighbors, the previous weekend the house had been occupied by a middle-aged couple who hadn't made a sound.

I lay awake deciding—or not deciding—what to do. My first impulse was to storm over indignantly and issue a lecture on consideration and manners, to shame the noisemakers into apologetic silence. It didn't take long to quash that impulse.

Then I considered reasoning with them. I would explain that I was trying to sleep and ask them to keep the noise down. Certainly they would respond to a reasonable request presented in a reasonable manner. At that moment the boisterous, cheerful voices were replaced by a single, angry one. It said, "Well, I've been living here for nine years and I make more money than you, you S.O.B." After that statement of manly defiance, the radio was turned off and the conversation level subsided, and I went back to sleep.

A couple of hours later, at breakfast, I heard familiar voices and looked   5
out to see five men in their 20s, each with a bottle of beer in his hand, walking past my house to the one next door. Soon they were on the deck, drinking and roughhousing until all but one got on bicycles and rode off, leaving the fifth man asleep in a chair.

A friend dropped by that afternoon, and I told her what had happened. I explained that I believed there was nothing to gain by confronting them directly. They were interested only in themselves, would not listen to reason, were the kind who would enjoy intimidating me physically, and I would be left helpless and in a rage. She said that I had done the sensible thing by doing nothing, and we agreed that in the event of a recurrence I would call the police and let them handle it.

Then, having resolved the problem in a mature, adult fashion, I said something that made no sense to her at all. I told her I felt like a coward.

When I was young, there was a story that all boys knew. It went something like this. On his way home from school, a boy is attacked by the neighborhood bully. He runs crying to his mother who comforts him and cleans his wounds, but when his father comes home, the boy is told he must fight back like a man. Then begins a period of surreptitious training in self-defense, a process which culminates with the ignominious and glorious defeat of the bully.

That was the myth, and, as every boy knows, it's a barefaced lie. In real life, the bully kills you.

But the truth is not important. What counts is that at some time and in   10
some way a boy is told to be a man, and he simply doesn't know how. Whether it's as blatant as being given boxing gloves for Christmas, as I was, or being pushed to play unwanted games, or urged to try one more time, or

any of the thousand coercions, all he knows is that somehow he has failed and he hasn't even taken the test.

There are two ways a boy can go at this critical moment in his life. He can become fearful and quit, get out of the game, or begin to create his own little swagger and try to start winning. In my case, I combined the two. Deep inside I was scared to death, and I knew it well, but I was big and a pretty fair mimic, and I developed an image that got me by. When physically confronted, I blustered and posed and did my imitation of tough and usually bluffed my way through. When that didn't work, I "chickened out" and suffered the torments of the damned.

As I grew older, the rules were modified, but the game remained the same. Being a man was still about winning, and when, in my early 20s, I dropped out of the race, it was a rejection of all that I was "supposed" to be. Later, when I became ambitious, it was acceptance of the very same things, and in each case I measured myself against the definition of manhood that I had carried since I was 3 or 4 or 5.

Though the game was not of my devising, when I chose to play, I did it well and accumulated the trophies that come with success. But the catch was that for a real man there is never enough. There's always a bigger prize, a greater challenge, a tougher test, and to stop winning is to lose.

Now all of us know that this is ridiculous—crazy, in fact—and no one need be so great a fool as to step into such a self-destructive trap. But I'm not talking about what makes sense. I'm talking about feelings, particularly the insidious feeling that is a part of every American male no matter how sane or intelligent or gentle or wise. The feeling deep in the pit of his stomach that says, "I'm not a man."

That is how I felt when I didn't go next door and challenge those guys   *15*
and force them to stop disturbing me. It didn't matter that it wouldn't have worked or that it didn't make sense or that there were other, more rational approaches. All that was head stuff, no match for the gnawing feeling, that remnant from my childhood, that once again I had failed the test.

A WHITE HERON

Sarah Orne Jewett

I

The woods were already filled with shadows one June evening, just before eight o'clock, though a bright sunset still glimmered faintly among the trunks of the trees. A little girl was driving home her cow, a plodding, dilatory, provoking creature in her behavior, but a valued companion for all that. They were going away from whatever light there was, and striking deep into the woods, but their feet were familiar with the path, and it was no matter whether their eyes could see it or not.

There was hardly a night the summer through when the old cow could be found waiting at the pasture bars; on the contrary, it was her greatest pleasure to hide herself away among the huckleberry bushes, and though she wore a loud bell she had made the discovery that if one stood perfectly still it would not ring. So Sylvia had to hunt for her until she found her, and call Co'! Co'! with never an answering Moo, until her childish patience was quite spent. If the creature had not given good milk and plenty of it, the case would have seemed very different to her owners. Besides, Sylvia had all the time there was, and very little use to make of it. Sometimes in pleasant weather it was a consolation to look upon the cow's pranks as an intelligent attempt to play hide and seek, and as the child had no playmates she lent herself to this amusement with a good deal of zest. Though this chase had been so long that the wary animal herself had given an unusual signal of her whereabouts, Sylvia had only laughed when she came upon Mistress Moolly at the swampside, and urged her affectionately homeward with a twig of birch leaves. The old cow was not inclined to wander farther, she even turned in the right direction for once as they left the pasture, and stepped along the road at a good pace. She was quite ready to be milked now, and seldom stopped to browse. Sylvia wondered what her grandmother would say because they were so late. It was a great while since she had left home at half-past five o'clock, but everybody knew the difficulty of making this errand a short one. Mrs. Tilley had chased the hornéd torment too many summer evenings herself to blame any one else for lingering, and was only thankful as she waited that she had Sylvia, nowadays, to give such valuable assistance. The good woman suspected that Sylvia loitered occasionally on her own account; there never was such a child for straying about out-of-doors since the world was made! Everybody said that it was a good change for a little maid who had tried to grow for eight years in a crowded manufacturing town, but, as for Sylvia herself, it seemed as if she never had been alive at all before she came to live at the farm. She thought often with wistful compassion of a wretched geranium that belonged to a town neighbor.

"'Afraid of folks,'" old Mrs. Tilley said to herself, with a smile, after she had made the unlikely choice of Sylvia from her daughter's houseful of children, and was returning to the farm. "'Afraid of folks,' they said! I guess she won't be troubled no great with 'em up to the old place!" When they reached the door of the lonely house and stopped to unlock it, and the cat came to purr loudly, and rub against them, a deserted pussy, indeed, but fat with young robins, Sylvia whispered that this was a beautiful place to live in, and she never should wish to go home.

The companions followed the shady woodroad, the cow taking slow steps and the child very fast ones. The cow stopped long at the brook to drink, as if the pasture were not half a swamp, and Sylvia stood still and waited, letting her bare feet cool themselves in the shoal water, while the great twilight moths struck softly against her. She waded on through the brook as the cow moved away, and listened to the thrushes with a heart that beat fast with pleasure. There was a stirring in the great boughs overhead. They were full of little birds and beasts that seemed to be wide awake, and going about their world, or else saying good-night to each other in sleepy twitters. Sylvia herself felt sleepy as she walked along. However, it was not much farther to the house, and the air was soft and sweet. She was not often in the woods so late as this, and it made her feel as if she were a part of the gray shadows and the moving leaves. She was just thinking how long it seemed since she first came to the farm a year ago, and wondering if everything went on in the noisy town just the same as when she was there; the thought of the great red-faced boy who used to chase and frighten her made her hurry along the path to escape from the shadow of the trees.

Suddenly this little woods-girl is horror-stricken to hear a clear whistle   5 not very far away. Not a bird's-whistle, which would have a sort of friendliness, but a boy's whistle, determined, and somewhat aggressive. Sylvia left the cow to whatever sad fate might await her, and stepped discreetly aside into the bushes, but she was just too late. The enemy had discovered her, and called out in a very cheerful and persuasive tone, "Halloa, little girl, how far is it to the road?" and trembling Sylvia answered almost inaudibly, "A good ways."

She did not dare to look boldly at the tall young man, who carried a gun over his shoulder, but she came out of her bush and again followed the cow, while he walked alongside.

"I have been hunting for some birds," the stranger said kindly, "and I have lost my way, and need a friend very much. Don't be afraid," he added gallantly. "Speak up and tell me what your name is, and whether you think I can spend the night at your house, and go out gunning early in the morning."

Sylvia was more alarmed than before. Would not her grandmother consider her much to blame? But who could have foreseen such an accident as this? It did not seem to be her fault, and she hung her head as if the stem of it were broken, but managed to answer "Sylvy," with much effort when her companion again asked her name.

Mrs. Tilley was standing in the doorway when the trio came into view. The cow gave a loud moo by way of explanation.

"Yes, you'd better speak up for yourself, you old trial! Where'd she   10 tucked herself away this time, Sylvy?" But Sylvia kept an awed silence; she knew by instinct that her grandmother did not comprehend the gravity of the situation. She must be mistaking the stranger for one of the farmer-lads of the region.

The young man stood his gun beside the door, and dropped a lumpy game-bag beside it; then he bade Mrs. Tilley good-evening, and repeated his wayfarer's story, and asked if he could have a night's lodging.

"Put me anywhere you like," he said. "I must be off early in the morn-ing, before day; but I am very hungry, indeed. You can give me some milk at any rate, that's plain."

"Dear sakes, yes," responded the hostess, whose long slumbering hos-pitality seemed to be easily awakened. "You might fare better if you went out to the main road a mile or so, but you're welcome to what we've got. I'll milk right off, and you make yourself at home. You can sleep on husks or feathers," she proffered graciously. "I raised them all myself. There's good pasturing for geese just below here towards the ma'sh. Now step round and set a plate for the gentleman, Sylvy!" And Sylvia promptly stepped. She was glad to have something to do, and she was hungry herself.

It was a surprise to find so clean and comfortable a little dwelling in this New England wilderness. The young man had known the horrors of its most primitive housekeeping, and the dreary squalor of that level of society which does not rebel at the companionship of hens. This was the best thrift of an old-fashioned farmstead, though on such a small scale that it seemed like a hermitage. He listened eagerly to the old woman's quaint talk, he watched Sylvia's pale face and shining gray eyes with ever growing enthusiasm, and insisted that this was the best supper he had eaten for a month, and afterward the new–made friends sat down in the door-way together while the moon came up.

Soon it would be berry-time, and Sylvia was a great help at picking.   15 The cow was a good milker, though a plaguy thing to keep track of, the hostess gossiped frankly, adding presently that she had buried four children, so Sylvia's mother, and a son (who might be dead) in California were all the children she had left. "Dan, my boy, was a great hand to go gunning," she explained sadly. "I never wanted for pa'tridges or gray squer'ls while he was to home. He's been a great wand'rer, I expect, and he's no hand to write letters. There, I don't blame him, I'd ha' seen the world myself if it had been so I could."

"Sylvy takes after him," the grandmother continued affectionately, after a minute's pause. "There ain't a foot o' ground she don't know her way over, and the wild creaturs counts her one o' themselves. Squer'ls she'll tame to come an' feed right out o' her hands, and all sorts o' birds. Last winter she got the jaybirds to bangeing° here, and I believe she'd 'a' scanted herself of her own meals to have plenty to throw out amongst 'em, if I had n't kep' watch. Anything but crows, I tell her, I'm willin' to help support—though Dan he had a tamed one o' them that did seem to have reason same as folks. It was round here a good spell after he went away. Dan an' his father they did n't hitch,—but he never held up his head ag'in after Dan had dared him an' gone off."

The guest did not notice this hint of family sorrows in his eager interest in something else.

----

bangeing: New England term for loafing

"So Sylvy knows all about birds, does she?" he exclaimed, as he looked round at the little girl who sat, very demure but increasingly sleepy, in the moonlight. "I am making a collection of birds myself. I have been at it ever since I was a boy." (Mrs. Tilley smiled.) "There are two or three very rare ones I have been hunting for these five years. I mean to get them on my own ground if they can be found."

"Do you cage 'em up?" asked Mrs. Tilley doubtfully, in response to this enthusiastic announcement.

"Oh no, they're stuffed and preserved, dozens and dozens of them,"   20
said the ornithologist, "and I have shot or snared every one myself. I caught a glimpse of a white heron a few miles from here on Saturday, and I have followed it in this direction. They have never been found in this district at all. The little white heron, it is," and he turned again to look at Sylvia with the hope of discovering that the rare bird was one of her acquaintances.

But Sylvia was watching a hop-toad in the narrow footpath.

"You would know the heron if you saw it," the stranger continued eagerly. "A queer tall white bird with soft feathers and long thin legs. And it would have a nest perhaps in the top of a high tree, made of sticks, something like a hawk's nest."

Sylvia's heart gave a wild beat; she knew that strange white bird, and had once stolen softly near where it stood in some bright green swamp grass, away over at the other side of the woods. There was an open place where the sunshine always seemed strangely yellow and hot, where tall, nodding rushes grew, and her grandmother had warned her that she might sink in the soft black mud underneath and never be heard of more. Not far beyond were the salt marshes just this side the sea itself, which Sylvia wondered and dreamed much about, but never had seen, whose great voice could sometimes be heard above the noise of the woods on stormy nights.

"I can't think of anything I should like so much as to find that heron's nest," the handsome stranger was saying. "I would give ten dollars to anybody who could show it to me," he added desperately, "and I mean to spend my whole vacation hunting for it if need be. Perhaps it was only migrating, or had been chased out of its own region by some bird of prey."

Mrs. Tilley gave amazed attention to all this, but Sylvia still watched the   25
toad, not divining, as she might have done at some calmer time, that the creature wished to get to its hole under the door-step, and was much hindered by the unusual spectators at that hour of the evening. No amount of thought, that night, could decide how many wished-for treasures the ten dollars, so lightly spoken of, would buy.

The next day the young sportsman hovered about the woods, and Sylvia kept him company, having lost her first fear of the friendly lad, who proved to be most kind and sympathetic. He told her many things about the birds and what they knew and where they lived and what they did with themselves. And he gave her a jack-knife, which she thought as great a treasure as if she were a desert-islander. All day long he did not once make her troubled or afraid except when he brought down some unsuspecting singing creature from its bough. Sylvia would have liked him vastly better without his gun; she could not understand why he killed the very birds he seemed to like so much. But as the day waned, Sylvia still watched the young man with loving admiration. She had never seen anybody so charming and delightful; the woman's heart, asleep in the child, was vaguely thrilled by a dream of love. Some premonition of that great power stirred and swayed these young creatures who traversed the solemn woodlands with soft-footed silent care. They stopped to listen to a bird's song; they pressed forward again eagerly, parting the branches—speaking to each other rarely and in whispers; the young man going first and Sylvia following, fascinated, a few steps behind, with her gray eyes dark with excitement.

She grieved because the longed-for white heron was elusive, but she did not lead the guest, she only followed, and there was no such thing as speaking first. The sound of her own unquestioned voice would have terrified her—it was hard enough to answer yes or no when there was need of that. At last evening began to fall, and they drove the cow home together, and Sylvia smiled with pleasure when they came to the place where she heard the whistle and was afraid only the night before.

II

Half a mile from home, at the farther edge of the woods, where the land was highest, a great pine-tree stood, the last of its generation. Whether it was left for a boundary mark, or for what reason, no one could say; the wood-choppers who had felled its mates were dead and gone long ago, and a whole forest of sturdy trees, pines and oaks and maples, had grown again. But the stately head of this old pine towered above them all and made a landmark for sea and shore miles and miles away. Sylvia knew it well. She had always believed that whoever climbed to the top of it could see the ocean; and the little girl had often laid her hand on the great rough trunk and looked up wistfully at those dark boughs that the wind always stirred, no matter how hot and still the air might be below. Now she thought of the tree with a new excitement, for why, if one climbed it at break of day could not one see all the world, and easily discover from whence the white heron flew, and mark the place, and find the hidden nest?

What a spirit of adventure, what wild ambition! What fancied triumph and delight and glory for the later morning when she could make known the secret! It was almost too real and too great for the childish heart to bear.

All night the door of the little house stood open and the whippoorwills came and sang upon the very step. The young sportsman and his old hostess were sound asleep, but Sylvia's great design kept her broad awake and watching. She forgot to think of sleep. The short summer night seemed as long as the winter darkness, and at last when the whippoorwills ceased, and she was afraid the morning would after all come too soon, she stole out of

30

the house and followed the pasture path through the woods, hastening toward the open ground beyond, listening with a sense of comfort and companionship to the drowsy twitter of a half-awakened bird, whose perch she had jarred in passing. Alas, if the great wave of human interest which flooded for the first time this dull little life should sweep away the satisfactions of an existence heart to heart with nature and the dumb life of the forest!

There was the huge tree asleep yet in the paling moonlight, and small and silly Sylvia began with utmost bravery to mount to the top of it, with tingling, eager blood coursing the channels of her whole frame, with her bare feet and fingers, that pinched and held like bird's claws to the monstrous ladder reaching up, up, almost to the sky itself. First she must mount the white oak tree that grew alongside, where she was almost lost among the dark branches and the green leaves heavy and wet with dew; a bird fluttered off its nest, and a red squirrel ran to and fro and scolded pettishly at the harmless housebreaker. Sylvia felt her way easily. She had often climbed there, and knew that higher still one of the oak's upper branches chafed against the pine trunk, just where its lower boughs were set close together. There, when she made the dangerous pass from one tree to the other, the great enterprise would really begin.

She crept out along the swaying oak limb at last, and took the daring step across into the old pine-tree. The way was harder than she thought; she must reach far and hold fast, the sharp dry twigs caught and held her and scratched her like angry talons, the pitch made her thin little fingers clumsy and stiff as she went round and round the tree's great stem, higher and higher upward. The sparrows and robins in the woods below were beginning to wake and twitter to the dawn, yet it seemed much lighter there aloft in the pine-tree, and the child knew she must hurry if her project were to be of any use.

The tree seemed to lengthen itself out as she went up, and to reach farther and farther upward. It was like a great main-mast to the voyaging earth; it must truly have been amazed that morning through all its ponderous frame as it felt this determined spark of human spirit wending its way from higher branch to branch. Who knows how steadily the least twigs held themselves to advantage this light, weak creature on her way! The old pine must have loved his new dependent. More than all the hawks, and bats, and moths, and even the sweet voiced thrushes, was the brave, beating heart of the solitary gray-eyed child. And the tree stood still and frowned away the winds that June morning while the dawn grew bright in the east.

Sylvia's face was like a pale star, if one had seen it from the ground, when the last thorny bough was past, and she stood trembling and tired but wholly triumphant, high in the treetop. Yes, there was the sea with the dawning sun making a golden dazzle over it, and toward that glorious east flew two hawks with slow-moving pinions. How low they looked in the air from that height when one had only seen them before far up, and dark against the blue sky. Their gray feathers were as soft as moths; they seemed only a little way from the tree, and Sylvia felt as if she too could go flying among the clouds. Westward, the woodlands and farms reached miles and miles into the distance; here and there were church steeples, and white villages, truly it was a vast and awesome world!

The birds sang louder and louder. At last the sun came up bewilderingly   *35*
bright. Sylvia could see the white sails of ships out at sea, and the clouds that were purple and rose-colored and yellow at first began to fade away. Where was the white heron's nest in the sea of green branches, and was this wonderful sight and pageant of the world the only reward for having climbed to such a giddy height? Now look down again, Sylvia, where the green marsh is set among the shining birches and dark hemlocks; there where you saw the white heron once you will see him again; look, look! a white spot of him like a single floating feather comes up from the dead hemlock and grows larger, and rises, and comes close at last, and goes by the landmark pine with steady sweep of wing and outstretched slender neck and crested head. And wait! wait! do not move a foot or a finger, little girl, do not send an arrow of light and consciousness from your two eager eyes, for the heron has perched on a pine bough not far beyond yours, and cries back to his mate on the nest and plumes his feathers for the new day!

The child gives a long sigh a minute later when a company of shouting cat-birds comes also to the tree, and vexed by their fluttering and lawlessness the solemn heron goes away. She knows his secret now, the wild, light, slender bird that floats and wavers, and goes back like an arrow presently to his home in the green world beneath. Then Sylvia, well satisfied, makes her perilous way down again, not daring to look far below the branch she stands on, ready to cry sometimes because her fingers ache and her lamed feet slip. Wondering over and over again what the stranger would say to her, and what he would think when she told him how to find his way straight to the heron's nest.

"Sylvy, Sylvy!" called the busy old grandmother again and again, but nobody answered, and the small husk bed was empty and Sylvia had disappeared.

The guest waked from a dream, and remembering his day's pleasure hurried to dress himself that might it sooner begin. He was sure from the way the shy little girl looked once or twice yesterday that she had at least seen the white heron, and now she must really be made to tell. Here she comes now, paler than ever, and her worn old frock is torn and tattered, and smeared with pine pitch. The grandmother and the sportsman stand in the door together and question her, and the splendid moment has come to speak of the dead hemlock-tree by the green marsh.

But Sylvia does not speak after all, though the old grandmother fretfully rebukes her, and the young man's kind, appealing eyes are looking straight in her own. He can make them rich with money; he has promised it, and they are poor now. He is so well worth making happy, and he waits to hear the story she can tell.

No, she must keep silence! What is it that suddenly forbids her and   *40*
makes her dumb? Has she been nine years growing and now, when the great

world for the first time puts out a hand to her, must she thrust it aside for a bird's sake? The murmur of the pine's green branches is in her ears, she remembers how the white heron came flying through the golden air and how they watched the sea and the morning together, and Sylvia cannot speak; she cannot tell the heron's secret and give its life away.

Dear loyalty, that suffered a sharp pang as the guest went away disappointed later in the day, that could have served and followed him and loved him as a dog loves! Many a night Sylvia heard the echo of his whistle haunting the pasture path as she came home with the loitering cow. She forgot even her sorrow at the sharp report of his gun and the sight of thrushes and sparrows dropping silent to the ground, their songs hushed and their pretty feathers stained and wet with blood. Were the birds better friends than their hunter might have been,—who can tell? Whatever treasures were lost to her, woodlands and summer-time, remember! Bring your gifts and graces and tell your secrets to this lonely country child!

TICKETS, PLEASE

D. H. Lawrence

There is in the Midlands a single-line tramway system which boldly leaves the county town and plunges off into the black, industrial countryside, up hill and down dale, through the long ugly villages of workmen's houses, over canals and railways, past churches perched high and nobly over the smoke and shadows, through stark, grimy cold little market-places, tilting away in a rush past cinemas and shops down to the hollow where the collieries are, then up again, past a little rural church, under the ash trees, on in a rush to the terminus, the last little ugly place of industry, the cold little town that shivers on the edge of the wild, gloomy country beyond. There the green and creamy coloured tram-cars seems to pause and purr with curious satisfaction. But in a few minutes—the clock on the turret of the Co-operative Wholesale Society's shops gives the time—away it starts once more on the adventure. Again there are the reckless swoops downhill, bouncing the loops: again the chilly wait in the hill-top market-place: again the breathless slithering round the precipitous drop under the church; again the patient halts at the loops, waiting for the outcoming car: so on and on, for two long hours, till at last the city looms beyond the fat gasworks, the narrow factories draw near, we are in the sordid streets of the great town, once more we sidle to a standstill at our terminus, abashed by the great crimson and cream-colored city cars, but still perky, jaunty, somewhat dare-devil, green as a jaunty sprig of parsley out of a black colliery garden.

To ride on these cars is always an adventure. Since we are in war-time, the drivers are men unfit for active service: cripples and hunchbacks. So they have the spirit of the devil in them. The ride becomes a steeplechase. Hurray! we have leapt in a clear jump over the canal bridge—now for the four-lane corner. With a shriek and a trail of sparks we are clear again. To be sure, a tram often leaps the rails—but what matter! It sits in a ditch till other trams come to haul it out. It is quite common for a car, parked with one solid mass of living people, to come to a dead halt in the midst of unbroken blackness, the heart of nowhere on a dark night, and for the driver and the girl conductor to call: "All get off—car's on fire!" Instead, however, of rushing out in a panic, the passengers stolidly reply: "Get on—get on! We're not coming out. We're stopping where we are. Push on, George." So till flames actually appear.

The reason for this reluctance to dismount is that the nights are howlingly cold, black, and windswept, and a car is a haven of refuge. From village to village, the miners travel, for a change of cinema, of girl, of pub. The trams are desperately packed. Who is going to risk himself in the black gulf outside, to wait perhaps an hour for another tram, then to see the forlorn notice 'Depot Only', because there is something wrong! Or to greet a unit of three bright cars all so tight with people that they sail past with a howl of derision. Trams that pass in the night.

This, the most dangerous tram-service in England, as the authorities themselves declare, with pride, is entirely conducted by girls, and driven by rash young men, a little crippled, or by delicate young men, who creep forward in terror. The girls are fearless young hussies. In their ugly blue uniform, skirts up to their knees, shapeless old peaked caps on their heads, they have all the *sang-froid*° of an old non-commissioned officer. With a tram packed with howling colliers,° roaring hymns downstairs and a sort of antiphony of obscenities upstairs, the lasses are perfectly at their ease. They pounce on the youths who try to evade their ticket-machine. They push off the men at the end of their distance. They are not going to be done in the eye—not they. They fear nobody—and everybody fears them.

"Hello, Annie!"   5

"Hello, Ted!"

"Oh, mind my corn, Miss Stone. It's my belief you've got a heart of stone, for you've trod on it again."

"You should keep it in your pocket," replies Miss Stone, and she goes sturdily upstairs in her high boots.

"Tickets, please."

She is peremptory, suspicious, and ready to hit first. She can hold her own against ten thousand. The step of that tram-car is her Thermopylæ.°   10

---

sang-froid: French for "cold blood," calm
colliers: coal miners
Thermopylæ: a pass in Greece where 300 Spartans delayed the Persian army under Xerxes

Therefore, there is a certain wild romance aboard these cars—and in the sturdy bosom of Annie herself. The time for soft romance is in the morning, between ten o'clock and one, when things are rather slack: that is, except market-day and Saturday. Thus Annie has time to look about her. Then she often hops off her car and into a shop where she has spied something, while the driver chats in the main road. There is very good feeling between the girls and the drivers. Are they not companions in peril, shipments aboard this careering vessel of a tram-car, for ever rocking on the waves of a stormy land.

Then, also, during the easy hours, the inspectors are most in evidence. For some reason, everybody employed in this tram-service is young: there are no grey heads. It would not do. Therefore the inspectors are of the right age, and one, the chief, is also good-looking. See him stand on a wet, gloomy morning, in his long oilskin, his peaked cap well down over his eyes, waiting to board a car. His face ruddy, his small brown moustache is weathered, he has a faint impudent smile. Fairly tall and agile, even in his waterproof, he springs aboard a car and greets Annie.

"Hello, Annie! Keeping the wet out?"

"Trying to."

There are only two people in the car. Inspecting is soon over. Then   15
for a long and impudent chat on the foot-board, a good, easy, twelve-mile chat.

The inspector's name is John Thomas Raynor—always called John Thomas, except sometimes, in malice, Coddy.° His face sets in fury when he is addressed, from a distance, with this abbreviation. There is considerable scandal about John Thomas in half a dozen villages. He flirts with the girl conductors in the morning, and walks out with them in the dark night, when they leave their tram-car at the depôt. Of course, the girls quit the service frequently. Then he flirts and walks out with the newcomer: always providing she is sufficiently attractive, and that she will consent to walk. It is remarkable, however, that most of the girls are quite comely, they are all young, and this roving life aboard the car gives them a sailor's dash and recklessness. What matter how they behave when the ship is in port? To-morrow they will be aboard again.

Annie, however, was something of a Tartar, and her sharp tongue had kept John Thomas at arm's length for many months. Perhaps, therefore, she liked him all the more: for he always came up smiling, with impudence. She watched him vanquish one girl, then another. She could tell by the movement of his mouth and eyes, when he flirted with her in the morning, that he had been walking out with this lass, or the other, the night before. A fine cock-of-the-walk he was. She could sum him up pretty well.

In this subtle antagonism they knew each other like old friends, they were as shrewd with one another almost as man and wife. But Annie

---

John Thomas, Coddy: slang terms for the male organ

had always kept him sufficiently at arm's length. Besides, she had a boy of her own.

The Statutes fair, however, came in November, at Bestwood. It happened that Annie had the Monday night off. It was a drizzling ugly night, yet she dressed herself up and went to the fair-ground. She was alone, but she expected soon to find a pal of some sort.

The roundabouts were veering round and grinding out their music,   20
the side-shows were making as much commotion as possible. In the co-coconut shies° there were no coconuts, but artificial war-time substitutes, which the lads declared were fastened into the irons. There was a sad decline in brilliance and luxury. None the less, the ground was muddy as ever, there was the same crush, the press of faces lighted up by the flares and the electric lights, the same smell of naphtha and a few potatoes, and of electricity.

Who should be the first to greet Miss Annie on the show-ground but John Thomas. He had a black overcoat buttoned up to his chin, and a tweed cap pulled down over his brows, his face between was ruddy and smiling and handy as ever. She knew so well the way his mouth moved.

She was very glad to have a 'boy'. To be at the Statutes without a fellow was no fun. Instantly, like the gallant he was, he took her on the Dragons, grim-toothed, roundabout switchbacks. It was not nearly so exciting as a tram-car actually. But, then, to be seated in a shaking, green dragon, uplifted above the sea of bubble faces, careering in a rickety fashion in the lower heavens, whilst John Thomas leaned over her, his cigarette in his mouth, was after all the right style. She was a plump, quick, alive little creature. So she was quite excited and happy.

John Thomas made her stay on for the next round. And therefore she could hardly for shame repulse him when he put his arm round her and drew her a little nearer to him, in a very warm and cuddly manner. Besides, he was fairly discreet, he kept his movement as hidden as possible. She looked down, and saw that his red, clean hand was out of sight of the crowd. And they knew each other so well. So they warmed up to the fair.

After the dragons they went on the horses. John Thomas paid each time, so she could but be complaisant. He, of course, sat astride on the outer horse—named 'Black Bess'—and she sat sideways, towards him, on the inner horse—named 'Wildfire'. But of course John Thomas was not going to sit discreetly on 'Black Bess', holding the brass bar. Round they spun and heaved, in the light. And round he swung on his wooden steed, flinging one leg across her mount, and perilously tipping up and down, across the space, half lying back, laughing at her. He was perfectly happy; she was afraid her hat was on one side, but she was excited.

---

coconut shies: a carnival attraction where people tried to knock over stacks of coconuts with thrown balls

He threw quoits on a table, and won for her two large, pale blue hat- 25
pins. And then, hearing the noise of the cinemas, announcing another performance, they climbed the boards and went in.

Of course, during these performances, pitch darkness falls from time to
time, when the machine goes wrong. Then there is a wild whooping, and a
loud smacking of simulated kisses. In these moments John Thomas drew
Annie towards him. After all, he had a wonderfully warm, cosy way of holding a girl with his arm, he seemed to make such a nice fit. And, after all, it
was pleasant to be so held: so very comforting and cosy and nice. He leaned
over her and she felt his breath on her hair; she knew he wanted to kiss her
on the lips. And, after all, he was so warm and she fitted in to him so softly.
After all, she wanted him to touch her lips.

But the light sprang up; she also started electrically, and put her hat
straight. He left his arm lying nonchalantly behind her. Well, it was fun, it
was exciting to be at the Statutes with John Thomas.

When the cinema was over they went for a walk across the dark, damp
fields. He had all the arts of love-making. He was especially good at holding
a girl, when he sat with her on a stile in the black, drizzling darkness. He
seemed to be holding her in space, against his own warmth and gratification.
And his kisses were soft and slow and searching.

So Annie walked out with John Thomas, though she kept her own boy
dangling in the distance. Some of the tram-girls chose to be huffy. But there,
you must take things as you find them, in this life.

There was no mistake about it, Annie liked John Thomas a good deal. 30
She felt so rich and warm in herself whenever he was near. And John Thomas really liked Annie, more than usual. The soft, melting way in which she
could flow into a fellow, as if she melted into his very bones, was something
rare and good. He fully appreciated this.

But with a developing acquaintance there began a developing intimacy.
Annie wanted to consider him a person, a man: she wanted to take an intelligent interest in him, and to have an intelligent response. She did not want
a mere nocturnal presence, which was what he was so far. And she prided
herself that he could not leave her.

Here she made a mistake. John Thomas intended to remain a nocturnal
presence; he had no idea of becoming an all-round individual to her. When
she started to take an intelligent interest in him and his life and his character,
he sheered off. He hated intelligent interest. And he knew that the only way
to stop it was to avoid it. The possessive female was aroused in Annie. So he
left her.

It is no use saying she was not surprised. She was at first startled, thrown
out of her count. For she had been so *very* sure of holding him. For a while
she was staggered, and everything became uncertain to her. Then she wept
with fury, indignation, desolation, and misery. Then she had a spasm of
despair. And then, when he came, still impudently, on to her car, still familiar, but letting her see by the movement of his head that he had gone away

to somebody else for the time being, and was enjoying pastures new, then
she determined to have her own back.

She had a very shrewd idea what girls John Thomas had taken out. She
went to Nora Purdy. Nora was a tall, rather pale, but well-built girl, with
beautiful yellow hair. She was rather secretive.

"Hey!" said Annie, accosting her; then softly: "Who's John Thomas on   35
with now?"

"I don't know," said Nora.

"Why, tha does," said Annie, ironically lapsing into dialect. "Tha
knows as well as I do."

"Well, I do, then," said Nora. "It isn't me, so don't bother."

"It's Cissy Meakin, isn't it?"

"It is, for all I know."   40

"Hasn't he got a face on him!" said Annie. "I don't half like his cheek.
I could knock him off the foot-board when he comes round at me."

"He'll get dropped on one of these days," said Nora.

"Ay, he will, when somebody makes up their mind to drop it on him.
I should like to see him taken down a peg or two, shouldn't you?"

"I shouldn't mind," said Nora.

"You've got quite as much cause to as I have," said Annie. "But we'll   45
drop on him one of these days, my girl. What? Don't you want to?"

"I don't mind," said Nora.

But as a matter of fact, Nora was much more vindictive than Annie.

One by one Annie went the round of the old flames. It so happened
that Cissy Meakin left the tramway service in quite a short time. Her mother
made her leave. Then John Thomas was on the *qui vive*.° He cast his eyes
over his old flock. And his eyes lighted on Annie. He thought she would be
safe now. Besides, he liked her.

She arranged to walk home with him on Sunday night. It so happened
that her car would be in the depôt at half-past nine: the last car would come
in at 10.15. So John Thomas was to wait for her there.

At the depôt the girls had a little waiting-room of their own. It was quite   50
rough, but cosy, with a fire and an oven and a mirror, and table and wooden
chairs. The half-dozen girls who knew John Thomas only too well had arranged to take service this Sunday afternoon. So, as the cars began to come
in, early, the girls dropped into the waiting-room. And instead of hurrying
off home, they sat around the fire and had a cup of tea. Outside was the
darkness and lawlessness of war-time.

John Thomas came on the car after Annie, at about a quarter to ten. He
poked his head easily into the girls' waiting-room.

"Prayer-meeting?" he asked.

"Ay," said Laura Sharp. "Ladies only."

---

qui vive: on the lookout; on the prowl

"That's me!" said John Thomas. It was one of his favourite exclamations.

"Shut the door, boy," said Muriel Baggaley.   55

"Oh, which side of me?" said John Thomas.

"Which tha likes," said Polly Birkin.

He had come in and closed the door behind him. The girls moved in their circle, to make a place for him near the fire. He took off his great-coat and pushed back his hat.

"Who handles the teapot?" he said.

Nora Purdy silently poured him out a cup of tea.   60

"Want a bit o' my bread and drippin'?" said Muriel Baggaley to him.

"Ay, give us a bit."

And he began to eat his piece of bread.

"There's no place like home, girls," he said.

They all looked at him as he uttered this piece of impudence. He   65
seemed to be sunning himself in the presence of so many damsels.

"Especially if you're not afraid to go home in the dark," said Laura Sharp.

"Me! By myself I am."

They sat till they heard the last tram come in. In a few minutes Emma Houselay entered.

"Come on, my old duck!" cried Polly Birkin.

"It *is* perishing," said Emma, holding her fingers to the fire.   70

"But—I'm afraid to, go home in, the dark," sang Laura Sharp, the tune having got into her mind.

"Who're you going with to-night, John Thomas?" asked Muriel Baggaley coolly.

"To-night?" said John Thomas. "Oh, I'm going home by myself to-night—all on my lonely-o."

"That's me!" said Nora Purdy, using his own ejaculation.

The girls laughed shrilly.   75

"Me as well, Nora," said John Thomas.

"Don't know what you mean," said Laura.

"Yes, I'm toddling," said he, rising and reaching for his overcoat.

"Nay," said Polly. "We're all here waiting for you."

"We've got to be up in good time in the morning," he said, in the   80
benevolent official manner.

They all laughed.

"Nay," said Muriel. "Don't leave us all lonely, John Thomas. Take one!"

"I'll take the lot, if you like," he responded gallantly.

"That you won't, either," said Muriel. "Two's company; seven's too much of a good thing."

"Nay—take one," said Laura. "Fair and square, all above board and say   85
which."

"Ay," cried Annie, speaking for the first time. "Pick, John Thomas; let's hear thee."

"Nay," he said. "I'm going home quiet to-night. Feeling good, for once."

"Whereabouts?" said Annie. "Take a good 'un, then. But tha's got to take one of us!"

"Nay, how can I take one," he said, laughing uneasily. "I don't want to make enemies."

"You'd only make *one*," said Annie.

"The chosen *one*," added Laura.   *90*

"Oh, my! Who said girls!" exclaimed John Thomas, again turning, as if to escape. "Well—good-night."

"Nay, you've got to make your pick," said Muriel. "Turn your face to the wall, and say which one touches you. Go on—we shall only just touch your back—one of us. Go on—turn your face to the wall, and don't look, and say which one touches you."

He was uneasy, mistrusting them. Yet he had not the courage to break away. They pushed him to a wall and stood him there with his face to it. Behind his back they all grimaced, tittering. He looked so comical. He looked around uneasily.

"Go on!" he cried.   *95*

"You're looking—you're looking!" they shouted.

He turned his head away. And suddenly, with a movement like a swift cat, Annie went forward and fetched him a box on the side of the head that sent his cap flying and himself staggering. He started round.

But at Annie's signal they all flew at him, slapping him, pinching him, pulling his hair, though more in fun than in spite or anger. He, however, saw red. His blue eyes flamed with strange fear as well as fury, and he butted through the girls to the door. It was locked. He wrenched at it. Roused, alert, the girls stood round and looked at him. He faced them, at bay. At that moment they were rather horrifying to him, as they stood in their short uniforms. He was distinctly afraid.

"Come on, John Thomas!" Come on! Choose!" said Annie.

"What are you after? Open the door," he said.   *100*

"We shan't—not till you've chosen!" said Muriel.

"Chosen what?" he said.

"Chosen the one you're going to marry," she replied.

He hesitated a moment.

"Open the blasted door," he said, "and get back to your senses." He   *105*
spoke with official authority.

"You've got to choose!" cried the girls.

"Come on!" cried Annie, looking him in the eye. "Come on! Come on!"

He went forward, rather vaguely. She had taken off her belt, and swinging it, she fetched him a sharp blow over the head with the buckle end. He sprang and seized her. But immediately the other girls rushed upon him, pulling and tearing and beating him. Their blood was now thoroughly up. He was their sport now. They were going to have their own back, out of him. Strange, wild creatures, they hung on him and rushed at him to bear him down. His tunic was torn right up the back, Nora had hold at the back of his collar, and was actually strangling him. Luckily the button burst. He struggled in a wild frenzy of fury and terror, almost mad terror. His tunic was simply torn off his back, his shirt-sleeves were torn away, his arms were naked. The girls rushed at him, clenched their hands on him and pulled at him: or they rushed at him and pushed him, butted him with all their might: or they struck him wild blows. He ducked and cringed and struck sideways. They became more intense.

At last he was down. They rushed on him, kneeling on him. He had neither breath nor strength to move. His face was bleeding with a long scratch, his brow was bruised.

Annie knelt on him, the other girls knelt and hung on to him. Their faces were flushed, their hair wild, their eyes were all glittering strangely. He lay at last quite still, with face averted, as an animal lies when it is defeated and at the mercy of the captor. Sometimes his eye glanced back at the wild faces of the girls. His breast rose heavily, his wrists were torn.

"Now, then, my fellow!" gasped Annie at length. "Now then—now—"

At the sound of her terrifying, cold triumph, he suddenly started to struggle as an animal might, but the girls threw themselves upon him with unnatural strength and power, forcing him down.

"Yes—now, then!" gasped Annie at length.

And there was a dead silence, in which the thud of heart-beating was to be heard. It was a suspense of pure silence in every soul.

"Now you know where you are," said Annie.

The sight of his white, bare arm maddened the girls. He lay in a kind of trance of fear and antagonism. They felt themselves filled with supernatural strength.

Suddenly Polly started to laugh—to giggle wildly—helplessly—and Emma and Muriel joined in. But Annie and Nora and Laura remained the same, tense, watchful, with gleaming eyes. He winced away from these eyes.

"Yes," said Annie, in a curious low tone, secret and deadly. "Yes! You've got it now. You know what you've done, don't you? You know what you've done."

He made no sound nor sign, but lay with bright, averted eyes, and averted, bleeding face.

"You ought to be *killed,* that's what you ought," said Annie, tensely. "You ought to be *killed.*" And there was a terrifying lust in her voice.

Polly was ceasing to laugh, and giving long-drawn Oh-h-hs and sighs as she came to herself.

"He's got to choose," she said vaguely.

"Oh, yes, he has," said Laura, with vindictive decision.

"Do you hear—do you hear?" said Annie. And with a sharp movement, that made him wince, she turned his face to her.

"Do you hear?" she repeated, shaking him.

110

115

120

125

But he was quite dumb. She fetched him a sharp slap on the face. He started, and his eyes widened. Then his face darkened with defiance, after all.

"Do you hear?" she repeated.

He only looked at her with hostile eyes.

"Speak!" she said, putting her face devilishly near his.

"What?" he said, almost overcome.   130

"You've got to *choose!*" she cried, as if it were some terrible menace, and as if it hurt her that she could not exact more.

"What?" he said, in fear.

"Choose your girl, Coddy. You've got to choose her now. And you'll get your neck broken if you play any more of your tricks, my boy. You're settled now."

There was a pause. Again he averted his face. He was cunning in his overthrow. He did not give in to them really—no, not if they tore him to bits.

"All right, then," he said, "I choose Annie." His voice was strange and   135
full of malice. Annie let go of him as if he had been a hot coal.

"He's chosen Annie!" said the girls in chorus.

"Me!" cried Annie. She was still kneeling, but away from him. He was still lying prostrate, with averted face. The girls grouped uneasily around.

"Me!" repeated Annie, with a terrible bitter accent.

Then she got up, drawing away from him with strange disgust and bitterness.

"I wouldn't touch him," she said.   140

But her face quivered with a kind of agony, she seemed as if she would fall. The other girls turned aside. He remained lying on the floor, with his torn clothes and bleeding, averted face.

"Oh, if he's chosen—" said Polly.

"I don't want him—he can choose again," said Annie, with the same rather bitter hopelessness.

"Get up," said Polly, lifting his shoulder. "Get up."

He rose slowly, a strange, ragged, dazed creature. The girls eyed him   145
from a distance, curiously, furtively, dangerously.

"Who wants him?" cried Laura, roughly.

"Nobody," they answered, with contempt. Yet each one of them waited for him to look at her, hoped he would look at her. All except Annie, and something was broken in her.

He, however, kept his face closed and averted from them all. There was a silence of the end. He picked up the torn pieces of his tunic, without knowing what to do with them. The girls stood about uneasily, flushed, panting, tidying their hair and their dress unconsciously, and watching him. He looked at none of them. He espied his cap in a corner, and went and picked it up. He put it on his head, and one of the girls burst into a shrill, hysteric laugh at the sight he presented. He, however, took no heed, but went straight to where his overcoat hung on a peg. The girls moved away from contact with him as if he had been an electric wire. He put on his coat and buttoned it down. Then he rolled his tunic-rags into a bundle, and stood before the locked door, dumbly.

"Open the door, somebody," said Laura.

"Annie's got the key," said one.   150

Annie silently offered the key to the girls. Nora unlocked the door.

"Tit for tat, old man," she said. "Show yourself a man, and don't bear a grudge."

But without a word or sign he had opened the door and gone, his face closed, his head dropped.

"That'll learn him," said Laura.

"Coddy!" said Nora.   155

"Shut up, for God's sake!" cried Annie fiercely, as if in torture.

"Well, I'm about ready to go, Polly. Look sharp!" said Muriel.

The girls were all anxious to be off. They were tidying themselves hurriedly, with mute, stupefied faces.

PHENOMENAL WOMAN

Maya Angelou

Pretty women wonder where my secret lies.
I'm not cute or built to suit a fashion model's size
But when I start to tell them,
They think I'm telling lies.
I say,   5
It's in the reach of my arms,
The span of my hips,
The stride of my step,
The curl of my lips.
I'm a woman   10
Phenomenally.
Phenomenal woman,
That's me.

I walk into a room
Just as cool as you please,   15
And to a man,
The fellows stand or
Fall down on their knees.
Then they swarm around me,

A hive of honey bees. *20*
I say,
It's the fire in my eyes,
And the flash of my teeth,
The swing in my waist,
And the joy in my feet. *25*
I'm a woman
Phenomenally.
Phenomenal woman,
That's me.

Men themselves have wondered *30*
What they see in me.
They try so much
But they can't touch
My inner mystery.
When I try to show them *35*
They say they still can't see.
I say,
It's in the arch of my back,
The sun of my smile,
The ride of my breasts, *40*
The grace of my style.
I'm a woman
Phenomenally.
Phenomenal woman,
That's me. *45*

Now you understand
Just why my head's not bowed.
I don't shout or jump about
Or have to talk real loud.
When you see me passing *50*
It ought to make you proud.
I say,
It's in the click of my heels,
The bend of my hair,
The palm of my hand, *55*
The need for my care.
'Cause I'm a woman
Phenomenally.
Phenomenal woman,
That's me. *60*

THIS IS JUST TO SAY

William Carlos Williams

I have eaten
the plums
that were in
the icebox

and which   *5*
you were probably
saving
for breakfast

Forgive me
they were delicious   *10*
so sweet
and so cold

ULYSSES

Alfred, Lord Tennyson

   It little profits that an idle king,
By this still hearth, among these barren crags,
Matched with an agéd wife,° I mete and dole
Unequal laws unto a savage race,
That hoard, and sleep, and feed, and know not me.   *5*
   I cannot rest from travel; I will drink
Life to the lees. All times I have enjoyed
Greatly, have suffered greatly, both with those
That loved me, and alone; on shore, and when
Through scudding drifts the rainy Hyades°   *10*
Vexed the dim sea. I am become a name;
For always roaming with a hungry heart
Much have I seen and known—cities of men
And manners, climates, councils, governments,

---

3. *agéd wife:* Penelope
10. *Hyades:* five stars in the constellation Taurus, supposed to predict rain when they rose
with the sun

Myself not least, but honored of them all—   15
And drunk delight of battle with my peers,
Far on the ringing plains of windy Troy.
I am a part of all that I have met;
Yet all experience is an arch wherethrough
Gleams that untraveled world, whose margin fades   20
For ever and for ever when I move.
How dull it is to pause, to make an end,
To rust unburnished, not to shine in use!
As though to breathe were life. Life piled on life
Were all too little, and of one to me   25
Little remains; but every hour is saved
From that eternal silence, something more,
A bringer of new things; and vile it were
For some three suns to store and hoard myself,
And this gray spirit yearning in desire   30
To follow knowledge like a sinking star,
Beyond the utmost bound of human thought.

    This is my son, mine own Telemachus,
To whom I leave the scepter and the isle—
Well-loved of me, discerning to fulfill   35
This labor by slow prudence to make mild
A rugged people, and through soft degrees
Subdue them to the useful and the good.
Most blameless is he, centered in the sphere
Of common duties, decent not to fail   40
In offices of tenderness, and pay
Meet adoration to my household gods,
When I am gone. He works his work, I mine.

    There lies the port; the vessel puffs her sail:
There gloom the dark, broad seas. My mariners,   45
Souls that have toiled, and wrought, and thought with me—
That ever with a frolic welcome took
The thunder and the sunshine, and opposed
Free hearts, free foreheads—you and I are old;
Old age hath yet his honor and his toil.   50
Death closes all; but something ere the end,
Some work of noble note, may yet be done,
Not unbecoming men that strove with Gods.
The lights begin to twinkle from the rocks;
The long day wanes; the slow moon climbs; the deep   55
Moans round with many voices. Come, my friends,
'Tis not too late to seek a newer world.
Push off, and sitting well in order smite
The sounding furrows; for my purpose holds

To sail beyond the sunset, and the baths   *60*
Of all the western stars, until I die.
It may be that the gulfs will wash us down;
It may be we shall touch the Happy Isles,°
And see the great Achilles,° whom we knew.
Though much is taken, much abides; and though   *65*
We are not now that strength which in old days
Moved earth and heaven, that which we are, we are:
One equal temper of heroic hearts,
Made weak by time and fate, but strong in will
To strive, to seek, to find, and not to yield.   *70*

----

63. *Happy Isles:* Elysium, a paradise thought to be reserved for heroes and to lie beyond the
sunset in the Atlantic Ocean
64. *Achilles:* the hero of the *Iliad*

16

Definition: Making Meanings for Your Reader

You are familiar with definitions. Every time you use a dictionary to look up the meaning of a word, you search for a definition. When you have to explain what you mean to another person, you may find yourself defining a term or an idea you've used or an object you've referred to. You can discover the aim and purpose of definition by examining the term itself. When you define, you try to make something *finite*. In other words, by telling what an object, an idea, a process, a person, a place, or an event is, you give it limits or boundaries to help your reader distinguish the subject of the definition from what it is not. In this way, definition is also a form of comparison or contrast as well as classification and analysis.

The definitions you find in a dictionary are called *formal* definitions. Here are two from *The Random House College Dictionary of the English Language:*

> **saw,** —n. **1.** a tool for cutting, typically a thin blade of metal with a series of sharp teeth. **2.** any similar tool or device, as a rotating disk, in which a sharp continuous edge replaces the teeth.
>
> **screwdriver,** —n. **1.** a hand tool for turning a screw, consisting of a specially formed shank rotated by a handle at one end.

Both definitions have the same structure. You find first the name of the class the object belongs to ("a tool" in both cases). Then you find the characteristics that differentiate this particular member of the class "tool" and its subclass from all the other members of the same class (for example, a screwdriver is a "hand *tool* for turning a screw" and a saw is "a *tool* for cutting"). In other words, a definition first classifies an object and then shows its differences from every other member of its class by analyzing it in terms of the parts that define that difference.

In looking at the possible approaches your dominant idea suggests, you might find that defining a technical or unfamiliar concept, term, or object might make your idea clearer. If you were to write a paper about the need for new oscilloscopes for your electronic engineering laboratory and your audience was composed primarily of persons who were not familiar with these instruments, you might find it useful to define the oscilloscope and its purpose in the lab to clarify your idea.

In other cases, you might find that your dominant idea suggests a definition as its central point. There might be a debate in your school regarding whether the students are being adequately educated. It might be necessary for you to define "adequate education" in order to take a position in response to the debate.

DEFINING ABSTRACT VERSUS CONCRETE SUBJECTS

When you examine your first exploration of your subject, you might find that it suggests a definition as the most useful approach to presenting your dominant idea or as part of the support for your idea. If you find yourself considering using definition, you need to think about the object you've chosen to define. Is it abstract or concrete? A concrete subject is an actual, material object or process: a machine, a physical activity, your car, your cat. The definition of a concrete subject often uses analysis to make itself clear because a material object or process is made up of specific parts that fit together in a certain way. Examples of that type of definition open this chapter.

Defining an abstract subject usually presents more of a challenge. An abstraction cannot be defined through an examination of its physical parts. It does not have a material, concrete existence; you cannot point to it, pick it up, or take it apart to show how it works. Concepts and qualities such as "courage" and "love" are abstract. So are ideas such as "existentialism," "liberal education," and "epistemology."

Defining by Example

There is always the danger that in attempting to define an abstract subject you will find yourself using equally abstract terms. Such an approach would present no problems if you were certain that your audience understood your terms in the same way you do. However, you usually cannot count on such a mutual understanding. Using concrete examples of what you mean through such organizational strategies as description or narration can help you make your dominant idea clear to your audience.

❧ Exercise

Gary Zukav has written a long book called *The Dancing Wu-Li Masters.* In that book he tells his readers about the nature and consequences of some of the discoveries that have been made in modern physics. However, because he could not count on his readers' knowing the nature of some of the concepts that underlie those discoveries, he had to establish the nature of those findings through definition. Here he defines the concept of "half life" by using an example:

> Suppose we put one gram of radium in a time vault and leave it there for sixteen hundred years. When we return, do we find one gram of radium? No! We find only half a gram. This is because radium atoms naturally disintegrate at a rate such that every sixteen hundred years half of them are gone. Therefore, physicists say that radium has a "half life of sixteen hundred years." If we put the radium back in the vault for another sixteen hundred years, only one fourth of the original gram would remain when we opened the vault again. Every sixteen hundred years one half of all the radium atoms in the world disappear.

In the essay "The Just-Right Wife," which appears in its entirety in Chapter 11 and from which the following paragraphs are taken, Ellen Goodman's dominant idea required her to define a familiar term in a special way. For her purposes, Goodman had to stipulate a definition; that is, she had to invent a definition of that term to suit her goals. Here is how she defines the "just-right wife":

> The upper-middle-class, middle-aged man of today wants a wife who won't make him feel guilty. He doesn't want to worry if she's happy. He doesn't want to hear her complain about her dusty American history degree. He doesn't want to know if she's crying at the psychiatrist's office. He most definitely doesn't want to be blamed. He wants her to fulfill herself already! He doesn't mean that maliciously.
>
> On the other hand, Lord knows, he doesn't want a wife who is too forward. The Saudi Arabian merchant believes that the Egyptian woman adapts more easily to his moods and needs. The American merchant also wants a woman who adapts herself to his moods and needs—his need for an independent woman and a traditional wife.
>
> He doesn't want to live with a "household drudge," but it would be nice to have an orderly home and well-scrubbed children. Certainly he wouldn't want a wife who got high on folding socks—he is not a Neanderthal—but it would be nice if she arranged for these things to get done.

1. In order to make his definition of "half life" clear, what other organizational approach does Zukav use?

2. In order to make her definition of the "just-right wife" clear, what other organizational approach does Goodman use?

3. Even though neither of these selections looks exactly like a formal definition, could you derive a formal definition from them?

Defining by Elimination

A writer discovering that his or her dominant idea suggests definition as the central approach might define by example, as both Zukav and Goodman do. A related approach is to define by elimination—by telling what the subject of the definition is not: a version of showing your reader a contrast. You probably noticed that Goodman takes this approach as well.

Here, e. e. cummings uses a special version of a definition that is a contrast to present his point of view:

> a politician is an arse upon
> which everyone has sat except a man

Working with a Reading

Here is another poet writing a highly personal definition of an abstract subject and trying to make the reader see what he sees. When you have read the poem, answer the questions that follow it, alone or with your group.

DOLOR

Theodore Roethke

> I have known the inexorable sadness of pencils,
> Neat in their boxes, dolor of pad and paper-weight,
> All the misery of manilla folders and mucilage,°
> Desolation in immaculate public places,
> Lonely reception room, lavatory, switchboard,   5
> The unalterable pathos of basin and pitcher,
> Ritual of multigraph, paper-clip, comma,
> Endless duplication of lives and objects.
> And I have seen dust from the walls of institutions,
> Finer than flour, alive, more dangerous than silica,   10
> Sift, almost invisible, through long afternoons of tedium,
> Dropping a fine film on nails and delicate eyebrows,
> Glazing the pale hair, the duplicate grey standard faces.

---

1. In writing his definition, what predominant organizational approach does Roethke use?

---

3. *mucilage:* a type of glue

2. On which aspects of the environment does Roethke focus your attention?

3. Examine the metaphors Roethke uses. Upon what feelings and ideas do they focus your attention?

4. Look up *dolor.* Is Roethke simply defining this term? Is he using it to lead you to a larger definition? What do you think he is defining in a larger sense?

5. Can you think of an environment that affected you as strongly as the environment that Roethke describes affected him? The effect could be positive as well as negative. Can you give this environment a one-word name that reflects the effect and leads to a larger definition? Now try to define that environment through examples of its effects upon you and others.

 Working with the Readings

The following two pieces are both extended definitions of relatively abstract concepts. Moreover, those concepts are connected to operations that are probably unfamiliar to you. Note the ways Tom Wolfe and Jack London make both the concepts and the operations clear to you. How do they account for an audience that knows very little about their subjects? How do they engage and hold your interest?

FROM THE RIGHT STUFF

Tom Wolfe

A young man might go into military flight training believing that he was entering some sort of technical school in which he was simply going to acquire a certain set of skills. Instead, he found himself all at once enclosed in a fraternity. And in this fraternity, even though it was military, men were not rated by their outward rank as ensigns, lieutenants, commanders, or whatever. No, herein the world was divided into those who had it and those who did not. This quality, this *it,* was never named, however, nor was it talked about in any way.

As to just what this ineffable quality was . . . well, it obviously involved bravery. But it was not bravery in the simple sense of being willing to risk your life. The idea seemed to be that any fool could do that, if that was all that was required, just as any fool could throw away his life in the process. No, the idea here (in the all-enclosing fraternity) seemed to be that a man should have the ability to go up in a hurtling piece of machinery and put his hide on the line and then have the moxie, the reflexes, the experience, the coolness, to pull it back in the last yawning moment—and then to go up again *the next day,* and the next day, and every next day, even if the series should prove infinite—and, ultimately, in its best expression, do so in a cause that means something to thousands, to a people, a nation, to humanity, to God. Nor was there *a test* to show whether or not a pilot had this righteous quality. There was, instead, a seemingly infinite series of tests. A career in flying was like climbing one of those ancient Babylonian pyramids made up of a dizzy progression of steps and ledges, a ziggurat, a pyramid extraordinarily high and steep; and the idea was to prove at every foot of the way up that pyramid that you were one of the elected and anointed ones who had *the right stuff* and could move higher and higher and even—ultimately, God willing, one day—that you might be able to join that special few at the very top, that elite who had the capacity to bring tears to men's eyes, the very Brotherhood of the Right Stuff itself.

None of this was to be mentioned, and yet it was acted out in a way that a young man could not fail to understand. When a new flight (i.e., a class) of trainees arrived at Pensacola, they were brought into an auditorium for a little lecture. An officer would tell them: "Take a look at the man on either side of you." Quite a few actually swiveled their heads this way and that, in the interest of appearing diligent. Then the officer would say: "One of the three of you is not going to make it!"—meaning, not get his wings. That was the opening theme, the *motif* of primary training. We already know that one-third of you do not have the right stuff—it only remains to find out who.

Furthermore, that was the way it turned out. At every level in one's progress up that staggeringly high pyramid, the world was once more divided into those men who had the right stuff to continue the climb and those who had to be *left behind* in the most obvious way. Some were eliminated in the course of the opening classroom work, as either not smart enough or not hardworking enough, and were left behind. Then came the basic flight instruction, in single-engine, propeller-driven trainers, and a few more—even though the military tried to make this stage easy—were washed out and left behind. Then came more demanding levels, one after the other, formation flying, instrument flying, jet training, all-weather flying, gunnery, and at each level more were washed out and left behind. By this point easily a third of the original candidates had been, indeed, eliminated . . . from the ranks of those who might prove to have the right stuff.

In the Navy, in addition to the stages that Air Force trainees went 5 through, the neophyte always had waiting for him, out in the ocean, a certain grim gray slab; namely, the deck of an aircraft carrier; and with it perhaps the most difficult routine in military flying, carrier landings. He was shown films about it, he heard lectures about it, and he knew that carrier landings were hazardous. He first practiced touching down on the shape of a flight deck painted on an airfield. He was instructed to touch down and gun right off. This was safe enough—the shape didn't move, at least—but it could do terrible things to, let us say, the gyroscope of the soul. *That shape!—it's so damned small!* And more candidates were washed out and left behind. Then came the day, without warning, when those who remained were sent out over the ocean for the first of many days of reckoning with the slab. The first day was always a clear day with little wind and a calm sea. The carrier was so steady that it seemed, from up there in the air, to be resting on pilings, and the candidate usually made his first carrier landing successfully, with relief and even *élan.* Many young candidates looked like terrific aviators up to that very point—and it was not until they were actually standing on the carrier deck that they first began to wonder if they had the proper stuff, after all. In the training film the flight deck was a grand piece of gray geometry, perilous, to be sure, but an amazing abstract shape as one looks down upon it on the screen. And yet once the newcomer's two feet were on it . . . *Geometry*—my God, man, this is a . . . skillet! It *heaved,* it moved up and down underneath his feet, it pitched up, it pitched down, it rolled to port (this great beast *rolled!*) and it rolled to starboard, as the ship moved into the wind and, therefore, into the waves, and the wind kept sweeping across, sixty feet up in the air out in the open sea, and there were no railings whatsoever. This was a *skillet!*—a frying pan!—a short-order grill!—not gray but black, smeared with skid marks from one end to the other and glistening with pools of hydraulic fluid and the occasional jet-fuel slick, all of it still hot, sticky, greasy, runny, virulent from God knows what traumas—still ablaze!—consumed in detonations, explosions, flames, combustion, roars, shrieks, whines, blasts, horrible shudders, fracturing impacts, as little men in screaming red and yellow and purple and green shirts with black Mickey Mouse helmets over their ears skittered about on the surface as if for their very lives (you've said it now!), hooking fighter planes onto the catapult shuttles so that they can explode their afterburners and be slung off the deck in a red-mad fury with a *kaboom!* that pounds through the entire deck—a procedure that seems absolutely controlled, orderly, sublime, however, compared to what he is about to watch as aircraft return to the ship for what is known in the engineering stoicisms of the military as "recovery and arrest." To say that an F-4 was coming back onto this heaving barbecue from out of the sky at a speed of 135 knots . . . that might have been the truth in the training lecture, but it did not begin to get across the idea of what the newcomer saw from the deck itself, because it created the notion that perhaps the plane was gliding in. On the deck one knew differently! As the aircraft came closer and the carrier heaved on into the waves and the plane's speed did not diminish and the deck did not grow steady—indeed, it pitched up and down five or ten feet per greasy heave—one experienced a neural alarm that no lecture could have prepared him for: This is not an *airplane* coming toward me, it is a brick with some poor sonofabitch riding it (*someone much like myself!*), and it is not *gliding,* it is *falling,* a thirty-thousand-pound brick, headed not for a stripe on the deck but for *me*—and with a horrible *smash!* it hits the skillet, and with a blur of momentum as big as a freight train's it hurtles toward the far end of the deck—another blinding storm!—another roar as the pilot pushes the throttle up to full military power and another smear of rubber screams out over the skillet—and this is nominal!—quite okay!—for a wire stretched across the deck has grabbed the hook on the end of the plane as it hit the deck tail down, and the smash was the rest of the fifteen-ton brute slamming onto the deck, as it tripped up, so that it is now straining against the wire at full throttle, in case it hadn't held and the plane had "boltered" off the end of the deck and had to struggle up into the air again. And already the Mickey Mouse helmets are running toward the fiery monster. . . .

And the candidate, looking on, begins to *feel* that great heaving sun-blazing deathboard of a deck wallowing in his own vestibular system—and suddenly he finds himself backed up against his own limits. He ends up going to the flight surgeon with so-called conversion symptoms. Overnight he develops blurred vision or numbness in his hands and feet or sinusitis so severe that he cannot tolerate changes in altitude. On one level the symptom is real. He really cannot see too well or use his fingers or stand the pain. But somewhere in his subconscious he knows it is a plea and a beg-off; he shows not the slightest concern (the flight surgeon notes) that the condition might be permanent and affect him in whatever life awaits him outside the arena of the right stuff.

Those who remained, those who qualified for carrier duty—and even more so those who later on qualified for *night* carrier duty—began to feel a bit like Gideon's warriors. *So many have been left behind!* The young warriors were now treated to a deathly sweet and quite unmentionable sight. They could gaze at length upon the crushed and wilted pariahs who had washed out. They could inspect those who did not have that righteous stuff.

The military did not have very merciful instincts. Rather than packing up these poor souls and sending them home, the Navy, like the Air Force and the Marines, would try to make use of them in some other role, such as flight controller. So the washout has to keep taking classes with the rest of his group, even though he can no longer touch an airplane. He sits there in the classes staring at sheets of paper with cataracts of sheer human mortification over his eyes while the rest steal looks at him . . . this man reduced to an ant, this untouchable, this poor sonofabitch. And in what test had he been found wanting? Why, it seemed to be nothing less than *manhood* itself. Naturally, this was never mentioned, either. Yet there it was. *Manliness, manhood, manly courage* . . . there was something ancient, primordial, irresistible about the challenge of this stuff, no matter what a sophisticated and rational age one might think he lived in.

1. In his essay, Wolfe defines a concept that is both abstract and probably unfamiliar to the greater part of his audience. How does he solve this problem through his choice of organizational strategies?

2. What do you think is Wolfe's attitude toward his subject? Why do you think he chose this attitude to speak with his audience?

3. Look again at the paragraph in which Wolfe describes landing on a carrier. What do you notice about the sentences that make it up? What effect do they have? How does the effect of these sentences work with Wolfe's subject in both the paragraph and the piece of writing as a whole?

TO BUILD A FIRE

Jack London

Day had broken cold and gray, exceedingly cold and gray, when the man turned aside from the main Yukon trail and climbed the high earth-bank, where a dim and little-travelled trail led eastward through the fat spruce timberland. It was a steep bank, and he paused for breath at the top, excusing the act to himself by looking at his watch. It was nine o'clock. There was no sun nor hint of sun, though there was not a cloud in the sky. It was a clear day, and yet there seemed an intangible pall over the face of things, a subtle gloom that made the day dark, and that was due to the absence of sun. This fact did not worry the man. He was used to the lack of sun. It had been days since he had seen the sun, and he knew that a few more days must pass before that cheerful orb, due south, would just peep above the sky line and dip immediately from view.

The man flung a look back along the way he had come. The Yukon lay a mile wide and hidden under three feet of ice. On top of this ice were as many feet of snow. It was all pure white, rolling in gentle undulations where the ice jams of the freeze-up had formed. North and south, as far as his eye could see, it was unbroken white, save for a dark hairline that curved and twisted from around the spruce-covered island to the south, and that curved and twisted away into the north, where it disappeared behind another spruce-covered island. This dark hairline was the trail—the main trail—that led south five hundred miles to the Chilcoot Pass, Dyea, and salt water; and that led north seventy miles to Dawson, and still on to the north a thousand miles to Nulato, and finally to St. Michael, on Bering Sea, a thousand miles and half a thousand more.

But all this—the mysterious, far-reaching hairline trail, the absence of sun from the sky, the tremendous cold, and the strangeness and weirdness of it all—made no impression on the man. It was not because he was long used to it. He was a newcomer in the land, a *chechaquo,* and this was his first winter. The trouble with him was that he was without imagination. He was quick and alert in the things of life, but only in the things, and not in the significances. Fifty degrees below zero meant eighty-odd degrees of frost. Such fact impressed him as being cold and uncomfortable, and that was all. It did not lead him to meditate upon his frailty as a creature of temperature, and upon man's frailty in general, able only to live within certain narrow limits of heat and cold; and from there on it did not lead him to the conjectural field of immortality and man's place in the universe. Fifty degrees below zero stood for a bite of frost that hurt and that must be guarded against by the use of mittens, ear flaps, warm moccasins, and thick socks. Fifty degrees below zero was to him just precisely fifty degrees below zero. That there should be anything more to it than that was a thought that never entered his head.

As he turned to go on, he spat speculatively. There was a sharp, explosive crackle that startled him. He spat again. And again, in the air, before it could fall to the snow, the spittle crackled. He knew that at fifty below spittle crackled on the snow, but this spittle had crackled in the air. Undoubtedly it was colder than fifty below—how much colder he did not know. But the temperature did not matter. He was bound for the old claim on the left fork of Henderson Creek, where the boys were already. They had come over across the divide from the Indian Creek country, while he had come the roundabout way to take a look at the possibilities of getting out logs in the spring from the islands in the Yukon. He would be in to camp by six o'clock; a bit after dark, it was true, but the boys would be there, a fire would be going, and a hot supper would be ready. As for lunch, he pressed his hand against the protruding bundle under his jacket. It was also under his shirt, wrapped up in a handkerchief and lying against the naked skin. It was the only way to keep the biscuits from freezing. He smiled agreeably to himself as he thought of those biscuits, each cut open and sopped in bacon grease, and each enclosing a generous slice of fried bacon.

He plunged in among the big spruce trees. The trail was faint. A foot of snow had fallen since the last sled had passed over, and he was glad he was without a sled, traveling light. In fact, he carried nothing but the lunch wrapped in the handkerchief. He was surprised, however, at the cold. It certainly was cold, he concluded, as he rubbed his numb nose and cheekbones with his mittened hand. He was a warm-whiskered man, but the hair on his face did not protect the high cheekbones and the eager nose that thrust itself aggressively into the frosty air.

At the man's heels trotted a dog, a big native husky, the proper wolf dog, gray-coated and without any visible or temperamental difference from its brother, the wild wolf. The animal was depressed by the tremendous cold. It knew that it was no time for travelling. Its instinct told it a truer tale than was told to the man by the man's judgment. In reality, it was not merely colder than fifty below zero; it was colder than sixty below, than seventy below. It was seventy-five below zero. Since the freezing point is thirty-two above zero, it meant that one hundred and seven degrees of frost obtained. The dog did not know anything about thermometers. Possibly in its brain there was no sharp consciousness of a condition of very cold such as was in the man's brain. But the brute had its instinct. It experienced a vague but menacing apprehension that subdued it and made it slink along at the man's heels, and that made it question eagerly every unwonted movement of the man as if expecting him to go into camp or to seek shelter somewhere and build a fire. The dog had learned fire, and it wanted fire, or else to burrow under the snow and cuddle its warmth away from the air.

The frozen moisture of its breathing had settled on its fur in a fine powder of frost, and especially were its jowls, muzzle, and eyelashes whitened by its crystalled breath. The man's red beard and mustache were likewise frosted, but more solidly, the deposit taking the form of ice and increasing with every warm, moist breath he exhaled. Also, the man was chewing tobacco, and the muzzle of ice held his lips so rigidly that he was unable to clear his chin when he expelled the juice. The result was that a crystal beard of the color and solidity of amber was increasing its length on his chin. If he fell down it would shatter itself, like glass, into brittle fragments. But he did not mind the appendage. It was the penalty all tobacco chewers paid in that country, and he had been out before in two cold snaps. They had not been so cold as this, he knew, but by the spirit thermometer at Sixty Mile he knew they had been registered at fifty below and at fifty-five.

He held on through the level stretch of woods for several miles, crossed a wide flat of nigger heads, and dropped down a bank to the frozen bed of a small stream. This was Henderson Creek, and he knew he was ten miles from the forks. He looked at his watch. It was ten o'clock. He was making four miles an hour, and he calculated that he would arrive at the forks at half-past twelve. He decided to celebrate that event by eating his lunch there.

The dog dropped in again at his heels, with a tail drooping discouragement, as the man swung along the creek bed. The furrow of the old sled trail was plainly visible, but a dozen inches of snow covered the marks of the last runners. In a month no man had come up or down that silent creek. The man held steadily on. He was not much given to thinking, and just then particularly he had nothing to think about save that he would eat lunch at the forks and that at six o'clock he would be in camp with the boys. There was nobody to talk to; and, had there been, speech would have been impossible because of the ice muzzle on his mouth. So he continued monotonously to chew tobacco and to increase the length of his amber beard.

Once in a while the thought reiterated itself that it was very cold and that he had never experienced such cold. As he walked along he rubbed *10* his cheekbones and nose with the back of his mittened hand. He did this automatically, now and again changing hands. But, rub as he would, the instant he stopped his cheekbones went numb, and the following instant the end of his nose went numb. He was sure to frost his cheeks; he knew that, and experienced a pang of regret that he had not devised a nose strap of the sort Bud wore in cold snaps. Such a strap passed across the cheeks, as well, and saved them. But it didn't matter much, after all. What were frosted cheeks? A bit painful, that was all; they were never serious.

Empty as the man's mind was of thoughts, he was keenly observant, and he noticed the changes in the creek, the curves and bends and timber jams, and always he sharply noted where he placed his feet. Once, coming around a bend, he shied abruptly, like a startled horse, curved away from the place where he had been walking, and retreated several paces back along the trail. The creek he knew was frozen clear to the bottom—no creek could contain water in that arctic winter—but he knew also that there were springs that bubbled out from the hillsides and ran along under the snow and on top the ice of the creek. He knew that the coldest snaps never froze these springs, and he knew likewise their danger. They were traps. They hid pools of water under the snow that might be three inches deep, or three feet. Sometimes a skin of ice half an inch thick covered them, and in turn was covered by the snow. Sometimes there were alternate layers of water and ice skin, so that when one broke through he kept on breaking through for a while, sometimes wetting himself to the waist.

That was why he had shied in such panic. He had felt the give under his feet and heard the crackle of a snow-hidden ice skin. And to get his feet wet in such a temperature meant trouble and danger. At the very least it meant delay, for he would be forced to stop and build a fire, and under its protection to bare his feet while he dried his socks and moccasins. He stood and studied the creek bed and its banks, and decided that the flow of water came from the right. He reflected awhile, rubbing his nose and cheeks, then skirted to the left, stepping gingerly and testing the footing for each step. Once clear of the danger, he took a fresh chew of tobacco and swung along at his four-mile gait.

In the course of the next two hours he came upon several similar traps. Usually the snow above the hidden pools had a sunken, candied appearance that advertised the danger. Once again, however, he had a close call; and once, suspecting danger, he compelled the dog to go on in front. The dog did not want to go. It hung back until the man shoved it forward, and then it went quickly across the white, unbroken surface. Suddenly it broke through, floundered to one side, and got away to firmer footing. It had wet its forefeet and legs, and almost immediately the water that clung to it turned to ice. It made quick efforts to lick the ice off its legs, then dropped down in the snow and began to bite out the ice that had formed between the toes. This was a matter of instinct. To permit the ice to remain would mean sore feet. It did not know this. It merely obeyed the mysterious prompting that arose from the deep crypts of its being. But the man knew, having achieved a judgment on the subject, and he removed the mitten from his right hand and helped tear out the ice particles. He did not expose his fingers more than a minute, and was astonished at the swift numbness that smote them. It certainly was cold. He pulled on the mitten hastily, and beat the hand savagely across his chest.

At twelve o'clock the day was at its brightest. Yet the sun was too far south on its winter journey to clear the horizon. The bulge of the earth intervened between it and Henderson Creek, where the man walked under a clear sky at noon and cast no shadow. At half-past twelve, to the minute, he arrived at the forks of the creek. He was pleased at the speed he had made. If he kept it up, he would certainly be with the boys by six. He unbuttoned his jacket and shirt and drew forth his lunch. The action consumed no more than a quarter of a minute, yet in that brief moment the numbness laid hold of the exposed fingers. He did not put the mitten on, but, instead, struck the fingers a dozen sharp smashes against his leg. Then he sat down on a snow-covered log to eat. The sting that followed upon the striking of his fingers against his leg ceased so quickly that he was startled. He had had no chance to take a bit of biscuit. He struck the fingers repeatedly and returned them to the mitten, baring the other hand for the purpose of eating. He tried to take a mouthful, but the ice muzzle prevented. He had forgotten to build a fire and thaw out. He chuckled at his foolishness, and as he chuckled he noted the numbness creeping into the exposed fingers. Also, he noted that the stinging which had first come to his toes when he sat down was already passing away. He wondered whether the toes were warm or numb. He moved them inside the moccasins and decided that they were numb.

He pulled the mitten on hurriedly and stood up. He was a bit frightened. He stamped up and down until the stinging returned into the feet. It certainly was cold, was his thought. That man from Sulphur Creek had spoken the truth when telling how cold it sometimes got in the country. And he had laughed at him at the time! That showed one must not be too sure of things. There was no mistake about it, it was cold. He strode up and down, stamping his feet and threshing his arms, until reassured by the returning warmth. Then he got out matches and proceeded to make a fire. From the undergrowth, where high water of the previous spring had lodged a supply of seasoned twigs, he got his firewood. Working carefully from a small beginning, he soon had a roaring fire, over which he thawed the ice from his face and in the protection of which he ate his biscuits. For the moment the cold of space was outwitted. The dog took satisfaction in the fire, stretching out close enough for warmth and far enough away to escape being singed.

When the man had finished, he filled his pipe and took his comfortable time over a smoke. Then he pulled on his mittens, settled the ear flaps of his cap firmly about his ears, and took the creek trail up the left fork. The dog was disappointed and yearned back toward the fire. This

15

man did not know cold. Possibly all the generations of his ancestry had been ignorant of cold, of real cold, of cold one hundred and seven degrees below freezing point. But the dog knew; all its ancestry knew, and it had inherited the knowledge. And it knew that it was not good to walk abroad in such fearful cold. It was the time to lie snug in a hole in the snow and wait for a curtain of cloud to be drawn across the face of outer space whence this cold came. On the other hand, there was no keen intimacy between the dog and the man. The one was the toil slave of the other, and the only caresses it had ever received were the caresses of the whip lash and of harsh and menacing throat sounds that threatened the whip lash. So the dog made no effort to communicate its apprehension to the man. It was not concerned in the welfare of the man; it was for its own sake that it yearned back toward the fire. But the man whistled, and spoke to it with the sound of whip lashes, and the dog swung in at the man's heels and followed after.

The man took a chew of tobacco and proceeded to start a new amber beard. Also, his moist breath quickly powdered with white his mustache, eyebrows, and lashes. There did not seem to be so many springs on the left fork of the Henderson, and for half an hour the man saw no signs of any. And then it happened. At a place where there were no signs, where the soft, unbroken snow seemed to advertise solidity beneath, the man broke through. It was not deep. He wet himself halfway to the knees before he floundered out to the firm crust.

He was angry, and cursed his luck aloud. He had hoped to get into camp with the boys at six o'clock, and this would delay him an hour, for he would have to build a fire and dry out his footgear. This was imperative at that low temperature—he knew that much; and he turned aside to the bank, which he climbed. On top, tangled in the underbrush about the trunks of several small spruce trees, was a highwater deposit of dry firewood—sticks and twigs, principally, but also larger portions of seasoned branches and fine, dry, last year's grasses. He threw down several large pieces on top of the snow. This served for a foundation and prevented the young flame from drowning itself in the snow it otherwise would melt. The flame he got by touching a match to a small shred of birch bark that he took from his pocket. This burned even more readily than paper. Placing it on the foundation, he fed the young flame with wisps of dry grass and with the tiniest dry twigs.

He worked slowly and carefully, keenly aware of his danger. Gradually, as the flame grew stronger, he increased the size of the twigs with which he fed it. He squatted in the snow, pulling the twigs out from their entanglement in the brush and feeding directly to the flame. He knew there must be no failure. When it is seventy-five below zero, a man must not fail in his first attempt to build a fire—that is, if his feet are wet. If his feet are dry, and he fails, he can run along the trail for half a mile and restore his circulation. But the circulation of wet and freezing feet cannot be restored by running when it is seventy-five below. No matter how fast he runs, the wet feet will freeze the harder. All this the man knew. The old-timer on Sulphur Creek had told him about it the previous fall, and now he was appreciating the advice. Already the sensation had gone out of his feet. To build the fire he had been forced to remove his mittens, and the fingers had quickly gone numb. His pace of four miles an hour had kept his heart pumping blood to the surface of his body and to all the extremities. But the instant he stopped, the action of the pump eased down. The cold of space smote the unprotected tip of the planet, and he, being on that unprotected tip, received the full force of the blow. The blood of his body recoiled before it. The blood was alive, like the dog, and like the dog it wanted to hide away and cover itself up from the fearful cold. So long as he walked four miles an hour, he pumped that blood, willy-nilly, to the surface; but now it ebbed away and sank down into the recesses of his body. The extremities were the first to feel its absence. His wet feet froze the faster, and his exposed fingers numbed the faster, though they had not yet begun to freeze. Nose and cheeks were already freezing, while the skin of all his body chilled as it lost its blood.

But he was safe. Toes and nose and cheeks would be only touched by the frost, for the fire was beginning to burn with strength. He was feeding it with twigs the size of his finger. In another minute he would be able to feed it with branches the size of his wrist, and then he could remove his wet footgear, and, while it dried, he could keep his naked feet warm by the fire, rubbing them at first, of course, with snow. The fire was a success. He was safe. He remembered the advice of the old-timer on Sulphur Creek, and smiled. The old-timer had been very serious in laying down the law that no man must travel alone in the Klondike after fifty below. Well, here he was; he had had the accident; he was alone; and he had saved himself. Those old-timers were rather womanish, some of them, he thought. All a man had to do was to keep his head, and he was all right. Any man who was a man could travel alone. But it was surprising, the rapidity with which his cheeks and nose were freezing. And he had not thought his fingers could go lifeless in so short a time. Lifeless they were, for he could scarcely make them move together to grip a twig, and they seemed remote from his body and from him. When he touched a twig, he had to look and see whether or not he had hold of it. The wires were pretty well down between him and his finger ends.

All of which counted for little. There was the fire, snapping and crackling and promising life with every dancing flame. He started to untie his moccasins. They were coated with ice; the thick German socks were like sheaths of iron halfway to the knees; and the moccasin strings were like rods of steel all twisted and knotted as by some conflagration. For a moment he tugged with his numb fingers, then, realizing the folly of it, he drew his sheath knife.

But before he could cut the strings, it happened. It was his own fault or, rather, his mistake. He should not have built the fire under the spruce tree. He should have built it in the open. But it had been easier to pull

20

the twigs from the brush and drop them directly on the fire. Now the tree under which he had done this carried a weight of snow on its boughs. No wind had blown for weeks, and each bough was fully freighted. Each time he had pulled a twig he had communicated a slight agitation to the tree—an imperceptible agitation, so far as he was concerned, but an agitation sufficient to bring about the disaster. High up in the tree one bough capsized its load of snow. This fell on the boughs beneath, capsizing them. This process continued, spreading out and involving the whole tree. It grew like an avalanche, and it descended without warning upon the man and the fire, and the fire was blotted out! Where it had burned was a mantle of fresh and disordered snow.

The man was shocked. It was as though he had just heard his own sentence of death. For a moment he sat and stared at the spot where the fire had been. Then he grew very calm. Perhaps the old-timer on Sulphur Creek was right. If he had only had a trail mate he would have been in no danger now. The trail mate could have built the fire. Well, it was up to him to build the fire over again, and this second time there must be no failure. Even if he succeeded, he would most likely lose some toes. His feet must be badly frozen by now, and there would be some time before the second fire was ready.

Such were his thoughts, but he did not sit and think them. He was busy all the time they were passing through his mind. He made a new foundation for a fire, this time in the open, where no treacherous tree could blot it out. Next he gathered dry grasses and tiny twigs from the highwater flotsam. He could not bring his fingers together to pull them out, but he was able to gather them by the handful. In this way he got many rotten twigs and bits of green moss that were undesirable, but it was the best he could do. He worked methodically, even collecting an armful of the larger branches to be used later when the fire gathered strength. And all the while the dog sat and watched him, a certain yearning wistfulness in its eyes, for it looked upon him as the fire provider, and the fire was slow in coming.

When all was ready, the man reached in his pocket for a second piece 25 of birch bark. He knew the bark was there, and, though he could not feel it with his fingers, he could hear its crisp rustling as he fumbled for it. Try as he would, he could not clutch hold of it. And all the time, in his consciousness, was the knowledge that each instant his feet were freezing. This thought tended to put him in a panic, but he fought against it and kept calm. He pulled on his mittens with his teeth, and threshed his arms back and forth, beating his hands with all his might against his sides. He did this sitting down, and he stood up to do it; and all the while the dog sat in the snow, its wolf brush of a tail curled around warmly over its forefeet, its sharp wolf ears pricked forward intently as it watched the man. And the man, as he beat and threshed with his arms and hands, felt a great surge of envy as he regarded the creature that was warm and secure in its natural covering.

After a time he was aware of the first faraway signals of sensation in his beaten fingers. The faint tingling grew stronger till it evolved into a stinging ache that was excruciating, but which the man hailed with satisfaction. He stripped the mittens from his right hand and fetched forth the birch bark. The exposed fingers were quickly going numb again. Next he brought out his bunch of sulphur matches. But the tremendous cold had already driven the life out of his fingers. In his effort to separate one match from the others, the whole bunch fell in the snow. He tried to pick it out of the snow, but failed. The dead fingers could neither touch nor clutch. He was very careful. He drove the thought of his freezing feet, and nose, and cheeks, out of his mind, devoting his whole soul to the matches. He watched, using the sense of vision in place of that of touch, and when he saw his fingers on each side the bunch, he closed them— that is, he willed to close them, for the wires were down, and the fingers did not obey. He pulled the mitten on the right hand, and beat it fiercely against his knee. Then, with both mittened hands, he scooped the bunch of matches, along with much snow, into his lap. Yet he was no better off.

After some manipulation he managed to get the bunch between the heels of his mittened hands. In this fashion he carried it to his mouth. The ice crackled and snapped when by a violent effort he opened his mouth. He drew the lower jaw in, curled the upper lip out of the way, and scraped the bunch with his upper teeth in order to separate a match. He succeeded in getting one, which he dropped on his lap. He was no better off. He could not pick it up. Then he devised a way. He picked it up in his teeth and scratched it on his leg. Twenty times he scratched before he succeeded in lighting it. As it flamed he held it with his teeth to the birch bark. But the burning brimstone went up his nostrils and into his lungs, causing him to cough spasmodically. The match fell into the snow and went out.

The old-timer on Sulphur Creek was right, he thought in the moment of controlled despair that ensued: after fifty below, a man should travel with a partner. He beat his hands, but failed in exciting any sensation. Suddenly he bared both hands, removing the mittens with his teeth. He caught the whole bunch between the heels of his hands. His arm muscles not being frozen enabled him to press the hand heels tightly against the matches. Then he scratched the bunch along his leg. It flared into flame, seventy sulphur matches at once! There was no wind to blow them out. He kept his head to one side to escape the strangling fumes, and held the blazing bunch to the birch bark. As he so held it, he became aware of sensation in his hand. His flesh was burning. He could smell it. Deep down below the surface he could feel it. The sensation developed into pain that grew acute. And still he endured it, holding the flame of the matches clumsily to the bark that would not light readily because his own burning hands were in the way, absorbing most of the flame.

At last, when he could endure no more, he jerked his hands apart. The blazing matches fell sizzling into the snow, but the birch bark was alight. He began laying dry grasses and the tiniest twigs on the flame. He could not pick and choose, for he had to lift the fuel between the heels of his hands. Small pieces of rotten wood and green moss clung to the twigs, and he bit them off as well as he could with his teeth. He cherished the flame carefully and awkwardly. It meant life, and it must not perish. The withdrawal of blood from the surface of his body now made him begin to shiver, and he grew more awkward. A large piece of green moss fell squarely on the little fire. He tried to poke it out with his fingers, but his shivering frame made him poke too far, and he disrupted the nucleus of the little fire, the burning grasses and tiny twigs separating and scattering. He tried to poke them together again, but in spite of the tenseness of the effort, his shivering got away with him, and the twigs were hopelessly scattered. Each twig gushed a puff of smoke and went out. The fire provider had failed. As he looked apathetically about him, his eyes chanced on the dog, sitting across the ruins of the fire from him, in the snow, making restless, hunching movements, slightly lifting one forefoot and then the other, shifting its weight back and forth on them with wistful eagerness.

The sight of the dog put a wild idea into his head. He remembered the tale of the man, caught in a blizzard, who killed a steer and crawled inside the carcass, and so was saved. He would kill the dog and bury his hands in the warm body until the numbness went out of them. Then he could build another fire. He spoke to the dog, calling it to him; but in his voice was a strange note of fear that frightened the animal, who had never known the man to speak in such way before. Something was the matter, and its suspicious nature sensed danger—it knew not what danger, but somewhere, somehow, in its brain arose an apprehension of the man. It flattened its ears down at the sound of the man's voice, and its restless, hunching movements and the liftings and shiftings of its forefeet became more pronounced; but it would not come to the man. He got on his hands and knees and crawled toward the dog. This unusual posture again excited suspicion, and the animal sidled mincingly away.

The man sat up in the snow for a moment and struggled for calmness. Then he pulled on his mittens, by means of his teeth, and got upon his feet. He glanced down at first in order to assure himself that he was really standing up, for the absence of sensation in his feet left him unrelated to the earth. His erect position in itself started to drive the webs of suspicion from the dog's mind; and when he spoke peremptorily, with the sound of whip lashes in his voice, the dog rendered its customary allegiance and came to him. As it came within reaching distance, the man lost his control. His arms flashed out to the dog, and he experienced genuine surprise when he discovered that his hands could not clutch, that there was neither bend nor feeling in the fingers. He had forgotten for the moment that they were frozen and that they were freezing more and more. All this happened quickly, and before the animal could get away, he encircled its

30

body with his arms. He sat down in the snow, and in this fashion held the dog, while it snarled and whined and struggled.

But it was all he could do, hold its body encircled in his arms and sit there. He realized that he could not kill the dog. There was no way to do it. With his helpless hands he could neither draw nor hold his sheath knife nor throttle the animal. He released it, and it plunged wildly away, with tail between its legs, and still snarling. It halted forty feet away and surveyed him curiously, with ears sharply pricked forward.

The man looked down at his hands in order to locate them, and found them hanging on the ends of his arms. It struck him as curious that one should have to use his eyes in order to find out where his hands were. He began threshing his arms back and forth, beating the mittened hands against his sides. He did this for five minutes, violently, and his heart pumped enough blood up to the surface to put a stop to his shivering. But no sensation was aroused in the hands. He had an impression that they hung like weights on the ends of his arms, but when he tried to run the impression down, he could not find it.

A certain fear of death, dull and oppressive, came to him. This fear quickly became poignant as he realized that it was no longer a mere matter of freezing his fingers and toes, or of losing his hands and feet, but that it was a matter of life and death with the chances against him. This threw him into a panic, and he turned and ran up the creek bed along the old, dim trail. The dog joined in behind and kept up with him. He ran blindly, without intention, in fear such as he had never known in his life. Slowly, as he plowed and floundered through the snow, he began to see things again—the banks of the creek, the old timber jams, the leafless aspens, and the sky. The running made him feel better. He did not shiver. Maybe, if he ran on, his feet would thaw out; and, anyway, if he ran far enough, he would reach camp and the boys. Without doubt he would lose some fingers and toes and some of his face; but the boys would take care of him, and save the rest of him when he got there. And at the same time there was another thought in his mind that said he would never get to the camp and the boys; that it was too many miles away, that the freezing had too great a start on him, and that he would soon be stiff and dead. This thought he kept in the background and refused to consider. Sometimes it pushed itself forward and demanded to be heard, but he thrust it back and strove to think of other things.

It struck him as curious that he could run at all on feet so frozen that he could not feel them when they struck the earth and took the weight of his body. He seemed to himself to skim along above the surface, and to have no connection with the earth. Somewhere he had once seen a winged Mercury, and he wondered if Mercury felt as he felt when skimming over the earth.

His theory of running until he reached camp and the boys had one flaw in it: he lacked the endurance. Several times he stumbled, and finally

35

he tottered, crumpled up, and fell. When he tried to rise, he failed. He must sit and rest, he decided, and next time he would merely walk and keep on going. As he sat and regained his breath, he noted that he was feeling quite warm and comfortable. He was not shivering, and it even seemed that a warm glow had come to his chest and trunk. And yet, when he touched his nose or cheeks, there was no sensation. Running would not thaw them out. Nor would it thaw out his hands and feet. Then the thought came to him that the frozen portions of his body must be extending. He tried to keep this thought down, to forget it, to think of something else; he was aware of the panicky feeling that it caused, and he was afraid of the panic. But the thought asserted itself, and persisted, until it produced a vision of his body totally frozen. This was too much, and he made another wild run along the trail. Once he slowed down to a walk, but the thought of the freezing extending itself made him run again.

And all the time the dog ran with him, at his heels. When he fell down a second time, it curled its tail over its forefeet and sat in front of him, facing him, curiously eager and intent. The warmth and security of the animal angered him, and he cursed it till it flattened down its ears appeasingly. This time the shivering came more quickly upon the man. He was losing in his battle with the frost. It was creeping into his body from all sides. The thought of it drove him on, but he ran no more than a hundred feet, when he staggered and pitched headlong. It was his last panic. When he had recovered his breath and control, he sat up and entertained in his mind the conception of meeting death with dignity. However, the conception did not come to him in such terms. His idea of it was that he had been making a fool of himself, running around like a chicken with its head cut off—such was the simile that occurred to him. Well, he was bound to freeze anyway, and he might as well take it decently. With this new-found peace of mind came the first glimmerings of drowsiness. A good idea, he thought, to sleep off to death. It was like taking an anesthetic. Freezing was not so bad as people thought. There were lots worse ways to die.

He pictured the boys finding his body next day. Suddenly he found himself with them, coming along the trail and looking for himself. And, still with them, he came around a turn in the trail and found himself lying in the snow. He did not belong with himself any more, for even then he was out of himself, standing with the boys and looking at himself in the snow. It certainly was cold, was his thought. When he got back to the States he could tell the folks what real cold was. He drifted on from this to a vision of the old-timer on Sulphur Creek. He could see him quite clearly, warm and comfortable, and smoking a pipe.

"You were right, old hoss; you were right," the man mumbled to the old-timer of Sulphur Creek.

Then the man drowsed off into what seemed to him the most comfortable and satisfying sleep he had ever known. The dog sat facing him

40

and waiting. The brief day drew to a close in a long, slow twilight. There were no signs of a fire to be made, and, besides, never in the dog's experience had it known a man to sit like that in the snow and make no fire. As the twilight drew on, its eager yearning for the fire mastered it, and with a great lifting and shifting of forefeet, it whined softly, then flattened its ears down in anticipation of being chidden by the man. But the man remained silent. Later the dog whined loudly. And still later it crept close to the man and caught the scent of death. This made the animal bristle and back away. A little longer it delayed, howling under the stars that leaped and danced and shone brightly in the cold sky. Then it turned and trotted up the trail in the direction of the camp it knew, where were the other food providers and fire providers.

---

1. Why do you think London has chosen to tell you this story? What do you think he has chosen to define? Is his subject abstract or concrete?

2. Does London ever tell you directly what it is that he defines? How does he make his idea clear?

3. Who is the protagonist in this story? Who or what is the antagonist(s)?

4. Are there other characters in the story? How do they make their presence known?

5. Would you call the dog a character? Why?

An Invitation to Write

In the examples of definition you've just read, the authors appear to be defining an abstract quality through their writing. Write a story, an essay, or a poem that uses your observations, experience, and feeling about your material to create a definition that reflects your views about a certain quality that seems important to you.

A Student Paper

When you have read this paper, answer the questions that follow it, alone or with your group.

WHAT A DEAL!

Paul Impellezzeri

Hello. How are we today?

Are you interested in any of these cars?

Well, Dick's my name, and deals are my game. For this week only I can send you home in one of these quality cars with no money down. I can do that because I trust you. I can tell, just by looking at you, that you want a quality car. Let me guess . . . You must be newlyweds.

Oh yes, I remember back to my newlywed days. "Only the best for the ones you love," that's what I always say. I saw the young lady eyeing the red beauty over there.

How much? With me, the price is not a problem. "Deal" is my middle name, and with our finance department anything is reasonable. Would you like to take it for a test drive?

Oh yes. I can certainly understand your desire to know the price. And believe me, here at Al's Autos we only want to serve you. I can tell that you're people who insist on quality, and this car matches your good judgment and high standards.

Because you're giving Al's Autos a chance at the deal, I'm gonna give you a great bargain. You see, I'm gonna have to level with you and tell you that here at Al's Autos we're overstocked. There's nothing I would love to see more than a fine couple like you drive this red beauty off the lot.

Oh, I hear you, and I agree totally. The price is very important. This car is a true value. This car looks expensive, but believe me, there is more value under this hood than in any other car, for any price. This car is a blend of performance, beauty, safety, and economy. This car was the most affordable one in its class in '87 while maintaining the best possible standards. Of course, as in any car, it requires limited maintenance, but as you can see, the previous owners kept the car in very good shape.

I admit the car shows a few flaws, nothing significant. I wouldn't lie to you and tell you the car is perfect when it's not. It takes a true knowledge of cars to pick these true values out from the imitators.

Well, if you really want to know the price, make me an offer. What would it take to put you in this car today?

You know, I'd really like to help you out, but you're gonna have to give me a more serious offer, something I can work with. Remember, this car is loaded with special features including an AM/FM stereo, front-wheel drive, power steering and anti-lock brakes. Folks, I'll tell you right now; there's no other dealer willing to sell this car at a lower price. Tomorrow we have a load of pickups coming in, and we need all the space we can get.

I'm perfectly willing to march right into that office and submit the deal of your life to my manager, but you're gonna have to give me something a little better than that. With the number you just gave me, he would laugh in my face. Won't you let me just make a little profit? How about coming inside? I'm sure we can work something out.

Sit right on down and make yourselves comfortable. Would either of you like a cup of coffee? Tea? How about a coke? Well, I think I'll have one too. It's an oven out there. Now that's another feature I'm sure you noticed. This car is equipped with an air conditioner and comprehensive heating system. No more chilly mornings or boiling afternoons.

Now, I'm a man of few words, so I'll get right to the point. Do you want to buy the car?

Well, like I said before, you are going to have to give me something a little more substantial. Do you have a trade-in? Are you a member of a credit union?

Well, maybe our finance department can arrange something. Over what time frame were you planning to pay for this car?

The price is not the important thing. The important thing is if it is affordable. What kind of payments can you make?

Well, now we're getting somewhere. If we stretch that over six years, we would have a more reasonable offer. Remember now, the first offer you gave me didn't even cover the invoice.

Well, I don't exactly recall the invoice price, but trust me; I could not sell my manager on your first offer. With this offer, we have a chance. It might be a little painful, but I'm willing to submit this offer. Are you willing to back me up on this? Are you willing to submit this offer?

Well, I haven't calculated the exact price, but it is in your target zone. You've made a wise choice. I'll be back with some papers to sign and the keys. A deal like this comes around only once a year.

---

1. How has the writer used point of view in this paper? What point of view has he chosen?

2. In this paper, the writer gives you one half of a dialogue. Has the writer managed his speaker's words clearly enough to let you know what the other persons say?

3. Who do you think is the protagonist? Who is the antagonist?

4. Granting the dominant idea in this paper defines something, what do you see as the central definition? How does the writer make that definition clear to you?

5. What other organizational strategies does the writer use to support his definition?

FURTHER READINGS

On the following pages you will find readings that use definition as their primary organizational strategy. If your teacher assigns some or all of these readings or if you are inclined to read them on your own, pay attention to the ways the writers use definition to support their dominant ideas. Also, note how the writers use voice and style to engage your feelings, your interest, and your intellect.

Remember, these writers are writing to you—a fellow human being. They have chosen to tell you something about coping with the effort of being human in their worlds. See how their examples and ideas speak to your experience. See how the combination of your experiences and those the writers offer you might lead you to your own ideas about your world.

BEAT ZEN, SQUARE ZEN, AND ZEN

Alan W. Watts

It is as difficult for Anglo-Saxons as for the Japanese to absorb anything quite so Chinese as Zen. For though the word "Zen" is Japanese and though Japan is now its home, Zen Buddhism is the creation of T'ang dynasty° China. I do not say this as a prelude to harping upon the incommunicable subtleties of alien cultures. The point is simply that people who feel a profound need to justify themselves have difficulty in understanding the viewpoints of those who do not, and the Chinese who created Zen were the same kind of people as Lao-tzu,° who, centuries before, had said, "Those who justify themselves do not convince." For the urge to make or prove oneself right has always jiggled the Chinese sense of the ludicrous. . . . To Confucius it seemed much better to be human-hearted than righteous, and to the great Taoists, Lao-tzu and Chuang-tzu,° it was obvious that one could not be right without also being wrong, because the two were as inseparable as back and front. As Chuang-tzu said, "Those who would have good government without its correlative misrule, and right without its correlative wrong, do not understand the principle of the universe."

T'ang dynasty: Lasted from about A.D. 618 to 906. It was distinguished by wide territorial expansion, great wealth, the invention of printing, and the flourishing of art and poetry.
Lao-tzu: the legendary founder (*ca.* 604–531 B.C.) of Taoism
Chuang-tzu (or Chuang-chou): a Taoist philosopher in China *ca.* 290 B.C.

To Western ears such words may sound cynical, and the Confucian admiration of "reasonableness" and compromise may appear to be a weak-kneed lack of commitment to principle. Actually they reflect a marvelous understanding and respect for what we call the balance of nature, human and otherwise—a universal vision of life is the Tao or way of nature in which the good and the evil, the creative and the destructive, the wise and the foolish are the inseparable polarities of existence. . . . At the roots of Chinese life there is a trust in the good-and-evil of one's own nature which is peculiarly foreign to those brought up with the chronic uneasy conscience of the Hebrew-Christian cultures. . . .

For rather different reasons, Japanese people tend to be as uneasy in themselves as Westerners, having a sense of social shame quite as acute as our more metaphysical sense of sin. This was especially true of the class most attracted to Zen, the *samurai*.° Ruth Benedict . . . was, I think, perfectly correct in saying that the attraction of Zen to the *samurai* class was its power to get rid of an extremely awkward self-consciousness induced in the education of the young. Part-and-parcel of this self-consciousness is the Japanese compulsion to compete with oneself—a compulsion which turns every craft and skill into a marathon of self-discipline. Although the attraction of Zen lay in the possibility of liberation from self-consciousness, the Japanese version of Zen fought fire with fire, overcoming the "self observing the self" by bringing it to an intensity in which it exploded. How remote from the regimen of the Japanese Zen monastery are the words of the great T'ang master Lin-chi:

> In Buddhism there is no place for using effort. Just be ordinary and nothing special. Eat your food, move your bowels, pass water, and when you're tired go and lie down. The ignorant will laugh at me, but the wise will understand.

. . . The Buddha or awakened man of Chinese Zen is "ordinary and nothing special"; he is humorously human. . . . We like this because here, for the first time, is a conception of the holy man and sage who is not impossibly remote, not superhuman but fully human, and, above all, not a solemn and sexless ascetic. . . . They are just like us, and yet much more at home in the world, floating much more easily upon the ocean of transience and insecurity.

Above all, I believe that Zen appeals to many in the post-Christian West   5
because it does not preach, moralize, and scold in the style of Hebrew-Christian prophetism. Buddhism does not deny that there is a relatively limited sphere in which human life may be improved by art and science, reason and good-will. However, it regards this sphere of activity as important but nonetheless subordinate to the comparatively limitless sphere in which things are as they are, always have been, and always will be—a sphere entirely beyond the categories of good and evil, success and failure, and indi-

---

samurai: warrior class of feudal Japan

vidual health and sickness. On the one hand, this is the sphere of the great universe. Looking out into it at night, we make no comparisons between right and wrong stars, nor between well and badly arranged constellations. Stars are by nature big and little, bright and dim. Yet the whole thing is a splendor and a marvel which sometimes makes our flesh creep with awe. On the other hand, this is also the sphere of human, everyday life which we might call existential.

For there is a standpoint from which human affairs are as much beyond right and wrong as the stars, and from which our deeds, experiences, and feelings can no more be judged than the ups and downs of a range of mountains. Though beyond moral and social valuation, this level of human life may also be seen to be just as marvelous and uncanny as the great universe itself. This feeling may become particularly acute when the individual ego tries to fathom its own nature, to plumb the inner sources of its own actions and consciousness. For here it discovers a part of itself—the inmost and greatest part—which is strange to itself and beyond its understanding and control. . . . Here I find my own inner workings functioning of themselves, spontaneously, like the rotation of the heavenly bodies and the drifting of the clouds. Strange and foreign as this aspect of myself at first seems to be, I soon realize that it *is* me, and much more me than my superficial ego. . . . The configuration of my nervous-system, like the configuration of the stars, happens of itself, and this "itself" is the real "myself."

From this standpoint—and here language reveals its limitations with a vengeance—I find that I cannot help doing and experiencing, quite freely, what is always "right," in the sense that the stars are always in their "right" places. As Hsiang-yen put it,

> There's no use for artificial discipline,
> For, move as I will, I manifest the ancient Tao.

At this level, human life is beyond anxiety, for it can never make a mistake. If we live, we live; if we die, we die; if we suffer, we suffer; if we are terrified, we are terrified. There is no problem about it. A Zen "master" was once asked, "Is it terribly hot, and how shall we escape the heat?" "Why not," he answered, "go to the place where it is neither hot or cold?" "Where is that place?" "In summer we sweat; in winter we shiver." In Zen one does not feel guilty about dying, or being afraid, or disliking the heat. At the same time, Zen does not insist upon this point of view as something which one *ought* to adopt; it does not preach it as an ideal. For if you don't understand it, your very not understanding is also IT. There would be no bright stars without dim stars, and, without the surrounding darkness, no stars at all.

The Hebrew-Christian universe is one in which moral urgency, the anxiety to be right, embraces and penetrates everything. God, the Absolute itself, is good as against bad, and thus to be immoral or in the wrong is to feel oneself an outcast not merely from human society but also from existence itself, from the root and ground of life. To be in the wrong therefore arouses a metaphysical anxiety and sense of guilt—a state of eternal damnation—utterly disproportionate to the crime. This metaphysical guilt is so insupportable that it must eventually issue in the rejection of God and of his laws—which is just what has happened in the whole movement of modern secularism, materialism, and naturalism. Absolute morality is profoundly destructive of morality, for the sanctions which it invokes against evil are far, far too heavy. One does not cure the headache by cutting off the head. The appeal of Zen, as of other forms of Eastern philosophy, is that it unveils behind the urgent realm of good and evil a vast region of oneself about which there need be no guilt or recrimination, where at last the self in indistinguishable from God.

But the Westerner who is attracted by Zen and who would understand it deeply must have one indispensable qualification: he must understand his own culture so thoroughly that he is no longer swayed by its premises unconsciously. He must really have come to terms with the Lord God Jehovah and with his Hebrew-Christian conscience so that he can take it or leave it without fear or rebellion. He must be free of the itch to justify himself. Lacking this, his Zen will be either "beat" or "square," either a revolt from the culture and social order or a new form of stuffiness and respectability. For Zen is above all the liberation of the mind from conventional thought, and this is something utterly different from rebellion against convention, on the one hand, or adapting foreign conventions, on the other. . . .

The "beat" mentality as I am thinking of it is something much more   10
extensive and vague than the hipster life of New York and San Francisco. It is a younger generation's nonparticipation in "the American Way of Life," a revolt which does not seek to change the existing order but simply turns away from it to find the significance of life in subjective experience rather than objective achievement. . . .

Beat Zen is a complex phenomenon. It ranges from a use of Zen for justifying sheer caprice in art, literature, and life to a very forceful social criticism and "digging of the universe" such as one may find in the poetry of Ginsberg, Whalen and Snyder, and, rather unevenly, in Kerouac, who is always a shade too self-conscious, too subjective, and too strident to have the flavor of Zen.

When Kerouac gives his philosophical final statement, "I don't know. I don't care. And it doesn't make any difference"—that cat is out of the bag, for there is a hostility in these words which clangs with self-defense. But just because Zen truly surpasses convention and its values, it has no need to say "To hell with it," nor to underline with violence the fact that anything goes.

It is indeed the basic intuition of Zen that there is an ultimate standpoint from which "anything goes." In the celebrated words of the master Yun-men, "Every day is a good day." Or as is said in the *Hsin-hsin Ming:*

> If you want to get the plain truth,
> Be not concerned with right and wrong.
> The conflict between right and wrong
> Is the sickness of the mind.

But this standpoint does not exclude and is not hostile towards the distinction between right and wrong at other levels and in more limited frames of reference. The world is seen to be beyond right and wrong when it is not framed: that is to say, when we are not looking at a particular situation by itself—out of relation to the rest of the universe. Within this room there is a clear difference between up and down; out in interstellar space there is not. Within the conventional limits of a human community there are clear distinctions between good and evil. But these disappear when human affairs are seen as part and parcel of the whole realm of nature. Every framework sets up a restricted field of relationships, and restriction is law or rule.

Now a skilled photographer can point his camera at almost any scene or object and create a marvelous composition by the way in which he frames and lights it. An unskilled photographer attempting the same thing creates only messes, for he does not know how to place the frame, the border of the picture, where it will be in relation to the contents. How eloquently this demonstrates that as soon as we introduce a frame anything does *not* go. But every work of art involves a frame. A frame of some kind is precisely what distinguishes a painting, a poem, a musical composition, a play, a dance, or a piece of sculpture from the rest of the world. Some artists may argue that they do not want their works to be distinguishable from the total universe, but if this be so they should not frame them in galleries and concert halls. Above all they should not sign them nor sell them. This is as immoral as selling the moon or signing one's name to a mountain. (Such an artist may perhaps be forgiven if he knows what he is doing, and prides himself inwardly, not on being a poet or painter, but a competent crook.) Only destructive little boys and vulgar excursionists go around initialling the trees.

Today there are Western artists avowedly using Zen to justify the indiscriminate framing of simply anything—blank canvases, totally silent music, torn up bits of paper dropped on a board and stuck where they fall, or dense masses of mangled wire. The work of the composer John Cage is rather typical of this tendency. In the name of Zen, he has forsaken his earlier and promising work with the "prepared piano," to confront audiences with eight Ampex tape-recorders simultaneously bellowing forth random noises. There is, indeed, a considerable therapeutic value in allowing oneself to be deeply aware of any sight or sound that may arise. For one thing, it brings to mind the marvel of seeing and hearing as such. For another, the profound willingness to listen to or gaze upon anything at all frees the mind from fixed preconceptions of beauty creating, as it were, a free space in which altogether new forms and relationships may emerge. But this is therapy; it is not yet art. It is on the level of the random ramblings of a patient on the analyst's couch: very important indeed as therapy, though it is by no means the aim of psychoanalysis to substitute such ramblings for conversation and literature. Cage's work would be redeemed if he framed and presented it as a kind of group session in audio-therapy, but as a concert it is simply absurd. One may hope, however, that *after* Cage has, by such listening, set his own mind free from the composer's almost inevitable plagiarism of the forms of the past, he will present us with the new musical patterns and relationships which he has not yet uttered.

Just as the skilled photographer often amazes us with his lighting and framing of the most unlikely subjects, so there are painters and writers in the West, as well as in modern Japan, who have mastered the authentically Zen art of controlling accidents. Historically this first arose in the Far-East in the appreciation of the rough texture of brush-strokes in calligraphy and painting, and in the accidental running of the glaze on bowls made for the tea-ceremony. One of the classical instances of this kind of thing came about through the shattering of a fine ceramic tea-caddy, belonging to one of the old Japanese tea-masters. The fragments were cemented together with gold, and its owner was amazed at the way in which the random network of thin gold lines enhanced its beauty. It must be remembered, however, that this was an *object trouvé*°—an accidental effect *selected* by a man of exquisite taste, and treasured as one might treasure and exhibit a marvelous rock or a piece of driftwood. For in the Zen-inspired art of *bonseki* or rock-gardening, the stones are selected with infinite care, and though the hand of man may never have changed them it is far from true that any old stone will do. Furthermore, in calligraphy, painting, and ceramics, the accidental effects of running glaze or of flying hair-lines of the brush were only accepted and presented by the artist when he felt them to be fortuitous and unexpected marvels within the context of the work as a whole.

What governed his judgment? What gives *certain* accidental effects in painting the same beauty as the accidental outlines of clouds? According to Zen feeling there is no precise rule, no rule, that is to say, which can be formulated in words and taught systematically. On the other hand, there is in all these things a principle of order which in Chinese philosophy is termed *li,* and which Joseph Needham has translated "organic pattern." *Li* originally meant the markings in jade, the grain in wood, and the fiber in muscle. It designates a type of order which is too multi-dimensional, too subtly inter-related, and too squirmingly vital to be represented in words or mechanical images. The artist has to know it as he knows how to grow his hair. He can do it again and again, but can never explain how. In Taoist philosophy this power is called *te,* or "magical virtue." It is the element of the miraculous which we feel both at the stars in heaven and at our own ability to be conscious.

It is the possession of *te,* then, which makes all the difference between mere scrawls and the "white writing" of Mark Tobey° which admittedly derived its inspiration from Chinese calligraphy.° It was by no means a purely haphazard drooling of paint or uncontrolled wandering of the brush,

---

object trouvé: an object discovered to have artistic merit even though not deliberately designed for that effect; literally, a "found" object
Mark Tobey: distinguished modern American painter
calligraphy: handwriting developed as an art in itself

for the character and taste of such an artist is visible in the grace (a possible equivalent of *te*) with which his strokes are formed even when he is not trying to represent anything except strokes. . . .

The real genius of Chinese and Japanese Zen artists in their use of controlled accidents goes beyond the discovery of fortuitous beauty. It lies in being able to express, at the level of artistry, the realization of that ultimate standpoint from which "anything goes" and at which "all things are of one suchness." The mere selection of any random shape to stick in a frame simply confuses the metaphysical and the artistic domains; it does not express the one in terms of the other. Set in a frame, any old mess is at once cut off from the totality of its natural context, and for this very reason its manifestation of the Tao is concealed. The formless murmur of night noises in a great city has an enchantment which immediately disappears when formally presented as music in a concert hall. A frame outlines a universe, a microcosm, and if the contents of the frame are to rank as art they must have the same quality of relationship to the whole and to each other as events in the great universe, the macrocosm of nature. In nature the accidental is always recognized in relation to what is ordered and controlled. The dark *yin* is never without the bright *yang*.° Thus the painting of Sesshu, the calligraphy of Ryokwan, and the ceramic bowls of the Hagi or Karatsu schools° reveal the wonder of accidents in nature through accidents in a context of highly disciplined art.

The realization of the unswerving "rightness" of whatever happens is   20
no more manifested by utter lawlessness in social conduct than by sheer caprice in art. As Zen has been used as a pretext for the latter in our times, its use as a pretext for the former is ancient history. Many a rogue has justified himself with the Buddhist formula, "Birth-and-death (*samsara*) is Nirvana; worldly passions are Enlightenment." This danger is implicit in Zen because it is implicit in freedom. Power and freedom can never be safe. They are dangerous in the same way that fire and electricity are dangerous. But it is quite pitiful to see Zen used as a pretext for license when the Zen in question is no more than an idea in the head, a simple rationalization. To some extent "Zen" is so used in the underworld which often attaches itself to artistic and intellectual communities. After all, the Bohemian way of life is primarily the natural consequence of artists and writers being so absorbed in their work that they have no interest in keeping up with the Joneses. It is also a symptom of creative changes in manners and morals which at first seem as reprehensible to conservatives as new forms in art. But every such community attracts a number of weak imitators and hangers-on, especially

---

yin and *yang*: the opposed forces whose balance underlies existence
Sesshu . . . Karatsu: Sesshu was a fifteenth-century Japanese master of black-ink (*sumi*) painting, and also a Zen priest; Ryokwan, a Japanese Zen priest and calligrapher (1758–1831); Hagi and Karatsu were schools of Japanese pottery celebrated for their "rough" naturalistic style.

in the great cities, and it is mostly in this class that one now finds the stereotype of the "beatnik" with his phony Zen. . . .

One of the most problematic characteristics of beat Zen, shared to some
extent both by the creative artists and their imitators, is the fascination for
marijuana and peyote, and the notion that the states of consciousness produced by these substances have some affinity with *satori*. That many of these
people "take drugs" naturally lays them wide open to the most extreme
forms of righteous indignation, despite the fact that marijuana and peyote
(or its derivative, mescaline) are far less harmful and habit-forming than
whiskey or tobacco. But while it is true that these drugs induce states of
great aesthetic insight and, perhaps, therapeutic value, the *satori*-experience
is so startlingly different from anything of this kind that no one who had
shared both could possibly confuse them. Both states of consciousness require an apparently paradoxical type of language to describe them, for which
reason one might easily confuse the drug-induced states with written accounts of *satori*. But *satori* is always marked by a kind of intense clarity and
simplicity from which complex imagery, jazzed-up sense perceptions, and
the strange "turned-on" feeling invariably produced by these drugs are absent. It is not by chance that *satori* is called *fu-sho* or "unproduced," which
means among other things, that there is no gimmick whether psychological
or chemical for bringing it about. *Satori* always remains inaccessible to the
mind preoccupied with its own states or with the search for ecstasy.

Now the underlying protestant lawlessness of beat Zen disturbs the
square Zennists very seriously. For square Zen is the Zen of established tradition in Japan with its clearly defined hierarchy, its rigid discipline, and its
specific tests of *satori*. More particularly, it is the kind of Zen adopted by
Westerners studying in Japan, who will before long be bringing it back
home. But there is an obvious difference between square Zen and the
common-or-garden squareness of the Rotary Club or the Presbyterian
Church. It is infinitely more imaginative, sensitive and interesting. But it is
still square because it is a quest for the *right* spiritual experience, for a *satori*
which will receive the stamp (*inka*) of approval and established authority.
There will even be certificates to hang on the wall.

If square Zen falls into any serious excess it is in the direction of spiritual
snobbism and artistic preciousness, though I have never known an orthodox
Zen teacher who could be accused of either. These gentlemen seem to take
their exalted office rather lightly, respecting its dignity without standing on
it. The faults of square Zen are the faults of any spiritual in-group with an
esoteric discipline and degrees of initiation. Students in the lower ranks can
get unpleasantly uppity about inside knowledge which they are not at liberty
to divulge—"and you wouldn't understand even if I could tell you"—and
are apt to dwell rather sickeningly on the immense difficulties and iron disciplines of their task. There are times, however, when this is understandable,
especially when someone who is just goofing-off claims that he is following
the Zen ideal of "naturalness."

The student of square Zen is also inclined at times to be niggling in his recognition of parallels to Zen in other spiritual traditions. Because the essentials of Zen can never be accurately and fully formulated, being an experience and not a set of ideas, it is always possible to be critical of anything anyone says about it, neither putting up nor shutting up. Any statement about Zen, or about spiritual experience of any kind, will always leave some aspect, some subtlety, unexpressed. No one's mouth is big enough to utter the whole thing. . . .

There was never a spiritual movement without its excesses and distortions. The experience of awakening which truly constitutes Zen is too timeless and universal to be injured. The extremes of beat Zen need alarm no one since, as Blake said, "the fool who persists in his folly will become wise." As for square Zen, "authoritative" spiritual experiences have always had a way of wearing thin, and thus of generating the demand for something genuine and unique which needs no stamp. 25

I have known followers of both extremes to come up with perfectly clear *satori* experiences, for since there is no real "way" to *satori* the way you are following makes very little difference. . . .

The old Chinese Zen masters were steeped in Taoism. They saw nature in its total interrelatedness, and saw that every creature and every experience is in accord with the Tao of nature just as it is. This enabled them to accept themselves as they were, moment by moment, without the least need to justify anything. They didn't do it to defend themselves or to find an excuse for getting away with murder. They didn't brag about it and set themselves apart as rather special. On the contrary, their Zen was *wu-shih,* which means approximately "nothing special" or "no fuss." But Zen is "fuss" when it is mixed up with Bohemian affectations, and "fuss" when it is imagined that the only proper way to find it is to run off to a monastery in Japan or to do special exercises in the lotus posture for five hours a day. And I will admit that the very hullabaloo about Zen, even in such an essay as this, is also fuss—but a little less so.

Having said that, I would like to say something for all Zen fussers, beat or square. Fuss is all right, too. If you are hung on Zen, there's no need to try to pretend that you are not. If you really want to spend some years in a Japanese monastery, there is no earthly reason why you shouldn't. Or if you want to spend your time hopping freight cars and digging Charlie Parker, it's a free country.

In the landscape of Spring there is neither better nor worse;
The flowering branches grow naturally, some long, some short.

PORNOGRAPHY

Margaret Atwood

When I was in Finland a few years ago for an international writers' conference, I had occasion to say a few paragraphs in public on the subject of pornography. The context was a discussion of political repression, and I was suggesting the possibility of a link between the two. The immediate result was that a male journalist took several large bites out of me. Prudery and pornography are two halves of the same coin, said he, and I was clearly a prude. What could you expect from an Anglo-Canadian? Afterward, a couple of pleasant Scandinavian men asked me what I had been so worked up about. All "pornography" means, they said, is graphic depictions of whores, and what was the harm in that?

Not until then did it strike me that the male journalist and I had two entirely different things in mind. By "pornography," he meant naked bodies and sex. I, on the other hand, had recently been doing the research for my novel *Bodily Harm,* and was still in a state of shock from some of the material I had seen, including the Ontario Board of Film Censors' "outtakes." By "pornography," I meant women getting their nipples snipped off with garden shears, having meat hooks stuck into their vaginas, being disemboweled; little girls being raped; men (yes, there are some men) being smashed to a pulp and forcibly sodomized. The cutting edge of pornography, as far as I could see, was no longer simple old copulation, hanging from the chandelier or otherwise: it was death, messy, explicit and highly sadistic. I explained this to the nice Scandinavian men. "Oh, but that's just the United States," they said. "Everyone knows they're sick." In their country, they said, violent "pornography" of that kind was not permitted on television or in movies; indeed, excessive violence of any kind was not permitted. They had drawn a clear line between erotica, which earlier studies had shown did not incite men to more aggressive and brutal behavior toward women, and violence, which later studies indicated did.

Some time after that I was in Saskatchewan, where, because of the scenes in *Bodily Harm,* I found myself on an open-line radio show answering questions about "pornography." Almost no one who phoned in was in favor of it, but again they weren't talking about the same stuff I was, because they hadn't seen it. Some of them were all set to stamp out bathing suits and negligees, and, if possible, any depictions of the female body whatsoever. God, it was implied, did not approve of female bodies, and sex of any kind, including that practised by bumblebees, should be shoved back into the dark, where it belonged. I had more than a suspicion that *Lady Chatterley's Lover,* Margaret Laurence's *The Diviners,* and indeed most books by most serious modern authors would have ended up as confetti if left in the hands of these callers.

For me, these two experiences illustrate the two poles of the emotionally heated debate that is now thundering around this issue. They also underline the desirability and even the necessity of defining the terms. "Pornography" is now one of those catchalls, like "Marxism" and "feminism," that have become so broad they can mean almost anything, ranging from certain verses in the Bible, ads for skin lotion and sex tests for children to the contents of *Penthouse,* Naughty '90s postcards and films with titles containing the word *Nazi* that show vicious scenes of torture and killing. It's easy to say that sensible people can tell the difference. Unfortunately, opinions on what constitutes a sensible person vary.

But even sensible people tend to lose their cool when they start talking about this subject. They soon stop talking and start yelling, and the name-calling begins. Those in favor of censorship (which may include groups not noticeably in agreement on other issues, such as some feminists and religious fundamentalists) accuse the others of exploiting women through the use of degrading images, contributing to the corruption of children, and adding to the general climate of violence and threat in which both women and children live in this society; or, though they may not give much of a hoot about actual women and children, they invoke moral standards and God's supposed aversion to "filth," "smut" and deviated *preversion,* which may mean ankles.

The camp in favor of total "freedom of expression" often comes out howling as loud as the Romans would have if told they could no longer have innocent fun watching the lions eat up Christians. It too may include segments of the population who are not natural bedfellows: those who proclaim their God-given right to freedom, including the freedom to tote guns, drive when drunk, drool over chicken porn and get off on videotapes of women being raped and beaten, may be waving the same anticensorship banner as responsible liberals who fear the return of Mrs. Grundy, or gay groups for whom sexual emancipation involves the concept of "sexual theater." *Whatever turns you on* is a handy motto, as is *A man's home is his castle* (and if it includes a dungeon with beautiful maidens strung up in chains and bleeding from every pore, that's his business).

Meanwhile, theoreticians theorize and speculators speculate. Is today's pornography yet another indication of the hatred of the body, the deep mind–body split, which is supposed to pervade Western Christian society? Is it a backlash against the women's movement by men who are threatened by uppity female behavior in real life, so like to fantasize about women done up like outsize parcels, being turned into hamburger, kneeling at their feet in slavelike adoration or sucking off guns? Is it a sign of collective impotence, of a generation of men who can't relate to real women at all but have to make do with bits of celluloid and paper? Is the current flood just a result of smart marketing and aggressive promotion by the money men in what has now become a multibillion-dollar industry? If they were selling movies about men getting their testicles stuck full of knitting needles by women with swastikas on their sleeves, would they do as well, or is this penchant somehow peculiarly male? If so, why? Is pornography a power trip rather than a sex one? Some say that those ropes, chains, muzzles and other restraining devices are an argument for the immense power female sexuality still wields in the male imagination; you don't put these things on dogs unless you're afraid of them. Others, more literary, wonder about the shift from the 19th-century Magic Woman or Femme Fatale image to the lollipop-licker, airhead or turkey-carcass treatment of women in porn today. The proporners don't care much about theory: they merely demand product. The antiporners don't care about it in the final analysis either: there's dirt on the street, and they want it cleaned up, now.

It seems to me that this conversation, with its *You're-a-prude/You're-a-pervert* dialectic, will never get anywhere as long as we continue to think of this material as just "entertainment." Possibly we're deluded by the packaging, the format: magazine, book, movie, theatrical presentation. We're used to thinking of these things as part of the "entertainment industry," and we're used to thinking of ourselves as free adult people who ought to be able to see any kind of "entertainment" we want to. That was what the First Choice pay-TV debate was all about. After all, it's only entertainment, right? Entertainment means fun, and only a killjoy would be antifun. What's the harm?

This is obviously the central question: *What's the harm?* If there isn't any real harm to any real people, then the antiporners can tsk-tsk and/or throw up as much as they like, but they can't rightfully expect more legal controls or sanctions. However, the no-harm position is far from being proven.

(For instance, there's a clear-cut case for banning—as the federal government has proposed—movies, photos and videos that depict children engaging in sex with adults: real children are used to make the movies, and hardly anybody thinks this is ethical. The possibilities for coercion are too great.)   10

To shift the viewpoint, I'd like to suggest three other models for looking at "pornography"—and here I mean the violent kind.

Those who find the idea of regulating pornographic materials repugnant because they think it's Fascist or Communist or otherwise not in accordance with the principles of an open democratic society should consider that Canada has made it illegal to disseminate material that may lead to hatred toward any group because of race or religion. I suggest that if pornography of the violent kind depicted these acts being done predominantly to Chinese, to blacks, to Catholics, it would be off the market immediately, under the present laws. Why is hate literature illegal? Because whoever made the law thought that such material might incite real people to do real awful things to other real people. The human brain is to a certain extent a computer: garbage in, garbage out. We only hear about the extreme cases (like that of American multimurderer Ted Bundy) in which pornography has contributed to the death and/or mutilation of women and/or men. Although pornography is not the only factor involved in the creation of such deviance, it certainly has upped the ante by suggesting both a variety of techniques and the social acceptability of such actions. Nobody knows yet what effect this stuff is having on the less psychotic.

Studies have shown that a large part of the market for all kinds of porn, soft and hard, is drawn from the 16-to-21-year-old population of young men. Boys used to learn about sex on the street, or (in Italy, according to Fellini movies) from friendly whores, or, in more genteel surroundings, from girls, their parents, or, once upon a time, in school, more or less. Now porn has been added, and sex education in the schools is rapidly being phased out. The buck has been passed, and boys are being taught that all women secretly like to be raped and that real men get high on scooping out women's digestive tracts.

Boys learn their concept of masculinity from other men: is this what most men want them to be learning? If word gets around that rapists are "normal" and even admirable men, will boys feel that in order to be normal, admirable and masculine they will have to be rapists? Human beings are enormously flexible, and how they turn out depends a lot on how they're educated, by the society in which they're immersed as well as by their teachers. In a society that advertises and glorifies rape or even implicitly condones it, more women get raped. It becomes socially acceptable. And at a time when men and the traditional male role have taken a lot of flak and men are confused and casting around for an acceptable way of being male (and, in some cases, not getting much comfort from women on that score), this must be at times a pleasing thought.

It would be naïve to think of violent pornography as just harmless entertainment. It's also an educational tool and a powerful propaganda device. What happens when boy educated on porn meets girl brought up on Harlequin romances? The clash of expectations can be heard around the block. She wants him to get down on his knees with a ring, he wants her to get down on all fours with a ring in her nose. Can this marriage be saved?

Pornography has certain things in common with such addictive substances as alcohol and drugs: for some, though by no means for all, it induces chemical changes in the body, which the user finds exciting and pleasurable. It also appears to attract a "hard core" of habitual users and a penumbra of those who use it occasionally but aren't dependent on it in any way. There are also significant numbers of men who aren't much interested in it, not because they're undersexed but because real life is satisfying their needs, which may not require as many appliances as those of users.

For the "hard core," pornography may function as alcohol does for the alcoholic: tolerance develops, and a little is no longer enough. This may account for the short viewing time and fast turnover in porn theatres. Mary Brown, chairwoman of the Ontario Board of Film Censors, estimates that for every one mainstream movie requesting entrance to Ontario, there is one porno flick. Not only the quantity consumed but the quality of explicitness must escalate, which may account for the growing violence: once the big deal was breasts, then it was genitals, then copulation, then that was no

r enough and the hard users had to have more. The ultimate kick is
, and after that, as the Marquis de Sade so boringly demonstrated, mul-
leath.

The existence of alcoholism has not led us to ban social drinking. On the
other hand, we do have laws about drinking and driving, excessive drunken-
ness and other abuses of alcohol that may result in injury or death to others.

This leads us back to the key question: what's the harm? Nobody
knows, but this society should find out fast, before the saturation point is
reached. The Scandinavian studies that showed a connection between depictions of sexual violence and increased impulse toward it on the part of
male viewers would be a starting point, but many more questions remain to
be raised as well as answered. What, for instance, is the crucial difference
between men who are users and men who are not? Does using affect a man's
relationship with actual women, and, if so, adversely? Is there a clear line
between erotica and violent pornography, or are they on an escalating con-
tinuum? Is this a "men versus women" issue, with all men secretly siding
with the proporners and all women secretly siding against? (I think not;
there *are* lots of men who don't think that running their true love through
the Cuisinart is the best way they can think of to spend a Saturday night, and
they're just as nauseated by films of someone else doing it as women are.) Is
pornography merely an expression of the sexual confusion of this age or an
active contributor to it?

Nobody wants to go back to the age of official repression, when even   20
piano legs were referred to as "limbs" and had to wear pantaloons to be
decent. Neither do we want to end up in George Orwell's *1984,* in which
pornography is turned out by the State to keep the proles in a state of torpor,
sex itself is considered dirty and the approved practice it only for reproduction. But Rome under the emperors isn't such a good model either.

If all men and women respected each other, if sex were considered joy-
ful and life-enhancing instead of a wallow in germ-filled glop, if everyone
were in love all the time, if, in other words, many people's lives were more
satisfactory for them than they appear to be now, pornography might just
go away on its own. But since this is obviously not happening, we as a society are going to have to make some informed and responsible decisions
about how to deal with it.

GIRL

Jamaica Kincaid

Wash the white clothes on Monday and put them on the stone heap;
wash the color clothes on Tuesday and put them on the clothesline to dry;
don't walk barehead in the hot sun; cook pumpkin fritters in very hot sweet

oil; soak your little clothes right after you take them off; when buying cotton to make yourself a nice blouse, be sure that it doesn't have gum on it, because that way it won't hold up well after a wash; soak salt fish overnight before you cook it; is it true that you sing benna° in Sunday School?; always eat your food in such a way that it won't turn someone else's stomach; on Sundays try to walk like a lady and not like the slut you are so bent on becoming; don't sing benna in Sunday School; you mustn't speak to wharf-rat boys, not even to give directions; don't eat fruits on the street—flies will follow you; *but I don't sing benna on Sundays at all and never in Sunday school;* this is how to sew on a button; this is how to make a buttonhole for the button you have just sewed on; this is how to hem a dress when you see the hem coming down and so to prevent yourself from looking like the slut I know you are so bent on becoming; this is how you iron your father's khaki shirt so that it doesn't have a crease; this is how you iron your father's khaki pants so that they don't have a crease; this is how you grow okra—far from the house, because okra tree harbors red ants; when you are growing dasheen, make sure it gets plenty of water or else it makes your throat itch when you are eating it; this is how you sweep a corner; this is how you sweep a whole house; this is how you sweep a yard; this is how you smile to someone you don't like too much; this is how you set a table for dinner with an important guest; this is how you smile to someone you don't like at all; this is how you smile to someone you like completely; this is how you set a table for tea; this is how you set a table for dinner; this is how you set a table for lunch; this is how you set a table for breakfast; this is how to behave in the presence of men who don't know you very well, and this way they won't recognize immediately the slut I have warned you against becoming; be sure to wash every day, even if it is with your own spit; don't squat down to play marbles—you are not a boy, you know; don't pick people's flowers—you might catch something; don't throw stones at blackbirds, because it might not be a blackbird at all; this is how to make a bread pudding; this is how to make doukona°; this is how to make pepper pot; this is how to make a good medicine for a cold; this is how to make a good medicine to throw away a child before it even becomes a child; this is how to catch a fish; this is how to throw back a fish you don't like, and that way something bad won't fall on you; this is how to bully a man; this is how a man bullies you; this is how to love a man, and if this doesn't work there are other ways, and if they don't work don't feel too bad about giving up; this is how to spit up in the air if you feel like it, and this is how to move quick so that it doesn't fall on you; this is how to make ends meet; always squeeze bread to make sure it's fresh; *but what if the baker won't let me feel the bread?*; you mean to say that after all you are really going to be the kind of woman who the baker won't let near the bread?

---

benna: calypso music
doukona: spicy plantain pudding

A NEW ENGLAND NUN

Mary E. Wilkins Freeman

It was late in the afternoon, and the light was waning. There was a difference in the look of the tree shadows out in the yard. Somewhere in the distance cows were lowing and a little bell was tinkling; now and then a farm-wagon tilted by, and the dust flew; some blue-shirted laborers with shovels over their shoulders plodded past; little swarms of flies were dancing up and down before the people's faces in the soft air. There seemed to be a gentle stir arising over everything for the mere sake of subsidence—a very premonition of rest and hush and night.

This soft diurnal commotion was over Louisa Ellis also. She had been peacefully sewing at her sitting-room window all the afternoon. Now she quilted her needle carefully into her work, which she folded precisely, and laid in a basket with her thimble and thread and scissors. Louisa Ellis could not remember that ever in her life she had mislaid one of these little feminine appurtenances, which had become, from long use and constant association, a very part of her personality.

Louisa tied a green apron round her waist, and got out a flat straw hat with a green ribbon. Then she went into the garden with a little blue crockery bowl, to pick some currants for her tea. After the currants were picked she sat on the back door-step and stemmed them, collecting the stems carefully in her apron, and afterwards throwing them into the hen-coop. She looked sharply at the grass beside the step to see if any had fallen there.

Louisa was slow and still in her movements; it took her a long time to prepare her tea; but when ready it was set forth, with as much grace as if she had been a veritable guest to her own self. The little square table stood exactly in the centre of the kitchen, and was covered with a starched linen cloth whose border pattern of flowers glistened. Louisa had a damask napkin on her tea-tray, where were arranged a cut-glass tumbler full of teaspoons, a silver cream-pitcher, a china sugar-bowl, and one pink china cup and saucer. Louisa used china every day—something which none of her neighbors did. They whispered about it among themselves. Their daily tables were laid with common crockery, their sets of best china stayed in the parlor closet, and Louisa Ellis was no richer nor better bred than they. Still she would use the china. She had for her supper a glass dish full of sugared currants, a plate of little cakes, and one of light white biscuits. Also a leaf or two of lettuce, which she cut up daintily. Louisa was very fond of lettuce, which she raised to perfection in her little garden. She ate quite heartily, though in a delicate, pecking way; it seemed almost surprising that any considerable bulk of the food should vanish.

After tea she filled a plate with nicely baked thin corncakes, and carried   5
them out into the back-yard.

"Cæsar!" she called. "Cæsar! Cæsar!"

There was a little rush, and the clank of a chain, and a large yellow-and-white dog appeared at the door of his tiny hut, which was half hidden among the tall grasses and flowers. Louisa patted him and gave him the corn-cakes. Then she returned to the house and washed the tea-things, polishing the china carefully. The twilight had deepened; the chorus of the frogs floated in at the open window wonderfully loud and shrill, and once in a while a long sharp drone from a tree-toad pierced it. Louisa took off her green gingham apron, disclosing a shorter one of pink and white print. She lighted her lamp, and sat down again with her sewing.

In about half an hour Joe Dagget came. She heard his heavy step on the walk, and rose and took off her pink-and-white apron. Under that was still another—white linen with a little cambric edging on the bottom; that was Louisa's company apron. She never wore it without her calico sewing apron over it unless she had a guest. She had barely folded the pink and white one with methodical haste and laid it in a table-drawer when the door opened and Joe Dagget entered.

He seemed to fill up the whole room. A little yellow canary that had been asleep in his green cage at the south window woke up and fluttered wildly, beating his little yellow wings against the wires. He always did so when Joe Dagget came into the room.

"Good-evening," said Louisa. She extended her hand with a kind of solemn cordiality. 10

"Good-evening, Louisa," returned the man, in a loud voice.

She placed a chair for him, and they sat facing each other, with the table between them. He sat bolt-upright, toeing out his heavy feet squarely, glancing with a good-humored uneasiness around the room. She sat gently erect, folding her slender hands in her white-linen lap.

"Been a pleasant day," remarked Dagget.

"Real pleasant," Louisa assented, softly. "Have you been haying?" she asked, after a little while.

"Yes, I've been haying all day, down in the ten-acre lot. Pretty hot work." 15

"It must be."

"Yes, it's pretty hot work in the sun."

"Is your mother well to-day?"

"Yes, mother's pretty well."

"I suppose Lily Dyer's with her now?" 20

Dagget colored. "Yes, she's with her," he answered, slowly.

He was not very young, but there was a boyish look about his large face. Louisa was not quite as old as he, her face was fairer and smoother, but she gave people the impression of being older.

"I suppose she's a good deal of help to your mother," she said, further.

"I guess she is; I don't know how mother'd get along without her," said Dagget, with a sort of embarrassed warmth.

"She looks like a real capable girl. She's pretty-looking too," remarked Louisa. 25

"Yes, she is pretty fair looking."

Presently Dagget began fingering the books on the table. There was a square red autograph album, and a Young Lady's Gift-Book, which had belonged to Louisa's mother. He took them up one after the other and opened them; then laid them down again, the album on the Gift-Book.

Louisa kept eying them with mild uneasiness. Finally she rose and changed the position of the books, putting the album underneath. That was the way they had been arranged in the first place.

Dagget gave an awkward little laugh. "Now what difference did it make which book was on top?" said he.

Louisa looked at him with a deprecating smile. "I always keep them that   30
way," murmured she.

"You do beat everything," said Dagget, trying to laugh again. His large face was flushed.

He remained about an hour longer, then rose to take leave. Going out, he stumbled over a rug, and trying to recover himself, hit Louisa's work-basket on the table, and knocked it on the floor.

He looked at Louisa, then at the rolling spools; he ducked himself awkwardly toward them, but she stopped him. "Never mind," said she; "I'll pick them up after you're gone."

She spoke with a mild stiffness. Either she was a little disturbed, or his nervousness affected her, and made her seem constrained in her effort to reassure him.

When Joe Dagget was outside he drew in the sweet evening air with a   35
sigh, and felt much as an innocent and perfectly well-intentioned bear might after his exit from a china shop.

Louisa, on her part, felt much as the kind-hearted, long-suffering owner of the china shop might have done after the exit of the bear.

She tied on the pink, then the green apron, picked up all the scattered treasures and replaced them in her work-basket, and straightened the rug. Then she set the lamp on the floor, and began sharply examining the carpet. She even rubbed her fingers over it, and looked at them.

"He's tracked in a good deal of dust," she murmured. "I thought he must have."

Louisa got a dust-pan and brush, and swept Joe Dagget's track carefully.

If he could have known it, it would have increased his perplexity and   40
uneasiness, although it would not have disturbed his loyalty in the least. He came twice a week to see Louisa Ellis, and every time, sitting there in her delicately sweet room, he felt as if surrounded by a hedge of lace. He was afraid to stir lest he should put a clumsy foot or hand through the fairy web, and he had always the consciousness that Louisa was watching fearfully lest he should.

Still the lace and Louisa commanded perforce his perfect respect and patience and loyalty. They were to be married in a month, after a singular courtship which had lasted for a matter of fifteen years. For fourteen out of the fifteen years the two had not once seen each other, and they had seldom exchanged letters. Joe had been all those years in Australia, where he had gone to make his fortune, and where he had stayed until he made it. He would have stayed fifty years if it had taken so long, and come home feeble and tottering, or never come home at all, to marry Louisa.

But the fortune had been made in the fourteen years, and he had come home now to marry the woman who had been patiently and unquestioningly waiting for him all that time.

Shortly after they were engaged he had announced to Louisa his determination to strike out into new fields, and secure a competency before they should be married. She had listened and assented with the sweet serenity which never failed her, not even when her lover set forth on that long and uncertain journey. Joe, buoyed up as he was by his sturdy determination, broke down a little at the last, but Louisa kissed him with a mild blush, and said good-by.

"It won't be for long," poor Joe had said, huskily; but it was for fourteen years.

In that length of time much had happened. Louisa's mother and brother   45
had died, and she was all alone in the world. But greatest happening of all—a subtle happening which both were too simple to understand—Louisa's feet had turned into a path, smooth maybe under a calm, serene sky, but so straight and unswerving that it could only meet a check at her grave, and so narrow that there was no room for any one at her side.

Louisa's first emotion when Joe Dagget came home (he had not apprised her of his coming) was consternation, although she would not admit it to herself, and he never dreamed of it. Fifteen years ago she had been in love with him—at least she considered herself to be. Just at that time, gently acquiescing with and falling into the natural drift of girlhood, she had seen marriage ahead as a reasonable feature and a probable desirability of life. She had listened with calm docility to her mother's views upon the subject. Her mother was remarkable for her cool sense and sweet, even temperament. She talked wisely to her daughter when Joe Dagget presented himself, and Louisa accepted him with no hesitation. He was the first lover she had ever had.

She had been faithful to him all these years. She had never dreamed of the possibility of marrying any one else. Her life, especially for the last seven years, had been full of a pleasant peace, she had never felt discontented nor impatient over her lover's absence; still she had always looked forward to his return and their marriage as the inevitable conclusion of things. However, she had fallen into a way of placing it so far in the future that it was almost equal to placing it over the boundaries of another life.

When Joe came she had been expecting him, and expecting to be married for fourteen years, but she was much surprised and taken aback as if she had never thought of it.

Joe's consternation came later. He eyed Louisa with an instant confirmation of his old admiration. She had changed but little. She still kept her

pretty manner and soft grace, and was, he considered, every whit as attractive as ever. As for himself, his stent° was done; he had turned his face away
from fortune-seeking, and the old winds of romance whistled as loud and
sweet as ever through his ears. All the song which he had been wont to hear
in them was Louisa; he had for a long time a loyal belief that he heard it still,
but finally it seemed to him that although the winds sang always that one
song, it had another name. But for Louisa the wind had never more than
murmured; now it had gone down, and everything was still. She listened for
a little while with half-wistful attention; then she turned quietly away and
went to work on her wedding clothes.

Joe had made some extensive and quite magnificent alterations in his   50
house. It was the old homestead; the newly-married couple would live
there, for Joe could not desert his mother, who refused to leave her old
home. So Louisa must leave hers. Every morning, rising and going about
among her neat maidenly possessions, she felt as one looking her last upon
the faces of dear friends. It was true that in a measure she could take them
with her, but, robbed of their old environments, they would appear in such
new guises that they would almost cease to be themselves. Then there were
some peculiar features of her happy solitary life which she would probably
be obliged to relinquish altogether. Sterner tasks than these graceful but half-
needless ones would probably devolve upon her. There would be a large
house to care for; there would be company to entertain; there would be
Joe's rigorous and feeble old mother to wait upon; and it would be contrary
to all thrifty village traditions for her to keep more than one servant. Louisa
had a little still, and she used to occupy herself pleasantly in summer weather
with distilling the sweet and aromatic essences from roses and peppermint
and spearmint. By-and-by her still must be laid away. Her store of essences
was already considerable, and there would be no time for her to distil for the
mere pleasure of it. Then Joe's mother would think it foolishness; she had
already hinted her opinion in the matter. Louisa dearly loved to sew a linen
seam, not always for use, but for the simple, mild pleasure which she took
in it. She would have been loath to confess how more than once she had
ripped a seam for the mere delight of sewing it together again. Sitting at her
window during long sweet afternoons, drawing her needle gently through
the dainty fabric, she was peace itself. But there was a small chance of such
foolish comfort in the future. Joe's mother, domineering, shrewd old matron
that she was even in her old age, and very likely even Joe himself, with his
honest masculine rudeness, would laugh and frown down all these pretty but
senseless old maiden ways.

Louisa had almost the enthusiasm of an artist over the mere order and
cleanliness of her solitary home. She had throbs of genuine triumph at the
sight of the window-panes which she had polished until they shone like
jewels. She gloated gently over her orderly bureau-drawers, with their ex-

---

stent: task

quisitely folded contents redolent with lavender and sweet clover and very purity. Could she be sure of the endurance of even this? She had visions, so startling that she half repudiated them as indelicate, of coarse masculine belongings strewn about in endless litter; of dust and disorder arising necessarily from a coarse masculine presence in the midst of all this delicate harmony.

Among her forebodings of disturbance, not the least was with regard to Cæsar. Cæsar was a veritable hermit of a dog. For the greater part of his life he had dwelt in his secluded hut, shut out from the society of his kind and all innocent canine joys. Never had Cæsar since his early youth watched at a woodchuck's hole; never had he known the delights of a stray bone at a neighbor's kitchen door. And it was all on account of a sin committed when hardly out of his puppyhood. No one knew the possible depth of remorse of which this mild-visaged, altogether innocent-looking old dog might be capable; but whether or not he had encountered remorse, he had encountered a full measure of righteous retribution. Old Cæsar seldom lifted up his voice in a growl or a bark; he was fat and sleepy; there were yellow rings which looked like spectacles around his dim old eyes; but there was a neighbor who bore on his hand the imprint of several of Cæsar's sharp white youthful teeth, and for that he had lived at the end of a chain, all alone in a little hut, for fourteen years. The neighbor, who was choleric and smarting with the pain of his wound, had demanded either Cæsar's death or complete ostracism. So Louisa's brother, to whom the dog had belonged, had built him his little kennel and tied him up. It was now fourteen years since, in a flood of youthful spirits, he had inflicted that memorable bite, and with the exception of short excursions, always at the end of the chain, under the strict guardianship of his master or Louisa, the old dog had remained a close prisoner. It is doubtful if, with his limited ambition, he took much pride in the fact, but it is certain that he was possessed of considerable cheap fame. He was regarded by all the children in the village and by many adults as a very monster of ferocity. St. George's dragon could hardly have surpassed in evil repute Louisa Ellis's old yellow dog. Mothers charged their children with solemn emphasis not to go too near to him, and the children listened and believed greedily, with a fascinated appetite for terror, and ran by Louisa's house stealthily, with many sidelong and backward glances at the terrible dog. If perchance he sounded a hoarse bark, there was a panic. Wayfarers chancing into Louisa's yard eyed him with respect, and inquired if the chain were stout. Cæsar at large might have seemed a very ordinary dog, and excited no comment whatever; chained, his reputation overshadowed him, so that he lost his own proper outlines and looked darkly vague and enormous. Joe Dagget, however, with his good-humored sense and shrewdness, saw him as he was. He strode valiantly up to him and patted him on the head, in spite of Louisa's soft clamor of warning, and even attempted to set him loose. Louisa grew so alarmed that he desisted, but kept announcing his opinion in the matter quite forcibly at intervals. "There ain't a better-natured dog in town," he would say, "and it's down-right cruel to keep him tied up there. Some day I'm going to take him out."

Louisa had very little hope that he would not, one of these days, when their interests and possessions should be more completely fused in one. She pictured to herself Cæsar on the rampage through the quiet and unguarded village. She saw innocent children bleeding in his path. She was herself very fond of the old dog, because he had belonged to her dead brother and he was always very gentle with her; still she had great faith in his ferocity. She always warned people not to go too near him. She fed him on ascetic fare of corn-mush and cakes, and never fired his dangerous temper with heating and sanguinary diet of flesh and bones. Louisa looked at the old dog munching his simple fare, and thought of her approaching marriage and trembled. Still no anticipation of disorder and confusion in lieu of sweet peace and harmony, no forebodings of Cæsar on the rampage, no wild fluttering of her little yellow canary, were sufficient to turn her a hair's-breadth. Joe Dagget had been fond of her and working for her all these years. It was not for her, whatever came to pass, to prove untrue and break his heart. She put the exquisite little stitches into her wedding-garments, and the time went on until it was only a week before her wedding-day. It was a Tuesday evening, and the wedding was to be a week from Wednesday.

There was a full moon that night. About nine o'clock Louisa strolled down the road a little way. There were harvest-fields on either hand, bordered by low stone walls. Luxuriant clumps of bushes grew beside the wall, and trees—wild cherry and old apple-trees—at intervals. Presently Louisa sat down on the wall and looked about her with mildly sorrowful reflectiveness. Tall shrubs of blueberry and meadow-sweet, all woven together and tangled with blackberry vines and horsebriers, shut her in on either side. She had a little clear space between them. Opposite her, on the other side of the road, was a spreading tree; the moon shone between its boughs, and the leaves twinkled like silver. The road was bespread with a beautiful shifting dapple of silver and shadow; the air was full of a mysterious sweetness. "I wonder if it's wild grapes?" murmured Louisa. She sat there some time. She was just thinking of rising, when she heard footsteps and low voices, and remained quiet. It was a lonely place, and she felt a little timid. She thought she would keep still in the shadow and let the persons, whoever they might be, pass her.

But just before they reached her the voices ceased, and the footsteps. 55 She understood that their owners had also found seats upon the stone wall. She was wondering if she could not steal away unobserved, when the voice broke the stillness. It was Joe Dagget's. She sat still and listened.

The voice was announced by a loud sigh, which was familiar as itself. "Well," said Dagget, "you've made up your mind, then, I suppose?"

"Yes," returned another voice; "I'm going day after to-morrow."

"That's Lily Dyer," thought Louisa to herself. The voice embodied itself in her mind. She saw a girl tall and full-figured, with a firm, fair face, looking fairer and firmer in the moonlight, her strong yellow hair braided in a close knot. A girl full of calm rustic strength and bloom, with a masterful way which might have beseemed a princess. Lily Dyer was a favorite with the village folk; she had just the qualities to arouse the admiration. She was good and handsome and smart. Louisa had often heard her praises sounded.

"Well," said Joe Dagget, "I ain't got a word to say."

"I don't know what you could say," returned Lily Dyer.

"Not a word to say," repeated Joe, drawing out the words heavily. Then there was a silence. "I ain't sorry," he began at last, "that that happened yesterday—that we kind of let on how we felt to each other. I guess it's just as well we knew. Of course I can't do anything any different. I'm going right on an' get married next week. I ain't going back on a woman that's waited for me fourteen years, an' break her heart."

"If you should jilt her to-morrow, I wouldn't have you," spoke up the girl, with sudden vehemence.

"Well, I ain't going to give you the chance," said he; "but I don't believe you would, either."

"You'd see I wouldn't. Honor's honor, an' right's right. An' I'd never think anything of any man that went against 'em for me or any other girl; you'd find that out, Joe Dagget."

"Well, you'll find out fast enough that I ain't going against 'em for you or any other girl," returned he. Their voices sounded almost as if they were angry with each other. Louisa was listening eagerly.

"I'm sorry you feel as if you must go away," said Joe, "but I don't know but it's best."

"Of course it's best. I hope you and I have got common-sense."

"Well, I suppose you're right." Suddenly Joe's voice got an undertone of tenderness. "Say, Lily," said he, "I'll get along well enough myself, but I can't bear to think—You don't suppose you're going to fret much over it?"

"I guess you'll find out I sha'n't fret much over a married man."

"Well, I hope you won't—I hope you won't, Lily. God knows I do. And—I hope—one of these days—you'll—come across somebody else—"

"I don't see any reason why I shouldn't." Suddenly her tone changed. She spoke in a sweet, clear voice, so loud that she could have been heard across the street. "No, Joe Dagget," said she, "I'll never marry any other man as long as I live. I've got good sense, an' I ain't going to break my heart nor make a fool of myself; but I'm never going to be married, you can be sure of that. I ain't that sort of a girl to feel this way twice."

Louisa heard an exclamation and a soft commotion behind the bushes; then Lily spoke again—the voice sounded as if she had risen. "This must be put a stop to," said she. "We've stayed here long enough. I'm going home."

Louisa sat there in a daze, listening to their retreating steps. After a while she got up and slunk softly home herself. The next day she did her house-work methodically; that was as much a matter of course as breathing; but she did not sew on her wedding-clothes. She sat at her window and medi-tated. In the evening Joe came. Louisa Ellis had never known that she had any diplomacy in her, but when she came to look for it that night she found it, although meek of its kind, among her little feminine weapons. Even now she could hardly believe that she had heard aright, and that she would not do Joe a terrible injury should she break her troth-plight.° She wanted to sound him without betraying too soon her own inclinations in the matter. She did it successfully, and they finally came to an understanding; but it was a difficult thing, for he was as afraid of betraying himself as she.

She never mentioned Lily Dyer. She simply said that while she had no cause of complaint against him, she had lived so long in one way that she shrank from making a change.

"Well, I never shrank, Louisa," said Dagget. "I'm going to be honest   75 enough to say that I think maybe it's better this way; but if you'd wanted to keep on, I'd have stuck to you till my dying day. I hope you know that."

"Yes, I do," said she.

That night she and Joe parted more tenderly than they had done for a long time. Standing in the door, holding each other's hands, a last great wave of regretful memory swept over them.

"Well, this ain't the way we've thought it was all going to end, is it, Louisa?" said Joe.

She shook her head. There was a little quiver on her placid face.

"You let me know if there's ever anything I can do for you," said he. "I ain't ever going to forget you, Louisa." Then he kissed her, and went down the path.

Louisa, all alone by herself that night, wept a little, she hardly knew why; but the next morning, on waking, she felt like a queen who, after fearing lest her domain be wrested away from her, sees it firmly insured in her possession.

Now the tall weeds and grasses might cluster around Cæsar's little hermit hut, the snow might fall on its roof year in and year out, but he never would go on a rampage through the unguarded village. Now the little canary might turn itself into a peaceful yellow ball night after night, and have no need to wake and flutter with wild terror against its bars. Louisa could sew linen seams, and distil roses, and dust and polish and fold away in lavender, as long as she listed. That afternoon she sat with her needle-work at the window, and felt fairly steeped in peace. Lily Dyer, tall and erect and blooming, went past; but she felt no qualm. If Louisa Ellis had sold her birthright she did not know it, the taste of the pottage° was so delicious, and had been her sole satisfaction for so long. Serenity and placid narrowness had become to her as the birthright itself. She gazed ahead through a long reach of future days strung together like pearls in a rosary, every one like the others, and all smooth and flawless and innocent, and her heart went up in thankfulness. Outside was the fervid summer afternoon; the air was filled with the sounds

---

troth-plight: pledge to marry
pottage: Thick soup. Esau sold his birthright to Jacob for a bowl of pottage (Genesis 25: 29–34).

of the busy harvest of men and birds and bees; there were halloos, metallic clatterings, sweet calls, and long hummings. Louisa sat, prayerfully numbering her days, like an uncloistered nun.

POEM FOR HALF-WHITE COLLEGE STUDENTS

Imamu Amiri Baraka

Who are you, listening to me, who are you
listening to yourself? Are you white or
black, or does that have anything to do
with it? Can you pop your fingers to no
music, except those wild monkies go on   5
in your head, can you jerk, to no melody,
except finger poppers get it together
when you turn from starchecking to checking
yourself? How do you sound, your words, are they
yours? The ghost you see in the mirror, is it really   10
you, can you swear you are not an imitation greyboy,
can you look right next to you in that chair, and swear,
that the sister you have your hand on is not really
so full of Elizabeth Taylor, Richard Burton is
coming out of her ears. You may even have to be Richard   15
with a white shirt and face, and four million negroes
think you cute, you may have to be Elizabeth Taylor, old lady,
if you want to sit up in your crazy spot dreaming about dresses,
and the sway of certain porters' hips. Check yourself, learn who it is
speaking, when you make some ultrasophisticated point, check yourself   20
when you find yourself gesturing like Steve McQueen, check it out, ask
in your black heart who it is you are, and is that image black or white,

you might be surprised right out the window, whistling dixie on the way

ARS POETICA

Archibald MacLeish

A poem should be palpable and mute
As a globed fruit,

Dumb
As old medallions to the thumb,

Silent as the sleeve-worn stone   5
Of casement ledges where the moss has grown—

A poem should be wordless
As the flight of birds.

A poem should be motionless in time
As the moon climbs,   10

Leaving, as the moon releases
Twig by twig the night-entangled trees,

Leaving, as the moon behind the winter leaves,
Memory by memory the mind—

A poem should be motionless in time   15
As the moon climbs.

A poem should be equal to:
Not true.

For all the history of grief
An empty doorway and a maple leaf.   20

For love
The leaning grasses and two lights above the sea—

A poem should not mean
But be.

CONSTANTLY RISKING ABSURDITY

Lawrence Ferlinghetti

Constantly risking absurdity
                and death
        whenever he performs
                above the heads
                      of his audience   5
the poet like an acrobat
          climbs on rime
             to a high wire of his own making
and balancing on eyebeams
            above a sea of faces   10
      paces his way
          to the other side of day
    performing entrechats
          and sleight-of-foot tricks
and other high theatrics   15
         and all without mistaking
         any thing
         for what it may not be

   For he's the super realist
             who must perforce perceive   20
      taut truth
         before the taking of each stance or step
  in his supposed advance
        toward that still higher perch
                      25
where Beauty stands and waits
          with gravity
            to start her death-defying leap
And he
      a little charleychaplin man
          who may or may not catch   30
    her fair eternal form
        spreadeagled in the empty air
   of existence

MUCH MADNESS IS DIVINEST SENSE

Emily Dickinson

Much Madness is divinest Sense—
To a discerning Eye—
Much Sense—the starkest Madness—
'Tis the Majority
In this, as All, prevail—   5
Assent—and you are sane—
Demur—you're straightway dangerous—
And handled with a Chain—

ODE ON A GRECIAN URN

John Keats

1

Thou still unravished bride of quietness,
    Thou foster-child of silence and slow time,
Sylvan historian, who canst thus express
    A flowery tale more sweetly than our rhyme:
What leaf-fringed legend haunts about thy shape   5
    Of deities or mortals, or of both,
        In Tempe° or the dales of Arcady?°
    What men or gods are these? what maidens loth?
What mad pursuit? What struggle to escape?
        What pipes and timbrels? What wild ecstasy?   10

2

Heard melodies are sweet, but those unheard
    Are sweeter; therefore, ye soft pipes, play on;
Not to the sensual ear, but, more endeared,
    Pipe to the spirit ditties of no tone:

---

7. *Tempe:* a beautiful valley in eastern Greece
7. *Arcady:* Arcadia, a place of rustic simplicity

Fair youth, beneath the trees, thou canst not leave   *15*
   Thy song, nor ever can those trees be bare;
     Bold Lover, never, never canst thou kiss,
Though winning near the goal—yet, do not grieve;
   She cannot fade, though thou hast not thy bliss,
     For ever wilt thou love, and she be fair!   *20*

3

Ah, happy, happy boughs! that cannot shed
   Your leaves, nor ever bid the Spring adieu;
And, happy melodist, unwearièd,
   For ever piping songs for ever new;
More happy love! more happy, happy love!   *25*
   For ever warm and still to be enjoyed,
     For ever panting, and for ever young;
All breathing human passion far above,
   That leaves a heart high-sorrowful and cloyed,
     A burning forehead, and a parching tongue.   *30*

4

Who are these coming to the sacrifice?
   To what green altar, O mysterious priest,
Lead'st thou that heifer lowing at the skies,
   And all her silken flanks with garlands drest?
What little town by river or sea shore,   *35*
   Or mountain-built with peaceful citadel,
     Is emptied of this folk, this pious morn?
And, little town, thy streets for evermore
   Will silent be; and not a soul to tell
     Why thou art desolate, can e'er return.   *40*

5

O Attic shape! Fair attitude! with brede
   Of marble men and maidens overwrought,
With forest branches and the trodden weed;
   Thou, silent form, dost tease us out of thought
As doth eternity: Cold Pastoral!   *45*
   When old age shall this generation waste,
     Thou shalt remain, in midst of other woe
Than ours, a friend to man, to whom thou say'st,
   "Beauty is truth, truth beauty—that is all
     Ye know on earth, and all ye need to know."   *50*

PART 5

Making a Logical Point

17

Argument and Persuasion

"Well, you may think you're right, but as far as I'm concerned, you couldn't possibly know what you're talking about."

"I do too know what I'm talking about, and if you had an ounce of sense, you'd see that."

"No, you're wrong."

"I'm right!"

"You're wrong!"

"Right!"

"Wrong!!"

"Right!!!"

When most people hear the word *argument,* they usually think of an exchange something like the preceding one: a battle of words in which each party is equally stubborn and neither listens to the other nor is prepared to give the other's point of view a hearing. However, in a formal sense, *argument* has a far different meaning: writing or speaking in a way that makes a logical case for your ideas.

Like everyone else, you have opinions about the events that create your day-to-day experience—events you see on the news or that you read about in newspapers, magazines, or your textbooks or that you hear about. Furthermore, you probably form opinions about novels, stories, poems, and plays that you read or about movies, plays, or TV shows that you see. In addition, you constantly encounter other people's opinions as you interact with them. Also, all of the various media usually reflect another person's opinion. Often you find yourself taking a position in response to another's version of an event because you experienced the same event, responded to it in a different way, and formed your own opinion about it.

YOU ALREADY HAVE SOME KNOWLEDGE OF ARGUMENT

When you express your opinion to another, you might find yourself anticipating or encountering that other person's disagreement or doubt and searching your experiences—your observations, the reading you've done, what you have heard from another person whom you trust—for ways of supporting your position. You may try to show how your idea makes sense by reporting the statements of others who have reached the same conclusions as you have or by pointing to an event you've experienced or read about that confirms your judgment. Argument, then, is a way of presenting your ideas in a form that appeals to your audience's reason, to their ability to think clearly and systematically.

Generally, argument is the process of creating a relationship between your opinion and your experience in order to support your position. Similarly, when you require another person to construct the same relationship to support his or her opinion, you use your idea of effective argument to test that person's conclusions.

In this chapter, you will meet ways of thinking consciously about your arguments as well as others' arguments. By learning to be aware of some of the elements of argument, you'll find you will become a better critic of your own—as well as of others'—opinions and their support. Also, you will be less easily fooled by such things as advertisements, political speeches, or other direct or hidden sources of opinion.

However, if pure argument were enough to convince everybody of the validity of a person's position, then written works and speeches would be much shorter than they are. As you already know, whenever you present your ideas in writing, you have an audience. Some ideas may be unpopular or distasteful to your audience; nevertheless, you believe that they are both reasonable and important. If you did not, why would you be wasting your time dealing with them? A substantial part of your audience is most likely composed of persons who may not agree with you, or who may hold values that could cause them to reject your ideas no matter how well argued they may be, or who are simply unfamiliar with your subject. As you can see, all but the most self-evident statement, such as "gravity causes objects to fall," creates the possibility of disagreement or even an emotional rejection of the assertion. If everyone in your audience agreed with you and knew what you were talking about, why would you need to make your case?

Because your audience is made up of persons who respond intellectually *and* emotionally to their worlds, you can make your argument more effective by taking into account the emotional as well as the intellectual nature of those in your audience. You can do this by using persuasion effectively.

Persuasion uses many of the techniques you've already worked with. Imagery, striking examples, metaphor and simile, connotation, the rhythm and length of your sentences, all of these are effective devices in moving your audience toward a response that supports your dominant idea. You can use persuasion as a resource to strengthen your argument by responding to what you expect to be your audience's reaction to your ideas. When you persuade, you recognize and write to your anticipation of your audience's emotions and assumptions. Most often you'll find yourself combining argument and persuasion in your argumentative writing.

This combination is a difficult one to create responsibly. Often, appealing to people's emotions as directly as possible seems simpler. A purely emotional appeal appears to take less effort, and often it's very effective. If persuasion alone were not effective, commercials and printed advertisements would be very different. However, if you think about what using persuasion alone implies about you and your attitude toward your audience and your own ideas, you might hesitate before choosing to use it exclusively. If you believe that you can influence your audience by appealing only to their emotions, then you are not crediting them with the ability to think effectively. Equally damaging, at some level you must be assuming that your argument does not have enough intellectual strength to carry its own weight. Finally, your audience will most likely find you out, feel manipulated, and reject or discount your ideas.

All in all, the best balance of argumentation and persuasion generally comes from devising the strongest, most responsible argument you can, then using persuasion to give your argument emotional heft by anticipating your audience's interests and responses to your ideas.

ARGUMENT: ARRANGING YOUR FACTS

Argument is the process by which you arrange your observations, your experiences, and information you have gotten from other sources into a series of larger statements that lead your reader to your conclusion. Argument develops its conclusions through two interacting ways of arranging facts, experiences, observations, and other people's findings: *inductive reasoning* and *deductive reasoning*. As you learn about these ways of thinking, remember that you are really learning nothing new. You must be reasonably good at these ways of thinking to function in the world.

Briefly, when you reason *inductively,* you move from specific observations—evidence—to larger ideas based upon those observations: your conclusion. An inductive conclusion is a statement that is more general than your observations but which is the result of those observations. For example, when you drive toward an intersection and see that the light is green, you continue through that intersection. You do so because repeated experiences have shown that chances are very good another driver won't enter the intersection from a cross street. You put a degree of faith in the generalization that where there is a green light, your passage won't be impeded by vehicles entering the intersection at right angles to your path.

When you reason *deductively,* you begin with a generalization: your major premise. A major premise is a more-or-less general statement based on inductive reasoning. In deductive reasoning you apply your major premise to a specific case: your minor premise. The minor premise is a smaller generalization also based on inductive reasoning, and you let these two statements lead you to your conclusion.

Here is an example of the way these two patterns of thinking work in everyday life. Usually, in order to sit in a chair, you must turn your back on it. You probably don't worry about the chair sneaking away from you while your back is turned. You don't fret about this because all your experience has shown you that chairs are inanimate objects; they don't move by themselves. That's a generalization based on experience: Chairs don't move by themselves. When you walk into a classroom, you sit down without worrying whether the chair is going to be there when you finish sitting down. You seat yourself with confidence because you have reasoned deductively about the classroom chair. You know that chairs don't move on their own; you know that the object you are about to turn your back on is a chair; therefore, you know it's safe to sit without worrying about whether the chair will be there. You've reasoned deductively about the chair by taking what you know generally about the ability of chairs to move by themselves and applying it to that particular chair. The real shock to a person subjected to the practical joke of someone's moving the chair as the person is about to sit does not happen when the victim hits the floor. It occurs when the victim passes through the space where he or she thought the chair was going to be. At that moment, the person's logical assumptions regarding the nature of chairs and their ability to move independently are destroyed.

INDUCTIVE REASONING

As you've seen, inductive reasoning moves from the specific case to the general conclusion—for example, sitting down again and again and learning that chairs don't move on their own. Inductive arguments always end with a general statement. To arrive at an effective generalization, you must have enough specific observations to support your conclusion, and those observations must be clearly linked to the conclusion. Because different generalizations may be more controversial or more complicated than others, it is impossible to say exactly how many specific examples you might need to effectively support a particular conclusion. In some cases, one instance might be enough. A child who grabs the flame at the end of a match because it looks pretty probably won't try that experiment again. In other cases, a large number of specific instances might be necessary to support a conclusion. Insurance companies set their rates based on many specific observations about certain groups of people. That's why you may find yourself paying a lot of money for your automobile insurance although you have had no accidents. If you are under twenty-five and male, your rates are the highest of all groups of insured individuals because a greater percentage of male drivers under twenty-five have accidents than do drivers in any other group.

When you use inductive reasoning, you can never be entirely certain of your conclusions no matter how many observations you collect. At a certain point you have to make what people who study logic call an "inductive leap." That leap is based on the fact that no matter how many times the same event occurs in the same way, it could be different the next time. (Next time, someone *could* pull that chair out from under you. Of course, the sun has risen every day you've been alive. But are you *absolutely certain* that it will rise tomorrow?) The best you can do is gather enough evidence so that you can arrive at relative certainty about your conclusion.

Sources of Evidence: Fact and Opinion

FACTS A *fact* is something that you know to have existed or happened or that you can verify by observing or measuring carefully. However, your observation or measurement of an event does not make that event a fact until it is tested further. This is so because one person can claim *any* event he or she believes has occurred to be a fact, whether or not that claim is true. The test of an accurate observation or measurement lies in another person's observing or measuring the same event and arriving at the same findings as those the first observer recorded.

Sometimes you cannot be present at an event because it is too distant from you or because it happened before you were around to observe it. If you limited yourself only to events you could observe and measure, most of the fields of study you're familiar with and upon which all of us have built modern thought would not exist. Sometimes you have to rely on another person's observations to help you along on your journey to your conclusions.

When you work with another person's observations, you have to establish that person's reliability before you decide to use his or her observations in your argument. In order to decide for yourself whether you can accept your source's observations, you should ask four questions about that person:

- *Was the observer physically present to record the event or its measurement?* This may seem like an obvious question, but people will sometimes repeat what they have heard from another person without having been present at the event themselves.

- *Was the observer capable of observing the event he or she reported to another?* It is not enough to be physically present at an event. An individual might report what *might have been seen* at an event—without actually seeing it—on the basis of what he or she *only heard* while there.

- *Was the observer capable of understanding the event he or she was present at and which he or she observed?* Would you believe the report of a five-year-old child with regard to a physics lecture even if that child had sat through the whole lecture?

- *Is the observer honest?* This is a much more difficult question to answer. It is best to depend on the behavior of the individual in the past. If the person has generally shown him- or herself to be honest before and has no special interest in the matter under discussion or reason to be prejudiced, you can accept his or her current observation with some degree of confidence.

These standards also apply to you. When you present a case to your reader that is based on your observations, you should assume that your reader will ask these same questions of you. Therefore, you should be sure to let your reader know that you were able to observe and could understand what you observed. If you are dealing with a controversial issue, it's also important to establish your integrity in your reader's mind.

OPINION As you work your way toward a conclusion, you may find that you have to rely on another person's opinion as evidence for your reasoning. Commercials often try to sway you toward a conclusion through another's opinion. Ballplayers or famous actors might be hired to recommend a product. The thought behind this approach is that if an individual is famous and respected, his or her opinion will sway you toward considering the product. If you think about such "testimonials," though, you might find yourself doubting the source. An individual's opinion carries more weight when he or she is an expert in the field. Unless your source knows what he or she is talking about, there is no reason to accept that source's opinion on the matter.

Assembling Your Evidence

Once you have chosen the evidence to support your conclusion, there are further points that you should consider to avoid the sorts of problems that will lead your audience to doubt your conclusion and the quality of your thinking.

- *Your evidence must be adequate.* Although, as you have learned, it is difficult to establish when you have enough evidence, it is often easy to tell when there isn't enough evidence. Not having enough evidence—enough examples to support your conclusion—leads to *overgeneralization.* Would you trust most conclusions based on a single observation?

- *Your evidence must be relevant to your conclusion.* Sometimes what appears to be evidence really addresses another issue that has nothing to do with the idea you are trying to support. For example, an editorial in your school newspaper argues in favor of supporting the continuation of football at your school because football is good for the players' characters. As evidence the editorial uses the fact that the sport generates significant amounts of money. Would you accept this argument, or do you think that the evidence has little to do with the conclusion?

- *Your evidence must be typical.* The facts or opinions you use to support your case must be typical of the situation you refer to. They must not be affected by special conditions. For example, if you judge that winter is coming because a tree standing in front of the exhaust of a refrigerating unit has dropped its leaves, you have probably not chosen a typical case.

- *Your evidence must be up-to-date.* A conclusion about an event that has just happened or is still occurring will be questionable if your evidence is drawn from a twenty-year-old observation or opinion.

- *Your evidence must be drawn from an unprejudiced source.* If your evidence comes from a special interest group or a person with a special case to plead, you must examine it very carefully to make certain it is not slanted in some way. You would not necessarily believe a child is brilliant just because his or her parent says so. When you suspect some of your evidence might come from a prejudiced source, you must remember to check it very carefully against other evidence.

- *Your evidence should not confuse sequence with cause and effect.* The name for this problem is *post hoc ergo propter hoc*—Latin for "after this, therefore because of this." It is easy to believe that sequence is the same as causality. Many superstitions are based on this type of reasoning. However, some intelligent-sounding arguments are really *post hoc* arguments. For example, people argue that the rate of murders declines after institution of the death penalty. However, this sequence of events does not demonstrate that one event *caused* the next one. The person making this argument would have to show the connection between the two. Remember the discussion of the cause-and-effect mode of organization in Chapter 15. It is just as important to show that there is a causal link between two events as it is to show that those two events really occurred.

- *Your conclusion must have a logical connection to your evidence.* If it does not, you have committed a fallacy called *non sequitur*—Latin for "it does not follow." This problem is like *post hoc ergo propter hoc* in that it confuses a cause-and-effect relationship with simple sequence. However, in this case, the conclusion simply has no logical connection with the evidence. If you were to assert that your campus needs more student parking spaces because more students drive their cars to school than before, your conclusion would not follow from your support. It ignores the possibilities of encouraging students to use public transportation, to carpool, or to bicycle.

- *If you are taking a position in conflict with another person's conclusion, question the other person's evidence, not his or her character.* If you attack the person instead of the argument, you have created an *ad hominem* (Latin for "to the person") argument. It is not an effective argument to state that your audience should not believe what Ms. Jones has to say about the upcoming election because she has led an immoral life. The facts of her life may have nothing to do with her intelligence or the depth and breadth of her knowledge of the issues.

• *When you present a comparison to support your conclusion, do not mistakenly assume that because two objects or events share some characteristics they are alike in every way.* Such an assumption is called a *false analogy*. People sometimes compare a philosophy or a political position to a disease eating away at the vitals of their country. They go on to say that when a person is ill, we cut out the disease or its source to cure the person. Therefore, we should ban or eliminate the type of thinking that causes the country's illness. For obvious reasons, such an argument will not work.

⇜ *Exercise*

Either on your own or with a group, examine each of the following statements and evaluate them in terms of how adequate they are as inductive statements. If you find a problem with the statement, identify it and examine ways of making the statement more effective as reasoning. In some cases, the statement may be beyond saving.

1. Your honor, before my client was arrested, he overheard the man who actually committed the crime of which my client has been accused. He says that he would recognize the man's voice again because of his strong southern accent. As soon as the Swedish-to-English translator arrives, I'll put my client on the stand.

2. Autumn is here. I took a walk through the woods yesterday, and I saw three trees whose leaves were changing color.

3. Professor Jones' exam was unfair. I know this because I spoke to sixteen out of the thirty students in his class. They all said so. They should know. None of them got higher than a D.

4. "Use Flower Breath mouthwash. I use it and my breath is fresh as spring all day," says Debby LaFox, the famous movie actor.

5. Every one of the thirty times I introduced alcohol into the distilled drinking water of mice they began to act erratically. However, when they drank distilled water alone, no behavioral changes occurred. I conclude from this set of circumstances that alcohol when ingested with distilled water causes erratic behavior in mice.

6. Nobody should take Dr. Kleinholtz's class. He's a terrible teacher because he wears dirty suits, smokes foul-smelling cigars, and speaks with a German accent.

7. We entered our last three wars just after we elected a Democrat as president. I'm not going to vote for the Democratic Party's candidate this year. The Democrats are the war party.

8. Since going to college is as much fun as having my teeth pulled, I think I'll go through the whole experience anaesthetized.

9. Arielle tripped and broke her leg as she was trying to avoid a black cat that had just run in front of her. It's true! If a black cat crosses your path, you'll have bad luck.

10. Nobody should accept Senator Ellison's word on anything. He is a

man who has been divorced three times, he runs around with
women half his age, and furthermore, he drinks.

 Working with the Readings

Read the three selections that follow: two poems and a document.
Alone or with your groups, answer the questions that follow each one.

OZYMANDIAS

Percy Bysshe Shelley

> I met a traveler from an antique land
> Who said: Two vast and trunkless legs of stone
> Stand in the desert . . . Near them, on the sand,
> Half sunk, a shattered visage lies, whose frown,
> And wrinkled lip, and sneer of cold command,   5
> Tell that its sculptor well those passions read
> Which yet survive, stamped on these lifeless things,
> The hand that mocked them and the heart that fed:
> And on the pedestal these words appear:
> "My name is Ozymandias, king of kings: 10
> Look on my works, ye Mighty, and despair!"
> Nothing beside remains. Round the decay
> Of that colossal wreck, boundless and bare
> The lone and level sands stretch far away.

---

1. What are the specific facts that the traveler gives the poet in this poem?

2. If you take all the facts that the traveler has chosen to relate to the poet, what conclusion can you reach about Ozymandias?

3. If you take your conclusions regarding Ozymandias and place them next to the physical observation that the traveler makes, what conclusion can you draw from the poem as a whole?

4. Because the poet invites you to move from specific observations to a conclusion, would you call this poem an inductive argument? Do the observations support the conclusion?

3. If you compare what Ozymandias has to say about himself through the statue and the inscription with what the traveler has found, what conclusion would you draw? Does this comparison lead you toward a sense of irony? Is the irony part of the argument itself?

IN A PROMINENT BAR IN SECAUCUS ONE DAY

X. J. Kennedy

To the tune of "The Old Orange Flute"
or the tune of "Sweet Betsy from Pike"

In a prominent bar in Secaucus° one day
Rose a lady in skunk with a topheavy sway,
Raised a knobby red finger—all turned from their beer—
While with eyes bright as snowcrust she sang high and clear:

"Now who of you'd think from an eyeload of me   5
That I once was a lady as proud as can be?
Oh I'd never sit down by a tumbledown drunk
If it wasn't, my dears, for the high cost of junk.

"All the gents used to swear that the white of my calf
Beat the down of a swan by a length and a half.   10
In a kerchief of linen I caught to my nose
Ah, there never fell snot, but a little gold rose.

"I had seven gold teeth and a toothpick of gold,
My Virginia cheroot° was a leaf of it rolled
And I'd light it each time with a thousand in cash—   15
Why the bums used to fight if I flicked them an ash.

"Once the toast of the Biltmore, the belle of the Taft,
I would drink bottle beer at the Drake, never draft,
And dine at the Astor° on Salisbury steak
With a clean tablecloth for each bite I did take.   20

"In a car like the Roxy° I'd roll to the track,
A steel-guitar trio, a bar in the back,
And the wheels made no noise, they turned over so fast,
Still it took you ten minutes to see me go past.

---

1. *Secaucus:* a decaying industrial town in western New Jersey
14. *cheroot:* a type of cigar
19. *Biltmore . . . Astor:* The Biltmore, Taft, Drake, and Astor were expensive hotels in New York City.
21. *Roxy:* a luxurious New York theater

"When the horses bowed down to me that I might choose,   *25*
I bet on them all, for I hated to lose.
Now I'm saddled each night for my butter and eggs
And the broken threads race down the backs of my legs.

"Let you hold in mind, girls, that your beauty must pass
Like a lovely white clover that rusts with the grass.   *30*
Keep your bottoms off barstools and marry you young
Or be left—an old barrel with many a bung.°

"For when time takes you out for a spin in his car
You'll be hard-pressed to stop him from going too far
And be left by the roadside, for all your good deeds,   *35*
Two toadstools for tits and a face full of weeds."

All the house raised a cheer, but the man at the bar
Made a phonecall and up pulled a red patrol car
And she blew us a kiss as they copped her away
From that prominent bar in Secaucus, N.J.   *40*

---

1. What do you think is Kennedy's dominant idea in this poem?

2. Kennedy's speaker reaches a conclusion, almost a moral, by the end of her speech. How does she lead herself and her audience to her conclusion? What would you say is her dominant organizational strategy? What others do you see?

3. The poem's story doesn't conclude with the lady's story. There is one more stanza. How do the actions of the bartender, the bar's patrons, and the police follow from everything that has preceded them? How does Kennedy's dominant idea, as you see it, result from everything he has told you?

4. Does this poem seem only comic to you, or do you have other responses to it by the end? How does your experience in combination with the poem create your response(s)?

---

32. *bung:* a hole for filling or tapping a barrel

THE DECLARATION OF INDEPENDENCE AS ADOPTED BY CONGRESS

Thomas Jefferson

In Congress, July 4, 1776.
THE UNANIMOUS DECLARATION OF THE
THIRTEEN UNITED STATES OF AMERICA,

When in the Course of human events, it becomes necessary for one people to dissolve the political bands which have connected them with another, and to assume among the powers of the earth, the separate and equal station to which the Laws of Nature and of Nature's God entitle them, a decent respect to the opinions of mankind requires that they should declare the causes which impel them to the separation. We hold these truths to be self-evident, that all men are created equal, that they are endowed by their Creator with certain unalienable Rights, that among these are Life, Liberty and the pursuit of Happiness. That to secure these rights, Governments are instituted among Men, deriving their just powers from the consent of the governed, That whenever any Form of Government becomes destructive of these ends, it is the Right of the People to alter or to abolish it, and to institute new Government, laying its foundation on such principles and organizing its powers in such form, as to them shall seem most likely to effect their Safety and Happiness. Prudence, indeed, will dictate that Governments long established should not be changed for light and transient causes; and accordingly all experience hath shewn, that mankind are more disposed to suffer, while evils are sufferable, than to right themselves by abolishing the forms to which they are accustomed. But when a long train of abuses and usurpations, pursuing invariably the same Object evinces a design to reduce them under absolute Despotism, it is their right, it is their duty, to throw off such Government, and to provide New Guards for their future security. Such has been the patient sufferance of these Colonies; and such is now the necessity which constrains them to alter their former Systems of Government. The history of the present King of Great Britain° is a history of repeated injuries and usurpations, all having in direct object the establishment of an absolute Tyranny over these States. To prove this, let Facts be submitted to a candid world. He has refused his Assent to Laws, the most wholesome and necessary for the public good. He has forbidden his Governors to pass Laws of immediate and pressing importance, unless suspended in their operation till his Assent should be obtained; and when so

---

King of Great Britain: George III

suspended, he has utterly neglected to attend to them. He has refused to pass other Laws for the accommodation of large districts of people, unless these people would relinquish the right of Representation in the Legislature, a right inestimable to them and formidable to tyrants only. He has called together legislative bodies at places unusual, uncomfortable, and distant from the depository of their public Records, for the sole purpose of fatiguing them into compliance with his measures. He has dissolved Representative Houses repeatedly, for opposing with manly firmness his invasions on the rights of the people. He has refused for a long time, after such dissolutions, to cause others to be elected; whereby the Legislative powers, incapable of Annihilation, have returned to the People at large for their exercise; the State remaining in the mean time exposed to all the dangers of invasion from without, and convulsions within. He has endeavoured to prevent the population of these States; for that purpose obstructing the Laws for Naturalization of Foreigners; refusing to pass others to encourage their migrations hither, and raising the conditions of new Appropriations of Lands. He has obstructed the Administration of Justice, by refusing his Assent to Laws for establishing Judiciary powers. He has made Judges dependent on his Will alone, for the tenure of their offices, and the amount and payment of their salaries. He has erected a multitude of New Offices, and sent hither swarms of Officers to harass our people, and eat out their substance. He has kept among us, in times of peace, standing Armies without the Consent of our legislatures. He has affected to render the Military independent of and superior to the Civil power. He has combined with others° to subject us to a jurisdiction foreign to our constitution, and unacknowledged by our laws; giving his Assent to their Acts of pretended Legislation: For Quartering large bodies of armed troops among us: For protecting them, by a mock Trial, from punishment for any Murders which they should commit on the Inhabitants of these States: For cutting off our Trade with all parts of the world: For imposing Taxes on us without our Consent; For depriving us in many cases of the benefits of Trial by Jury: For transporting us beyond Seas to be tried for pretended offences: For abolishing the free System of English Laws in a neighbouring Province,° establishing therein an Arbitrary government, and enlarging its Boundaries so as to render it at once an example and fit instrument for introducing the same absolute rule into these Colonies; For taking away our Charters, abolishing our most valuable Laws, and altering fundamentally the Forms of our Governments: For suspending our own Legislatures, and declaring themselves invested with power to legislate for us in all cases whatsoever. He has abdicated Government here, by declaring us out of his Protection and waging War against us. He has plundered our seas, ravaged our Coasts, burnt our towns, and

---

others: the British Parliament
Province: Quebec

destroyed the Lives of our people. He is at this time transporting large Armies of foreign Mercenaries° to compleat the works of death, desolation and tyranny, already begun with circumstances of Cruelty & perfidy scarcely paralleled in the most barbarous ages, and totally unworthy the Head of a civilized nation. He has constrained our fellow Citizens taken Captive on the high Seas to bear Arms against their Country, to become the executioners of their friends and Brethren, or to fall themselves by their Hands. He has excited domestic insurrections amongst us, and has endeavoured to bring on the inhabitants of our frontiers, the merciless Indian Savages, whose known rule of warfare, is an undistinguished destruction of all ages, sexes and conditions. In every stage of these Oppressions We have Petitioned for Redress in the most humble terms: Our repeated Petitions have been answered only by repeated injury. A Prince, whose character is thus marked by every act which may define a Tyrant, is unfit to be the ruler of a free people. Nor have We been wanting in attentions to our British brethren. We have warned them from time to time of attempts by their legislature to extend an unwarrantable jurisdiction over us. We have reminded them of the circumstances of our emigration and settlement here. We have appealed to their native justice and magnanimity, and we have conjured them by the ties of our common kindred to disavow these usurpations, which, would inevitably interrupt our connections and correspondence. They too have been deaf to the voice of justice and of consanguinity. We must, therefore, acquiesce in the necessity, which denounces° our Separation, and hold them, as we hold the rest of mankind, Enemies in War, in Peace Friends.

We, therefore, the Representatives of the United States of America, in General Congress, Assembled, appealing to the Supreme Judge of the world for the rectitude of our intentions, do, in the Name, and by Authority of the good People of these Colonies, solemnly publish and declare, That these United Colonies are, and of right ought to be Free and Independent States; that they are Absolved from all Allegiance to the British Crown, and that all political connection between them and the State of Great Britain, is and ought to be totally dissolved; and that as Free and Independent States, they have full Power to levy War, conclude Peace, contract Alliances, establish Commerce, and to do all other Acts and Things which Independent States may of right do. And for the support of this Declaration, with a firm reliance on the protection of divine Providence, we mutually pledge to each other our Lives, our Fortunes and our sacred Honor.

---

1. What is the dominant idea of this document? Where does Jefferson place that idea?

Mercenaries: German soldiers hired by the British
denounces: announces

2. How does Jefferson support that idea? What material does he use for support?

3. What does Jefferson do at the conclusion of this document? How do you know where the conclusion begins?

4. What is the tone and voice of this document? How does Jefferson create that tone?

5. What other tones and voices might Jefferson have created, given the circumstances under which this document was written? Do you think the voice and tone he chose was the most effective? Why?

❧ *An Invitation to Write*

As you go through your daily life, look about you for an issue that is important to you and that you can present to your reader as a generalization. That issue might involve your life, the life or lives of people around you, or events you have heard or read about. Write a short story, a poem, or an essay in which you assemble specific examples to support your conclusion.

DEDUCTIVE REASONING

Deduction takes your thinking in a direction that appears to be the opposite of induction. As you've seen, induction moves you from specific facts—observations, measurements, and opinions—to general statements. Deduction moves you from a general statement to the application of that statement to a specific case. The full study of deductive reasoning is far too broad and complicated for a text such as this. However, there are a number of simple principles of deduction that you will find useful in critically examining your own and other people's arguments.

The *syllogism* is the essential tool of deduction. Usually a three-part statement, a syllogism takes two inductively truthful statements—one general and one more specific—and puts them together to create a new truth.

The first part of a syllogism is called the *major premise*. The major premise is a more-or-less general statement that is either self-evidently true or that finds its support in a sufficient number of specific pieces of evidence—in other words, in inductive reasoning. Here is a major premise:

Evergreen trees do not lose their needles in the fall.

The second part of a syllogism is called the *minor premise*. The minor premise is most usually a statement about a member of a class to which the major premise will be applied. This statement is also the result of applying careful observation to arrive at a fact: inductive reasoning. Here is a minor premise that speaks to the example major premise:

This tree in my yard is an evergreen.

The final part of a syllogism is called the *conclusion*. If the syllogism is valid (more on this later), the conclusion is the *only* possible result of the major and minor premises. Here is the conclusion that follows from the example major and minor premises:

This tree in my yard won't lose its needles in the fall.

Validity and the Syllogism

When people discuss whether or not a syllogism is *valid,* they are asking whether or not the conclusion is the *only* possible result of the major and minor premises. Problems that keep some syllogisms from being valid may be in the major premise or the minor premise.

Some major premises may be *exclusive;* that is, they restrict an action or a characteristic to a certain group:

Only science majors study physics.

Other major premises may be *nonexclusive;* that is, they make a general statement about a group but do not exclude individuals who are not members of that group:

All science majors study physics. (but so do other people)

On the basis of the exclusive statement, you can say that because Josephine studies physics, she must be a science major. However, on the basis of the nonexclusive statement, you cannot conclude that Josephine is a science major because she studies physics. That statement does not exclude other people from studying that subject.

Exclusive:

Only science majors study physics.
Josephine studies physics.
Josephine must be a science major.

Nonexclusive:

All science majors study physics. (but so do others)
Josephine studies physics.
Josephine may or may not be a science major.

Other premises may apply only to *some* members of a group, and so you can only arrive at a possibility, not a certainty, in your conclusion. For example, if you begin by saying that

Some dogs like to swim. (but not every dog does)

and your minor premise is

Fluffy is a dog.

then the best conclusion you can reach is that

> Fluffy may like to swim.

If your premise applies to *all* the members of a certain class, and you apply your premise to an object or a person who is *not necessarily* part of that class, all you can develop as a conclusion is a possibility. If you start by saying that

> All dogs like to eat meat. (but so do other creatures)

and your minor premise is

> Myrtle likes to eat meat.

you cannot conclude that Myrtle is a dog. However, you can say that

> Myrtle *may be* a dog.

Sometimes your premise might be a negative statement. If your minor premise is also a negative statement, you cannot reach a definite conclusion. For example, if you begin by stating that

> No students like to study grammar. (but nonstudents might)

and your minor premise is

> Eleanor is not a student.

you can't conclude that Eleanor likes to study grammar. The most you can say is that

> Eleanor *may* like to study grammar.

However, if your minor premise is

> Eleanor likes to study grammar.

you can say with certainty that

> Eleanor is not a student.

Sometimes your major premise is not a *declarative* statement but a *conditional* statement that tells your reader that if A is so, then B must also be so. Such a statement is made up of an "if" clause (the *condition*) and a "then" clause (the *consequence*). When you use or read syllogisms based on these statements, you must make sure that the minor premise either affirms the condition (the "if") or denies the consequence (the "then"). If the minor premise does neither of these, then the conclusion is not certain.

For example, if your major premise is

> If there is smoke, then there is fire.

then you can say

> There is smoke. (confirming the "if" statement)

and conclude with certainty that

> There is fire.

Or you can say

> There is no fire. (denying the "then" statement)

and conclude with certainty that

> There is no smoke.

But if you say

> There is no smoke. (denying the "if" statement)

you can't be certain that there is no fire. (If you were a scout, you probably learned how to make a smokeless fire.) The best conclusion you can arrive at is that

> There may or may not be fire.

One other type of syllogism that you may find useful is the kind that presents two or more alternatives to your reader. For example, if you see a person driving erratically, you might think:

> That driver is either careless or drunk or on medication or not wearing his glasses or there's something wrong with his car.

Once you have made certain that your major premise covers *all* the possible reasons for the event you witnessed, you can methodically begin to eliminate each of the possibilities by testing them against your observations until you arrive at the one (or more) that remains.

You must also test your and other persons' reasoning to see that the language is unambiguous: that the words are concrete enough to be clear and that the words mean the same thing each time you use them. For example, consider this syllogism:

> The holder of one hand in this poker game will win.
> I hold one hand in this poker game.
> I will win.

If you play poker or any other card game, you have probably convinced yourself of the truth of this syllogism from time to time. The problem is that "one hand" means something different each time it is used. To use a word with two different meanings in the same argument is called *equivocation* (to have equal voices).

Truth in Syllogisms

Validity and *truth* are entirely different matters when you consider deductive argument and syllogisms. Remember, to determine validity, you consider the relationship between the major and minor premises of the syllogism and the precision of the language; you only consider whether the conclusion is the only possible one that could result from the premises. The issue of whether the major and minor premises are true is irrelevant to the question of validity. Look at this syllogism:

> All dogs can fly.
> This animal is a dog.
> This animal can fly.

Of course, the major premise is false, but that fact does not make any difference as far as the *validity* of the syllogism is concerned. The conclusion is the only one that you can reach from the premises.

The *truth* of a syllogism is the point at which inductive and deductive thinking connect most clearly with each other. Major and minor premises are more-or-less general statements. Therefore, they are most likely the products of inductive reasoning. When you consider your own or other persons' chains of reasoning, you must test their statements—the links in the chain—against the evidence that supports them. If the evidence fails, then the truth of the idea and of the conclusion that it leads to is questionable at best, even though the argument is perfectly valid.

✑ *Exercise*

In your group or on your own, examine each of these syllogisms and test them for both truth and validity. Remember that a syllogism can be valid (that is, the conclusion is the only one that could result from the premises) and still be untrue. When you find a syllogism that you believe has problems, first identify the problems and then see if there are ways you can rearrange the form or rewrite the statements so as to help them make sense. In some cases, there may be no way to repair the syllogism.

1. All athletes eat Zingg cereal for breakfast.
   Rachel eats Zingg cereal for breakfast.
   Rachel is an athlete.

2. Any golfer who makes a hole-in-one is lucky.
   I made a hole-in-one.
   I am one lucky golfer.

3. All cats have nine lives.
   Fluffy is a cat.
   Fluffy has nine lives.

4. No dog has two heads.
   One dog has one more head than no dog.
   One dog has three heads.

5. If you study hard, you'll get a good grade.
   You got a good grade.
   You studied hard.

6. If you study hard, you'll get a good grade.
   You studied hard.
   You will get a good grade.

7. If you study hard, you'll get a good grade.
   You didn't study hard.
   You probably won't get a good grade.

8. Man is the only creature that we know of that is capable of reason.
   Mary is not a man.
   Mary is not reasonable.

9. Either you are alive or you're dead.
   You are living.
   You're not dead.

10. Money is the root of all evil.
    Time is money.
    Time is the root of all evil.

Syllogisms in the Real World

Everyday life is full of examples of deductive thinking. However, you'll rarely find people expressing every part of the syllogism underlying their statements. Usually, a person presenting his or her argument will leave out one part of the reasoning chain. For example, if a professor says to you: "You can't take this class because you haven't registered for it," he or she is not stating the major premise of the argument. That premise looks something like this: "Anyone who has not registered for this class can't take this class."

Sometimes, you'll find the major premise stated but the minor premise missing. A person might tell you, "Of course you have to pay taxes. Everybody has to pay taxes." The missing minor premise is something like "You are a person" (part of "everybody").

It is equally possible to come across a statement that is missing the conclusion. Instead, the major and minor premises imply the conclusion. You might say to a friend who has made a mistake: "You're only human. Everyone can make a mistake now and then." The missing conclusion might look like this: "You can make a mistake."

When you read another person's written argument, you'll find the reasoning stated in a far less formal way than it would be were that person to write a syllogism. You can analyze the person's argument more accurately and systematically if you resolve it into its premises. When you have seen the premises, examined the language, and tested to see whether that person's conclusion is the only conclusion that could possibly result from the premises, you can judge the truth and the validity of that person's argument as well as find ways of refuting his or her position.

~~≈ *Exercise*

The following are "real-world" statements which reflect syllogisms missing one of the parts. With your group or on your own, read these statements and break them down into syllogisms, supplying the missing part. After you have done that, examine each syllogism to see if the conclusion follows as the only result of the premises and if the premises themselves appear to be true. If you find a problem with the argument, see if you can restate the syllogism so as to make it valid.

1. We should rely exclusively on the opinions of young people because everyone over thirty is untrustworthy.
2. Students, like all people with active minds, are easily influenced by any idea, like Communism, which seems advanced and may hold out hope for the impractical idealist. It is easy to see why our colleges are full of communists.
3. People who are poor lack ambition. If they did not lack ambition, they would not be poor.
4. The editorial in today's issue of the student newspaper states that only a student can understand the need for growth at this university. Well, I'm a student, and I think that the college should grow no larger.
5. All governments must deceive the public from time to time for reasons of security. This bulletin issued by the government is a lie.
6. Houses with shallow foundations should be avoided at all costs. You should buy this house.
7. Anyone traveling in the African mail boat will be three days late. Don't expect Mr. Smith today just because the boat is scheduled to arrive.
8. Great art is dying out. There are few great artists in the world at any time because they are so rare and so special. This move in many countries toward democracy is destroying art.
9. Of course Susan is a poor driver. What do you expect from a woman?
10. Sam Jones' book on divorce should be pretty informative. Jones has been married and divorced five times.
11. Anyone old enough to serve in the armed forces and fight for our country is old enough to drink. Eighteen-year-olds should be allowed to drink.

Another Way of Looking at Deduction

Breaking a deductive argument down into its premises and its conclusion is often a useful way of examining its basic elements. Another useful tool for examining the effectiveness of your own or another person's argument involves examining its major premise directly. Of course, you've

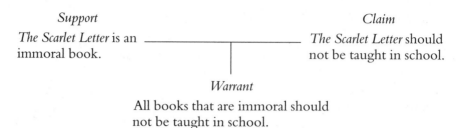

Support

The Scarlet Letter is an
immoral book.

Claim

The Scarlet Letter should
not be taught in school.

Warrant

All books that are immoral should
not be taught in school.

Figure 17.1 Toulmin's Analysis of Argument

learned by now that a major premise depends on inductive reasoning, the collection and examination of evidence that leads the arguer to a general conclusion that he or she will apply to a specific case.

The approach Stephen Toulmin has developed to crafting and analyzing arguments is equally useful for focusing your attention on the support for an argument as well as on the argument itself.

Let's say we begin with the following syllogism:

All books that are immoral should not be taught in school.
The Scarlet Letter is an immoral book.
The Scarlet Letter should not be taught in school.

Figure 17.1 shows how the argument would look using Toulmin's approach. From Toulmin's angle, the major premise becomes the *warrant,* the minor premise becomes the *support,* and the conclusion becomes the *claim.* Looked at in this way, the warrant acts like a bridge that takes you from the support (minor premise) to the claim (conclusion).

This way of critically examining your or another person's argument is effective for two reasons. First, unless your assumptions leading to your conclusion are absolutely obvious, your audience will be more likely to accept your conclusion if they know what your warrant is. Approaching your argument from the Toulmin angle focuses your attention on the support for your conclusion and invites you to make certain that your warrant is true and has inductive support.

The second reason that Toulmin's approach might be useful for you is the way it focuses your attention on the warrant for a conclusion and works backwards from it. We're presented with arguments from one source or another every day. We read editorials in newspapers, listen to teachers in our classes, and sometimes argue with our friends. With Toulmin's approach in mind, you have a tool that takes you right to the center of another person's argument. It focuses your attention on the assumptions that the individual begins with and invites you to test them against facts. It leads you to ask another person, "What is the basis of your argument? How did you get to it? What is your evidence?"

You can interrogate your own argument by asking yourself these questions based on Toulmin's approach:

What is the evidence I have used to support my claim (conclusion)? Is there enough? Is all of it relevant to my claim?

Have I made my warrant clear to my audience? Have I backed it up with enough evidence?

Does my claim make too general an assertion? Do I have to qualify it by using words such as "some," "most," or "many"?

PERSUASION

Persuasion eliminates disagreement by eliminating conflict. When you write an argument, you present a dominant idea that you cannot be certain your audience will accept even if your generalizations are well supported and your deductive argument is valid and true. As a result, almost all argumentative writing contains an element of persuasion. When you persuade, you convince your audience that any disagreement is really the result of a misunderstanding. You show your readers that you and they really have the same interests and concerns.

When you persuade your audience to consider your dominant idea or controversial elements of its support, you try to define the greatest amount of common ground that you and your readers share. To do so, you first need to know your readers so that you can speak to them in terms of their interests, their attitudes toward what you urge, and the goals that you can show them you and they share.

Advertising is one of the most common, skillful forms of pure persuasion without any regard for valid argument. Studying this pure, and often tremendously effective, way of influencing choices helps you understand how persuasion works. Many advertising copywriters write ads that appeal to what they believe to be their audience's interests, feelings, and fantasies. Many advertisements don't sell the product as much as what the product will supposedly do for the purchaser and his or her self-image or what he or she hopes to become or avoid becoming. Others don't address the quality of the product, but they speak to what the copywriter believes are the concerns of the audience; those concerns may have nothing to do with the quality of the product. For example, consider the following advertisement:

> AT TOYOTA we believe in the importance of investing in the economies where we do business. That's why we've invested over $5 billion in our operations here in America. That's why since 1988 we've increased our purchasing of U.S. made parts by 357% to over $4 billion per year. And that's why almost half the Toyota passenger cars sold in America are manufactured right here in Kentucky and California. *IN-VESTING IN THE THINGS WE ALL CARE ABOUT.* **TOYOTA**

This advertisement says nothing about the usefulness or reliability of this company's product. Instead, it speaks to the resentment and fear many Americans feel regarding Japanese industry and the balance of trade. It responds to the tendency on the part of many prospective buyers to think in terms of buying an American product. Thus it assures the reader that Toyota is a company that has sunk economic roots in America.

Here is another example:

> Business travelers depend on Thai Airways International for convenient daily departures to Tokyo or Seoul and beyond. But there's so much more. The discerning traveler appreciates the luxurious service and unparalleled amenities that only one airline can offer. It's all part of Thai Airways' exclusive, award-winning Royal Orchid Service. From the moment you come aboard Thai Airways, the experience begins. Enjoy international cuisine, champagne, fine wines and spirits. All the while, you'll be pampered by our gracious service as you luxuriate in spacious seating. So, when your travels take you to Tokyo, Seoul or one of 70 other destinations worldwide, let it all begin on Thai Airways where business is always a pleasure.

Most airlines usually arrive and depart according to schedule and make every attempt to get their passengers to their destinations safely. And if you examine the statistics with regard to safety and on-time performance, in most cases the differences are so small as to make one airline pretty much the same as another. It follows that one airline is about as good as another in these essential characteristics. Thus this airline sells amenities such as good food, good wine, and gracious service. Added to this is the fact that many business travelers resent sitting with tourists and individuals paying economy fares. Therefore, Thai Airways tries to attract its business travelers by telling them that they will be pampered in a way that *sounds* very much like the way first-class travelers are treated. Finally, although "Royal Orchid Service" sounds both expensive and exotic, it means nothing.

❧ Exercise

Read the following texts of advertisements. Meeting with your group or alone, analyze these texts in terms of the sort of audience the writer has in mind and the attitudes to which the writer has chosen to appeal.

Example 1
HAIR DO'S
Suit yourself.
Take a risk occasionally.
Keep the cut fresh. The cut is everything.
Run your fingers through it.
Let him run his fingers through it.
Color it, curl it, change it now and then.
Have fun with it.
Be kind to it.
WE DO IT RIGHT.
REGIS
HAIRSTYLISTS

Example 2

There it is. The highway stretched out in front of you. Yellow on black. It looks so . . . serious. But that's no reason to take it that way. Try the 1993 Ford Escort GT.

Fire up the 16-valve dual overhead cam engine and feel the twisting road curve into a smile on your face. With responsive handling and nimble sport suspension, the Escort GT will make getting there fun in itself. And this car looks as spirited as it is—with a cool asymmetrical grille and an aerodynamic rear spoiler.

The 1993 Ford Escort GT. A car that proves even serious driving can be fun.

Example 3

Is it true that, as you age, your funny bone starts to deteriorate?

Why does the world automatically get so serious when you grow up? Aren't there still strawberries to be stolen? Lakes to skinny dip in? Cigars to smoke? Waiters to flirt shamelessly with? When exercised regularly, your funny bone's the last to go.

KEDS   They feel good

Example 4

Out here, the laws of the land do not apply.

The rhythms
of life at sea are
different.

Norwegian Cruise Line takes you not only to the most exotic places on earth, but in your own mind—serene, unexplored places. This serenity is assured by a staff dedicated to service, ships that are among the newest at sea, menus that reflect the best of the world's cuisines and Chocoholic buffets, gracious amenities and even innovations like non-smoking cabins.

⤳ *An Invitation to Write*

Alone or in your group, find a common product that hardly anyone thinks about and that is sold in your bookstore. Write a persuasive advertisement that you believe will make customers *want* to buy this product.

In order to write a successful, persuasive advertisement, the copywriter needs to know his or her audience and something of their psychology. One way of seeing how knowledge of an audience affects persuasive writing is to look at an assortment of magazines and note which products are advertised in which magazines. For example, you will probably never find cosmetics advertised in a magazine such as *The Sporting News* or *Field and Stream,* nor will you find off-road vehicles advertised in *Vogue* or *Sassy.* Furthermore, the same product is often advertised in different magazines that have entirely different readers. The ads will often vary according to the audience the writers intend them for.

For the purposes of defining your audience, you might find the audience dialogue in Chapter 6 (page 115) useful. Using this tool, you should be able to define your audience closely enough to make intelligent choices about what sort of examples and language to use, how much your audience knows about your subject, and what probable feelings and assumptions your audience might have about your discussion of your topic and your conclusions.

Knowing your audience is not enough, however. Your audience also needs to know something of you. What you show them of yourself depends upon what attitude you want them to have toward you. Usually you want your audience to see you as someone who shares their interests, who knows more than they do about your subject, and who accepts them on their own terms. Consider: Would you be inclined to agree with someone whose aims were different from yours? Would you be inclined to give an open-minded hearing to the ideas of a person who presents him- or herself as superior or inferior to you? As you revise your argumentative writing, think about whether you have used your choice of language and voice to create a character that is effective for the subject of your argument and for the readers you have imagined as your audience.

When you read that you have to create a character to suit your audience, you may feel that you are being asked to be dishonest. However, if you think a little more about this issue, you'll probably discover that you constantly pick and choose among all the ways of presenting yourself that are available to you. You learned about presenting yourself to an audience earlier in this book, and much of what you learned is relevant to your goal of persuading your audience. Consider: You would never dress casually for a job interview, even though you might feel more comfortable in casual clothes. You would never use slang in a formal speech before a group of people you intend to impress, although you often use it in less-formal situations. If you were making a speech at a political rally, you probably would not consider using long, involved sentences, nor would you assemble a detailed argument with specific evidence. If you did so, you would probably lose your audience. Most people attend such speeches expecting to be moved by emotional language and phrases such as "civic responsibility" or "a thousand points of light." On the other hand, individuals attending a scholarly conference on the same political issues will reject such phrases immediately and expect a tight, unified, coherent, logical argument with specific, detailed evidence. Like everyone, you have learned many ways of acting. Each of them is no more or less a part of you than any of the others. Like most people, you probably choose the way of acting that seems most appropriate to you in a specific situation.

Ideally, when you revise your written argument, you'll choose to use persuasion responsibly, as a way of reinforcing your conclusion with appeals to your audience's human and humane concerns. Effective, principled persuasion depends on remembering that your audience is made up of people who live their lives at both an intellectual and an emotional level and who are most effectively spoken to at both those levels. Your responsible use of persuasion also depends upon your respect for your audience. Although you might be able to move them with pure persuasion, by doing so, you refuse to recognize their ability to make decisions through their ability to reason. If you do that, you treat them as something less than your equals: reasonable, mature human beings.

Working with the Readings

Read the selections that follow and, alone or in your group, answer the questions that follow each one.

TO HIS COY MISTRESS

Andrew Marvell

  Had we but world enough, and time,
This coyness, lady, were no crime.
We would sit down, and think which way
To walk, and pass our long love's day,
Thou by the Indian Ganges'° side   *5*
Shoudst rubies find; I by the tide
Of Humber° would complain. I would
Love you ten years before the flood,
And you should, if you please, refuse
Till the conversion of the Jews.°   *10*
My vegetable love should grow
Vaster than empires and more slow;
An hundred years should go to praise
Thine eyes, and on thy forehead gaze;
Two hundred to adore each breast,   *15*
But thirty thousand to the rest;
An age at least to every part,
And the last age should show your heart.
For, lady, you deserve this state,
Nor would I love at lower rate.   *20*

---

5. *Ganges:* the holy river of India
7. *Humber:* a river in England
10. *conversion of the Jews:* supposedly to occur on Judgment Day

But at my back I always hear
Time's wingéd chariot hurrying near;
And yonder all before us lie
Deserts of vast eternity.
Thy beauty shall no more be found;   25
Nor, in thy marble vault, shall sound
My echoing song; then worms shall try
That long-preserved virginity,
And your quaint° honor turn to dust,
And into ashes all my lust: 30
The grave's a fine and private place,
But none, I think, do there embrace.
    Now therefore, while the youthful hue
Sits on thy skin like morning dew
And while thy willing soul transpires°   35
At every pore with instant fires,
Now let us sport us while we may,
And now, like amorous birds of prey,
Rather at once our time devour
Than languish in his slow-chapped° power.   40
Let us roll all our strength and all
Our sweetness up into one ball,
And tear our pleasures with rough strife
Thorough the iron gates of life:
Thus, though we cannot make our sun   45
Stand still, yet we will make him run.

----

1. Note that this poem is written in three paragraphs. Looking at each paragraph, reduce it to its core statement. Arrange these statements in order. What kind of argument does Marvell's speaker use? What kind of a syllogism is it? What is the major premise, the minor premise, and the conclusion?

2. What is the situation that creates this syllogism? Imagine a scene with a setting and characters that reflects this situation. What does it look like? What are the characters like?

3. What is the speaker's support for each part of his argument? What examples does he use for evidence? How do you think he intends these examples to affect his audience?

----

29. *quaint:* overcareful
35. *transpires:* breathes forth
40. *slow-chapped:* slow-jawed

4. How does the speaker use language, imagery, and figures of speech to express his evidence and support his argument? What effect upon his audience do you think he intends to have?

5. Look again at the results of your having reduced the poem to a major premise, a minor premise, and a conclusion. Is this argument valid or invalid? True or untrue? How do the answers to these questions affect your judgment of the speaker?

6. If you are working on your own, take the role of the lady in the poem and prepare an answer to the speaker. (Your answer need not be in verse.)

   If you are working in a group, split the group. Have one part of the group take the role of the lady and prepare a logical and persuasive answer to the speaker. Then have the other part of the group answer the lady's statement from the point of view of the speaker.

YOUNG GOODMAN BROWN

Nathaniel Hawthorne

Young Goodman° Brown came forth at sunset into the street at Salem village; but put his head back, after crossing the theshold, to exchange a parting kiss with his young wife. And Faith, as the wife was aptly named, thrust her own pretty head into the street, letting the wind play with the pink ribbons of her cap while she called to Goodman Brown.

"Dearest heart," whispered she, softly and rather sadly, when her lips were close to his ear, "prithee put off your journey until sunrise and sleep in your own bed to-night. A lone woman is troubled with such dreams and such thoughts that she's afeard of herself sometimes. Pray tarry with me this night, dear husband, of all nights in the year."

"My love and my Faith," replied young Goodman Brown, "of all nights in the year, this one night must I tarry away from thee. My journey, as thou callest it, forth and back again, must needs be done 'twixt now and sunrise. What, my sweet, pretty wife, dost thou doubt me already, and we but three months married?"

"Then God bless you!" said Faith, with the pink ribbons; "and may you find all well when you come back."

"Amen!" cried Goodman Brown. "Say thy prayers, dear Faith, and 5 go to bed at dusk, and no harm will come to thee."

Goodman: form of address for commoners; the equivalent of Mr.

So they parted; and the young man pursued his way until, being about to turn the corner by the meeting-house, he looked back and saw the head of Faith still peeping after him with a melancholy air, in spite of her pink ribbons.

"Poor little Faith!" thought he, for his heart smote him. "What a wretch am I to leave her on such an errand! She talks of dreams, too. Methought as she spoke there was trouble in her face, as if a dream had warned her what work is to be done to-night. But no, no; 'twould kill her to think it. Well, she's a blessed angel on earth; and after this one night I'll cling to her skirts and follow her to heaven."

With this excellent resolve for the future, Goodman Brown felt himself justified in making more haste on his present evil purpose. He had taken a dreary road, darkened by all the gloomiest trees of the forest, which barely stood aside to let the narrow path creep through, and closed immediately behind. It was all as lonely as could be; and there is this peculiarity in such a solitude, that the traveller knows not who may be concealed by the innumerable trunks and the thick boughs overhead; so that with lonely footsteps he may yet be passing through an unseen multitude.

"There may be a devilish Indian behind every tree," said Goodman Brown to himself; and he glanced fearfully behind him as he added, "What if the devil himself should be at my very elbow!"

His head being turned back, he passed a crook of the road, and, look-   10 ing forward again, beheld the figure of a man, in grave and decent attire, seated at the foot of an old tree. He arose at Goodman Brown's approach and walked onward side by side with him.

"You are late, Goodman Brown," said he. "The clock of the Old South° was striking as I came through Boston, and that is full fifteen minutes agone."

"Faith kept me back a while," replied the young man, with a tremor in his voice, caused by the sudden appearance of his companion, though not wholly unexpected.

It was now deep dusk in the forest, and deepest in that part of it where these two were journeying. As nearly as could be discerned, the second traveller was about fifty years old, apparently in the same rank of life as Goodman Brown, and bearing a considerable resemblance to him, though perhaps more in expression than features. Still they might have been taken for father and son. And yet, though the elder person was as simply clad as the younger, and as simple in manner too, he had an indescribable air of one who knew the world, and who would not have felt abashed at the governor's dinner table or in King William's° court, were

---

Old South: Old South Church in Boston
King William: William III, king of England (1689–1708)

it possible that his affairs should call him thither. But the only thing about him that could be fixed upon as remarkable was his staff, which bore the likeness of a great black snake, so curiously wrought that it might almost be seen to twist and wriggle itself like a living serpent. This, of course, must have been an ocular deception, assisted by the uncertain light.

"Come, Goodman Brown," cried his fellow-traveller, "this is a dull pace for the beginning of a journey. Take my staff, if you are so soon weary."

"Friend," said the other, exchanging his slow pace for a full stop, 15 "having kept covenant by meeting thee here, it is my purpose now to return whence I came. I have scruples touching the matter thou wot'st° of."

"Sayest thou so?" replied he of the serpent, smiling apart. "Let us walk on, nevertheless, reasoning as we go; and if I convince thee not thou shalt turn back. We are but a little way in the forest yet."

"Too far! too far!" exclaimed the goodman, unconsciously resuming his walk. "My father never went into the woods on such an errand, nor his father before him. We have been a race of honest men and good Christians since the days of the martyrs;° and shall I be the first of the name of Brown that ever took this path and kept—"

"Such company, thou wouldst say," observed the elder person, inter-preting his pause. "Well said, Goodman Brown! I have been as well ac-quainted with your family as with ever a one among the Puritans; and that's no trifle to say. I helped your grandfather, the constable, when he lashed the Quaker woman so smartly through the streets of Salem;° and it was I that brought your father a pitch-pine knot, kindled at my own hearth, to set fire to an Indian village, in King Philip's war.° They were my good friends, both; and many a pleasant walk have we had along this path, and returned merrily after midnight. I would fain be friends with you for their sake."

"If it be as thou sayest," replied Goodman Brown, "I marvel they never spoke of these matters; or, verily, I marvel not, seeing that the least rumor of the sort would have driven them from New England. We are a people of prayer, and good works to boot, and abide no such wickedness."

"Wickedness or not," said the traveller, with the twisted staff, "I have 20 a very general acquaintance here in New England. The deacons of many a church have drunk the communion wine with me; the selectmen° of

---

wot'st: knowest
days of the martyrs: the time of the persecution of the Protestants in England
lashed . . . Salem: A law of 1661 required that Quakers be stripped naked "from the middle upwards," tied to the rear of a cart, and whipped through the town.
King Philip's war: uprising of New England Indians (1675–1676)
selectmen: town officers

divers towns make me their chairman; and a majority of the Great and General Court° are firm supporters of my interest. The governor and I, too—But these are state secrets."

"Can this be so?" cried Goodman Brown, with a state of amazement at his undisturbed companion. "Howbeit, I have nothing to do with the governor and council; they have their own ways, and are no rule for a simple husbandman° like me. But, were I to go on with thee, how should I meet the eye of that good old man, our minister, at Salem village? Oh, his voice would make me tremble both Sabbath day and lecture day."°

Thus far the elder traveller had listened with due gravity; but now burst into a fit of irrepressible mirth, shaking himself so violently that his snake-like staff actually seemed to wriggle in sympathy.

"Ha! ha! ha!" shouted he again and again; then composing himself, "Well, go on, Goodman Brown, go on; but, prithee, don't kill me with laughing."

"Well, then, to end the matter at once," said Goodman Brown, considerably nettled, "there is my wife, Faith. It would break her dear little heart; and I'd rather break my own."

"Nay, if that be the case," answered the other, "e'en go thy ways,   25
Goodman Brown. I would not for twenty old women like the one hobbling before us that Faith should come to any harm."

As he spoke he pointed his staff at a female figure on the path, in whom Goodman Brown recognized a very pious and exemplary dame, who had taught him his catechism in youth, and was still his moral and spiritual adviser, jointly with the minister and Deacon Gookin.

"A marvel, truly, that Goody° Cloyse should be so far in the wilderness at nightfall," said he. "But with your leave, friend, I shall take a cut through the woods until we have left this Christian woman behind. Being a stranger to you, she might ask whom I was consorting with and whither I was going."

"Be it so," said his fellow-traveller. "Betake you to the woods, and let me keep the path."

Accordingly the young man turned aside, but took care to watch his companion, who advanced softly along the road until he had come within a staff's length of the old dame. She, meanwhile, was making the best of her way; with singular speed for so aged a woman, and mumbling some indistinct words—a prayer, doubtless—as she went. The traveller put forth his staff and touched her withered neck with what seemed the serpent's tail.

"The devil!" screamed the pious old lady.   30

General Court: the legislature of the Puritan colony
husbandman: farmer
lecture day: midweek lecture on Scripture
Goody: contraction of "Goodwife," the feminine equivalent of "Goodman"

"Then Goody Cloyse knows her old friend?" observed the traveller, confronting her and leaning on his writhing stick.

"Ah, forsooth, and is it your worship indeed?" cried the good dame. "Yea, truly is it, and in the very image of my old gossip, Goodman Brown, the grandfather of the silly fellow that now is. But—would your worship believe it?—my broomstick hath strangely disappeared, stolen, as I suspect, by that unhanged witch, Goody Cory, and that, too, when I was all anointed with the juice of smallage and cinquefoil and wolf's bane"°—

"Mingled with fine wheat and the fat of a new-born babe," said the shape of old Goodman Brown.

"Ah, your worship knows the recipe," cried the old lady, cackling aloud. "So, as I was saying, being all ready for the meeting, and no horse to ride on, I made up my mind to foot it; for they tell me there is a nice young man to be taken into communion to-night. But now your good worship will lend me your arm, and we shall be there in a twinkling."

"That can hardly be," answered her friend. "I may not spare you my arm, Goody Cloyse; but here is my staff, if you will."   *35*

So saying, he threw it down at her feet, where, perhaps, it assumed life, being one of the rods which its owner had formerly lent to the Egyptian magi.° Of this fact, however, Goodman Brown could not take cognizance. He had cast up his eyes in astonishment, and, looking down again, beheld neither Goody Cloyse nor the serpentine staff, but his fellow-traveller alone, who waited for him as calmly as if nothing had happened.

"That old woman taught me my catechism," said the young man; and there was a world of meaning in this simple comment.

They continued to walk onward, while the elder traveller exhorted his companion to make good speed and persevere in the path, discoursing so aptly that his arguments seemed rather to spring up in the bosom of his auditor than to be suggested by himself. As they went, he plucked a branch of maple to serve for a walking stick, and began to strip it of the twigs and little boughs, which were wet with evening dew. The moment his fingers touched them they became strangely withered and dried up as with a week's sunshine. Thus the pair proceeded, at a good free pace, until suddenly, in a gloomy hollow of the road, Goodman Brown sat himself down on the stump of a tree and refused to go any farther.

"Friend," said he, stubbornly, "my mind is made up. Not another step will I budge on this errand. What if a wretched old woman do choose to go to the devil when I thought she was going to heaven: is that any reason why I should quit my dear Faith and go after her?"

---

smallage . . . wolf's bane: smallage, wild celery; cinquefoil, a member of the rose family; wolf's bane, a poisonous herb thought to have magical powers
magi: The rods of the magicians of Egypt were turned into serpents (*Exodus* 7).

"You will think better of this by and by," said his acquaintance, composedly. "Sit here and rest yourself a while; and when you feel like moving again, there is my staff to help you along."   40

Without more words, he threw his companion the maple stick, and was as speedily out of sight as if he had vanished into the deepening gloom. The young man sat a few moments by the roadside, applauding himself greatly, and thinking with how clear a conscience he should meet the minister in his morning walk, nor shrink from the eye of good old Deacon Gookin. And what calm sleep would be his that very night, which was to have been spent so wickedly, but so purely and sweetly now, in the arms of Faith! Amidst these pleasant and praiseworthy meditations, Goodman Brown heard the tramp of horses along the road, and deemed it advisable to conceal himself within the verge of the forest, conscious of the guilty purpose that had brought him thither, though now so happily turned from it.

On came the hoof tramps and the voices of the riders, two grave old voices, conversing soberly as they drew near. These mingled sounds appeared to pass along the road, within a few yards of the young man's hiding-place; but, owing doubtless to the depth of the gloom at that particular spot, neither the travellers nor their steeds were visible. Though their figures brushed the small boughs by the wayside, it could not be seen that they intercepted, even for a moment, the faint gleam from the strip of bright sky athwart which they must have passed. Goodman Brown alternately crouched and stood on tiptoe, pulling aside the branches and thrusting forth his head as far as he durst without discerning so much as a shadow. It vexed him the more, because he could have sworn, were such a thing possible, that he recognized the voices of the minister and Deacon Gookin, jogging along quietly, as they were wont to do, when bound to some ordination or ecclesiastical council. While yet within hearing, one of the riders stopped to pluck a switch.

"Of the two, reverend sir," said the voice like the deacon's, "I had rather miss an ordination dinner° than to-night's meeting. They tell me that some of our community are to be here from Falmouth° and beyond, and others from Connecticut and Rhode Island, besides several of the Indian powwows,° who, after their fashion, know almost as much deviltry as the best of us. Moreover, there is a goodly young woman to be taken into communion."

"Mighty well, Deacon Gookin!" replied the solemn old tones of the minister. "Spur up, or we shall be late. Nothing can be done, you know, until I get on the ground."

---

ordination dinner: celebration when a Puritan minister was ordained
Falmouth: a village on Cape Cod
powwows: priests

The hoofs clattered again; and the voices, talking so strangely in the   *45*
empty air, passed on through the forest, where no church had ever been
gathered, nor solitary Christian prayed. Whither, then, could these holy
men be journeying so deep into the heathen wilderness? Young Goodman Brown caught hold of a tree for support, being ready to sink down
on the ground, faint and overburdened with the heavy sickness of his
heart. He looked up to the sky, doubting whether there really was a
heaven above him. Yet there was the blue arch, and the stars brightening
in it.

"With heaven above and Faith below, I will yet stand firm against the
devil!" cried Goodman Brown.

While he still gazed upward into the deep arch of the firmament and
had lifted his hands to pray, a cloud, though no wind was stirring, hurried
across the zenith and hid the brightening stars. The blue sky was still
visible, except directly overhead, where this black mass of cloud was
sweeping swiftly northward. Aloft in the air, as if from the depths of the
cloud, came a confused and doubtful sound of voices. Once the listener
fancied that he could distinguish the accents of towns-people of his own,
men and women, both pious and ungodly, many of whom he had met at
the communion table, and had seen others rioting at the tavern. The next
moment, so indistinct were the sounds, he doubted whether he had heard
aught but the murmur of the old forest, whispering without a wind.
Then came a stronger swell of those familiar tones, heard daily in the
sunshine at Salem village, but never until now from a cloud of night.
There was one voice, of a young woman, uttering lamentations, yet with
an uncertain sorrow, and entreating for some favor, which, perhaps, it
would grieve her to obtain; and all the unseen multitude, both saints and
sinners, seemed to encourage her onward.

"Faith!" shouted Goodman Brown, in a voice of agony and desperation; and the echoes of the forest mocked him, crying, "Faith! Faith!" as
if bewildered wretches were seeking her all through the wilderness.

The cry of grief, rage, and terror was yet piercing the night, when
the unhappy husband held his breath for a response. There was a scream,
drowned immediately in a louder murmur of voices, fading into far-off
laughter, as the dark cloud swept away, leaving the clear and silent sky
above Goodman Brown. But something fluttered lightly down through
the air and caught on the branch of a tree. The young man seized it, and
beheld a pink ribbon.

"My Faith is gone!" cried he, after one stupefied moment. "There is   *50*
no good on earth; and sin is but a name. Come, devil; for to thee is this
world given."

And, maddened with despair, so that he laughed loud and long, did
Goodman Brown grasp his staff and set forth again, at such a rate that he
seemed to fly along the forest path rather than to walk or run. The road
grew wilder and drearier and more faintly traced, and vanished at length,

leaving him in the heart of the dark wilderness, still rushing onward with the instinct that guides mortal man to evil. The whole forest was peopled with frightful sounds—the creaking of the trees, the howling of wild beasts, and the yell of Indians; while sometimes the wind tolled like a distant church bell, and sometimes gave a broad roar around the traveller, as if all Nature were laughing him to scorn. But he was himself the chief horror of the scene, and shrank not from its other horrors.

"Ha! ha! ha!" roared Goodman Brown when the wind laughed at him. "Let us hear which will laugh loudest. Think not to frighten me with your deviltry. Come witch, come wizard, come Indian powwow, come devil himself, and here comes Goodman Brown. You may as well fear him as he fear you."

In truth, all through the haunted forest there could be nothing more frightful than the figure of Goodman Brown. On he flew among the black pines, brandishing his staff with frenzied gestures, now giving vent to an inspiration of horrid blasphemy, and now shouting forth such laughter as set all the echoes of the forest laughing like demons around him. The fiend in his own shape is less hideous than when he rages in the breast of man. Thus sped the demoniac on his course, until, quivering among the trees, he saw a red light before him, as when the felled trunks and branches of a clearing have been set on fire, and throw up their lurid blaze against the sky, at the hour of midnight. He paused, in a lull of the tempest that had driven him onward, and heard the swell of what seemed a hymn, rolling solemnly from a distance with the weight of many voices. He knew the tune; it was a familiar one in the choir of the village meet-inghouse. The verse died heavily away, and was lengthened by a chorus, not of human voices, but of all the sounds of the benighted wilderness pealing in awful harmony together. Goodman Brown cried out, and his cry was lost to his own ear by its unison with the cry of the desert.

In the interval of silence he stole forward until the light glared full upon his eyes. At one extremity of an open space, hemmed in by the dark wall of the forest, arose a rock, bearing some rude, natural resemblance either to an altar or a pulpit, and surrounded by four blazing pines, their tops aflame, their stems untouched, like candles at an evening meeting. The mass of foliage that had overgrown the summit of the rock was all on fire, blazing high into the night and fitfully illuminating the whole field. Each pendent twig and leafy festoon was in a blaze. As the red light arose and fell, a numerous congregation alternately shone forth, then disappeared in shadow, and again grew, as it were, out of the darkness, peopling the heart of the solitary woods at once.

"A grave and dark-clad company," quoth Goodman Brown.   55

In truth they were such. Among them, quivering to and fro between gloom and splendor, appeared faces that would be seen next day at the council board of the province, and others which, Sabbath after Sabbath, looked devoutly heavenward, and benignantly over the crowded pews, from the holiest pulpits in the land. Some affirm that the lady of the governor° was there. At least there were high dames well known to her, and wives of honored husbands, and widows, a great multitude, and ancient maidens, all of excellent repute, and fair young girls, who trembled lest their mothers should espy them. Either the sudden gleams of light flashing over the obscure field bedazzled Goodman Brown, or he recognized a score of the church members of Salem village famous for their especial sanctity. Good old Deacon Gookin had arrived, and waited at the skirts of that venerable saint, his revered pastor. But, irreverently consorting with these grave, reputable, and pious people, these elders of the church, these chaste dames and dewy virgins, there were men of dissolute lives and women of spotted fame, wretches given over to all mean and filthy vice, and suspected even of horrid crimes. It was strange to see that the good shrank not from the wicked, nor were the sinners abashed by the saints. Scattered also among their pale-faced enemies were the Indian priests, or powwows, who had often scared their native forest with more hideous incantations than any known to English witchcraft.

"But where is Faith?" thought Goodman Brown; and, as hope came into his heart, he trembled.

Another verse of the hymn arose, a slow and mournful strain, such as the pious love, but joined to words which expressed all that our nature can conceive of sin, and darkly hinted at far more. Unfathomable to mere mortals is the lore of fiends. Verse after verse was sung; and still the chorus of the desert swelled between like the deepest tone of a mighty organ; and with the final peal of that dreadful anthem there came a sound, as if the roaring wind, the rushing streams, the howling beasts, and every other voice of the unconverted wilderness were mingling and according with the voice of guilty man in homage to the prince of all. The four blazing pines threw up a loftier flame, and obscurely discovered shapes and visages of horror on the smoke wreaths above the impious assembly. At the same moment the fire on the rock shot redly forth and formed a glowing arch above its base, where now appeared a figure. With reverence be it spoken, the figure bore no slight similitude, both in garb and manner, to some grave divine of the New England churches.

"Bring forth the converts!" cried a voice that echoed through the field and rolled into the forest.

At the word, Goodman Brown stepped forth from the shadow of the trees and approached the congregation, with whom he felt a loathful brotherhood by the sympathy of all that was wicked in his heart. He could have well-nigh sworn that the shape of his own dead father beckoned him to advance, looking downward from a smoke wreath, while a woman, with dim features of despair, threw out her hand to warn him back. Was it his mother? But he had no power to retreat one step, nor to

60

---

the lady of the Governor: The wife of Sir William Phips. According to contemporary accounts, Phips' wife was charged with but not tried for witchcraft at Salem.

resist, even in thought, when the minister and good old Deacon Gookin seized his arms and led him to the blazing rock. Thither came also the slender form of a veiled female, led between Goody Cloyse, that pious teacher of the catechism, and Martha Carrier,° who had received the dev- il's promise to be queen of hell. A rampant hag was she. And there stood the proselytes beneath the canopy of fire.

"Welcome, my children," said the dark figure, "to the communion of your race! Ye have found thus young your nature and your destiny. My children, look behind you!"

They turned; and flashing forth, as it were, in a sheet of flame, the fiend worshippers were seen; the smile of welcome gleamed darkly on every visage.

"There," resumed the sable° form, "are all whom ye have reverenced from youth. Ye deemed them holier than yourselves, and shrank from your own sin, contrasting it with their lives of righteousness and prayerful aspirations heavenward. Yet here are they all in my worshipping assembly. This night it shall be granted you to know their secret deeds: how hoary- bearded elders of the church have whispered wanton words to the young maids of their households; how many a woman, eager for widow's weeds, has given her husband a drink at bedtime and let him sleep in her bosom; how beardless youths have made haste to inherit their fathers' wealth; and how fair damsels—blush not, sweet ones—have dug little graves in the garden, and bidden me, the sole guest, to an infant's funeral. By the sym- pathy of your human hearts for sin ye shall scent out all the places— whether in church, bed-chamber, street, field, or forest—where crime has been committed, and shall exult to behold the whole earth one stain of guilt, one mighty blood spot. Far more than this. It shall be yours to penetrate in every bosom, the deep mystery of sin, the fountain of all wicked arts, and which inexhaustibly supplies more evil impulses than human power—than my power at its utmost—can make manifest in deeds. And now, my children, look upon each other."

They did so; and, by the blaze of the hell-kindled torches, the wretched man beheld his Faith, and the wife her husband, trembling be- fore that unhallowed altar.

"Lo, there ye stand, my children," said the figure, in a deep and solemn tone, almost sad with its despairing awfulness, as if his once an- gelic nature could yet mourn for our miserable race. "Depending upon one another's hearts, ye had still hoped that virtue were not all a dream. Now are ye undeceived. Evil is the nature of mankind. Evil must be your only happiness. Welcome again, my children, to the communion of your race."

65

Martha Carrier: hanged as a witch at Salem
sable: black

"Welcome," repeated the fiend worshippers, in one cry of despair and triumph.

And there they stood, the only pair, as it seemed, who were yet hesitating on the verge of wickedness in this dark world. A basin was hollowed, naturally, in the rock. Did it contain water, reddened by the lurid light? or was it blood? or, perchance, a liquid flame? Herein did the shape of evil dip his hand and prepare to lay the mark of baptism upon their foreheads, that they might be partakers of the mystery of sin, more conscious of the secret guilt of others, both in deed and thought, than they could now be of their own. The husband cast one look at his pale wife, and Faith at him. What polluted wretches would the next glance show them to each other, shuddering alike at what they disclosed and what they saw!

"Faith! Faith!" cried the husband, "look up to heaven, and resist the wicked one."

Whether Faith obeyed he knew not. Hardly had he spoken when he found himself amid calm night and solitude, listening to a roar of the wind which died heavily away through the forest. He staggered against the rock, and felt it chill and damp; while a hanging twig, that had been all on fire, besprinkled his cheek with the coldest dew.

The next morning young Goodman Brown came slowly into the   *70* street of Salem village, staring around him like a bewildered man. The good old minister was taking a walk along the graveyard to get an appetite for breakfast and meditate his sermon, and bestowed a blessing, as he passed, on Goodman Brown. He shrank from the venerable saint as if to avoid an anathema.° Old Deacon Gookin was at domestic worship, and the holy words of his prayer were heard through the open window. "What God doth the wizard pray to?" quoth Goodman Brown. Goody Cloyse, that excellent old Christian, stood in the early sunshine at her own lattice, catechizing a little girl who had brought her a pint of morning's milk. Goodman Brown snatched away the child as from the grasp of the fiend himself. Turning the corner by the meeting-house, he spied the head of Faith, with the pink ribbons, gazing anxiously forth, and bursting into such joy at sight of him that she skipped along the street and almost kissed her husband before the whole village. But Goodman Brown looked sternly and sadly into her face, and passed on without a greeting.

Had Goodman Brown fallen asleep in the forest and only dreamed a wild dream of a witch–meeting?

Be it so if you will; but, alas! it was a dream of evil omen for young Goodman Brown. A stern, a sad, a darkly meditative, a distrustful, if not a desperate man did he become from the night of that fearful dream. On

---

anathema: curse

the Sabbath day, when the congregation were singing a holy psalm, he could not listen because an anthem of sin rushed loudly upon his ear and drowned all the blessed strain. When the minister spoke from the pulpit with power and fervid eloquence, and, with his hand on the open Bible, of the sacred truths of our religion, and of saint-like lives and triumphant deaths, and of future bliss or misery unutterable, then did Goodman Brown turn pale, dreading lest the roof should thunder down upon the gray blasphemer and his hearers. Often, awakening suddenly at midnight, he shrank from the bosom of Faith; and at morning or eventide, when the family knelt down at prayer, he scowled and muttered to himself, and gazed sternly at his wife, and turned away. And when he had lived long, and was borne to his grave a hoary corpse, followed by Faith, an aged woman, and children and grandchildren, a goodly procession, besides neighbors not a few, they carved no hopeful verse upon his tombstone, for his dying hour was gloom.

---

1. In terms of his religious beliefs, at the last minute Brown makes the right choice. Why, then, does it appear that he has been punished for his choice?

2. In this story, Hawthorne gives you a character who seems to be the Devil (see his dialogue with Goody Cloyse). If this character is the Devil, how does he fall short of what you would expect to see if the Devil were to appear? Why do you think Hawthorne does this?

3. What are the premises (assumptions) about his world and the people in it that Brown begins with?

4. When Brown and the Devil speak about Brown's premises, what does the Devil do?

5. Aside from the dialogue with the Devil, what events occur in the story that reflect upon Brown's premises?

6. Does Brown's decision to "look up to heaven and resist the wicked one" result from a change in his premises? Has Brown learned from what he has seen and heard?

7. Use what you understand of Brown's premises to reconstruct the reasoning he uses to reject the Devil. Is his reasoning true? Does your answer to this explain the problem raised in Question 1?

8. Given what you've learned from your answers to these questions, do you think it's important to know whether Brown dreamed every-thing that happened in this story or not? Why doesn't Hawthorne give you a definitive answer after he has asked the question?

9. What do you think is Hawthorne's dominant idea?

THE ISLAND OF PLENTY

Johnson C. Montgomery

The United States should remain an island of plenty in a sea of hunger. The future of mankind is at stake. We are not responsible for the rest of humanity. We should not accept responsibility for all humanity. We owe more to the hundreds of billions of *Homo futurans* than we do to the hungry millions—soon to be billions—of our own generation.

Ample food and resources exist to nourish man and all other creatures indefinitely into the future. This planet is indeed an Eden—to date our only Eden. Admittedly our Eden is plagued by pollution. Some of us have polluted the planet by reproducing too many of us. Too many people have made excessive demands on the long-range carrying capacity of our garden; and during the last 200 years there has been dramatic, ever-increasing destruction of the web of life on earth. If we try to save the starving millions today, we will simply destroy what's left of Eden.

The problem is not that there is too little food. The problem is there are too many people—many too many. It is not that the children should never have been born. It is simply that we have mindlessly tried to cram too many of us into too short a time span. Four billion humans are fine—but they should have been spread over several hundred years.

But the billions are already here. What should we do about them? Should we send food, knowing that each child saved in Southeast Asia, India or Africa will probably live to reproduce and thereby bring more people into the world to live even more miserably? Should we eat the last tuna fish, the last ear of corn and utterly destroy the garden? That is what we have been doing for a long time and all the misguided efforts have merely increased the number who go to bed hungry each night. There have never been more miserable, deprived people in the world than there are right now.

It was obvious even in the late 1950s that the famine the world now faces was coming unless people immediately began exercising responsibility for reducing population levels. It was also obvious that too many people contributed to the risk of nuclear war, global pestilence, illiteracy and even to many problems that are usually classified as purely economic. For example, unemployment is having too many people for the available jobs. Inflation is in part the result of too much demand from too many people. But in the 1950s, population control was taboo and those who warned of impending disasters received a cool reception.

By the time Zero Population Growth, Inc., was formed, those of us who wanted to do something useful decided to concentrate our initial efforts on our own families and friends and then on the white American

5

middle and upper classes. Our belief was that by setting an example, we could later insist that others pay attention to our proposals.

I think I was the first in the original ZPG group to have had a vasectomy. Nancy and I had two children—each doing superbly well and each getting all the advantages of the best nutrition, education, attention, love and other resources available. I think Paul Ehrlich° (one child) was the next. Now don't ask me to cut my children back to the same number of calories that children from large families eat. In fact, don't ask me to cut my children back on anything. I won't do it without a fight; and in today's world, power is in knowledge, not numbers. Nancy and I made a conscious decision to limit the number of our children so each child could have a larger share of whatever we could make available. We intend to keep the best for them.

The future of mankind is indeed with the children. But it is with the nourished, educated and loved children. It is not with the starving, uneducated and ignored. This is of course a highly elitist point of view. But that doesn't make the view incorrect. As a matter of fact, the lowest reproductive rate in the nation is that of one of the most elite groups in the world—black, female Ph.D.'s. They had to be smart and effective to make it. Having made it, they are smart enough not to wreck it with too many kids.

We in the United States have made great progress in lowering our birth rates. But now, because we have been responsible, it seems to some that we have a great surplus. There is, indeed, waste that should be eliminated, but there is not as much fat in our system as most people think. Yet we are being asked to share our resources with the hungry peoples of the world. But why should we share? The nations having the greatest needs are those that have been the least responsible in cutting down on births. Famine is one of nature's ways of telling profligate peoples that they have been irresponsible in their breeding habits.

Naturally, we would like to help; and if we could, perhaps we should.   10
But we can't be of any use in the long run—particularly if we weaken ourselves.

Until we have at least a couple of years' supply of food and other resources on hand to take care of our own people and until those asking for handouts are doing at least as well as we are at reducing existing excessive population-growth rates, we should not give away our resources—not so much as one bushel of wheat. Certainly we should not participate in any programs that will increase the burden that mankind is already placing on the earth. We should not deplete our own soils to save those who will only die equally miserably a decade or so down the line—and in many cases only after reproducing more children who are inevitably doomed to live and die in misery.

Paul Ehrlich: biology professor at Stanford and past president of ZPG

We know the world is finite. There is only so much pie. We may be able to expand the pie, but at any point in time, the pie *is* finite. How big a piece each person gets depends in part on how many people there are. At least for the foreseeable future, the fewer of us there are, the more there will be for each. That is true on a family, community, state, national and global basis.

At the moment, the future of mankind seems to depend on our maintaining the island of plenty in a sea of deprivation. If everyone shared equally, we would all be suffering from protein-deficiency brain damage— and that would probably be true even if we ate every last animal on earth.

As compassionate human beings, we grieve for the condition of mankind. But our grief must not interfere with our perception of reality and our planning for a better future for those who will come after us. Someone must protect the material and intellectual seed grain for the future. It seems to me that that someone is the U.S. We owe it to our children—and to their children's children's children's children.

These conclusions will be attacked, as they have been within Zero   *15* Population Growth, as simplistic and inhumane. But truth is often very simple and reality often inhumane.

---

1. What is Montgomery's argument here? Try to break it down into a major premise, a minor premise, and a conclusion. Don't worry if you have to rephrase some statements and use your own words to do this.

2. What persuasive techniques does Montgomery use here? How does he appeal to his audience? What emotions does he speak to? What images does he use to activate those emotions?

3. What information does Montgomery present to define himself for his audience?

4. Now that you've decided what emotions Montgomery tries to evoke in his audience and how he defines himself to his audience, how would you describe or define that audience?

5. If you are working on your own, prepare a statement in which you disagree with Montgomery. Try to counter his arguments with your own. If you were writing to the same audience as Montgomery is, what steps would you take to persuade your audience that your point should be considered as seriously as his?

    If you are working in a group, divide your group into a pro-Montgomery and an anti-Montgomery faction. The anti-Montgomery faction should prepare a logical and persuasive statement representing its position. Then the pro-Montgomery faction should prepare an equally logical and persuasive statement answering the first group's objections.

A Student Paper

After you have read this paper, answer the questions that follow it, alone or with your group.

THE COMMERCIALIZATION OF HEALTH AND FITNESS

Brigitte Doane

When I was young, maintaining my weight and becoming physically fit were not issues that I thought about every day. In fact, rarely did I think of them at all. When I was hungry, I found something in the house to eat, and when I exercised, it was as a form of play or a way to spend time with my friends. I didn't count calories, I didn't measure my fat intake, and under no circumstances would I ever have considered wasting any of my precious afternoon sun to jump around in front of a Jane Fonda workout video because I wanted to lose a few inches around my middle. Fitness was not something I read about, worried about, or scheduled into my day. It was a way of living that seemed to envelop everything I did. It was something that came naturally because I was happy and had to do something to expend my energy.

Nevertheless, as I got older, my behavior seemed to change. Looking around, I began to notice titles like "How to Lose Those Stubborn Last Pounds" and "Discover the Miracle Diet That Saved Oprah Winfrey" glaring at me from the cover of nearly every magazine. Turning on the television, I was bombarded with slogans to "Just do it" and "Drink milk," for, after all, "It does a body good." I saw ads for diet centers, fitness centers, and quick-fix diet shakes. Even restaurants began to offer low-calorie salad dressings and fat-free desserts. Everywhere I looked someone was trying to get me to lose weight or get into shape. Nonetheless, something within me kept me from jumping onto the bandwagon right away. Even though it was something I needed to do, the whole process just didn't seem natural.

To begin with, let's take a look at the entire health club phenomenon. I must admit that once I realized exercising was not a choice, I, too, handed over the few hundred dollars necessary to get myself in through the doors of one of these fitness temples. I have donned the little leotards with the perfectly matching leggings and have spent the money necessary for just the right pair of tennis shoes.

However, I'm not sure the experience was all it was cracked up to be. To begin with, the whole idea of spending my entire day at work insulated from Nature by four walls and a porthole just to spend my last few precious hours of daylight behind another four walls was more than a little depressing. Rather than getting the fresh air and sunshine I absolutely craved by taking a walk around my neighborhood or riding my bike to and from work, I would hastily jump in my car and drive directly to the gym just to breathe the same ventilated, overused air I breathed in all day at work.

In addition, despite claims to the contrary, the gym did not turn out   5
to be the ideal place to relieve all my physical and emotional tensions. In fact, it is amazing to me that with all the hoopla I keep hearing about stress in the American workplace and the drive for success, here was just one more place for the average person (myself included) to compare himself or herself to others with larger biceps, thinner thighs, and more shapely torsos. As if it isn't enough that all day long we are already entrenched in the common American battle for prestige, appearance, and material gain, then we have to subject ourselves to the stress of comparison and competition when it comes to doing something that should ultimately make us feel good about ourselves and make our lives more enjoyable.

Nonetheless, the problem I see with the Western idea of health maintenance is not centered solely on the fitness club. Even the workout video, although it eliminates the humiliating aspects of comparison, has its drawbacks. The other night I was sweating enthusiastically with the latest video guru. Although I was benefiting my body tremendously with oxygen and muscular strengthening, I realized I was also missing out on what I see now as some of the fundamental benefits of exercise. Exercise is supposed to be something that gets a person outside and in touch with the world. It is something that should allow a person to enjoy the environment as he or she walks through the neighborhood or feels the air change from warm to cool during a hike up a short hill. It should allow a person to see other people living or to see children playing in their yards. And a person should have the opportunity to ponder his or her life and thoughts during a long bike ride through the back roads of the community or while canoeing quietly across a lake. Needless to say, I experienced none of this trapped in my living room in front of a 40-minute workout tape. Currently, it seems that the whole concept of "working out" has become so centered on building bulk and dropping inches that people have forgotten that the original purpose of exercise was to add something to one's life and to make living more enjoyable.

And what about nutrition? The entire weight-loss industry has thought up countless ways to lose those lingering pounds. There are pre-canned liquid diets, pre-packaged frozen foods, weekly motivational meetings, diet centers, summer camps for forced weight loss, nutritional magazines, conferences, and motivational audiotapes. Weight loss has become too complex. Having gone on a weight-loss crusade myself a couple of years ago, I remember having to plan my meals a week in advance to ensure that I would get all the nutritional requirements I needed each day. I would have to follow little meal charts with allotted portions, and I would schedule my workout regimens to be sure I'd get in at least four of them a week for no less than 20 minutes each. I reluctantly started to count the calories, measure the grams of fat, and spend much more time than I should have reading articles on the benefits of vegetarianism, wheat grass, and taking various vitamin supplements. And having actually done all of this, I have to admit there were times I quietly wondered to myself why on earth I did it. Although it certainly was of benefit to watch what and how much I ate, the whole reason for losing weight is to be happy and live a healthier, more pleasurable life. With all the complexity built into my regimen, I was hardly able to enjoy even one day.

Nevertheless, I do realize that fitness and weight-loss programs are valuable. Having been overweight and out of shape in the past, I know that in this condition it is hard to enjoy even the simplest of life's little pleasures. I do wonder, however, if the commercialized emphasis on health and fitness has not brought us further from, rather than closer to, its very intentions. Much more than physical prowess, the entire motivation behind the health industry is supposed to be the improvement of the quality of life. The theory of the diet gurus is that the more time I spend and the more effort I expend in planning a fat-free, salt-free, pesticide-free diet, the longer and more fulfilling my life will be. I will have more energy and motivation to do the things I want to do and will enjoy my life more. Despite this, I can't help but think that Americans have segregated health and happiness into so many little categories that they will never see the overall picture. I have learned that health is about much more than working out four times a week and staying thin. It is about being able to carry out the plans and achieve the goals I have set for my life without being hindered by weakness, frailty, bad health, and lagging stamina.

I'm definitely not opposed to health and fitness, and I'm not opposed to achieving my dreams or being all I can be if that includes being thin or muscular. I do believe, however, that I need to keep my life in focus. I need to remember that if I think too much about achieving and becoming, I'm going to lose out on the thrill of just being.

---

1. What is the writer's argument in this paper?

2. What facts and observations does the writer use to support her argument?

3. How does the writer sequence the ideas she uses to support her conclusion?

4. What voice and tone does the writer use to persuade her audience?

5. What other persuasive elements do you find the writer using in this paper?

6. If you were in this writer's group or if you were editing her paper for her, what suggestions would you offer to help her make her paper more effective? Why do you think your suggestions would be useful?

An Invitation to Write

As you walk around your campus, pay attention to what people are arguing about; read the opinion-editorial section of your campus newspaper; become aware of problems that you encounter as you pursue your education. (Please define your "education" *very* broadly. It's more than classes.)

When you find an issue that is important to you (watch for your "felt sense"), discover what your position is with regard to that issue. Draft an argumentative piece of writing that represents your position to an audience.

Putting it All Together: Working with a Reading

Read the following piece of writing, noticing how Reed combines all of the elements that have been covered so far—organizational strategies, voice, figurative language, rhythm, and sound—to make his position and his attitude clear to his audience. Then, alone or with your group, answer the questions that follow this selection.

A VETERAN WRITES

Fred Reed

I begin to weary of the stories about veterans that are now in vogue with the newspapers, the stories that dissect the veteran's psyche as if prying apart a laboratory frog—patronizing stories written by style-section reporters who know all there is to know about chocolate mousse, ladies' fashions, and the wonderful desserts that can be made with simple jello. I weary of seeing veterans analyzed and diagnosed and explained by people who share nothing with veterans, by people who, one feels intuitively, would regard it as a harrowing experience to be alone in a backyard.

Week after week the mousse authorities tell us what is wrong with the veteran. The veteran is badly in need of adjustment, they say—lacks balance, needs fine tuning to whatever it is in society that one should be attuned to. What we have here, all agree, with omniscience and veiled condescension, is a victim: The press loves a victim. The veteran has bad dreams, say the jello writers, is alienated, may be hostile, doesn't socialize well—isn't, to be frank, quite right in the head.

But perhaps it is the veteran's head to be right or wrong in, and maybe it makes a difference what memories are in the head. For the jello writers the war was a moral fable on Channel Four, a struggle hinging on Nixon and Joan Baez and the inequities of this or that. I can't be sure. The veterans seem to have missed the war by having been away in Vietnam at the time and do not understand the combat as it raged in the internecine cocktail parties of Georgetown.°

Still, to me Vietnam was not what it was to the jello writers, not a ventilation of pious simplisms, not the latest literary interpretation of the domino theory. It left me memories the fashion writers can't imagine. It was the slums of Truong Minh Ky, where dogs' heads floated in pools of green water and three-inch roaches droned in sweltering back-alley rooms and I was happy. Washington knows nothing of hot, whorerich, beery Truong Minh Ky. I remember riding the bomb boats up the Mekong to Phnom Penh, with the devilish brown river closing in like a vise and rockets shrieking from the dim jungle to burst against the sandbagged wheelhouse, and crouching below the waterline between the diesel tanks. The mousse authorities do not remember this. I remember the villa on Monivong in Phnom Penh, with Sedlacek, the balding Australian hippie, and Naoki, the crazy freelance combat photographer, and Zoco, the Frenchman, when the night jumped and flickered with the boom of artillery and we listened to Mancini on shortwave and watched Nara dance. Washington's elite did not know Nara. They know much of politicians and of furniture.

If I try to explain what Vietnam meant to me—I haven't for years,   5
and never will again—they grow uneasy at my intensity. *My God,* their eyes say, *he sounds as though he liked it over there. Something in the experience clearly snapped an anchoring ligament in his mind and left him with odd cravings, a perverse view of life—nothing dangerous, of course, but. . . . The war did that to them,* they say. *War is hell.*

Well, yes, they may have something there. When you have seen a peasant mother screaming over three pounds of bright red mush that, thanks to God and a Chicom 107,° is no longer precisely her child, you see that Sherman° may have been on to something. When you have eaten fish with Khmer troops in charred Cambodian battlefields, where the heat beats down like a soft rubber truncheon and a wretched stink comes from shallow graves, no particular leap of imagination is necessary to notice that war is no paradise. I cannot say that the jello writers are wrong

---

Georgetown: a well-to-do section of Washington, D.C., where many high government officials reside
Chicom 107: Chinese Communist rocket used by the Viet Cong
Sherman: General William Tecumseh Sherman, who said, "War is hell."

in their understanding of war. But somehow I don't like hearing pieties about the war from these sleek, wise people who never saw it. It offends propriety.

There were, of course, veterans and veterans. Some hated the war, some didn't. Some went around the bend down in IV Corps, where leeches dropped softly down collars like green sausages and death erupted unexpected from the ungodly foliage. To the men in the elite groups— the Seals, Special Forces, Recondos, and Lurps who spent years in the Khmer bush, low to the ground where the ants bit hard—the war was a game with stakes high enough to engage their attention. They liked to play.

To many of us there, the war was the best time of our lives, almost the only time. We loved it because in those days we were alive, life was intense, the pungent hours passed fast over the central event of the age and the howling jets appeased the terrible boredom of existence. Psychologists, high priests of the mean, say that boredom is a symptom of maladjustment; maybe, but boredom has been around longer than psychologists have.

The jello writers would say we are mad to remember fondly anything about Nixon's war that Kennedy started. They do not remember the shuddering flight of a helicopter high over glowing green jungle that spread beneath us like a frozen sea. They never made the low runs a foot above treetops along paths that led like rivers through branches that clawed at the skids, never peered down into murky clearings and bubbling swamps of sucking snake-ridden muck. They do not remember monsoon mornings in the highlands, where dragons of mist twisted in the valleys, coiling lazily on themselves, puffing up and swallowing whole villages in their dank breath. The mousse men do not remember driving before dawn to Red Beach, when the headlights in the blackness caught ghostly shapes, maybe VC,° thin yellow men mushroom-headed in the night, bicycling along the alien roads. As nearly as I can tell, jello writers do not remember anything.

Then it was over. The veterans came home. Suddenly the world   *10* seemed to stop dead in the water. Suddenly the slant-eyed hookers were gone, as were the gunships and the wild drunken nights in places that the jello writers can't picture. Suddenly the veterans were among soft, proper people who knew nothing of what they had done and what they had seen, and who, truth to be told, didn't much like them.

Nor did some of us much like the people at home—though it was not at first a conscious distaste. Men came home with wounds and terrible memories and dead friends to be greeted by that squalling she-ass of Tom Hayden's,° to find a country that viewed them as criminals. Slowly, to

---

VC: Viet Cong
Tom Hayden: Hayden was married to Jane Fonda, who, at the time, was an antiwar activist.

more men than will admit to it, the thought came: *These are the people I fought for?* And so we lost a country.

We looked around us with new eyes and saw that, in a sense the mousse people could never understand, we had lost even our dignity. I remember a marine corporal at Bethesda Naval Hospital who, while his wounds healed, had to run errands for the nurses, last year's co-eds. "A hell of a bust," he said with the military's sardonic economy of language. "Machine gunner to messenger boy."

It wasn't exactly that we didn't fit. Rather, we saw what there was to fit with—and recoiled. We sought jobs, but found offices where countless bureaucrats shuffled papers at long rows of desks, like battery hens awaiting the laying urge, their bellies billowing over their belts. Some of us joined them but some, in different ways, fled. A gunship pilot of my acquaintance took to the law, and to drink, and spent five years discovering that he really wanted to be in Rhodesia. Others went back into the death-in-the-bushes outfits, where the hard old rules still held. I drifted across Asia, Mexico, Wyoming, hitchhiking and sleeping in ditches a lot until I learned that aberrant behavior, when written about, is literature.

The jello writers were quickly upon us. We were morose, they said, sullen. We acted strangely at parties, sat silently in corners and watched with noncommittal stares. Mentally, said the fashion experts, we hadn't made the trip home.

It didn't occur to them that we just had nothing to say about jello.   *15*
Desserts mean little to men who have lain in dark rifle pits over Happy Valley in rainy season, watching mortar flares tremble in low-lying clouds that flickered like the face of God, while in the nervous evening safeties clicked off along the wire and amtracs rumbled into alert idles, coughing and waiting.

Once, after the GIs had left Saigon, I came out of a bar on Cach Mang and saw a veteran with a sign on his jacket: VIET NAM: IF YOU HAVEN'T BEEN THERE, SHUT THE FUCK UP. Maybe, just maybe, he had something.

---

1. What do you think Reed's dominant idea is?
2. What dominant organizational strategy do you see Reed using?
3. What supporting organizational strategies do you see Reed using?
4. What voice does Reed choose?
5. What resources of language, repetition, and rhythm does Reed use to create his voice?
6. What audience does Reed have in mind? How do his choices of organizational strategy and voice take his audience into account?
7. What relationship does Reed create between himself and his audience with these choices? Do you think it's the most effective choice for his purposes? Why do you think so?

8. In his last paragraph Reed uses a word that readers rarely see in a formal essay. Does Reed "earn" his use of that word? Why do you think he chooses to use it?

_____

❧ *An Invitation to Write*

Find a subject based in your experience that you feel as strongly about as Reed feels about his subject. Write an essay, a story, a poem, or a short play that communicates that feeling to your reader. Use as many of the devices you've learned about as you think appropriate, taking into account your readers, what you believe their relationship to your subject to be, and how you feel about that relationship.

FURTHER READINGS

On the following pages you will find readings that present and support arguments. If your teacher assigns some or all of these readings or if you are inclined to read them on your own, pay attention to the ways the writers use argument to support their dominant ideas. Also, note how the writers use voice and style to engage your feelings, your interest, and your intellect.

Remember, these writers are writing to you—a fellow human being. They have chosen to tell you something about coping with the effort of being human in their worlds. See how their examples and ideas speak to your experience. See how the combination of your experiences and those the writers offer you might lead you to your own ideas about your world.

A MODEST PROPOSAL

For Preventing the Children of Poor People in Ireland from Being a Burden to Their Parents or Country, and for Making Them Beneficial to the Public

Jonathan Swift

It is a melancholy object to those who walk through this great town° or travel in the country, when they see the streets, the roads, and cabin doors, crowded with beggars of the female-sex, followed by three, four, or six children, all in rags and importuning every passenger for an alms. These mothers, instead of being able to work for their honest livelihood, are forced to employ all their time in strolling to beg sustenance for their helpless infants, who, as they grow up, either turn thieves for want of work, or leave their dear native country to fight for the Pretender° in Spain, or sell themselves to the Barbadoes.°

I think it is agreed by all parties that this prodigious number of children in the arms, or on the backs, or at the heels of their mothers, and frequently of their fathers, is in the present deplorable state of the kingdom a very great additional grievance; and therefore whoever could find out a fair, cheap, and easy method of making these children sound, useful members of the

---

town: Dublin
Pretender: claimant to the English throne, who was barred from succeeding to the throne in a Protestant revolution
Barbadoes: Many poor Irish tried to escape poverty by emigrating to the Barbadoes.

commonwealth would deserve so well of the public as to have his statue set up for a preserver of the nation.

But my intention is very far from being confined to provide only for the children of professed beggars; it is of a much greater extent, and shall take in the whole number of infants at a certain age who are born of parents in effect as little able to support them as those who demand our charity in the streets.

As to my own part, having turned my thoughts for many years upon this important subject, and maturely weighed the several schemes of other projectors,° I have always found them grossly mistaken in their computation. It is true, a child just dropped from its dam may be supported by her milk for a solar year, with little other nourishment; at most not above the value of two shillings,° which the mother may certainly get, or the value in scraps, by her lawful occupation of begging; and it is exactly at one year old that I propose to provide for them in such a manner as instead of being a charge upon their parents or the parish, or wanting food and raiment for the rest of their lives, they shall on the contrary contribute to the feeding, and partly to the clothing, of many thousands.

There is likewise another great advantage in my scheme, that it will prevent those voluntary abortions, and that horrid practice of women murdering their bastard children, alas, too frequent among us, sacrificing the poor innocent babes, I doubt, more to avoid the expense than the shame, which would move tears and pity in the most savage and inhuman breast.

The number of souls in this kingdom being usually reckoned one million and a half, of these I calculate there may be about two hundred thousand couples whose wives are breeders; from which number I subtract thirty thousand couples who are able to maintain their own children, although I apprehend there cannot be so many under the present distresses of the kingdom; but this being granted, there will remain an hundred and seventy thousand breeders. I again subtract fifty thousand for those women who miscarry, or whose children die by accident or disease within the year. There only remain an hundred and twenty thousand children of poor parents annually born. The question therefore is, how this number shall be reared and provided for, which, as I have already said, under the present situation of affairs, is utterly impossible by all the methods hitherto proposed. For we can neither employ them in handicraft or agriculture; we neither build houses (I mean in the country) nor cultivate land. They can very seldom pick up a livelihood by stealing till they arrive at six years old, except where they are of towardly parts,° although I confess they learn the rudiments much earlier, during which time they can however be looked upon only as probationers, as I have been informed by a principal gentleman in the county

5

---

projectors: people with projects, schemes
two shillings: about fifty cents
towardly parts: promising abilities

of Cavan, who protested to me that he never knew above one or two instances under the age of six, even in a part of the kingdom so renowned for the quickest proficiency in that art.

I am assured by our merchants that a boy or a girl before twelve years old is no salable commodity; and even when they come to this age they will not yield above three pounds, or three pounds and half a crown° at most on the Exchange; which cannot turn to account either to the parents or the kingdom, the charge of nutriment and rags having been at least four times that value.

I shall now therefore humbly propose my own thoughts, which I hope will not be liable to the least objection.

I have been assured by a very knowing American of my acquaintance in London, that a young healthy child well nursed is at a year old a most delicious, nourishing, and wholesome food, whether stewed, roasted, baked, or boiled; and I make no doubt that it will equally serve in a fricassee or a ragout.

I do therefore humbly offer it to public consideration that of the hundred and twenty thousand children, already computed, twenty thousand may be reserved for breed, whereof only one fourth part to be males, which is more than we allow to sheep, black cattle, or swine; and my reason is that these children are seldom the fruits of marriage, a circumstance not much regarded by our savages, therefore one male will be sufficient to serve four females. That the remaining hundred thousand may at a year old be offered in sale to the persons of quality and fortune through the kingdom, always advising the mother to let them suck plentifully in the last month, so as to render them plump and fat for a good table. A child will make two dishes at an entertainment for friends; and when the family dines alone, the fore or hind quarter will make a reasonable dish, and seasoned with a little pepper or salt will be very good boiled on the fourth day, especially in winter.

I have reckoned upon a medium that a child just born will weigh twelve pounds, and in a solar year if tolerably nursed increaseth to twenty-eight pounds.

I grant this food will be somewhat dear, and therefore very proper for landlords, who, as they have already devoured most of the parents, seem to have the best title to the children.

Infant's flesh will be in season throughout the year, but more plentiful in March, and a little before and after. For we are told by a grave author, an eminent French physician,° that fish being a prolific diet, there are more children born in Roman Catholic countries about nine months after Lent than at any other season; therefore, reckoning a year after Lent, the markets will be more glutted than usual, because the number of popish infants is at

10

---

half a crown: five shillings
French physician: François Rabelais, a sixteenth-century comic writer

least three to one in this kingdom; and therefore it will have one other collateral advantage, by lessening the number of Papists° among us.

I have already computed the charge of nursing a beggar's child (in which list I reckon all cottagers, laborers, and four fifths of the farmers) to be about two shillings per annum, rags included; and I believe no gentleman would repine to give ten shillings for the carcass of a good fat child, which, as I have said, will make four dishes of excellent nutritive meat, when he hath only some particular friend or his own family to dine with him. Thus the squire will learn to be a good landlord, and grow popular among the tenants; the mother will have eight shillings net profit, and be fit for work till she produces another child.

Those who are more thrifty (as I must confess the times require) may   *15* flay the carcass; the skin of which artificially° dressed will make admirable gloves for ladies, and summer boots for fine gentlemen.

As to our city of Dublin, shambles° may be appointed for this purpose in the most convenient parts of it, and butchers we may be assured will not be wanting; although I rather recommend buying the children alive, and dressing them hot from the knife as we do roasting pigs.

A very worthy person, a true lover of his country, and whose virtues I highly esteem, was lately pleased in discoursing on this matter to offer a refinement upon my scheme. He said that many gentlemen of this kingdom, having of late destroyed their deer, he conceived that the want of venison might be well supplied by the bodies of young lads and maidens, not exceeding fourteen years of age nor under twelve, so great a number of both sexes in every county being now ready to starve for want of work and service; and these to be disposed of by their parents, if alive, or otherwise by their nearest relations. But with due deference to so excellent a friend and so deserving a patriot, I cannot be altogether in his sentiments; for as to the males, my American acquaintance assured me from frequent experience that their flesh was generally tough and lean, like that of our schoolboys, by continual exercise, and their taste disagreeable; and to fatten them would not answer the charge. Then as to the females, it would, I think with humble submission, be a loss to the public, because they soon would become breeders themselves; and besides, it is not improbable that some scrupulous people might be apt to censure such a practice (although indeed very unjustly) as a little bordering upon cruelty; which, I confess, hath always been with me the strongest objection against any project, how well soever intended.

But in order to justify my friend, he confessed that this expedient was put into his head by the famous Psalmanazar,° a native of the island Formosa,

---

Papists: Catholics
artificially: skillfully
shambles: slaughterhouses
Psalmanazar: a Frenchman who passed himself off as a native of Formosa (Taiwan)

who came from thence to London above twenty years ago, and in conversation told my friend that in his country when any young person happened to be put to death, the executioner sold the carcass to persons of quality as a prime dainty; and that in his time the body of a plump girl of fifteen, who was crucified for an attempt to poison the emperor, was sold to his Imperial Majesty's prime minister of state, and other great mandarins of the court, in joints from the gibbet, at four hundred crowns. Neither indeed can I deny that if the same use were made of several plump young girls in this town, who without one single groat° to their fortunes cannot stir abroad without a chair,° and appear at the playhouse and assemblies in foreign fineries which they never will pay for, the kingdom would not be the worse.

Some persons of a desponding spirit are in great concern about that vast number of poor people who are aged, diseased, or maimed, and I have been desired to employ my thoughts what course may be taken to ease the nation of so grievous an encumbrance. But I am not in the least pain upon that matter, because it is very well known that they are every day dying and rotting by cold and famine, and filth and vermin, as fast as can be reasonably expected. And as to the younger laborers, they are now in almost as hopeful a condition. They cannot get work, and consequently pine away for want of nourishment to a degree that if at any time they are accidentally hired to common labor, they have not strength to perform it; and thus the country and themselves are happily delivered from the evils to come.

I have too long digressed, and therefore shall return to my subject. I think the advantages by the proposal which I have made are obvious and many, as well as of the highest importance.   20

For first, as I have already observed, it would greatly lessen the number of Papists, with whom we are yearly overrun, being the principal breeders of the nation as well as our most dangerous enemies; and who stay at home on purpose to deliver the kingdom to the Pretender, hoping to take their advantage by the absence of so many good Protestants, who have chosen rather to leave their country than to stay at home and pay tithes against their conscience to an Episcopal curate.

Secondly, the poorer tenants will have something valuable of their own, which by law may be made liable to distress,° and help to pay their landlord's rent, their corn and cattle being already seized and money a thing unknown.

Thirdly, whereas the maintenance of an hundred thousand children, from two years old and upwards, cannot be computed at less than ten shillings a piece per annum, the nation's stock will be thereby increased fifty thousand pounds per annum, besides the profit of a new dish introduced to the tables of all gentlemen of fortune in the kingdom who have any refine-

---

groat: a coin worth about four pennies
chair: a sedan chair, carried by servants
distress: seizure for payment of debts

ment in taste. And the money will circulate among ourselves, the goods being entirely of our own growth and manufacture.

Fourthly, the constant breeders, besides the gain of eight shillings sterling per annum by the sale of their children, will be rid of the charge of maintaining them after the first year.

Fifthly, this food would likewise bring great custom to taverns, where the vintners will certainly be so prudent as to procure the best receipts for dressing it to perfection, and consequently have their houses frequented by all the fine gentlemen, who justly value themselves upon their knowledge in good eating; and a skillful cook, who understands how to oblige his guests, will contrive to make it as expensive as they please.

Sixthly, this would be a great inducement to marriage, which all wise nations have either encouraged by rewards or enforced by laws and penalties. It would increase the care and tenderness of mothers toward their children, when they were sure of a settlement for life to the poor babes, provided in some sort by the public, to their annual profit instead of expense. We should see an honest emulation among the married women, which of them could bring the fattest child to the market. Men would become as fond of their wives during the time of their pregnancy as they are now of their mares in foal, their cows in calf, or sows when they are ready to farrow; nor offer to beat or kick them (as is too frequent a practice) for fear of a miscarriage.

Many other advantages might be enumerated. For instance, the addition of some thousand carcasses in our exportation of barreled beef, the propagation of swine's flesh, and improvement in the art of making good bacon, so much wanted among us by the great destruction of pigs, too frequent at our tables, which are no way comparable in taste or magnificence to a well-grown, fat, yearling child, which roasted whole will make a considerable figure at a lord mayor's feast or any other public entertainment. But this and many others I omit, being studious of brevity.

Supposing that one thousand families in this city would be constant customers for infants' flesh, besides others who might have it at merry meetings, particularly weddings and christenings, I compute that Dublin would take off annually about twenty thousand carcasses, and the rest of the kingdom (where probably they will be sold somewhat cheaper) the remaining eighty thousand.

I can think of no one objection that will possibly be raised against this proposal, unless it should be urged that the number of people will be thereby much lessened in the kingdom. This I freely own, and it was indeed one principal design in offering it to the world. I desire the reader will observe, that I calculate my remedy for this one individual kingdom of Ireland and for no other that ever was, is, or I think ever can be upon earth. Therefore let no man talk to me of other expedients: of taxing our absentees at five shillings a pound: of using neither clothes nor household furniture except what is of our own growth and manufacture: of utterly rejecting the materials and instruments that promote foreign luxury: of curing the expensiveness of pride, vanity, idleness, and gaming in our women: of introducing a vein of parsimony, prudence, and temperance: of learning to love our country, in the want of which we differ even from Laplanders and the inhabitants of Topinamboo:° of quitting our animosities and factions, nor acting any longer like the Jews, who were murdering one another at the very moment their city was taken: of being a little cautious not to sell our country and conscience for nothing: of teaching landlords to have at least one degree of mercy toward their tenants: lastly, of putting a spirit of honesty, industry, and skill into our shopkeepers; who, if a resolution could now be taken to buy only our native goods, would immediately unite to cheat and exact upon us in the price, the measure, and the goodness, nor could ever yet be brought to make one fair proposal of just dealing, though often and earnestly invited to it.

Therefore I repeat, let no man talk to me of these and the like expe-   *30* dients, till he hath at least some glimpse of hope that there will ever be some hearty and sincere attempt to put them in practice.

But as to myself, having been wearied out for many years with offering vain, idle, visionary thoughts, and at length utterly despairing of success, I fortunately fell upon this proposal, which, as it is wholly new, so it hath something solid and real, of no expense and little trouble, full in our own power, and whereby we can incur no danger in disobliging England. For this kind of commodity will not bear exportation, the flesh being of too tender a consistence to admit a long continuance in salt, although perhaps I could name a country° which would be glad to eat up our whole nation without it.

After all, I am not so violently bent upon my own opinion as to reject any offer proposed by wise men, which shall be found equally innocent, cheap, easy, and effectual. But before something of that kind shall be advanced in contradiction to my scheme, and offering a better, I desire the author or authors will be pleased maturely to consider two points. First, as things now stand, how they will be able to find food and raiment for an hundred thousand useless mouths and backs. And secondly, there being a round million of creatures in human figure throughout this kingdom, whose sole subsistence put into a common stock would leave them in debt two millions of pounds sterling, adding those who are beggars by profession to the bulk of farmers, cottagers, and laborers, with their wives and children who are beggars in effect; I desire those politicians who dislike my overture, and may perhaps be so bold to attempt an answer, that they will first ask the parents of these mortals whether they would not at this day think it a great happiness to have been sold for food at a year old in the manner I prescribe, and thereby have avoided such a perpetual scene of misfortunes as they have

---

Topinamboo: a district in Brazil
a country: England

since gone through by the oppression of landlords, the impossibility of paying rent without money or trade, the want of common sustenance, with neither house nor clothes to cover them from the inclemencies of the weather, and the most inevitable prospect of entailing the like or greater miseries upon their breed forever.

I profess, in the sincerity of my heart, that I have not the least personal interest in endeavoring to promote this necessary work, having no other motive than the public good of my country, by advancing our trade, providing for infants, relieving the poor, and giving some pleasure to the rich. I have no children by which I can propose to get a single penny; the youngest being nine years old, and my wife past childbearing.

WHY NOT USE FOOD AS FOOD?

George Will

The federal government is nibbling at the cheese glut. The Agriculture Department has proposed requiring that frozen pizzas contain a certain minimum amount of cheese and that the use of cheese substitutes be clearly confessed on packages.

The frozen pizza industry regards this proposal as the kind of Leninism that Ronald Reagan was elected to stop. But the cheese glut (which is just a portion of the dairy products surplus, which is just a bit of the agriculture surplus) demands boldness.

Jeffrey Birnbaum, a *Wall Street Journal* reporter, recently toured a dormant limestone mine in Missouri. There, the government "stores so much surplus cheese, butter and powdered milk that a visitor would be hard pressed to walk past it all in one day." A tour by golf cart reveals canyons of cheddar cheese in 500-pound barrels, towers of frozen butter in 68-pound boxes, endless aisles of 100-pound sacks of dried milk—61 million pounds of dairy products, enough to cover 13 football fields 17 feet deep, or fill a train stretching from Manhattan to Toledo.

This is just two percent of the 2.9 billion pounds of dairy products that taxpayers have bought. In recent years they have paid $3 billion, or $13,000 for every dairy farmer. Taxpayers are currently paying $275,000 an hour to buy more surpluses, and are paying $5 million a month to store the stuff.

Well, now. Perhaps a dozen-trillion pizzas would cut the current cheese glut, but that many pizzas would lead to a terrible pepperoni shortage. We need another idea. 5

Perhaps we should sell frozen pizzas to the Soviet Union. Moscow might send some of our pizzas, as it sends grain, to Nicaragua, but that is commerce in fungible goods. If Moscow cannot afford pizzas, we can do what we do regarding grain: give them credits and generally fiddle things so that pizzas (like the grain) cost Moscow less than it costs Americans to produce them.

Here is another whimsical idea: we could stop paying farmers to inundate markets and limestone mines with dairy products. Today the government is taxing consumers (everyone) to pay farmers to produce food that is, because of price supports, unnecessarily expensive when taxpayers buy it at supermarkets and is expensive when taxpayers pay to store it.

One study says that a $1-per-hundredweight reduction in the support price would knock nine cents off a gallon of milk and a pound of cheese, and 11 cents off a pound of butter, and $1.2 billion off consumers' food bills in a year. Furthermore, dairy products, being cheaper, would be more exportable, so there would be less to store.

But here is a better idea: use the food as food. America does not have enough productivity. Government should not pay people, as it today is paying farmers, to produce less—less of something that parts of the world need desperately. Surely it is not beyond the capacity of public policy to make America's agricultural bounty an asset to American policy. Indeed, it is a scandal not to.

Today in 18 black African countries (Morocco and Algeria, too, have   10
desperate needs), 20 million persons face starvation unless 600,000 tons of extra food reach them. Since 1960, Africa's food production has increased less than 2 percent a year—less than population growth. In nine countries, food production is more than 10 percent below 1960 levels.

The World Bank estimates that nearly 200 million persons—60 percent of all Africans—eat fewer calories daily than the United Nations considers a survival diet.

Drought is only part of the problem. Governments have made Africa unnecessarily vulnerable to such natural phenomena. Urban mobs demand food at artificially low prices, thus discouraging production. Government planners have tried to spur industrialization by holding down food prices in the hope that this would hold down urban wages. If someone could leash Africa's governments and unleash American farmers on Africa, the continent could produce 100 times more food than it does today.

Logistical problems (including problems posed by African bureaucracies) involved in even distributing food are staggering, and there is the danger that American food could produce dependency and further depress African agriculture. But an American attempt to solve these problems is as close as one can come in this world to an absolute moral imperative.

I am staring at a photograph of what looks, at first glance, to be a bold, wizened old man. Actually, it is a child. The child is sucking the withered breast of a woman who could be 19 years old. It is a sight to concentrate the mind on limestone mines full of food.

THE IMP OF THE PERVERSE

Edgar Allan Poe

In the consideration of the faculties and impulses—of the *prima mobilia*°
of the human soul, the phrenologists° have failed to make room for a propensity which, although obviously existing as a radical, primitive, irreduc-
ible sentiment, has been equally overlooked by all the moralists who have
preceded them. In the pure arrogance of the reason, we have all overlooked
it. We have suffered its existence to escape our senses, solely through want
of belief—of faith;—whether it be faith in Revelation, or faith in the Kabbala.° The idea of it has never occurred to us, simply because of its supererero-
gation.° We saw no *need* of the impulse—for the propensity. We could not
perceive its necessity. We could not understand, that is to say, we could not
have understood, had the notion of this *primum mobile* ever obtruded itself;
—we could not have understood in what manner it might be made to further the objects of humanity, either temporal or eternal. It cannot be denied
that phrenology, and in good measure, all metaphysicianism have been concocted *à priori.*° The intellectual or logical man, rather than the understanding or observant man, set himself to imagine designs—to dictate purposes
to God. Having thus fathomed to his satisfaction the intentions of Jehovah,
out of these intentions he built his innumerable systems of mind. In the
matter of phrenology, for example, we first determined, naturally enough,
that it was the design of the Deity that man should eat. We then assigned to
man an organ of alimentiveness,° and this organ is the scourge with which
the Deity compels man, will-I, nill-I, into eating. Secondly, having settled
it to be God's will that man should continue his species, we discovered an
organ of amativeness,° forthwith. And so with combativeness, with ideality, with causality, with constructiveness,—so, in short, with every organ,
whether representing a propensity, a moral sentiment, or a faculty of the
pure intellect. And in these arrangements of the *principia* of human action,
the Spurzheimites,° whether right or wrong, in part, or upon the whole,
have but followed, in principle, the footsteps of their predecessors; deducing

---

prima mobilia: Latin for "prime movers"
phrenologists: those who study the human skull as indicative of character and intellect
Kabbala: a Jewish tradition of mystical interpretation of the Old Testament
supererogation: beyond what is necessary
à priori: deductive reasoning
alimentiveness: from phrenology, having to do with eating
amativeness: from phrenology, having to do with love
Spurzheimites: followers of Johannes Spurzheim (1776–1832), a German phrenologist

and establishing every thing from the preconceived destiny of man, and upon the ground of the objects of his Creator.

It would have been wiser, it would have been safer to classify (if classify we must,) upon the basis of what man usually or occasionally did, and was always occasionally doing, rather than upon the basis of what we took it for granted the Deity intended him to do. If we cannot comprehend God in his visible works, how then in his inconceivable thoughts, that call the works into being! If we cannot understand him in his objective creatures, how then in his substantive moods and phases of creation?

Induction, _à posteriori,_° would have brought phrenology to admit, as an innate and primitive principle of human action, a paradoxical something, which we may call _perverseness,_ for want of a more characteristic term. In the sense I intend, it is, in fact, a _mobile_ without motive, a motive not _motivirt._° Through its promptings we act without comprehensible object; or, if this shall be understood as a contradiction in terms, we may so far modify the proposition as to say, that through its promptings we act, for the reason that we should _not._ In theory, no reason can be more unreasonable; but, in fact, there is none more strong. With certain minds, under certain conditions, it becomes absolutely irresistible. I am not more certain that I breathe, than that the assurance of the wrong or error of any action is often the one unconquerable _force_ which impels us, and alone impels us to its prosecution. Nor will this overwhelming tendency to do wrong for the wrong's sake, admit of analysis, or resolution into ulterior elements. It is a radical, a primitive impulse—elementary. It will be said, I am aware, that when we persist in acts because we feel we should _not_ persist in them, our conduct is but a modification of that which ordinarily springs from the _combativeness_ of phrenology. But a glance will show the fallacy of this idea. The phrenological combativeness has for its essence, the necessity of self-defence. It is our safeguard against injury. Its principle regards our well-being; and thus the desire to be well, is excited simultaneously with its development. It follows, that the desire to be well must be excited simultaneously with any principle which shall be merely a modification of combativeness, but in the case of that something which I term _perverseness,_ the desire to be well is not only not aroused, but a strongly antagonistical sentiment exists.

An appeal to one's own heart is, after all, the best reply to the sophistry just noticed. No one who trustingly consults and thoroughly questions his own soul, will be disposed to deny the entire radicalness of the propensity in question. It is not more incomprehensible than distinctive. There lives no man who at some period has not been tormented, for example, by an earnest desire to tantalize a listener by circumlocution. The speaker is aware that he displeases; he has every intention to please; he is usually curt, precise, and clear; the most laconic and luminous language is struggling for utterance

---

à posteriori: reasoning from evidence—inductive reasoning
motivirt: motivated

upon his tongue; it is only with difficulty that he restrains himself from giving it flow; he dreads and deprecates the anger of him whom he addresses; yet, the thought strikes him, that by certain involutions and parentheses, this anger may be engendered. That single thought is enough. The impulse increases to a wish, the wish to a desire, the desire to an uncontrollable longing, and the longing, (to the deep regret and mortification of the speaker, and in defiance of all consequences,) is indulged.

We have a task before us which must be speedily performed. We know that it will be ruinous to make delay. The most important crisis of our life calls, trumpet-tongued, for immediate energy and action. We glow, we are consumed with eagerness to commence the work, with the anticipation of whose glorious result our whole souls are on fire. It must, it shall be undertaken to-day, and yet we put it off until to-morrow; and why? There is no answer, except that we feel *perverse,* using the word with no comprehension of the principle. To-morrow arrives, and with it a more impatient anxiety to do our duty, but with this very increase of anxiety arrives, also, a nameless, a positively fearful, because unfathomable, craving for delay. This craving gathers strength as the moments fly. The last hour for action is at hand. We tremble with the violence of the conflict within us,—of the definite with the indefinite—of the substance with the shadow. But, if the contest have proceeded thus far, it is the shadow which prevails,—we struggle in vain. The clock strikes, and is the knell of our welfare. At the same time, it is the chanticleer-note to the ghost that has so long overawed us. It flies—it disappears—we are free. The old energy returns. We will labor *now.* Alas, it is *too late!*

We stand upon the brink of a precipice. We peer into the abyss—we grow sick and dizzy. Our first impulse is to shrink from the danger. Unaccountably we remain. By slow degrees our sickness, and dizziness, and horror, become merged in a cloud of unnameable feeling. By gradations, still more imperceptible, this cloud assumes shape, as did the vapor from the bottle out of which arose the genius in the Arabian Nights. But out of this *our* cloud upon the precipice's edge, there grows into palpability, a shape, far more terrible than any genius, or any demon of a tale, and yet it is but a thought, although a fearful one, and one which chills the very marrow of our bones with the fierceness of the delight of its horror. It is merely the idea of what would be our sensations during the sweeping precipitancy of a fall from such a height. And this fall—this rushing annihilation—for the very reason that it involves that one most ghastly and loathsome of all the most ghastly and loathsome images of death and suffering which have ever presented themselves to our imagination—for this very cause do we now the most vividly desire it. And because our reason violently deters us from the brink, *therefore,* do we the most impetuously approach it. There is no passion in nature so demoniacally impatient, as that of him, who shuddering upon the edge of a precipice, thus meditates a plunge. To indulge for a moment, in any attempt at *thought,* is to be inevitably lost; for reflection but urges us to forbear, and *therefore* it is, I say, that we *cannot.* If there be no friendly arm to check us, or if we fail in a sudden effort to prostrate ourselves backward from the abyss, we plunge, and are destroyed.

Examine these and similar actions as we will, we shall find them resulting solely from the spirit of the *Perverse*. We perpetrate them merely because we feel that we should *not*. Beyond or behind this, there is no intelligible principle: and we might, indeed, deem this perverseness a direct instigation of the arch-fiend, were it not occasionally known to operate in furtherance of good.

I have said thus much, that in some measure I may answer your question—that I may explain to you why I am here—that I may assign to you something that shall have at least the faint aspect of a cause for my wearing these fetters, and for my tenanting this cell of the condemned. Had I not been thus prolix, you might either have misunderstood me altogether, or, with the rabble, have fancied me mad. As it is, you will easily perceive that I am one of the many uncounted victims of the Imp of the Perverse.

It is impossible that any deed could have been wrought with a more thorough deliberation. For weeks, for months, I pondered upon the means of the murder. I rejected a thousand schemes, because their accomplishment involved a *chance* of detection. At length, in reading some French memoirs, I found an account of a nearly fatal illness that occurred to Madam Pilau, through the agency of a candle accidentally poisoned. The idea struck my fancy at once. I knew my victim's habit of reading in bed. I knew, too, that his apartment was narrow and ill-ventilated. But I need not vex you with impertinent details. I need not describe the easy artifices by which I substituted, in his bed-room candle-stand, a wax-light of my own making, for the one which I there found. The next morning he was discovered dead in his bed, and the coroner's verdict was,—"Death by the visitation of God."

Having inherited his estate, all went well with me for years. The idea of detection never once entered my brain. Of the remains of the fatal taper, I had myself carefully disposed. I had left no shadow of a clue by which it would be possible to convict, or even to suspect, me of the crime. It is inconceivable how rich a sentiment of satisfaction arose in my bosom as I reflected upon my absolute security. For a very long period of time, I was accustomed to revel in this sentiment. It afforded me more real delight than all the mere worldly advantages accruing from my sin. But there arrived at length an epoch, from which the pleasurable feeling grew, by scarcely perceptible gradations, into a haunting and harassing thought. It harassed because it haunted. I could scarcely get rid of it for an instant. It is quite a common thing to be thus annoyed with the ringing in our ears, or rather in our memories, of the burthen of some ordinary song, or some unimpressive snatches from an opera. Nor will we be the less tormented if the song itself be good, or the opera air meritorious. In this manner, at last, I would perpetually catch myself pondering upon my security, and repeating, in a low under-tone, the phrase, "I am safe."

One day, while sauntering along the streets, I arrested myself in the act of murmuring, half aloud, these customary syllables. In a fit of petulance, I

10

re-modelled them thus:—"I am safe—I am safe—yes—if I be not fool enough to make open confession!"

No sooner had I spoken these words, than I felt an icy chill creep to my heart. I had had some experience in these fits of perversity, (whose nature I have been at some trouble to explain,) and I remembered well, that in no instance, I had successfully resisted their attacks. And now my own casual self-suggestion, that I might possibly be fool enough to confess the murder of which I had been guilty, confronted me, as if the very ghost of him whom I had murdered—and beckoned me on to death.

At first, I made an effort to shake off this nightmare of the soul. I walked vigorously—faster—still faster—at length I ran. I felt a maddening desire to shriek aloud. Every succeeding wave of thought overwhelmed me with new terror, for, alas! I well, too well, understood that to *think,* in my situation, was to be lost. I still quickened my pace. I bounded like a madman through the crowded thoroughfares. At length, the populace took the alarm, and pursued me. I felt *then* the consummation of my fate. Could I have torn out my tongue, I would have done it—but a rough voice resounded in my ears—a rougher grasp seized me by the shoulder. I turned—I gasped for breath. For a moment, I experienced all the pangs of suffocation; I became blind, and deaf, and giddy; and then, some invisible fiend, I thought, struck me with his broad palm upon the back. The long-imprisoned secret burst forth from my soul.

They say that I spoke with a distinct enunciation, but with marked emphasis and passionate hurry, as if in dread of interruption before concluding the brief but pregnant sentences that consigned me to the hangman and to hell.

Having related all that was necessary for the fullest judicial conviction, I   *15*
fell prostrate in a swoon.

But why shall I say more? To-day I wear these chains, and am *here!* To-morrow I shall be fetterless!—*but where?*

A VERY OLD MAN WITH ENORMOUS WINGS: A TALE FOR CHILDREN

Gabriel García Márquez

Translated by Gregory Rabassa

On the third day of rain they had killed so many crabs inside the house that Pelayo had to cross his drenched courtyard and throw them into the sea, because the newborn child had a temperature all night and they thought it was due to the stench. The world had been sad since Tuesday. Sea and sky were a single ash-gray thing and the sands of the beach, which on March nights glimmered like powdered light, had become a stew of mud and rotten shellfish. The light was so weak at noon that when Pelayo was coming back to the house after throwing away the crabs, it was hard for him to see what it was that was moving and groaning in the rear of the courtyard. He had to go very close to see that it was an old man, a very old man, lying face down in the mud, who, in spite of his tremendous efforts, couldn't get up, impeded by his enormous wings.

Frightened by that nightmare, Pelayo ran to get Elisenda, his wife, who was putting compresses on the sick child, and he took her to the rear of the courtyard. They both looked at the fallen body with mute stupor. He was dressed like a ragpicker. There were only a few faded hairs left on his bald skull and very few teeth in his mouth, and his pitiful condition of a drenched great-grandfather had taken away any sense of grandeur he might have had. His huge buzzard wings, dirty and half-plucked, were forever entangled in the mud. They looked at him so long and so closely that Pelayo and Elisenda very soon overcame their surprise and in the end found him familiar. Then they dared speak to him, and he answered in an incomprehensible dialect with a strong sailor's voice. That was how they skipped over the inconvenience of the wings and quite intelligently concluded that he was a lonely castaway from some foreign ship wrecked by the storm. And yet, they called in a neighbor woman who knew everything about life and death to see him, and all she needed was one look to show them their mistake,

"He's an angel," she told them. "He must have been coming for the child, but the poor fellow is so old that the rain knocked him down."

On the following day everyone knew that a flesh-and-blood angel was held captive in Pelayo's house. Against the judgment of the wise neighbor woman, for whom angels in those times were the fugitive survivors of a celestial conspiracy, they did not have the heart to club him to death. Pelayo watched over him all afternoon from the kitchen, armed with his bailiff's club, and before going to bed he dragged him out of the mud and locked him up with the hens in the wire chicken coop. In the middle of the night, when the rain stopped, Pelayo and Elisenda were still killing crabs. A short time afterward the child woke up without a fever and with a desire to eat. Then they felt magnanimous and decided to put the angel on a raft with fresh water and provisions for three days and leave him to his fate on the high seas. But when they went out into the courtyard with the first light of dawn, they found the whole neighborhood in front of the chicken coop having fun with the angel, without the slightest reverence, tossing him things to eat through the openings in the wire as if he weren't a supernatural creature but a circus animal.

Father Gonzaga arrived before seven o'clock, alarmed at the strange news. By that time onlookers less frivolous than those at dawn had already arrived and they were making all kinds of conjectures concerning the captive's future. The simplest among them thought that he should be named

5

mayor of the world. Others of sterner mind felt that he should be promoted to the rank of five-star general in order to win all wars. Some visionaries hoped that he could be put to stud in order to implant on earth a race of winged wise men who could take charge of the universe. But Father Gonzaga, before becoming a priest, had been a robust woodcutter. Standing by the wire, he reviewed his catechism in an instant and asked them to open the door so that he could take a close look at that pitiful man who looked more like a huge decrepit hen among the fascinated chickens. He was lying in a corner drying his open wings in the sunlight among the fruit peels and breakfast leftovers that the early risers had thrown him. Alien to the impertinences of the world, he only lifted his antiquarian eyes and murmured something in his dialect when Father Gonzaga went into the chicken coop and said good morning to him in Latin. The parish priest had his first suspicion of an imposter when he saw that he did not understand the language of God or know how to greet His ministers. Then he noticed that seen close up he was much too human: he had an unbearable smell of the outdoors, the back side of his wings was strewn with parasites and his main feathers had been mistreated by terrestrial winds, and nothing about him measured up to the proud dignity of angels. Then he came out of the chicken coop and in a brief sermon warned the curious against the risks of being ingenuous. He reminded them that the devil had the bad habit of making use of carnival tricks in order to confuse the unwary. He argued that if wings were not the essential element in determining the difference between a hawk and an airplane, they were even less so in the recognition of angels. Nevertheless, he promised to write a letter to his bishop so that the latter would write to his primate so that the latter would write to the Supreme Pontiff in order to get the final verdict from the highest courts.

His prudence fell on sterile hearts. The news of the captive angel spread with such rapidity that after a few hours the courtyard had the bustle of a marketplace and they had to call in troops with fixed bayonets to disperse the mob that was about to knock the house down. Elisenda, her spine all twisted from sweeping up so much marketplace trash, then got the idea of fencing in the yard and charging five cents admission to see the angel.

The curious came from far away. A traveling carnival arrived with a flying acrobat who buzzed over the crowd several times, but no one paid any attention to him because his wings were not those of an angel but, rather, those of a sidereal bat. The most unfortunate invalids on earth came in search of health: a poor woman who since childhood had been counting her heartbeats and had run out of numbers; a Portuguese man who couldn't sleep because the noise of the stars disturbed him; a sleepwalker who got up at night to undo the things he had done while awake; and many others with less serious ailments. In the midst of that shipwreck disorder that made the earth tremble, Pelayo and Elisenda were happy with fatigue, for in less than a week they had crammed their rooms with money and the line of pilgrims waiting their turn to enter still reached beyond the horizon.

The angel was the only one who took no part in his own act. He spent his time trying to get comfortable in his borrowed nest, befuddled by the hellish heat of the oil lamps and sacramental candles that had been placed along the wire. At first they tried to make him eat some mothballs, which, according to the wisdom of the wise neighbor woman, were the food prescribed for angels. But he turned them down, just as he turned down the papal lunches that the penitents brought him, and they never found out whether it was because he was an angel or because he was an old man that in the end he ate nothing but eggplant mush. His only supernatural virtue seemed to be patience. Especially during the first days, when the hens pecked at him, searching for the stellar parasites that proliferated in his wings, and the cripples pulled out feathers to touch their defective parts with, and even the most merciful threw stones at him, trying to get him to rise so they could see him standing. The only time they succeeded in arousing him was when they burned his side with an iron for branding steers, for he had been motionless for so many hours that they thought he was dead. He awoke with a start, ranting in his hermetic language and with tears in his eyes, and he flapped his wings a couple of times, which brought on a whirlwind of chicken dung and lunar dust and a gale of panic that did not seem to be of this world. Although many thought that his reaction had been one not of rage but of pain, from then on they were careful not to annoy him, because the majority understood that his passivity was not that of a hero taking his ease but that of a cataclysm in repose.

Father Gonzaga held back the crowd's frivolity with formulas of maidservant inspiration while awaiting the arrival of a final judgment on the nature of the captive. But the mail from Rome showed no sense of urgency. They spent their time finding out if the prisoner had a navel, if his dialect had any connection with Aramaic, how many times he could fit on the head of a pin, or whether he wasn't just a Norwegian with wings. Those meager letters might have come and gone until the end of time if a providential event had not put an end to the priest's tribulations.

It so happened that during those days, among so many other carnival attractions, there arrived in town the traveling show of the woman who had been changed into a spider for having disobeyed her parents. The admission to see her was not only less than the admission to see the angel, but people were permitted to ask her all manner of questions about her absurd state and to examine her up and down so that no one would ever doubt the truth of her horror. She was a frightful tarantula the size of a ram and with the head of a sad maiden. What was most heart-rending, however, was not her outlandish shape but the sincere affliction with which she recounted the details of her misfortune. While still practically a child she had sneaked out of her parents' house to go to a dance, and while she was coming back through the woods after having danced all night without permission, a fearful thunderclap rent the sky in two and through the crack came the lightning bolt of brimstone that changed her into a spider. Her only nourishment came from

10

the meatballs that charitable souls chose to toss into her mouth. A spectacle like that, full of so much human truth and with such a fearful lesson, was bound to defeat without even trying that of a haughty angel who scarcely deigned to look at mortals. Besides, the few miracles attributed to the angel showed a certain mental disorder, like the blind man who didn't recover his sight but grew three new teeth, or the paralytic who didn't get to walk but almost won the lottery, and the leper whose sores sprouted sunflowers. Those consolation miracles, which were more like mocking fun, had already ruined the angel's reputation when the woman who had been changed into a spider finally crushed him completely. That was how Father Gonzaga was cured forever of his insomnia and Pelayo's courtyard went back to being as empty as during the time it had rained for three days and crabs walked through the bedrooms.

The owners of the house had no reason to lament. With the money they saved they built a two-story mansion with balconies and gardens and high netting so that crabs wouldn't get in during the winter, and with iron bars on the windows so that angels couldn't get in. Pelayo also set up a rabbit warren close to town and gave up his job as bailiff for good, and Elisenda bought some satin pumps with high heels and many dresses of iridescent silk, the kind worn on Sunday by the most desirable women in those times. The chicken coop was the only thing that didn't receive any attention. If they washed it down with creolin and burned tears of myrrh inside it every so often, it was not in homage to the angel but to drive away the dungheap stench that still hung everywhere like a ghost and was turning the new house into an old one. At first, when the child learned to walk, they were careful that he not get too close to the chicken coop. But then they began to lose their fears and got used to the smell, and before the child got his second teeth he'd gone inside the chicken coop to play, where the wires were falling apart. The angel was no less standoffish with him than with other mortals, but he tolerated the most ingenious infamies with the patience of a dog who had no illusions. They both came down with chicken pox at the same time. The doctor who took care of the child couldn't resist the temptation to listen to the angel's heart, and he found so much whistling in the heart and so many sounds in his kidneys that it seemed impossible for him to be alive. What surprised him most, however, was the logic of his wings. They seemed so natural on that completely human organism that he couldn't understand why other men didn't have them too.

When the child began school it had been some time since the sun and rain had caused the collapse of the chicken coop. The angel went dragging himself about here and there like a stray dying man. They would drive him out of the bedroom with a broom and a moment later find him in the kitchen. He seemed to be in so many places at the same time that they grew to think that he'd been duplicated, that he was reproducing himself all through the house, and the exasperated and unhinged Elisenda shouted that it was awful living in that hell full of angels. He could scarcely eat and his antiquarian eyes had also become so foggy that he went about bumping into posts. All he had left were the bare cannulae of his last feathers. Pelayo threw a blanket over him and extended him the charity of letting him sleep in the shed, and only then did they notice that he had a temperature at night, and was delirious with the tongue twisters of an old Norwegian. That was one of the few times they became alarmed, for they thought he was going to die and not even the wise neighbor woman had been able to tell them what to do with dead angels.

And yet he not only survived his worst winter, but seemed improved with the first sunny days. He remained motionless for several days in the farthest corner of the courtyard, where no one would see him, and at the beginning of December some large, stiff feathers began to grow on his wings, the feathers of a scarecrow, which looked more like another misfortune of decrepitude. But he must have known the reason for those changes, for he was quite careful that no one should notice them, that no one should hear the sea chanteys that he sometimes sang under the stars. One morning Elisenda was cutting some bunches of onions for lunch when a wind that seemed to come from the high seas blew into the kitchen. Then she went to the window and caught the angel in his first attempts at flight. They were so clumsy that his fingernails opened a furrow in the vegetable patch and he was on the point of knocking the shed down with the ungainly flapping that slipped on the light and couldn't get a grip on the air. But he did manage to gain altitude. Elisenda let out a sigh of relief, for herself and for him, when she saw him pass over the last houses, holding himself up in some way with the risky flapping of a senile vulture. She kept watching him even when she was through cutting the onions and she kept on watching until it was no longer possible for her to see him, because then he was no longer an annoyance in her life but an imaginary dot on the horizon of the sea.

HOLY SONNET 6

John Donne

Death be not proud, though some have called thee
Mighty and dreadful, for, thou art not so,
For, those whom thou think'st, thou dost overthrow,
Die not, poor death, nor canst thou kill me;
From rest and sleep, which but thy pictures be,   5
Much pleasure, then from thee, much more must flow,
And soonest our best men with thee do go,
Rest of their bones, and soul's delivery.
Thou art slave to fate, chance, kings, and desperate men,

And dost with poison, war, and sickness dwell,   *10*
And poppy° or charms can make us sleep as well,
And better than thy stroke; why swell'st° thou then?
One short sleep past, we wake eternally,
And death shall be no more, Death thou shalt die.

THE MOTHER

Gwendolyn Brooks

Abortions will not let you forget.
You remember the children you got that you did not get,
The damp small pulps with a little or with no hair,
The singers and workers that never handled the air.
You will never neglect or beat   *5*
Them, or silence or buy with a sweet.
You will never wind up the sucking-thumb
Or scuttle off ghosts that come.
You will never leave them, controlling your luscious sigh,
Return for a snack of them, with gobbling mother-eye.   *10*

I have heard in the voices of the wind the voices of my dim killed children.
I have contracted. I have eased
My dim dears at the breasts they could never suck.
I have said, Sweets, if I sinned, if I seized
Your luck   *15*
And your lives from your unfinished reach,
If I stole your births and your names,
Your straight baby tears and your games,
Your stilted or lovely loves, your tumults, your marriages, aches, and your
       deaths,
If I poisoned the beginnings of your breaths,   *20*
Believe that even in my deliberateness I was not deliberate.
Though why should I whine,
Whine that the crime was other than mine?—
Since anyhow you are dead.
Or rather, or instead,   *25*
You were never made.

___

11. *poppy:* opium
12. *swell'st:* puff yourself up

But that too, I am afraid,
Is faulty: oh, what shall I say, how is the truth to be said?
You were born, you had body, you died.
It is just that you never giggled or planned or cried.   *30*

Believe me, I loved you all.
Believe me, I knew you, though faintly, and I loved, I loved you
All.

THE GROUNDHOG

Richard Eberhart

In June, amid the golden fields,
I saw a groundhog lying dead.
Dead lay he; my senses shook,
And mind outshot our naked frailty.
There lowly in the vigorous summer   *5*
His form began its senseless change,
And made my senses waver dim
Seeing nature ferocious in him.
Inspecting close his maggots' might
And seething caldron of his being,   *10*
Half with loathing, half with a strange love,
I poked him with an angry stick.
The fever arose, became a flame
And Vigor circumscribed the skies,
Immense energy in the sun,   *15*
And through my frame a sunless trembling.
My stick had done nor good nor harm.
Then stood I silent in the day
Watching the object, as before;
And kept my reverence for knowledge   *20*
Trying for control, to be still,
To quell the passion of the blood;
Until I had bent down on my knees
Praying for joy in the sight of decay.
And so I left; and I returned   *25*
In Autumn strict of eye, to see
The sap gone out of the groundhog,
But the bony sodden hulk remained.
But the year had lost its meaning,
And in intellectual chains   *30*

I lost both love and loathing,
Mured° up in the wall of wisdom.
Another summer took the fields again
Massive and burning, full of life,
But when I chanced upon the spot   35
There was only a little hair left,
And bones bleaching in the sunlight
Beautiful as architecture;
I watched them like a geometer,
And cut a walking stick from a birch.   40
It has been three years, now.
There is no sign of the groundhog.
I stood there in the whirling summer,
My hand capped a withered heart,
And thought of China and of Greece,   45
Of Alexander° in his tent;
Of Montaigne° in his tower,
Of Saint Theresa° in her wild lament.

---

32. *Mured:* walled
46. *Alexander:* Alexander the Great (356–323 B.C.), Macedonian king famous for conquering much of the world
47. *Montaigne:* Michel de Montaigne (1533–1592), French essayist who commented on human affairs
48. *Saint Theresa:* Saint Theresa of Avila (1515–1582), a mystic who founded a religious order

PART 6

Using Sources

18

The Research Paper

PREPARING TO WRITE YOUR PAPER

The idea of writing a research paper makes many students nervous or impatient. Writing a long paper and assembling support for your dominant idea by sifting through other people's ideas to judge which of them offer the most effective evidence can be intimidating. Or based on your experience with research and research papers, you may think there is little point to them. You may have considered many of them tedious exercises—digging up boring information in the library just to complete an assignment that didn't particularly interest you in the first place.

On the other hand, think of the times you wanted to know about something for your own good reasons. Perhaps you had some money to spend and you were looking forward to buying yourself a good camera, a computer, or even a car. Before you spent your money, you probably wanted to know if you were spending it intelligently on a good product or wasting it on a shoddy piece of equipment. You probably did research in consumer magazines and magazines dealing specifically with the product you wanted to buy, or you borrowed or bought books that dealt with that product. There might have been other times when you became interested in a particular subject or a field of study. Perhaps you were considering a career or thinking about changing your major, or you had discovered a hobby or sport that interested you. In any case, you wanted to know more about something. Most likely you went to the library or to a bookstore and got some books on the subject. Perhaps you subscribed to magazines because you wanted to keep up with new ideas in that area.

In all those cases, you did research. Any time you go beyond your own experience—into books, magazines, specialized journals, or even when you speak to another person who knows more about a subject than you do—you are doing research.

In fact, the word *research* comes from the French *rechercher,* which means "to seek." And that is exactly what you do whenever you do research: you seek out information. And when you search for knowledge about a subject that interests you, your expenditure of time and energy doesn't seem to be an empty exercise.

These facts lead to the same truth regarding writing research papers as they do about any act of writing. If you feel a reason to write and a need to know about your subject as well as a sense that it is important to you to communicate what you've learned to others, then you will find yourself interested in collecting and arranging the material that leads you and your reader to your conclusion.

When you work on a research paper dealing with events and ideas that mean something to you, you not only learn more about an area that interests you, you also develop writing and critical thinking skills that will lead to success in almost any area. By writing a research paper, you learn to test your ideas against existing evidence; you learn to evaluate and choose between conflicting opinions; you develop the ability to analyze your material carefully and effectively. All these skills are essential to success in almost every field.

Discovering the Limits of the Job

It's always a good idea to find out as much as you can about the requirements of any project before you start it. Gathering this information can save you a lot of wasted effort as well as keep you from doing an inadequate job. This is as true in writing a research paper as it is in undertaking any task.

Before you begin a research paper, be certain you know what is required of you. Your instructor may give you a set of specifications. Among them might be the length of the paper and the types and number of sources. In addition, your instructor might limit you to scholarly sources, or he or she might allow you to use popular magazines, interviews, films, or television shows as well. If you are not certain what you are being asked to do, be sure to ask your teacher to clarify any confusing elements for you *before* you begin.

Choosing Your Subject

When you understand the requirements for your paper, you can begin to choose a general subject. If your teacher has provided you with a list of general subjects for your paper, choose the one that seems most interesting to you. If, as is often the case, the subject is up to you, you will generally find that you'll give yourself the chance to write a more successful paper if you begin with a general area that interests you and that you want to know something more about. This area may grow out of your experiences or what you have learned in your class at the time you write the paper. For example, you might find that a critical situation at your school directly affects you. The effects of a change in the course requirements of your major might offer you an opportunity to uncover more information. You might have come across some information in one of your courses that you would like to follow further. The newspaper might provide you with a subject. Or you might find an area of research that directly and immediately benefits you. You might be in the market for a product, such as a motorcycle. Or you might be investigating moving into an apartment off campus and see a way of using this opportunity to find out enough to make an intelligent decision and to record your discoveries for others.

At this point, you should think only in terms of a general area of investigation. As you learn more about the subject through your research, you can narrow your scope as well as begin to formulate a dominant idea.

PRELIMINARY RESEARCH: DISCOVERING AND LIMITING YOUR SUBJECT

Your research will be much easier if you begin with a preliminary idea of what issues or events you intend to concentrate on. Having a general sense of what you want to investigate helps you decide what information is important and what questions you need to ask.

Earlier in this book you discovered the difference between foreground and background. That difference is especially important as you begin to collect material for your research paper. What you find in the foreground and what recedes into the background are usually determined by what you have chosen to focus your attention on. Unless you have an area of investigation to focus your attention, you cannot distinguish what is important to observe and what is not, what serves as a background for the important facts and what is irrelevant. Once you know the general area of your concern—your subject—you can begin to make intelligent choices as to what you should pay attention to and what you can let go.

Unless you're already very familiar with your subject, you'll have trouble narrowing it until you know enough about it to see it as a whole and in a very general way. To get that sort of view of your material, you begin with preliminary research. This sort of research does not concern itself with highly specialized books covering a very narrow part of your subject, nor does it necessarily require very close reading. Instead, it's often a good idea to begin with books that deal generally with your subject or with articles in popular magazines or in the newspapers. Read through them quickly to get an idea of what the primary issues or themes are and to see which of them appeals to you.

As you do preliminary reading and research, more limited ideas for a paper will probably occur to you. Make sure to note them so that you will have a list you can refer to after you have finished your preliminary reading. These limited subjects will give you a foundation for your later work.

When you've finished your preliminary research, look at your list of subjects. Approach this list as if it were the result of one of the discovery strategies you used when you worked on a shorter paper. Keep your attention primed _ɔr the subject that seems to suggest the greatest reason to write to you. Once you have found it, begin to quiz yourself. Ask yourself why this subject appears to have the most interest for you. Most likely you will find that it leaps out at you because it suggests a dominant idea, possibly one that makes an assertion that something is so, not so, or must be done. That is, this subject strikes your felt sense that something is wrong and needs to be corrected or that something is right and that your audience needs to know about it.

Having at least a preliminary sense of your dominant idea is especially important in the process of research. As you begin to dig more and more deeply into your subject, you need a sieve to sort what is important from what is not. That sieve is your provisional dominant idea.

However, you should not settle on a final version of your dominant idea too quickly. Writing a research paper is in many ways like all the other writing discussed in this book. As you write and revise, as you add more material through your research, and as you learn more and think more about your subject, you may very quickly find your dominant idea changing. What you begin with at this point is a working, or provisional, dominant idea. As you absorb more information, you will move toward a final dominant idea that may look very different from the one you started with. For example, it is possible that as you read further in the field, you will discover material that contradicts your working dominant idea, especially if the idea is based on a controversial issue. It would be dishonest to ignore that material. You have to account for it either by showing how the position that material represents is not a valid one or, if you discover that the contradiction is valid, by modifying your dominant idea.

PRIMARY AND SECONDARY RESEARCH: USING THE LIBRARY

Your paper is bound to contain both *primary* and *secondary* research and sources. Primary research is based upon your own experience or observations. Primary sources are accounts by individuals who directly witnessed the material covered by your subject, or, if your research is in literature, primary sources are the work or works that are themselves the subject of your writing. However, you cannot do a complete job of supporting your dominant idea without examining relevant secondary information. You do secondary research when you consult what others have said about your subject—for example, a commentary on the account of an event another has reported or critical commentary on a work of literature. You will most likely do some of your primary research and the bulk of your secondary research by consulting material held in a library.

A library is a collection of books, periodicals, audiotapes, videotapes, microfilms, and microfiches. Each subject in any of these classifications is called a "holding." All of the information contained in the holdings is available to you for your research. Learning how to find that information as quickly and as accurately as possible helps you conduct the best sort of research. If you're not yet familiar with your library, sign up for a library tour if the library offers one. In addition, you can usually find informative handouts near the central desk where books are checked out.

The material held by your library is arranged according to one of two systems of classification: the Dewey Decimal System or the Library of Congress System. Both of these systems assign a call number to each library holding. The material is then arranged in the library according to the number it has been assigned. Figure 18.1 illustrates both cataloging systems.

Your library has a card catalog, which is a database of all the material the library holds. The card catalog is a collection of index card–sized cards. Usually, the information is classified according to three different principles, each having its own collection of cards. One set of files contains cards arranged alphabetically by the last names of the authors of the various holdings; in another set, the cards are arranged alphabetically by subject matter. The third arranges the cards alphabetically by the titles of the holdings.

Figure 18.1 Cataloging systems: Dewey Decimal and Library of Congress

Dewey Decimal System		*Library of Congress System*	
000–099	General Works	A	General Works
100–199	Philosophy	B	Philosophy, Psychology, Religion
200–299	Religion		
300–399	Social Sciences	C	History and Auxiliary Sciences
400–499	Language	D	History and Topography (except North and South America)
500–599	Pure Science		
600–699	Technology (Applied Sciences)	E–F	History and Topography (North and South America)
700–799	The Arts	G	Geography and Anthropology
800–899	Literature	H	Social Sciences
900–999	History	J	Political Science
		K	Law
		L	Education
		M	Music
		N	Fine Arts
		P	Language and Literature
		Q	Science
		R	Medicine
		S	Agriculture
		T	Technology
		U	Military Science
		V	Naval Science
		Z	Bibliography and Library Science

Some libraries now keep the card catalog in a computer database as well. Usually, you can access this information through terminals placed throughout the building. If this is the case in your library, make certain that you learn how to use these terminals. They are a tremendously powerful searching tool that can save you a lot of time compared with the old card catalogs.

When you begin your research, you'll probably have a fairly clear general idea of the subject of your paper. Therefore, it's best to begin your work in the library with the subject heading section of the card catalog. If you don't find as many books as you would like under the subject heading you start with, look for books under related subject headings. Often the last line of each card listing a book under a given subject heading lists related subject headings. Sometimes you can find related subject headings listed on a separate card at the front of each section of the catalog devoted to a major subject heading.

If your subject is the work of a single writer, you might want to begin with the catalog arranged by authors' last names to see what your library's holdings of your author's work look like. Remember, however, that if your subject is an author, quite possibly that person has been the subject of another writer's work. You must also look up your author's name in the subject catalog.

You most likely will not have much use for the catalog arranged by titles of works at the beginning of your research. However, once you have begun to dig more deeply into your subject, you might find one writer referring to a work by another writer. At that point, the title catalog is as useful as the author catalog for locating the book.

Figure 18.2 shows an example of a card—in this case, a subject card. Author and title cards contain the same information once you get past the

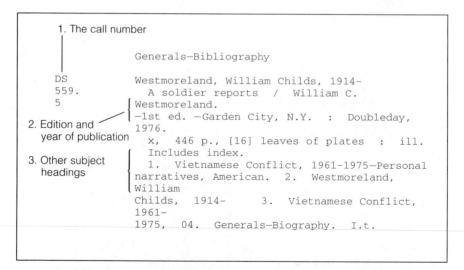

Figure 18.2 A Card-Catalog Subject Card

heading. Study the example carefully. The most useful parts of the card for you (numbered in the illustration) are these:

1. *The call number.* In the upper left corner of the card you'll find the call number. This number tells you the book's location in the library. Your library probably has a map or directory that tells you where to find the books under a particular call number. When you find the call number grouping, you might not find the book you are looking for. Look on adjacent shelves. Sometimes people are careless about returning books to their proper places.

2. *The edition and year of publication.* Sometimes a library will have copies of every edition and revision of a book. Unless you have a good reason not to do so, be certain you use the most recent edition of the book. It will contain the most up-to-date information about your subject. You can find yourself looking very silly when you've used out-of-date information and your reader knows it.

3. *Other subject headings.* To repeat: Sometimes books that are important to your subject are cataloged under other headings. You should exhaust all the possibilities that you can.

Reference Works

Because reference works help you do your preliminary research and help you define the limits of your subject, they are very useful for beginning your exploration. But all reference works condense and limit their information to such a degree that they are not appropriate for serious, intelligent research. Reference works rarely have much more than basic facts. They lack the interpretive material that makes a serious book or article important and interesting. They will, however, point you in useful directions. Here is a list of common, important reference works.

Biography

International Who's Who
Who's Who in America

Business and Economics

Dictionary of Banking and Finance
Encyclopedia of Economics

Ethnic and Feminist Studies

Encyclopedia of Feminism
Harvard Encyclopedia of American Ethnic Groups

Fine Arts

New Grove Dictionary of American Music
The New Harvard Dictionary of Music
The Oxford Companion to Art
The Thames and Hudson Dictionary of Art Terms

Literature and Film

The Oxford Companion to American Literature
The Oxford Companion to English Literature
World Encyclopedia of the Film

History and Political Science

Editorials on File
Encylopedia of American Political History
Facts on File
A Political Handbook of the World

Philosophy and Religion

A Dictionary of Non-Christian Religions
The Encyclopedia of American Religions
An Encyclopedia of Philosophy

Science, Technology, and Mathematics

A Dictionary of Mathematics
Encylopedia of Medical History
McGraw-Hill Encyclopedia of Science and Technology
The Merck Index of Chemicals and Drugs
The Physician's Desk Reference

Psychology and Education

Encyclopedia of Education
Encyclopedia of Psychology
Encyclopedia of Special Education

Social Sciences

Dictionary of Anthropology
Encyclopedia of Crime and Justice
International Encyclopedia of the Social Sciences

Almost certainly, your libary has other works of equal or greater useful-ness. You'll find reference holdings in the subject card catalog with the no-tation "REF" on the card. Some libraries keep a separate card catalog of reference works. In the reference room itself, you might find that your li-brary keeps the reference works arranged alphabetically by subject; or you might find the books arranged by call number. (In the Library of Congress System, the call numbers of all reference works begin with "Z," but each work has a unique number.) If you become lost or confused, find a person who works in the reference section. He or she will be happy to help you in your search. Don't hesitate to ask for help.

Periodicals

Periodicals are magazines or journals that are published at regular or intermittent intervals throughout the year. There are three types of period-icals: general, serious, and scholarly.

General periodicals are written for the average reader. Among this type of publication you can find newspapers; news magazines, such as *Time* or *U.S. News and World Report;* magazines that make scientific or technical issues accessible to the average reader, such as *Psychology Today* or *Discover;* and magazines for people who are interested in a particular subject, such as *Car and Driver* or *Gourmet.*

Articles in these publications use an informal, often personal, writing style and present their subjects generally. These articles are useful for background information and an overview of a subject. However, they rarely examine their subjects deeply or comprehensively enough to be useful for a research paper. In addition, because these articles rarely cite their sources completely, you often cannot establish the reliability of the information they contain.

Serious periodicals fall somewhere between the general and the scholarly periodicals. They contain articles written for well-educated laypersons rather than experts in a field. *Scientific American* is a good example of a serious periodical. Although the articles in serious periodicals provide you with documentation, it is not as comprehensive as that provided in scholarly periodicals.

Scholarly periodicals are written for readers with specialized knowledge in a particular field who want to follow the information contained in the articles to its sources. Such journals include the *Journal of the American Psychoanalytic Association* or the *Journal of English and Germanic Philology.* Articles in these publications pursue their topics to the greatest depth possible. They are written by experts in their fields. These articles develop their ideas with facts; references to previous studies; and clear, logical argument. They thoroughly cite the ideas they borrow, allowing you to pursue those ideas and the lines of reasoning the authors used.

Indexes, Abstracts, and Bibliographies

Indexes are cumulative listings of articles published in a specific group of journals and magazines. Major newspapers, such as the *New York Times* or the *San Francisco Chronicle,* also print annual subject directories.

Many libraries have moved away from keeping some of these directories in bound volumes. Instead, the material arrives on microfilm, computer disks, or CD-ROM, or it may be accessed through a computer and a modem. If your library has moved in this direction, ask a reference librarian which of these indexes and directories are on-line and which years they cover. If you are inexperienced with computer database searches, be certain to ask a librarian how to use the on-line directories *before* you try to do so. If you don't know the structure of the directory or how to conduct a search, you'll take far more time than is necessary to find the information you need. (However, chances are very slim that you will hurt the computer.) Trying to find information without knowing how to retrieve it can also be so frustrating that you will give up. Libraries often post written instructions near every terminal. Some provide pamphlets with complete instructions for using the computer terminals.

If your library does not yet have a computerized system, you'll have to find the bound indexes and bibliographies, which are usually in the periodicals room or in the reference room. Normally, if they are in the periodicals room, they are arranged alphabetically. If they are in the reference room, they are arranged by call number. Rarely, bibliographies or indexes are shelved in the stacks with books in the same field of study under the call number for that field. In any case, you can look up the bibliography or index you need in the card catalog.

Here is a sampling of indexes and bibliographies that you can find in most college libraries. This list does not begin to cover specialized publications within most fields. It is probably a good idea to speak with a professor who teaches in your field of interest to learn of other indexes and bibliographies that are available.

General

Biography Index
Humanities Index
New York Times *Index*
Reader's Guide to Periodical Literature
Social Sciences Index
Speech Index

Arts and Literature

Art Index
Book Review Index
Film Literature Index
Modern Language Association International Bibliography
Music Index
New York Times Book Review *Index*
Play Index

Business and Economics

Business Periodicals Index
Instructional Bibliography of Economics
Wall Street Journal *Index*

Education

Education Abstracts
Education Index
ERIC Research in Education

History, Political Science, and Government

Historical Abstracts
Monthly Guide to United States Government Publications
Political Science Bibliographies

Philosophy and Religion

Philosopher's Index
Religion Index

Sciences

Applied Science and Technology Index
Biological Abstracts
Botanical Bibliographies
Chemical Abstracts
Engineering Index Annual
Environment Index
International Computer Bibliography

THE WORKING BIBLIOGRAPHY

As you read books and articles on your subject, you will find that some of them are not as useful as you had hoped and that others are clearly promising and contain information that you think you might want to include in your paper. As you begin to discover these sources, prepare a working bibliography for yourself: a master list of potential sources. Begin a working bibliography early in your research and keep it up-to-date as you work. Nothing is quite as frustrating as finding yourself in the middle of writing your paper and vaguely remembering a source of information that you can no longer track down.

Because you cannot be certain how your paper is going to turn out until you finish it and because you cannot be certain what your dominant idea will finally be when you draft your paper, it is a good idea to include in your working bibliography every source that you think might possibly be useful. This means that your working bibliography will contain far more sources than you will use in your paper. But, again, it is more difficult to discover toward the end of your writing that a source you originally thought was not quite relevant enough to record has suddenly become essential to your paper than it is to note sources that you don't ultimately use.

Recording Bibliographic Information

The easiest way to arrange your working bibliography is to keep each source on a separate index card. You will find that four-by-six-inch or, better yet, five-by-seven-inch index cards will be more useful than three-by-five-inch cards. The larger card allows you to record all the information necessary to identify your source while leaving you room to jot brief notes to yourself about why a source looks promising or about the information it contains.

Whatever else you put on your index card, be certain to include the following pieces of information:

If your source is a book, write down its author (last name first), title, edition (if relevant), city of publication, publisher's name, date of publication, and library call number.

If your source is an article in a reference text, write down the author's name (last name first) if the article is signed, the title of the article, the name of the reference work, the edition, the page numbers covered by the article, and the reference work's call number.

If your source is an article in a periodical, write down the name of the author (last name first), the title of the article, and the title of the periodical; also record the date, the volume and issue numbers, or the month or season and year of publication of the periodical, as well as the pages on which the article appears.

In all cases, record the name(s) of the author(s) of the work exactly as it or they appear on the title page because, in the case of more than one author, the author listed first is considered to be the primary author. If the work is credited to an organization, a university, or an institute, assume that the organization itself is the author.

Here is a summary of the elements to list on the working bibliography card for various types of publications.

A Book

1. The author's name, last name first.
2. The complete title.
3. The publisher's location and name. (If more than one location is listed, use the city listed first or most prominently on the title page.)
4. The most recent year of copyright.
5. The edition (if relevant).
6. The volume number (for multivolume works).

Zukav, Gary. *The Dancing Wu-Li Masters.* New York: Bantam, 1979.

A General Periodical

1. The author's name (if one is given).
2. The title of the article.
3. The title of the periodical.
4. The date (both month and year—and day if the magazine is published more than once a month).
5. The pages the article appears on.

Shapiro, Andrew L. "Giving Cons and Ex-Cons the Vote." *The Nation* 20 December 1993. 767–68.

A Newspaper Article

1. The author's name (if one is given).
2. The title of the article.

3. The name of the newspaper and the edition.
4. The section in which the article appears.
5. The pages the article appears on.

Karys, April. "Prize Hog Dies of Heat Prostration at County Fair."
San Luis Obispo Telegram-Tribune 2 Aug. 1993, sec. A: 1.

An Article in a Book-Length Anthology

1. The author's name.
2. The title of the article.
3. The title of the book.
4. The editor of the book.
5. The edition (if relevant).
6. The publisher's location and the publisher.
7. The copyright date.
8. The pages on which the article appears.

Shippey, T. A. "The Cold War in Science Fiction." *Science Fiction:
A Critical Guide*. Ed. Patrick Parrinder. New York: Longman, 1979.
90–109.

An Article in a Scholarly Journal

1. The author's name.
2. The title of the article.
3. The title of the journal.
4. The date of publication. (Include volume and issue numbers as well
   as year, or the month or season if no issue number is given.)
5. The pages on which the article appears.

Holland, Norman N. "Literary Interpretation and the Three Phases of
Psychoanalysis." *Critical Inquiry* 3.2 (1976): 221–34.

Figure 18.3 shows sample bibliography cards for a book, an article in a
reference text, and an article in a periodical.

Narrowing Your Working Bibliography

Now that you have skimmed the material in your field and you have
your working bibliography on index cards, you should think about narrowing your working bibliography down to those sources you think will be the
most useful for your paper. Review the sources in your working bibliography and judge them by the following standards:

Relevance. In putting your working bibliography together, you might
have worked solely from the title of a book or an article, or you might
have skimmed the piece. Now take a close look at the material and see
if it really contains anything important to your idea.

Timeliness. How long ago was this source published? The subject you
have chosen and the type of research you are doing will influence your

Book

Hoffman, Abbie
Woodstock Nation: A Talk-Rock Album
New York: Random, 1969
HN65
H55

Reference Text

Bender, Paul
"Obscenity"
Encyclopedia Americana
1981 ed.

Journal

Peut, Daoud
"How to Write a Composition Textbook"
The Journal of Esoteric Information
27.3 (1994)
21-56

Figure 18.3 Bibliography Cards: Book, Article in Reference Text, and Periodical Article.

judgment in this area. If, for example, you are researching a historical subject, sources published at the time of the event are probably just as important as those that have been published recently. On the other hand, if you have chosen to work with a modern development in your field, you will probably want to restrict your research to current material.

Objectivity. Is this source biased? The fact that a writer reaches a conclusion and that he or she states it strongly is not evidence of bias. As you read, ask yourself whether the writer has taken other points of view into account, especially those that oppose his or her conclusions. Has the writer answered those opposing positions logically?

Once you have filtered from your working bibliography those entries that are not relevant or that are not adequate, put those cards aside and save the ones that you need. However, don't throw the discards away. You might find later in your writing that a source you thought you didn't need has suddenly become essential to your argument.

TAKING NOTES

Taking notes as you read your primary and secondary sources is the way you save information and ideas that you might use in developing your dominant idea. One of the most important elements of writing a research paper is the ability to retrieve information effectively. As you consult your sources, you'll gather a lot of information. When you get down to writing, you'll need a way of organizing and retrieving this material as quickly as possible.

Organizing Information for Retrieval

It's normally impossible to have all your sources available to refer to as you draft your paper. You may need to return a source to the library before you start writing, and some sources cannot be removed from the library. When you discover you need one of your sources, it might have been borrowed by someone else, the library might be closed, or you might not be within reach of the library where the source is held.

It is possible to note all your information in a loose-leaf binder or on a notepad. But then you face the problem of having to leaf through loose pages in search of a single piece of information—a frustrating and unnecessarily time-consuming process.

As it was for your working bibliography, the most effective way to record and arrange your information is to use index cards. Again, it is probably best to use the largest cards you can. It's easier—and there's less chance of error—to record all the material reflecting one piece of information on a single index card than to staple or paper-clip two or three cards together. When you use index cards and confine yourself to noting one—and only one—piece of information on each card, then you can retrieve that piece of information easily.

As you read your primary and secondary sources, make certain that you are following the writers' arguments clearly and that you record all the important facts and the way the writers have reasoned from those facts. Also be sure that you have grasped the writers' central ideas. Trace the relationship between the supporting points and the writers' conclusions and see how the supporting details develop and define the supporting points. In short, be aware of the connection between a general concept and the subordinate material that gives that concept unity and logical sense. Use the same approaches to reading another person's statement that you have developed in revising your own writing.

As you read your sources, stay conscious of the ways each source's ideas and their support speak to and connect with your working dominant idea as well as to what you already know about your material. When you find a source presenting material you already know or that you have already recorded from another source, you might not need to take notes. However, if the source presents new material that is relevant and important to your ideas, take full notes. It is always better to overdo the job. Take notes on anything that you think *just might* have something to do with your idea or that you suspect *might possibly* be important to your paper. When you finish your paper, you will probably find yourself with a stack of note cards containing information that you never used. However, you have already discovered in your writing that you cannot be sure what your dominant idea will be, what the relevant supporting material will be, and what your major organizational strategy will be until your writing is finished. You do not want to find yourself discovering that your dominant idea, its support, or its shape is changing and you have not taken the notes necessary to support that new dominant idea.

To repeat, buy the largest cards you can and make certain that you record *only one source* and *only one piece of information* on each card. Also, make it easy to recall, retrieve, and arrange your information by giving each card a heading at the top that accurately reflects the information it contains. If you record your information in a binder or a notebook, you will probably find yourself having to cut and paste your material to make sense of it. Furthermore, sheets of paper tempt you to fill each piece, recording as many bits of information as each sheet will hold. Finding a single piece of information will be frustrating at best.

To increase the usefulness of your notes during the writing process, you should record on each information card:

A key word or short phrase at the top of the card that tells you what the note is about. As you begin to recognize subtopics to your key words or phrases, be certain to record the subtopic after the main heading.

Complete information. If you have written down the author's exact words, be certain to enclose the portion of your note that is a direct quotation in quotation marks. If you fill up a card, finish on another one and staple the two together. (Don't use paper clips. They have a habit of getting detached.)

The source of the information. Write the author's last name and the title of his or her work on the card. (Your working bibliography card for the source contains the publication data.)

The page or pages in the source where the information can be found. If the material extends over several pages in the source, show clearly where the page breaks occur.

Figure 18.4 is a sample of an information card.

Kinds of Notes

DIRECT QUOTATIONS Notes that reproduce another author's statement word for word are direct quotations. It's best to use a direct quotation when the source's ideas are unusual or controversial. When you directly quote the source, you show that you have represented your source's viewpoint accurately. It is also a good idea to quote a source directly when the author's words are especially effective or striking.

If you record a direct quotation on your note card, be certain to record the author's statement *exactly* as it appears in the source, including the punctuation. As long as you don't change the meaning of the original, you can eliminate a phrase or a sentence from the quotation if it's not relevant to your point. You show your reader that you have omitted a phrase or a

> Eastern Mysticism: Unity and Individuality
>
> "When the Eastern mystics tell us that they experience all things and events as manifestations of a basic oneness, this does not mean that they pronounce all things to be equal. They recognize the individuality of things, but at the same time they are aware that all differences and contrasts are relative within an all-embracing unity."
>
> Capra. *The Tao of Physics*, 145.

Figure 18.4 Sample Information Card

sentence by inserting an ellipsis—three spaced periods—where the deleted words would have occurred. For example, here is an original quotation:

> A biography is constructed from ruins, but, as any archaeologist will tell you, there is never the means to unearth all the rooms, or follow the buried roads, or dig into every cistern for treasure.

Here is the quotation with an ellipsis to show that material has been omitted:

> A biography is constructed from ruins, but . . . there is never the means to unearth all the rooms, or follow the buried roads, or dig into every cistern for treasure.

If you eliminate material from the end of a sentence, place the period that ends the sentence in its usual place—immediately after the last letter of the sentence—and follow it with three spaced periods that signal your reader that something has been omitted.

> A biography is constructed from ruins, but, as any archaeologist will tell you, there is never the means to unearth all the rooms. . . .

If you eliminate material from the beginning of a quotation, you don't need an ellipsis. Just place the quotation marks where you start quoting directly, and, unless the first word ordinarily requires capitalization, you don't have to capitalize it.

SUMMARIES When you summarize, you condense somebody else's ideas and put them into your own words. Summaries usually present a central idea and its main supporting points and key details. When you take notes, you can sometimes record this type of material in outline form, to be expanded into your own words later. Or you may want to record the summary material as a brief paragraph. When you summarize, be certain that you use the author's major terms to maintain the precision of his or her idea, or, if you choose to put the idea entirely into your own words, make certain the words you choose mean *exactly* the same thing as the author intended.

Here is a direct quotation:

> Drug laws greatly increase the price of illegal drugs, often forcing users to steal to get the money to obtain them. Although difficult to estimate, the black market prices of heroin and cocaine appear to be about 100 times greater than their pharmaceutical prices. For example, a hospital-dispensed dose of morphine (a drug from which heroin is easily derived) costs only pennies; legal cocaine costs about $20 per ounce. It is frequently estimated that at least 40 percent of all property crime in the United States is committed by drug users so that they can maintain their habits. That amounts to about 4 million crimes per year and $7.5 billion in stolen property.

And here is a summary:

Four million crimes and $7.5 billion in stolen property every year in the United States are the result of drug laws. Because drugs are not legal, the black market prices of heroin and cocaine appear to be 100 times greater than the pharmaceutical prices. Thus, users are forced to steal in order to get money for these drugs.

COMBINED NOTES As you take notes, you may discover that much of the material in a source is best summarized but that some of the source's exact wording makes the point so well that you want to keep it. In that case, you can summarize the bulk of the material, including only a few words from the source. Be certain to put quotation marks around the source's language.

Here is a direct quotation from a source:

It is the rarest thing in the world to hear a rational discussion of vivisection. Those who disapprove of it are commonly accused of "sentimentality," and very often their arguments justify the accusation. They paint pictures of pretty little dogs on dissecting tables. But the other side lies open to exactly the same charge. They also defend the practice by drawing pictures of suffering women and children whose pain can be relieved (we are assured) only by the fruits of vivisection. The one appeal, quite as clearly as the other, is addressed to emotion, to the particular emotion we call pity. And neither appeal proves anything. If the thing is right—and if right at all, it is a duty—then pity for the animal is one of the temptations we must resist in order to perform that duty. If the thing is wrong, then pity for human suffering is precisely the temptation which will lure us into doing that wrong thing. But the real question—*whether* it is right or wrong—remains meanwhile just where it was.

And here is the combined note:

People rarely discuss vivisection rationally. Both sides appeal to their audience's emotions through sentimentality. Either "they paint pictures of pretty little dogs on dissecting tables," or they speak of relieving human suffering. Since both appeals are addressed to emotion, neither proves anything. The question of whether vivisection is right or wrong never gets addressed rationally.

Plagiarism

Both copyright law and the ethics of scholarship require that you credit another person for his or her ideas *whether you directly quote that person's words or you put his or her ideas into your own words*. If you fail to give credit to a source, you have plagiarized. If you plagiarize, you undermine your credibility with your reader by showing him or her that you are probably dishonest, not to be trusted. In addition, one purpose of acknowledging your sources is to allow your readers to follow up in those sources if they want to learn more about your topic. Failure to cite your sources or to cite them accurately keeps your reader from discovering additional information.

You must provide documentation in the following cases:

When you *quote directly, word for word,* from a source.

When you *summarize in your own words* ideas or information from a source. The only exception to this rule is material that is commonly known and accepted (whether or not you were aware of it) or material that is a matter of historical or scientific record.

When you *combine a summary and a quotation.*

There are specific formats for citing material from outside sources; they will be covered later in this chapter. But as you take notes, it is important that you know the definition of plagiarism. Recording citation information properly, completely, and clearly in your notes makes it much easier to avoid plagiarism. Make certain that each note includes its source and its page number and that each bibliography card is complete.

WRITING YOUR PAPER

Now that you have completed your research, you're ready to begin writing your paper. However, keep in mind that the process of writing a research paper can turn back on itself just as easily as the process of writing a shorter piece can. As you write, you may discover that you need to follow an idea a little further and that you might have to do more research.

Reexamining Your Dominant Idea

When you began your research, you had a preliminary sketch of your dominant idea. It is possible, even probable, that as you did your research you found your dominant idea changing. You might have discovered that your dominant idea oversimplified the issue. Or your research might have altered your original dominant idea in some way.

Now is the time to reconsider your dominant idea and to revise it, if necessary, in terms of the information you have discovered through your research. This new or revised dominant idea is the beginning point for your first draft. Remember, though, that as you write, you may discover reasons to change your dominant idea again.

Preparing a Preliminary Outline for Your Paper

For many people writing a research paper, an outline is a useful tool. It may also help you. An outline allows you to group and sequence your major points and the supporting material. When you have an outline, you have a very general plan for your paper that you can follow or modify as you write. In addition, making an outline may help you focus your attention on such issues as where your support is strong and where it might need some further development. It may also help you decide whether your main ideas follow each other in a logical sequence.

It is important to remember that an outline is only a temporary plan for your paper. It might change as you write your paper and discover better ways of arranging your material. When you show your plan to your group or to your instructor (if he or she has asked to see it), you might get suggestions for revising it. Don't feel that you *must* follow your first outline simply because you wrote it down.

When you put your outline together, concentrate on the body of your paper. Remember that introductions and conclusions are best written at the end—when you know what you are introducing and concluding. Generally, the most effective way to arrange an outline is to write your provisional dominant idea at the top of the page. Then:

List your main topics in the order you plan to discuss them, giving each of them a roman numeral.

List relevant subtopics under the main topics in the order in which you plan to present them. Indent the subtopics under the main topics. Give each subtopic a capital letter.

List supporting points in order under each of the subtopics. Indent the supporting points under the subtopics. Give each supporting point an arabic number.

List specific details in order under each of the supporting points. Indent the details under the supporting points. Label each specific detail with a lowercase letter. Instead of writing the complete specific detail in your outline, make a clear note of what you intend to do. For example, instead of the full quote from Smith, write, "Smith quote here."

Here is how part of an effective outline might look:

Dominant Idea

I. Main Topic
   A. Subtopic.
      1. Supporting point.
         a. Specific detail.
         b. Specific detail.
      2. Supporting point.
         a. Specific detail.
         b. Specific detail.
   B. Subtopic.
      1. Supporting point.
         a. Specific detail.
      2. Supporting point.
         a. Specific detail.
         b. Specific detail.

II. Main Topic
   A. Subtopic.
      1. Supporting point.
         a. Specific detail.
         b. Specific detail.
         c. Specific detail.
      2. Supporting point.
         a. Specific detail.
         b. Specific detail.
   B. Subtopic, etc.

Sorting Your Note Cards

Once you have your provisional outline completed, you can sort your note cards. The simplest way to do this is to first group the cards by main topic. Then work with each main topic, grouping the cards by subtopics and supporting points until your arrangement matches the outline. This will not be difficult if you have remembered to clearly note each card's contents at the top. Use rubber bands to keep each group of cards together. Then you won't have to shuffle through all your cards to find the specific card you need as you write your first draft.

Writing Your First Draft

As you do with any other piece of writing, you begin a research paper with a first draft. Remember, even though you have note cards reflecting your research ideas, you are still exploring your subject when you draft. As in the case of any first draft, your job is to get the ideas down on the page without censoring your writing. You are still exploring the dimensions of your dominant idea and your thoughts about it. You need not be concerned about issues of grammar, spelling, or style at this stage. On the other hand, the draft for a research paper requires you to make decisions as to what sources you intend to include and where you want to place that material. Use your outline, but don't be its slave. You might discover a more effective sequence for your material, find that some material doesn't fit, or realize that information you thought you weren't going to use has suddenly become very important. As you write, refer to your note cards. Don't count on your memory for the correct piece of information every time you need it. Include appropriate quotations or summaries in your draft. Rather than losing your train of thought by recopying this material into your draft, clip or staple the card containing the information in the appropriate place on the page or write yourself a clear note that directs you to the appropriate card.

As you write your draft, it is probably better to write more than you might need. Explain each of your points as completely as possible; include alternative ways of making your point if they occur to you. If you do not do this as you draft, you might not be able to recall the idea if you need it when you begin to revise.

While you write your draft, remember that the purpose of your paper is not simply to string together other people's ideas and facts you have gained through your research. You are presenting *your* dominant idea. You must interpret and comment upon the material you are including as the result of your research to lead your audience to your conclusion, to show how that material supports your dominant idea, and to keep your paper unified and coherent.

REVISING, EDITING, AND PROOFREADING

When you have completed your first draft, it's often a good idea to get away from it for a day or so. Remember, the most effective way to read your draft is to read it as if you were a critic or its audience. You have to judge the draft in terms of its logic, its unity, and its coherence. If you have it too freshly in your mind, you may not be able to get enough distance from it to see it as objectively as you should. Even better, form a critique group with some of your classmates and trade papers to get a fresh reading of your work.

When you return to your draft, reread all of it and get a sense of how well it hangs together. Try outlining your draft as you read it, without referring to your preliminary outline; then look at the two together. Make certain as you look at the outline of your draft that you have not created problems in unity and coherence—that every point refers to your dominant idea and that the connections between points are clear and not confusing. Be certain that each point in support of your dominant idea adds to the unity and coherence of your paper and that you have stated each point accurately and completely. If one seems weak, you might have to return to your note cards and uncover some more material to support that point. You may find that you need to go back to the library to get additional information.

If you feel confident that your paper is unified and coherent and that all of your major points and subtopics are adequately supported, write your introduction and conclusion. You might want to review Chapter 8, on openings and closings.

DOCUMENTING YOUR RESEARCH

At the end of your paper, you are expected to provide your readers with a list of your primary and secondary sources. There are many different formats for documenting your research. The two primary ones are the MLA (Modern Language Association) style and the APA (American Psychological Association) style. Other fields of study have slightly different formats. Here are the sources for some of them.

Biology
Council of Biology Editors. *CBE Style Manual: A Guide for Authors, Editors, and Publishers in the Biological Sciences.* 5th ed. Bethesda, MD: Council of Biology Editors, 1983.

Chemistry

American Chemical Society. *The ACS Style Guide: A Manual for Authors and Editors.* 2nd ed. Washington, DC: American Chemical Society Publishing, 1986.

English and the Humanities

Gibaldi, Joseph, and Walter S. Achtert. *MLA Handbook for Writers of Research Papers.* 3rd ed. New York: Modern Language Association of America, 1988.

Geology

Bates, Robert L., Rex Buchanan, and Marla Adkins–Heljeson, eds. *Geowriting: A Guide to Writing, Editing, and Printing in Earth Science.* 5th ed. Alexandria, VA: American Geological Institute, 1992.

Law

Columbia Law Review. *A Uniform System of Citation.* 15th ed. Cambridge, MA: Harvard Law Review, 1991.

Linguistics

Linguistic Society of America. "LSA Style Sheet." Published annually in the December issue of the *LSA Bulletin.*

Mathematics

American Mathematical Society. *A Manual for Authors of Mathematical Papers.* 8th ed. Providence, RI: American Mathematical Society, 1984.

Medicine

International Steering Committee of Medical Editors. "Uniform Requirements for Manuscripts Submitted to Biomedical Journals." *Annals of Internal Medicine* 90 (Jan. 1979): 95–99.

Physics

American Institute of Physics. *Style Manual for Guidance in the Preparation of Papers.* 4th ed. New York: American Institute of Physics, 1990.

Psychology and the Social Sciences

American Psychological Association. *Publication Manual of the American Psychological Association.* 4th ed. Washington, DC: American Psychological Association, 1994.

When you write papers in your major field, ask a professor in that field what the preferred citation style is and learn it.

Remember, whenever you use somebody else's ideas, whether or not you quote them directly, you must acknowledge your source by doing two things. You must identify the author; you must specify the page in that author's work where the material appears.

Using Parentheses

Perhaps in high school you were required to use footnotes or endnotes in your research papers. Most likely, you'll be happy to learn that the parenthetical documentation style is the one that is preferred in most fields of study. Unless otherwise indicated, instructions and examples in this textbook follow the style of the Modern Language Association of America (MLA). When you prepare your research paper, check with your teacher to find out what his or her preference is.

Documenting your sources requires parenthetical insertions identifying both author and page reference. Here is a paragraph from *The Firmament of Time* by Loren Eiseley that illustrates this approach:

> It is necessary in surveying the human quest for certainty to consider death before life. I have not done this out of perversity. Rather I have done it because in the sequence of ideas we have been studying, it is necessary to understand certain aspects of death before we can comprehend the nature of life and its changes (Eiseley 33).

You might want to use Eiseley's idea regarding the necessity of understanding death in order to understand life. However, you don't want to quote the whole paragraph. You might write:

> To understand life and how it changes, "it is necessary to understand certain aspects of death . . ." (Eiseley 33).

Or you might write:

> One essential factor in studying the nature of life is "to understand certain aspects of death" (Eiseley 33) as a way of examining humanity's need for certainty.

In looking at these examples, notice these elements of the parenthetic citation:

> Only the author's last name appears.

> The page number comes immediately after the author's last name, with no punctuation between the two. If the quotation covers more than one page, give the full page range: for example, (Eiseley 45–47).

> If the quotation ends the sentence, the period comes *after* the parenthetical citation.

Attributions and Parentheses

When you write, it is important to indicate clearly where your ideas stop and your source's ideas begin. To make this distinction clear, writers provide attributions for their readers. Attributions identify sources within your writing. Logically, if you name the source's author in your text, you don't have to place his or her name inside the parentheses; only the page number is necessary. For example:

Loren Eiseley states that to understand the human search for certainty it is necessary to study death before the nature of life becomes clear (33).

Special Problems with Authors' Names

It's quite possible that in your research you will use more than one source by the same author. If that is the case, your citation or your attribution must include the title of the work along with the page reference. If you give the title of one of the author's works as part of your attribution, use the full title. However, if the title is part of your parenthetic citation, use a shortened form unless the title is only one or two words: for example, (Eiseley Firmament 92). As a convention, book titles are underlined whereas article titles appear in quotation marks. In the same manner, poem titles and those of short stories appear in quotation marks; the titles of novels and plays are underlined.

If your source has more than one author, use the following conventions: If there are two or three authors, give all the authors' last names in either the attribution or the parenthetical citation. If there are more than three authors, give the last name of the first author followed by *et al.,* which means "and others."

If, among the works you are citing, there are two or more authors with the same last name, you must include in either the attribution or the parentheses each author's first name (or initials if the author—for instance, T. S. Eliot—normally uses only initials).

If you come across a source with no author named, your parenthetic reference may include either the title of the work you are quoting from or the name of the organization that published the work (not necessarily the name of the publisher).

Special Problems with Pagination

If your source has no page numbers, your parenthetic citation will have no page numbers. If you attribute the source in your text, no parenthetical citation is necessary.

If your source has more than one volume, indicate the volume number and then the page number with a colon between them: for example, (Smith 3: 87).

If your source is not a print source—for example, if it is a television show, an interview, or a lecture—give in your parenthetical citation only the first item (the speaker or the person interviewed, for example) that you intend to use in your list of works cited.

The Format for Long Quotations

If your quotation is longer than four lines, it should start on a new line and should be indented ten spaces from the left margin throughout its length. This arrangement is called the "block format." Since the block already shows the reader that you are quoting, you don't need quotation marks. However, if the quotation itself contains a quotation, the internal quotation should be enclosed by quotation marks. Block quotations should be double-spaced, as is the rest of your paper. When you use a block quotation, the parenthetical citation *follows* the period that ends the quotation.

The List of Works Cited: MLA Format

As you write your paper, keep track of the works you cite. You should have a stack of bibliography cards you prepared as you did your research. Now, as you revise your paper, find the cards for the works you have referenced in your paper. After you have finished the body of your paper, arrange these cards alphabetically according to the authors' last names.

The list of works cited appears at the end of your paper. It should contain *only* those works you actually quote, summarize, or refer to in your paper. No other works should appear in this list.

Your list of works cited should be double-spaced, and there should not be extra spaces between the entries. Lists of works cited use the hanging indent format. That is, the first line of an entry begins at the left margin. If the entry extends beyond one line, all additional lines in that entry should be indented five spaces from the left margin. Each major element in the entry should be separated from the next one with a period. Here are some general rules for setting up your citations:

Begin with the author's name, last name first. Then enter the first name and middle initial, if any. Put a comma between the last and first names. Put a period after the full name.

Give the complete title of the book or article. If the book has a subtitle, separate it from the title with a colon. Underline the full title and follow it with a period.

Give the city of publication and follow it with a colon. If more than one location is listed for the publisher, use the city listed first. If the book is published in the United States, give only the name of the city. If the city of publication is in another country and is not well known, follow the name of the city with the name of the country, separating the two with a comma. Place a colon after the city of publication.

Give the publisher's name. Use only key words, omitting "Company," "Press," and other words of that sort. If the publisher is a university press, use UP. Put a comma after the publisher's name.

Give the publication date. Use the most recent year of copyright, not the year of the most recent printing.

SAMPLE BOOK ENTRIES

A book with one author

Watt, Ian. The Rise of the Novel: Studies in

    Defoe, Richardson, and Fielding. Berkeley:

    California UP, 1967.

More than one work by the same author

Eiseley, Loren. The Firmament of Time. New York:

    Atheneum, 1968.

---. The Unexpected Universe. New York: Harcourt,

    1969.

When you use more than one work by the same author, list each book separately. The author's name begins only the first entry. For all other entries by the same author, three hyphens followed by a period take the place of the author's name. Books by the same author are arranged alphabetically by title.

Books with two or more authors

Anderson, T. W., and Stanley L. Sclove. An

    Introduction to the Statistical Analysis of Data.

    Boston: Houghton, 1978.

In the case of books with two or three authors, give all the authors' names. However, reverse only the name of the first author. If there are more than three authors, record only the first author's name; follow it with a comma and *et al.*

Revised edition of a book

Anastasi, Anne. Psychological Testing. 4th ed. New

    York: Macmillan, 1976.

A book with an editor or a translator

Irving, Washington. Selected Writings of Washington

    Irving. Ed. Saxe Commins. New York: Random, 1945.

The editor's or translator's name comes after the title, and it is identified by the abbreviation *Ed.* or *Trans.* preceding it. Don't reverse the order of the editor's or translator's name.

A book that is an anthology

```
Plimpton, George, ed. Writers at Work: The Paris

    Review Interviews, Third Series. New York:

    Viking, 1967.
```

If you used the edited book (not just one article or selection in it) as a reference in your paper, give the editor's name in the author's-name position and follow the name with a comma and the abbreviation *ed.*

An article in an anthology

```
Sweetman, Bill. ''The A-10 Thunderbolt.'' The Great

    Book of Modern Warplanes. Ed. Bernard Fitzsimins,

    et al. New York: Portland, 1987. 9-72.
```

If you use a selection from an anthology, first list the author of the selection, then the selection title in quotation marks, the title of the book, the name of the editor, publication data, and the selection's page numbers without *p.* or *pp.* End each main element with a period.

A chapter in a book by one author

```
Flesch, Rudolf. ''Is Grammar Necessary?'' How to Make

    Sense. New York: Harper, 1954. 22-45.
```

A book by an institution or a corporation

```
Boston Children's Medical Center. Child Health

    Encyclopedia: The Complete Guide for Parents. New

    York: Delacorte, 1975.
```

The name of the institution or corporation is placed in the author position even if the same group is the publisher as well.

SAMPLE PERIODICAL ENTRIES The basic MLA format for listing articles that appeared in periodicals has many of the same elements as those for books. However, there are some important differences:

If there is an author for the article, begin the entry with the author's last name. If the article is unsigned, begin the entry with its title. When placing such an entry in the list of works cited, alphabetize it by the first word in the article's title.

Enclose the article's title in quotation marks. Follow the title with a period, inside the final quotation mark.

Follow with the name of the periodical, underlined. Omit the article (for example, *the*) if the title begins with one. Don't use any punctuation after the name.

Give the date of publication. If your entry comes from a newspaper or weekly magazine, include the day, month (abbreviated), and year, in that order. If your source is a scholarly journal, give the volume number, issue number (if there is one), and the year. This section is closed by a colon.

Give the page numbers. Don't use *p.*, *pp.*, or *page*.

Article from a weekly or biweekly magazine

Dvorak, John C. ''Kiss your ASCII Goodbye.'' PC

    Magazine 15 Sept. 1992: 93.

Article from a monthly or bimonthly magazine

Oliveri, Frank. ''The Bone.'' Air Force Magazine Sept.

    1992: 35-40.

Article from a newspaper

Rosenberg, Howard. ''Bigotry on TV: The Stain Still

    Lingers.'' Los Angeles Times 16 Dec. 1992,

    sec. F: 1, 12.

Cite the name of the newspaper, but omit *The* at the head of the title. If the location is not given in the title, put the city in brackets after the title: for example, Five Cities Times-Press Recorder [Grover Beach, CA]. Follow this with the day, month (abbreviated), and year of publication. If the newspaper prints more than one edition, indicate the edition you have taken the article from by abbreviating that information and placing it after the date. If the newspaper has sections, indicate the section with the appropriate letter or number. Place a colon between the section and the page.

Editorial or letter to the editor

''Why We Need More Rapid Transit.'' Editorial.

    Telegram Tribune [San Luis Obispo, CA] 31 Apr.

    1991, sec. 1: 8.

Editorials or letters are listed in the same way as any unsigned article, but you should indicate the nature of the piece by adding *Editorial* or *Letter* after the article's title.

Article from a scholarly journal

Lu, Min-Zhan. ''Conflict and Struggle: The Enemies or

    Preconditions of Basic Writing?'' College English

    54 (1992): 887–913.

Some journals have continuous pagination. That is, the volume for each year begins with page 1, and the pages are numbered continuously through the end of the volume for a given year. Other journals begin each issue at page 1. If the journal you cite is paged continuously, use numbers to indicate the volume and follow that with the year of publication in parentheses. If the journal you cite pages each issue separately, use numbers to show the volume and issue numbers. Separate the two with a period. Leave no space after the period.

NONPRINT SOURCES

Television or radio program

''The DC-3.'' Narr. Alexander Scourby. Nova. PBS.

    KCET, Los Angeles. 15 Dec. 1992.

Movie, videotape, filmstrip, or slide program

Willy Wonka and the Chocolate Factory.   Dir. Mel

    Stuart. With Gene Wilder. Warner Brothers, 1971.

Give the title, director, distribution company, and the year. You may list the main performer(s) after the director. If the work is a videotape, filmstrip, or slide program, note the medium right after the title.

Computer software

Arkanoid. Computer software. Taito, 1988. PC.

If you know the program's author, place it in the author's position.

Personal interview

Lant, Katherine M.   Personal interview. 30 Feb. 1991.

Lecture

Cushing, James. ''Camille Paglia and Emily

Dickinson.'' Lecture. California Polytechnic

State University Books at High Noon Lecture

Series. California State Polytechnic University.

San Luis Obispo, 11 Nov. 1992.

The APA Documentation Format

Whereas the MLA format is used in most fields in the humanities, papers written in the social sciences and education normally use the American Psychological Association (APA) format. However, as the Fourth Edition of the *Publication Manual of the American Psychological Association* (1994) states, for undergraduate papers (and even for graduate theses and dissertations) the APA format typically is modified to suit individual departments' or instructors' preferences: "The *Publication Manual* is not intended to cover scientific writing at an undergraduate level, because preferences for style at that level are diverse" (p. 332). Accordingly, the guidelines for using APA style stated here and illustrated in the sample paper on pages 790–808 present a model that is accurate as far as it goes but does not exhaust the possibilities. For example, although a separate title page is permissible and may be required by individual instructors, the sample paper omits such a page. As the list of style manuals on pages 765–766 suggests, other disciplines employ still other formats; check with your instructor to find which format he or she requires.

LIST OF REFERENCES   In the APA style, as in the MLA style, the list of sources is arranged alphabetically and appears at the end of the research paper. However, whereas the MLA format calls the list "Works Cited," APA style calls the list "References."

Although both styles include the same information, they shape it in different ways. Here are some of the main contrasting features of APA entries:

The date of publication comes immediately after the author's name. It is placed in parentheses and followed by a period.

All author's names are given in the reference. However, in the textual citation, *et al.* is used after the first citation for works having from three to five authors and on all citations for works having six or more authors.

All authors' names are inverted, and authors' first and middle names are reduced to initials.

An ampersand (&) rather than the word *and* precedes the last author's name (in the References list but not in parenthetical citations).

Two or more works by the same author are arranged not alphabetically but by the date of publication, beginning with the earliest.

Multiple works by one author published in the same year are distinguished by lowercase letters—for example: (1988a), (1988b).

Only the first letter of a book or article title (and its subtitle) is capitalized, except for any proper names included within the title.

The first line of each entry is indented as for a paragraph of text; all additional lines begin at the left margin.

Periods separating elements within an entry are followed by one space rather than two.

PARENTHETIC CITATIONS   Like the MLA format, the APA format requires that citations be enclosed in parentheses within the text and provide the author's last name. The important difference between the two formats is that the APA parenthetic note also contains the year of publication and provides the page number only with a quotation. APA citations are also punctuated, with commas between the author's name and the year and between the year and the page number. In addition, *p.* or *pp.* appears before the page number(s).

In the APA format, if you begin a quotation with an attribution to the author, the year of publication follows the author's name and the page number appears at the end of the quotation.

TWO STUDENT RESEARCH PAPERS

The two research papers that follow were written by first-year composition students. The first uses the MLA citation format, and the second uses the format specified by the APA. As you read these papers, note how these writers have used their sources to support their arguments without letting those sources *become* their arguments. Also, take note of how the writers account for the audiences for their papers, how they make choices with regard to voice and style, and how they think about what their audiences may know and what they need to be told.

MLA Style

Yvette Acord

Professor ————————————

English ——————

———— November 1994

Flush the Five-Gallon Toilet Goodbye

Few subjects in our modern, open culture are
excluded or forbidden from mention. Many topics
which were not widely discussed ten years ago
and even five years ago are today considered
progressive, and almost fashionable. Such former
unspokens as incest, homosexuality and AIDS, bulimia
and anorexia, teen pregnancy, and alcohol and drug
dependency are frequent features in newspapers and
on television. It might appear that there are few
taboos left to expose. One taboo perpetuated by
social custom and emotional aversion still exists:
the toilet. This is evidenced in our reluctance
either to talk about the subject or to change our
attitudes regarding it. Yet if the toilet were to
become a subject of conversation, we would discover
that this common bathroom fixture is an environmental
threat as well as poorly designed for the function
for which it is intended. It is wasteful of one
of our most precious natural resources: water.
In addition, the design of the toilet is
physiologically inefficient.

Acord 2

The standard flush toilet in our so-called
advanced Western society uses far more water than
is necessary, placing a huge financial burden on
cities and taxpayers to operate expensive sewage
treatment plants. Our repressive and backward views
about toilets and the associated activities of
urinating and defecating not only promote a normal
bodily function as undesirable but preclude our
examination and design of toilets for physiological
efficiency.

There are few other topics which, upon studying,
could lead to more benefit for a greater number of
people. Change is rarely easy or fast, but it is
almost always necessary, as well as inevitable.
I hope that this paper will be a small catalyst
leading to such change.

The history of the forerunners of our flush
toilet is scant and sometimes conflicting, but what
exists is certainly interesting. There is no clear
evidence that the "first attempt at water borne
disposal occurred when some primitive man stuck his
backside over a convenient stream" (Palmer 13).
However, there is archaeological evidence that a
means of disposing of human wastes with the aid of
piped water existed in India in the period around
3000 B.C. (Palmer 13). Other ancient examples of

Acord 3

toilets have been discovered in remains of Minoan,
Sumerian, Cretan, and Egyptian cultures (Palmer
13-15; Kira 11). The Romans seem to have
developed public urinals. The Emperor Vespasian
had them constructed in large cities, but not for
the purpose of promoting public health. The urine
was sold to dye-makers as a mordant and was a
source of income for the Emperor (Palmer 15).

In later centuries in Europe, toilets were a
possibility only for the nobility and the clergy.
The majority of people simply "retired a bow's
shot away" (Palmer 16). Sewage removal was not
thought of further. When toilets were located
inside buildings, there were no means of removing
the waste. It built up until it necessitated
entire households' moving to a second residence for
a season while peasant laborers removed the refuse
(Palmer 20-21).

In the 1590s in England, Sir John Harrington,
a godson of Elizabeth I, developed a type of
"water closet" which the queen liked so much that
she reportedly had one installed in her palace.
Sir John even wrote a book upon the subject which
contained poetry and jokes and gave practical
instructions for building a water closet. His
contemporaries, however, seemed not to have read

Acord 4

the work, and his advice went unheeded (Palmer 26-31).

The first patent for a water closet was taken out by Alexander Cummings in 1775, but for the most part, human wastes were dumped into open gutters on streets below residences. There began to be concern for sanitation as a result of awareness of diseases, such as typhoid, dysentery, and cholera, caused by waterborne infections. Various publications urged the adoption of sewage facilities and clean water supplies for all citizens (Palmer 22-23). The increasing population density in cities and the rise of an affluent middle-class population resulting from the Industrial Revolution necessitated toilets as an item of household equipment for more than just the nobility and upper classes.

The water closets of that time worked by opening and closing valves which controlled the flow of water. Often these valves leaked or were simply left open all the time, causing a continuous flow of water. The Board of Trade in England was responsible for the water supply, and they were greatly concerned about the water waste occurring as a result of the water closets (Reborn 9-11).

In the early 1870s the Board of Trade called

Acord 5

for someone to evolve a ''Water Waste Preventer''
(Reborn 12-13). Many plumbers directed their
efforts to this challenge, but it was Thomas
Crapper, a prominent London plumber, who perfected
the flush toilet as we know it today. His toilet
made use of siphonic action to trigger water down
the flush pipe and automatically shut off the water
supply, refilling the tank by means of a float
attached to a metal arm. As water refilled the
tank, the float rose and brought the arm to a
position that closed the water inlet. This
prevented the waste of water that occurred in the
case of a perpetual flow (Reborn 13-15). Crapper
had a large plumbing company in London and later
became the Royal plumber, updating the residences
of Queen Victoria and Edward VII.

The water tanks (cisterns) for those early
toilets were placed well above the bowl in order to
make use of the force of water generated over a
distance. But as improvements in tanks and bowls
were made, it was possible to place the tank next
to the bowl. This seems to have become prevalent
by the 1930s. The toilets in most homes today are
basically the same as Crapper's ''Water Waste
Preventer.'' The materials may vary, and most
feature a handle on the tank instead of a pull
chain, but the design is the same.

Acord 6

It is ironic that an appliance invented to
save water in fact wastes a great deal of it. The
standard toilet in most American homes uses five
gallons of water for each flush. It is ludicrous
in times of concern over depleting water tables
that people will try to conserve water by less
frequent lawn sprinkling, installing water-saving
showerheads, and buying water-saving dishwasher
models, yet overlook one of the larger sources of
water waste in their homes, the toilet.

It is estimated that 40% of the water
consumption in a North American home is allocated
to flushing the toilet (McGill University 3). That
turns out to be a lot of water. For one person,
about 13,000 gallons of water is contaminated each
year to move an average of 165 gallons of bodily
wastes (Stoner vii). Perhaps only a severe water
shortage, or increased taxes and local water rates,
or both will motivate individuals to reconsider the
subject of toilets. In a world where more than 70%
of the population does not even have access to
piped water (McGill University 1), we certainly
take our supply for granted.

In addition, toilets require sewer systems.
In urban areas there are underground networks of
pipes which carry sewage to a centralized location
for treatment and disposal. This method of waste

Acord 7

processing requires immense quantities of water,
mainly as a transporting medium, and a lot of money
to implement and maintain. Also, the purification
of the water for reuse after transporting the waste
has an immense cost. Estimates for providing
traditional disposal systems for all urban areas
in our country range from the tens of billions to
hundreds of billions of dollars. Not only do our
sewer systems cost a lot to build and operate, they
also require a lot of energy (electricity and fuel
oil) to run (Stoner 20-21).

Furthermore, there are a number of negative
side effects resulting from our present sewage
system. In all fairness, today's system is
certainly preferable to tossing household-pail
contents into open gutters on the street, as was
the practice until less than two centuries ago, but
our modern sewers have problems that we cannot
afford to overlook.

One of the serious problems that exists is
that when too much water is taken from subsurface
sources to get rid of wastes, wells and other
surface waters, such as lakes and rivers, start to
dry up and the groundwater table is lowered. Also,
discharging treated wastes into the sea instead of
returning them to groundwater supplies contributes
to this same condition. Other problems that can

Acord 8

occur are the leakage of sewage from pipes into
groundwater, the premature death of lakes, landfill
space shortages, and air pollution from sewage
incineration (Stone 22-25).

These are only a few of the serious
repercussions of our supposedly modern sewage
disposal system. It is important to keep in mind
that many of these problems are directly related to
our use of water-greedy flush toilets.

In the concern over environmental damage
caused by human wastes, it is easy to forget that
they are a potentially beneficial substance. In
centuries past and even as recently as the 1890s,
wastes were commonly either converted to manure
and sold to farmers as fertilizers or transported
directly to "sewage farms" for treatment and
use (Sweetener 16). Today in many cultures this
recycling still goes on. The law of thermodynamics,
which states that matter is neither created nor
destroyed, takes on a new, but appropriate,
perspective when applied to the subject of human
wastes. Feces and urine contain many plant- and
crop-nourishing components, such as nitrogen,
phosphorus, potassium, carbon, and calcium (Stoner
47). It is amazing that we spend so much time,
effort, and money trying to break down sewage while
overlooking its potential as a valuable resource.

Acord 9

Fortunately, we are not limited to just the five-gallon flush toilet. There are many other types of toilets--including pit latrines, aqua privies, septic tanks, chemical and incinerating toilets, composting privies, and vacuum toilets, to name a few. And there are literally hundreds of variations available within these categories.

What should we do about our water-wasting toilets? For most people living in urban areas, it is not practical or possible to switch to alternative types of toilets. We are prisoners of our existing sewer systems. What we can do, however, is use more efficient flush toilets that use far less water than the standard five gallons. There is a model which uses three gallons of water per flush available in the 1987 Spring/ Summer Sears Catalog (p. 883) and which only costs $49.99. That would mean a 40% savings in water. Another water-saving model is manufactured by an English firm and is called the Dual Flush Cistern. It is a tank that fits onto your toilet which releases one or two gallons of water depending on how long the flushing handle is held down (McGill University 42).

Since so many types of more efficient toilets are available, it is puzzling that the standard five-gallon flush variety remains prevalent.

Acord 10

Although we consider retiring our refrigerators, vacuums, and other household appliances after a number of years of use, we rarely, if ever, think about getting a new style of toilet. As consumers, we must demand that alternatives be made available. It is as easy to imagine a corporate monopoly in the toilet-manufacturing industry, which is inflexible and unresponsive to consumer need, as it is to imagine a lack of concern and input regarding this subject on the part of the general population. It may be a combination of both these factors and still others which have contributed to the lack of change in our society with regard to toilets.

In the long run, our attitudes toward toilets may be the key factor precluding change. Unfortunately, this seems to be the aspect of toilets least researched. (Even in researching this subject, our own library's card catalog does not include a listing for "toilet" but directs one to "See water closet.") It is difficult to find the origins of our negative feelings about urinating and defecating since they have varied widely over the centuries and from culture to culture. These negative feelings are, however, "a learned response rather than rooted in our instincts" (Kira 94). Very young children exhibit no disgust over feces or urine.

Acord 11

Not only are these negative attitudes learned, they are of fairly recent origin. Urine has been one of the oldest known components of soap. Oxidized urine produces ammonia compounds that are a standard agent for dissolving fats. It has also been used to set dyes at least from the time of the Roman Empire to that of American Indian tribes. And it is even drunk as a pick-me-up for salts and trace minerals that might otherwise be seriously depleted in very hot climates. It has played an important role in many religious rituals and is thought to be the origin of holy water. Feces also have a long history of practical and symbolic uses. They have been used for fertilizer, fuel, and even curing tobacco. The feces of the Dalai Lama were considered sacred and worn as an amulet (Kira 94-96).

One of the most noticeable indicators of our negative feelings toward bodily wastes, especially feces, is in our language. The terms "piss" and "shit" almost always have a negative connotation, as does "asshole," from whence feces originate. Even "fart" is an embarrassing word for many people. Often these and other related terms are used in an insulting or humiliating context.

There are probably many reasons contributing to the negative connotation of terms having to do

Acord 12

with normal bodily functions. According to Kira,
religious dictates play a large role (97). The
association of sexual anatomy with that of
elimination probably has also been a factor.
Secrecy and misinformation concerning sex have
persisted until recently in our society and in
many cases still persist. It is also that lack
of knowledge about physiology that gave rise to
our negative mythology concerning urinating and
defecating. And habit or custom is responsible for
a lot. We take for granted most of our culturally
conditioned assumptions, and some of the most
deeply ingrained have to do with this subject.

Reflection upon these culturally conditioned
assumptions might lead to more direct and useful
discussion of these appliances, which would allow
the redesign of toilets for greater physiological
efficiency, comfort, and health.

Research done by Kira shows that the squatting
position is the best for defecation. At the very
least, the feet need to touch the floor, and there
should be flexion of the thighs against the
abdomen. The omnipresent high "throne" design is
highly inadequate for this purpose. Toilet seats
need to be lower and, perhaps, to have footrests
for shorter persons and children. In many Eastern
cultures, toilets often do not even have seats, but

Acord 13

consist of markings for feet placement and a bowl
set into and even with the floor. This way the
user assumes a squatting position (Kira 123). The
assumption that Western societies are more advanced
is highly questionable in this regard.

     There is much to gain from changing our attitudes
about elimination processes. Much embarrassment
and humiliation on the part of individuals could be
spared, water could be saved, pollution reduced.
This change should start with education.
Youngsters should be taught about elimination
the way they are taught about nutrition: that it is
an everyday matter essential to good health. And
we should also make a conscious effort not to
inflict our own negative attitudes on very young
children. The subject of urine and feces should be
talked about and not hidden. They are as much a
crucial part of us as breathing or eating or
sleeping. Through education and communication,
change is possible. And when it comes to toilets--
the kind we use and our attitudes toward them--
change is for the better.

Acord 14

Works Cited

Kira, Alexander. The Bathroom. New York: Viking,
     1976.
McGill University, Montreal School of Architecture.
     Stop the Five Gallon Flush! 5th ed.
     Montreal: McGill UP, 1976.
Palmer, Roy. The Water Closet, A New History.
     London: David & Charles, 1973.
Reborn, Wallace. Flushed with Pride. London:
     McDonald, 1969.
Sears, Roebuck and Co. Catalog. Spring/Summer
     1987
Stoner, Carol Hupping, ed. Goodbye to the Flush
     Toilet. Emmaus, PA: Rodale, 1977.

APA Style

Kathie McReynolds

Professor _____

English _____

_____ December 1994

Fetal Tissue Research: Is It Beneficial?

Fetal tissue obtained from elective abortions has proven its effectiveness in the treatment of otherwise incurable diseases such as Parkinson's disease and juvenile-onset diabetes. But several questions and concerns still remain as to how this tissue should be obtained and used and whether or not it should be used at all. The use of fetal tissue from elective abortions in research into the cure of certain diseases is essential. Without it, there would be little hope for those who suffer from conditions such as Parkinson's disease and juvenile-onset diabetes.

This paper will cover the history of fetal tissue research, with special attention to the political problems fetal tissue research has encountered in the past several years as well as the multiple uses of fetal tissue in the treatment of previously incurable disorders. The arguments against the use of fetal tissue from elective abortions and the alternatives suggested by its opponents will be presented and commented on.

Fetcl Tissue Research

2

Finally, the ethical concerns surrounding fetal
tissue will be raised along with some suggestions
that have been offered by researchers in this
field.

Fetal tissue has been used for research
purposes since the 1930s. From the outset, fetal
tissue research has proven time and time again to
be an invaluable tool for science (Greeley et al.,
1989). Cell lines derived from fetal tissue have
been used to develop immunization treatments for
polio, rubella, and Rh disease (Bigly, Hager, &
Glick, 1993). Also to emerge from fetal tissue
research was the understanding of chromosomal
abnormalities, cancer, and cellular immunology.

Research into the use of fetal tissue was
advancing rapidly when one small request to the
National Institutes of Health brought it to a
halt. In 1987 the NIH was asked to fund a study of
fetal tissue transplants into Parkinson's disease
patients. This request led to the formation of
an NIH advisory panel by Assistant Secretary Dr.
Robert Windom. The panel was made up of experts,
both proponents of and opponents to such research.
This panel was formed to provide guidelines for the
Fethical use of fetal tissue in research, if they
decided to recommend the practice at all. As it

Fetal Tissue Research

3

happened, the formation of the panel was all for
naught. While the panel was still deliberating
upon the guidelines, the White House, then under
President Reagan, sent a letter to the Secretary
of Health and Human Services proposing the complete
prohibition of the use of federal funds for fetal
tissue research involving tissue from elective
abortions. In May 1988, a moratorium on federal
funding of fetal tissue research using tissue from
elective abortions was enacted (Annas & Elias,
1989).

The Bush administration decided to continue
the ban in 1989, arguing that if the transplants of
fetal tissue from elective abortions proved to be
successful in the treatment of incurable disease,
more abortions could result (Revenuer, 1991). In
other words, fetal tissue research was linked to
the debate over elective abortions.

The opponents of elective abortions made their
feelings clear regarding the use of tissue derived
from elective abortions for research. For example,
Matt Clark, a writer for Newsweek, noted that the
right-to-life movement paints a Brave New World
scenario of "embryos fertilized and growing on
racks like house plants . . ." (Clark, Gosnell,
& Hager, 1993, p. 62). Also, Douglas Johnson, the

legislative director of the National Right-to-
Life Committee, stated: "It is unworthy of us
as a nation to kill our unborn children and
then cannibalize them for spare parts" (qtd.
in Revenuer, 1991, p. 2077). These opinions are
based on emotion and religious or moral positions
and not on scientific fact. In order for good,
rational decisions to be made about the use of
this tissue, emotion needs to be removed, and the
facts need to be recognized for what they are.
These facts show that fetal tissue research is a
viable tool that has limitless possibilities and
capabilities to provide people presently afflicted
with debilitating diseases the chance to lead a
normal life.

    Fetal tissue research has uncovered many
possibilities for the treatment of many presently
incurable diseases. Daniel Koshland, the editor of
Science, said that "to the non-scientist, fetal
tissue may seem like any other, but fetal cells are
less developed and are more malleable and willing
to grow than mature cells" (1988, p. 1733). Fetal
cells grow rapidly and are adaptable. Since the
cells are immature, they have little possibility
of evoking an immune response from the recipient
(Greely et al., 1989). Fetal cells are also

"plastic." An immature fetal cell has the potential for becoming anything from a liver cell to a kidney (Bigly et al., 1993).

The treatment of Parkinson's disease is one avenue that researchers are exploring. Parkinson's disease is a debilitating disease afflicting mainly the elderly. Sufferers do not have enough dopamine secreted by the substantia nigra of their brains to be able to move properly. The disease is progressive. Ultimately, their minds become trapped within their bodies.

Until about ten years ago, researchers had had no success in pursuing research in using fetal tissue transplants in Parkinson's patients. The major reason was that there was no way of inducing parkinsonism in animals for testing such a treatment. Then the illicit use of the designer drug MPTP lent some hope. MPTP caused parkinsonism in some users by destroying the dopamine-producing cells of the substantia nigra. This gave researchers a way of inducing parkinsonism in laboratory animals. After the parkinsonism had been achieved in monkeys, fetal cells were transplanted into their brains. As a result, the parkinsonism was decreased, behavioral improvement occurred, and dopamine was being synthesized in the monkeys'

brains due to integration of the fetal cells
(Hanson & Sladek, 1989).

After the successful treatment of the monkeys,
the transplant process was tried on two MPTP
drug abusers who were suffering greatly from
parkinsonism. This avenue was taken because MPTP-
induced parkinsonism was static. This eliminated
the complications of the ongoing disease process of
Parkinson's disease in the elderly. The operations
took place in Sweden, and the benefits to the two
patients were impressive. These patients needed
less of the drug L-dopa, which was the only
available treatment for Parkinson's disease until
transplantation became a feasible possibility
(Fahn, 1992).

Further research in Sweden has shown that
brain stem tissue from 6- to 8-week fetuses has
given rise to fully functioning dopamine-secreting
cells in the brains of Parkinson's disease sufferers
(Bigly et al., 1993). Dr. Anders Bjorklund, of the
University of Lund, Sweden, said that the treatment
brings patients back to where they were 5-7 years
earlier (Bigly et al., 1993). In the United States,
the first fetal cell transplant into a Parkinson's
patient was performed in 1988 under a privately
funded study by Dr. Charles Freed of the University

Fetal Tissue Research

7

of Colorado Health Science Center. He performed
the procedure on Don Nelson, 52. Mr. Nelson could
barely walk before surgery. After the procedure,
he found he could enjoy woodworking again as well
as take less medication (Bigly et al., 1993).

As a result of this research, even abortion
foes agree that the treatment is invaluable.
Morris Udall, formerly of the House of Representatives,
had to retire due to Parkinson's disease. Mark
Hatfield (R, Ore.), an ardent abortion foe, had the
following to say of Morris Udall and his condition:
"After watching what Mo and his family have gone
through, I have to ask this question, again: Can we
deny this opportunity of hope to millions of others
who suffer from debilitating diseases?" (qtd. in
Revenuer, 1992, p. 879).

Fetal tissue transplantation is not only
useful in the treatment of Parkinson's disease, but
also juvenile-onset diabetes. Juvenile-onset
diabetes is caused by an autoimmune response
against the person's own pancreatic cells, which
are responsible for insulin production in the body.
There is new hope for these people now due to fetal
tissue transplantation of pancreatic cells into the
patient. Dr. Ken Lafferty, of the University of
Colorado, implanted insulin-producing cells from a

Fetal Tissue Research

8

fetal pancreas into diabetes sufferers. Out of his
patients, five need less insulin therapy than
before, which means a more normal life for them
(Clark et al., 1993). A normal life is exactly
what Julie Thurmond, daughter of Senator Strom
Thurmond (R, S.C.) and a diabetic, desires.
Senator Thurmond, a strong abortion opponent, had
this to say about his daughter and the use of fetal
tissue for treatment of disease: "I believe that
for the sake of Julie and those individuals who
suffer from diabetes and other serious diseases, we
cannot afford to lose this opportunity to develop a
cure" (qtd. in Revenuer, 1992, p. 879).

    Fetal-to-fetal transplantation is another
important development in fetal tissue research.
This technique can cure a condition in someone who
isn't even born yet, thus eliminating long-term
suffering and medical bills. Daniel Koshland,
editor of Science, had this to say: "Fetal tissue
may be of particular benefit to those women who are
agonizing over the heart-rending decision between
abortion and bringing a child with predictable
life-long difficulties into the world" (1992,
p. 174). In other words, the use of tissue from
one abortion can actually prevent the abortion of
another child.

Fetal Tissue Research

9

In a specific example of a fetal-to-fetal transplant, Hurler's syndrome, an inherited enzymatic disorder of the liver, was treated in utero. The parents of the unborn child, Rev. Guy Walden and wife, Tarryl, had already lost one child and were losing another to this fatal disease. Even though they were strong antiabortionists, they decided to go ahead with the transplant instead of risking the loss of a third child. A fetal-to-fetal transplant of liver cells from an ectopic pregnancy was performed with the hope that the cells would implant in the bone marrow of the Waldens' unborn child and begin producing the absent enzyme. Six months after the child was born, adequate levels of the enzyme were being synthesized to deter the effects of the disorder (Bigly et al., 1993). The child has a chance for life now through the help of an ended one.

The potential uses of fetal tissue in the treatment of disease are endless. In addition to its known usefulness in Parkinson's disease, juvenile-onset diabetes, and Hurler's syndrome, fetal tissue may prove to be helpful in the eradication of female sterility, radiation sickness, cancer, Huntington's disease, Alzheimer's disease, and many others. Now that federal funds

are available for such research because President
Clinton lifted the moratorium on fetal tissue
research, maybe more information will be forthcoming
regarding the viability of fetal tissue in the
treatment of the above diseases and others.
Already there is a proposal to the NIH for funding
to transplant fetal tissue into 40 elderly
Parkinson's disease patients' brains.

Other possible uses of fetal tissue for
transplantation are many and varied. Female
sterility may be remedied through the transplantation
of fetal ovaries, which are viable in a two-month
fetus. Such a transplant might give a woman born
without ovaries a chance to conceive. ''The
abortion of one fetus could give life to a whole
family of babies'' (Bigly et al., 1993, p. 51).

Radiation sickness and its destruction of bone
marrow and red blood cells, like that seen in the
Chernobyl disaster, could potentially be treated
with fetal liver cells. Dr. Richard Gale, of UCLA,
tried this procedure in three Chernobyl victims.
Unfortunately, all of them died of burns before
the effects could be noted. However, Gale still
believes that such treatment is possible and
would be better than the other alternative, the
transplantation of adult bone marrow. Fetal tissue

Fetal Tissue Research

11

has a decreased possibility of rejection by the
recipient (Clark et al., 1993).

The pro-life movement is not against the use
of fetal tissue in the treatment of disease.
However, they oppose the use of fetal tissue from
elective abortions in the treatment of disease.
Their position is that fetal tissue from other
sources--namely, ectopic pregnancies (pregnancies
in which the fetus implants in the fallopian tube
or elsewhere outside of the uterus), spontaneous
abortions, and stillbirths--can provide viable
tissue in the treatment of disease without the
stigma of elective abortion attached to it. This
position is invalid due to the abnormalities of
the tissue. Spontaneous abortions and stillbirths
happen for a reason. These events generally occur
as the result of an abnormality on the part of
the developing fetus. As a result, there is risk
attached to the use of such tissue to treat
disease.

The pro-lifers maintain that tissue obtained
from ectopic pregnancies is absolutely usable for
transplantation purposes. The tissue is acceptable
to them because it was obtained through a favorable
means of abortion, abortion to save the life of the
mother. From a medical standpoint, however, this

Fetal Tissue Research

12

tissue is rarely usable in transplantations.
Ectopic pregnancies rarely produce tissue that is
viable or even recognizable (Garry, Kaplan, Vawter,
& Kearney, 1992). In one study of the tissue from
65 ectopic pregnancies, 33 samples were structurally
abnormal: 18 had a chorionic sac and no embryo, 8
had no differentiation of the organs, and 7 had
systemic abnormalities, such as spina bifida (Garry
et al., 1992).

    The story is much the same for spontaneous
abortions. The editor of Science, Daniel Koshland,
had the following to say about tissue from
spontaneous abortions: "Such tissue is usually
received in poor condition and is frequently
inherently unusable for the reason that natural
miscarriage is caused by fetal malfunctions that
might be viewed as nature's way of eliminating a
potentially defective child" (1992, p. 1741). The
statistics back up his claim. Of spontaneously
aborted fetuses, about one-half that aborted during
the first trimester and one-fifth that aborted
during the second trimester were shown to be
chromosomally abnormal. Another potential hazard
of this tissue is the possibility that it may be
infected with such agents as herpes simplex 1 and
2, rubella, toxoplasma, or cytomegalovirus (Annas &

Fetal Tissue Research

13

Elias, 1989). Finally, the tissue may be unusable
due to the conditions surrounding the actual
expulsion of the tissue. There is hemorrhaging,
followed by necrosis and degradation of the tissue,
and finally expulsion of the tissue up to 2 to
3 weeks after the fetus has died (Garry et al.,
1992).

Stillbirths have been offered as another
option in fetal tissue research by the pro-life
faction. There are several reasons why this
tissue is unusable. For one, the tissue is rarely
culturable, so it is not viable. For another,
stillbirths yield tissue that is beyond the realm
of usefulness in transplantation. Stillbirths
occur later in the pregnancy, and by then the
fetal cells have lost most of their potential
to be "plastic." For example, for a neural
transplantation of fetal cells, the cells have to
be less than 12 weeks of age to be viable (Garry
et al., 1992). A stillbirth occurs after 20 weeks
of gestation, far beyond the time of therapeutic
usefulness.

The only material that is suitable for
transplantation is tissue obtained from elective
abortions. This tissue is not abnormal, can be

Fetal Tissue Research

14

checked for infection, and can be chosen for the
correct stage of development. All the evidence
shows that these benefits by far outweigh those of
obtaining potentially hazardous tissue in order to
prevent elective abortion.

While it is true that there is no other viable
tissue available for fetal tissue transplantation
than that of elective abortions, it is also true
that the practice of using such tissue should be
heavily regulated to prevent misuse. Abortions
should not be performed so that the tissue can be
donated; the decision to abort should be made
before, and separately from, the decision to
donate; a woman should not benefit from donating
her abortion to science; and the fetal cadaver
should be treated with respect, like a human
cadaver. These are the main ethical concerns of
the scientific community and the federal government.
Arthur Kaplan, director of the Center of Biomedical
Ethics at the University of Minnesota, stated that
"the worst potential ethical evil of all this
would be to create lives simply to end them and
take parts" (qtd. in Clark et al., 1993, p. 63).
His opinion echoes the position of all scientists
who agree with the practice of using fetal tissue

Fetal Tissue Research

15

from elective abortions--one of optimism and hope
for curing disease, but including reservations with
respect to the ethical issue.

A woman should not be allowed to have an
abortion for the sole purpose of donating
the tissue. The researchers want to prevent
encouragement of aborting fetuses for the purpose
of donating because "conception should not be
undertaken for a purpose other than bearing
children" (Greely et al., 1989). The NIH advisory
panel formed in 1988 recommended that the decisions
to abort and to donate be kept separate (Annas &
Elias, 1989). This decision would serve to prevent
a woman from being able to designate a recipient
for her fetus. If this practice were allowed, a
woman could become pregnant just so she could abort
the fetus and donate the parts to an ailing
relative. This would be ethically disastrous,
because the value of a human life would diminish
drastically.

Another concern is that a woman who chooses to
donate her fetus may financially benefit from the
procedure. Just as the practice of paying donors
for their blood was outlawed, the practice of
paying a woman for undergoing an abortion should be
unlawful. If it is not, there could be a potential

for a woman to get pregnant just so she could get rid of the fetus to collect a payoff. Greely and his associates agree by stating that "patients should not derive any benefit from the use of tissue from fetuses they have chosen to abort" (1989, p. 1094).

Fetal tissue transplantation involving elective abortion tissue is essential. The potential for treating incurable diseases and conditions seems endless. As Dr. Abraham Lee Berman of the New York University Medical Center stated: "This [fetal tissue research] is to medicine what superconductivity is to physics" (qtd. in Clark et al., 1993, p. 62). Diseases that are presently incurable might be eradicated in the future. Parkinson's disease, juvenile-onset diabetes, Hurler's syndrome, female sterility, Alzheimer's disease, and many others are candidates for more research due to the enormous influence they have on society.

Abortion opponents don't question the research itself. However, they have serious reservations about the use of tissue from elective abortions in the research. The tissues they suggest as alternatives to that from elective abortions, such as tissue from spontaneous abortions and ectopic

Fetal Tissue Research

17

pregnancies, are not viable because they have
the potential to do more harm than good to the
recipient. Therefore, the only tissue that should
be used in fetal tissue transplantation is that
obtained from the elective abortion.

      Fetal tissue from elective abortions can be
used in an ethical manner that benefits lifetime
sufferers of disease by giving them a new lease on
life. As long as abortion is legal in this
country, we should be able to use a resource that
otherwise would go to waste. Daniel Koshland said
it best when he stated that "fetal tissue is
discarded tissue that cannot live on its own,
cannot do the mother any good, and may provide us
with research knowledge or medical therapy" (1988,
p. 1733). Let something good come out of one of a
woman's toughest decisions.

References

Annas, G. J., & Elias, S. (1989). Sounding board: The politics of transplantation of human fetal tissue. New England Journal of Medicine, 320, 1079-82.

Bigly, S., Hager, M., & Glick, D. (1993, Feb. 22). Cures from the womb. Newsweek, pp. 49-51.

Clark, M., Gosnell, M., & Hager, M. (1993, Feb. 22). Should medicine use the unborn? Newsweek, pp. 62-63.

Fahn, S. (1992). Fetal-tissue transplants in Parkinson's disease. New England Journal of Medicine, 327, 1589-90.

Garry, D. J., Kaplan, A. R., Vawter, D. E., & Kearney, W. (1992). Sounding board: Are there really alternatives to the use of fetal tissue from elective abortions in transplantation research? New England Journal of Medicine, 327, 1592-95.

Greely, H. T., Hamm, T., Johnson, R., Price, C. R., Weingarten, R., & Raffin (1989). The ethical use of human fetal tissue in research. New England Journal of Medicine, 320, 1093-96.

Hanson, J. T., & Sladek, J. R. (1989). Fetal research. Science, 246, 775-79.

Fetal Tissue Research

19

Koshland, D. E. (1988). Fetal tissue in research [Editorial]. Science, 241, 1773.

Koshland, D. E. (1992). Fetal tissue research [Editorial]. Science, 256, 1741.

Revenuer, J. (1991, July 27). House vote overturns ban on fetal tissue research. CQ Weekly Report, 2077-79.

Revenuer, J. (1992, Apr. 4). Vote to end fetal tissue ban hinged on personal stakes. CQ Weekly Report, 879-81.

Glossary

Act In Burke's Pentad, act is what the agent does. An act in a pentad must be willed by the actor and not automatic or reflexive.

***Ad Hominem* Fallacy** *Ad hominem* (to the person) attacks the person as a way of countering that person's argument instead of confronting the argument itself.

Agency In Burke's Pentad, the agency is how the act was performed or the means by which it was brought into being.

Agent In Burke's Pentad, the agent is the individual who performs the act.

Alliteration The repetition of consonant sounds in a line of poetry or in prose, usually, but not always, initial consonant sounds.

Analogy An extended comparison of two similar things. It is a way of using the familiar or simple to explain the unfamiliar or complex. It is important to remember that you can use an analogy to clarify an idea but not to prove a point.

Analysis The organizational strategy based on dividing a whole into its component parts by using a consistent principle of analysis.

Anapest A metrical foot consisting of two unaccented syllables followed by an accented syllable ($\smile\smile\prime$).

Antagonist The individual(s), object(s), or circumstance(s) that oppose the protagonist in a work of literature.

Argument The use of logic through deductive and inductive reasoning to support an assertion, a thesis, or a proposition. Argument appeals to an audience's reasoning power.

Assonance The repetition of vowel sounds.

Audience The individual or individuals at whom you direct your piece of writing. It is important to know the nature of your audience in order to make intelligent decisions with regard to your choice of supporting material, voice, and organizational strategy.

Cause and Effect The organizational strategy by which you can show how something happened or what its results were.

Character A person that a writer creates through description, action, and dialogue.

Classification The organizational strategy by which you take a number of objects and organize them into groups according to a single principle.

Clustering A discovery strategy that produces a map of your ideas and experiences and the connections between them from which you can create a first written draft of your piece of writing.

Coherence Coherence in writing is the effect of having each paragraph or sentence clearly relate to the one that precedes it and to the one that follows it.

Comparison and Contrast The organizational strategy that supports a dominant idea by showing the similarities and the differences between objects, events, persons, or ideas.

Connotation The implications or associations of a word that extends beyond its literal meaning.

Dactyl A metrical foot containing an accented syllable followed by two unaccented syllables ($'\smile\smile$).

Deductive Reasoning The form of reasoning that moves from a generalization (see inductive reasoning) to a conclusion by applying that generalization to a specific fact. A deduction is built on a three-part structure called a syllogism. (See also validity.)

Definition The organizational strategy that presents the basic nature, meaning, or characteristics of an object, a living thing, or an idea.

Denotation The literal meaning of a word as found in the dictionary, as opposed to connotation which is the range of associations and emotions evoked by a word.

Denouement French for "untying a knot," the final action of a plot that resolves the conflict.

Description Representing an object or a location through words that make the subject of the description clear to your audience.

Dialogue The conversation between persons reflected through the writing in drama, poetry, and both fiction and nonfiction prose.

Dimeter A line of poetry containing two feet (units) of a meter.

Dominant Idea The particular focus you take toward your subject. A dominant idea can be a thesis or argumentative conclusion, but it may also be an attitude or an emotion evoked by the subject.

Draft The first exploration of your writing. Drafting is the stage at which you work at getting your ideas, examples, attitudes, and feelings on paper in order to see how they might connect with each other and where they might lead.

Dramatic Irony The contrast between what a character wants and what he or she gets, usually as the result of circumstances that are beyond the character's control.

Editing The process by which you make certain that your language says precisely what you want it to say without vagueness and without unnecessary repetition.

Essay A short piece of nonfiction prose that reflects a dominant idea about a relatively limited topic.

Fact An event that is known to exist or to have existed because it can be or has been verified by careful observation or measurement.

Figurative Language The imaginative use of words. (See simile, metaphor, and personification.)

First-Person Point of View The point of view in which a character tells his or her story. The reader can only know what that character knows and can only experience what that character experiences.

Foot In poetry, a single unit of meter.

Free Verse Poetry that arranges itself according to the rhythm of its words rather than regular meter.

Freewriting A discovery strategy that asks you to write without stopping to revise, correct, edit, or think about your writing. It helps you discover what you might use as a dominant idea as well as effective language and support.

General A general term includes many specific instances of that term. A generalization covers a lot of territory. How general you can be in your writing depends on how much information your audience has.

Grammar The study of the arrangement of words into phrases and sentences, the forms and structures of the words themselves, and the corresponding relationships between ideas and their arrangements.

Iamb A metrical foot composed of an unaccented foot followed by an accented foot (˘ ′).

Imagery Writing that appeals directly to the senses.

Inductive Reasoning Reaching a conclusion by reasoning from specific examples to general conclusions. While valid deduction always produces certain conclusions, you can never be entirely certain of an inductive conclusion.

Irony A statement or situation in which something that is said or that occurs is contradicted by the way things really are and of which the audience and possibly some of the characters are aware.

Limited Point of View The point of view in which a narrator relates the experiences and thoughts of a single character. The narrator may comment upon the character and his or her thoughts, but the thoughts of the other characters are closed to the narrator.

Metaphor The imaginative comparison of two unlike things that does not use the terms "like" or "as."

Meter The rhythmic pattern in poetry that is created by the regular arrangement of patterns of stressed and unstressed syllables, for example, iambic pentameter or anapestic tetrameter.

Monometer A line of poetry composed of one metrical foot.

Narration An organizational strategy that arranges events in a sequence, usually chronological. Narration tells a story.

***Non Sequitur* Fallacy** *Non sequitur* (it does not follow) means that while a conclusion follows an observation, that conclusion has no clear relationship to the observation.

Objective Point of View The point of view in which the narrator takes no part, makes no judgments, formulates no conclusions. In effect, the narrator functions like a camera, recording only what happens at the time and place the events occur.

Occasion The time, place, and conditions under which a piece of writing happens.

Octameter A line of poetry composed of eight metrical feet.

Omniscient Point of View The point of view that can shift in and out of the minds of more than one of the characters in a piece of writing as well as move freely through time and space.

Opinion A person's interpretation of events he or she asserts to be facts.

Pentad A discovery strategy developed by Kenneth Burke. It considers an event from the standpoint of act, agent, agency, scene, and purpose, and the relationships between these elements.

Personification A form of figurative language in which nonhuman objects are given human characters or attitudes.

Persuasion The use of language and examples to appeal to your audience's emotion to influence its members to think a certain way or to reach a certain conclusion.

Plagiarism The use of another's ideas and words as if they were the writer's own, without acknowledging the source of those words and ideas.

Plot The sequence of events in a story, poem, play, narrative essay, or the narrative part of an essay.

Point of View The angle from which a writer tells a story. Point of view is either omniscient, limited, first-person, or objective.

Post Hoc Fallacy. *Post hoc ergo propter hoc* (after this, therefore because of this) is the fallacy that confuses sequence with causation and draws conclusions as a result of that confusion.

Prewriting The stage of discovering ideas that might develop themselves into a dominant idea in a piece of writing, also the discovery of effective supporting material that clarifies the ideas. Prewriting may also include, but does not require, drafting.

Process The organizational strategy based on showing how to do something or how something had been or might be done.

Proofreading The process by which you make certain you have followed the conventions of grammar and spelling in your writing. You should not worry about these issues until you have completed drafting, revising, and editing.

Protagonist The leading character in a narration. Usually, the protagonist's aims are opposed by the antagonist(s).

Punctuation The system of marks such as commas and periods that reflect the relationships between words, phrases, and the ideas they express.

Research Paper A piece of writing that uses reference to the ideas and discoveries of others as steps to reaching and supporting its dominant idea. It does not use research as its conclusion, only as a means of reaching its conclusion.

Revision The process of "re-seeing" your writing with the aim of sharpening its focus, narrowing your dominant idea, making sure your writing is unified and coherent, and seeing that you've accounted for what your audience needs to know and what it assumes.

Rhetoric The discovery of the best available means of persuasion, or the study of the methods of finding the best available means of persuasion.

Rhyme The similarity of sounds between words, most usually the final sounds of lines of poetry.

Rhythm The regular occurrence of stressed syllables in poetry.

Scene The part of Burke's Pentad concerned with the physical and time-defined surroundings where the agent performed the act.

Simile The imaginative comparison of two things by means of "like" or "as."

Specific A specific term is limited to one or a few instances of a general word or phrase. While a general term covers a lot of territory, a specific term is far more limited.

Spondee A metrical foot that contains two stressed syllables.

Stance The attitude you take toward your subject.

Stress The accent or emphasis a word or a syllable receives in speech or in a line of poetry.

Style The characteristic way in which a writer uses his or her words and their rhythms.

Subject The general area covered by your paper. Subject differs from the dominant idea; the dominant idea is the writer's particular focus on the subject or the writer's stance in relation to the subject.

Subplot A subordinate plot within a play or a piece of fiction that resembles the main plot or contrasts directly with the main plot in such a way as to comment upon the main plot.

Syllogism The three-part structure of a syllogism: The major premise is the generalization. The minor premise is the specific statement to which the major premise is applied. The conclusion is the statement that follows from the major and minor premises.

Symbol Something that stands for something else.

Symbolism The use of one thing to represent something else.

Tetrameter A line of poetry that contains four metrical feet.

Theme A synonym for the dominant idea but more usually applied to a literary work.

Tone The use of language, especially in its connotative form, to express the writer's or speaker's attitude toward his or her subject.

Trimeter A line of poetry that contains three metrical feet.

Trochee A metrical foot which has an accented syllable followed by an unaccented syllable ($'\smile$).

Unity Unity is the effect of having all your supporting, specific instances related to your dominant idea.

Validity A valid argument is a deductive argument whose conclusion must follow from its major and minor premises.

Verbal Irony The difference between events or situations as they are stated and the way the audience sees that they are.

Vocabulary The words over which you have enough control to use effectively or to understand.

Voice Your choice of words to reflect your emotions or to create corresponding emotions in your audience.

Acknowledgments

SHERWOOD ANDERSON, "Discovery of a Father." Copyright 1939 by The Reader's Digest. Copyright renewed 1966 by Eleanor Copenhaver Anderson. Reprinted by permission of Harold Ober Associates Incorporated.

MAYA ANGELOU, "Phenomenal Woman" from *And Still I Rise* by Maya Angelou. Copyright © 1978 by Maya Angelou. Reprinted by permission of Random House, Inc.

MARGARET ATWOOD, "you fit into me," "Pornography" from *Power Politics* by Margaret Atwood. Copyright © 1971, House of Anansi Press, Toronto. Reprinted with the permission of Stoddart Publishing Co. Limited, Don Mills, Ontario, Canada.

W. H. AUDEN, "The Unknown Citizen" and "Musee des Beaux Arts" from *Collected Poems* by W. H. Auden. Copyright © 1940 and renewed 1968 by W. H. Auden. Reprinted by permission of Random House, Inc.

AMIRI BARAKA, "Poem For Half-White College Students" from *Black Magic Poetry*. Copyright by Amiri Baraka. Reprinted by permission of Sterling Lord Literistic, Inc.

ELIZABETH BISHOP, "Filling Station" and "The Fish" from *The Complete Poems 1927–1979* by Elizabeth Bishop. Copyright © 1979, 1983 by Alice Helen Methfessel. Reprinted by permission of Farrar, Straus & Giroux, Inc.

ROBERT BLY, "Taking the hands of someone you love," from *Silence in the Snowy Fields*. Copyright © 1960, 1961, 1962 by Robert Bly. Wesleyan University by permission of University Press of New England.

T. CORAGHESSAN BOYLE, "Greasy Lake," from *Greasy Lake and Other Stories* by T. Coraghessan Boyle. Copyright © 1979, 1981, 1983, 1984, 1985 by R. Coraghessan Boyle. Used by permission of Viking Penguin, a division of Penguin Books USA Inc.

EDMUND BRILL, Excerpt from *The Interpretation of Dreams*. Translated and edited by Dr. A. A. Brill in THE BASIC WRITINGS OF SIGMUND FREUD, Random House, Inc., New York. Copyright 1938, © renewed 1965 by Gioia B. Bernheim and Edmund Brill. Reprinted with permission.

GWENDOLYN BROOKS, "Sadie and Maud" and "The Mother" reprinted by permission of the author.

CHARLES BUKOWSKI, "dogfight." Copyright © 1974 by Charles Bukowski. Reprinted from *Burning in Water Drowning in Flame: Selected Poems 1955–1973* with the permission of Black Sparrow Press.

RAYMOND CARVER, "Popular Mechanics," from *What We Talk About When We Talk About Love* by Raymond Carver. Copyright © 1981 by Raymond Carver. Reprinted by permission of Alfred A. Knopf Inc.

NORMAN COUSINS, "Who Killed Benny Paret?" from *Present Tense* by Norman Cousins, McGraw-Hill, Inc.

STEPHEN CRANE, "The Open Boat," from *The Complete Works of Stephen Crane, Volume V: Tales of Adventure* edited by Fredson Bowers (Charlotte: Virginia, 1970). Used by permission of the University Press of Virginia.

COUNTEE CULLEN, "Incident" from *On These I Stand* by Countee Cullen. Copyright © 1925 by Harper & Brothers. Copyright renewed 1953 by Ida M. Cullen. Reprinted by permission of GRM Associates, Inc., agents for the Estate of Ida M. Cullen.

E. E. CUMMINGS, "1(a" reprinted from COMPLETE POEMS, 1904–1962, by E. E. Cummings, edited by George J. Firmage, by permission of Liveright Publishing Corporation. Copyright © 1958, 1986, 1991 by the Trustees for the E. E. Cummings Trust.

JAMES DICKEY, "Cherrylog Road," from *Helmets*, published by Wesleyan University Press. Copyright 1964 by James Dickey. Reprinted by permission of University Press of New England.

EMILY DICKINSON, "He preached upon Breadth," "Much Madness," and "I Heard a Fly Buzz" from *The Poems of Emily Dickinson*, Thomas H. Johnson, ed., Cambridge, Mass.: The Belknap Press of Harvard University Press. Copyright © 1951, 1955, 1979, 1983 by the President and Fellows of Harvard College. Reprinted by permission of the publishers and the Trustees of Amherst College.

ANNIE DILLARD, "Sojourner," from *Teaching a Stone to Talk* by Annie Dillard. Copyright © 1982 by Annie Dillard. Reprinted by permission of HarperCollins Publishers, Inc.

RICHARD EBERHART, "The Groundhog" from *Collected Poems 1930–1986* by Richard Eberhart. Copyright © 1988 by Richard Eberhart. Reprinted by permission of Oxford University Press, Inc.

LOREN EISELEY, "The Judgement of the Birds," from *The Immense Journey* by Loren Eiseley. Copyright © 1956 by Loren Eiseley. Reprinted by permission of Random House, Inc.

T. S. ELIOT, "The Love Song of J. Alfred Prufrock" from *Collected Poems 1909–1962* by T. S. Eliot, published by Harcourt Brace, Inc. Copyright © 1964, 1963 by T. S. Eliot.

NORA EPHRON, "A Few Words about Breasts" from *Crazy Salad: Some Things About Women* by Nora Ephron. Copyright 1972 by Nora Ephron. Reprinted by permission of International Creative Management, Inc.

WILLIAM FAULKNER, "That Evening Sun," from *Collected Stories of William Faulkner* by William Faulkner. Copyright © 1959 by William Faulkner. Reprinted by permission of Random House, Inc.

LAWRENCE FERLINGHETTI, "Constantly Risking Absurdity" from *A Coney Island of the Mind* by Lawrence Ferlinghetti. Copyright © 1958 by Lawrence Ferlinghetti. Reprinted by permission of New Directions Publishing Corp.

ROBERT FROST, "Design," "The Road Not Taken," and "The Most of It," from *The Poetry of Robert Frost* edited by Edward Connery Lathem. Copyright 1936, 1942 by Robert Frost. Copyright © 1964, 1970 by Lesley Frost Ballantine. Copyright © 1969 by Henry Holt and Company, Inc. Reprinted by permission of Henry Holt and Company, Inc.

SUSAN GLASPELL, *Trifles*. Copyright 1951 by Walter H. Baker Company. Reprinted by permission of Baker's Plays, Boston, MA 02111.

TOM GODWIN, "The Cold Equations," copyright 1954 by Street & Smith Publications, Inc. Reprinted by permission of the author and the author's agents, Scott Meredith Literary Agency, L.P., 845 Third Avenue, New York, NY 10022.

ELLEN GOODMAN, "The Just-Right Wife." Copyright © 1994, The Boston Globe Company. Reprinted with permission.

ROBERT GRAVES, "The Naked and the Nude," from *Collected Poems 1975* by Robert Graves. Copyright © 1975 by Robert Graves. Reprinted by permission of Oxford University Press, Inc.

ROBERT HAYDEN, "Those Winter Sundays," reprinted from *Angle of Ascent, New and Selected Poems* by Robert Hayden, by permission of Liveright Publishing Corporation. Copyright © 1975, 1972, 1970, 1966 by Robert Hayden.

ERNEST HEMINGWAY, "Hills Like White Elephants," reprinted with permission of Scribners, an imprint of Simon & Schuster, from *Men Without Women* by Ernest Hemingway. Copyright 1927 by Charles Scribner's Sons. Copyright renewed 1955 by Ernest Hemingway.

LANGSTON HUGHES, "Dream Deferred," from *The Panther and the Lash* by Langston Hughes. Copyright 1951 by Langston Hughes. Reprinted by permission of Alfred A. Knopf Inc.

ROBINSON JEFFERS, "Hurt Hawks," from *Selected Poetry of Robinson Jeffers*. Copyright © 1928 and renewed 1956 by Robinson Jeffers. Reprinted by permission of Random House, Inc.

GARRISON KEILLOR, "School," from *Lake Wobegon Days* by Garrison Keillor. Copyright ©

1985 by Garrison Keillor. Used by permission of Viking Penguin, a division of Penguin Books USA Inc.

X. J. KENNEDY, "In a Prominent Bar in Secaucus One Day" from *Nude Descending a Staircase*. Reprinted by permission of Curtis Brown, Ltd. Copyright © 1961 by X. J. Kennedy.

JAMAICA KINCAID, "Girl," from *At The Bottom of the River* by Jamaica Kincaid. Copyright © 1978, 1983 by Jamaica Kincaid. Reprinted by permission of Farrar, Straus & Giroux, Inc.

MARTIN LUTHER KING, JR., "I Have a Dream." Reprinted by arrangement with The Heirs to the Estate of Martin Luther King, Jr., c/o Joan Daves Agency as agent for the proprietor. Copyright 1963 by Martin Luther King, Jr., copyright renewed 1991 by Coretta Scott King.

MAXINE HONG KINGSTON, "No Name Woman," from *The Woman Warrior* by Maxine Hong Kingston. Copyright © 1975, 1976 by Maxine Hong Kingston. Reprinted by permission of Alfred A. Knopf Inc.

GALWAY KINNELL, "Blackberry Eating," from *Mortal Acts, Mortal Words* by Galway Kinnell. Copyright © 1980 by Galway Kinnell. Reprinted by permission of Houghton Mifflin Company. All rights reserved.

HAROLD KRENTS, "Darkness at Noon," from The New York Times, May 26, 1976. Copyright © 1976 by The New York Times Company. Reprinted by permission.

PÄR LAGERKVIST, "Father and I," from *The Eternal Smile and Other Stories* (1952), copyright by the estate of Pär Lagerkvist 1992; published in agreement with Albert Bonniers Forlag AB.

D. H. LAWRENCE, "Tickets, Please," copyright 1922 by Thomas Seltzer, Inc., renewal copyright 1950 by Frieda Lawrence, from *Complete Short Stories of D. H. Lawrence* by D. H. Lawrence. Used by permission of Viking Penguin, a division of Penguin Books USA Inc.

BARRY LOPEZ, "My Horse," from *Crossing Open Ground*. Copyright © 1978, 1979, 1980, 1981, 1982, 1983, 1984, 1985, 1986, 1988 by Barry Lopez. Reprinted by permission of Sterling Lord Literistic, Inc.

ARCHIBALD MACLEISH, "Ars Poetica," from *Collected Poems 1917–1982* by Archibald MacLeish. Copyright © 1985 by The Estate of Archibald MacLeish. Reprinted by permission of Houghton Mifflin Co. All rights reserved.

HAKI R. MADHUBUTI, "But He Was Cool . . . he even stopped for green lights," from *Don't Cry, Scream* (Chicago: Third World Press, 1969). By permission.

NORMAN MAILER, "The Death of Benny Paret," from *The Presidential Papers*. Copyright 1960, 1962, 1963 by Norman Mailer. Reprinted by permission of the author and the author's agents, Scott Meredith Literary Agency, Inc.

BERNARD MALAMUD, "The Magic Barrel," from *The Magic Barrel* by Bernard Malamud. Copyright © 1954, 1958 and copyright renewed © 1982, 1986 by Bernard Malamud. Reprinted by permission of Farrar, Straus & Giroux, Inc.

MALCOLM X, "My First Conk," from *The Autobiography of Malcolm X*. Copyright © 1964 by Alex Haley and Malcolm X and copyright © 1965 by Alex Haley and Betty Shabazz. Reprinted by permission of Random House, Inc.

GABRIEL GARCIA MARQUEZ, "A Very Old Man With Enormous Wings," from *Leaf Storm and Other Stories* by Gabriel Garcia Marquez. Copyright © 1971 by Gabriel Garcia Marquez. Reprinted by permission of HarperCollins Publishers, Inc.

MARK MATHABANE, "My Father's Tribal Rule," from *Kaffir Boy* by Mark Mathabane. Copyright © 1986 by Mark Mathabane. Reprinted with the permission of Macmillan Publishing Company.

CHEROKEE PAUL MCDONALD, "A View from the Bridge." Reprinted by permission of the author.

STANLEY MILGRAM, "The Perils of Obedience," abridged and adapted from *Obedience to Authority* by Stanley Milgram. Published in *Harper's Magazine*. Copyright © 1974 by Stanley Milgram. Reprinted by permission of HarperCollins Publishers. "Some Conditions of Obedience and Disobedience to Authority" in *Human Relations,* Vol. 18, No. 1, 1965, pp. 57–76. Copyright © 1972 by Stanley Milgram. Reprinted by permission of Alexandra Milgram.

YUKIO MISHIMA, "Patriotism," from *Death in Midsummer.* Copyright © 1966 by New Directions Publishing Corp. Reprinted by permission of New Directions Publishing Corp.

JESSICA MITFORD, "Mr. Jones' Ordeal," from *The American Way of Death* by Jessica Mitford. Copyright © 1963, 1978 by Jessica Mitford. Reprinted by permission of Jessica Mitford. All rights reserved.

JOHNSON C. MONTGOMERY, "Island of Plenty," *Newsweek,* December 23, 1974.

SHARON OLDS, "The Victims," from *The Dead and the Living* by Sharon Olds. Copyright © 1983 by Sharon Olds. Reprinted by permission of Alfred A. Knopf Inc.

TILLIE OLSEN, "I Stand Here Ironing," from *Tell Me A Riddle* by Tillie Olsen. Copyright © 1956, 1957, 1960, 1961 by Tillie Olsen. Used by permission of Delacorte Press/Seymour Lawrence, a division of Bantam Doubleday Dell Publishing Group, Inc.

GEORGE ORWELL, "Shooting an Elephant," from *Shooting An Elephant and Other Essays* by George Orwell. Copyright 1950 by Sonia Brownell Orwell and renewed 1978 by Sonia Pitt-Rivers. Reprinted by permission of Harcourt Brace & Company.

WILFRED OWEN, "Dulce et Decorum Est" from *Collected Poems of Wilfred Owen.* Copyright © 1963 by Chatto & Windus, Ltd. Reprinted by permission of New Directions Publishing Corp.

MARGE PIERCY, "Barbie Doll" and "The Secretary Chant," from *Circles on the Water* by Marge Piercy. Copyright © 1982 by Marge Piercy. Reprinted by permission of Alfred A. Knopf Inc.

SYLVIA PLATH, "metaphors," from *Crossing the Water* by Sylvia Plath. Copyright © 1960 by Red Hughes. Copyright renewed. Reprinted by permission of HarperCollins Publishers, Inc.

ROBERT RAGAINI, "A Question of Manhood," *Newsday,* March 29, 1987.

FRED REED, "A Veteran Writes." Copyright © 1980 by Harper's Magazine. All rights reserved. Reprinted from the December issue by special permission.

HENRY REED, "Naming of Parts," from *Collected Poems,* edited by Jon Stalworthy (1991). Reprinted by permission of Oxford University Press.

TOMAS RIVERA, "And the Earth Did Not Devour Him" is reprinted with permission from the publisher of *And the Earth Did Not Devour Him* (Houston: Art Publico Press-University of Houston, 1987).

EDWIN ARLINGTON ROBINSON, "Richard Cory," from *The Children of the Night* by Edwin Arlington Robinson (New York: Charles Scribner's Sons, 1897). "Mr. Flood's Party" reprinted with permission of Simon & Schuster from *Collected Poems of Edwin Arlington Robinson.* Copyright 1921 by Edwin Arlington Robinson, renewed 1949 by Ruth Nivison.

RICHARD RODRIGUEZ, "Children of a Marriage." Copyright © 1974 by Richard Rodriguez. Reprinted by permission of Georges Borchardt, for the author.

THEODORE ROETHKE, "Dolor," copyright 1943 by Modern Poetry Association, Inc. "My Papa's Waltz," copyright 1946 by Hearst Magazines, Inc. "Root Cellar," copyright 1943 by Modern Poetry Association, Inc., from *The Collected Poems of Theodore Roethke* by Theodore Roethke. Used by permission of Doubleday, a division of Bantam Doubleday Dell Publishing Group, Inc.

IRMA S. ROMBAUER and MARION ROMBAUER BECKER, Recipe for Duckling Rouennaise from *The Joy of Cooking,* Revised edition, 1973. The New American Library, Inc.

OLIVER SACKS, "Rebecca," from *The Man Who Mistook His Wife for a Hat* by Oliver Sacks. Copyright © 1970, 1981, 1983, 1984, 1985, by Oliver Sacks. Reprinted by permission of Simon & Schuster, Inc.

DEBORAH SALAZAR, "My Abortion." Reprinted by permission of *Exquisite Corpse: A Journal of Books and Ideas,* editor, Andrei Codrescu.

PHYLLIS SCHLAFLY, "Understanding the Difference," from *The Power of the Positive Woman* by Phyllis Schlafly. Copyright © 1977 by Phyllis Schlafly. Reprinted by permission of Crown Publishers, Inc.

RICHARD SELZER, "The Discus Thrower," from *Confession of a Knife* by Richard Selzer. Copyright © 1979 by Richard Selzer. Reprinted by permission of John Hawkins & Associates, Inc.

Index